# ART
## Connections

## Arts Education for the 21st Century

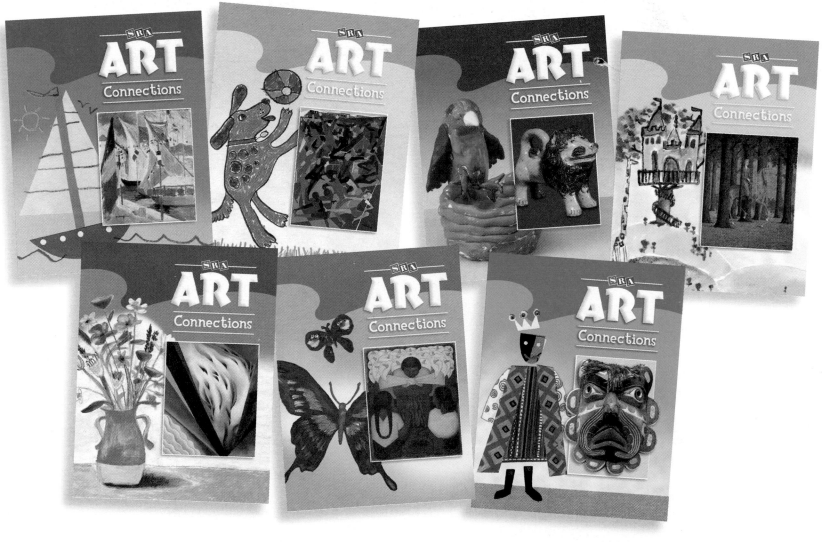

Culture    Personal Expression    Creativity

History    Beauty    Critical Thinking

**Art encourages different ways of learning, knowing, and communicating.**

i

# All the Resources you Need for Great Art Teaching!

**Art Connections** provides everything teachers need to offer meaningful art education.

## Student Edition K–6

Comprehensive student materials in two formats:

**Student Edition**

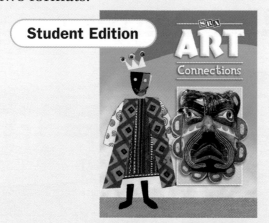

LEVEL 6

**Big Book**

LEVEL 6

## Teacher Edition

Everything classroom and art teachers need to teach art effectively

LEVEL 4

- Complete lesson plans to teach
  - elements and principles of art
  - art history and culture
  - art criticism
  - art production
- Art background
- Cross-curricular connections
- Program resources guide

## Technology Components

**e-Presentation for students and teachers**

LEVEL K

**e-Presentation** offers the complete Student Edition as a presentation tool for teachers, complete with multimedia experiences, assessments, teacher materials, and a gallery of all artworks in the entire program.

This electronic gallery allows immediate access to all the artwork in the **Art Connections** program.

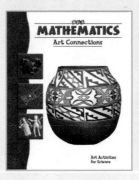

***Cross-Curricular Art Connections*** include practical art projects for the classroom to help meet subject-area guidelines in

- Social Studies
- Mathematics
- Language Arts and Reading
- Science

**LEVEL 3**

***Reading and Writing Test Preparation*** that reinforces art content

**LEVEL 1**

***Home and After-School Connections*** for every unit, in English and Spanish

***Professional Development Guide*** for both classroom teachers and art specialists

**LEVEL 5**

***Assessment*** with tests in English and Spanish for every lesson

***Art Around the World CD-ROM*** includes 150 works of art from the *Art Around the World Collection,* representing a variety of thought-provoking perspectives and activities.

***The National Museum of Women in the Arts Collection CD-ROM*** dynamically explores the 200-print collection to introduce students to key women artists.

# Enrich students' lives with exposure to the great masters and cultures of the world.

## Fine-Art Resources

***Transparencies*** Overhead transparency study prints for all lesson artwork allow for up-close examination.

**LEVEL 5**

***Large Prints*** for each unit provide exemplary artwork to develop unit concepts.

**LEVEL 2**

**LEVEL 1**

***Artist Profiles*** Pictures, background information, and profiles for every artist in the program provide valuable historical and cultural information at your fingertips.

***Literature and Art Videos and DVD*** develop art connections to literature.

**The Polar Express**

***Art Around the World*** 150-print resource explores the art of the world's cultures.

# Elements and Principles of Art Teaching Resources

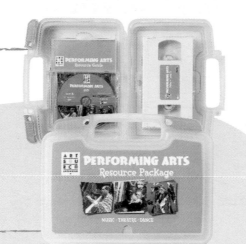

**LEVEL 3**

*Artsource® Performing Arts Resource Package (Video and DVD)* integrates the performing arts of dance, music, and theatre.

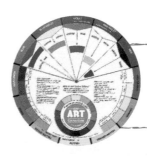

*The National Museum of Women in the Arts Collection* This 200-print resource provides famous artwork from famous women artists.

**Elements of Art** poster reinforces line, shape, color, value, form, space, and texture.

**Principles of Art** poster develops concepts of rhythm, balance, movement, harmony, variety, emphasis, and unity.

Use the **Color Wheel** to explore color concepts.

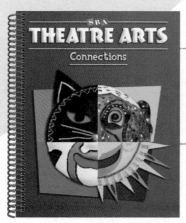

**LEVEL 4**

*Theatre Arts Connections* is a complete dramatic arts program that ties to *Art Connections*.

*Flash Cards* provide a quick review of the elements and principles of art.

v

# Build a foundation in the elements and principles of art.

**36 Lessons** at every grade level develop the elements and principles of art in six-lesson units.

◄ **Rembrandt van Rijn.**
*Portrait of Rembrandt.*

◄ **Frida Kahlo.**
*Frida y Diego Rivera.*

**LEVEL 6**

---

**Unit Openers** introduce students to unit concepts and master artists.

Unit 5

# Space, Proportion, and Distortion

Artists use accurate proportions to realistically depict people and objects.

Copley painted this realistic portrait of the Pepperrell family in 1778. The Pepperrell family lived in New England until about the time of the American Revolution, when they moved to England. At about the same time, Sir William Pepperrell lost most of his wealth. Notice that Copley used correct proportions to make the painting realistic.

▲ **John Singleton Copley.**
(American).
*Sir William Pepperrell
and His Family.* 1778.

Oil on canvas. 90 × 108 inches
(228.6 × 274.32 cm.). North
Carolina Museum of Art, Raleigh,
North Carolina.

Artists use space in paintings to give the appearance of depth on a flat surface.
➤ How do you think John Singleton Copley created space in *Sir William Pepperrell and His Family*?
➤ Which objects in the painting look closer to you? Which objects look farther away?

Artists use accurate **proportions** to show people or things realistically.
➤ Do you think the people in Copley's painting look like they have been painted with accurate proportions? Explain.

**In This Unit** you will learn about different ways that artists show size and placement. Here are the topics you will study:
➤ Foreground, middle ground, and background
➤ Perspective techniques
➤ Point of view
➤ Face proportion
➤ Body proportions
➤ Distortion

*Master Artist Profile*

## John Singleton Copley

(1738–1815)

John Singleton Copley was a popular portrait painter during the eighteenth century. When he was seventeen years old he created a portrait of George Washington. In his attempt to capture details and to make his subjects appear natural, Copley sometimes required fifteen or sixteen sittings for a single portrait. Copley moved to England during the American Revolution and did not return to America.

154 Unit 5

Unit 5 155

**LEVEL 4**

---

**Unit Wrap-Ups** review concepts, explore Art Museums or Art Careers and allow students to experience Artsource® connections to dance, theatre, and music.

Wrapping Up Unit 5

Space, Proportion, and Distortion

▲ **Jacob Lawrence.** (American). *Study for the Munich Olympic Games Poster.* 1971.

Gouache on paper. 35⅝ × 27 inches (90.17 × 68.58 cm.).
Seattle Art Museum, Seattle, Washington.

180 Unit 5

Wrapping Up Unit 5
Space, Proportion, and Distortion, continued

**Show What You Know**

VISIT A MUSEUM
**The Smithsonian**

Answer these questions...

🎨 **Art Criticism** Critical Thinking

**Describe** What do you see?
During this step you will collect information about the subject of the work.
➤ How many people do you see? What kinds of facial expressions do they have?
➤ What are the people doing? What are they wearing?
➤ What is the setting?

**Analyze** How is this work organized?
Think about how the artist used the elements and principles of art.
➤ Which people or objects look closest to you? Which look farthest away?
➤ What is in the foreground, the middle ground, and the background?
➤ Where do you see a part of someone's body that overlaps and covers part of another person or object?
➤ What is the point of view of this painting?
➤ Where do you see distortion?

**Interpret** What is the artist trying to say?
Use the clues you discovered during your analysis to find the message the artist is trying to show.
➤ Which runner do you think will win the race? Why?
➤ What is the mood of this painting?
➤ What sounds would you hear if you could go into the painting?

**Decide** What do you think about the work?
Use all the information you have gathered to decide whether this is a successful work of art.
➤ Is the work successful because it is realistic, because it is well-organized, or because it has a strong message?

ART
S
O
U
R
C
E
**Space and Proportion in Music**

...born in Cuba. ...ld he moved to ...ard harp music. ...from his friend ...master harpist, ...but eventually ...fe to the harp.

...make a simple ...nd. Vibration is ...nsation caused in ...of air. You can hear ...a string tightly ...ack the string.

...tch rubber bands ...re that rubber ...cknesses.

...e if you get ...s. The thickness, ...e strings will

...thicknesses of ...igher or lower

▲ Ortiz. *"Joropo Azul."*

🎨 **Art Criticism**

**Describe** Describe how you made your instrument.

**Analyze** What did you do to get a higher or lower tone or pitch?

**Interpret** What did you feel as you created an instrument and heard the sounds it made?

**Decide** Were you able to get a satisfying musical sound from your simple instrument?

Unit 5 181

Unit 5 183

**LEVEL 4**

vi

# Integrate the four disciplines of art into every lesson for well-rounded exposure to all the dimensions of art.

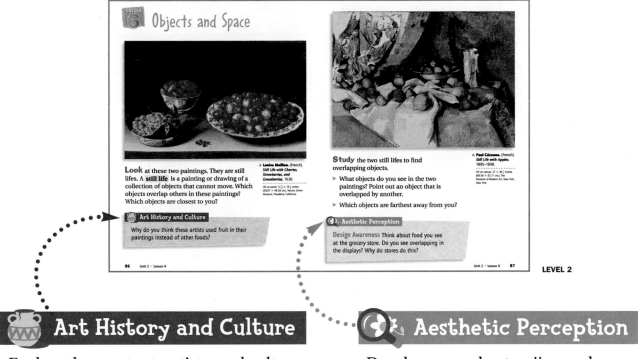

## Art History and Culture

Explore the great art, artists, and cultures of the world.

## Aesthetic Perception

Develop an understanding and appreciation for art.

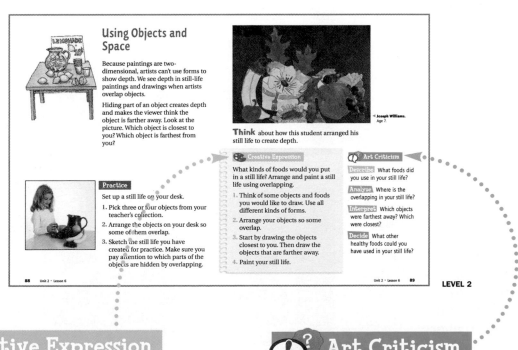

## Creative Expression

Encounter a broad range of art media in a variety of hands-on art activities that give students an avenue for self-expression and self-esteem.

## Art Criticism

Enrich critical-thinking skills as students learn about the elements and principles of art by examining their own and others' artwork.

# Add dimension to all subjects with meaningful art connections.

Connect Art to Mathematics, Social Studies, Science, Language Arts and Reading.

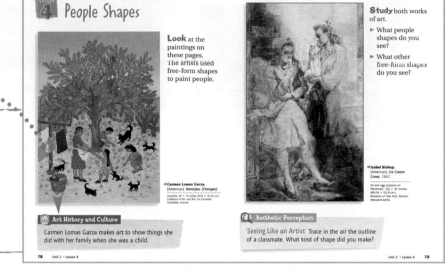

**LEVEL 1**

*History*
Develop historical understanding as students explore art history and culture in every lesson.

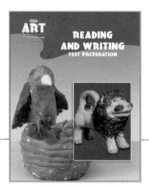

**LEVEL 2**

*Reading and Writing Test Preparation*
Use art content, information about artists, art concepts, and art history to practice reading and writing skills in every unit.

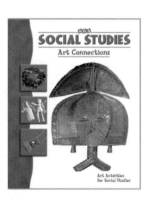

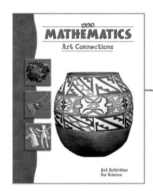

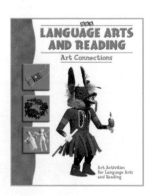

*Cross-Curricular Art Connections*
These books provide a wealth of exciting art activities designed specifically to support subject-area studies in Science, Mathematics, Social Studies, Language Arts and Reading as they reinforce art concepts.

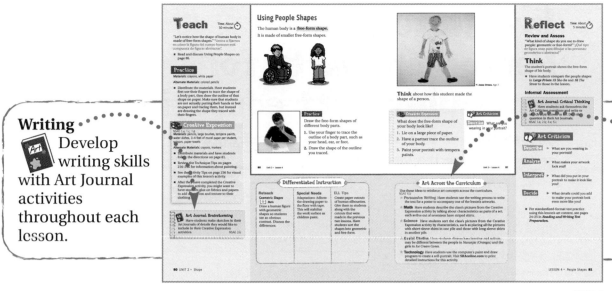

LEVEL 1

## Writing

Develop writing skills with Art Journal activities throughout each lesson.

## Cross-Curricular Ideas

Show students how artwork and concepts relate to science, mathematics, social studies, reading/language arts, and technology in every lesson.

LEVEL 2

## Cross-Curricular Integration

Integrate language arts and reading, math, science, and social studies concepts naturally as students work through each art lesson.

LEVEL 4

## Vocabulary Development

Key vocabulary terms are highlighted, defined, and reviewed to develop the language of art.

LEVEL 3

## Literature Integration

Integrate literature with Illustrator Profiles and Literature and Art video experiences at the beginning of every unit.

Research has shown that incorporating the arts into core curriculum areas in a way that actively involves students in the learning process produces "significant positive effects on student achievement, motivation, and engagement in learning, and notable changes in classroom practices" ("Different Ways of Knowing: 1991–94 National Longitudinal Study Final Report" in Schools, Communities, and the Arts: A Research Compendium).

# Integrate all the Performing Arts for a complete Art education.

**Expose children to music, dance, and theatre as they explore the visual arts.**

LEVEL 2

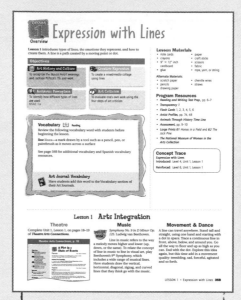

LEVEL 5

 **Music Connections** in every Unit Opener translate the visual arts elements and principles into music.

 **Music Experiences** in every lesson from Macmillan/McGraw-Hill's *Spotlight on Music* expand creativity and develop music appreciation.

 **Artsource®** music performances on video and DVD explore the elements and principles of art through the performing arts.

LEVEL 4

## Dance

LEVEL 3

**Artsource®** dance performances on video and DVD explore the elements and principles of art through the performing arts.

## Theatre

LEVEL 5

**Artsource®** theatre performances on video and DVD explore the elements and principles of art through the performing arts.

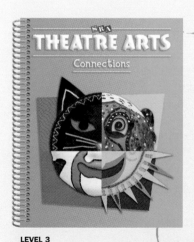

LEVEL 3

**Theatre Arts Connections** for grades K–6 lessons explore the elements and principles of theatre arts as students develop the elements and principles of visual arts.

Case studies have indicated that students perceive "that the arts facilitate their personal and social development." It also appears that to gain the full benefit of arts education, students should be exposed to all of the arts, including fine arts, dance, theatre, and music ("Arts Education in Secondary School: Effects and Effectiveness" in Critical Links, p. 76).

# Meet Today's Standards for Art Education.

*Art Connections* exceeds the national standards for art education.

## National Standards for Arts Education

**Content Standard #1:**

Understanding and applying media, techniques, and processes

The Creative Expression activity in every lesson of *Art Connections* develops understanding and experience with a wide variety of media, techniques, and processes. Practice activities in every lesson focus specifically on techniques.

**Content Standard #2:**

Using knowledge of structures and functions

*Art Connections* develops the elements and principles of art in every grade level, K–6. Units and lessons are organized to explore the elements and principles in exemplary art and then to practice techniques and create works of art that employ specific structures and functions of art.

**Content Standard #3:**

Choosing and evaluating a range of subject matter, symbols, and ideas

*Art Connections* introduces students to subject matter and symbols at the beginning of every grade level and then uses that knowledge throughout every lesson in the Aesthetic Perception questions and Creative Expression activities as students explore content to develop meaning in artwork.

**Ali M. Forbes.** Age 7.

**Jasmine Krasel.** Age 9.

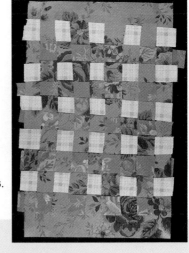

**Briana Kittle.** Age 6.

**Content Standard #4:**

Understanding the visual arts in relation to history and cultures

Every lesson in *Art Connections* has a specific objective related to the understanding of art history and culture. These objectives are met as students analyze and interpret exemplary artwork and develop their own artwork.

**Content Standard #5:**

Reflecting upon and assessing the characteristics and merits of one's own work and the work of others

The four steps of art criticism are explored in every lesson throughout the program as students analyze their own artwork and the work of others.

**Content Standard #6:**

Making connections between visual arts and other disciplines

Theatre, Dance, and Music are integrated into every unit of *Art Connections*. The elements and principles of visual art are translated into Dance, Theater, and Music through the Artsource® lessons and experiences. In addition, *Theatre Arts Connections* lessons and Music connections throughout the program develop a comprehensive understanding of the connections between visual arts and the performing arts.

Cross-curricular connections are built into every lesson through teaching strategies and ideas that integrate language arts and reading, math, science, and social studies concepts. Art Projects for each of the different subject areas are also included in the program.

# Let the experts bring the best practices to your classroom.

**Rosalind Ragans**, Ph.D., Senior Author

Artist, Associate Professor Emerita

Georgia Southern University

## Authors

**Willis "Bing" Davis**

Artist, Art Consultant

Associate Professor Emeritus,

Central State University, Ohio

**Tina Farrell**

Assisstant Superintendant, Curriculum and Instruction

Clear Creek Independent School District, Texas

**Jane Rhoades Hudak,** Ph.D.

Professor of Art

Georgia Southern University

**Gloria McCoy**

Former President, Texas Art Education Association

K–12 Art Director

Spring Branch Independent School District, Texas

**Bunyan Morris**

Art Teacher

Effingham County School System

Springfield, Georgia

**Nan Yoshida**

Art Education Consultant

Los Angeles, California

## Contributors

**Jackie Ellet**

Elementary Art Teacher

Duncan Creek Elementary School

Georgia

**Artsource® Music, Dance, and Theatre Lessons**

Education Division

The Music Center of Los Angeles County

**National Museum of Women in the Arts Collection**

National Museum of Women in the Arts

Washington, D.C.

xiv

# Your Fine-Arts Partner for K–12 Art, Theatre, Dance and Music

**McGraw-Hill offers textbook programs to build, support, and extend an enriching fine-arts curriculum from kindergarten through high school.**

**Senior Author
Rosalind Ragans**

## Start with Art  SRA

SRA/McGraw-Hill presents *Art Connections* for Grades K–6. *Art Connections* builds the foundations of the elements and principles of art across the grade levels as the program integrates art history and culture, aesthetic perception, creative expression in art production, and art criticism into every lesson.

*Art Connections* also develops strong cross-curricular connections and integrates the arts with literature, *Theatre Arts Connections* lessons, *Artsource*® experiences, and integrated music selections from Macmillan/McGraw-Hill's *Spotlight on Music*.

**Author
Rosalind Ragans
and Gene Mittler**

## Integrate with Art  Glencoe

Glencoe/McGraw-Hill offers comprehensive middle and high school art programs that encourage students to make art a part of their lifelong learning. All Glencoe art programs interweave the elements and principles of art to help students build perceptual skills, promote creative expression, explore historical and cultural heritage, and evaluate artwork.

- Introduce students to the many themes artists express.
- Explore the media, techniques, and processes of art.
- Understand the historical and cultural contexts of art.

**Author
Rosalind Ragans**

*ArtTalk* offers high school students opportunities to perceive, create, appreciate, and evaluate art as it develops the elements and principles of art.

## Motivate with Music  Macmillan McGraw-Hill

Macmillan/McGraw-Hill's *Spotlight on Music* offers an exiting and comprehensive exposure to music foundations and appreciation.

## Sing with Style Glencoe

Glencoe/McGraw-Hill introduces *Experiencing Choral Music* for Grades 6–12. This multilevel choral music program includes instruction in the basic skills of vocal production and music literacy, and provides expertly recorded music selections in many different styles and from various periods of history.

# Getting Started
# The very basics...

**Here are some tips for Getting Started with Art Connections.**

## Before School Begins

1. Explore the components you have (student materials, **Overhead Transparencies**, **Large Prints**, and so on). Consider uses and alternative uses for each of the components.

2. Plan your year.
   - Consider how often you meet with students.
   - Decide how many lessons you can present.
   - Examine your curriculum requirements.
   - Select the lessons that best meet your curriculum requirements.

3. Organize art materials.
   - Identify the *Creative Expression* activities you will have students develop.
   - Determine how you will budget materials to last the entire year.
   - Compile a list of materials and order them.
   - Arrange classroom space to store materials.

4. Arrange classroom space to create and store student artwork.

## The First Day of School

1. Give an overview of your expectations, objectives, and what you want students to accomplish.

2. Introduce the artroom to students. Show them where things are kept.

3. Establish and communicate:
   - rules for behavior.
   - rules for handling art materials.
   - rules for cleaning up.

4. Begin the ***Art Connections*** introductory lessons, including *What Is Art?*, *About Art Criticism*, *About Aesthetic Perception*, and *About Art History and Culture*.

## Planning a Lesson

1. Review the lesson in the *Teacher's Edition*, including lesson objectives, in-text questions, *Practice*, and *Creative Expression* activities.

2. Assemble program components, such as **Transparencies, Large Prints,** and the **Big Book**.

3. Make any copies of activities or assessments that will be needed for the lesson.

4. Assemble art materials.

5. Determine how you will assess the lesson.

# TEACHER'S EDITION

**SRA**

# ART
## Connections

## Level 4

### Authors

Rosalind Ragans, Ph.D., Senior Author

Willis "Bing" Davis     Jane Rhoades Hudak, Ph.D.     Bunyan Morris
Tina Farrell           Gloria McCoy           Nan Yoshida

### Contributing Author

Jackie Ellett

ART
S O U
RC
ARTSOURCE

Education Division
The Music Center of Los Angeles County

**SRA**

*Columbus, OH*

*The McGraw·Hill Companies*

# Authors

**Senior Author**
Dr. Rosalind Ragans, Ph.D.
Associate Professor Emerita
Georgia Southern University

Willis "Bing" Davis
Associate Professor Emeritus
Central State University - Ohio
President & Founder of SHANGO:
The Center for the Study of
African American
Art & Culture

Tina Farrell
Assistant Superintendent,
Curriculum and Instruction
Clear Creek Independent School
District,
League City, Texas

Jane Rhoades Hudak, Ph.D.
Professor of Art
Georgia Southern University

Gloria McCoy
Former President,
Texas Art Education Association
Spring Branch Independent
School District, Texas

Bunyan Morris
Art Teacher
Effingham County School System,
Springfield, Georgia

Nan Yoshida
Art Education Consultant
Retired Art Supervisor,
Los Angeles Unified School
District
Los Angeles, California

**Photo Credit** **Cover,** Georgia O'Keeffe, *Blue and Green Music.* Alfred Stieglitz Collection, gift of Georgia O'Keeffe, 1969.835. Image ©The Art Institute of Chicago. ©2004 The Georgia O'Keeffe Foundation/Artist Rights Society (ARS), New York.

**SRAonline.com**

Send all inquiries to:
SRA/McGraw-Hill
8787 Orion Place
Columbus, OH  43240-4027

Printed in the United States of America.

ISBN  0-07-600394-9

3 4 5 6 7 8 9 BCM 10 09 08 07 06

The **McGraw·Hill** Companies

# Contributors

**Contributing Author**
Jackie Ellett, Ed.S
Elementary Art Teacher
Duncan Creek Elementary School
Hoschton, Georgia

**Contributing Writer**
Lynda Kerr, NBCT
Ed. D. Candidate, Art Teacher
Henry County, Georgia

 **Artsource® Music, Dance, Theatre Lessons**
Mark Slavkin, Vice President for Education
The Music Center of Los Angeles County
Michael Solomon, Managing Director
Music Center Education Division
Melinda Williams, Concept Originator and Project Director
Susan Cambigue-Tracey, Project Coordinator and Writer
Madeleine Dahm, Movement and Dance Connection Writer
Keith Wyffels, Staff Assistance
Maureen Erbe, Logo Design

**Music Connections**
Kathy Mitchell
Music Teacher
Eagan, Minnesota

**More about Aesthetics**
Richard W. Burrows, Executive Director
Institute for Arts Education
San Diego, California

**Art History**
Gene A. Mittler, Ph.D.
Professor Emeritus
Texas Tech University

**Resources for Students with Disabilities**
Mandy Yeager
Ph.D. Candidate
The University of North Texas
Denton, Texas

**Brain-Based Learning in the Arts**
Jamye Ivey
K-12 Art Supervisor
Dougherty County School System, Georgia

**Safe Use of Art Materials**
Mary Ann Boykin

Director, The Art School for Children and Young Adults
University of Houston–Clear Lake
Houston, Texas

**Integrating the Four Art Forms**
Susan Cambigue-Tracey
The Music Center of Los Angeles County

**Using Writing to Enhance Your Art Curriculum**
Mary Lazzari, EdS
Elementary Art Teacher
Clarke County School District
Athens, Georgia

**Museum Education**
Marilyn J. S. Goodman
Director of Education
Solomon R. Guggenheim Museum
New York, New York

**Displaying Student Artwork**
Jackie Ellett
Duncan Creek Elementary School
Hoschton, Georgia

## Student Activities

Cassie Appleby
Glen Oaks Elementary School
McKinney, Texas

Maureen Banks
Kester Magnet School
Van Nuys, California

Christina Barnes
Webb Bridge Middle School
Alpharetta, Georgia

Beth Benning
Willis Jepson Middle School
Vacaville, California

Chad Buice
Craig Elementary School
Snellville, Georgia

Beverly Broughton
Gwinn Oaks Elementary School
Snellville, Georgia

Missy Burgess
Jefferson Elementary School
Jefferson, Georgia

Marcy Cincotta-Smith
Benefield Elementary School
Lawrenceville, Georgia

Joanne Cox
Kittredge Magnet School
Atlanta, Georgia

Carolyn Y. Craine
McCracken County Schools
Paducah, Kentucky

Jackie Ellett
Duncan Creek Elementary School
Hoschton, Georgia

Tracie Flynn
Home School
Rushville, Indiana

Phyllis Glenn
Malcom Bridge Elementary
Bogart, Georgia

Dallas Gillespie
Dacula Middle School
Dacula, Georgia

Dr. Donald Gruber
Clinton Junior High School
Clinton, Illinois

Karen Heid
Rock Springs Elementary School
Lawrenceville, Georgia

Alisa Hyde
Southwest Elementary
Savannah, Georgia

Kie Johnson
Oconee Primary School
Watkinsville, Georgia

Sallie Keith, NBCT
West Side Magnet School
LaGrange, Georgia

Letha Kelly
Grayson Elementary School
Grayson, Georgia

Diana Kimura
Amestoy Elementary School
Gardena, California

Desiree LaOrange
Barkley Elementary School
Fort Campbell, Kentucky

Deborah Lackey-Wilson
Roswell North Elementary
Roswell, Georgia

Dawn Laird
Goforth Elementary School
Clear Creek, Texas

Mary Lazzari
Timothy Road Elementary School
Athens, Georgia

Michelle Leonard
Webb Bridge Middle School
Alpharetta, Georgia

Lynn Ludlam
Spring Branch ISD
Houston, Texas

Mark Mitchell
Fort Daniel Elementary School
Dacula, Georgia

Martha Moore
Freeman's Mill Elementary School
Dacula, Georgia

Connie Niedenthal
Rushville Elementary
Rushville, Indiana

Barbara Patisaul
Oconee County Elementary School
Watkinsville, Georgia

Elizabeth Paulos-Krasle
Social Circle Elementary
Social Circle, Georgia

Jane Pinneau
Rocky Branch Elementary School
Watkinsville, Georgia

Marilyn Polin
Cutler Ridge Middle School
Miami, Florida

Michael Ramsey
Graves County Schools
Mayfield, Kentucky

Rosemarie Sells
Social Circle Elementary
Social Circle, Georgia

Jean Neelen-Siegel
Baldwin School
Alhambra, California

Debra Smith
McIntosh County School System
Darien, Georgia

Patricia Spencer
Harmony Elementary School
Buford, Georgia

Melanie Stokes
Smiley Elementary School
Ludowici, Georgia

Rosanne Stutts
Davidson Fine Arts School
Augusta, Georgia

Fran Sullivan
South Jackson Elementary School
Athens, Georgia

Kathy Valentine
Home School
Burkburnett, Texas

Debi West
Rock Springs Elementary School
Lawrenceville, Georgia

Sherry White
Bauerschlag Elementary School
League City, Texas

Patricia Wiesen
Cutler Ridge Middle School
Miami, Florida

Deayna Woodruff
Loveland Middle School
Loveland, Ohio

Gil Young
El Rodeo School
Beverly Hills, California

Larry A. Young
Dacula Elementary School
Dacula, Georgia

# Table of Contents

◀ **Natalia Goncharova.**
*Maquillage.*

# Unit 1 Line

➍ **indicates Core Lessons**

**5**

---

**Reading Comprehension Skills and Strategies**

❶ Vocabulary, Using Literature, Comparing and Contrasting

❷ Vocabulary, Using Literature, Purpose

❸ Vocabulary, Using Literature, Point of View

❹ Vocabulary, Using Literature, Asking Questions

❺ Vocabulary, Using Literature, Fact and Opinion

❻ Vocabulary, Using Literature, Summarizing

▲ **Stuart Davis.**
*Composition.*

# Unit 2 Shape, Pattern, Rhythm, and Movement

•❖ **Indicates Core Lessons**

**Reading Comprehension Skills and Strategies**
❶ Vocabulary, Using Literature, Purpose
❷ Vocabulary, Using Literature, Comparing and Contrasting
❸ Vocabulary, Using Literature
❹ Vocabulary, Using Literature, Summarizing
❺ Vocabulary, Using Literature, Fact and Opinion
❻ Vocabulary, Using Literature, Making Inferences

◀ **Miriam Schapiro.**
*Pas de Deux.*

# Unit 3 Color and Value

◗ indicates Core Lessons                                                      **7**

---

**Reading Comprehension Skills and Strategies**
❶ Vocabulary, Using Literature, Main Idea and Details
❷ Vocabulary, Using Literature, Fact and Opinion
❸ Vocabulary, Using Literature
❹ Vocabulary, Using Literature, Comparing and Contrasting
❺ Vocabulary, Using Literature, Cause and Effect
❻ Vocabulary, Using Literature, Thematic Connection: Imagination

◀ **Michelangelo.**
*Pietà.*

# Unit 4 Form, Texture, and Emphasis

**8**

➥ indicates Core Lessons

**Reading Comprehension Skills and Strategies**

❶ Vocabulary, Using Literature
❷ Vocabulary, Using Literature

❸ Vocabulary, Using Literature
❹ Vocabulary, Using Literature, Comparing and Contrasting

❺ Vocabulary, Using Literature, Fact and Opinion
❻ Vocabulary, Using Literature, Summarizing

▲ **John Singelton Copley.**
*Sir William Pepperrell and His Family.*

# Unit 5 Space, Proportion, and Distortion

•◆ indicates Core Lessons

**9**

Reading Comprehension Skills and Strategies
❶ Vocabulary, Using Literature
❷ Vocabulary, Using Literature
❸ Vocabulary, Using Literature
❹ Vocabulary, Using Literature
❺ Vocabulary, Using Literature, Mood
❻ Vocabulary, Using Literature

9

▲ **Judith Leyster.**
*The Concert.*

# Unit 6 Balance, Harmony, Variety, and Unity

**10**

➥ indicates Core Lessons

Reading Comprehension Skills and Strategies
① Vocabulary, Using Literature, Summarizing
② Vocabulary, Using Literature, Comparing and Contrasting
③ Vocabulary, Using Literature
④ Vocabulary, Using Literature
⑤ Vocabulary, Using Literature
⑥ Vocabulary, Using Literature

# Technique Tips

# Activity Tips

# Overview

The purpose of these pages is to open students' minds to the idea that visual arts include many components and take many forms. The arts satisfy the human need for display, celebration, personal expression, and communication. We use the visual arts to enhance our innermost feelings and to communicate ideas. Art is made by people. Even people who are not professional artists can enjoy the creative process.

## Activating Prior Knowledge

- Ask students what they think art is. Encourage creative, divergent thinking. In visual art, there are many answers to a question.

## Questions to Discuss

- Have students look at the images on pages 12 and 13 and name the things that are visual art. Then ask the following questions.

  ▶ Which of these things could you hold in your hands?

  ▶ Which one could you walk inside?

  ▶ Which ones would you hang on a wall?

  ▶ Which ones could you wear?

- Encourage students to think about things they have at home that fit the categories on these pages. The building they live in is architecture. They have dishes and other containers. Many of them have things hanging on the walls to enhance their visual environments. A few may have sculpture in the home. Many will have seen sculptures in and around public buildings.

---

## What Is Art?

## Art is . . .

**Painting** is color applied to a flat surface.

▲ **Vincent Van Gogh.** (French). *Houses at Auvers.* 1890.

Oil on canvas. 29¾ × 24⅜ inches (75.56 × 61.93 cm.). Museum of Fine Arts, Boston, Massachusetts.

**Drawing** is the process of making art with lines.

▲ **Pablo Picasso.** (Spanish). *Portrait of Dora Maar.* 1938.

Pencil on paper mounted on fiberboard. 30 9/16 × 22 7/16 inches (77.62 × 57 cm.). Hirshhorn Museum and Sculpture Garden, Smithsonian Institution, Washington, D.C.

**Sculpture** is art that fills up space.

▲ **David Bates.** (American). *Seated Man #4.* 1995.

Painted wood. 88 × 37½ × 45½ inches (223.52 × 95.25 × 115.57 cm.). Dallas Museum of Art, Dallas, Texas.

**Architecture** is the art of designing and constructing buildings.

▲ **Jørn Oberg Utzon.** (Danish). *Opera House.* 1957–1973.

Sydney, Australia.

## Printmaking is the process of transferring an original image from one prepared surface to another.

▲ **Katsushika Hokusai.** (Japanese.) *Winter Loneliness,* from *One Hundred Poems Explained by the Nurse.* 1839.

Woodcut. 10⅛ × 14½ inches (25.5 × 36.8 cm.). Honolulu Academy of Art, Honolulu, Hawaii

## Photography is the act of capturing an image on film.

◀ **Eliot Elisofon.** (American). *Asante Paramount Chief Nana Akyanfuo Akowuah Dateh II, Akwamuhene of Kumase.* 1970.

Photograph. National Museum of African Art, Smithsonian Institution, Washington, D.C.

## Ceramics is the art of making objects with clay.

▲ **Artist Unknown.** (Kongo peoples, Congo and Democratic Republic of Congo.) **Bowl.** Late-nineteenth to early-twentieth century.

Ceramic and resin. 5⅞ × 4⅛ × 5⅞ inches (14.9 × 10.49 × 14.94 cm.). National Museum of African Art, Smithsonian Institution, Washington, D.C.

## A mask is a covering for the face to be used in ceremonies and other events.

▲ **Charlie James.** (Southern Kwakiutl.) *Sun Tranformation Mask.* Early nineteenth century.

Royal British Columbia Museum, British Columbia, Canada.

# Art is created by people

▶ to communicate ideas.

▶ to express feelings.

▶ to give us well-designed objects.

What Is Art? **13**

## Using the Credit Line

The credit line is a list of important facts about the work of art that appears below or next to the work. For example, you can help students understand the size of an artwork and how it relates to their own size. Most credit lines contain the following information.

- Name of the artist.
- Title of the work. This always appears in italics. If the word *detail* follows the title, it means that the image is part of a larger work of art.
- Year the work was created. A *c* before the date indicates that the piece was made around the year given.
- Medium used by the artist.
- Size of the work. The first number is the height, the second is the width, and a third number indicates depth for three-dimensional works.
- Location of the work. This tells the museum, gallery, or collection in which the work is housed.

## Art Studios, Galleries, and Museums

Works of art are created in ***studios.*** A studio is an artist's workplace, much like a classroom is a studio for students. Almost everything an artist needs to create an artwork will be found in his or her studio. It is possible for people to visit artist studios, but an invitation from the artist is usually required.

***Art galleries*** are private businesses where art dealers display and sell works of art. Art galleries are typically open to the public, and the works of art may be viewed even if the patrons do not intend to buy anything.

A ***museum*** is a public or private building where valuable and important artwork is cared for and displayed for the public to view. *Curators* are people who supervise the museum and organize exhibitions. *Docents* are special tour directors who help explain the art to visitors.

# Overview

These pages introduce students to the three components that define a work of art: the subject, the composition, and the content.

## Subject

The subject is the image that the viewer can easily identify in a work of art. The subject may be one person or many people. It may be a thing. It can be an event, such as a party. In recent years, some artists have chosen to create nonobjective art. This is art that has no recognizable subject matter. In this type of art, the elements of art become the subject.

## Composition

The composition is the way the principles of art are used to organize the elements of art. Notice how Benny Andrews uses color and shape to portray the image of a family dinner.

## Content

The content is the message the work communicates to the viewer. The message may be an idea, such as family unity, or an emotion or feeling, such as joy or loneliness. If the work of art is functional, such as *Habitat,* then the function is the meaning. Does the work of art look like it could perform the function it is supposed to?

# What Is Art?

Every work of art has three parts.

## Subject

The objects you can recognize are the subject matter of a work of art. When a work has no recognizable objects, the elements of art such as lines, shapes, colors, and so on become the subject of the work.

## Composition

The composition of the work is the way the artist has used the principles to organize the elements of art.

## Content

The content is the message the artwork communicates. Content is the meaning of the work. If the work is functional, such as a chair or clothing, then the content is the function of the object.

- ▶ In which work of art do you think the subject matter is very important?
- ▶ In which artwork do you think composition is most important?
- ▶ Which work seems to have the strongest message? Explain.
- ▶ Which artwork's meaning relates to its function?

▲ **Benny Andrews.** (American).
*Grandmother's Dinner.* 1992.

Oil on canvas. 72 × 52 inches (182.88 × 132.08 cm.).
Ogden Museum of Southern Art, New Orleans, Louisiana.

▲ **William Sharp.** (English/American). *Great
Water Lily of America.* 1854.

Chromolithograph on woven white paper. 21¼ × 27 inches
(53.98 × 68.58 cm.). Amon Carter Museum, Fort Worth, Texas.

▲ **Artist Unknown.** (Maya/Huipil). *Huipil Weaving.*
c. 1950.

Backstrap woven plain weave with supplementary-weft pattern, silk on
cotton. 50 × 14½ inches (127 × 36.83 cm.). Museum of International
Folk Art, Santa Fe, New Mexico.

▲ **Mosche Safdie.** (Israeli). *Habitat.* 1967.

Concrete. Montreal, Canada.

What Is Art?    **15**

## Activating Prior Knowledge

- Ask students to say the first thing they
look for when they look at a work of art.
Students may say they look at color, size,
or what the work is about. Some may say
they look for the feeling or message they
get from the artwork. Give students time
to explore this question. It will provide a
good context for the discussion on these
pages.

## Questions to Discuss

- Read with students the text on page 14
and look at the images on page 15. Share
with them some of the information above.
Encourage students to think about their
responses during the Activating Prior
Knowledge discussion as they look at
these images and think about the
information you have shared with them.

▶ Read the questions on page 14 and discuss
the answers. The subject matter is
important in *Grandmother's Dinner* and
*Great Water Lily of America.* Composition
is important in *Huipil Weaving. Huipil
Weaving* and *Habitat* are works in which
the meaning relates to function. Most
students will think that *Grandmother's
Dinner* has the strongest message.
However, it is important to point out that
the function of a work is an important
message *(Huipil Weaving* and *Habitat).*

# Overview

In art, subject means something an artist has depicted or represented in an artwork. For example, the subject matter of Paul Cézanne's painting of fruit is called a still life. Some subject matter, like the objects in Cézanne's still life, is easy to identify. Others are more difficult because the artwork may be symbolic or nonobjective. Artists create works of art on a variety of subjects: the natural world, literature, religion, the constructed world, history, and so on. These pages deal with several of the most common subject-matter topics—people, objects, everyday life, stories, things outside, colors and shapes, and things that have a deeper meaning.

Talk with students about each subject-matter topic description below. Encourage them to look for examples of different subject matter in the lessons. By helping them to look at each subject in greater detail and by asking thoughtful questions, your students will begin to develop an understanding for differences among subject matter in art.

## Still Life

Artists create works of art that show a variety of objects. Traditional still lifes are bowls, vases, bottles, pitchers, fruit, flowers, food on a table, and/or musical instruments (among other things) that are artfully arranged.

▶ **Question:** What are the objects in this still life?

# Subject Matter

Artists make art about many subjects. *Subject matter* is the content of an artist's work. For example, the subject of a painting can be a vase of flowers or a self-portrait. This subject matter is easy to see. The subject matter is harder to understand when the artwork stands for something beyond itself. Look at the artwork on these pages. Notice the different kinds of subject matter.

## Still Life

▲ **Paul Cézanne.** (French). *Still Life with Basket of Apples.* 1895.
Oil on canvas. 23⅗ × 31½ inches (60 × 80 cm.). The Art Institute of Chicago, Chicago, Illinois.

## Landscape

▲ **Z. Vanessa Helder.** (American). *Rocks and Concrete.* c. 1940.

Watercolor on paper. 19 × 15⅞ inches (48.26 × 40.34 cm.). Cheney Cowles Museum, Spokane, Washington.

## Landscape

This area includes the natural world—plants, animals, or other things outside. The suffix *-scape* means "a view of." For example, a *cityscape* is buildings and city life seen in an artwork. A *seascape* is a scene of the sea.

▶ **Question:** What objects do you see in this landscape?

## Genre

In art, the term *genre* is used to indicate subjects that have to do with ordinary people engaged in everyday activities.

▶ **Question:** What everyday activities is this boy doing?

▲ **Winslow Homer.** (American.) *Nooning.* c. 1872.
Oil on canvas. $13\frac{5}{16} \times 19\frac{5}{8}$ inches (33.02 × 48.26 cm.). Wadsworth Atheneum, Hartford, Connecticut.

## Nonobjective

◄ **Natalya Goncharova.** (Russian). *Maquillage.* 1913.
Gouache on paper. $4\frac{3}{8} \times 6\frac{3}{8}$ inches (11.13 × 16.21 cm.). Dallas Museum of Art, Dallas, Texas.

## Portrait

◄ **Elizabeth Catlett.** (American). *Sharecropper.* 1970.
Color linocut. 26 × 22 inches (66.04 × 55.88 cm.). Smithsonian American Art Museum, Washington, D.C.

What Is Art?     **19**

## Nonobjective

Sometimes artwork is nonobjective. It does not have an identifiable subject matter—no familiar subjects are shown. People respond to the way the artwork has been organized and designed. Nonobjective art focuses specifically on the elements and principles of art: line, shape, color, and so on.

▶ **Question:** The artwork does not use a subject we can identify. What are some of the lines, shapes, and colors you see in this picture?

## Portrait

This category includes portraits, self-portraits, and group portraits. Portraits are one of the oldest subjects in art history. Artists try to present both an accurate depiction and also other aspects of a person's character in a portrait.

▶ **Question:** What do you think the artist is telling us about this person?

## Stories

A story is an account of some incident from a real person's life, a historic event, or from a myth, legend, or other piece of symbolic literature.

▶ **Question:** What story do you think is being told in this artwork?

# What Is Art?

## Allegory

▲ **Jan van Eyck.** (Flemish.) *Portrait of Giovanni Arnolfini and His wife Giovanna Cenami.* 1434.
Oil on wood panel. 32 x 23 inches. The National Gallery, London, England.

**20** What Is Art?

**20** What Is Art?

# Symbolism

▲ **Artist Unknown.** (Huichol People/Mexico). *Mother of the Eagles.* 1991.
Braided yarn embedded in vegetable wax on wood. $15\frac{3}{4} \times 19\frac{1}{2}$ inches (40 × 49.53 cm.). Private collection.

## Symbols

Sometimes works of art contain symbols—visual signs of something invisible. For example, a dove can be a symbol of peace, or an hourglass may represent the passing of time. Symbols represent a broader idea or sometimes have a secret meaning.

▶ **Question:** What symbols do you see in this work? What do you think they mean?

# Overview

Each language has its own system of words and rules of grammar. To learn a new language, you need to learn new words and a new set of rules for putting the words together. The language of visual art also has its own system. The words of the language are the **elements** of art. They are the basic visual symbols in the language of art. Just as there are basic kinds of words such as nouns, verbs, adjectives, and adverbs, there are basic kinds of art elements. These are line, shape, color, value, space, form, and texture. These elements are the visual building blocks that the artist puts together to create a work of art. No matter what materials are used, the artwork will contain all of the visual elements. Sometimes one element will be more important than the others.

Visual images are organized according to rules. In language, these are the rules of grammar. In visual art, the rules for organizing the elements of art are called the **principles** of art. These principles include pattern, rhythm, balance, emphasis, harmony, variety, and unity.

## Activating Prior Knowledge

- Ask students what they think of when they hear each of the following words: *line, shape, color.* Encourage them to look around the classroom for examples.

## Questions to Discuss

- Have students examine the images on pages 22 and 23. Ask them what they can tell about each photo. What stands out in each image? How does each image help explain the element or principle?

# Elements of Art

Art is a language. The words of the language are the elements of art.

Line

Shape

Form

Space

Color

Value

Texture

# Principles of Art

Artists organize their artwork using the principles of art.

Pattern

Rhythm

Balance

Emphasis

Harmony

Variety

Unity

## The Language of Art

The elements and principles of art are the concepts or ideas that artists use to organize their artwork. Artists use a variety of media and materials to make art. *Media* are types of art such as photography, watercolor, and so on. *Materials* are the things used to make the art, such as markers, paint, paper, clay, fabric, wood, metal, or glass.

There are specific techniques and processes that artists use to manipulate the materials. For example, the proper way to hold a brush to create a thin line with watercolor paint is a specific technique unique to watercolor painting. The process of creating a finished watercolor painting consists of many interwoven steps, such as thinking about what to paint, sketching several ideas, deciding which elements and principles will enhance the work, choosing the best sketch, deciding which watercolor techniques to use, and finally, producing the finished work.

Special techniques and procedures are used with each material. You will need to learn different techniques and follow different procedures for modeling clay than you will for creating paper sculpture. Drawing with crayons requires different techniques and procedures from drawing with oil pastels or chalk. Using the computer to make original art requires that you learn how to use specific computer hardware and software.

# Overview

Art history is the record of art from the past to the present. By looking at art from the past, we learn what the people who lived before us were like—their feelings and beliefs, clothes, food, houses, and how they viewed the world around them.

## Questions to Discuss:

### Knowledge
▶ Who created the artwork?

▶ When was the artwork created?

▶ What is the artwork's title?

▶ Have you ever seen an artwork like this? Where?

### Comprehension
▶ Is this artwork useful? How is it used?

▶ Compare this artwork with another work from a similar time period. How are the works alike and different?

▶ What interests you most about this artwork?

▶ What is the major theme of this artwork?

### Application
▶ What types of materials were used to create this artwork?

▶ Demonstrate how the artwork was created.

▶ Explain how this artwork could have a different use today.

### Analysis
▶ What are the main elements in this artwork?

▶ Compare this painting with another painting in this book. How are they alike? How are they different?

▶ What does this artwork mean?

## About Art

▲ **Frida Kahlo.** (Mexican). *Frida y Diego Rivera.* 1931.
Oil on canvas. 39⅜ × 31 inches (100.01 × 78.74 cm.). San Francisco Museum of Modern Art, San Francisco, California.

**Art History and Culture**

## Look at the artwork.
▶ What people or objects do you see?

▶ Do they look like people and objects you see around you today? Explain.

## Look at the caption.
▶ When was the artwork created?

▶ What can you learn about the artist?

## Learn more.
▶ Do some research to find out more about the artist, the art-work, and the time period.

### Synthesis
▶ How many titles can you create for this artwork? Name them.

▶ Name a person you would like to give this artwork to as a gift. Why?

▶ Imagine that two people in this room are having a conversation. What would they say to each other? Why?

### Evaluation
▶ Do you think this artwork is interesting? Why?

▶ Summarize this artwork's unique qualities.

## What to Do
▪ Have students research to find out information about the life and times of Frida Kahlo. Students may write a biography of the artist or dress up as the artist and tell the artist's story to classmates.

▪ Have students research Kahlo and another artist who lived at the same time. Students should research information about the media, styles, techniques, and procedures the artists used. Have pairs of students role-play a discussion between the two artists about media, style, and personal beliefs about art.

▪ Have students work in groups to act out this painting. They should write a script for what happened before, during, and after the moment shown in the painting.

# Overview

 **Aesthetic Perception**

Aesthetic perception encourages students to make choices rather than give "correct answers." By understanding the process of aesthetic perception, students can see something from a new perspective and ultimately realize that art is all around them.

Journal writing is an integral part of aesthetic perception. It is an ongoing record of what a student does, notices, and thinks. Journals track the evolution of thoughts and experiences over time. Through this recorded journey, the student has the ability to reflect on where one has been and where one is going. Writing thoughts, reactions, perceptions, new information, and questions intensifies each student's life experiences.

## Guidelines for Aesthetic Perception

Students like to know what is important about a work of art and what was important to the artist. They are fascinated with information, questions, and descriptions. There are some guiding principles in the development of aesthetic perception at this level that can profoundly influence teaching practice.

1. All aesthetic perception actively involves the learner.

2. All aesthetic perception involves reflection.

3. The works of art have substance. Their tools and a working vocabulary are vital to empower the learner.

4. Aesthetic perception is a process based upon examination of the artist's choices and the choices in response made by the viewer.

5. All responses are valid. Right and wrong are irrelevant issues when viewing works of art.

6. All works of art relate to each other, and each relates to all other areas of life.

## About Art

▲ **Frida Kahlo.** (Mexican). *Frida y Diego Rivera.* 1931.
Oil on canvas. 39⅜ × 31 inches (100.01 × 78.74 cm.). San Francisco Museum of Modern Art, San Francisco, California.

## Look

▶ Look at the work of art. What sounds, smells, or feelings are in this work of art?

▶ What happened just before and just after in this work of art?

▶ What kind of music would be playing in this work of art?

## Look Inside

▶ Imagine you are one of these people. Who are you? What are you thinking? How do you feel?

▶ If you could add yourself to the painting, what would you look like? What would you be doing?

▶ Act out or tell the story in this work of art with a beginning, a middle, and an end.

▶ Draw what you can't see in this work of art. Are there hidden images that should be revealed?

## Look Outside

▶ How is this like or different from your own world?

▶ What does the artist want you to know or think about in this work of art?

▶ Describe your journey in viewing this work of art. Include your thoughts, ideas, and changes in thinking.

▶ What will you remember about this work?

## Questions to Discuss

▶ What is happening in this work of art?

▶ What is this work of art about?

▶ What is your favorite part of this work of art?

▶ What is most important in this artwork?

▶ What happened just before and just after in this work of art?

▶ If you were in this work of art, what would you be doing?

▶ What have you learned about the work of art?

▶ What does the artist want you to know or think about in this work of art?

▶ How do you feel about the work of art? What does it make you feel?

▶ What will you remember about this work of art?

▶ Has this work of art changed your thinking?

## Things to Do

▪ Draw yourself into the work of art.

▪ Draw what you can't see in the work of art.

▪ Act out or show the story in the work of art.

▪ Collect objects that are similar to the objects in the work of art and make aesthetic judgments about them.

▪ Role-play an interview with the artist about how the work of art was made.

# Overview

Art criticism is an organized system for looking at and talking about art. The purpose of art criticism is to get the viewer involved in a perception process that delays judgment until all aspects of the image have been studied. Learning art criticism also gives each viewer the confidence to discuss a work of art without worrying what other people might think.

**Describe** **What do I see?**

During this step, the viewer lists all the obvious things in the artwork. Objectivity is important.

## Questions to Discuss

▶ List and describe everything you see in the artwork. Answers may include: We see the full figures of a man and a woman standing on a plain, brown floor. Above Frida's head flies a tan dove with blue-tipped wings. Frida looks tiny. She is wearing a floor-length, ruffled, dark blue-green skirt and a red scarf that is trimmed with diamond shapes and fringe. Diego is wearing a plain, dark blue suit (and so on).

**Analyze** **How is the work organized?**

During this step the viewer examines how the elements and principles of art are used in the artwork.

## Questions to Discuss

▶ Describe the elements of art that you see. Answers may include: **Line**—There are horizontal lines where the floor meets the wall, on the wall, and in the rug. **Shape**—The tabletops, bookcase, lamp, doilies, and picture frames are geometric. The chairs, vase, flowers, leaves, and pitchers are free-form shapes (and so on).

▶ How has the artist used the principles of design? Answers may include: **Balance**—Informal balance; the large, plain shape of Diego is balanced by the small, busy shape and bright color of Frida. **Emphasis**—The bright red scarf leads our eyes to the clasped hands (and so on).

## About Art

▲ **Frida Kahlo.** (Mexican). *Frida y Diego Rivera.* 1931.
Oil on canvas. 39⅜ × 31 inches (100.01 × 78.74 cm.). San Francisco Museum of Modern Art, San Francisco, California.

 **Art Criticism**

## Describe

▶ List everything you see in this painting. Be sure to describe the people and their clothing.

## Analyze

▶ How has the artist used line, shape, color, value, space, and texture?

▶ What kind of balance has the artist used?

▶ Has the artist used emphasis to make us notice one thing more than others?

## Interpret

▶ What is happening?

▶ What is the artist telling us about these two people?

## Decide

▶ Have you ever seen another artwork like this?

▶ Is it successful because it is realistic?

▶ Is it successful because it is well-organized?

▶ Is it successful because you have strong feelings when you study it?

## More About Aesthetic Judging

You can use art criticism to make aesthetic judgments about functional objects such as cars or shoes. Follow the first two steps (**Describe** and **Analyze**) as described. During **Interpret,** consider the purpose of the object as its meaning. (Does a pitcher look like it will pour liquid without spilling?) As you **Decide,** consider whether the object works when it is used. (If a chair is not comfortable to sit in, it is not functioning properly and is not successful as a chair.)

## Interpret — What is the artist saying to me?

During interpretation, viewers will make inferences about the message in the work of art. Each interpretation can be different because each is based upon the feelings and life experiences of the viewer.

### Questions to Discuss

▶ What do I think about this work?

▶ What is the artist trying to tell us about these people and their lives? The clasped hands of these two people represent the link between them. They are married, and this is their wedding portrait. She leans toward him, but he turns away from her to the outside world. She shows her need for him; he shows his independence.

## Decide

This is when the viewer decides whether or not the work is successful. There are two levels of judgment to be made. The first is personal: do you like the work?

The second level is also subjective, but it uses aesthetic theories to help the viewer decide whether the work is successful. More than one theory may be used to judge a work.

▪ Some critics think that the most important thing about a work of art is the realistic presentation of the subject matter. This aesthetic theory is called **imitationalism** or **realism.**

▪ Other critics think that composition is the most important factor in a work of art. This aesthetic theory, called **formalism** or **composition,** emphasizes the design qualities and the arrangement of the elements of art using the principles of art.

▪ Some critics claim that no object should be considered art if it fails to arouse an emotional response in the viewer. **Emotionalism** or **expressionism** is a theory concerned with the content or the meaning of the work of art.

### Questions to Discuss

▶ Have you seen any works in this book that look similar to the style of this artist?

▶ Which aesthetic theories would you use to judge the success of this work? The two people and the objects are realistic. The artist has used informal balance to organize the work, and has used the red scarf as a point of emphasis. The artist has shown the feelings of these two people.

# Overview

## Creative Expression

The creative process, like the writing process or the scientific method, is an organized approach to creative problem solving that can be used by professional artists and students alike. Throughout *Art Connections,* the Creative Expression activities are presented as problems to be solved. Remind students of the steps in the creative process as they work on the activities.

### Get an idea.

- Inspiration can come from many places. In the *Art Connections* Creative Expression activities, the idea comes from the activity instructions. Professional artists may get ideas from a client who has commissioned a piece of art from nature, from a historical event, from everyday life, or from the available media and materials.

- Try the following to help students when they have trouble getting an idea.

  1. As a class, brainstorm about where to get ideas for artwork: works by other artists, personal experiences, stories students have read, and so on.

  2. Encourage students to write ideas in the Ideas section of their Art Journals. Remind students that they can make notes for ideas anytime, not just in art class.

  3. Pair students who are having trouble thinking of ideas with students who have many ideas. One student can model getting ideas for the other student.

### Plan your work.

- Once students have an idea, they must decide the best way to execute that idea. Would a two-dimensional or three-dimensional artwork best convey the idea that students are trying to show? Should students use watercolor or pencil?

### Make a sketch.

- Just like professional writers, professional artists do not make a perfect work on the first try. They may make several sketches, evaluate those sketches, and revise them before deciding on a final vision for the artwork.

- Encourage students to make sketches in the Ideas section of their Art Journals.

## About Art

▲ **Frida Kahlo.** (Mexican). *Frida y Diego Rivera.* 1931.
Oil on canvas. 39⅜ × 31 inches (100.01 × 78.74 cm.). San Francisco Museum of Modern Art, San Francisco, California.

# How does an artist create a work of art?

Art is a process. You can follow the same steps to create your own work of art.

1. Get an idea.
   - ▶ Artists get inspiration from many places. Look around you. People, objects, and scenes may provide inspiration for a work of art.

2. Plan your work.
   - ▶ Do you want your artwork to be two-dimensional or three-dimensional?
   - ▶ Decide what media you want to use.
   - ▶ What materials will you need?

3. Make a sketch.
   - ▶ Think about how you want your artwork to look. Sketch several ideas.
   - ▶ If your artwork will be three-dimensional, sketch it from different points of view.
   - ▶ Then choose the best idea.

4. Use the media.
   - ▶ Make an artwork based on your best idea. You may want to practice using the materials first.
   - ▶ When making your composition, remember the elements and principles of art. How can you use them to make your artwork say what you want it to say?

5. Share your final work.
   - ▶ Evaluate your work using the four steps of art criticism. What do you like best about your work? What would you do differently next time?

## Use the media.

- In this stage of the creative process, students make their artwork based on their plans. Encourage students to practice using unfamiliar media, and to try new techniques on a small practice piece before using those techniques on their artwork.

- Even during this stage of the process, students may get new ideas. Encourage them to be flexible.

## Share your final work.

- Art is meant to be shared with and viewed by others. Encourage students to share their artwork with family or friends, display it in the classroom, or display it in the school display area. This is also a good time for students to self-evaluate their work using the four steps of art criticism.

## More About Art Journals

- Art Journals are a wonderful way to work through ideas. At the beginning of the school year, help students set up an Art Journal. This can be a spiral notebook or a three-ring binder with pages for writing and sketching. The Art Journal will be divided into sections for Concepts, Ideas, Critical Thinking (Art Criticism), Vocabulary.

  1. Encourage students to use the Concepts section of their journals for summarizing unit and lesson concepts, writing questions they have, and listing other things they want to learn.

  2. Students can use the Ideas section of their Art Journals for brainstorming, organizing, planning, and sketching. Remind students that they can write ideas in their journals any time; they do not need to wait until a designated time in art class.

  3. Students can use the Critical Thinking section of their journals to self-evaluate their work using the four steps of Art Criticism. In *Art Connections,* students are asked to self-evaluate after each Creative Expression activity. This can be a valuable tool to help students review art concepts and get ideas for their next work.

  4. Encourage students to use the Vocabulary section of their Art Journals to record unfamiliar words, summarize or explain definitions, and so on. Developing vocabulary is an important step in being able to think about and communicate about art.

# Overview

Elementary teachers are responsible for the safety of their students. Specific guidelines have been established by the Center for Safety in the Arts, and these guidelines should be followed to ensure that both students and teachers use art materials safely. Following are some general tips for using art materials safely. For more detailed information, see "Safe Use of Art Materials" on page T12 of this book.

## Safe Art Materials

- Use only water-soluble AP- or CP-designated markers. Never use permanent or scented markers.

- Use only dustless chalk.

- Make sure that crayons have the AP or CP label to ensure that they do not contain lead.

- When using tempera paint, use only liquid tempera, not powdered tempera. Do not use any spray paints or fixatives.

- Use only water-soluble printers' inks.

- Use pencils to carve into soft surfaces for printing blocks. Do not use mat knives or other sharp instruments.

- Do not allow young children to use sharp scissors; blunt points are safe.

- Do not use rubber cement unless it bears the AP or CP label. Do not use solvent-based glues.

## Safety

- ▶ Use art materials only on your artwork.
- ▶ Keep art materials out of your mouth, eyes and ears.
- ▶ Use scissors and other sharp tools carefully. Keep your fingers away from the cutting blades.
- ▶ Wash your hands after using the art materials.
- ▶ Wear an art shirt or smock to protect your clothes.
- ▶ Use only art materials with a "nontoxic" label.

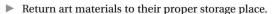

- ▶ Return art materials to their proper storage place.
- ▶ Be careful not to breathe chalk or clay dust.
- ▶ Use only new and clean foam trays.
- ▶ Do not walk around the room with sharp tools in your hand.
- ▶ Be aware of others in your work space.
- ▶ Always follow your teacher's directions when using the art materials.

## General Safety Precautions

■ Read the labels on all materials used in the art room. Look carefully for the AP/CP labels. If these are not present, be suspicious. Imported art materials should be looked upon with extreme caution. Other countries have not developed the rigid safety codes adopted by the United States.

■ Do not accept or use old art materials that may have been left in the school or donated by some well-meaning adult. If the materials do not bear the current safety codes, toss them out.

■ Never allow food or drink in the room where art activities are being conducted. Dust and even fibers float freely in the air and can readily contaminate food or drink.

■ Practice cleanliness. Have children wash their hands thoroughly with soap after using art materials.

■ Use absolutely no permanent markers or solvent-based materials in the art room. If a material stains the clothes or hands and does not clean up with simple soap and water, it is not appropriate or safe for young children to use.

■ Use plastic containers for washing paintbrushes; glass is dangerous in the hands of young children.

■ Paper cutters should not be used by elementary-school children. The paper cutter should be kept out of the students' reach, and left in a locked position always with the blade turned to the wall.

■ Do not use commercial dyes around children; use vegetable or natural dyes (flowers, teas, onion skins).

■ Do not allow children in a room where a kiln is firing; both the heat and the fumes are dangerous.

# Unit 1 Planning Guide

| | Lesson Title | Suggested Pacing | Creative Expression Activity |
|---|---|---|---|
| **Lesson 1** | **Types of Lines** | 1 hour | Design a poster for a cause. |
| **Lesson 2** | **Gesture Drawing** | 1 hour | Create a gesture drawing. |
| **Lesson 3** | **Observation Drawing** | 1 hour | Make an observation drawing. |
| **Lesson 4** | **Contour Lines** | 1 hour | Create a contour drawing. |
| **Lesson 5** | **Flowing Lines** | 1 hour | Create a plant drawing using Chinese painting techniques. |
| **Lesson 6** | **Shading Techniques** | 1 hour | Create a still-life drawing. |
| **ARTSOURCE** | **Line in Dance and Music** | 35 minutes | Create a circle dance. |

| Materials | Program Resources | Fine Art Resources | Literature Resources |
|---|---|---|---|
| newsprint, white drawing paper, pencils, erasers, color markers | *Assessment,* pp. 9–10 *Reading and Writing Test Preparation,* pp. 6–7 *Home and After-School Connections Flash Cards* 1–6 | *Transparency 1 Artist Profiles,* pp. 36, 64 *Large Prints 49* and *50 The National Museum of Women in the Arts Collection* | *Stranded at Plimoth Plantation 1626* by Gary Bowen |
| white paper, crayons | *Assessment,* pp. 11–12 *Reading and Writing Test Preparation,* pp. 8–9 *Flash Cards* 4, 6 | *Transparency 2 Artist Profiles,* pp. 20, 69 *Large Prints 49* and *50 The National Museum of Women in the Arts Collection* | *Better Than a Lemonade Stand* by Daryl Bernstein |
| white paper, pencils, erasers | *Assessment,* pp. 13–14 *Reading and Writing Test Preparation,* pp. 10–11 *Flash Cards* 1–6 | *Transparency 3 Artist Profiles,* pp. 9, 24 *Large Prints 49* and *50 Art Around the World Collection* | *The Fantastic Journey of Pieter Bruegel* by Anders C. Shafer |
| white paper, pencils | *Assessment,* pp. 15–16 *Reading and Writing Test Preparation,* pp. 12–13 *Flash Cards* 1–6 | *Transparency 4 Artist Profiles,* pp. 3, 42 *Large Prints 49* and *50 The National Museum of Women in the Arts Collection* | *Harry the Poisonous Centipede* by Lynne Reid Banks |
| paper, bamboo limb, black India ink, no. 5 round pointed watercolor brushes | *Assessment,* pp. 17–18 *Reading and Writing Test Preparation,* pp. 14–15 *Flash Cards* 1–6 | *Transparency 5 Artist Profiles,* pp. 31, 44 *Large Prints 49* and *50 Art Around the World Collection* | *Prairie Dogs Kiss and Lobsters Wave* by Marilyn Singer |
| white paper, soft lead pencils, erasers | *Assessment,* pp. 19–20 *Reading and Writing Test Preparation,* pp. 16–17 *Flash Cards* 1–3 | *Transparency 6 Artist Profiles,* pp. 48, 71 *Large Prints 49* and *50 The National Museum of Women in the Arts Collection* | *Kids to the Rescue! First Aid Techniques for Kids* by Maribeth and Darwin Boelts |
| "Suite of Appalachian Music and Dance" | | | |

# Unit Overview

## 1 Line

**Lesson 1:** A **line** is a path created by a moving point or dot.

**Lesson 2: Gesture drawings** are quick sketches in which the actions of people, animals, or objects are captured.

**Lesson 3: Observation drawings** are sketches in which figures or objects are drawn in relation to their environment.

**Lesson 4: Contour lines** are lines that show the edges and ridges of objects.

**Lesson 5: Flowing lines** create a feeling of calm and gracefulness.

**Lesson 6: Shading techniques** are used to darken areas by repeating lines or dots.

# Introduce Unit Concepts

"In paintings, drawings, and sculptures, artists use lines to control the way we see a work of art." "Los artistas en las pinturas, los dibujos y las esculturas usan las líneas para controlar la manera en que vemos una obra de arte".

## Line
- Have students look around the classroom for examples of different types of lines, such as zigzag, curved, horizontal, and vertical lines.

## Cross-Curricular Projects
- See the *Language Arts and Reading, Mathematics, Science,* and *Social Studies Art Connections* books for activities that further develop line concepts.

# Line

◄ **Natalya Goncharova.** (Russian). *Maquillage.* 1913.
Gouache on paper. $4\frac{3}{8} \times 6\frac{3}{8}$ inches (11.13 × 16.21 cm.). Dallas Museum of Art, Dallas, Texas.

## Artists use a variety of lines to create artwork.

*Maquillage* is a nonobjective painting by Natalya Goncharova. She used a variety of lines in this painting. In French, the word *maquillage* refers to makeup. This may be a clue to the meaning of this painting.

**34** Unit 1

# Fine Art Prints

Display *Large Prints 49 Bedroom at Arles* and *50 Sawamura Kodenji as Tsuyu no Mae.* Refer to the prints throughout the unit as students learn about line.

**Large Print 49**

**Large Print 50**

Artists use **lines** in drawings, paintings, and sculptures to create shapes and movement.

▶ What types of lines do you see in the painting by Natalya Goncharova?

▶ What type of line do you see more than once?

▶ Does this painting seem like a close-up or a faraway view?

▶ What do the lines in the center of the painting indicate?

**In This Unit** you will learn about and practice techniques used to create lines in artwork.

Here are the topics you will study:
▶ Types of Lines
▶ Gesture Drawing
▶ Observation Drawing
▶ Contour Lines
▶ Flowing Lines
▶ Shading Techniques

*Self Portrait with Yellow Lilies*

## Natalya Goncharova
(1881–1962)

Natalya Goncharova was born in central Russia. She studied sculpture at the Moscow School of Painting, Sculpture, and Architecture. After her studies, Goncharova devoted her full attention to painting. She was one of a group of artists who led the movement from traditional to nonobjective art in Russia. In 1917 Goncharova settled permanently in Paris, where she designed for the theater and continued to paint until the end of her life.

Unit 1    **35**

# Examine the Artwork

"Let's look closely at the painting." "Vamos a observar detalladamente la pintura".

■ Have students closely examine the painting. Ask them to describe what they see.

■ Have students answer the questions about lines on page 35.

▶ There are zigzag lines; straight lines that move up and down, from side to side, and at a slant; and parallel lines that overlap.

▶ Zigzag lines, overlapping parallel lines, and straight lines appear more than once.

▶ Viewers feel like they are standing next to the scene. The outline of a face appears to be in the background of the painting.

▶ The lines in the center of the painting suggest the features of a face.

# Unit Pretest

Display *Transparency 43* as a pretest. Answers: 1.B, 2.C, 3.C, 4.A, 5.B

# Home Connection

■ See *Home and After School Connections* for family newsletters and activities for this unit.

## Art History and Culture

### Natalya Goncharova

Natalya Goncharova (na tal´ ya gən chär´ə və) (1881–1962) was a Russian painter and theatrical designer. In 1917 Goncharova settled permanently in Paris, where she continued to paint, exhibit, and design for the theater. *Maquillage* is an abstract painting. The word *maquillage* is a French word that means "theatrical makeup." *Maquillage* was created using gouache on paper. Gouache is an opaque watercolor paint.

See pages 24–25 and 16–21 for more about art history and subject matter.

**Artist Profiles, pp. 23**

◀ Artist Profile ▶

#### Natalya Sergeevna Goncharova
1881–1962

Natalya Goncharova (nä täl´ ē ä gon´ chä rô vä) was a member of the second generation of Russian women to receive art education. She became a leader of this generation of artists, taking part in the social, political, and aesthetic upheavals of the early twentieth century. After studying history and science—as well as sculpture and painting in Moscow—Goncharova joined other avant-garde artists in developing new forms of Russian art. They used native Russian peasant art, religious icons, and traditional folk culture in their work. She exhibited her paintings until the end of her life.

ILLUSTRATOR PROFILE

# Robert McCloskey

(1915–2003)

As a child growing up in Hamilton, Ohio, Robert McCloskey's first loves were music and inventing. When he reached high school, however, McCloskey developed a passion for art. In 1932 he attended Boston's Vesper George Art School on a scholarship and later went on to the National Academy of Design in New York.

McCloskey's first meeting with a children's book editor in New York left him without a contract, but with some sound advice. The editor suggested that McCloskey get more in touch with what was real to him, so McCloskey returned to Ohio, where he began to draw and paint images that reflected his Midwestern life. At this time, McCloskey wrote and illustrated his first book, *Lentil.*

McCloskey's later works were also drawn from personal experience. For example, his classic *Make Way for Ducklings* was inspired by a scene that McCloskey observed on the streets of Boston. During the making of this Caldecott Medal winner, McCloskey shared his apartment with four mallard ducks, whose movements he studied as they waddled around his studio and swam in his bathtub. Several of his other books portray life on Scott Island in Maine, where McCloskey lived with his wife and two daughters. This was the setting for his first full-color book, *Time of Wonder* (1958), which earned McCloskey a second Caldecott Medal.

Throughout Unit 1, share McCloskey's illustrations with the class and discuss the use of line in his books. Which types of lines does he use? Does McCloskey use gesture or flowing lines?

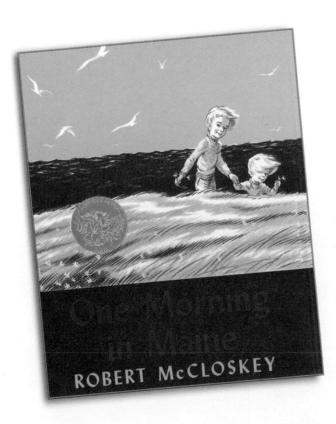

## Music

*Line* in music refers to the way a melody moves higher and lower. Have students sing a song and show higher and lower movement of the melody with their hands. Draw lines in several different shapes on the board, then create sounds that match one of the lines. The class can decide which line matches the sound.

## Literature

Show the video or DVD *The Dancing Skeleton* by Cynthia DeFelice to introduce the concept of line. Students can identify different kinds of lines and recognize how lines communicate movement in the steps of the dancing skeleton.

**Literature and Art**

## Performing Arts

ARTSOURCE Show "Suite of Appalachian Music and Dance." Have students pay attention to the dancer's movements.

**Artsource®**

## Lesson 1 Overview

# Types of Lines

**Lesson 1** introduces lines in art. Lines are used by artists to control the movement of the viewer's eyes. A line is a path created by a moving point or dot.

## Objectives

### Art History and Culture
To Identify and compare the subject matter in both works of art.

### Creative Expression
To use a variety of lines to create a poster for a cause

### Aesthetic Perception
To define and identify a variety of lines that artists use in their works of art

### Art Criticism
To evaluate own work using the four steps of art criticism

### Vocabulary ⭐ Reading

Review the following vocabulary words with students before beginning the lesson.

**line** línea—a path created by a moving point or dot

**vertical line** línea vertical—a line that moves up and down

**horizontal line** línea horizontal—a line that moves from side to side or left to right

See page 59B for additional vocabulary and Spanish vocabulary resources.

### Art Journal: Vocabulary
Have students add these words to the Vocabulary section of their Art Journals.

## Lesson Materials
- 9" × 12" newsprint for practice drawings
- 9" × 12" white drawing paper
- pencils
- erasers
- colored markers
- 12" × 18" white drawing paper

**Alternate Materials:**
- premixed tempera paints and oil pastels
- pencils

## Program Resources
- *Reading and Writing Test Prep.*, pp. 6–7
- *Transparency 1*
- *Flash Cards* 1–6
- *Artist Profiles*, pp. 36, 64
- *Animals Through History Time Line*
- *Assessment,* pp. 9–10
- *Large Prints 49* Bedroom at Arles and *50* Sawamura Kodenji as Tsuyu no Mae
- *The National Museum of Women in the Arts Collection*

### Concept Trace
Types of Lines
**Introduced:** Level 3, Unit 1, Lesson 1

**Reinforced:** Level 5, Unit 1, Lesson 1

---

## Lesson 1 Arts Integration

### Theatre

Complete Unit 1, Lesson 1, on pages 18–19 of *Theatre Arts Connections.*

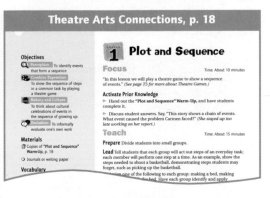

Theatre Arts Connections, p. 18

### Music

SPOTLIGHT on MUSIC

*Miniwanka, or The Moments of Water.* R. Murray Schafer.

Line in music refers to the way a melody moves higher and lower (up, down, or the same). To relate the concept of line in music to line in visual art, play Schafer's *Miniwanka, or The Moments of Water,* which includes sounds of raindrops, trills, and hissing. Have students draw the vertical, horizontal, diagonal, zigzag, and curved lines that they think go with the music.

### Movement & Dance

A line goes somewhere. Have students stand tall and straight. Using one hand and starting with a dot in space, have them trace a continuous line through space. They should go all the way to floor, up as high as they can, and around themselves. Have students end back at the dot. Have them explore this idea with straight lines and diagonal lines, and then repeat with curved lines.

# Focus

**Time:** About 10 minutes

## Activate Prior Knowledge

"Name the different types of lines that make up various objects in our classroom." "Nombren diferentes tipos de líneas que forman varios objetos de nuestro salón de clases".

■ Discuss student responses by verifying whether their identification of lines in objects are correct.

### Using Literature ⭐ Reading

■ Have students read *Stranded at Plimoth Plantation 1626* by Gary Bowen. Encourage students to identify the different types of lines used in the illustrations.

### Thematic Connection ⭐ Social Studies

■ **A Question of Value:** Use the paintings to discuss how artists use their work to portray their values. National Standards for Arts Education in Visual Arts (NSAE) 5.b

## Introduce the Art

# Look

"Let's take a close look at the two works of art." "Vamos a observar detalladamente estas dos obras de arte".

### Comparing and Contrasting ⭐ Reading

■ Have students list the similarities and differences in the two works of art. Both paintings show a variety of lines and incorporate bright colors. Smith's painting contains words and uses rough and expressionistic lines. Kandinsky's painting shows broad, flat areas of bright colors as well as lines.

## Art History and Culture

Possible answer: The subject in an image can be easily identified. It may be people, an event, or an object. There are usually no identifiable shapes in works of art with no subject matter.

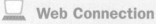 **Web Connection**

To view works of art by Jaune Quick-to-See Smith, visit **www.artmissoula.org**.

---

# Types of Lines

▲ **Jaune Quick-to-See Smith.** (American). *Rainbow.* 1989.
•••••••••••••••••••••••••••••
Oil and mixed-media on canvas.
66 × 84 inches (167.64 × 213.36 cm.).
Private Collection.

**Look** at the art on these pages. Jaune Quick-to-See Smith created her painting using loose brushstrokes to reflect her feelings about the environment. The symbols in her painting are similar to symbols in ancient Native American petroglyphs (rock drawings). Kandinsky's painting is nonobjective: it has no subject matter. Kandinsky painted colors and shapes as his subjects, which expressed his feelings.

## Art History and Culture

How can you tell when an artwork has a subject matter, such as Smith's painting, or no subject matter, such as Kandinsky's painting?

---

## Art History and Culture

### Jaune Quick-to-See Smith

Jaune Quick-to-See Smith (zhŏn kwik tōō sē smith) (1941– ) was born into a large family on a Montana reservation. Smith, who has worked as a curator, lecturer, and environmental activist, is one of the best-known Native American artists of her generation. Her art carries on the Native American legacy of reverence for nature and the land by expressing concerns about the damage caused by the mining, drilling, and logging industries. Smith has attempted to use art to bridge the gap between Native American and European American culture.

See pages 24–25 and 16–21 for more about art history and subject matter.

**Artist Profiles, p. 64**

**Artist Profile**

**Jaune Quick-to-See Smith**
b. 1941

Jaune Quick-to-See Smith (zhŏn kwik tōō sē smith) was born into a large family on a Montana reservation. She often went hungry as a child. Her Shoshone grandmother gave her the name "Quick-to-See" because Smith was quick to understand things. When Smith was in first grade, she already knew she wanted to be an artist. Later she was told that she was not college material and that a woman could not have a career in art. Smith spent 22 years supporting herself, raising three children, finishing college, and completing a master's degree in painting. She now paints as frequently as possible in a remodeled stable

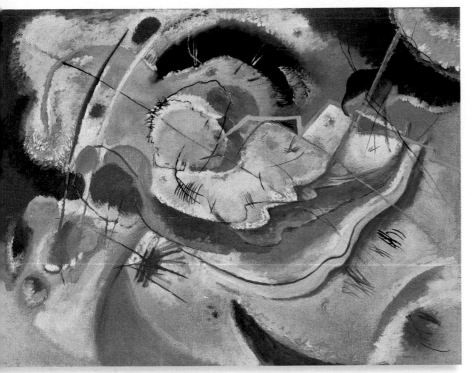

**Study** both works of art to find the different types of lines.

▶ Identify line directions.

▶ Look for thick and thin lines.

▶ Where do you see rough and smooth lines?

▶ Can you find broken and solid lines?

▲ **Wassily Kandinsky.** (Russian).
*Little Painting with Yellow (Improvisation).* 1914.

Oil on canvas. 31 × 39⅝ inches
(78.74 × 100.64 cm.). Philadelphia Museum
of Art, Philadelphia, Pennsylvania.

## Aesthetic Perception

**Design Awareness** Think of line designs on clothing, or look for various line designs on objects in the room.

## Art History and Culture

### Wassily Kandinsky

Wassily Kandinsky (va sēl´ ē kan din´ skē) (1866–1944) was a Russian-born artist who studied art in Munich. Kandinsky lived in Germany for many years and eventually settled in France during the 1930s. He devoted much of his time to the relationship between art and music. He gave many of his paintings music-related names such as *Improvisation* or *Composition*. After looking at one of his paintings resting on its side, he discovered that colors and shapes can stand on their own as subjects in art. As a result, he was arguably the first artist to abandon recognizable reality and paint abstract canvases.

See pages 24–25 and 16–21 for more about art history and subject matter.

**Artist Profiles, p. 36**

◀ Artist Profile ▶
**Wassily Kandinsky**
1866-1944

Wassily Kandinsky (va sēl´ ē kan din´ skē) first tried painting as a teenager in his native Russia. Even then he felt that each color had a mysterious life of its own. He was still drawn to colors and painting while he studied law and economics in college, but he believed that art was "a luxury forbidden to a Russian." In time, he moved to Germany, studied art, and began his career. Throughout his life Kandinsky moved back and forth between Russia and Germany. In 1933 he settled in France after Nazi storm troopers labeled his painting style "degenerate."

## Study

▶ Both: rounded lines create curves; Kandinsky: diagonal lines in the center

▶ Smith: Thick-lined brushstrokes represent the rainbow. Kandinsky: Thick-lined brushstrokes throughout the painting, thin-lined brush strokes in the center.

▶ Both: The brushwork creates rough lines. Kandinsky: Smooth lines in the center of the painting.

▶ Smith: Solid lines create the rainbow; rough lines create texture. Kandinsky: Solid lines all over

■ For more examples of abstract and nonobjective art, see *The National Museum of Women in the Arts Collection.*

### Art Journal: Writing

Encourage students to define and illustrate different types of lines in the Concepts section of their Art Journals. What else do they want to know about line?

## Aesthetic Perception

**Design Awareness** Lines in clothing and on objects could include vertical lines, horizontal lines, diagonal lines, zigzag lines, and curved lines. Have students point out different types of lines.

**Developing Visual Literacy** Invite students to look for clues in the paintings that contribute to their understanding of the works of art. For example, the words and symbols in Smith's painting reflect her feelings about the environment.

### Web Connection

For more information about Kandinsky paintings, visit **www.philamuseum.org** (Philadelphia Museum of Art).

each

"How can you illustrate the five different kinds of lines?" "¿Cómo pueden ilustrar los cinco tipos diferentes de líneas?"

- Read and discuss the types of lines shown on page 38.

## Practice

**Materials:** 12″ × 18″ white drawing paper, markers

**Alternate Materials:** pencils

- Distribute the materials and have students follow the directions on page 38.

### Creative Expression

**Materials:** 9″ × 12″ newsprint for practice drawings, 9″ × 12″ white drawing paper, pencils, erasers, color markers

**Alternate Materials:** premixed tempera paints and oil pastels

- Distribute the materials and have students follow the directions on page 39.
- See page 228 in the Activity Tips for visual examples of techniques.

### Art Journal: Brainstorming

Have students brainstorm ideas for causes that concern them and list their ideas in their Art Journals. Then have students write slogans for their favorite causes. Students should also plan how they will portray these causes in their posters in the Creative Expression activity.
NSAE 2.c

## Using Lines

A **line** is a mark drawn by a tool such as a pencil, pen, or paintbrush as it moves across a surface. Artists use lines to define how an object looks.

Here are some different types of lines:

 A **vertical line** moves up and down.

 A **horizontal line** moves from side to side or from left to right.

 A **diagonal line** is slanted.

 **Zigzag lines** are diagonal lines that connect.

 **Curved lines** bend and change direction slowly.

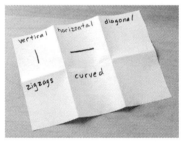

### Practice

Draw each line and its variation. Use markers.

1. Fold a sheet of paper into six equal boxes. Print the name of each of the five types of lines at the top of each box, leaving one box empty.

2. Using a black marker, create the type of line indicated.

3. In the empty box, create a design using all five types of lines.

### Differentiated Instruction

**Reteach**
Lead students in a "Simon Says" manner, having them use their arms to mimic the directional lines.

**Special Needs**
For students with moderate-to-severe cognitive disabilities, it is important to remember that the primary objective of this lesson is not the printing of the slogan, but the creation of a personally relevant picture using different types of lines.

**ELL**
Students may find it helpful to see examples of different types of lines on the board before they identify them in the paintings.

◀ **Christopher Cornelison.**
Age 8.

**Think** about what kinds of lines the student artist used in the poster.

### Creative Expression

What emotions do you feel when you think about a cause that concerns you? Create a poster. Use different kinds of lines and a slogan to represent your cause.

1. Think about a cause that concerns you, such as pollution. Write a short slogan or message that expresses your concerns.

2. Design a poster about your cause. Use the different kinds of lines and line variations that you saw in the artwork. Plan a way to work your slogan into a design, like Jaune Quick-to-See Smith did.

### Art Criticism

**Describe** Name the objects and the slogan in your poster.

**Analyze** List the different lines you used. How did you make your slogan fit the design?

**Interpret** Does your poster express your concerns? Do your friends understand what you are trying to say?

**Decide** Did you use the five different kinds of lines in your poster? Explain.

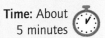

# Reflect

**Time:** About 5 minutes

## Review and Assess

"Let's review what we've learned about lines."
"Vamos a repasar lo que hemos aprendido acerca de las lineas".

## Think

The artist used all five line types.

- Use *Large Prints 49* Bedroom at Arles and *50* Sawamura Kodenji as Tsuyu no Mae to have students identify different types of lines.

## Informal Assessment

- For standardized-format test practice using this lesson's art content, see pages 6–7 in *Reading and Writing Test Preparation.*

### Art Journal: Critical Thinking

Have students answer the four art criticism questions—Describe, Analyze, Interpret, and Decide—in their Art Journals. In small groups, have students discuss the use of lines in their artwork. Also have students describe their intents and form conclusions about their posters.
NSAE 5.a

---

## Art Across the Curriculum

Use these simple ideas to reinforce art concepts across the curriculum.

★ **Persuasive Writing** Have students use the writing process to write persuasive paragraphs to convince classmates to support a cause important to them, like Jaune Quick-to-See Smith used painting to convince people to support a cause important to her.

★ **Math** Discuss points, lines, and line segments.

★ **Science** Use the painting *Rainbow* to discuss environmental conditions that destroy plants and animals.

★ **Social Studies** Mapmakers use lines to draw maps. Have students learn about lines (longitude and latitude) used in maps.

★ **Technology** Have students use the drawing feature in a computer's word processing program to practice making different types of lines. Visit **SRAonline.com** to print detailed instructions for this activity.
NSAE 6.b

# Types of Lines

## Extra! For the Art Specialist

Time: About 45 minutes

### Focus

Study **Large Print 49** *Bedroom at Arles* and ask students to point out different types of lines. Ask students which direction the lines are moving.

### Teach

Explain to students that they will be creating a mixed-media project using different types of lines. They will combine oil pastel resist with paper collage. Demonstrate making an oil-pastel resist. Color a variety of lines and select one color to paint over the drawn lines. Then have students complete the alternate activity.

### Reflect

Have students use the four steps of art criticism to evaluate their work. Did they use a variety of lines in their project? Have students describe the lines they used.

### Alternate Activity

**Materials:**

- sketchbook
- pencils, erasers
- oil pastels
- watercolor paints
- various types of paper $4\frac{1}{2} \times 6''$ (construction, wrapping paper, etc.)
- scissors
- glue

1. Have students review the different types of lines. Have them use oil pastels to draw a design using different lines. Some lines should be thick, others thin.

2. Students should select one color and paint a wash over the lines.

3. While the resist is drying, students should cut a variety of lines from paper.

4. Have students glue the lines to the background paper. Some of the cut lines should pop up from the paper.

## Research in Art Education

There is a link among "arts education and creative thinking, academic self-concept, and school climate" ("Learning In and Through the Arts: The Question of Transfer" in *Critical Links*, p. 66). Students in schools with quality arts programs tend to use more creativity, take more risks, and view themselves as academically competent. As students learn about different types of lines, encourage them to think about how lines relate to different areas of the arts.

## Assessment

Use the following rubric to evaluate the artwork that students make in the Creative Expression activity and to assess students' understanding of types of lines.

Have students complete page 9 or 10 in their *Assessment* books.

| | Art History and Culture | Aesthetic Perception | Creative Expression | Art Criticism |
|---|---|---|---|---|
| **3 POINTS** | The student can identify and compare the subject matter in both works of art. | The student accurately defines *line* and identifies types of lines in a work of art. | The student incorporates a variety of lines in his or her drawing. | The student thoughtfully and honestly evaluates own work using the four steps of art criticism. |
| **2 POINTS** | The student's identification or comparison is weak or incomplete. | The student shows emerging awareness of the different types of lines, but cannot consistently identify them. | The student's drawing shows some awareness of different types of lines. | The student attempts to evaluate own work, but shows an incomplete understanding of evaluation criteria. |
| **1 POINT** | The student cannot identify or compare the subject matter in the works of art. | The student cannot identify different types of lines. | The student's drawing shows no understanding of different types of lines. | The student makes no attempt to evaluate own work. |

**Assessment, p. 9**

Name _____ Date _____ Lesson **1** UNIT 1

**Types of Lines**

**A** Drawing
Draw each kind of line in the box above the label.

| | |
|---|---|
| zigzag line | curved line |

**B** Short Answer
Answer the question.
What are the three directions in which a line moves?
1. _____
2. _____
3. _____

**C** Writing
Look at Wassily Kandinsky's *Little Painting with Yellow.* Briefly describe the types of lines the artist used in his painting.

_____
_____
_____

Level 4     Unit 1 • Line     9

# Lesson 2 Overview

# Gesture Drawing

**Lesson 2** introduces gesture drawing. A gesture is an expressive movement. Gesture lines are quickly drawn to capture the movement of a person, animal, or object in a painting or drawing.

## Objectives

 **Art History and Culture**

To demonstrate knowledge of the lives and work of Audrey Flack and Paolo Veronese

 **Creative Expression**

To use loose lines to create gesture drawings

 **Aesthetic Perception**

To define and identify gestural techniques used in art

**Art Criticism**

To evaluate own work using the four steps of art criticism

## Vocabulary  Reading

Review the following vocabulary words with students before beginning the lesson.

**gesture** *gesto*—an expressive movement

**gesture sketch** *pintura gestual*—a quick sketch that captures the movement or action of an object

See page 59B for additional vocabulary and Spanish vocabulary resources.

### Art Journal: Vocabulary

Have students add these words to the Vocabulary section of their Art Journals.

## Lesson Materials
- 9" × 12" white drawing paper
- crayons

**Alternate Materials:**
- pencils
- conte crayons

## Program Resources
- *Reading and Writing Test Prep.,* pp. 8–9
- *Transparency 2*
- *Flash Cards* 4, 6
- *Artist Profiles,* pp. 20, 69
- *Animals Through History Time Line*
- *Assessment,* pp. 11–12
- *Large Prints 49 Bedroom at Arles* and **50** *Sawamura Kodenji as Tsuyu no Mae*
- *The National Museum of Women in the Arts Collection*

### Concept Trace
Gesture Drawing
**Introduced:** Level 3, Unit 1, Lesson 1
**Reinforced:** Level 5, Unit 1, Lesson 2

---

## Lesson 2 Arts Integration

### Theatre

Complete Unit 1, Lesson 2, on pages 20–21 of *Theatre Arts Connections.*

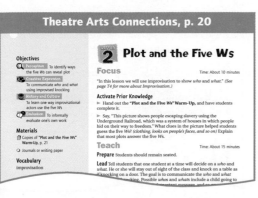

### Music

*The Loco-Motion.* Gerry Goffin and Carole King.

Gesture lines are quickly drawn to capture the movement of a person, animal, or object. Minimal details and repeated lines and shapes help to create the sense of expressive movement. Play and/or have students sing *The Loco-Motion* while they complete the Practice activity in which they illustrate the three gesture techniques. Encourage them to use the repeated lines in the music to develop their gesture drawings.

### Movement & Dance

Use quick voice prompts to initiate movement sketches. Name an object and give students ten seconds to do a movement sketch of the idea.

# Focus

## Activate Prior Knowledge

"What are some ways that artists show movement?" "¿Cuáles son algunas de las maneras en que los artistas muestran movimiento?"

- Discuss students' answers. Give examples of stop-action photography and slow-motion film.

### Using Literature ⭐ Reading

- Have students read *Better Than a Lemonade Stand* by Daryl Bernstein. The illustrations show expressive movements or gestures.

### Thematic Connection ⭐ Social Studies

- **People:** Use the paintings to discuss the use of gesture sketches to portray people.

## Introduce the Art

# Look

"Let's take a close look at the two works of art." "Vamos a observar detalladamente estas dos obras de arte".

### Purpose ⭐ Reading

- Have students list possible reasons why the works of art were created. *Self-Portrait (the Memory)* was created in 1958, when the artist was in her twenties. It may have been created as a way to keep a record of what the artist looked like at that age. *Sheet of Studies for "The Martyrdom of Saint George"* is a page full of gesture sketches created in preparation for a painting.

## 🏺 Art History and Culture

Possible answer: A portrait of a person living in the sixteenth century would illustrate clothes that were worn during that period.

## 💻 Web Connection

To learn more about women artists, visit **www.nmwa.org** (National Museum of Women in the Arts).

---

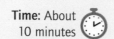
# Gesture Drawings

**Look** at the works of art on these two pages. *Self-Portrait (the Memory)* was painted by Audrey Flack in 1958, when she was an art student. *Sheet of Studies for "The Martyrdom of Saint George"* was created in Italy around 1566. It is a full page of gesture sketches used as a study for a painting. Artists make many studies of models before they begin their final compositions.

◀ **Audrey Flack.** (American). *Self-Portrait (the Memory).* 1958.
Oil on canvas. 50 × 34 inches (127 × 86.36 cm.). Art Museum of Miami University, Oxford, Ohio.

## 🏺 Art History and Culture

Notice the nationality of each artist and the year each artwork was created. How would Flack's self-portrait be different if she had been a woman living in the sixteenth century?

## 🏺 Art History and Culture

### Audrey Flack

Audrey Flack (ô´ drē flak) (1931– ) had always longed to paint in a realistic manner, and in the early 1950s Flack became famous for her superrealistic, photorealistic paintings. Since 1981 she has sculpted powerful images of women and continued her work as a photorealist. Flack's self-portrait is a realistic painting of herself. She communicates her ideas through vibrant colors, textures, and a unique sense of space. Flack was one of the first artists to make paintings based on photographs.

See pages 24–25 and 16–21 for more about art history and subject matter.

**Artist Profiles, p. 20**

◆ Artist Profile ◆

**Audrey Flack**
b. 1931

Audrey Flack (ô´ drē flak) grew up in New York City and lives there still. She earned a fine arts degree from Yale. She also studied anatomy, the structure of the human body. This helps her make her paintings more realistic. Flack is married to a musician. Early in her career she painted while raising two daughters. She has also taught at Pratt Institute and New York University.

**Study** both works of art and find the lines that show movement.

▶ Find a repeated line that represents movement.

▶ Which figure seems to be the most lively? Which figure seems to be the calmest?

▶ Describe how detail is used or not used in each work of art.

▶ Compare the works of art. What similarities do you see? What differences do you see?

▲ **Paolo Veronese.** (Italian). *Sheet of Studies for "The Martyrdom of Saint George."* c. 1566.

Pen and brown ink and brown wash. 11⅜ × 8⁹⁄₁₆ inches (28.9 × 21.7 cm.). J. Paul Getty Museum, Los Angeles, California.

## Aesthetic Perception

**Seeing Like an Artist** Look around the classroom. Observe how everyone is moving. Notice the variety of gestures around you. What do these gestures represent?

## Art History and Culture

### Paolo Veronese

Paolo Veronese (pä´ ō lō  ver ə nā´ sē) (1528–1588) was born Paolo Caliari in Verona, Italy. Veronese belonged to a family of artists. Much of his work was wall and ceiling paintings. He created *Sheet of Studies for "The Martyrdom of Saint George"* as a preparatory study for a painting in Verona. It established the basic compositional features of the painting as well as the arrangements and character of the individual figures. *Sheet of Studies for "The Martyrdom of Saint George"* is a page full of gesture sketches. Veronese used both drawings and oil sketches in preparing paintings.

See pages 24–25 and 16–21 for more about art history and subject matter.

**Artist Profiles, p. 69**

• Artist Profile •

**Paolo Veronese**
1528–1588

Born Paolo Caliari in Verona, Italy, the name *Paolo Veronese* (pä´ ō lō  ver ə nā´ sē) was created from the city of his birth. When he was 14, Veronese was apprenticed to a Venetian painter, and by the time he was in his early twenties, he was painting at the Palazzo Ducale. Veronese worked in Venice and other nearby towns for the rest of life. He operated a workshop in Venice, and hired his brothers and sons. After his death Veronese's family continued to make works under the label *Haeredes Pauli*, making it difficult for historians to discern whether Veronese was the true artist behind some works.

## Study

▶ Veronese: The repeated lines in the figures represent movement.

▶ Flack: The gesture lines in the self-portrait indicate inner excitement—the excitement of creation. Veronese: The figures in the sketches appear to be lively.

▶ The moods are those of excitement, expressed by the gestural lines.

▶ Flack: Oil on canvas is used to create minimal detail on the figure. Veronese: Pen and brown ink and brown wash are used to show the movement of the story.

■ For more examples of portraits, see *The National Museum of Women in the Arts Collection.*

### Art Journal: Writing

Encourage students to write their own explanations of gesture drawing in the Concepts section of their Art Journals. What else do they want to know about gesture drawing?

## Aesthetic Perception

**Seeing Like an Artist** Gestures are movements of the hands or head that show what a person is thinking or feeling. For example, holding out your hand with the palm up is a gesture that means you want something.

**Developing Visual Literacy** Discuss what each artwork "says." What meaning was the artist trying to convey? Explain to students that *Sheet of Studies for "The Martyrdom of Saint George"* is a narrative. The artist was attempting to tell a story. Have students view Audrey Flack's portrait and list reasons why an artist would create a self-portrait. NSAE 5.a

### Web Connection

Search the collections at **www.getty.edu** to find works of art by Paolo Veronese.

# Teach

**Time:** About 45 minutes

"Can you illustrate a gesture?" "¿Pueden ilustrar las tres técnicas gestuales?"

- Discuss gesture drawings on page 42.

## Practice

**Materials:** 9" × 12" white drawing paper, crayons

**Alternate Materials:** pencils

- Distribute the materials and have students follow the directions on page 42.
- Have volunteers pose for the gesture sketches.

##  Creative Expression

**Materials:** 9" × 12" white drawing paper, crayons

**Alternate Materials:** conte crayons

- Distribute the materials and have students follow the directions on page 43.
- See page 228 in the Activity Tips for visual examples of techniques.

### Art Journal: Brainstorming

Have students brainstorm ideas for gestures and list their ideas in their Art Journals. Then have them plan their poses for the gesture drawings in the Creative Expression activity.


# Using Gesture Drawings

A **gesture** is an expressive movement. **Gesture lines** are quickly drawn to capture the movement of a person, an animal, or an object in a painting or drawing.

A **gesture sketch** is a quick sketch. To capture the gesture of an object, quick sketches or action drawings are used. The idea is to capture the movement or action of the object.

**Repeated lines** are used to give the feeling of movement or motion.

**Repeated shapes,** like hands or legs, also give the feeling of motion. The more times that shapes are repeated, the faster the motion looks.

Because gesture lines are used to capture movement, **minimal details** are used in the rest of the drawing. Often details are only suggested; for example, a few lines can suggest a mouth or an eye.

## Practice

Illustrate the three gesture techniques. Use crayon.

1. Make quick sketches capturing the gestures of several of your classmates.
2. Make sure your sketches have repeated lines, shapes, and very little detail.

**42** Unit 1 • Lesson 2

## Differentiated Instruction

### Reteach
Have students pair up and take turns "freezing" in a movement. Ask students to draw their partner, making sure to bend the lines at joints, like the elbows and knees.

### Special Needs
The use of supplemental resources may reinforce lesson objectives for students with disabilities. Drawing workbooks that show gesture drawings of animals, people, and cartoon characters would be a helpful resource for guided practice.

### ELL
Students may find it difficult to describe what they see in artwork without first hearing some appropriate vocabulary. Consider examining pictures as a group and modeling some of the possible words students might use to describe their experiences.

◀ **Hayden Verner.**
Age 9.

**Think** about how the student artist created the feeling of movement in the drawing.

 **Creative Expression**

How can you capture the look of movement in a drawing? Create the feeling of movement in a gesture drawing.

1. Think about how action is captured in a drawing. Use quick, sketchy lines.

2. Take turns with classmates freezing in a movement. Hold poses for 30 seconds. Each time you draw someone new, change the crayon color.

3. Repeat lines and shapes and let your figures overlap to fill the entire page.

**Art Criticism**

**Describe** Describe the figures in your drawing.

**Analyze** Talk about the various gesture techniques that you used.

**Interpret** What type of feeling have you created in your drawing? What kinds of lines seem to represent action?

**Decide** Do you feel that you successfully caught the gestures of your classmates? Explain.

# Reflect
**Time:** About 5 minutes

## Review and Assess

"What have you learned about how artists draw gestures?" "¿Qué han aprendido acerca de cómo los artistas dibujan los gestos?"

## Think

The artist used repeated lines and shapes to create the feeling of movement.

■ Use *Large Print 50* Sawamura Kodenji as *Tsuyu no Mae* to have students examine how lines are used to create a gesture drawing.

## Informal Assessment

■ For standardized-format test practice using this lesson's art content, see pages 8–9 in *Reading and Writing Test Preparation.*

**Art Journal: Critical Thinking**

Have students answer the four art criticism questions—Describe, Analyze, Interpret, and Decide—in their Art Journals. In small groups, have students discuss the use of quickly drawn lines to create gesture sketches in the Creative Expression activity.

## Art Across the Curriculum

Use these simple ideas to reinforce art concepts across the curriculum.

★ **Narrative Writing** Have students use the writing process to write a biographical paragraph (or written picture) about the person sitting next to them.

★ **Math** Discuss horizontal, vertical, and parallel lines.

★ **Science** Discuss the structure of the human body, and give examples of gestures humans are capable and incapable of performing.

★ **Social Studies** Use the Flack painting to discuss how historical records are kept through paintings, photographs, videos, and pictures.

★ **Technology** Have students use the drawing feature in a computer's word processing program to create gesture sketches. Visit **SRAonline.com** to print detailed instructions for this activity.
NSAE 6.b

Lesson 2 Wrap-Up

# Gesture Drawing

## Extra! For the Art Specialist

**Time:** About 45 minutes

### Focus

Study **Large Print 50** *Sawamura Kodenji as Tsuyu no Mae* and ask students to point out the different types of lines that show or capture a movement or pose. What area has the most movement in it? Which area has the least amount of movement?

### Teach

Explain to students that they will be creating a series of gesture drawings using white chalk. Then have students complete the alternate activity.

### Reflect

Have students use the four steps of art criticism to evaluate their work. Did they effectively create a gesture drawing? What is the gesture or pose that is captured in their artwork?

### Alternate Activity

**Materials:**
- black construction paper
- white chalk
- color chalk
- pencil, eraser
- sketchbook

1. Have students create several gesture drawings following the Creative Expression directions on page 39.

2. Students should select their best gesture drawing and use color chalk to emphasize areas of importance, such as the face or the clothing.

3. Have students create an exhibition of their drawings so they can interpret the moods in each of the works of art.
   NSAE 5.c

## Research in Art Education

"The purposes of Art Education are to build awareness of the aesthetic components in human experience: the feeling of kinship between the young 'artist-analyst' and the traditions of artistic creation and comprehension of the language of visual form as embodied and as experienced through the visual impact of everyday objects." (*Report of the Commission on Art Education*, 1965, NAEA.)

## Assessment
Use the following rubric to evaluate the artwork that students make in the Creative Expression activity and to assess students' understanding of gesture drawing.

Have students complete page 11 or 12 in their **Assessment** books.

|  | Art History and Culture | Aesthetic Perception | Creative Expression | Art Criticism |
|---|---|---|---|---|
| **3 POINTS** | The student demonstrates knowledge of the lives and work of Flack and Veronese. | The student can define gesture drawing and identify the gestural techniques in art. | The student uses loose lines to create gesture drawings. | The student thoughtfully and honestly evaluates own work using the four steps of art criticism. |
| **2 POINTS** | The student demonstrates some awareness of the lives and work of Flack and Veronese but cannot consistently identify them. | The student shows some understanding of gesture drawing and emerging awareness of gestural techniques. | The student's drawings show some attempt to use loose lines. | The student attempts to evaluate own work, but shows an incomplete understanding of evaluation criteria. |
| **1 POINT** | The student cannot demonstrate knowledge of the lives and work of Flack and Veronese. | The student cannot define gesture drawing and cannot identify gestural techniques. | The student did not use loose lines in his or her drawings. | The student makes no attempt to evaluate own work. |

### Assessment, p. 11

Name _____ Date _____

Lesson 2 UNIT 1

**Gesture Drawing**

**A. Vocabulary**
Write the answer.
What is a gesture sketch? _____

**B. Short Answer**
List three techniques used to create gesture drawings.
1. _____
2. _____
3. _____

**C. Writing**
Study *Self-Portrait (the Memory)* by Audrey Flack. Briefly describe how the artist used gesture lines.
_____
_____
_____
_____
_____
_____
_____
_____

Level 4                    Unit 1 • Line    11

# Lesson 3 Overview

# Observation Drawing

**Lesson 3** introduces observation drawing. An observation drawing is a drawing made while looking at a person or object.

## Objectives

 **Art History and Culture**

To identify and compare the periods and cultures reflected in paintings by sixteenth- and twentieth- century artists

**Creative Expression**

To use a specific point of view to create a drawing of people in relation to their environment

**Aesthetic Perception**

To define how artists use observational sketches and different viewpoints in their work

**Art Criticism**

To evaluate own work using the four steps of art criticism

## Vocabulary  Reading

Review the following vocabulary word with students before beginning the lesson.

**observation drawing** dibujo de observación—a drawing created from direct observation

See page 59B for additional vocabulary and Spanish vocabulary resources.

 **Art Journal: Vocabulary**

Have students add this word to the Vocabulary section of their Art Journals.

## Lesson Materials

- 9" × 12" white drawing paper
- pencils
- erasers

### Alternate Materials
- black felt-tip markers

## Program Resources
- *Reading and Writing Test Prep.,* pp. 10–11
- *Transparency 3*
- *Flash Cards* 1–6
- *Artist Profiles,* pp. 9, 24
- *Animals Through History Time Line*
- *Assessment,* pp. 13–14
- *Large Prints 49* Bedroom at Arles and *50* Sawamura Kodenji as Tsuyu no Mae
- *Art Around the World Collection*

### Concept Trace
Observation Drawing
**Introduced:** Level 3, Unit 1, Lesson 2

**Reinforced:** Level 5, Unit 1, Lesson 2

---

# Lesson 3 Arts Integration

## Theatre

Complete Unit 1, Lesson 3 on pages 22–23 of *Theatre Arts Connections.*

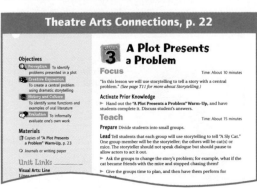

## Music

*My Home's in Montana.* Cowboy Song.

An observation drawing is made while looking at a person or object. It can be from a bird's-eye, aerial, ant's, eye-level, or close-up view. Play and/or have students sign the cowboy song *My Home's in Montana,* which includes landscape and close-up images. Have students make a quick 2-minute observation drawing after listening to the song. Compare the different points of view students chose to draw.

## Movement & Dance

Have students work a with partner to create observational sketches. One student creates a shape, and the other student stands next to him or her. The student who is drawing should make large, quick-motion sketches. Have each students create three observational movement sketches.

ocus

**Time:** About 10 minutes

### Activate Prior Knowledge

"What do you notice when you are far away from, close to, or looking down on a scene?"

"¿Qué notan cuando están lejos, cerca o mirando una escena desde arriba?"

■ Discuss the responses given by the students about various points of view.

**Using Literature** ⭐ Reading

■ Have students read *The Fantastic Journey of Pieter Bruegel* by Anders C. Shafer to learn more about the life and art of Pieter Bruegel the Elder.

**Thematic Connection** ⭐ Social Studies

■ **Heritage:** Use the paintings to discuss the concept of heritage. Point out that the artists are from different backgrounds. Have students compare and contrast the cultural settings in the works of art.
NSAE 4.a; 4.b

### Introduce the Art

## Look

■ "Let's take a close look at the two works of art." "Vamos a observar de cerca las dos obras de arte".

**Point of View** ⭐ Reading

■ Have students discuss the points of view used in each work of art. Have students discuss how the images would be different if the artists had used different points of view. In Bruegel's painting the viewer is looking down on the scene. Goodnight used a close-up point of view in his painting.

 **Art History and Culture**

Possible answer: *Children's Games* suggests fun, happy moments. *Endangered Species* suggests a dangerous situation or unhappy moments. The children are not happy.

Visit **www.metmuseum.org** (the Metropolitan Museum of Art) for more information about works of art by Pieter Bruegel the Elder.

🖥 **Web Connection**

---

 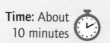

**Look** at the paintings on these pages. *Children's Games* shows children in the sixteenth century playing games. At least 80 games are portrayed in this painting. *Endangered Species* by Paul Goodnight also focuses on children. However, they are in a completely different environment. Both *Children's Games* and *Endangered Species* are genre paintings, showing everyday life.

▲ **Pieter Bruegel the Elder.** (Flemish). *Children's Games.* 1560.

Oil on oakwood panel. 46¼ × 63⅜ inches (118.11 × 160.99 cm.). Kunsthistorisches Museum, Gemaldegalerie, Vienna, Austria.

 **Art History and Culture**

Notice the title of each artwork and the movement of the children. Use descriptive words to compare the environments portrayed in each painting.

---

🏺 **Art History and Culture**

### Pieter Bruegel the Elder

Pieter Bruegel the Elder (pē ter broo´ gəl) (1525–1569) concentrated on painting landscapes and scenes of peasant life. His ability to paint peasant life earned him the nickname "Peasant Bruegel." Bruegel is generally considered the greatest Flemish painter of the sixteenth century. *Children's Games* shows the life of European peasant children during the 1500s and the variety of games that they commonly played. There are at least eighty games portrayed in this painting. Most of Bruegel's paintings, including his many landscapes, have some narrative content. Bruegel produced a great many drawings, engravings, and paintings.

See pages 24–25 and 16–21 for more about art history and subject matter.

**Artist Profiles, p. 9**

▸ Artist Profile

**Pieter Bruegel the Elder**
1525–1569

Pieter Bruegel (pē´ ter broi gəl) the Elder was born in Holland. He studied art in Antwerp, Belgium, and later married his teacher's daughter. They had two sons, who also became painters. Pieter the Younger was a portrait painter. The other son, Jan, painted flowers. Bruegel the Elder was educated and wealthy. However, he often dressed like a poor farmer so that he could closely observe the lives of peasants. He made them the subjects of many of his paintings. Bruegel even attended weddings of strangers. He brought gifts so that he would be welcome. Bruegel died at age 44.

**Study**

> Goodnight: The three children playing up front are seen from a straight-ahead, close-up viewpoint. Bruegel: The viewer is looking down on the scene to take in the numerous activities.

> Answers will vary.

> Goodnight: The innocent children are endangered by the environment. Bruegel: The multitude of children playing games creates a busy, energetic, and overwhelming feeling of activity.

■ For more examples of art from Europe, see the *Art Around the World Collection.*

**Study** both works of art and notice how they show different ways of seeing action.

▶ What point of view did each artist use?

▶ How many different games can you find in Bruegel's painting?

▶ Both artists portrayed children moving very differently in their environments. What different messages do you think the artists were sending? What feelings do you get when you look at each painting?

▲ **Paul Goodnight.**
(American). *Endangered Species.* c. 1970.
..............................
Acrylic. 2½ × 5 feet (.76 × 1.52 meters).
Private collection.

**Art Journal: Writing**

Encourage students to write their own explanations of observation drawing in the Concepts section of their Art Journals. What else do they want to know about observation drawing?

 **Aesthetic Perception**

**Design Awareness** Look around the room at your classmates. How do the students close to you look in relation to students right behind them and to those even farther away?

 **Aesthetic Perception**

**Design Awareness** People in the foreground (close to the viewer) appear larger. People in the middle appear smaller than people in the front but larger than those in the back. People in the back appear to be smaller than those in the middle and the front.

**Developing Visual Literacy** Invite students to compare the two paintings. Point out that both paintings show children interacting, but in two different environments. What are the similarities and differences in the activities and movements of the children portrayed in the paintings?

## Art History and Culture

### Paul Goodnight

Paul Goodnight (pôl good´ nīt) (1946– ) began a career in art when he used his childhood hobby of art as a way to communicate the horrors he experienced during the Vietnam War. He later received a bachelor's degree and a master's in fine art from the Massachusetts College of Art. Goodnight is a contemporary artist who paints images that reflect pride in his African heritage. Goodnight's paintings are images of everyday situations. His art has been featured on popular television shows and collected by prominent people such as Maya Angelou and Bill Cosby.

See pages 24–25 and 16–21 for more about art history and subject matter.

**Artist Profiles, p. 24**

◀ Artist Profile ▶
**Paul Goodnight**
b. 1946

Paul Goodnight (paul gud´ nit) was born in Chicago and raised by his grandparents in New London, Connecticut. As a child he was happy but often in trouble. After serving in the Vietnam War, Goodnight was so devastated he could no longer speak clearly. He turned to painting and drawing as a way to work through the horrors he experienced during the war. After earning a bachelor's degree from Massachusetts College of Art, Goodnight worked as a commercial artist, creating album covers and package designs. His art has become very popular and has been featured on movie and television sets, including *The Fresh Prince of Bel Air, Seinfeld,* and *ER.* One of Goodnight's images was chosen for an

 **Web Connection**
Visit **www.paulgoodnight.com** to view works of art by Paul Goodnight. (This site is for teacher use only.)

# Teach

**Time:** About 30 minutes

"Can you illustrate different points of view of your classroom by creating observation drawings?" "¿Pueden ilustrar diferentes puntos de vista de su salón de clases creando dibujos de observación?"

- Read and discuss the definition of *observation drawing* and the four types of viewpoints on page 46.

## Practice

**Materials:** 9" × 12" white paper, pencils

**Alternate Materials:** felt-tip markers

- Distribute the materials and have students follow the directions on page 46.

## Creative Expression

**Materials:** 9" × 12" white drawing paper, pencils, erasers

**Alternate Materials:** black felt-tip markers

- Distribute the materials and have students follow the directions on page 47.

- See page 229 in Activity Tips for visual examples of techniques.

- Have students invent new ways to produce observation drawings using a variety of art media and materials.
NSAE 5.a

 **Art Journal: Brainstorming**
Have students brainstorm different points of view in the Ideas section of their Art Journals. Then have students select a specific point of view for their observation drawings in the Creative Expression activity.

# Using Observation Drawings

An observation drawing is a drawing made while looking at a person or object. Artists draw figures or objects in relation to their surroundings, but a painting can often show different points of view.

In a **bird's-eye view or aerial view** viewers feel they are looking down on a scene.

In an **ant's view** viewers feel they are looking up, toward an object or figure.

In a **faraway or eye-level view** viewers feel they are standing far away from the scene.

In a **close-up view** viewers feel they are right next to an object, or are a part of the action in a picture.

## Practice

Create an observation drawing. Use pencil.

1. Draw a scene from the room. Use one of the points of view listed above.

2. Look at the points of view in *Children's Games* and *Endangered Species* for ideas.

## Differentiated Instruction

**Reteach**
Have students take an object from their desks. Ask them to observe it from beneath, above, close up, and far away and to explain their observations. If you have a telescope in the classroom, allow students to use it to observe their objects.

**Special Needs**
The use of technology such as digital cameras can help students with disabilities achieve lesson objectives in alternate ways. Students can go outside and take a picture of people in action, immediately view the picture, and describe the types of lines they see in the image.

**ELL**
Students may benefit from hearing descriptions of each of the four viewpoints described in this lesson so that they may develop language to describe their own works of art later. Consider using a visual aid, such as a quick sketch, to reinforce your discussion.

◄ Graham Bennett.
Age 9.

**Think** about how the student artist created the observation drawing.

 **Creative Expression**

How can you best capture the action of a group of children running and playing? Draw a sketch by observing children at play.

1. Think about repeating lines and shapes to draw gestures.

2. Go to the school playground and watch all the action that is taking place.

3. Sketch a variety of gestures from a specific point of view. Show the gestures of the children and some of their environment. Fill the entire page. Be sure to overlap your objects and use a variety of lines.

**Art Criticism**

**Describe** Describe the children and their environment.

**Analyze** Explain how you captured the children's gestures in relation to their environment.

**Interpret** Decide how your selected viewpoint creates a certain feeling in your picture.

**Decide** Did you successfully draw the gestures of the children in relation to their environment? Explain.

Unit 1 • Lesson 3    **47**

---

# Reflect    Time: About 5 minutes

## Review and Assess

"Let's review how artists use different viewpoints." "Vamos a repasar cómo los artistas usan diferentes puntos de vista".

## Think

The artist included some details in the drawings but they are not close-up details. Only a portion of the field can be seen by the viewer.

■ Use **Large Prints 49** *Bedroom at Arles* and **50** *Sawamura Kodenji as Tsuyu no Mae* to have students identify the point of view each artist used.

## Informal Assessment

■ For standardized-format test practice using this lesson's art content, see pages 10–11 in *Reading and Writing Test Preparation.*

**Art Journal: Critical Thinking**
Have students answer the four art criticism questions—Describe, Analyze, Interpret, and Decide—in their Art Journals. In small groups, have students discuss the use of viewpoints in their observation drawings in the Creative Expression activity.

---

**Art Across the Curriculum**

Use these simple ideas to reinforce art concepts across the curriculum.

★ **Descriptive Writing** Have students use the writing process to write a descriptive paragraph about the painting *Children's Games.*

★ **Math** Have students learn about rays and angles by examining the ones used in *Children's Games.*

★ **Science** Use the painting *Endangered Species* to discuss endangered species of plants and animals.

★ **Social Studies** Have students learn about peasant life in the sixteenth century by examining the subjects in *Children's Games.*

★ **Technology** Have students use the clip art in a computer's word processing program to illustrate different points of view. Visit **SRAonline.com** to print detailed instructions for this activity.
NSAE 6.b

# Observation Drawing

## Extra! For the Art Specialist

**Time:** About 45 minutes

### Focus

Study *Large Print 49* *Bedroom at Arles* and ask students to discuss the point of view the artist depicted in this work. Where are you, the viewer, standing in relation to the image in this artwork?

### Teach

Review the concepts of observation drawing and points of view. Collect a variety of objects for students to select. Place the objects in a centralized location. Explain to students that they will select one object and create a drawing of it from four different points of view. Have students complete the alternate activity.

### Reflect

Have students use the four steps of art criticism to evaluate their work. Did they effectively create an observation drawing from four points of view?

### Alternate Activity

**Materials:**
- sketchbook or 9" × 12" drawing paper
- pencils
- erasers

1. Have students select one object that interests them and observe its details. Have students begin with drawing a close-up view. The image should fill the page.

2. The second drawing of the object should be a faraway view. The basic shape of the object should be included, but no details. Students should also include objects that are in the background or foreground.

3. The third drawing should be from an ant's view. The object should be placed so that it is above eye level.

4. The final drawing is from a bird's eye-view. Have students place the object on the floor.

## Research in Art Education

Research has shown that incorporating the arts in education can lead to positive school change. Pilot projects demonstrate that "the arts do contribute to the general school curriculum, to learning for all students, to school and professional culture, to educational and instructional practices, and to the schools' neighborhoods and communities" ("The Arts and Education Reform: Lessons from a Four-Year Evaluation of the A+ Schools Program, 1995–1999" in *Critical Links*, p. 84). As students learn about observation drawing, encourage them to think about how people and objects relate to their environment.

## Assessment

Use the following rubric to evaluate the artwork that students make in the Creative Expression activity and to assess students' understanding of observation drawing.

Have students complete page 13 or 14 in their *Assessment* books.

| | Art History and Culture | Aesthetic Perception | Creative Expression | Art Criticism |
|---|---|---|---|---|
| **3 POINTS** | The student can identify differences in the periods and cultures reflected in the works of art. | The student accurately defines *observation drawing* and identifies the four types of viewpoints. | The student depicts a specific viewpoint in his or her drawing. | The student thoughtfully and honestly evaluates own work using the four steps of art criticism. |
| **2 POINTS** | The student's identification of differences is weak or incomplete. | The student shows emerging awareness of the differences among the four types of viewpoints and some understanding of observation drawing. | The student's drawing shows an attempt to depict a specific viewpoint. | The student attempts to evaluate own work but shows an incomplete understanding of evaluation criteria. |
| **1 POINT** | The student cannot identify or compare the periods and cultures reflected in the works of art. | The student does not understand what an observation drawing is and cannot identify the four types of viewpoints. | The student's drawing does not show a specific viewpoint. | The student makes no attempt to evaluate own work. |

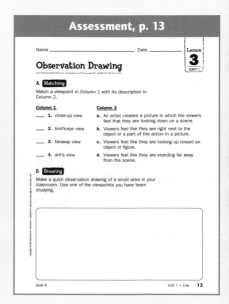

**Assessment, p. 13**

Name _____ Date _____

Lesson 3 UNIT 1

**Observation Drawing**

**A. Matching**

Match a viewpoint in Column 1 with its description in Column 2.

Column 1
___ 1. close-up view
___ 2. bird's-eye view
___ 3. faraway view
___ 4. ant's view

Column 2
a. An artist creates a picture in which the viewers feel that they are looking down on a scene.
b. Viewers feel like they are right next to the object or a part of the action in a picture.
c. Viewers feel like they are looking up toward an object or figure.
d. Viewers feel like they are standing far away from the scene.

**B. Drawing**

Make a quick observation drawing of a small area in your classroom. Use one of the viewpoints you have been studying.

Level 4          Unit 1 • Line   **13**

# Contour Lines

Lesson 4 introduces contour lines. Contour lines are lines that show the edges and surface ridges of an object.

## Objectives

 **Art History and Culture**

To demonstrate knowledge of the lives and work of Benny Andrews and Henri Matisse

 **Creative Expression**

To draw pictures to illustrate the differences between regular contour and blind contour drawings

**Aesthetic Perception**

To discriminate between how artists use contour lines and how they use blind contours to see and record objects

 **Art Criticism**

To evaluate own work using the four steps of art criticism

### Vocabulary  Reading

Review the following vocabulary word with students before beginning the lesson.

**blind contour drawing** **contorno a ciegas**—a drawing created by keeping one's eyes on the object being drawn and concentrating on directions and curves without looking at the paper or lifting the pencil or pen from the paper

See page 59B for additional vocabulary and Spanish vocabulary resources.

 **Art Journal: Vocabulary**

Have students add this word to the Vocabulary section of their Art Journals.

## Lesson Materials

- 9″ × 12″ white drawing paper
- 12″ × 18″ white drawing paper
- black felt-tip markers

**Alternate Materials**
- pencils

## Program Resources

- *Reading and Writing Test Prep.,* pp. 12–13
- *Transparency 4*
- *Flash Cards* 1–6
- *Artist Profiles,* pp. 3, 42
- *Animals Through History Time Line*
- *Assessment,* pp. 15–16
- *Large Prints 49* Bedroom at Arles and *50* Sawamura Kodenji as Tsuyu no Mae

### Concept Trace
Contour Lines
**Introduced:** Level 3, Unit 1, Lesson 3
**Reinforced:** Level 5, Unit 1, Lesson 2

---

## Lesson 4 Arts Integration

### Theatre

Complete Unit 1, Lesson 4, on pages 24–25 of *Theatre Arts Connections.*

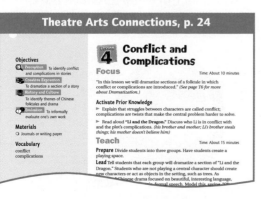

Theatre Arts Connections, p. 24

### Music

SPOTLIGHT on MUSIC

*Big Bunch of Roses.* John Wesley Work.

The contour of an object or figure is its edges and surface ridges. Play Work's charming *Big Bunch of Roses* as student practice contour drawing. As the music plays, have students close their eyes and envision a bunch of roses and without lifting pencil from paper, create a contour drawing of the roses.

### Movement & Dance

Divide students into groups of four. Each person will take a turn being the model. The model will pose, while the other members of the group keep their eyes on the pose at all times in order to trace the outline of the model. Have the students start at top of head or at the feet going clockwise.

 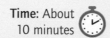

# Focus

**Time:** About 10 minutes

## Activate Prior Knowledge

"Describe the edges and lines that make up a drinking glass." "Describan los bordes y las líneas que forman un vaso".

- Show students a glass as you read the above instruction.

- Discuss students' responses. They will probably mention that vertical and curved lines make up a glass.

### Using Literature ⭐ Reading

- Read *Harry the Poisonous Centipede* by Lynne Reid Banks. The illustrations of insects and human body parts are examples of contour drawings.

### Thematic Connection ⭐ Social Studies

- **Neighborhoods/Communities:** Use the paintings to discuss things that symbolize a community (food, dress, objects, patriotism, architecture, and so on). NSAE 3.a

## Introduce the Art

# Look

"Let's take a close look at the two works of art." "Vamos a observar de cerca las dos obras de arte".

### Asking Questions ⭐ Reading

- Have students ask and answer questions to learn about the message in each artwork. What is the subject matter of each artwork? Andrews: Narrative portrait. Matisse: portrait. Could the Matisse drawing also be considered a genre? Yes. What is a patriot? A person who loves his or her country and defends and supports it.

 **Art History and Culture**

Possible answer: *Patriots* is considered a contemporary artwork, meaning that the artist is still living and that the artwork was created during or close to the lifetimes of the viewers.

 **Web Connection**

Visit **www.nga.gov** (National Gallery of Art) to view exhibitions of works of art by African American artists.

---

**Look** at the works of art on these pages. Matisse made this pen-and-ink drawing in 1939. His drawing is a portrait. Andrews's drawing is a reflection of his experiences with everyday people. His drawing is a narrative. Notice how both artists used contour lines to define the edges and ridges of the subjects in their drawings.

◀ **Benny Andrews.** (American). *Patriots.* 1991.

Pen and ink on paper. $22\frac{1}{2}$ × 15 inches (57.15 × 38.1 cm.). Cumberland Gallery, Nashville, Tennessee.

 **Art History and Culture**

Notice the years that the works of art were created. *Patriots* is considered a contemporary work of art. What does *contemporary* mean?

---

**Art History and Culture**

## Benny Andrews

Benny Andrews (ben´ ē an´ drōoz) (1930– ) reflects his personal experiences with the farmers, workers, and everyday people of his world in paintings, drawings, and collages. Andrews's art often focuses on people and places that were part of his Southern upbringing. His art makes the viewer think about his subjects and the social fabric and conditions of today's society. Andrews was born the second of ten children of sharecroppers George and Viola Andrews. He began drawing at the age of three and attended the Art Institute of Chicago during his adulthood. His works have been displayed in many prestigious galleries.

See pages 24–25 and 16–21 for more about art history and subject matter.

**Artist Profiles, p. 3**

▸ Artist Profile ◂

**Benny Andrews**
b. 1930

Benny Andrews (ben´ ē an´ drūz) was born in rural Georgia during the Great Depression. His parents were farmers. They raised ten children. Andrews grew up watching his father George paint pictures on every available surface. Benny himself scratched pictures in the dirt with sticks. After high school, he served in the United States Air Force. At the time, Georgia did not permit African American students to attend its art schools. A federal law forced the state to pay part of Andrews's tuition to an out-of-state school. Andrews was able to earn a degree at the Art Institute of Chicago. But even there, the work of African American students was not included in student shows. After a long struggle, Andrews finally

**▲ Henri Matisse.** (French). *Portrait of a Woman with a Hood.* 1939.

Lead pencil. 13⅛ × 10⅛ inches (33.2 × 25.6 cm.). State Hermitage Museum, St. Petersburg, Russia.

**Study** both works of art to see how lines flow throughout them.

▶ Describe some of the lines you see.

▶ What areas are emphasized more than others? What techniques did the artists use to emphasize these areas?

▶ Think of three adjectives to describe the couple in Andrews's drawing. Then list three adjectives to describe Matisse's woman.

## Aesthetic Perception

**Design Awareness** Closely observe objects in your environment. Notice changes in surface areas that would be defined as contours in a drawing.

# Art History and Culture

## Henri Matisse

Henri Matisse (än´ rē ma tēs´) (1869–1954) was an accomplished painter, sculptor, and graphic designer. Matisse was the leader of an art movement called fauvism. Members of this movement were called *Fauves,* meaning "wild beasts," because they rejected traditional styles and painted with brilliant colors and bold distortions of reality. Matisse experimented with color and line throughout his art career. Some of Matisse's contour drawings were studies that were made in preparation for paintings. He is considered one of the most influential artists of the 1900s.

See pages 24–25 and 16–21 for more about art history and subject matter.

**Artist Profiles, p. 42**

*Artist Profile*
**Henri Matisse**
1869–1954

Henri Matisse (än´ rē ma tēs´) was the son of a middle-class couple in the north of France. He was not interested in art while he was in school. After high school his father sent him to law school in Paris. When he was 21 an appendicitis attack changed his life. Because he had to spend a long time in the hospital, his mother brought him a paint box to help him pass the time. Matisse eventually convinced his father to let him drop out of law school and study art. Matisse married and started a family soon after. His paintings were not selling, so he worked for a decorator and his wife opened a hat shop. During the last years of his life he suffered from arthritis. Unable to hold a brush in his hands, he devoted his efforts to

# Study

▶ The lines used in both works of art are contour lines, representing only the edges and surface ridges of each image.

▶ Matisse: Smooth contour lines draw emphasis to the face. Andrews: Dark contour lines draw emphasis to the people's upper torsos.

▶ Both drawings use thin contour lines, with the only thickness being used to create depth and show variation.

■ For more examples of portraits, see *The National Museum of Women in the Arts Collection.*

### Art Journal: Writing

Encourage students to write their own explanations of contour lines in the Concepts section of their Art Journals. What else do they want to know about contour lines?

## Aesthetic Perception

**Design Awareness** Lots of changes in surface areas could be defined as a contour in a drawing, for example, fold lines in clothing or open spaces in objects such as scissors or a crate.

**Developing Visual Literacy** Invite students to share any personal experiences that contribute to their understanding of the works of art. For example, what do students think is the most important thing about their culture? (patriotism, clothes, architecture, and so on)

### Web Connection

Visit **www.musee-matisse-nice.org** (the Henri Matisse Museum of Nice) to learn more about the life and art of Henri Matisse.

each

**Time:** About 45 minutes

"Can you create a blind contour drawing of your hand?" "¿Pueden crear un contorno a ciegas de su mano?"

- Read and discuss the definitions of *contour* and *blind contour* on page 50.

## Practice

**Materials:** 9" × 12" white drawing paper, felt-tip markers

**Alternate Materials:** pencils

- Distribute the materials and have students follow the directions on page 50.

## Creative Expression

**Materials:** 12" × 18" white drawing paper, pencils

**Alternate Materials:** black felt-tip pen

- Distribute the materials and have students follow the directions on page 51.

- See page 229 in Activity Tips for visual examples of techniques.

 **Art Journal: Brainstorming**

Have students create a list in their Art Journals of things they need to remember when creating a blind contour drawing. Have them refer to this list before they begin the Creative Expression activity.

---

# Using Contour Lines

The **contour** of an object or figure is its edges and surface ridges. Artists often make contour drawings of objects and use them as studies before making a painting or drawing. Artists also make blind contour drawings, which help them to become more perceptive. Even if these drawings are not very accurate, making them develops an artist's ability to observe.

**Contour lines** are lines that show the edges and surface ridges of an object.

A **blind contour drawing** is a drawing that is made by looking at the object being drawn, not at the paper. You make a blind contour drawing by following the edges and ridges of an object with your eyes as you slowly draw it with your pen. Try not to look at your paper; instead, concentrate on the object you are drawing. Do not lift your pen from the paper. Try to draw one continuous line

## Practice

Create a blind contour drawing of your hand. Use a felt-tip pen.

1. Look closely at your hand. Notice all the contours, the outer edges, the folds where you close your hand, and the lines around your knuckles.

2. Draw a blind contour of your hand, looking at it from one angle. Try to make your drawing one continuous line.

**50** Unit 1 • Lesson 4

---

## Differentiated Instruction

**Reteach**

Have students use their fingers to slowly trace along the outside edges of a simple object as their eyes follow the object. Then have them draw the object with their fingers on their palms as their eyes slowly follow the contours of the object.

**Special Needs**

Students may have difficulty letting their eyes follow the contour lines of a person or object. You may facilitate closer examination by standing near the person or object and slowly air-tracing the contour lines for students to observe.

**ELL**

You may want students to experience a concrete example of the lesson's vocabulary before asking them to describe their own work. You might create a blind contour drawing on the board while describing the process aloud for the group.

◄ **Maizie Pfizenmeyer.**
Age 9.

**Think** about how the student artist used blind contour and regular contour in the drawing.

## Creative Expression

How can you develop your ability to observe? Create both a blind contour and a regular contour drawing of a person.

1. Observe the edges and ridges of objects and of people around you.

2. Create a blind contour drawing of the model. Do not lift the chalk from the construction paper as you work.

3. On a new sheet of construction paper, make a slower, regular contour drawing of the model. You may look at your paper, but do not pick up the chalk. The line must be one continuous line.

4. Add several objects to your drawing.

## Art Criticism

**Describe** What objects did you include with the person in your drawing?

**Analyze** Explain the types of lines you used to create your drawings.

**Interpret** What similarities and differences do you see between your regular contour and your blind contour drawings?

**Decide** What strategies did you use to make your drawings successful? Did you improve in your second contour drawing?

Unit 1 • Lesson 4 **51**

# Reflect

Time: About 5 minutes

## Review and Assess

"What have you learned about contour drawings?" "¿Qué han aprendido acerca de los dibujos de contornos?"

## Think

The shape of the model looks like it is part of a blind contour. The details on the face and clothes look like a contour drawing.

■ Use *Large Prints 49 Bedroom at Arles* and *50 Sawamura Kodenji as Tsuyu no Mae* to have students identify contour lines.

## Informal Assessment

■ For standardized-format test practice using this lesson's art content, see pages 12–13 in *Reading and Writing Test Preparation.*

### Art Journal: Critical Thinking

Have students answer the four art criticism questions—Describe, Analyze, Interpret, and Decide—in their Art Journals. In small groups, have students discuss the use of continuous lines in their regular contour and blind contour drawings in the Creative Expression activity.

## Art Across the Curriculum

Use these simple ideas to reinforce art concepts across the curriculum.

★ **Poetry Writing** Have students use the writing process to write a poem about why it is important to be loyal to your country.

★ **Math** Have students learn about right angles and perpendicular lines by examining the straight lines in *Patriots*.

★ **Science** India ink is indelible (cannot be erased). Have students research the purposes of various types of inks.

★ **Social Studies** Use the drawing *Patriots* to discuss traditions of celebrating patriotism in different countries.

★ **Technology** Have students find suitable clip art in a computer's word processing program to illustrate contour drawing. Visit **SRAonline.com** to print detailed instructions for this activity.
NSAE 6.b

# Contour Lines

## Extra! For the Art Specialist

**Time:** About 45 minutes

### Focus

Study **Large Print 50** *Sawamura Kodenji as Tsuyu no Mae.* Ask students to point out the outlines of the shapes. Have students describe the shapes and where they think the lines begin and end.

### Teach

Demonstrate making a blind contour drawing. Explain that your hand moves along the edges of the object as your eyes move along the edges. Demonstrate drawing a contour drawing of the same object. Discuss the differences and similarities. Have students complete the alternate activity.

### Reflect

Have students use the four steps of art criticism to evaluate their work. Did they effectively create a contour drawing of their shoe? Did they encounter any difficulties?

### Alternate Activity

**Materials:**
- sketchbook
- newspaper
- 9" × 12" or smaller drawing paper
- pencils, erasers
- fine-tipped pen
- color pencils and/or watercolor paints (optional)

1. Have students create a contour drawing of their shoe. Have them notice the ridges and edges. Have students begin by creating several blind contours of the shoe. Have them use newspaper to drape over their hands as they make the blind contour drawing. This will keep them from looking.

2. On drawing paper, have students create a contour drawing of a shoe.

3. Have students use a pen to outline their drawings and to add details such as stitching lines.

4. As an option, students can use either color pencils or watercolor paints to add color.

## Research in Art Education

Some researchers suggest that studying art helps students develop critical-thinking and problem-solving skills. Certain aspects of art education may encourage these skills: "Art history and art criticism . . . are probably more responsible than studio courses for producing measured improvements in vocabulary, writing, and critical thinking skills." ("Theories and Research That Support Art Instruction for Instrumental Outcomes" in *Schools, Communities, and the Arts: A Research Compendium*). The purpose of a contour drawing is to improve perception, or the way you look or think about what you see. As students create contour drawings, encourage them to become aware of changes in their perceptions.

## Assessment

Use the following rubric to evaluate the artwork that students make in the Creative Expression activity and to assess students' understanding of contour lines.

Have students complete page 15 or 16 in their *Assessment* books.

| | Art History and Culture | Aesthetic Perception | Creative Expression | Art Criticism |
|---|---|---|---|---|
| **3 POINTS** | The student demonstrates knowledge of the lives and work of Andrews and Matisse. | The student accurately defines and discriminates between contour lines and blind contour. | The student's drawings clearly illustrate the differences between regular contour and blind contour. | The student thoughtfully and honestly evaluates own work using the four steps of art criticism. |
| **2 POINTS** | The student's knowledge of the lives and work of Andrews and Matisse is weak or incomplete. | The student shows emerging awareness of the differences between contour lines and blind contour but cannot consistently identify them. | The student's drawings show a weak or incomplete understanding of the differences between regular contour and blind contour drawings. | The student attempts to evaluate own work but shows an incomplete understanding of evaluation criteria. |
| **1 POINT** | The student cannot demonstrate knowledge of the lives and work of Andrews and Matisse. | The student cannot identify contour lines and blind contour. | The student's drawings show no understanding of the differences between regular contour and blind contour. | The student makes no attempt to evaluate own artwork. |

### Assessment, p. 15

Name _____ Date _____

**Contour Lines**

Lesson **4** UNIT 1

**A.** Drawing
Use a crayon or marker to draw a blind contour of your hand.

**B.** Writing
Write step-by-step directions for making a blind-contour drawing.

_____
_____
_____

**C.** Short Answer
1. What is the purpose of a regular contour drawing? _____
2. What is the purpose of a blind contour drawing? _____

Level 4

Unit 1 • Line **15**

# Lesson 5 Overview

# Flowing Lines

**Lesson 5** introduces flowing lines. Artists use flowing lines to create a mood or feeling.

## Objectives

### Art History and Culture

To recognize the focus on nature in works of art by Asian artists

### Creative Expression

To use flowing lines to create a painting of bamboo

### Aesthetic Perception

To identify flowing lines in a work of art

### Art Criticism

To evaluate own work using the four steps of art criticism

## Vocabulary ⭐ Reading

Review the following vocabulary word with students before beginning the lesson.

**flowing lines** *líneas que fluyen*—curved lines with no sudden breaks in the movement, used to create a feeling of calm and gracefulness

See page 59B for additional vocabulary and Spanish vocabulary resources.

### Art Journal: Vocabulary

Have students add this word to the Vocabulary section of their Art Journals.

## Lesson Materials

- 12" × 18" newsprint
- 12" × 18" white paper
- watercolors
- round pointed watercolor brushes
- water container half filled with water
- bamboo limb
- black India ink, no. 5
- paper towels

**Alternate Materials**
- rice paper
- No. 2 Chinese brushes
- watercolor paper

## Program Resources

- *Reading and Writing Test Prep.*, pp. 14–15
- *Transparency 5*
- *Flash Cards* 1–6
- *Artist Profiles*, pp. 31, 44
- *Animals Through History Time Line*
- *Assessment*, pp. 17–18
- *Large Prints 49* Bedroom at Arles and *50* Sawamura Kodenji as Tsuyu no Mae
- *Art Around the World Collection*

### Concept Trace
**Flowing Lines**
Introduced: Level 3, Unit 1, Lesson 2

Reinforced: Level 5, Unit 1, Lesson 2

---

# Lesson 5 Arts Integration

## Theatre

Complete Unit 1, Lesson 5, on pages 26–27 of *Theatre Arts Connections.*

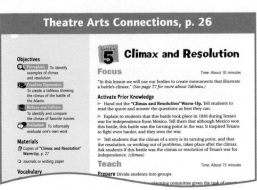

## Music

*Walking in the Air.* Howard Blake.

Flowing lines create a feeling of calm and gracefulness. Play Howard Blake's *Walking in the Air* from the popular animated film *The Snowman* as students complete the Practice activity in which they create flowing lines. Encourage them to use the flowing musical lines and images they create in their paintings.

## Movement & Dance

Have students use different parts of their bodies, hands, noses, elbows, and knees to write their first names in large cursive motions in space. Students should demonstrate a sense of flow and complete their name without any stops. Students can also explore running the pattern of their name on the floor, using a smooth flowing motion.

# Focus

**Time:** About 10 minutes

## Activate Prior Knowledge

"Can you name the types of lines you used in previous works of art?" "Pueden nombrar los tipos de líneas que usaron anteriormente en obras de arte?"

- Discuss students' answers and draw the lines.

### Using Literature ⭐ Reading

- Read *Prairie Dogs Kiss and Lobsters Wave* by Marilyn Singer. Flowing lines are used to create different environmental settings.

### Thematic Connection ⭐ Science

- **Living Things:** Use the paintings to discuss living things and note that plants, animals, and people are classified as living things.

## Introduce the Art

# Look

"Let's take a close look at the two works of art." "Vamos a observar detalladamente las dos obras de arte".

### Fact and Opinion ⭐ Reading

- Have students list facts and opinions about each artwork. (Possible Answers: Facts: Both works of art were created by Asian artists. Both artists worked directly on paper with ink. Mei's artwork is a landscape painting of orchids and rocks. Hokusai's painting is a portrait of a boy playing a flute. Opinions: The boy in the Hokusai painting must enjoy playing the flute. The orchids in the Mei painting would look better if there were more color.)

###  Art History and Culture

Possible answer: Both works of art were created with ink on paper. Both also have thick and thin lines.

 **Web Connection**
For more information on Asian art, visit
**www.clevelandart.org** (the Cleveland Museum of Art).

**52** UNIT 1 • Line

---

 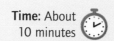

# Flowing Lines

▲ **Gu Mei.** (Chinese). *Orchids and Rocks.* 1644. Ming Dynasty.

Detail of handscroll ink on paper. $10\frac{5}{8} \times 67\frac{1}{4}$ inches (27 × 170.8 cm). Arthur M. Sackler Gallery, Smithsonian Institution, Washington, D.C.

**Look** closely at the ink paintings on these pages. Mei used flowing lines in her landscape painting. Hokusai used repeated lines and concentrated on the contours of the objects in his portrait. The lines are of various thickness. *Boy with a Flute* is a portrait. Both artists worked directly on paper with ink.

###  Art History and Culture

Look at the captions and elements in the paintings, such as the writing in both and the features of the child in *Boy with a Flute*. What do the artists' works have in common?

---

### Art History and Culture

## Gu Mei

Gu Mei (gōō mā) (1619–1664) was a musician, a poet, and a painter of landscapes and orchids. *Orchids and Rocks,* created in 1644, is a scene from nature. In the first and last sections of the painting, the orchids grow upward in a normal way. The orchids in the middle section overhang a cliff. *Orchids and Rocks* is a landscape.

See pages 24–25 and 16–21 for more about art history and subject matter.

**Artist Profiles, p. 44**

◆ Artist Profile ◆

**Gu Mei**
1619-1664

Gu Mei (gōō mā) was born in Nanjing, China. She held a unique place among the intellectuals of the time because she was not only a talented musician and poet, but also a painter. Gu Mei married a respected poet, Gong Dingzi.

▲ **Gu Mei.** (Chinese). *Orchids and Rocks.* 1644. Ming Dynasty.

Detail of handscroll ink on paper. $10\frac{5}{8} \times 67\frac{1}{4}$ inches (27 × 170.8 cm). Arthur M. Sackler Gallery, Smithsonian Institution, Washington, D.C.

▲ **Katsushika Hokusai.** (Japanese).
*Boy with a Flute.* Edo Period.
••••••••••••••••••••••••••••••
Ink on paper. 4½ × 6¼ inches (11.43 × 15.88 cm.).
Freer Gallery of Art, Smithsonian Institution,
Washington, D.C.

**Study** both works of art to see how the artists
used lines to create flowing contours.

▶ Describe how lines are used in the paintings.

▶ Are the lines all the same? Are some thicker
than others?

▶ How do you think the boy in Hokusai's
painting is feeling?

### Aesthetic Perception

**Design Awareness** Examine objects with line patterns. How do
you use lines to create emphasis in a work of art? What type of
brush would you use to make the thinnest lines?

## Art History and Culture

### Katsushika Hokusai

Katsushika Hokusai (kät sōō´ shē kä  hō´ kōō sī) (1760–1849)
produced a vast number of prints, sketches, and paintings. He may
have produced about 30,000 works of art over a period of 70 years.
Hokusai was one of the main artists of the Edo period. Much of his
work was done in a style called *ukiyo-e*, meaning "floating world."
This style focused on nature and people doing everyday things.
Hokusai's portrait reflects the transition from portraiture of the
wealthy to scenes of common people. *Boy with a Flute* is an
ink-wash painting. Ink is
used as if it were watercolor.

See pages 24–25 and 16–21
for more about art history
and subject matter.

**Artist Profiles, p. 31**

◆ Artist Profile ◆
**Katsushika Hokusai**
1760-1849
Katsushika Hokusai (kät sōō´ shē kä  hō´ kōō
sī) was born in the city that is now Tokyo.
He changed his name more than 30 times.
No one knows why. When his home became
dirty, he moved. He lived in 93 different
places! Hokusai supported himself
by illustrating comic books, greeting cards,
and novels. During his lifetime he had two
wives and seven children.

Hokusai was not interested in money.
To pay his bills he would hand over an
envelope of money he had received for
a painting. Sometimes it was enough, and
sometimes it wasn't. When he was broke,
he bought art supplies after dark, hoping
to avoid people he owed. Hokusai painted

## Study

▶ Hokusai: The folds of fabric and strands of
hair give a softer feeling and texture to the
thin contours of the figure. Mei: The
flowing lines in the orchids create a
calm feeling.

▶ Hokusai: Repeated zigzag lines on the
drum. Mei: Smooth and broken lines in
the orchids.

▶ Hokusai: The flowing lines of the boy's
casual pose create a sense of happiness
and peace (or thoughtfulness and quiet).

■ For more examples of art from Asia, see
the *Art Around the World Collection.*

### Art Journal: Writing

Encourage students to define and
illustrate flowing lines in the Concepts
section of their Art Journals. What else do
they know about flowing lines?

### Aesthetic Perception

**Design Awareness** Discuss students' answers.
Artists often vary the thickness of their lines
for emphasis. Use a thin, pointed brush to
paint thin lines and details. For thick lines
and large areas, press firmly on the tip or use
a wide brush.

**Developing Visual Literacy** Have students
create visuals that could be used to
complement the main idea of the works of
art. For example, for *Orchids and Rocks,*
students should create visuals that would
appear in an environment in which
orchids grow.

### Web Connection

Visit **www.cjn.or.jp/ukiyo-e/index-j.html** (the
Japanese Ukiyo-e Museum) to view paintings
done in the ukiyo-e style.

 **Teach**

"Can you paint flowing thick and thin lines?"
"¿Pueden pintar líneas corridas gruesas y finas?"

- Discuss flowing lines and line variation on page 54.

## Practice

**Materials:** 12" × 18" white paper, watercolors, round pointed watercolor brushes, water container half filled with water, paper towels

**Alternate Materials:** watercolor paper

- Distribute the materials and have students follow the directions on page 54.

 **Creative Expression**

**Materials:** paper, bamboo limb, black India ink, no. 5 round pointed watercolor brushes

**Alternate Materials:** rice paper, no. 2 Chinese brushes

- Before students complete the Creative Expression activity, have them view the portfolios of Asian artists. Have students interpret the ideas and moods represented in the works of art, if possible.
NSAE 4.c
- Distribute the materials and have students follow the directions on page 55.
- See page 230 in Activity Tips for visual examples of techniques.

### Art Journal: Brainstorming
Have students brainstorm points of view they could use to draw their plants in the Creative Expression activity. Students should create practice sketches of their plants in the Plans/Sketches section of their Art Journals.

# Using Flowing Lines

**Flowing lines** create a feeling of calm and gracefulness. Flowing lines are fluid; they change direction and size.

 You can create **light lines** by adding more water to your watercolor paints, and **dark lines** by using less water. The amount of water you mix with the paint will control the strength of your color.

 To create a **thin line,** hold the brush vertically to the paper and touch the paper lightly with the tip of the brush.

To make a **flowing line,** begin with a thin line and gradually press the brush down. Pull up the brush again to make the line become thinner.

## Practice

Create flowing lines. Use watercolors and a pointed brush.

1. Dip your brush in the paint. Use the point of your brush for thin lines and press gently on your brush for thick lines.
2. Practice using different amounts of pressure on your brush to make lines change.

**54** Unit 1 • Lesson 5

## Differentiated Instruction

### Reteach
Have students use a pencil and draw a continuous line following your cues to create line variation. When you say "soft," students should apply very light pressure with the pencil. When you say "hard," they should increase the pressure.

### Special Needs
Students having difficulty grasping small paintbrushes may benefit from a foam-rubber cylinder taped around the brush. Students with cognitive disabilities will need guided practice with painting and brush techniques before beginning the lesson activity.

### ELL
Students may have a need to expand their vocabulary about emotions so that they can respond to the art presented. You might illustrate emotions or moods with quick sketches of faces. Post the sketches with the words they illustrate for ongoing reference.

◀ **Shirley Paul.**
Age 9.

**Think** about how the student artist used flowing lines in the drawing.

### Creative Expression

How would you draw a plant using a brush?

1. Examine a piece of bamboo. Notice how it grows.

2. Watch your teacher demonstrate two Chinese brush-painting hand positions. Practice these positions. Then practice the brushstrokes on newsprint using watered-down black ink.

3. Using the same black ink, paint several pieces of bamboo on white paper. Sit straight and hold your breath while making each brushstroke. Remember to breathe before the next stroke.

### Art Criticism

**Describe** Describe the plant in your drawing.

**Analyze** Did you use flowing lines? Explain.

**Interpret** Were you successful in drawing your plant? Explain.

**Decide** If you were to do it over, what would you change?

# Reflect

**Time:** About 10 minutes

### Review and Assess
"What have you learned about line variation?" "¿Qué han aprendido sobre la variación líneal?"

## Think
The artist used flowing lines in the leaves and thin stems in the bamboo plant.

- Use *Large Prints 49 Bedroom at Arles* and *50 Sawamura Kodenji as Tsuyu no Mae* to have students identify line variation.

### Informal Assessment

- For standardized-format test practice using this lesson's art content, see pages 14–15 in *Reading and Writing Test Preparation.*

### Art Journal: Critical Thinking
Have students answer the four art criticism questions—Describe, Analyze, Interpret, and Decide—in their Art Journals. In small groups, have students discuss the use of flowing lines in their pictures in the Creative Expression activity.

### Art Across the Curriculum

Use these simple ideas to reinforce art concepts across the curriculum.

★ **Expository Writing** Have students use the writing process to write an expository paragraph about plants while examining the plants in *Orchids and Rocks.*

★ **Math** Use the paintings to discuss lines of symmetry.

★ **Science** Use the painting *Orchids and Rocks* to discuss various environments in which plants grow.

★ **Social Studies** Discuss Asian influences in the United States such as food, fashion, and architecture and note that both works of art were created by Asian artists.

★ **Technology** Have students use a computer word processing program to demonstrate flowing lines and line variation. Visit **SRAonline.com** to print detailed instructions for this activity.
NSAE 6.b

# Flowing Lines
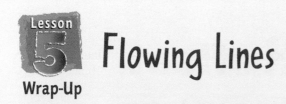

## Extra! For the Art Specialist

### Focus

Study **Large Print 50** *Sawamura Kodenji as Tsuyu no Mae*. Have the students study the variations of lines used by the artist. Which lines flow easily? Which lines give the feeling of calmness?

### Teach

Discuss how artists create observation-brush drawings. They bring the drawing back to the studio and make it into a more detailed painting, often in oil or acrylic. It is not unusual for artists today to create observation-brush drawings as a final artwork. Explain that students will create a landscape based on direct observation of an area outside. They will be using line variation to produce flowing lines that give a feeling of calmness. Have students complete the alternate activity.

### Reflect

Have students use the four steps of art criticism to evaluate their work. Did they effectively use flowing lines to create a landscape?

### Alternate Activity

**Materials:**
- sketchbook or heavy drawing paper 9" × 12" or larger
- pencils, erasers
- drawing boards
- watercolor paints
- brushes in various sizes
- water containers
- paper towels

1. Have students carefully observe the area they will be painting.

2. Have students create several quick sketches showing various points of view. Have them select their best sketch.

3. On drawing paper, have students lightly sketch a few of the most important contour lines. They will use these as guidelines when painting begins.

4. Have students use watercolor paints to draw shapes and go over the contours. Have them use line variation. By varying the pressure that is applied to the brush, they can make lines move from thick to thin.

### Research in Art Education

Research has shown that assessing knowledge through a combination of drawing and writing can lead to higher scores for content knowledge. This applies to native English speakers and limited English speakers alike. It also suggests that "drawing may be one way to reveal what students know but cannot put into words" ("The Arts, Language, and Knowing: An Experimental Study of the Potential of the Visual Arts for Assessing Academic Learning by Language Minority Students" in *Critical Links,* page 141). As students learn about using flowing lines in drawings, encourage them to use drawing as a form of communication.

## Assessment
Use the following rubric to evaluate the artwork that students make in the Creative Expression activity and to assess students' understanding of the lesson concepts.

Have students complete page 17 or 18 in their *Assessment* books.

|  | Art History and Culture | Aesthetic Perception | Creative Expression | Art Criticism |
|---|---|---|---|---|
| **3 POINTS** | The student can identify and compare the focus of both works of art. | The student accurately identifies flowing lines in a work of art. | The student's painting includes flowing lines. | The student thoughtfully and honestly evaluates own work using the four steps of art criticism. |
| **2 POINTS** | The student's comparison is weak or incomplete. | The student shows some awareness of flowing lines but cannot consistently identify them. | The student's painting shows an attempt to use flowing lines. | The student attempts to evaluate own work, but shows an incomplete understanding of evaluation criteria. |
| **1 POINT** | The student cannot identify or compare the focus in the works of art. | The student cannot identify flowing lines in a work of art. | The student's painting shows no understanding of flowing lines. | The student makes no attempt to evaluate own artwork. |

**Assessment, p. 17**

Name _____ Date _____

Lesson **5** UNIT 1

**Flowing Lines**

**A. Short Answer**
Explain what the term *flowing lines* means.

**B. Drawing**
Use either a set of watercolors or markers to demonstrate what a flowing drawing looks like. Select an object in the room that you can easily see from your seat, and draw it.

**C. Writing**
Katsushika Hokusai painted *Boy with a Flute*. Notice how he used brushstrokes to create a variety of lines. Write a short paragraph describing the different types of lines he used.

Level 4

Unit 1 • Line     17

# Lesson 6 Overview

# Shading Techniques

**Lesson 6** introduces shading techniques. Artists use shading techniques to darken an area by repeating several lines close together.

## Objectives

 **Art History and Culture**

To demonstrate knowledge of the lives and work of James McNeill Whistler and Giorgio Morandi

 **Creative Expression**

To use shading techniques to create light and dark values in a drawing

 **Aesthetic Perception**

To define and identify shading techniques

**Art Criticism**

To use the four steps of art criticism to evaluate own work

### Vocabulary  Reading

Review the following vocabulary words with students before beginning the lesson.

**shading** *sombreado*—a technique for darkening areas by repeating marks such as lines or dots

**value** *valor*—the lightness or darkness of a color or object

See page 59B for additional vocabulary and Spanish vocabulary resources.

 **Art Journal: Vocabulary**

Have students add these words to the Vocabulary section of their Art Journals.

## Lesson Materials

- art paper
- pencils
- 12″ × 18″ white drawing paper
- soft lead pencils
- erasers

### Alternate Materials
- pens
- markers

## Program Resources
- *Reading and Writing Test Prep.,* pp. 16–17
- *Transparency 6*
- *Flash Cards* 1–3
- *Artist Profiles,* pp. 48, 71
- *Animals Through History Time Line*
- *Assessment,* pp. 19–20
- *Large Prints 49 Bedroom at Arles* and **50** *Sawamura Kodenji as Tsuyu no Mae*
- *The National Museum of Women in the Arts Collection*

### Concept Trace
**Shading Techniques**
Introduced: Level 2, Unit 3, Lesson 4

Reinforced: Level 5, Unit 2, Lesson 4

---

## Lesson 6 Arts Integration

### Theatre

Complete Unit 1, Lesson 6, on pages 28–33 of *Theatre Arts Connections.*

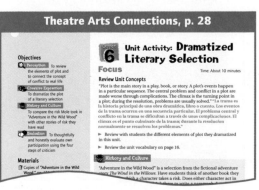

Theatre Arts Connections, p. 28

### Music

*Octopus's Garden.* Richard Starkey.

Shading is a technique for creating dark values or darkening an area. To provide context for shading, play the Beatle song *Octopus's Garden.* Encourage students to think about the different values they could see under the sea, below the storm, beneath the waves, and near a cave.

### Movement & Dance

Have students work with a partner to explore the idea of lightness, darkness, and shadowing. Have one partner stand in front and create a series of slow, fluid movements that reach out in different directions. The other partner will be the shading behind them, echoing their movements.

# Focus

## Activate Prior Knowledge

"Have you ever tried to show light and dark areas or shadows in your drawings? How did you do it?" "¿Alguna vez han tratado de mostrar áreas claras y oscuras o sombras en sus dibujos? ¿Cómo lo hicieron?"

■ Discuss student answers.

**Using Literature** ⭐ Reading

■ Read *Kids to the Rescue! First Aid Techniques for Kids* by Maribeth and Darwin Boelts. The illustrations in this book incorporate shading techniques.

**Thematic Connection** ⭐ Science

■ **Shadows:** Artists use shading techniques to create light values, dark values, and shadows in a work of art. Invite students to find shadows in the artwork.

## Introduce the Art

# Look

"Let's look closely at the two works of art." "Vamos a observar detalladamente las dos obras de arte".

**Summarizing** ⭐ Reading

■ Have students summarize the subject matter in each artwork. Whistler's etching is a portrait of a man wearing a jacket with his arms folded across his chest. Morandi's artwork is a still life of several objects, including jars.

## 🏺 Art History and Culture

The time and place during which an artwork is created does affect the type of media used to create the artwork.

 **Web Connection**
Visit **www.whistlerhouse.org/galleries.htm** (Whistler House Museum of Art) to view works of art by James McNeill Whistler.

---

# Shading Techniques

**Look** at both works of art. Notice the shading techniques used by the two artists. In *Drouet* notice how the area around the face is done with short controlled lines, while the body is created with loose lines. The loose lines create a light value. In his still-life etching, Morandi used closely drawn lines to create a darker value.

◀ **James McNeill Whistler** (American). *Drouet.* 1859.

Etching and drypoint. $8\frac{7}{8} \times 6$ inches (22.54 × 15.24 cm.). Los Angeles County Museum of Art, Los Angeles, California.

## 🏺 Art History and Culture

Notice that both etchings were created during different centuries. Do the time and place during which an artwork is created affect the type of media used to create the artwork?

## 🏺 Art History and Culture

### James McNeill Whistler

James McNeill Whistler (jāmz mək nēl´ hwis´ lər) (1834–1903) was an American artist who produced etchings, paintings, and furniture designs during his art career. He was also known as an interior decorator and a writer. Whistler began his formal art training at the Imperial Academy of Fine Art in Russia. His family lived in Russia during the 1840s. Whistler later attended West Point where he excelled in drawing but flunked mathematics and science. He moved to Europe during the 1850s and spent the rest of his life mostly in France and England.

See pages 24–25 and 16–21 for more about art history and subject matter.

**Artist Profiles, p. 71**

*Artist Profile*

**James McNeill Whistler**
1834–1903

Although James McNeill Whistler (jāmz mak nēl´ hwis´ lər) was born in Lowell, Massachusetts, he often claimed that he was born somewhere in Europe. Whistler did spend part of his childhood in Russia—his father, an engineer, helped construct the St. Petersburg-Moscow railroad—and he studied at the Imperial Academy of Fine Arts for one year. After returning to America, Whistler attended West Point Military Academy, and then he traveled to Paris to study art. Throughout his career Whistler worked experimentally and refused to be associated with any one style of painting.

▲ **Giorgio Morandi.** (Italian). *Still Life with Coffee Pot.* 1933.

.................................
Etching on paper. 11⅛ × 16⅜ inches (29.8 × 39 cm.). The Museum of Modern Art, New York, New York.

**Study** both works of art to see how the artists used lines in shading techniques.

▶ What types of lines do you see?

▶ Where are lines close together or far apart?

▶ Where are the darkest and lightest areas in each etching?

▶ How did the artists make certain objects look realistic?

### Aesthetic Perception

**Seeing Like an Artist** Slowly turn your hand and observe how the light and dark areas change as your hand turns.

### Art History and Culture

#### Giorgio Morandi

Giorgio Morandi (jor´jē ō mo rän´dē) (1890–1964) was a recluse who spent almost his entire life in Bologna, Italy. His artwork revolves around still lifes and landscapes in which there is no room for human figures. The arrangements of bottles, jugs, plates, and bowls are common in his still-life works of art. Morandi, who gained worldwide recognition for his work after World War II, spent many years teaching drawing and printmaking in public schools in Bologna. A large-scale retrospective of Morandi's work was held in several important museums in the United States during the early 1980s.

See pages 24–25 and 16–21 for more about art history and subject matter.

**Artist Profiles, p. 48**

● Artist Profile ●
#### Giorgio Morandi
1890-1964

Giorgio Morandi (jor´ jē ō mo rän´ dē) was born in Bologna, Italy, and became one of the most respected masters in modern Italian art. After displaying an artistic talent at a very young age, Morandi in 1907 enrolled in the Academy of Fine Arts in Bologna. His scholastic performance was excellent at first, but conflicts arose with his professors when his changing interests led him to develop his own artistic language. Morandi began to exhibit his work in 1914 and taught for many years in the municipally-run drawing schools. After World War II broke out in 1943, he moved to Grizzana and began producing exceptional still lifes and landscapes. Morandi continued to paint until he

## Study

▶ Whistler: parallel lines, diagonal lines, horizontal and vertical parallel lines, curved lines; Morandi: diagonal lines

▶ Whistler: Lines in the hair, beard, and underneath the folded hands are close together, while lines that form the body are far apart; Morandi: Lines are consistently close together.

▶ Whistler: The lightest area is the body, and the darkest areas are the beard and hair. Morandi: The lightest areas are the objects in the foreground, and the darkest areas are the shadows.

▶ Both artists made objects look realistic by using shading and highlights.

■ For more examples of still lifes, see *The National Museum of Women in the Arts Collection.*

### Art Journal: Writing

Encourage students to write their own explanations of shading techniques in the Concepts section of their Art Journals. What else do they want to know about shading techniques?

### Aesthetic Perception

**Seeing Like an Artist** Have students watch you demonstrate holding your hand under a light source and turning it so that they can see how light affects the value of your hand.

**Developing Visual Literacy** Invite students to compare how the choice of media and point of view affect the portrayal of the subject in each artwork. For example, in *Drouet* we get a close-up view of the subject so we can make out the details of his face. The media (etching and drypoint) accurately illustrate details such as the hair.

### Web Connection

Visit **www.museomorandi.it/english/sec_pag.htm** (Museo Morandi) to learn more about the life and art of Giorgio Morandi.

# Teach

**Time:** About 10 minutes

"How are lines used to create a value scale going from light to dark values?" *"Cómo se usan las líneas para crear una escala de valores desde valores más claros a más oscuros?"*

- Discuss shading techniques on page 58.

## Practice

**Materials:** art paper, pencils

**Alternate Materials:** pens or markers

- Distribute the materials and have students follow the directions on page 58.

## Creative Expression

**Materials:** 12" × 18" white drawing paper, soft lead pencils (4B), erasers

**Alternate Materials:** pens and markers

- Distribute the materials and have students follow the directions on page 59.
- Have students integrate ideas about themselves and family in their still lives.
  NSAE 3.b
- See page 230 in Activity Tips for visual examples of techniques.

### Art Journal: Brainstorming

Have students brainstorm ways to portray the light and dark values of their still-life drawings in the Ideas section of their Art Journals. Then have them select a point of view for their still-life drawing in the Creative Expression activity.

---

# Using Shading Techniques

**Shading** is a technique for creating dark values or darkening an area by repeating marks such as lines or dots. **Value** is the lightness or darkness of a color or object. Hatching, crosshatching, and contour hatching are shading techniques.

**Hatching** is a pattern of parallel lines.

In **cross-hatching,** the parallel lines overlap each other.

**Contour hatching** follows the form of an object. If you are creating a shadow on a ball, the hatch lines will curve around the surface of the ball.

Lines or dots placed close together create a dark value. Lines or dots placed far apart create a light value.

Hatching     Cross-hatching     Contour hatching

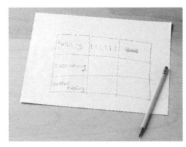

## Practice

Use shading techniques to draw a value scale. Use a soft lead pencil and white paper.

1. Divide a sheet of paper into three columns and three rows. Print the name of each shading technique in each box in the first column.

2. Draw lines far apart in the second column to show the lightest value. In the third column, show the darkest value by drawing lines as close as you can without having them touch.

3. Practice hatching in the first row, crosshatching in the second row, and contour hatching in the third row.

**58**   Unit 1 • Lesson 6

---

## Differentiated Instruction

**Reteach**

Have students draw three shapes. Have them use the shading techniques taught in this lesson to shade the three shapes.

**Special Needs**

Students with disabilities may benefit from guided practice before the lesson. Have students complete a value drawing of just one object to check for understanding.

**ELL**

Frequent comprehension checks can help you monitor students' ability to follow the lesson. You can ask students for physical responses or short verbal responses to indicate their understanding; for example, *Point to the darkest section of the Whistler etching.*

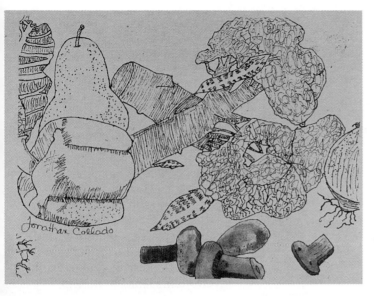

◄ **Jonathan Collado.**
Age 9.

**Think** about how the student artist used shading techniques in the drawing.

### Creative Expression

How can you use shading techniques to show light and dark values? Use shading techniques to show light and dark values in a still-life drawing.

1. Think about ways to portray the value (lightness or darkness) of objects in your classroom.

2. Arrange a still life. Use five or more objects. Set up a lamp or spotlight so the light is coming from one side.

3. Using a pencil, lightly sketch the shapes of the objects. Use a variety of hatching techniques to represent the light and dark areas of your composition.

### Art Criticism

**Describe** Describe the shading techniques you used.

**Analyze** Do any areas have highlights or shadows? Explain.

**Interpret** Select a name for your still life.

**Decide** Were you successful in using shading techniques to create different values? Explain.

Unit 1 • Lesson 6     **59**

---

# Reflect
Time: About 10 minutes

### Review and Assess

"Were you able to use lines to create values in your drawing?" "¿Pudieron usar líneas para crear valores en sus dibujos?"

## Think

The artist used hatching on the stems of the vegetables and contour hatching on the bell pepper.

■ Use *Large Prints 49* Bedroom at Arles and *50 Sawamura Kodenji as Tsuyu no Mae* to have students identify how the artists used shading techniques.

### Informal Assessment

■ For standardized-format test practice using this lesson's art content, see pages 16–17 in *Reading and Writing Test Preparation.*

### Art Journal: Critical Thinking

Have students answer the four art criticism questions—Describe, Analyze, Interpret, and Decide—in their Art Journals. In small groups, have students discuss the use of shading techniques in their pictures in the Creative Expression activity.

---

### Art Across the Curriculum

Use these simple ideas to reinforce art concepts across the curriculum.

★ **Personal Writing** Have students explain their personal values in journal entries and point out that the word *value* is also important in art.

★ **Math** Discuss how the word *value* relates to math.

★ **Science** Have students research and discuss printmaking. Use the etching by Giorgio Morandi as an example of printmaking.

★ **Social Studies** Have students discuss cultural issues that immigrants may experience, and point out that James McNeill Whistler was an American who spent about half of his life living in Europe.

★ **Technology** Have students use the line tool in a computer drawing program to illustrate different types of shading techniques. Visit **SRAonline.com** to print detailed instructions for this activity.
NSAE 6.b

# Shading Techniques

 **For the Art Specialist**

**Time:** About 45 minutes

## Focus

Study **Large Print 49** *Bedroom at Arles* and have the students study the various shading techniques used. Where do they see repeated lines used to create value?

## Teach

Review techniques for creating light and dark values, using lines. Collect and display various textured fabrics. Have students make a group set-up at their tables. Have each group use three fabrics. Explain that they will be creating a contour drawing of their arrangement and will use various shading techniques to add a range of values to the drawing. Then have students complete the alternate activity.

## Reflect

Have students use the four steps of art criticism to evaluate their work. Did they effectively create a contour drawing using a variety of shading techniques?

### Alternate Activity

**Materials:**
- sketchbook
- drawing paper 9" × 12" or larger
- pencils, erasers
- medium ink pen (optional)
- variety of fabrics in different textures

1. Arrange three different fabrics in the center of the table. The fabrics should have interesting folds to create a three-dimensional form.

2. Have students create several quick sketches to help decide on the point of view they like best.

3. On drawing paper, have students lightly compose their drawings. The contours of the shapes should be large enough to fill the page.

4. Students can use a pen to complete the drawing. They can capture the different textures of the fabrics in the drawing by using the three shading techniques.

## Research in Art Education

" . . . the kind of deliberately designed tasks students are offered in school help define the kind of thinking they will learn to do. The kind of thinking students learn to do will influence what they come to know and the kind of cognitive skills they acquire." (Eisner, Elliot W. *The Arts and the Creation of Mind.* New Haven: Yale Univ. Press, 2002.)

## Assessment

Use the following rubric to evaluate the artwork students make in the Creative Expression activity and to assess students' understanding of shading techniques.

Have students complete page 19 or 20 in their *Assessment* books.

| | Art History and Culture | Aesthetic Perception | Creative Expression | Art Criticism |
|---|---|---|---|---|
| **3 POINTS** | The student demonstrates knowledge of the lives and work of Whistler and Morandi. | The student accurately defines and identifies shading techniques. | The student's artwork clearly illustrates shading techniques. | The student thoughtfully and honestly evaluates own work using the four steps of art criticism. |
| **2 POINTS** | The student's knowledge of the lives and work of Whistler and Morandi is weak or incomplete. | The student shows emerging awareness of shading techniques but cannot consistently identify them. | The student's artwork shows some awareness of shading techniques. | The student attempts to evaluate own work but shows an incomplete understanding of evaluation criteria. |
| **1 POINT** | The student cannot demonstrate knowledge of the lives and work of Whistler and Morandi. | The student cannot define or identify shading techniques. | The student's artwork shows no understanding of shading techniques. | The student makes no attempt to evaluate own artwork. |

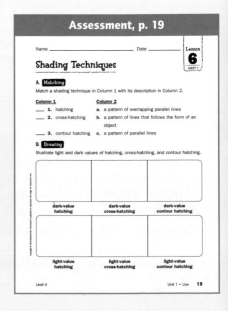

**ant's view**—viewers feel they are looking up, toward an object or figure. **vista de hormiga**—los espectadores sienten que están observando un objeto o una figura desde abajo hacia arriba

**bird's-eye view**—or aerial view; viewers feel they are looking down on a scene. **vista panorámica**—o vista aérea; los espectadores sienten que están observando una escena desde arriba hacia abajo

**blind-contour drawing**—a drawing that is made by looking at the object being drawn, not at the paper **dibujo de contorno a ciegas**—un dibujo que se hace mirando el objeto que se dibuja en vez del papel

**close-up view**—viewers feel they are right next to an object or are a part of the action in a picture **vista de primer plano**—los espectadores sienten que están al lado de un objeto, o que son parte de la acción en una pintura

**contour hatching**—a shading technique that follows the form of an object **sombreado de contorno**—o rayado; una técnica de sombreado que sigue la forma de un objeto

**contour line**—defines the edges and surface ridges of an object **línea de contorno**—define los bordes y los surcos de la superficie de un objeto

**cross-hatching**—a shading technique created when sets of parallel lines cross or intersect **rayado con líneas entrecruzadas**—una técnica de sombreado que se logra cuando grupos de líneas paralelas se cruzan o intersecan

**curved**—lines that bend and change gradually or turn inward to form spirals **curva**—líneas que se doblan o cambian gradualmente o dan la vuelta hacia adentro para formar espirales

**diagonal**—lines that move on a slant **diagonal**—líneas inclinadas

**faraway view**—or eye-level view; viewers feel they are standing far away from the scene. **vista de lejos**—o a nivel de la vista; los espectadores sienten que están lejos de la escena

**flowing lines**—create a feeling of calm and gracefulness. Flowing lines are fluid; they change direction and size. **líneas que fluyen**—crean un sentimiento de calma y delicadeza. Estas líneas son fluidas; cambian de dirección y tamaño

**gesture sketch**—quick drawings used to capture the position or pose of the body **dibujo gestual**—dibujos rápidos usados para captar la posición o postura del cuerpo

**hatching**—a shading technique that looks like a series of parallel lines **rayado**—una técnica de sombreado que se ve como una serie de líneas paralelas

**horizontal**—lines that move from side to side **horizontal**—líneas que se mueven de lado a lado

**line**—a mark drawn by a tool such as a pencil, pen, or paintbrush as it moves across a surface **línea**—una marca trazada con un instrumento como un lápiz, una pluma o un pincel al desplazarlo por una superficie

**point of view**—the angle at which the viewer sees an object **punto de vista**—el ángulo desde donde el espectador observa un objeto

**portrait**—a two- or three-dimensional artwork created in the image of a person or animal **retrato**—una obra de arte bidimensional o tridimensional creada a imagen de una persona o un animal

**shading**—a technique for creating dark values or darkening an area by repeating marks such as lines or dots **sombreado**—una técnica para crear valores oscuros u oscurecer un área repitiendo marcas como líneas o puntos

**still life**—the arrangement of common inanimate objects from which artists draw or paint **naturaleza muerta**—el arreglo de objetos comunes inanimados de los cuales los artistas dibujan o pintan

**value**—the lightness or darkness of a hue **valor**—lo claro u oscuro de un matiz

**vertical**—lines that move from top to bottom **vertical**—líneas que se mueven de arriba a abajo

**zigzag**—lines that are made by joining diagonal lines **en zigzag**—líneas que se hacen al unir líneas diagonales

## Vocabulary Practice

T Display *Transparency 37* to review unit vocabulary words.

**Reference Skills** [★] Vocabulary

Have students look up *line* in a dictionary. Do any of the definitions refer to art? Explain. Repeat the process for other unit vocabulary words.

**Parts of Speech** [★] Vocabulary

Have volunteers select a vocabulary word, such as *gesture*, and explain whether it has more than one part of speech. Repeat for other unit vocabulary words.

**Syllables** [★] Vocabulary

Have volunteers divide unit vocabulary words into syllables.

# Wrapping Up Unit 1

## Line

▲ **Emily Carr.** (Canadian). *Self-Portrait.* 1939.
..................................................
Oil on wove paper mounted on plywood. 33⅝ × 22¾ inches
(85.5 × 57.7 cm.). National Gallery of Canada, Ottawa,
Canada.

**60**    Unit 1

## Art Criticism

**Critical Thinking** Art criticism is an organized system for looking at and talking about art. You can criticize art without being an expert. The purpose of art criticism is to get the viewer involved in a perception process that delays judgment until all aspects of the artwork have been studied.

■ See pages 28–29 for more about art criticism.

### Describe

▶ The viewer sees the head, torso, and left arm of a seated person. The torso is slightly slanted; the arm is relaxed and bent as if it is resting on something. The body is sideways; the head is turned to face the viewer. The person wears glasses. The eyes turn to look at the viewer. The expression is neutral. The person wears a brown hat and an apron.

▶ The lines create a background. There is no recognizable object in the background.

### Analyze

▶ Vertical lines: background. Diagonal lines: outlining the arm, back, and side of the face. Curved lines: lines on the arm, the torso, the neckline of the clothing, the edge of the hat, the glasses, the hair, and the ear.

▶ The lines in the background and the lines behind the arm look like loose, gesture lines.

▶ This painting shows a close-up view. The top portion of the figure fills the space.

Where do you see contour lines?

▶ Thick contour lines outline the back of the head, the edge of the hat, the back of the arm, and the front of the lower torso. Thin contour lines outline the frames of the glasses and the side of the face. The lines around the arm and the lines on the apron are contour shading lines.

## Art History and Culture

### Emily Carr

Emily Carr (em´ ə lē  kär) (1871–1945) was born in Victoria, British Columbia, where she lived for most of her life. Two distinct themes run through her work: nature and the cultural heritage of the indigenous people of the Canadian West Coast. She was noted for her detailed landscape paintings and her writings. Carr spent many years away from her native Canada pursuing an education. Her first public exhibition was held in 1944 in Montreal, Canada. She created *Self-Portrait* in 1938, seven years before she died.

See pages 24–25 and 16–21 for more about art history and subject matter.

**Artist Profiles, p. 10**

**Artist Profile**

**Emily Carr**
1871–1945

Emily Carr (em´ ə lē  kär) was born in British Columbia, Canada. She liked to paint and draw as a child, but her family did not encourage her. Her parents died when she was a teenager. Struggling to establish herself as an artist, she taught art, grew fruit, raised animals, and made pottery and rugs.

Carr visited many Native American reservations. She admired the people and their art and used them as subjects in her paintings. The head of an art museum in Ottawa recognized her skills. Carr later met the Group of Seven—young Canadian artists who were experimenting with painting. At last she belonged to a community and began to paint full time. Carr was in her late

 **Art Criticism** Critical Thinking

**Describe** **What do you see?**
During this step you will collect information about the subject of the work.
- ▶ Describe the person you see.
- ▶ Describe the background.

**Analyze** **How is this work organized?**
Think about how the artist used the elements and principles of art.
- ▶ Where do you see vertical, diagonal, and curved lines?
- ▶ Do you see any lines that look like loose gesture lines?
- ▶ What kind of view did the artist use for this painting? Explain.
- ▶ Where do you see contour lines and shading lines?

**Interpret** **What is the artist trying to say?**
Use the clues you discovered during your analysis to find the message the artist is trying to show.
- ▶ Does the artist's use of lines make this an active or a calm picture?
- ▶ Would you like to meet the person in the painting? Why?

**Decide** **What do you think about the work?**
Use all the information you have gathered to decide whether this is a successful work of art.
- ▶ Is this painting successful because it is realistic, because it is well-organized, or because it has a strong message? Explain.

## Interpret

- ▶ The repeated lines in the background, the repeated lines on the body, as well as the gesture lines, create an active look even though the figure is sitting in a calm pose.
- ▶ Answers will vary. Some will say the person looks intelligent. Others may say the person looks serious or unfriendly. Some may see this person as lonely.

## Decide

- ▶ Answers will vary. Some will say it is realistic, some will say it is well organized, and some will say it has a strong message about the person in the work.

**Art Journal: Writing**
Have students write answers to Aesthetic Perception in their Art Journals.

 **Aesthetic Perception**

**Seeing Like an Artist** Have students think about a friend or family member, or bring in a picture of a friend or family member to display. How does each picture compare to Emily Carr's *Self-Portrait?* Discuss the pictures on display.

**Describe** ▶ List and describe everything you see in the picture.

**Analyze** ▶ Where do you see lines and shapes in the picture?
▶ How do they contribute to the look of the person?

**Interpret** ▶ How does the picture make you feel?
▶ What name would you give the person? Why?

**Decide** ▶ Do you have strong feelings when you look at the picture?

"A variety of lines, gestures, and shading techniques are used by artists to create artwork." "Los artistas usan una variedad de líneas, gestos y técnicas de sombreado para crear las pinturas".

**T** Review the unit vocabulary with students using *Transparency 37.*

### Art Journal: Writing

Have students answer the questions on page 62 in their Art Journals or on a separate sheet of paper. 1. C, 2. B, 3. A, 4. C, 5. A

**T** For further assessment, have students complete the unit test on *Transparency 43.*

## VISIT A MUSEUM
## The Wadsworth Atheneum

► Have students write to a museum (such as the Wadsworth Atheneum) or an art gallery in their community, city, or state to find out whether it has an educational department and, if so, what services this department provides for its patrons and visitors.

"There is no must in art because art is free."
—Wassily Kandinsky

---

Line, continued

## Show What You Know

Answer these questions on a separate sheet of paper.

❶ Which of the following is not a type of line?
  A. flowing
  B. horizontal
  C. observation

❷ A(n) _____ is a quick sketch or action drawing of an object or person.
  A. observation drawing
  B. gesture sketch
  C. diagonal line

❸ A(n) _____ drawing is made while looking at an object.
  A. observation
  B. parallel
  C. contour

❹ A(n) _____ is the outline or edges of an object or figure.
  A. observation
  B. gesture
  C. contour

❺ _____ are used to create light and dark values in a drawing.
  A. Shading techniques
  B. Gesture techniques
  C. Observation techniques

---

## VISIT A MUSEUM
## The Wadsworth Atheneum

The Wadsworth Atheneum, in Hartford, Connecticut, is the oldest public art museum in America. It has about 50,000 works of art from the United States and other countries. Bronze pieces from ancient Egypt, Greece, and Rome, and paintings from the past 400 years can be found there. The museum also has the Amistad Collection, which is a history of African American culture. The museum has programs and activities for people of all ages and interests who love art.

▲ The Wadsworth Atheneum

---

## Unit Assessment Options

### Aesthetic Perception

**Practice** Have students list the techniques on pages 42 and 54 and then find examples of each technique in the classroom.

### Creative Expression

**Student Portfolio** Have students review all the artwork they have created during this unit and select the pieces they wish to keep in their portfolios.

### Art Criticism

**Activity** Have students select an artwork from this unit and study it using the four steps of art criticism. (See pages 28–29 for more information about art criticism.) Have students work alone or in pairs and present their findings aloud or in writing.

# Line in Dance and Music

The AMAN International Folk Ensemble performs traditional dances from different ethnic groups who live in America. This photo shows a circle dance from a geographical area of the United States called *Appalachia*. The choreographer uses lines on the dance floor to create a dance.

**What to Do** Create a circle dance.

1. Form either one large circle or several smaller ones. Hold hands and create a dance. Choose four of these ideas and combine them into a dance using eight counts for each:

   ▶ Walk into the center, decreasing the circle.

   ▶ Walk out from the center, increasing the circle.

   ▶ Walk to the right. Walk to the left.

   ▶ Drop hands and turn in place.

   ▶ Jump in place.

   ▶ Two people drop hands and follow the leader in a snakelike path.

2. Perform your dance to music.

▲ AMAN International Folk Ensemble. "Suite of Appalachian Music and Dance."

 **Art Criticism**

**Describe** Describe the four movement ideas you chose.

**Analyze** What did you do to put the movements together into a dance?

**Interpret** How did it feel to move in unison with others?

**Decide** Were you successful in creating a circle dance?

 **Art History and Culture**

## Appalachian Dance and Music

The "Suite of Appalachian Music and Dance," choreographed by Jerry Duke, is intended to be a collage of different dance forms found in the Appalachians. Big circle dance is a style that was brought to the Appalachian Mountain region of the eastern United States by settlers from the British Isles. The dancers also do rhythmic footwork called "clogging." This type of body movement is also inspired by West African dance.

 **Line in Dance and Music**

**Objective:** To work with a group to create a circle dance

**Materials:** "Suite of Appalachian Music and Dance" performed by AMAN International Folk Ensemble, running time 7:24; "Big Circle Dance" Appalachian music

# Focus

Time: About 5 minutes

■ Discuss the information on page 63.

**Art History and Culture**

■ Have students discuss dances from different cultures.

# Teach

Time: About 20 minutes

**Aesthetic Perception**

■ Have students discuss what images come to mind when they watch the video clip.

**Creative Expression**

■ Have students make one large circle or several small circles. Guide them in different movement choices to make a circle dance. Play the "Big Circle Dance" music when students are ready to perform.

■ **Informal Assessment** Provide positive feedback and encourage refinement.

# Reflect

Time: About 10 minutes

**Art Criticism**

■ Have students answer the four art criticism questions on page 63 aloud or in writing.

■ Were students able to successfully create a group circle dance?

# Unit 2 Planning Guide

| | Lesson Title | Suggested Pacing | Creative Expression Activity |
|---|---|---|---|
| **Lesson 1** | **Geometric Shapes** | 1 hour | Design a collage. |
| **Lesson 2** | Free-Form Shapes | 1 hour | Create a fantasy painting. |
| **Lesson 3** | **Pattern** | 1 hour | Make a paper quilt. |
| **Lesson 4** | **Visual Rhythm** | 1 hour | Illustrate an event. |
| **Lesson 5** | **Rhythm and Movement** | 1 hour | Create an illustration of music. |
| **Lesson 6** | **Flowing Rhythm** | 1 hour | Create a flowing rhythm design. |
| ▲ R T S ● U R C ▇ ARTSOURCE | **Shape, Rhythm, and Movement in Theatre** | 50 minutes | Create a tableau. |

| Materials | Program Resources | Fine Art Resources | Literature Resources |
|---|---|---|---|
| newsprint, white paper, pencils, magazines, colored tissue paper, wallpaper, fabric scraps, scissors, glue, oil pastels | *Assessment,* pp. 21–22 **Reading and Writing Test Preparation,** pp. 18–19 **Home and After-School Connections** **Flash Cards** 7, 9–11 | *Transparency 7* *Artist Profiles,* pp. 7, 66 *Large Prints 51* and *52* *The National Museum of Women in the Arts Collection* | *Going Back Home* by Toyomi Igus |
| computer, paint or draw program, printer, paper | *Assessment,* pp. 23–24 **Reading and Writing Test Preparation,** pp. 20–21 **Flash Cards** 8, 18–19 | *Transparency 8* *Artist Profiles,* pp. 19, 50 *Large Prints 51* and *52* *Art Around the World Collection* | *Poppy* by Avi |
| pencils, color construction paper, plastic foam, brayer, printing ink, fine-tipped marker, color pencils, crayons | *Assessment,* pp. 25–26 **Reading and Writing Test Preparation,** pp. 22–23 **Flash Cards** 10–12 | *Transparency 9* *Artist Profiles,* pp. 18, 43 *Large Prints 51* and *52* *Art Around the World Collection* | *My Grandmother's Journey* by John Cech |
| color dustless chalk, sketch paper, pencils, large white drawing paper, oil pastels | *Assessment,* pp. 27–28 **Reading and Writing Test Preparation,** pp. 24–25 **Flash Cards** 9–11 | *Transparency 10* *Artist Profiles,* pp. 12, 46 *Large Prints 51* and *52* *The National Museum of Women in the Arts Collection* | *Here Is the African Savanna* by Madeleine Dunphy |
| classical music, color construction paper, oil pastels, watercolor paints, large brushes, jars of water | *Assessment,* pp. 29–30 **Reading and Writing Test Preparation,** pp. 26–27 **Flash Cards** 9–11 | *Transparency 11* *Artist Profiles,* pp. 55, 67 *Large Prints 51* and *52* *The National Museum of Women in the Arts Collection* | *Germs Make Me Sick* by Melvin Berger |
| white drawing paper, 12" × 12" squares of color construction paper, scissors, glue, oil pastels | *Assessment,* pp. 31–32 **Reading and Writing Test Preparation,** pp. 28–29 **Flash Card** 6 | *Transparency 12* *Artist Profiles,* pp. 31, 32 *Large Prints 51* and *52* *Art Around the World Collection* | *Runner in the Sun: A Story of Indian Maize* by D'Arcy McNickle |
| "Long Haired Girl," a simple story, notecards, pencils | | | |

# Unit Overview

# 2 Shape, Pattern, Rhythm, and Movement

**Lesson 1: Geometric shapes** can be described and measured in mathematical terms.

**Lesson 2: Free-form shapes** are irregular and uneven shapes that are not geometric. They are often found in nature.

**Lesson 3: Pattern** When artists repeat a line, shape, or color, they create a pattern.

**Lesson 4: Visual rhythm** is used to pull the viewer's eyes through a work of art.

**Lesson 5: Rhythm** is used in many ways to create visual **movement.**

**Lesson 6: Flowing rhythm** is visual rhythm created by repeating curved lines and shapes.

# Introduce Unit Concepts

"Artists use the elements of shape, pattern, rhythm, and movement in creating all types of art." "Los artistas usan los elementos de forma, patrón, ritmo y movimiento al crear todo tipo de arte."

## Shape and Pattern
- Discuss how geometric and free-form shapes are different.
- Ask students to use their bodies to form patterns.

## Rhythm and Movement
- Clap out a rhythm, and have students illustrate that rhythm using colors and shapes.
- Have students look through their textbooks for examples of movement, and discuss the similarities and differences.

## Cross-Curricular Projects
- See the *Language Arts and Reading, Mathematics, Science,* and *Social Studies Art Connections* books for activities that further develop shape, pattern, rhythm, and movement concepts.

---

# Shape, Pattern, Rhythm, and Movement

▲ **Stuart Davis.** (American). *Composition.* 1935.

Oil on canvas. $22\frac{1}{4} \times 30\frac{1}{8}$ inches (56.515 × 76.51 cm.). Smithsonian American Art Museum, Washington, D.C.

**Shape, pattern, rhythm, and movement add variety and interest to art.**

Stuart Davis painted this still life, *Composition,* in 1935. He simplified what he saw and created geometric and free-form shapes. Davis effectively used shape, pattern, rhythm, and movement in this painting.

**64**    Unit 2

## Fine Art Prints

Display **Large Prints 51** *Chiwana (The Big River)* and **52** *Nightingale.* Refer to the prints throughout the unit as students learn about shape, pattern, rhythm, and movement.

**Large Print 51**

**Large Print 52**

Artists use **shapes** to represent forms in nature and forms created by people.

▶ What types of shapes do you see most often in the painting?

Artists often repeat shapes, lines, or colors to create a **pattern.**

▶ Where do you see repeated shapes in the painting?

When **rhythm** is used, it creates the illusion of **visual movement.**

▶ Notice how Davis repeated diagonal lines across the work to create visual movement.

**In This Unit** you will learn and practice techniques to create patterns and the feeling of rhythm and movement in art. You also will review types of shapes. Here are the topics you will study:

▶ Geometric shapes
▶ Free-form shapes
▶ Pattern
▶ Visual rhythm
▶ Rhythm and movement
▶ Flowing rhythm

## Stuart Davis
(1894–1964)

Stuart Davis was a painter, printmaker, cartoonist, and graphic designer. Davis was born in Philadelphia in 1894. His mother was a sculptor, and his father was an editor for the *Philadelphia Press.* Davis's paintings often reflect his love of jazz music. His art also displays the influence of cubism, a style in which artists created paintings with split objects, whose various sides were seen at the same time.

Unit 2    **65**

# Examine the Artwork

"Let's look closely at the painting." "Vamos a observar detalladamente la pintura."

■ Have students closely examine the painting. Ask them to describe what they see.

■ Have students answer the questions about shape, pattern, rhythm, and movement on page 65.

▶ The artwork includes circles, triangles, and free-form shapes. Ovals are found in the palette and in the wheel with the shovel through it. The edge of the wheel has a triangular pattern.

▶ There are repeated spots in the left and right corners and in the top-center portion of the painting. There are repeated triangles around the wheel in the left corner and repeated diamonds in the triangle in the center of the painting.

▶ A fast-paced motion is created. The objects and the person in the image appear to be racing toward the viewer.

# Unit Pretest

**T** Display *Transparency 44* as a pretest. Answers: 1. B, 2. A, 3. C, 4. C, 5. A

# Home Connection

■ See *Home and After-School Connections* for family newsletters and activities for this unit.

 ## Art History and Culture

### Stuart Davis

Stuart Davis (stoō´ ərt dā´ vəs) (1894–1964) is known as one of America's greatest modern painters. Davis created a variety of artwork, including drawings, watercolors, gouaches, and still-life paintings. Davis sought to find the right arrangement of visual elements in his artwork. When creating still lifes, he would sometimes nail down his objects. He also displayed his love of jazz in some of his artwork. *Composition* is a still life. This artwork includes fine-art tools and various other tools, including a shovel.

See pages 24–25 and 16–21 for more about art history and the subject matter.

**Artist Profiles, p. 16**

Artist Profile
**Stuart Davis**
1894-1964
Stuart Davis (stū´ art dā´ vəs) was born in Philadelphia. He left high school when he was only 16 years old and went to New York City to study art. His long career began when he showed some paintings in the Armory Show in New York City in 1913. This large and important show introduced modern art to many Americans. Afterward Davis's career took off. By the 1920s, he was studying cubism. Through the 1940s, many of his paintings showed his love of jazz music. He even gave some of his paintings musical titles.

### ILLUSTRATOR PROFILE
# Susan Guevara

When Susan Guevara was eleven years old, her family took a three-month tour of Europe, visiting seventeen countries in a camper. The languages, foods, and magical buildings and castles would later provide inspiration for Susan's art.

Susan studied at the Academy of Art College in San Francisco and at the Royal academy of Fine Art in Belgium before beginning her career as a professional illustrator. She has stated that no two of her books are done in the same style. Because each story is unique, she tries to make the illustrations unique as well.

When Susan speaks to students, she tells them that learning about new places through travel and reading helps her describe the world of the stories she illustrates. Students learn that combining this knowledge with imagination is an essential step in illustrating picture books.

Throughout Unit 2, share Guevara's illustrations with the class and discuss her use of shape, pattern, rhythm, and movement. What shapes have patterns on them? Where are there examples of rhythm? Where and how does Guevara create visual movement?

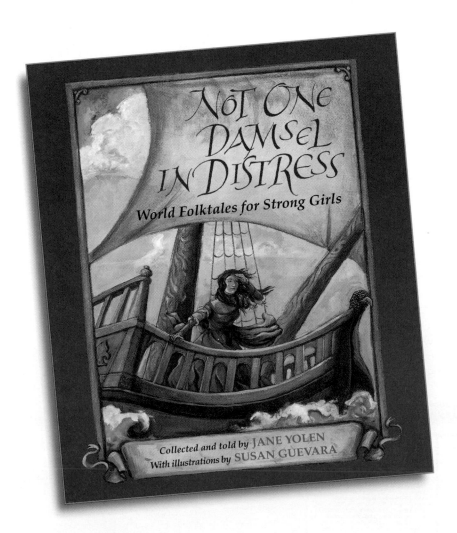

## Music

In music, the effect of movement is created primarily through the elements of beat, rhythm, and tempo (the speed of the beat). If possible, listen to music that depicts movement and discuss how musical elements are used to create the effect of the activity.

## Literature

Use the video or DVD *Kachina Spirit* to introduce the unit concepts. Students will recognize the use of shape, rhythm, and movement in the Kachina dolls. Different types of shapes can be identified, as well as rhythm with repeating elements.

**Literature and Art**

## Performing Arts

 Show "Long Haired Girl." Point out how the performers create rhythm.

**Artsource®**

# Lesson 1 Geometric Shapes

## Overview

**Lesson 1** introduces geometric shapes in art. Geometric shapes are shapes that can be described and measured in mathematical terms.

## Objectives

 **Art History and Culture**

To identify and compare the subject matter in works by American and Uruguayan artists

 **Creative Expression**

To use a variety of two-dimensional shapes to create a collage

 **Aesthetic Perception**

To define and identify different types of geometric shapes

 **Art Criticism**

To evaluate own work using the four steps of art criticism

### Vocabulary ⭐ Vocabulary

Review the following vocabulary words with students before beginning the lesson.

**geometric shapes** figuras geométricas—shapes that can be described and measured in mathematical terms

**two-dimensional shapes** figuras bidimensionales—shapes that are flat and can be measured by height and width

See page 89B for additional vocabulary and Spanish vocabulary resources.

 **Art Journal: Vocabulary**

Have students add these words to the Vocabulary section of their Art Journals.

## Lesson Materials

- 9" × 12" white drawing paper
- 12" × 18" white drawing paper
- 9" × 12" newsprint
- black felt-tip markers, pencils, oil pastels
- magazines, colored tissue paper
- wallpaper, fabric scraps
- scissors, glue

**Alternate Materials:**
- markers
- fine-line felt-tip pens

## Program Resources

- *Reading and Writing Test Prep.,* pp. 18–19
- *Transparency 7*
- *Flash Cards* 7, 9–11
- *Artist Profiles,* pp. 7, 66
- *Animals Through History Time Line*
- *Assessment,* pp. 21–22
- *Large Prints 51 Chiwana (The Big River)* and *52 Nightingale*
- *The National Museum of Women in the Arts Collection*

### Concept Trace

Geometric Shapes

**Introduced:** Level 3, Unit 1, Lesson 3

**Reinforced:** Level 5, Unit 1, Lesson 3

---

## Lesson 1 Arts Integration

### Theatre

Complete Unit 2, Lesson 1, on pages 36–37 of *Theatre Arts Connections.*

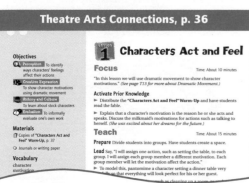

### Music

 Listen to "Tinikling." This music accompanies a dance from the Philippines that symbolizes the movement of a crane. Have students imagine the movements that accompany the music. What geometric shapes can they visualize?

### Movement & Dance

Use Chinese jump ropes (or large circular pieces of elastic) to help students understand geometric shapes. Each student should have a jump rope. Have them place their feet and hands on it. Students should explore ways to stretch the rope into various geometric shapes. Have them find three variations on each shape by changing planes or using different sizes and positions in space.

LESSON 1 • Geometric Shapes **65B**

# Focus

**Time:** About 10 minutes

## Activate Prior Knowledge

"Can you think of any geometric shapes that represent symbols of communication?"

"¿Pueden pensar en alguna figura geométrica que represente símbolos de comunicación?"

■ Discuss student answers. They may mention the hexagon shape of stop signs and the shapes of other traffic signals.

### Using Literature ☆ Reading

■ Have students read *Going Back Home* by Toyomi Igus. Encourage students to identify geometric shapes used in the illustrations of clothing and houses.

### Thematic Connection ☆ Social Studies

■ **Storytelling:** Encourage students to talk about storytelling in art. What are the stories that Biggers and Torres-García are telling?

## Introduce the Art

# Look

"Study the paintings on these pages closely."

"Estudien detalladamente las pinturas de estas páginas."

### Purpose ☆ Reading

■ Have students suggest the purpose for creating both works of art. *Shotguns, Fourth Ward* may have been created to document the history of an African American community. Torres-García may have created his painting to tell his life story, including the city of his birth (Montevideo).

 ## Art History and Culture

Students might suggest that John Biggers illustrated his culture, and Joaquin Torres-García illustrated things about himself or his family.

### 💻 Web Connection

Visit **www.museum.oas.org** (Art Museum of the Americas) to view the Geometric Art Exhibition in the permanent collection.

---

# Geometric Shapes

◀ **John Biggers.** (American). *Shotguns, Fourth Ward.* 1987.
Acrylic and oil on board. 41¼ × 31 inches (104.78 × 78.74 cm.). Hampton University Museum, Hampton, Virginia.

**Look** at the art on these pages. *Shotguns, Fourth Ward* represents one of the earliest settlements of an African American community in the city of Houston, Texas. Notice the repeated triangular shapes of the roofs and the repeated rectangular shapes on the railroad tracks. Torres-García's painting is an abstract painting. It contains many geometric shapes.

 ## Art History and Culture

Both artists used paint to tell a story about something that was important to them. After viewing the paintings, name something that was important to each artist.

## Art History and Culture

### John Biggers

John Biggers (jän big´ərz) (1924–2000) created murals, drawings, paintings, and sculptures. Biggers was an art professor and head of the art department at Texas Southern University from 1949 to 1983. Much of his work explores the meaning of family and community to African Americans. Biggers created a series of paintings about shotgun houses in 1987. Shotgun houses have a long hall down the middle with a door at each end and rooms on each side of the hall. Shotgun houses can be traced from West Africa to the Caribbean to the United States.

See pages 24–25 and 16–21 for more about art history and subject matter.

**Artist Profiles, p. 7**

*Artist Profile*

**John Biggers**
1924-2000

John Biggers (jon big´ ərs) was born in South Carolina. He was the youngest of seven children. Biggers greatly admired his father, who had lost a leg as a child while working at a plantation sawmill. As an adult, his father became the principal of a three-room school. To pay his own tuition at a private school, Biggers got up every morning at 4 A.M. to start the school's furnaces. After graduating, he began to paint. In 1943, Biggers was drafted into World War II. He soon discovered that African American soldiers were shown less respect than German prisoners of war. He became so depressed that he was hospitalized. In time Biggers went back to school and earned his degree at

▲ **Joaquin Torres-Garcia.** (Uruguayan). *Abstract Art in Five Tones and Complementaries.* 1943.

........................................

Oil on board mounted on panel. $20\frac{1}{2} \times 26\frac{5}{8}$ inches (52.07 × 67.62 cm). Albright-Knox Art Gallery, Buffalo, New York.

**S**tudy both works of art to find different geometric shapes.

▶ Where are the circles and triangles?

▶ What other geometric shapes do you see?

▶ What things do these shapes represent?

### Aesthetic Perception

**Design Awareness** Look out a window or around your classroom. Notice how the objects are made of shapes. Make a list of three objects, and describe the geometric shapes needed to draw them.

## Art History and Culture

### Joaquín Torres-García

Joaquín Torres-García (wäh kēn´ tor´ res gär sē´ ä) (1874–1949) often created works of art that included symbols and words that communicate his life story. For example, in the painting above, Torres-García used geometric shapes to create symbolic objects. He included words including his initials, JTG; MONTEVIDEO, his birthplace; and SIGLO XX, the twentieth century. Torres-García's grandfather and father were carpenters, and the saw at the upper left represents carpentry. On the lower left is an hour glass that represents intellect. The pot on the right is often grouped with a hammer or compass; it represents culture and labor.

See pages 24–25 and 16–21 for more about art history and the subject matter.

**Artist Profiles, p. 66**

> Artist Profile
> **Joaquín Torres-Garcia**
> 1874–1949
>
> Joaquin Torres-Garcia (wäh kēn´ tor´ res gär sē´ ä) was born in Uruguay. His family moved to Spain when he was 17 years old. An eager student and deep thinker, he studied many subjects, including art. As a young man, Torres-Garcia illustrated magazines, created murals, and taught art classes to support himself. In 1915 Torres-Garcia designed wooden toys with interchangeable parts to amuse his three children. He moved to New York City, where he hoped to sell the toys. However, they were difficult to manufacture. After trying to sell his toys in Italy, Torres-Garcia and his family settled in Paris. He began to use

## Study

▶ Biggers: Triangular-shaped roofs, circles on the roofs. Torres-García: circles in the upper-left and lower-left corners

▶ Biggers: The front part of the house is a square, and the railroad tracks are rectangles. Torres-García: Rectangles and squares all over the painting

▶ Biggers: Triangles are used to form the roof, rectangles form the railroad tracks, and squares form the porch. Torres-García: Upper-left circles and triangles represent a saw; lower-left triangles, rectangles, and squares are used to form an hourglass, and a circle used to represent a pot.

■ For more examples of abstract and nonobjective art, see *The National Museum of Women in the Arts Collection.*

### Art Journal: Writing

Encourage students to define and illustrate *geometric shapes* in the Concepts section of their Art Journals. What else do they want to know about geometric shapes?

### Aesthetic Perception

**Design Awareness** List examples of classroom objects that have different geometric shapes. For example, a door might have a rectangular shape, a desk might have a square shape, and a clock and a plate might have circular shapes.
NSAE 2.a.
**Developing Visual Literacy** Encourage students to speculate on the time periods represented in the works of art. For example, the houses in *Shotguns, Fourth Ward* are not from the twenty-first century, so this painting must represent earlier times in history.

### Web Connection

Search **www.museum.oas.org** (Art Museum of the Americas) to view works of art by Joaquín Torres-García.

# Teach

**Time:** About 45 minutes

"Can you draw a picture of your hand using only geometric shapes?" "¿Pueden hacer un dibujo de su mano usando sólo figuras geométricas?"

- Discuss geometric shapes on page 68.

## Practice

**Materials:** one sheet of 9" × 12" white drawing paper, black felt-tip markers

**Alternate Materials:** fine-line felt-tip pens

- Distribute the materials and have students follow the directions on page 68.

 ## Creative Expression

**Materials:** 9" × 12" newsprint for practice drawings, 12" × 18" white drawing paper, pencils, magazines, colored tissue paper, wallpaper, fabric scraps, scissors, glue, oil pastels

**Alternate Materials:** markers

- Distribute the materials and have students follow the directions on page 69.

- Have students integrate a variety of ideas about themselves and community in their collages. NSAE 3.a; 3.b

- See page 231 in the Activity Tips for visual examples of techniques.

### Art Journal: Brainstorming

Have students brainstorm themes for collages and list items that might be included in their illustrations in the Ideas section of their Art Journals. Then have students plan how they will show this theme in their collages in the Creative Expression activity.

# Using Geometric Shapes

**Geometric shapes** can be described and measured in mathematical terms. They can be drawn with a ruler or compass. The geometric shapes in this lesson are **two-dimensional,** which means they are flat. You can measure the length and width of a rectangle and a square, and the circumference and diameter of a circle.

Here are five geometric shapes:

Circle        Square        Triangle

Oval        Rectangle

## Practice

Create a drawing of your hand, using only geometric shapes. Use a marker.

1. Notice how each area of your hand can be represented with a geometric shape. For instance, a part of your finger could be drawn as a rectangle.

2. Using geometric shapes, create two drawings of your hand in different positions.

## Differentiated Instruction

**Reteach**
Have students create geometric shapes using a ruler. Ask them to create as many shapes as possible.

**Special Needs**
Encouraging students with disabilities to try many different arrangements of collage elements before gluing any items down will increase their confidence.

**ELL**
You may wish to provide specific, concrete modeling of each step of the collage process, supported with visual clues in abbreviated form. After students have finished, you might guide partners' oral discussion, for example, "Ask your partner, 'What materials did you use? Newspapers? Magazines?'"

◀ **Chris Gunter.**
Age 9.

**Think** about three geometric shapes this student artist used in the collage.

 **Creative Expression**

What shapes are the people, places, and things around you? Create a collage based on a theme.

1. Think about a theme for your collage. Make some quick sketches. Use mostly geometric shapes.

2. Draw your best sketch. Add collected materials to make your collage.

3. Before you glue the materials to the paper, arrange your collage until you find a design you like. Use as many geometric shapes as you can. Fill the background with color.

**Art Criticism**

**Describe** Describe the subject matter and materials of your collage.

**Analyze** Where did you use geometric shapes? Why did you choose the colors and shapes you used in your collage?

**Interpret** Give your work a title.

**Decide** Do you feel you were successful in using shapes to create objects in your collage? If you were to do it over, what would you change?

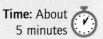 Time: About
5 minutes

## Review and Assess

"Let's review what we've learned about geometric shapes." "Vamos a repasar lo que hemos aprendido acerca de las figuras geométricas."

## Think

The artist used squares, rectangles, and circles in his artwork.

■ Use *Large Prints 51 Chiwana (The Big River)* and *52 Nightingale* to have students identify geometric shapes.

## Informal Assessment

■ Have students interpret moods in their classmates' collages. Do they see any similarities in their collages?
NSAE 5.a; 5.c

■ For standardized-format test practice using this lesson's art content, see pages 18–19 in *Reading and Writing Test Preparation.*

**Art Journal: Critical Thinking**

Have students answer the four art criticism questions—Describe, Analyze, Interpret, and Decide—in their Art Journals. In small groups, have students discuss the use of geometric shapes in their collages in the Creative Expression activity.

## Art Across the Curriculum

Use these simple ideas to reinforce art concepts across the curriculum.

★ **Expository Writing** After students complete the Creative Expression activity, have them write an explanation of how to create a collage.

★ **Math** Discuss how to find the area of geometric shapes such as a rectangle and a square.

★ **Science** Discuss shapes that can be found on an animal's coat. A dalmatian, for example, may have many circular spots on its coat.

★ **Social Studies** Use the painting *Shotguns, Fourth Ward* to have students learn about and discuss shotgun houses.

★ **Technology** Have students use the automatic shapes in the computer's draw program to illustrate geometric shapes. Have them experiment using the Fill tool. Visit **SRAonline.com** to print detailed instructions for this activity.
NSAE 6.b

# Geometric Shapes

## Extra! For the Art Specialist

**Time:** About 45 minutes

### Focus

Have students study **Large Print 52** *Nightingale* and ask them how geometric shapes are used. Does the use of geometric shapes affect the mood of the artwork?

### Teach

Ask students to look around the room and point out the various geometric shapes. Explain that they will create a small fabric collage depicting a place where they have lived or visited. Some type of building must be included in the collage. Prior to the activity collect fabric scraps, buttons, ribbon, lace, and yarn. Have students complete the Alternate Activity.

### Reflect

Have students use the four steps of art criticism to evaluate their work. Did they use a variety of geometric shapes in their collages? Have students describe the shapes they used.

### Alternate Activity

**Materials:**
- sketchbooks
- pencils, erasers
- 9″ × 12″ felt squares in a variety of colors
- scissors, craft glue
- variety of items with different textures

1. Have students create several quick sketches of the place they want to use in their collage. They should use mainly geometric shapes, even for things that are not always made of geometric shapes.

2. Have students select a colored felt background. Then they should begin selecting and cutting fabric into geometric shapes to create their images.

3. Students should cut objects such as windows, doors, trees, and cars and overlap them at least two times.

4. Once all of the basic shapes have been cut, have students glue them in place. They can use ribbon, yarn, lace, or buttons as details to complete the collage.

## Research in Art Education

"The general goal of art criticism is to try to understand mankind and the human condition. But beyond that, it seeks to discover and communicate the 'meaning' of art—usually of modern or contemporary art because it can be examined in the context of the present." Risatti, H. "Art Criticism in Discipline-Based Art Education." (*Journal of Aesthetic Education.* Summer. 1987. 217–225.)

## Assessment

Use the following rubric to evaluate the artwork students make in the Creative Expression activity and to assess students' understanding of geometric shapes.

Have students complete page 21 or 22 in their **Assessment** books.

| | Art History and Culture | Aesthetic Perception | Creative Expression | Art Criticism |
|---|---|---|---|---|
| **3 POINTS** | The student identifies and compares the subject matter in works by American and Uruguayan artists. | The student accurately defines and identifies different types of geometric shapes. | The student included a variety of geometric shapes in his or her collage. | The student thoughtfully and honestly evaluates own work using the four steps of art criticism. |
| **2 POINTS** | The student's identification and comparison are weak or incomplete. | The student shows emerging awareness of geometric shapes but cannot consistently identify them. | The student's collage shows some awareness of geometric shapes. | The student attempts to evaluate own work but shows an incomplete understanding of evaluation criteria. |
| **1 POINT** | The student cannot identify or compare the subject matter in works by American or Uruguayan artists. | The student cannot define or identify different geometric shapes. | The student did not include geometric shapes in his or her collage. | The student makes no attempt to evaluate own work. |

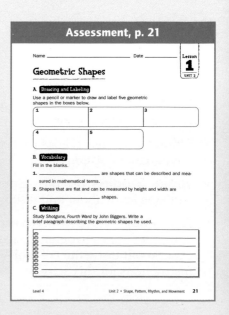

**Assessment, p. 21**

Name _____ Date _____

**Lesson 1** UNIT 2

**Geometric Shapes**

**A.** Drawing and Labeling
Use a pencil or marker to draw and label five geometric shapes in the boxes below.

**B.** Vocabulary
Fill in the blanks.

1. _____ are shapes that can be described and measured in mathematical terms.
2. Shapes that are flat and can be measured by height and width are _____ shapes.

**C.** Writing
Study *Shotguns, Fourth Ward* by John Biggers. Write a brief paragraph describing the geometric shapes he used.

Level 4    Unit 2 • Shape, Pattern, Rhythm, and Movement    21

# Free-Form Shapes

Lesson 2 introduces free-form shapes. Free-form shapes are organic shapes that are irregular or uneven, with outlines that are curved, angular, or both. They are often found in nature.

## Objectives

###  Art History and Culture

To identify and compare themes reflected in works by American artists

### Creative Expression

To use a variety of free-form shapes to create a fantasy painting

### Aesthetic Perception

To define and identify free-form shapes

### Art Criticism

To evaluate own work using the four steps of art criticism

## Lesson Materials

- 9″ × 12″ paper for sketches, pencils
- felt-tip markers
- computer
- paint or draw program
- paper

**Alternate Materials:**
- markers, pencils, crayons
- construction paper

## Program Resources

- *Reading and Writing Test Prep.,* pp. 20–21
- *Transparency 8*
- *Flash Cards* 8, 18–19
- *Artist Profiles,* pp. 19, 50
- *Animals Through History Time Line*
- *Assessment,* pp. 23–24
- *Large Prints 51* Chiwana (The Big River) and *52* Nightingale
- *Art Around the World Collection*

### Concept Trace
Free-Form Shapes
**Introduced:** Level 3, Unit 1, Lessons 5–6

**Reinforced:** Level 5, Unit 1, Lesson 3

## Vocabulary  Vocabulary

Review the following vocabulary words with students before beginning the lesson.

**free-form shapes** figuras abstractas—organic shapes, often found in nature, that are irregular or uneven, with outlines that are curved, angular, or both.

**silhouette** silueta—the shape of a shadow

See page 89B for additional vocabulary and Spanish vocabulary resources.

###  Art Journal: Vocabulary

Have students add these words to the Vocabulary section of their Art Journals.

## Lesson 2 Arts Integration

### Theatre

Complete Unit 2, Lesson 2, on pages 38–39 of *Theatre Arts Connections.*

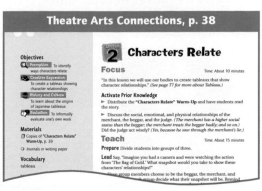

### Music

 The shapes found in Western music generally contain patterns both large and small. The melodies of Native Americans, however, are less predictable; they are more free-form. Listen to "Tekanionton'neha." The melodic contour is generally downward, but the length of the melodies is not regular.

### Movement & Dance

Divide students into groups of four. Have the first person make a free-form shape with his or her body and freeze. Have the rest of the students take four counts each and add themselves to the free-form shape to create a group shape. Then have the first student leave the group shape; the other students should also leave one by one.

# Focus

Time: About 10 minutes

## Activate Prior Knowledge

"Where have you seen shapes that are not geometric?" "¿Dónde han visto figuras que no sean geométricas?"

- Discuss students' answers. Then ask them to draw some of the free-form shapes on the board.

**Using Literature** ⭐ Reading

- Have students read *Poppy* by Avi. The illustrations of animals, trees, and leaves are examples of free-form shapes.

**Thematic Connection** ⭐ Science

- **Communication:** Discuss the message in each work of art. Minnie Evans communicated her dream world, and Elizabeth Murray implied the outdoors.

## Introduce the Art

# Look

"Let's take a close look at the two works of art." "Vamos a observar detalladamente las dos obras de arte."

**Comparing and Contrasting** ⭐ Reading

- Have students list the similarities and differences in the two works of art. Both have circular shapes. Evans's artwork includes flowers. Murray's artwork implies the outdoors through colors and shapes. Both include red, blue, and green.

 **Art History and Culture**

Give students examples of recurring themes in artworks. Wassily Kandinsky often used paint to illustrate music. Wayne Thiebaud created many works of art depicting bakeshop goodies. Have students look through their textbooks to find works by these artists.

🖥 **Web Connection**

Visit **www.whitney.org/welcome.html** (The Whitney Museum of American Art) to learn more about American art. NOTE: This site is for teacher use only.

**70** UNIT 2 • Shape, Pattern, Rhythm, and Movement

---

 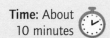 Free-Form Shapes

Lesson 2

▲ **Minnie Evans.** (American). *Design Made at Airlie Gardens.* 1967.
......................................
Oil and mixed media on canvas. $19\frac{7}{8} \times 23\frac{7}{8}$ inches (50.5 × 60.6 cm). Smithsonian American Art Museum, Washington, D.C.

**Look** at the art on these pages. Minnie Evans used free-form shapes in her narrative painting to communicate her dreams. Elizabeth Murray's painting is an abstract work that implies the outdoors through colors and shapes. Look for the free-form shapes in these paintings. Also look for geometric shapes.

 **Art History and Culture**

Minnie Evans often used flowers as a theme in her artwork. Can you name other themes that could be shown in several works by an artist?

**70** Unit 2 • Lesson 2

 **Art History and Culture**

## Minnie Evans

Minnie Evans (min´ ē e´ vənz) (1890–1987) was an African American artist who created artwork that reflected her private dream world. Much of her work includes the flowers of Airlie Gardens, where she worked as a gatekeeper for twenty-five years. Evans was in her forties when she started drawing in earnest. She went on to draw and paint for the next fifty years. Evans created her mixed media compositions by cutting out the faces and flora from her crayon drawings, gluing them to either canvas or cardboard backing, and then combining them with either oil or watercolor paints.

See pages 24–25 and 16–21 for more about art history and the subject matter.

**Artist Profiles, p. 19**

*Artist Profile*
**Minnie Evans**
1890–1987

Minnie Evans (min´ ē ev´ənz) was born in North Carolina. She left the state only once in her life. She went to school through the sixth grade, and had no training in art. Yet she said, "Something told me to draw or die." She started drawing in 1925 and continued for the rest of her life. Evans first used crayons and later created collages. All of her work expressed her vision of the relationship between God, people, and nature. She worked as a maid and a gatekeeper at Airlie Gardens in Wilmington, North Carolina. Her art hangs in the permanent collections of museums as far away as Switzerland.

**Study** both paintings to find a variety of shapes.

▶ What types of shapes do you see most often in each painting?

▶ Describe some of the free-form shapes that you see.

▶ Do these paintings remind you of anything you have seen or experienced before? If so, what?

 **Aesthetic Perception**

**Seeing Like an Artist** Think about the various objects in nature that are made of free-form shapes. Use examples to explain the differences between free-form and geometric shapes.

▲ **Elizabeth Murray.** (American). *Riverbank.* 1997.
··························
Oil on canvas and wood. 112 × 120 inches (284.48 × 304.8 cm). Albright-Knox Art Gallery, Buffalo, New York.

# Art History and Culture

## Elizabeth Murray

Elizabeth Murray (ē li´zə bəth  mûr´ ē) (1940– ) sold drawings of elephants, cowboys, and stage coaches to her elementary school classmates for twenty-five cents apiece. After attending the Art Institute of Chicago, where she took classes in drawing, landscape painting, and traditional techniques, Murray used her artistic abilities to explore unknown territories. She developed a style that combines painting and sculpture and is considered a master of the shaped canvas. Murray's art often includes images of domestic objects in a state of disarray. In *Riverbank,* Murray overlapped shaped canvases to create a small amount of depth.

See pages 24–25 and 16–21 for more about art history and the subject matter.

**Artist Profiles, p. 50**

**Artist Profile**
**Elizabeth Murray**
b. 1940

Elizabeth Murray (ē lī´ zə bəth  mûr´ē) was born in Chicago, Illinois. Her artistic abilities were evident during elementary school when she sold drawings of elephants, cowboys, and stagecoaches to her classmates for 25 cents apiece. Murray attended the Art Institute of Chicago, where she took classes in figure drawing, landscape painting, and traditional techniques. She attended Mills College in Oakland, California and moved to New York City in 1967. Her first solo exhibition was held in 1976, and now her paintings and prints are found in major collections throughout the United States.

# Study

▶ Both use circles combined with free-form shapes. Evans: Many triangles are found in the leaf designs, and circles are found in the petals and rounded shapes. Murray: Squares are found on the fingernail tips.

▶ Evans: Face shapes, leaf shapes, hearts, and flowers are all free-form shapes. Murray: A finger is a free-form shape.

▶ Both paintings might remind students of collages.

■ For more examples of art from North America, see the *Art Around the World Collection.*

**Art Journal: Writing**
Encourage students to define and illustrate *free-form shapes* in the Concepts section of their Art Journals. What else do they want to know about free-form shapes?

 **Aesthetic Perception**

**Seeing Like an Artist** Mountains, clouds, oceans, and flowers are some examples of free-form shapes. Geometric shapes are usually found in human-made objects, such as buildings, furniture, and road signs. Free-form shapes include things that are not made by people.

**Developing Visual Literacy** Have students select, organize, or produce visuals to complement and extend the meanings of the artwork. For example, for Elizabeth Murray's painting, students should select images that illustrate the theme of the outdoors. The images should be consistent with the color and shape patterns included in the artwork.
NSAE 5.a

**Web Connection**
Visit **www.baldwingallery.com** to view artwork by Elizabeth Murray.

# Teach

Time: About 45 minutes

"Can you create a silhouette using free-form shapes?" "¿Pueden crear una silueta usando figuras abstractas?"

- Discuss the free-form shapes on page 72.

## Practice

**Materials:** 9" × 12" white drawing paper, felt-tip markers

**Alternate Materials:** pencils, crayons, cut construction paper

- Distribute the materials and have students follow the directions on page 72.

## Creative Expression

**Materials:** computer, paint or draw program, printer, paper

**Alternate Materials:** markers, construction paper

- Distribute the materials and have students follow the directions on page 73.

- See page 231 in the Activity Tips for visual examples of techniques.

### Art Journal: Brainstorming

Have students brainstorm objects for their fantasy drawings in the Creative Expression activity and list the objects in the Ideas section of their Art Journals. Then have students sketch some of the objects in the Plans/Sketches section of their Art Journals.

# Using Free-Form Shapes

Free-form shapes are irregular and uneven. A **free-form shape** is any shape that is not a geometric shape. Free-form shapes are sometimes called organic shapes because they occur in nature. They also can be created from the imagination. These are examples of solid and outlined free-form shapes.

## Practice

Use free-form shapes to draw a silhouette. Use a felt-tip marker.

1. A **silhouette** is the shape of a shadow. Many silhouettes are free-form shapes.

2. Look at objects that are made of free-form shapes. Draw a silhouette of one of those objects. Color it solid.

## Differentiated Instruction

**Reteach**
Have students close their eyes and draw shapes with curved lines and with combinations of curved and straight lines.

**Special Needs**
Help students understand how to transform real objects into free-form shapes by changing a wire sculpture of a recognizable object into a free-form shape.

**ELL**
For the Study section, you might want to restate questions using more familiar vocabulary or grammatical structures. For example, "What kinds of shapes do you see? Are they mostly geometric? Are they mostly irregular?

◀ **Brittany Blanton.**
Age 9.

**Think** about how this student artist used free-form shapes in the painting.

### Creative Expression

Have you ever pretended to be in a different world—maybe a city under the sea? Use free-form shapes to create a fantasy painting.

1. Use the computer airbrush tool to create an ocean-like background of blues and greens, with a sand-colored bottom.
2. Use the paintbrush tool to create free-form shapes that look like seaweed and shells.
3. Color the free-form drawings with bright colors, using the paintbrush tool.
4. Save and print a copy of your undersea fantasy painting.

### Art Criticism

**Describe** Describe the objects in your painting. Was it easy to use free-form shapes to create them?

**Analyze** Did you change geometric shapes to free-form shapes?

**Interpret** Give your work a title that expresses its mood.

**Decide** Were you successful in using free-form shapes to represent objects?

**eflect**     Time: About 5 minutes

### Review and Assess
"What have we learned about free-form shapes?" "¿Qué hemos aprendido acerca de las figuras abstractas?"

## Think
The artist used free-form shapes to illustrate the plant life on the ocean floor.

■ Use *Large Prints 51* Chiwana *(The Big River)* and *52* Nightingale to have students identify free-form shapes.

### Informal Assessment
■ For standardized-format test practice using this lesson's art content, see pages 20–21 in *Reading and Writing Test Preparation.*

### Art Journal: Critical Thinking
Have students answer the four art criticism questions—Describe, Analyze, Interpret, and Decide—in their Art Journals. In small groups, have students discuss how they used free-form shapes to illustrate objects in the Creative Expression activity.

### Art Across the Curriculum

Use these simple ideas to reinforce art concepts across the curriculum.

★ **Descriptive Writing** Have students write descriptive paragraphs about Elizabeth Murray's painting.

★ **Math** Use the circles in the painting by Minnie Evans to discuss how to find the circumference of a circle.

★ **Science** Have students discuss different types of vegetation that would grow along a riverbank.

★ **Social Studies** Have students use reference books to learn more about the lives of Evans and Murray.

★ **Technology** Have students select appropriate clip art in the computer's word processing program to illustrate free-form shapes. Visit **SRAonline.com** to print detailed instructions for this activity.
NSAE 6.b

# Free-Form Shapes

 **Extra!** For the Art Specialist

**Time:** About 45 minutes

## Focus

Have students study **Large Print 51** **Chiwana (The Big River)** and ask them how free-form shapes are used. What types of shape do they see most often? Have them describe these shapes.

## Teach

Explain to the students that they will create pictures of themselves, but will incorporate shapes from nature as their hair and clothing. Point out how the face in Minnie Evans's work looks like a person, but the floral decorations make the image more of a fantasy. Demonstrate blending and overlapping colors. Show students that if they make their colorings waxy they can use tissues to polish them. Have the students complete the Alternate Activity.

## Reflect

Have students use the four steps of art criticism to evaluate their work. Did they overlap and blend colors?

### Alternate Activity

**Materials:**
- sketchbook
- pencils, erasers
- 12" × 12" white drawing paper
- crayons
- tissues
- collected images of natural objects

1. Have students create quick sketches of themselves. Have them practice drawing their hair as if it were made up of natural objects.

2. Once they are satisfied with the natural objects they have drawn, have students lightly draw in the shape of their face. It should be larger than their hand. Have students draw in natural objects for their hair and shirt.

3. Have students use crayon to color the picture, overlapping and blending colors. Have them color in the background so that no white from the paper is showing.

4. Once the image is completely colored, have students use tissues to polish the crayon.

## Research
### in Art Education

"There is more to learning about art than learning to do it. Most people will not actually seek to make art in their lifetime, but all of us have daily contact with visual stimuli that deliberately (in package design, fashion, or good building) or accidentally (a pattern of leaves on snow or an unexpected bright color against a faded doorway) appeal to our aesthetic sense and offer a bit of visual order in the bustle of the everyday." (Elizabeth Vallance. "Criticism as Subject Matter in Schools and in Art Museums." *Journal of Aesthetic Education*.1988. 69–81.)

## Assessment
Use the following rubric to evaluate the artwork students make in the Creative Expression activity and to assess students' understanding of free-form shapes.

Have students complete page 23 or 24 in their **Assessment** books.

| | Art History and Culture | Aesthetic Perception | Creative Expression | Art Criticism |
|---|---|---|---|---|
| **3 POINTS** | The student identifies and compares themes reflected in works by American artists. | The student accurately defines and identifies free-form shapes. | The student uses a variety of free-form shapes to create a fantasy painting. | The student thoughtfully and honestly evaluates own work using the four steps of art criticism. |
| **2 POINTS** | The student's comparison is weak or incomplete. | The student shows emerging awareness of free-form shapes but cannot consistently identify them. | The student's fantasy painting shows some awareness of free-form shapes. | The student attempts to evaluate own work, but shows an incomplete understanding of evaluation criteria. |
| **1 POINT** | The student cannot identify or compare themes reflected in works by American artists. | The student does not understand what free-form shapes are. | The student's fantasy painting does not include free-form shapes. | The student makes no attempt to evaluate own artwork. |

**Assessment, p. 23**

Name _____ Date _____

**Lesson 2** UNIT 2

**Free-Form Shapes**

**A. Drawing**
Draw a design below using free-form shapes.

**B. Vocabulary**
Fill in the blanks.
A _____, a _____, and a _____ are three examples of free-form shapes found in nature.

**C. Writing**
Write a paragraph describing how Minnie Evans used free-form shapes in her drawing *Design Made at Airlie Gardens*.

Level 4    Unit 2 • Shape, Pattern, Rhythm, and Movement    23

# Pattern

Lesson 3 introduces pattern. When artists repeat a line, shape, or color, they create patterns.

## Objectives

### Art History and Culture
To understand that colors and shapes in a fiber artwork may be representative of the artist's culture

### Creative Expression
To create a motif to print a pattern

### Aesthetic Perception
To learn how to create patterns

### Art Criticism
To evaluate own work using the four steps of art criticism

## Vocabulary  ⭐ Vocabulary

Review the following vocabulary words with students before beginning the lesson.

**pattern** patrón—occurs when an artist repeats lines, shapes, or colors in an artwork to create a feeling of movement

**motif** motivo—the unit of repetition in a pattern or visual rhythm

See page 89B for additional vocabulary and Spanish vocabulary resources.

### Art Journal: Vocabulary
Have students add these words to the Vocabulary section of their Art Journals.

## Lesson Materials
- classroom objects such as pens, pencils, crayons
- pencils, colored construction paper
- plastic foam (from meat trays or plates with the edges trimmed off)
- brayer, printing ink, fine-tip markers
- color pencils, crayons

**Alternate Materials:**
- 12″ × 18″ white paper
- tempera paints
- paintbrushes

## Program Resources
- *Reading and Writing Test Prep.,* pp. 22–23
- *Transparency 9*
- *Flash Cards* 10–12
- *Artist Profiles,* pp. 18, 43
- *Animals Through History Time Line*
- *Assessment,* pp. 25–26
- *Large Prints 51* Chiwana (The Big River) and *52* Nightingale
- *Art Around the World Collection*

### Concept Trace
Pattern
**Introduced:** Level 3, Unit 5, Lesson 1
**Reinforced:** Level 5, Unit 3, Lesson 5

---

## Lesson 3  Arts Integration

### Theatre
Complete Unit 2, Lesson 3, on pages 40–41 of *Theatre Arts Connections.*

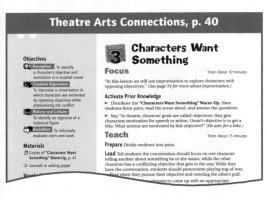
**Theatre Arts Connections, p. 40**

### Music
 Sing or listen to "Mongolian Night Song." One melodic pattern is repeated; however, the speed of the melody changes. This is called *diminution* when the melody is sped up and *augmentation* when it is stretched out. Where do students hear augmentation?

### Movement & Dance
In small groups, have students create a visual pattern using level (high, medium, and low). Have them create four different patterns that can be repeated using actions, such as standing, kneeling, lunging, and sitting.

 **ocus**

## Activate Prior Knowledge

"Make a list of words usually associated with the word *pattern*." "Hagan una lista de palabras que por lo general se asocian con la palabra *patrón*."

- Discuss students' answers. Students may list such things as a wallpaper pattern and a spelling pattern. Elicit from students their understanding that patterns result from repetition.

**Using Literature**  Reading

- Have students read *My Grandmother's Journey* by John Cech. The illustrator included patterns on the clothes and on the borders around the text.

**Thematic Connection**  Social Studies

- **About Me:** Use the artwork to discuss how artists use motifs, colors, and shapes to illustrate things about themselves.

## Introduce the Art

# Look

"Let's take a close look at the two works of art." "Vamos a observar detalladamente las dos obras de arte."

**Asking Questions**  Science

- Have students list questions they could ask to learn about the symbolism in works of art made with fiber. What does the mask in Mazloomi's quilt imply? Where have I seen masks before? Could the kente cloth design or the hat design be some sort of official dress for a chief?

 ## Art History and Culture

Have students identify what the colors and shapes represent in each work of art. Ask students if they have seen cloths like these in American society. NSAE 3.b; 4.a

**Web Connection**
Visit www.mindspring.com/~mazloomi/ to view works of art by Carolyn Mazloomi.

---

 **Pattern**

▲ **Carolyn Mazloomi.** (American). *Mask Communion.* 1998.

Quilted cotton and silk. 7 × 7 feet (2.1 × 2.1 meters). Private collection.

**Look** at the art on these pages. Mazloomi's artwork is a symbolic quilt made from cotton and silk. Elisofon's photograph is a portrait of a man wearing a kente cloth wrapped in the traditional manner. Can you find the repeated shapes on the quilt and the kente cloth?

 ## Art History and Culture

Fiber works of art, such as quilts and kente cloths, may include colors and shapes that represent something important in the artist's culture.

---

## Art History and Culture

### Carolyn Mazloomi

Carolyn Mazloomi (ka´ rə lin maz lōō´ mē) (1948– ) has created many quilts that display her African American heritage. Her work has been featured in many museums, including the Smithsonian Institution and the Wadsworth Atheneum. In 1983 Mazloomi founded the Women of Color Quilters' Network, which promotes fiber artwork by African Americans. The organization currently has 1,700 members and chapters around the country. Mazloomi, who holds a doctorate in aerospace engineering, has been quilting for about forty years.

See pages 24–25 and 16–21 for more about art history and the subject matter.

**Artist Profiles, p. 43**

▸ Artist Profile ◂
**Carolyn Mazloomi**
b. 1948

Fiber artist, author, lecturer, and historian Carolyn Mazloomi (ka´ rə lin maz lōō´ mē) is considered one of America's leading quilters and is recognized for founding the Women of Color Quilters' Network, an international organization that promotes the fiber art creations of African Americans. Mazloomi is also the author of *Spirits of the Cloth*, a book celebrating the quilts and stories of contemporary African American fiber artists. Her work has been exhibited across the United States and internationally, and her book *Spirits of the Cloth* earned the Best Nonfiction Book of the Year award from the American Library Association.

**Study** both works of art to find examples of patterns.

▶ Where are lines or shapes repeated in the works of art?

▶ Where do your eyes look first in each artwork, and where do they look last?

▶ How do you think the patterns in the quilt and the kente cloth were created?

◀ **Eliot Elisofon.** (American). *Asante Paramount Chief Nana Akyanfuo Akowuah Dateh II, Akwamuhene of Kumase.* 1970.

Photograph. National Museum of African Art, Smithsonian Institution, Washington, D.C.

## Aesthetic Perception

**Design Awareness** Look at the clothes and other fabrics in your classroom. Find repeated lines, shapes, or colors that form a pattern.

# Study

▶ Mazloomi: Motif on the border of the quilt, on the row barriers, on the row and column barriers, the mask, and the object beside it. Elisofon: Motif on headgear, kente cloth, and geometric shapes

▶ Possible answers: Mazloomi: the masks at the top of the quilt. Elisofon: the man's face

▶ Possible answers: Mazloomi: sewing or knitting. Elisofon: weaving or stamping

■ For more examples of art from Africa, see the *Art Around the World Collection.*

### Art Journal: Writing

Encourage students to write their own explanations for *pattern* and *motif* in the Concepts section of their Art Journals. What else do they want to know about pattern?

## Aesthetic Perception

**Design Awareness** Have students take note of stripes, polka dots, plaids, and checkerboard patterns in their environment.

**Developing Visual Literacy** Ask students to interpret and evaluate the various ways in which visual image makers, such as graphic artists, illustrators, and news photographers represent meanings. For example, Eliot Elisofon's photograph shows the kente cloth wrapped and worn in the traditional manner. Have students list other reasons why Elisofon might have taken this picture.
NSAE 5.a

# Art History and Culture

## Eliot Elisofon

Eliot Elisofon (1911–1973) was a photographer, filmmaker, author, and painter. The Eliot Elisofon Photographic Archives are kept at the Smithsonian National Museum of African Art. The archives include African materials (photographs, transparencies, and film) with images of African culture that Elisofon bequeathed to the museum. The photograph above is of a man wearing a kente cloth. The word *kente* comes from the term *kenten*, which means "basket." Kente cloths can be identified by their vibrant colors, multicolored patterns, geometric shapes, and bold designs. The cloths' designs often resemble the woven design of a basket.

See pages 24–25 and 16–21 for more about art history and the subject matter.

**Artist Profiles, p. 18**

**◆ Artist Profile ◆**
**Eliot Elisofon**
1911-1973
Born in New York, Eliot Elisofon led a richly multifaceted life, primarily as a photographer and photojournalist. He worked for *LIFE* and *National Geographic*, created television productions, and was a war photographer and correspondent. He traveled throughout six continents, completing assignments on architecture, celebrities, food, African life, and social subjects. In addition to photography he was a color consultant for films, a painter of watercolors, and a famous collector of primitive art. He shared his knowledge with others by lecturing at museums, colleges, and clubs around the country, and wrote many essays, articles, and books about his experiences.

**Web Connection**
Visit **www.nmafa.si.edu** (Smithsonian National Museum of African Art) to view exhibitions of artwork by Africans.

**Time:** About 45 minutes

"Can you use classroom objects to illustrate a random, regular, and alternating pattern?"

"¿Pueden usar objetos del salón de clases para ilustrar un patrón al azar, regular y alterno?"

- Discuss the definitions of *pattern* and *motif* on page 76.

- Have students choose appropriate vocabulary to discuss the use of art principles, such as pattern.
  NSAE 2.c

## Practice

**Materials:** classroom objects such as pens, pencils, crayons

- Distribute the materials and have students follow the directions on page 76.

## Creative Expression

**Materials:** pencils, colored construction paper, plastic foam (from meat trays or plates with the edges trimmed off) brayer, printing ink, fine-tip markers, color pencils, crayons

**Alternate Materials:** 12" × 18" white paper, tempera paints, paintbrushes

- Distribute the materials and have students follow the directions on page 77.

- See page 232 in the Activity Tips for visual examples of techniques.

### Art Journal: Brainstorming

Have students brainstorm and sketch ideas for their motifs for the Creative Expression activity in the Ideas section of their Art Journals.

---

# Recognizing Pattern

A **pattern** is a decorative design on the surface of something. Patterns are decorative. The part of a pattern that repeats is called a motif.

A **motif** is something visual that is repeated in a pattern. The motif can be the same each time, or it may vary. In a grocery store, each can on a shelf full of canned goods is a motif, even if the labels vary.

A **random pattern** has motifs that appear in no apparent order, with irregular spaces in between.

A **regular pattern** has identical motifs and equal amounts of space between them.

An **alternating pattern** occurs when the motif is changed in some way or a second motif is introduced.

One Motif                    Two Motifs

## Practice

Arrange classroom objects into patterns.

1. In small groups, collect classroom objects such as pencils, markers, and crayons.

2. Use the classroom objects to illustrate random, regular, and alternating patterns.

---

## Differentiated Instruction

**Reteach**

Use a piece of patterned material to illustrate patterns. Have students identify the colors and shapes that are repeated in the design of the material. Elicit from students that a motif is a unit of repetition in a pattern.

**Special Needs**

Some students with physical disabilities may benefit form having their plastic foam taped down as they are printing. Also, an inking tray or container with raised edges may help students with poor motor control as they roll ink onto the brayer.

**ELL**

To help students with the language in the lesson, you may want to focus on descriptive words such as *small, large,* and *equal.* These words, along with examples, will help students describe their work as they progress through the activities.

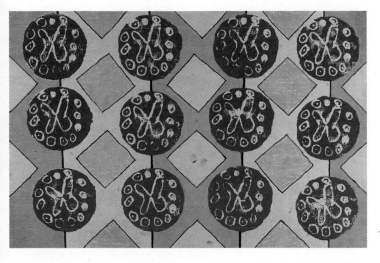

◀ **Thomas Garcia.**
Age 9.

**Think** about what kinds of patterns the student artist used in the artwork.

 **Creative Expression**

Create a paper quilt with a random, regular, or alternating pattern.

1. Cut plastic foam into a shape. With pencil, draw a design on the foam.
2. Choose where you will place the print on the construction paper.
3. Roll a thin layer of ink onto the foam.
4. Lay the foam on the construction paper. Gently rub to transfer the design.
5. Repeat the design as many times as you want.
6. Let the paper dry, then draw and color geometric shapes in the background.

**Art Criticism**

**Describe** Describe the motif that you created.

**Analyze** What kind of pattern did you use?

**Interpret** Name your paper quilt.

**Decide** Did you illustrate the pattern correctly?

 **Reflect**    Time: About 5 minutes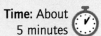

## Review and Assess
"Let's review what we've learned about pattern." "Vamos a repasar lo que aprendimos sobre el patrón."

## Think
The artist used a repeating pattern in the artwork.

■ Use *Large Prints 51 Chiwana (The Big River)* and *52 Nightingale* to have students identify motifs and patterns.

## Informal Assessment
■ Have students interpret ideas in their classmates' paper quilts. Ask students if the patterns created a certain mood.
   NSAE 5.a
■ For standardized-format test practice using this lesson's art content, see pages 22–23 in *Reading and Writing Test Preparation.*

**Art Journal: Critical Thinking**
Have students answer the four art criticism questions—Describe, Analyze, Interpret, and Decide—in their Art Journals. In small groups, have students discuss the motifs they used to print different patterns in the Creative Expression Activity.

---

## Art Across the Curriculum

Use these simple ideas to reinforce art concepts across the curriculum.

★ **Poetry Writing** Have students each create a pattern poem by rewriting one they already know.

★ **Math** Have students study patterns in sets of numbers.

★ **Science** Discuss patterns found in nature, such as those on tree bark, and patterns formed by leaves.

★ **Social Studies** Discuss patterns and motifs displayed in the national flags of different countries. Students should note that certain patterns or motifs are symbolic.

★ **Technology** Have students use a shape in the draw feature of the computer's word processing program to illustrate different types of rhythm. Visit **SRAonline.com** to print detailed instructions for this activity.
NSAE 6.b

## Lesson 3 Wrap-Up

# Pattern

---

## Extra! For the Art Specialist

**Time:** About 45 minutes

### Focus

Have students study the works of art from this lesson and have them point out and describe the patterns used. Do they see a set of colors repeated? Do they see a pattern made of shapes or lines?

### Teach

Explain to students that they will be drawing three costumed figures. The costumes can be for a parade, a dance, the circus, or a special event. All three costumes will have different patterns. Have the students complete the Alternate Activity.

### Reflect

Have students use the four steps of art criticism to evaluate their work. Did they use different patterns on their costumes? Have students describe the patterns.

### Alternate Activity

**Materials:**
- sketchbooks
- pencils, erasers
- 12" × 18" white drawing paper
- color markers
- multicultural markers
- watercolor paints
- paintbrushes, water containers

1. Have students create six different patterns made of lines, shapes, and colors. Then have them sketch some ideas for costumes.

2. On paper, have students draw three figures in costume. Have them think about using basic shapes and overlapping the figures.

3. Have students select patterns from their sketches to begin decorating the costumes. Have them use markers to color in the figures and their costumes.

4. Once the figures are completely colored, have students paint the background.

### Research in Art Education

One case study showed that students who were "learning disabled and who were 'reluctant' readers" were better able to engage in reading when the creation and analysis of visual art was incorporated in their discussions of stories. This suggests that combining visual art with reading may help certain readers ("Reading *Is* Seeing: Using Visual Response to Improve the Literary Reading of Reluctant Readers" in *Critical Links,* p. 144). As students learn about patterns in art, encourage them to think about how understanding word patterns will improve their reading skills.

---

## Assessment

Use the following rubric to evaluate the artwork students make in the Creative Expression activity and to assess students' understanding of pattern.

Have students complete page 25 or 26 in their *Assessment* books.

| | Art History and Culture | Aesthetic Perception | Creative Expression | Art Criticism |
|---|---|---|---|---|
| **3 POINTS** | The student understands that colors and shapes used in a fiber artwork may be representative of the artist's culture. | The student accurately explains how patterns are created. | The student's artwork incorporates a regular, random, or alternating pattern. | The student thoughtfully and honestly evaluates own work using the four steps of art criticism. |
| **2 POINTS** | The student shows some awareness that the colors and shapes in a fiber artwork may be representative of the artist's culture. | The student shows some awareness of how patterns are created. | The student's artwork shows some attempt to incorporate a regular, random, or alternating pattern. | The student attempts to evaluate own work but shows an incomplete understanding of evaluation criteria. |
| **1 POINT** | The student does not understand that the colors and shapes used in a fiber artwork may be representative of the artist's culture. | The student does not understand how patterns are created. | The student's artwork does not include a regular, random, or alternating pattern. | The student makes no attempt to evaluate own work. |

### Assessment, p. 25

Name _____ Date _____

**Pattern** — Lesson 3 UNIT 2

**A. Drawing**
Use a motif to draw a regular pattern, an alternating pattern, and a random pattern.

| | | |
|---|---|---|
| Regular Pattern | Alternating Pattern | Random Pattern |

**B. Writing**
Study *Mask Communion* by Carolyn Mazloomi. Write a brief paragraph describing the motif and type of pattern she used.

Level 4     Unit 2 • Shape, Pattern, Rhythm, and Movement     **25**

# Lesson 4 Visual Rhythm Overview

Lesson 4 introduces visual rhythm. Visual rhythm is created by repeated positive shapes separated by negative spaces.

## Objectives

 **Art History and Culture**

To identify and compare the subject matter in art by Native American and Spanish artists

 **Creative Expression**

To use visual rhythm in a work of art

 **Aesthetic Perception**

To identify how artists create visual rhythm in a work of art

 **Art Criticism**

To evaluate own work using the four steps of art criticism

### Vocabulary  Vocabulary

Review the following vocabulary words with students before beginning the lesson.

**rhythm** *ritmo*—a feeling of movement created by using the same types of lines, shapes, or colors several times in a work of art

**visual rhythm** *ritmo visual*—rhythm in art that is visible and is created by repetition

See page 89B for additional vocabulary and Spanish vocabulary resources.

 **Art Journal: Vocabulary**

Have students add these words to the Vocabulary section of their Art Journals.

## Lesson Materials

- pencils, erasers
- 9" × 12" white drawing paper
- colored dustless chalk, oil pastels
- sketch paper

**Alternate Materials:**
- crayons
- color pencils

## Program Resources

- *Reading and Writing Test Prep.,* pp. 24–25
- *Transparency 10*
- *Flash Cards* 9–11
- *Artist Profiles,* pp. 12, 46
- *Animals Through History Time Line*
- *Assessment,* pp. 27–28
- *Large Prints 51 Chiwana (The Big River)* and *52 Nightingale*
- *The National Museum of Women in the Arts Collection*

### Concept Trace
Visual Rhythm
**Introduced:** Level 3, Unit 5, Lesson 4

**Reinforced:** Level 5, Unit 5, Lesson 2

---

# Lesson 4 Arts Integration

## Theatre

Complete Unit 2, Lesson 4, on pages 42–43 of *Theatre Arts Connections.*

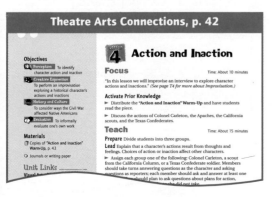

## Music

 Rhythm in music combines pulse and subdivisions of the beat into patterns of long and shorter sounds. As students examine *Crow Men in Ceremonial Dress,* have them listen to "Dakota Flute Song." Have them listen for pulse and rhythm.

## Movement & Dance

Clap a steady, continuous rhythmic beat. Select one student to be the class leader. The leader (working with the rhythm of the claps) should take four counts to do a movement. Then the group takes four counts to copy his or her movement. Have students repeat, and each time the leader must explore a range of movement ideas. If the first four counts are movements that are high, then the next four counts should be movements that are low.

# Focus

**Time:** About 10 minutes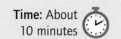

## Activate Prior Knowledge

"Can you make a list of at least three events that are a part of your daily rhythm?"

"¿Pueden hacer una lista de por lo menos tres eventos que sean parte de su ritmo diario?"

- Discuss students' answers. Students may list events such as eating breakfast, walking the dog, and combing their hair. Elicit from students the understanding that rhythm results from repetition.

**Using Literature** ⭐ Reading

- Have students read the book *Here Is the African Savanna* by Madeleine Dunphy, illustrated by Tom Leonard. The illustrations of the animals and the trees contain examples of visual rhythm.

**Thematic Connection** ⭐ Social Studies

- **Cooperation and Competition:** Discuss how objects in the paintings either cooperate or compete to create rhythm.

## Introduce the Art

# Look

"Let's take a close look at the two works of art." "Vamos a observar detalladamente las dos obras de arte."

**Summarizing** ⭐ Reading

- Have students summarize the subject matter in each artwork. Chief Black Hawk's painting is narrative. It depicts men dressed in ceremonial dress. Miró's painting is nonobjective. It has no recognizable subject matter. There are several recognizable objects in the painting, however, including eyes, stars, and a moon.

 **Art History and Culture**

Discuss cultural influences such as food, clothing, and architecture.

🖥 **Web Connection**

Visit **www.nmai.si.edu** (National Museum of the American Indian) to view works of art by Native Americans.

**78** UNIT 2 • Shape, Pattern, Rhythm, and Movement

---

 Lesson 4

# Visual Rhythm

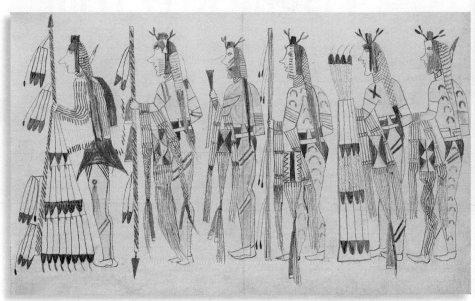

▲ **Chief Black Hawk.** (American). *Crow Men in Ceremonial Dress.* 1880–1881.
............................
Ink and pencil on paper. 10¼ × 16½ inches (26 × 41.9 cm.). Fenimore Art Museum, Cooperstown, New York.

**Look** at the artwork on these pages. The painting by Chief Black Hawk is a narrative. It was created to illustrate the details of rituals and dress in Lakota culture. Joan Miró's painting is nonobjective. Can you find repeated shapes in these works of art?

 **Art History and Culture**

Chief Black Hawk used art to teach others about his culture. What can artists include in their work that would teach others about their culture?

**78** Unit 2 • Lesson 4

---

 **Art History and Culture**

## Chief Black Hawk

Chief Black Hawk (blak hôk) (nineteenth century) used art to illustrate the details of rituals and dress in Lakota culture. Black Hawk, a Native American artist, is believed to have been born in the 1830s and died in 1890 at the Battle of Wounded Knee. His collection of seventy-six drawings was discovered during the 1990s in a file cabinet donated to charity. Black Hawk's drawings were commissioned in 1880 by a Cheyenne Agency trader, William Edward Caton. Caton furnished Black Hawk with paper and pencils and paid him fifty cents a sheet for each drawing.

See pages 24–25 and 16–21 for more about art history and the subject matter.

**Artist Profiles, p. 12**

*Artist Profile*

**Chief Black Hawk**
c. 1830–1890

▲ **Chief Black Hawk.** (American). *Crow Men in Ceremonial Dress.* c. 1880–1881.
Ink and pencil on paper. 10¼ × 16½ inches (26 × 41.9 cm.). Fenimore Art Museum, Cooperstown, New York.

Plains Indian artist Chief Black Hawk (blak hôk) was a member of the Lakota tribe of the Sans Arc band who lived on the Cheyenne River Sioux Reservation. He was a medicine man who acted as a mediary between his Lakota people and the non-Lakota domain, and he used his artwork to express the strength and heritage of his culture. While the Plains Indians were fighting for their land and independence Black Hawk created commissioned drawings of his people, which served to explain their world to outside forces. His numerous sketches addressed the ceremonial, spiritual, and physical aspects of the Lakota, and provided a means for their world to be remembered in history.

◀ **Joan Miró.** (Spanish). *Symbols and Love Constellations of a Woman.* 1941.
...........................................
Watercolor and gouache. 18 × 15 inches (45.6 × 38 cm.). Art Institute of Chicago, Chicago, Illinois.

**Study** both works of art to find examples of rhythm.

▶ Can you identify the beats and the rests in the paintings?

▶ Where is the repetition in the paintings?

▶ Visual rhythms create the feeling of movement as the viewer's eyes follow the visual beats through a work of art. How do these artists create the feeling of movement?

**Aesthetic Perception**

**Seeing Like an Artist** List examples of visual rhythm in your environment.

## Art History and Culture

### Joan Miró

Joan Miró (zhô än´ mē rō´) (1893–1983) was inspired by the landscapes and people of Catalonia, the region of Spain where he was born. Miró began to draw at age eight. His style developed from traditional painting to surreal fantasy. Surrealism proposes that dreams, fantasy, and the subconscious serve as inspiration to the artist. During the late 1930s and early 1940s, Miró painted a series of twenty-three gouaches titled *Constellations*. Miró gave many of the paintings in the *Constellations* series elaborate names, such as *Beautiful Bird Revealing the Unknown to a Pair of Lovers.*

See pages 24–25 and 16–21 for more about art history and the subject matter.

**Artist Profiles, p. 46**

♦ Artist Profile ♦

**Joan Miró**
1893-1983

Joan Miró (hô´ än´ mē rō´) entered art school in his native Spain when he was a teenager. His teachers introduced him to modern art, but in time he developed his own style, moving from traditional painting to surreal fantasy. Miró lived in Spain and France and focused entirely on his art. By the end of World War II he was very famous. He painted a wall-sized mural for Harvard University, and created two ceramic walls for the UNESCO building in Paris, France. Both the cities of Houston, Texas, and Chicago, Illinois, asked him to create huge sculptures. Miró received numerous awards for his artwork. He lived a quiet life, and although his work received much attention, Miró remained in the background. Creating

## Study

▶ Chief Black Hawk: The men are the beats, and the spaces between them are the rests. Miró: The little circles are the beats, and the spaces between them are the rests.

▶ Chief Black Hawk: repetition of men, headgear, the pattern in the device held by the first and third men; the pattern in the hand cloth. Miró: repetition of circles, stars, and lines

▶ Chief Black Hawk: the men facing one direction and having almost equal amounts of spaces between them; They appear to be walking toward something. Miró: A random pattern of shapes and sizes connected by thin threads of line to follow the path of the implied lines

■ For more examples of abstract and nonobjective art, see *The National Museum of Women in the Arts Collection.*

**Art Journal: Writing**

Encourage students to define and illustrate *visual rhythm* in the Concepts section of their Art Journals. What else do they want to know about visual rhythm?

**Aesthetic Perception**

**Design Awareness** The books in a bookcase and the cars in a parking lot have visual rhythm, as does a line of people in a cafeteria. Each person is a positive beat, and the space between each person is a negative beat, or rest.

**Developing Visual Literacy** Invite students to share any personal experiences that contribute to their understanding of the artwork. For example, relative to the painting *Crow Men in Ceremonial Dress,* what do they know about Native Americans? Do students have ceremonial clothes in their cultures?

**Web Connection**

Search through the collection of the Guggenheim Museum (www.guggenheimcollection.org) for works of art by Joan Miró.

each
**Time:** About 45 minutes

"Can you use a shape to illustrate visual rhythm?" "¿Pueden usar una figura para ilustrar el ritmo visual?"

- Discuss the definition of visual rhythm on page 80.

## Practice

**Materials:** pencil, 9" × 12" white drawing paper

**Alternate Materials:** colored pencils or crayons

- Distribute the materials, and have students follow the directions on page 80.

### Creative Expression

**Materials:** colored dustless chalk, sketch paper, pencils, large white drawing paper, oil pastels

**Alternate Materials:** crayons

- Distribute the materials and have students follow the directions on page 81.

- Have students integrate a variety of ideas about themselves and life events in their pictures. NSAE 3.b

- See page 232 in the Activity Tips for visual examples of techniques.

### Art Journal: Brainstorming

Have students brainstorm possible events or activities for the Ideas section of their Art Journals. Then have students plan how they will illustrate the selected event or activity in the Creative Expression activity.

# Using Visual Rhythm

Just as in music, a **visual rhythm** has a beat—the positive shape or form—and a rest—the negative space between the beats. In Chief Black Hawk's work, the men are the beats and the spaces between them are the rests. In Miró's artwork the little circles are the beats and the spaces between them are the rests.

The flowers are the beats. The spaces are the rests.

## Practice

Create a design that demonstrates visual rhythm.

1. Using construction paper, cut ten free-form shapes.

2. On another piece of construction paper, arrange your shapes to form a design that creates visual rhythm. Remember that the shapes are the beats in your design.

## Differentiated Instruction

**Reteach**

Have students use lines and geometric shapes to illustrate visual rhythm. Students should identify the beats in their illustrations.

**Special Needs**

Help students make learning connections by asking them to sound out their visual rhythms by clapping, snapping, or making other sounds.

**ELL**

To promote students' acquisition of the art terminology used in this lesson, you might ask students to check their Practice and Creative Expression activity works with a partner before moving to the final product. They can ask each other questions that you provide for them on a chart about rhythm.

◀ **J. T. Harrison.**
Age 9.

**Think** about how this student artist created visual rhythm.

 **Creative Expression**

Create a picture of an exciting event by using visual rhythm to demonstrate the visual movement in your work.

1. Think about an activity that has rhythmic movement. The event or activity should involve people, for example, a parade, a sports activity, or a dance performance.

2. Make sketches of people participating in the event. Place the people in uniforms.

3. Plan a composition that will have visual beats (the people) and rests (negative spaces).

4. Draw your figures with chalk on the paper. Finish with oil pastel colors.

 **Art Criticism**

**Describe** What is the subject of your drawing?

**Analyze** Describe the beats and rests in your artwork.

**Interpret** Give your work a title.

**Decide** Would your artwork have been better if you had illustrated a different activity or event?

 **Reflect**    Time: About 5 minutes

### Review and Assess

"Let's review what we've learned about visual rhythms." "Vamos a repasar lo que hemos aprendido acerca de los ritmos visuales."

## Think

The artist created visual rhythm by drawing similar ballerinas, but spacing them differently.

■ Use *Large Prints 51* Chiwana (*The Big River*) and *52 Nightingale* to have students identify visual rhythm.

### Informal Assessment

■ For standardized-format test practice using this lesson's art content, see pages 24–25 in *Reading and Writing Test Preparation.*

**Art Journal: Critical Thinking**

Have students answer the four art criticism questions—Describe, Analyze, Interpret, and Decide—in their Art Journals. In small groups, have students discuss the use of visual movement in the Creative Expression activity.

## Art Across the Curriculum

Use these simple ideas to reinforce art concepts across the curriculum.

★ **Personal Writing** Have students write invitations to the principal of your school asking him or her to come view the artwork created by the class.

★ **Math** Discuss how even and odd numbers can be used to create a rhythm.

★ **Science** Have students identify rhythms that occur in nature, such as the rhythmic cycle of the seasons and the phases of the moon.

★ **Social Studies** Ask each student to make a list of six events that are a part of their cultural rhythms such as celebrating birthdays and eating turkey on Thanksgiving.

★ **Technology** Have students use the computer's draw program to illustrate visual rhythm. Visit **SRAonline.com** to print detailed instructions for this activity.
NSAE 6.b

# Visual Rhythm

---

## Extra! For the Art Specialist

**Time:** About 45 minutes

### Focus

Have students study *Large Print 51 Chiwana (The Big River)* and discuss how the artist used rhythm. What art elements were repeated to create rhythm?

### Teach

Explain to students that they will be creating nonobjective paintings based on the art elements. They will use visual movement by repeating one or more of the art elements. Have students complete the Alternate Activity.

### Reflect

Have students use the four steps of art criticism to evaluate their work. Did they effectively create a nonobjective painting showing visual rhythm? Which colors did they use?

### Alternate Activity

**Materials:**
- pencils, erasers
- canvas (any size), acrylic paints
- mixing tray, various size paintbrushes
- water containers, paper towels, newspapers

1. Have students look at the work of Chief Black Hawk and Joan Miró on pages 78–79. Discuss how rhythm was used in their paintings.

2. In their Art Journals, have students create several sketches, using one or more of the art elements to create nonobjective compositions. Have them select their best sketch to transfer onto canvas.

3. Have students select a color scheme to complete the nonobjective paintings.

## Research in Art Education

Research has shown that the "looking and reasoning skills" learned during visual-arts training can also be applied to scientific images ("Investigating the Educational Impact and Potential of the Museum of Modern Art's Visual Thinking Curriculum" in *Critical Links,* p. 142). Students involved in visual arts training showed less circular reasoning and more evidential reasoning when evaluating both fine-art images and scientific images. Encourage students to use evidential reasoning as they identify visual rhythm in artwork.

---

## Assessment

Use the following rubric to evaluate the artwork students make in the Creative Expression activity and to assess students' understanding of visual rhythm.

Have students complete page 27 or 28 in their *Assessment* books.

| | Art History and Culture | Aesthetic Perception | Creative Expression | Art Criticism |
|---|---|---|---|---|
| **3 POINTS** | The student can identify and compare the subject matter in works by Native American and Spanish artists. | The student identifies how artists create rhythm in a work of art. | The student's artwork shows visual rhythm. | The student thoughtfully and honestly evaluates own work using the four steps of art criticism. |
| **2 POINTS** | The student's comparison is weak or incomplete. | The student shows emerging awareness of visual rhythm but cannot consistently identify how it was created in a work of art. | The student's artwork shows some awareness of visual rhythm. | The student attempts to evaluate own work but shows an incomplete understanding of evaluation criteria. |
| **1 POINT** | The student cannot identify or compare the subject matter in works by Native American and Spanish artists. | The student cannot identify how artists create rhythm in a work of art. | The student's artwork does not show visual rhythm. | The student makes no attempt to evaluate own work. |

### Assessment, p. 27

Name _____ Date _____

Lesson **4** UNIT 2

**Visual Rhythm**

**A** Drawing
Create a design to illustrate visual rhythm.

**B** Writing
Write a brief paragraph describing the beats and the rests in your design.

Level 4     Unit 2 • Shape, Pattern, Rhythm, and Movement     27

# Lesson 5 Overview

# Rhythm and Movement

**Lesson 5** introduces rhythm and movement. Artists use rhythm in many ways to create visual movement.

## Objectives

###  Art History and Culture

To identify moods created in paintings by American artists

###  Creative Expression

To use line, shape, and color to represent rhythm and movement

###  Aesthetic Perception

To define and identify visual movement in a work of art

###  Art Criticism

To evaluate own work using the four steps of art criticism

## Vocabulary  Vocabulary

Review the following vocabulary words with students before beginning the lesson.

**visual movement** movimiento visual—a sense of movement created by the use of repeated lines, shapes, and colors

**nonobjective painting** pintura abstracta—a painting that contains no recognizable subject matter

See page 89B for additional vocabulary and Spanish vocabulary resources.

### Art Journal: Vocabulary

Have students add these words to the Vocabulary section of their Art Journals.

## Lesson Materials

- classical music, CD or tape player
- 12" × 18" colored construction paper
- oil pastels, watercolor paints
- large paintbrushes, jars of water

**Alternate Materials:**
- acrylic paints

## Program Resources

- *Reading and Writing Test Prep.,* pp. 26–27
- *Transparency 11*
- *Flash Cards* 9–11
- *Artist Profiles,* pp. 55, 67
- *Animals Through History Time Line*
- *Assessment,* pp. 29–30
- *Large Prints 51* Chiwana (The Big River) and *52* Nightingale
- *The National Museum of Women in the Arts Collection*

### Concept Trace
Rhythm and Movement
**Introduced:** Level 3, Unit 5, Lesson 5

**Reinforced:** Level 5, Unit 5, Lesson 3

---

## Lesson 5 Arts Integration

### Theatre

Complete Unit 2, Lesson 5, on pages 44–45 of *Theatre Arts Connections.*

**Theatre Arts Connections, p. 44**

**Objectives**
☑ Perception To identify problems faced by certain characters
☑ Creative Expression To explore the way characters solve a problem through dramatization
☑ History and Culture To compare radio and television news
☑ Evaluation To informally evaluate one's own work

**Materials**
☐ Journals or writing paper

### Lesson 5 Characters Solve a Problem

**Focus** Time: About 10 minutes
"In this lesson we will invent and dramatize the outcome of some unsolved problems." *(See page T6 for more about Dramatization.)*

**Activate Prior Knowledge**
▶ Read aloud "The Golden Goose."
▶ Discuss some of the problems characters encounter in the story. Explain that a main character usually faces a problem; the more difficult this problem is to solve, the more interesting the play is.

**Teach** Time: About 10 minutes
**Prepare** Divide students into small groups.
**Lead** Say, "Dumming solved the princess's problem. Whose problems were not solved at the story's end? *(The other people stuck in the goose.)* What happened to those people? Did they remain stuck?"
▶ Tell students each group will create a nightly news report explaining the logical sequence of events that happened to these people the week after the story's end. Remind them to focus on the characters' problem.

### Music

 SPOTLIGHT on MUSIC Listen to "Winter," by Antonio Vivialdi. This piece is a set of four concertos for violin and orchestra. In each piece, Vivialdi uses rhythms and tone colors to create the feelings of the different seasons. In "Winter," the music suggests cold weather, stamping of feet, and resting somewhere warm. Have students imagine an event for the last section.

### Movement & Dance

Have students create nonverbal, rhythmic conversations with a partner. Assign students the number one or two. The ones have four counts to move using gesture, shape, body percussion, and axial movements, such as swing, turn, and push. Have the ones hold their last position. The twos should respond to them in a gesture and rhythmic movement for four counts. Have students repeat this sequence three times.

 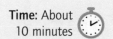
## Activate Prior Knowledge

"Think about the ways people move. Describe some of these movements." "Piensen en las maneras en que se mueve la gente. Describan algunos de estos movimientos."

- Discuss and list students' responses on the board. Have students identify the movements of different people at school.

**Using Literature** ⭐ Reading

- Have students read *Germs Make Me Sick* by Melvin Berger. Encourage students to identify examples of visual movement in the illustrations.

**Thematic Connection** ⭐ Science

- **Shapes:** Have students discuss what happens to the shape of an object when it is moving quickly through space.

## Introduce the Art

# Look

"Let's look closely at the two paintings." "Vamos a observar detalladamente estas dos pinturas."

**Fact and Opinion** ⭐ Reading

- Have students compare and contrast the paintings as they list facts and opinions about them. Answers may vary. Facts: The titles of both works of art incorporate the word *room*. *The Magic Room* is a narrative. *Within the Room* has no recognizable subject matter. Opinions: I think anyone would have fun playing in a room like the one in the painting *The Magic Room*. It must have taken a long time to create all the shapes in the painting *Within the Room*.

 **Art History and Culture**

Valdez's painting has a happy feeling conveyed by the colors and objects, such as the bouncing balls and gymnast swings. Pousette-Dart's painting conveys warm, crowded, serious emotions.
NSAE 5.c

 **Web Connection**

Visit **www.molaa.com** (Museum of Latin American Art) to view works of art by Latin Americans.

---

# Rhythm and Movement

▲ **Patssi Valdez.** (American). *The Magic Room.* 1994.
Acrylic on canvas. 96 × 119⅜ inches (243.8 × 303.8 cm.). Smithsonian American Art Museum, Washington, D.C.

**Look** at the art on these pages. *The Magic Room* is a narrative. This painting includes bouncing balls, gymnastic swings, chairs, a window, and a door. *Within the Room* is a nonobjective work about the lines, colors, shapes, and textures in a room. When your eyes follow rhythm in a work of art, you experience visual movement.

 **Art History and Culture**

Artists often use their works to create a mood or a feeling. What is the mood of each painting?

**82** Unit 2 • Lesson 5

---

 **Art History and Culture**

## Patssi Valdez

Patssi Valdez (1951– ) creates paintings that are examinations of herself and her surroundings. Valdez, a Chicana artist who grew up in east Los Angeles, has used painting as therapy to work through unhappy emotions. Early in her career, she painted unsettling images of domestic disorder. Her later works portray more tranquil scenes. Valdez continued to paint off and on while working as a photographer, performance artist, and makeup artist. More than fifty of her paintings are displayed at the Laguna Art Museum in Laguna Beach, California.

See pages 24–25 and 16–21 for more about art history and the subject matter.

**Artist Profiles, p. 67**

◆ Artist Profile ◆
**Patssi Valdez**
b. 1951
Patssi Valdez was born in California and grew up in Los Angeles, where she became involved in politically active performance art. Her present work includes large, brightly colored paintings that address themes of self-realization and the borderline between an inner personal world and a vibrant public world. She often paints rooms with expressive patterns and movement, drawing attention to windows or doors that look out on a richly colored landscape.

▲ **Richard Pousette-Dart.**
(American). *Within the Room.* 1942.
......................................
Oil on canvas. 36 × 60 inches
(91.44 × 152.4 cm.). Whitney Museum
of American Art, New York, New York.

**S**tudy both paintings to see how rhythm was used to create the feeling of movement.

▶ What types of lines and shapes do you see? What colors do you see?

▶ Explain how the artists created rhythm in the paintings.

▶ When rhythm is used, it creates the feeling of movement, which can be fast or slow. Explain the way the movement feels as you study these paintings.

### Aesthetic Perception

**Seeing Like an Artist** Look around you. Notice the number of things that look as if they are about to move.

### Art History and Culture

#### Richard Pousette-Dart

Richard Pousette-Dart (ri shâr´ pū set´ där) (1916–1992) was the second of three children born to Nathaniel Poussette, a painter, writer, and art lecturer, and Flora Louise Dart, a poet. Pousette-Dart lived in New York where he worked as an office clerk from 1936 to 1940. He had two children, Jonathan, born in 1952 and Joanna, born in 1947. Joanna also became a painter. Pousette-Dart was a self-taught artist who created many works of art. He appropriated many ideas, symbols, and forms for his artwork from his interest in world cultures.
Pousette-Dart received a National Endowment for the Arts award for individual artists in 1967.

See pages 24–25 and 16–21 for more about art history and the subject matter.

**Artist Profiles, p. 55**

*Artist Profile*
**Richard Pousette-Dart**
1916–1992

Richard Pousette-Dart (ri shâr´ pū set´ där) was born in Minnesota. His parents encouraged his interest in the arts. His father was an artist and writer, and his mother was a poet and musician. His family moved near New York City when he was two. Pousette-Dart dropped out of college to live in New York City. He worked as a secretary during the day and painted only at night, struggling for recognition. After he became successful he moved to a rural area so he could work alone. In 1959 he returned to the city to teach other artists to use self-discovery in their works. Pousette-Dart married a poet, and they had two children.

### Study

▶ **Shapes** Valdez: circles, square, vertical lines; Pousette-Dart: curved lines and shapes. **Colors** Valdez: green, blue, gold, orange; Pousette-Dart: dark red, blue, yellow, white

▶ Valdez: repeated swirling shapes on the ground; Pousette-Dart: alternating free-form shapes with the same swirling feel

▶ Valdez: slow movement leading into another room; Pousette-Dart: swirling feel creates a fast movement

■ For more examples of abstract and nonobjective art, see *The National Museum of Women in the Arts Collection.*

### Art Journal: Writing
Encourage students to define and illustrate visual movement in the Concepts section of their Art Journals. What else do they want to know about visual movement?

### Aesthetic Perception

**Seeing Like an Artist** Students should list objects such as books, pencils, desks, chairs, and so on. Give students examples of movements that are not caused by humans, such as ocean waves, a flowing river, and leaves swaying in the wind.

**Developing Visual Literacy** Have students select, organize, or produce visuals to complement and extend meanings in the paintings. For example, for *The Magic Room* students should select images that illustrate a lighthearted and fun mood. The images should be consistent with the patterns of colors and shapes included in the artwork. NSAE 5.a

### Web Connection
Visit **artarchives.si.edu/exhibits/exonline.htm** to view works of art by American artists. NOTE: This site is for teacher use only.

 each

**Time:** About 45 minutes

"Let's use music to illustrate rhythm and movement." "*Vamos a usar música para ilustrar el ritmo y el movimiento.*"

- Discuss visual movement on page 84.

## Practice

**Materials:** classical music, CD or tape player

**Alternate Materials:** none

- Distribute the materials and have students follow the directions on page 84.

##  Creative Expression

**Materials:** classical music, 12" × 18" color construction paper, oil pastels, watercolor paints, large brushes, jars of water

**Alternate Materials:** acrylic paints

- Distribute the materials and have students follow the directions on page 85.

- See page 233 in the Activity Tips for visual examples of techniques.

### Art Journal: Brainstorming

Have students brainstorm different shapes that might represent the beats of the music and lines that might represent the movement of the melody. Have them list their ideas in the Ideas section of their Art Journals.

---

# Using Visual Movement

**Visual movement** occurs when the eye is pulled through a work by a rhythm of beats and rests. Visual rhythm is used to create visual movement.

The beats of the rhythm (used to create the movement) can be shapes, colors, lines, or textures, as well as objects such as people or trees. As in music, visual rhythm can have primary beats and secondary beats.

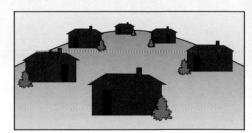

The beats are the trees, and the negative spaces are the rests.

The houses are the major beats. The doors and bushes are secondary beats.

## Practice

Use music to illustrate rhythm and movement.

1. Listen to a piece of classical music, such as a piece by Beethoven or Mozart.

2. Listen for the beat. Clap quietly to the beat.

3. Then listen to the melody line and move your arms in the air to represent the movement of the melody.

**84** Unit 2 • Lesson 5

---

## Differentiated Instruction

### Reteach
Have the students trace their fingers along repeated lines and shapes in the two paintings in this lesson. Ask them to describe the ways the lines and shapes move.

### Special Needs
To ensure success in project execution, involve students in guided practice of the steps involved in watercolor painting.

### ELL
Students may benefit from making an oral-to-print connection with the language in the textbook before they read. You can establish this link by describing procedures as you demonstrate them step by step.

◄ **Aubrey Silva.**
Age 9.

**Think** about how the student artist created visual movement.

 **Creative Expression**

Use shapes, colors, and lines to represent rhythm and movement in a piece of music.

1. Listen to music and imagine the shape and placement of the beats. Visualize the line movement to represent the melody.

2. Select related oil pastel colors to represent the beat and the melody. Select dark watercolors to use in the background.

3. Listen again and draw the beats using one color. Press heavily.

4. Listen again, and using a second color, draw the melody lines. Again, press hard.

5. Paint the background using the watercolors that you selected.

**Art Criticism**

**Describe** What are some of the lines, shapes, and colors that you used? Are some lines or shapes overlapping?

**Analyze** What did you repeat to create the feeling of visual movement?

**Interpret** Do the colors express the mood of the music?

**Decide** Do you feel your painting successfully illustrates visual movement?

Unit 2 • Lesson 5     **85**

**Review and Assess**

"What have we learned about rhythm and movement?" "¿Qué hemos aprendido acerca del ritmo y el movimiento?"

# Think

The artist used curved lines to make a spiral shape.

■ Use *Large Prints 51 Chiwana (The Big River)* and *52 Nightingale* to have students identify rhythm and movement.

## Informal Assessment

■ Have students exchange their works of art and interpret the moods created by their classmates. NSAE 5.b

■ For standardized-format test practice using this lesson's art content, see pages 26–27 in *Reading and Writing Test Preparation.*

**Art Journal: Critical Thinking**

Have students answer the four art criticism questions—Describe, Analyze, Interpret, and Decide—in their Art Journals. In small groups, have students discuss the use of lines, shapes, and colors to show movement in their artwork.

## Art Across the Curriculum

Use these simple ideas to reinforce art concepts across the curriculum.

★ **Narrative Writing** Have students use the painting *The Magic Room* as the setting of a one-paragraph story.

★ **Math** Discuss how musicians use math, such as counting the beats and rests in a rhythm.

★ **Science** Discuss energy as it relates to movement. For example, the wind is a source of energy, flying animals use the wind to travel, and the wind spreads plant seeds for pollination.

★ **Social Studies** Discuss the word *movement* as it relates to history, as in the Civil Rights Movement.

★ **Technology** Have students use the lines in the computer's draw program to illustrate rhythm and movement. Visit **SRAonline.com** to print detailed instructions for this activity. NSAE 6.b

# Rhythm and Movement

 **For the Art Specialist**

Time: About 45 minutes

## Focus

Have students study *Large Print 51 Chiwana (The Big River)* and point out and describe the lines and shapes they see. When they look at the lines and shapes, do they feel that the movement is slow and easy, or fast?

## Teach

Explain to the students that they will be creating black-and-white designs using repeated lines and shapes to create the feeling of movement. Have them complete the Alternate Activity.

## Reflect

Have students use the four steps of art criticism to evaluate their work. Did they use a variety of lines and shapes? Have students explain how they decided to color their designs.

### Alternate Activity

**Materials:**
- pencils, erasers
- 9″ × 12″ white paper
- fine-point black markers

1. On paper, have students draw a continuous horizontal curved or zigzag line. The line needs to touch both ends of the paper. Then have them continue drawing lines that parallel the first line, varying the distance between lines.

2. Once the page is filled with horizontal lines, have students draw a vertical line from the top of the paper to the bottom. The line can be straight, curved, or zigzag.

3. Have students space the vertical lines across the paper, varying the distance between each.

4. Have students use black markers to color in black and white patterns. The same colored shapes should not touch.

## Research
### in Art Education

An overview of research concerning the arts in education shows that high arts involvement leads to outcomes "central to the goals society typically articulates for public education—productive social membership, critical and higher-order thinking, and commitment to the skills for lifelong learning" ("Promising Signs of Positive Effects: Lessons from the Multi-Arts Studies" in *Critical Links,* p. 99). As students learn about rhythm and movement, encourage them to think about the goal of public education: progress or movement toward creating a better society.

## Assessment
Use the following rubric to evaluate the artwork students make in the Createive Expression activity and to assess students' understanding of visual movement.

Have students complete page 29 or 30 in their *Assessment* books.

| | Art History and Culture | Aesthetic Perception | Creative Expression | Art Criticism |
|---|---|---|---|---|
| **3 POINTS** | The student identifies the moods created by both artists in the paintings. | The student accurately defines and identifies visual movement in a work of art. | The student's artwork shows the use of lines and shapes to illustrate visual movement. | The student thoughtfully and honestly evaluates own work using the four steps of art criticism. |
| **2 POINTS** | The student's identification is weak or incomplete. | The student shows some awareness of visual movement but cannot consistently identify it in a work of art. | The student's artwork shows some attempt to use lines and shapes to create visual movement. | The student attempts to evaluate own work, but shows an incomplete understanding of evaluation criteria. |
| **1 POINT** | The student cannot identify the moods created in the paintings. | The student cannot define or identify visual movement. | The student did not use lines and shapes to create visual movement in his or her artwork. | The student makes no attempt to evaluate own work. |

### Assessment, p. 29

Name _____ Date _____

**Rhythm and Movement**

Lesson **5** UNIT 2

**A.** Drawing
Create a design to illustrate visual movement.

**B.** Writing
Write a brief paragraph describing how you created movement in your design.

Level 4     Unit 2 • Shape, Pattern, Rhythm, and Movement    **29**

# Lesson 6 Overview

# Flowing Rhythm

Lesson 6 introduces flowing rhythm. Flowing rhythm is visual rhythm created by repeating curved lines or shapes.

## Objectives

 **Art History and Culture**

To identify how Native American and Japanese artists reflect their cultures in their artwork

 **Creative Expression**

To use a cut-paper design to illustrate the concept of flowing rhythm

 **Aesthetic Perception**

To recognize elements used to create flowing rhythm

 **Art Criticism**

To evaluate own work using the four steps of art criticism

## Vocabulary  Vocabulary

Review the following vocabulary words with students before beginning the lesson.

**flowing rhythm** ritmo continuo—visual rhythm created by repeating curved lines or shapes

**curved lines** líneas curvas—rounded, flowing lines

See page 89B for additional vocabulary and Spanish vocabulary resources.

 **Art Journal: Vocabulary**

Have students add these words to the Vocabulary section of their Art Journals.

## Lesson Materials

- 9″ × 12″ white drawing paper
- 12″ × 12″ squares of colored construction paper
- scissors, glue
- oil pastels
- felt-tip black markers or pens

**Alternate Materials:**
- crayons
- pencils

## Program Resources

- *Reading and Writing Test Prep.*, pp. 28–29
- *Transparency 12*
- *Flash Card 6*
- *Artist Profiles*, pp. 31, 32
- *Animals Through History Time Line*
- *Assessment*, pp. 31–32
- *Large Prints 51* Chiwana (The Big River) and *52* Nightingale
- *Art Around the World Collection*

## Concept Trace
Flowing Rhythm
**Introduced:** Level 3, Unit 5, Lesson 5

**Reinforced:** Level 5, Unit 5, Lesson 2

---

# Lesson 6 Arts Integration

## Theatre

Complete Unit 2, Lesson 6, on pages 46–51 of *Theatre Arts Connections.*

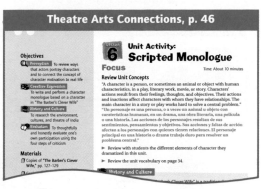

## Music

 Listen to "Largo from Symphony No. 9 in E Minor, Op.95." The rhythm in the melody, dotted eighth-sixteenth quarter, is very slow in this piece but has a driving feel to it. The sixteenth note seems to need to get to the next beat. This same rhythm, used at a faster tempo, provides the bouncy feel in the song "Fascinating Rhythm" by George Gershwin.

## Movement & Dance

Have students practice breathing in different ways, trying to match their breathing with movement. Have them pay attention to the duration of breath, the depth of the breath, and the quality of the breath.

 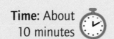
## Activate Prior Knowledge

"What happens when you throw a stone into a pond?" "¿Qué pasa cuando lanzas una piedra en un pozo?"

- Discuss the answers given by the students. They may mention ocean waves lapping on the shore or a view of hills or mountains.

### Using Literature ⭐ Reading

- Have students read *Runner in the Sun: A Story of Indian Maize* by D'Arcy McNickle, illustrated by Allan Houser. Point out illustrations that demonstrate flowing rhythm.

### Thematic Connection ⭐ Science

- **Wind:** Use both works of art to discuss how the wind shapes and changes lines in nature.

## Introduce the Art

# Look

"Let's take a close look at the two works of art." "Vamos a observar detalladamente las dos obras de arte."

### Making Inferences ⭐ Reading

- Have students find clues they can use to infer what is being portrayed in the works of art. *Coming of Age* refers to youths. The strands of hair suggest motion and running. Houser may be suggesting that coming of age is a confusing time in people's lives, and they may want to run in different directions. The title *Winter Loneliness* might suggest that the people on the mountain are lonely because they are trapped by the snow.

###  Art History and Culture

Students' responses will vary but might include Kandinsky's *Little Painting with Yellow* and Valdez's *The Magic Room*.

 **Web Connection**

Visit **www.mongersongalleries.com** (Mongerson Galleries) to view sculptures by Allan Houser.

---

▲ **Allan Houser.** (American). *Coming of Age.* 1977.
Bronze. 12½ × 15½ inches (31.75 × 39.37 cm). Denver Art Museum, Denver, Colorado.

**Look** at the art on these pages. *Coming of Age* was created to celebrate female youth and beauty. Notice the flowing rhythm of the lines in the girl's hair. In Hokusai's painting the smoke creates a flowing rhythm. Also the edge of the snow on the roof of the hut forms a flowing rhythm. This is a landscape painting.

###  Art History and Culture

Can you think of other works of art with lines that create a flowing rhythm?

### Art History and Culture

#### Allan Houser

Allan Houser (aˊlən houˊzər) (1915–1994) was a Native American artist who created many lasting images of Native American people. Houser's art was first shown in 1939 at the World's Fair. Houser, who produced drawings, woodcarvings, paintings, and sculptures throughout his career, was also an illustrator of children's books. *Coming of Age* is a narrative. This sculpture was created to celebrate feminine youth and beauty. The upturned head symbolizes the girl's desire to run to the four directions of Earth. The feather worn in her hair signifies a long life.

See pages 24–25 and 16–21 for more about art history and the subject matter.

**Artist Profiles, p. 32**

Artist Profile
**Allan Houser**
1915-1994
Born in Oklahoma, Allan Houser (aˊlən houˊzər) was the great-nephew of the Apache chief Geronimo. In 1929, he left high school to help out on his family's farm, but he was also able to study his passion—art. In 1936, his paintings were shown at the World's Fair in New York. After he painted several large murals for government buildings in Washington, D.C. In 1939 and 1940, he began to explore sculpture. Houser made small wood carvings while he taught art and worked as a pipe fitter's assistant.

▲ **Katsushika Hokusai.** (Japanese). *Winter Loneliness,* from *One Hundred Poems Explained by the Nurse.* 1839.

Woodcut. $10\frac{1}{16} \times 14\frac{1}{2}$ inches (25.5 × 36.8 cm.). Honolulu Academy of Art, Honolulu, Hawaii.

## Study both works of art to find flowing rhythms.

▶ What kinds of lines do you see most often in both works of art? Where are the lines located?

▶ Where do you see flowing rhythms in the works of art?

▶ Describe the subject of each artwork.

### Aesthetic Perception

**Seeing Like an Artist** Think of places in nature where you can find flowing rhythms.

## Art History and Culture

### Katsushika Hokusai

Katsushika Hokusai (kät soo´ shē kä hō´ koo sī) (1760–1849) was a Japanese artist whose work covered a spectrum of art forms, including woodblock prints and book illustrations. Between the ages of fifteen and eighteen, Hokusai worked as an apprentice, engraving wooden mirrors. He later applied his carving skills to woodblocks. Hokusai lived his life restlessly and unconventionally. He changed his name several times and moved about ninety-three times. Hokusai created works of art for over seventy years.

See pages 24–25 and 16–21 for more about art history and the subject matter.

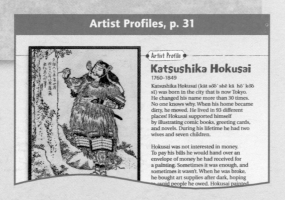

**Artist Profiles, p. 31**

● Artist Profile ●

**Katsushika Hokusai**
1760–1849

Katsushika Hokusai (kät soo´ shē kä hō´ koo sī) was born in the city that is now Tokyo. He changed his name more than 30 times. No one knows why. When his home became dirty, he moved. He lived in 93 different places! Hokusai supported himself by illustrating comic books, greeting cards, and novels. During his lifetime he had two wives and seven children.

Hokusai was not interested in money. To pay his bills he would hand over an envelope of money he had received for a painting. Sometimes it was enough, and sometimes it wasn't. When he was broke, he bought art supplies after dark, hoping would people he owed. Hokusai painted

## Study

▶ Houser: Curved lines form the hair and features of the face. Hokusai: Curved lines form the smoke and the roof of the hut; vertical lines form the trees.

▶ Houser: hair. Hokusai: smoke, the edge of the snow on the roof of the hut

▶ Houser: portrait of a young girl. Hokusai: narrative view of a winter scene with mountains covered in deep snow where hunters and foresters warm their hands at a fire outside a mountain hut

■ For more examples of Asian art, see the *Art Around the World Collection.*

### Art Journal: Writing

Encourage students to define and illustrate *flowing rhythm* in the Concepts section of their Art Journals. What else do they want to know about flowing rhythm?

### Aesthetic Perception

**Seeing Like an Artist** Flowing rhythms can be found in curved lines, such as those of ocean waves and rolling hills. Mountain ridges are an example of repeated free-form shapes that create a flowing rhythm.

**Developing Visual Literacy** Have students create drawings to illustrate the meaning each artist wanted to convey. For example, for *Winter Loneliness,* students might draw objects that would be present on a snow-covered mountain in Japan.

### Web Connection

To view works of art by Japanese artists, browse the Asian Collection of the Smithsonian at **www.asia.si.edu/collections/japaneseHome.htm.**

 # Teach

**Time:** About 45 minutes

"Let's create an original design using flowing rhythm." "Vamos a crear un diseño original usando ritmo continuo."

- Discuss the definition of *flowing rhythm* and the two elements used to create it on page 88.

## Practice

**Materials:** 9" × 12" white drawing paper, felt-tip black markers or pens

**Alternate Materials:** crayons or pencils

- Distribute the materials and have students follow the directions on page 88.

## Creative Expression

**Materials:** 9" × 12" white drawing paper, 12" × 12" squares of colored construction paper, scissors, glue, oil pastels

**Alternate Materials:** crayons

- Distribute the materials and have students follow the directions on page 89.

- See page 233 in the Activity Tips for visual examples of techniques.

### Art Journal: Brainstorming

Have students brainstorm ways they could use lines to show rhythm in the Ideas section of their Art Journals. Then have students select the colors for their flowing rhythm designs in the Creative Expression activity.

---

# Creating Rhythm

One way to create rhythm in a work of art is by repeating curved lines or shapes. This type of rhythm is known as **flowing rhythm.** There are no sudden changes in lines or breaks in the movement. Ocean waves are an example of flowing rhythm.

Curved lines, like the hair in Houser's sculpture, create a flowing rhythm.

Free-form shapes that are repeated can sometimes create a flowing rhythm.

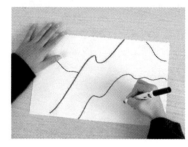

## Practice

Create an original design using a flowing rhythm. Use a black marker.

1. Flowing rhythms can be the change of tides, the bark on a tree, or rolling hills. Think about flowing rhythms in nature.

2. Choose an item with a flowing rhythm and create a close-up of a part of that item using repeated lines. Think about how it might look under a microscope and try to reproduce the image.

---

## Differentiated Instruction

**Reteach**
Have students clap out a beat or rhythm with their hands. Ask them to describe the sound of the rhythm and how it was achieved.

**Special Needs**
Students who have difficulty cutting may benefit from the use of adaptive scissors for this lesson activity.

**ELL**
Students who are hesitant or not ready to speak in long sentences may find it helpful to respond physically or with one- or two-word responses to questions. These students can identify lines in the paintings and respond to questions such as, "Are the lines straight or curved? Is there just one line?"

◀ **Schansa Blackburn.**
Age 9.

**Think** about how the student artist used flowing lines to create the rhythm.

 **Creative Expression**

How does the wind shape and change lines and forms in nature? Create a flowing-rhythm design.

1. Think about how lines can show rhythm. Cut a variety of curving lines and long, flowing free-form shapes from paper.

2. Arrange the cut shapes on the paper until you get a flowing-rhythm design you like. Then glue down the shapes.

 **Art Criticism**

**Describe** Name the types of lines and shapes you used.

**Analyze** What did you repeat to create visual movement?

**Interpret** What would be a good title to explain your work?

**Decide** Did you successfully create a flowing rhythm?

 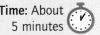
# Reflect
Time: About 5 minutes

## Review and Assess
"Let's review what we have learned." "Vamos a repasar lo que hemos aprendido."

## Think
There are two different directions of flowing rhythm, one moves horizontally on the left and the other moves vertically on the right.

- Use **Large Prints 51** *Chiwana (The Big River)* and **52** *Nightingale* to have students identify flowing rhythm.

- Have students create portfolios of their artwork. Have students exchange their portfolios to interpret ideas and moods in the works of art created by their peers.
NSAE 5.a; 5.b

## Informal Assessment
- For standardized-format test practice using this lesson's art content, see pages 28–29 in *Reading and Writing Test Preparation.*

### Art Journal: Critical Thinking
Have students answer the four art criticism questions—Describe, Analyze, Interpret, and Decide—in their Art Journals. In small groups, have students discuss the use of flowing rhythm in the Creative Expression activity.

---

## Art Across the Curriculum

Use these simple ideas to reinforce art concepts across the curriculum.

⭐ **Persuasive Writing** Have students write persuasive paragraphs to convince you that they have an idea for a Creative Expression activity that is better than the one listed in the textbook.

⭐ **Math** Discuss the reasons why the heights of mountains are estimated rather than being measured exactly.

⭐ **Science** Have students discuss mountains. Use the mountain depicted in *Winter Loneliness* to direct the discussion.

⭐ **Social Studies** Discuss the distinguishing characteristics of Japan, home to Hokusai, and China, a neighboring country.

⭐ **Technology** Have students find appropriate clip art to illustrate flowing rhythm. Visit **SRAonline.com** to print detailed instructions for this activity.
NSAE 6.b

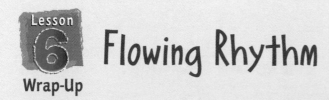
# Flowing Rhythm

---

## Extra! For the Art Specialist

### Focus

Have students study **Large Print 52** *Nightingale*, especially the curves used to create flowing rhythm. When they look at the repeated curves, how do they feel? Why?

### Teach

Explain to students that they will create nonobjective drawings in which the subject matter include lines, colors, and shapes. They will use oil pastels on black paper and will repeat curved lines and small repeated shapes to create flowing rhythm. Have the students complete the Alternate Activity.

### Reflect

Have students use the four steps of art criticism to evaluate their work. Did they successfully create a nonobjective design with a flowing rhythm?

### Alternate Activity

**Materials:**
- sketchbooks
- pencils, erasers
- 12″ × 18″ black construction paper
- oil pastels

1. Have students practice making flowing lines. Have them continue making curved lines until they get the feel of flowing rhythm.

2. Using oil pastels, have students draw a flowing, curved line along the paper. Then have them create a design with curving lines, using thick and thin lines.

3. Have students color some of the spaces between the lines. Have them keep the feeling of flowing rhythm by blending white into their colored oil pastels.

4. Students should use small, repeated shapes along some of the lines. They may want to gradually change the sizes of the shapes. Have students leave some areas of the paper black.

## Research
### in Art Education

"The making of art is an essential activity for elementary children. They need and want hands-on experiences in this 'other language.' Art lessons must include cycles of experiences with basic media and techniques, allowing students to acquire and then build upon skills fundamental to creative expression." (Kay Alexander, "Art Curricula by and for Art Educators," in *Art Education: Elementary* ed. Andra Johnson, 1992.)

---

## Assessment
Use the following rubric to evaluate the artwork students make in the Creative Expression activity and to assess students' understanding of flowing rhythm.

Have students complete page 31 or 32 in their *Assessment* books.

| | Art History and Culture | Aesthetic Perception | Creative Expression | Art Criticism |
|---|---|---|---|---|
| **3 POINTS** | The student identifies how Native American and Japanese artists reflected their cultures in their artwork. | The student recognizes elements used to create flowing rhythm. | The student applies the concept of flowing rhythm to the cut-paper design. | The student thoughtfully and honestly evaluates own work using the four steps of art criticism. |
| **2 POINTS** | The student's identification is weak or incomplete. | The student shows emerging awareness of flowing rhythm but cannot consistently identify elements used to create it. | The student's cut-paper design shows some awareness of flowing rhythm. | The student attempts to evaluate own work, but shows an incomplete understanding of evaluation criteria. |
| **1 POINT** | The student cannot identify how Native American and Japanese artists reflected their cultures in their artwork. | The student cannot identify elements used to create flowing rhythm. | The student's cut-paper design does not show flowing rhythm. | The student makes no attempt to evaluate own work. |

### Assessment, p. 31

Name _____ Date _____

Lesson **6** UNIT 2

**Flowing Rhythm**

**A. Short Answer**
Write the answer to the question.
What types of lines and shapes are often used to create flowing rhythms?

**B. Drawing**
In the boxes below, use a pencil to illustrate two ways to create flowing rhythms.

| 1 | 2 |
|---|---|
| | |

**C. Writing**
Look closely at *Winter Loneliness* by Katsushika Hokusai. Write a brief paragraph that describes how the artist used lines and shapes to create flowing rhythm.

Level 4      Unit 2 • Shape, Pattern, Rhythm, and Movement    **31**

**alternating pattern**—can repeat a motif, but change position; alter spacing between motifs or add a second motif **patrón alterno**—se puede repetir un motivo, pero se cambia la posición; alterar el espacio entre los motivos o agregar otro

**free-form shapes**—two-dimensional images made of straight or curved lines or a combination of both **figuras abstractas**—imágenes bidimensionales hechas de líneas rectas o curvas o una combinación de ambas

**geometric shapes**—mathematically precise shapes: circle, square, and triangle **figuras geométricas**—figuras matemáticas precisas: círculo, cuadrado y triángulo

**motif**—a unit that is made up of objects or art elements which is repeated **motivo**—una unidad compuesta de objetos o elementos artísticos que se repite

**nonobjective**—art that has no recognizable subject matter **subjetivo**—arte que no posee un tema reconocible

**pattern**—a repeated surface decoration **patrón**—una decoración de superficie repetida

**random pattern**—occurs when the motif is repeated in no apparent order **patrón al azar**—ocurre cuando se repite el motivo sin un orden aparente

**regular pattern**—occurs when identical motifs are repeated with an equal amount of space between them **patrón regular**—ocurre cuando se repiten motivos idénticos con igual cantidad de espacio entre ellos

**shape**—a two-dimensional area that is measured by height and width **figura**—un área bidimensional que se mide según su altura y su ancho

**visual movement**—occurs when the eye is pulled through a work of art by the rhythm of beats and rests **movimiento visual**—ocurre cuando se atrae la vista por una obra de arte por medio del ritmo de compases y pausas

**rhythm**—the principle of design that organizes the elements in a work of art by repeating elements or objects **ritmo**—el principio de diseño que organiza los elementos en una obra de arte al repetir elementos u objetos

## Vocabulary Practice

**T** Display **Transparency 38** to review unit vocabulary words.

**Similes** ⭐ Vocabulary

Have students create a simile for the word *pattern*. Repeat the process for other unit vocabulary words.

**Prefixes and Suffixes** ⭐ Vocabulary

Have students add or remove prefixes and suffixes using the unit vocabulary words. Then have them discuss what the meanings of these words are.

**Word Origins** ⭐ Vocabulary

Have a volunteer look up the word *rhythm* in a dictionary and explain where the word originated. Repeat the process for other unit vocabulary words.

# Wrapping Up Unit 2
## Shape, Pattern, Rhythm, and Movement

 **Art Criticism**

**Critical Thinking** Art criticism is an organized system for looking at and talking about art. A person can criticize art without being an expert. The purpose of art criticism is to get the viewer involved in a perception process that delays judgment until all aspects of the artwork have been studied.

■ See pages 28–29 for more about art criticism.

## Describe

▶ There are three seated African American women. They are sitting close together. The center woman is further back than the others. Each is wearing a different, turban-like headdress. Their shirts are different but they all have the same stiff, long skirts with similar designs on them.

▶ The wall and the floor seem to be covered with a continuous fabric. The floor is a different color from the wall, but it has the same design. The stars behind the women's heads make a crown shape. There is a long, flat object on the ground to the right of the women.

## Analyze

▶ There are triangles on the floor, the wall, and the women's dresses. There are squares on the skirts and the headdresses. The triangles on the floor and the wall join to make squares. The shapes that surround the women are circles.

▶ The women and the shadow are free-form shapes.

▶ There are patterns on the floor, the wall, the skirts, and the headdresses. The square on the headdress is a simple motif. The square motif on the floor is made of four large triangles and is surrounded by a border of triangles.

▶ The repetition of the women's heads and feet pull the viewer's eyes to the center. The stars create a flowing rhythm behind the heads of the women.

▲ **John Biggers.** (American)
*Starry Crown.* 1987.
Acrylic on canvas. 61 × 49 inches (154.9 × 124.5 cm.).
Dallas Museum of Art, Dallas, Texas.

## Art History and Culture

### John Biggers

John Biggers (jän big´ ərz) (1924–2000) created murals, drawings, paintings, and sculptures. Biggers was an art professor and head of the art department at Texas Southern University from 1949 to 1983. Much of his work explores the meaning of family and community to African Americans. Biggers used the language of murals and his interest in sacred geometry to combine influences from American regionalism, African American figurative tradition, and African and Native American sources into fascinating works of art. Biggers is an alumnus of Hampton University.

See pages 24–25 and 16–21 for more about art history and the subject matter.

**Artist Profiles, p. 7**

◆ Artist Profile ◆
**John Biggers**
1924–2000
John Biggers (jon big´ ars) was born in South Carolina. He was the youngest of seven children. Biggers greatly admired his father, who had lost a leg as a child while working at a plantation sawmill. As an adult, his father became the principal of a three-room school. To pay his own tuition at a private school, Biggers got up every morning at 4 A.M. to start the school's furnaces. After graduating, he began to paint. In 1943, Biggers was drafted into World War II. He soon discovered that African American soldiers were shown less respect than German prisoners of war. He became so depressed that he was hospitalized. In time Biggers went back to school and earned his degree at

 **Art Criticism** Critical Thinking

**Describe** **What do you see?**

During this step you will collect information about the subject of the work.

▶ Describe the people you see.

▶ Describe the setting and the objects in the picture.

**Analyze** **How is this work organized?**

Think about how the artist has used the elements and principles of art.

▶ Where do you see geometric shapes?

▶ Where do you see free-form shapes?

▶ Where do you see decorative patterns? Where do you see a simple motif? Where is a complex motif?

▶ Where do you see rhythmic repetitions in this work?

**Interpret** **What is the artist trying to say?**

Use the clues you discovered during your analysis to find the message the artist is trying to show.

▶ Who are these women? What are they doing?

▶ What do you think these women represent?

**Decide** **What do you think about the work?**

Use all the information you have gathered to decide whether or not this is a successful work of art.

▶ Is this painting successful because it is realistic, because it is well organized, or because it has a strong message? Explain.

 **Interpret**

▶ Answers will vary. Because of the regal posture and their isolation, some may guess the women are royalty or goddesses. Others may see women sewing.

▶ Answers will vary. Some students may say the past because the women look as if they are dressed in native costumes.

**Decide**

▶ Answers will vary. Some students will say the message or story is important. Some may cite realism. Others may also like the composition.

**Art Journal: Writing**

Have students write answers to Aesthetic Perception in their Art Journals.

▶ Have students visit a local art gallery or museum, if possible. Encourage them to interpret moods and ideas in exhibitions by professional artists. NSAE 4.c; 5.c

 **Aesthetic Perception**

**Seeing Like An Artist** Have students think about groups of people interacting with each other. Have they ever seen a group like the one depicted in *Starry Crown*?

**Describe**

▶ List and describe everything you see in the artwork.

**Analyze**

▶ Where do you see shape, pattern, rhythm, and movement in the artwork?

▶ How do these elements contribute to the look of the women?

**Interpret**

▶ How does the artwork make you feel?

▶ Why did Biggers choose the title *Starry Crown*?

**Decide**

▶ Do you have strong feelings when you look at the artwork?

"A variety of shapes, patterns, rhythm, and movement lines are used by artists to create pictures." "Los artistas usan una variedad de figuras, patrones, ritmo y líneas de movimiento para crear sus pinturas".

**T** Review the unit vocabulary with students using *Transparency 38.*

### Art Journal: Writing

Have students answer the questions on page 92 in their Art Journals or on a separate sheet of paper. 1. A, 2. B, 3. A, 4. A, 5. B

**T** For further assessment, have students complete the unit test on *Transparency 44.*

### CAREERS IN ART
## Photography

► Encourage students to compare pictures they have taken (or family pictures) to pictures in magazines. How are the pictures similar or different? Do they think the pictures in the magazines look better than their own pictures? What techniques could the photographer have used to make his or her pictures better?

"I try to apply colors like words that shape poems, like notes that shape music."

–Joan Miró

---

Shape, Pattern, Rhythm, and Movement, continued

## Show What You Know

Answer these questions on a separate sheet of paper.

**1** _____ shapes are shapes based on mathematical terms.
A. Geometric
B. Free-form
C. Alternating

**2** _____ shapes are shapes that occur in nature.
A. Geometric
B. Free-form
C. Alternating

**3** A motif is used to create a _____.
A. pattern
B. rhythm
C. movement

**4** _____ has beats—the positive shapes or forms—and rests—the negative spaces between the beats.
A. Visual rhythm
B. Pattern
C. Flowing rhythm

**5** In _____ rhythm, there are no sudden changes in lines or breaks in movement.
A. movement
B. flowing
C. visual

---

### CAREERS IN ART
## Photography

Photographers use cameras to create pictures.

**Advertising photographers** use pictures to illustrate the layout of an advertisement. They must think about how to make products appealing to viewers.

**Photojournalists** use pictures to tell stories. They go where news events are occurring.

**Fashion photographers** use pictures to show the latest fashions. Their work most often appears in magazines and catalogs.

▲ **Photojournalist**

---

## Unit Assessment Options

### Aesthetic Perception

**Practice** Have students select one of the concepts in the Show What You Know section on page 92, then find examples of each concept in the classroom.

### Creative Expression

**Student Portfolio** Have students review all the artwork they have created during this unit and select the pieces they wish to keep in their portfolios.

### Art Criticism

**Activity** Have students select an artwork from this unit and study it using the four steps of art criticism. (See pages 28–29 for more information about art criticism.) Have students work alone or in pairs and present their findings aloud or in writing.

# Shape, Rhythm, and Movement in Theatre

Eth-Noh-Tec, an Asian American theatre company, combines music, movement, and words in their performances. They use rhythmic dialogue, body poses, comic facial expressions, and hand gestures to create flowing rhythm. This theatre style comes from ancient Chinese and Japanese traditions. They perform Asian stories with morals about the lives of common people.

**What to Do** Create a tableau, or frozen picture, of a scene from a class story.

1. Divide into small groups. Your teacher will give you a card that describes one event from a story.

2. Discuss your event and create the event as a tableau. Create visual rhythm with beats and rests in your tableau.

3. Have one person be the director. Other people can be the characters, as well as objects in the setting, such as a tree.

4. Each group presents their tableau in the story sequence.

▲ Eth-Noh-Tec. "Long Haired Girl."

 **Art Criticism**

**Describe** What kind of visual rhythm did you create in your tableau?

**Analyze** Explain the decisions you made in order to create the tableau.

**Interpret** How does your tableau express the main idea of the scene?

**Decide** How well did you capture the mood of the scene? Explain.

Unit 2    **93**

 **Art History and Culture**

## Asian American Theatre

The Eth-Noh-Tec performance style reflects ancient Asian theatre styles. These include Chinese opera, which has highly moral stories about the lives of common people, and Japanese *Kyogen*, which are comic plays written in everyday language. They also incorporate musical sounds of the *ditze*, a Chinese flute, and *taiko*, Japanese drums. Eth-Noh-Tec combines three different types of performing arts: theatre, dance/movement, and music. They can each be used separately to tell stories, but when combined they touch all of the senses. Dance tells a story primarily through movement, although it is often accompanied by music. Theatre tells a story through spoken words and staged images. Music tells a story through sound and rhythm.

# Shape, Rhythm, and Movement in Theatre

**Objective:** Use lines to create a tableau that shows a specific scene from a story

**Materials:** "Long Haired Girl" performed by Eth-Noh-Tec Running time: 10:35; a simple story with each scene summarized on a card

## Focus
**Time:** About 5 minutes

■ Discuss the information on page 93.

 **Art History and Culture**

■ As a class, create a list of plays students have watched. Have them explain what they liked about each performance.

## Teach
**Time:** About 35 minutes

**Aesthetic Perception**

■ Have students watch "Long Haired Girl" and identify movements that look like flowing rhythm.

**Creative Expression**

■ Select a story for the class to interpret. Divide the story into four or five scenes. Explain what a tableau is and demonstrate one.

■ **Informal Assessment** Comment positively on each group's interpretation of their scene.

## Reflect
**Time:** About 10 minutes

 **Art Criticism**

■ Have students answer the four art criticism questions on page 93 aloud or in writing.

■ Did students effectively create tableaux that showed specific scenes and used flowing rhythm? Have them discuss what they like and what they would change.

# Unit 3 Planning Guide

| | Lesson Title | Suggested Pacing | Creative Expression Activity |
|---|---|---|---|
| **Lesson 1** | The Color Wheel | 1 hour | Design a color wheel on the computer. |
| **Lesson 2** | Neutral Colors | 1 hour | Create an outdoor drawing. |
| **Lesson 3** | Complementary Colors | 1 hour | Make a nine-patch quilt design. |
| **Lesson 4** | Low-Intensity Colors | 1 hour | Create a desert landscape. |
| **Lesson 5** | Tints and Shades | 1 hour | Create a direct-observation painting. |
| **Lesson 6** | Color Moods | 1 hour | Paint an imaginary scene. |
| **ART SOURCE** | Color and Value in Music | 45 minutes | Create a bottle orchestra. |

| Materials | Program Resources | Fine Art Resources | Literature Resources |
|---|---|---|---|
| computer with draw and paint applications, color printer, paper | *Assessment,* pp. 33–34 *Reading and Writing Test Preparation,* pp. 30–31 *Flash Cards* 7, 8 *Home and After-School Connections* | *Transparency 13 Artist Profiles,* pp. 16, 30 *Large Prints 53* and *54 Art Around the World Collection* | *Sleds on Boston Common: A Story of the American Revolution* by Louise Borden |
| sandpaper, chalk in various colors, pencils, sketch paper | *Assessment,* pp. 35–36 *Reading and Writing Test Preparation,* pp. 32–33 *Flash Card* 11 | *Transparency 14 Artist Profiles,* pp. 4, 27 *Large Prints 53* and *54 Art Around the World Collection* | *Pasteur's Fight Against Microbes* by Beverly Birch and Christian Birmingham |
| 9" × 9" primary color paper, 3" squares of its complementary color, pencils, scissors, glue | *Assessment,* pp. 37–38 *Reading and Writing Test Preparation,* pp. 34–35 *Flash Cards* 12–14 | *Transparency 15 Artist Profiles,* pp. 75, 81 *Large Prints 53* and *54 The National Museum of Women in the Arts Collection* | *Island of the Blue Dolphins* by Scott O'Dell |
| newsprint for sketches, white paper, pencils, liquid tempera paints, paintbrushes, water containers | *Assessment,* pp. 39–40 *Reading and Writing Test Preparation,* pp. 36–37 *Flash Card* 20 | *Transparency 16 Artist Profiles,* pp. 37, 76 *Large Prints 53* and *54 The National Museum of Women in the Arts Collection* | *Brainstorm! The Stories of Twenty American Kid Inventors* by Tom Tucker |
| plants, oil pastels, paint, brushes, water containers, mixing trays, paper towels, newspaper, construction paper | *Assessment,* pp. 41–42 *Reading and Writing Test Preparation,* pp. 38–39 *Flash Cards* 9–10 | *Transparency 17 Artist Profiles,* pp. 53, 65 *Large Prints 53* and *54 The National Museum of Women in the Arts Collection* | *Frozen Fire: A Tale of Courage* by James Houston |
| white drawing paper, pencils, sketch paper, paper towels, liquid tempera paints, newspaper, brushes, water containers, mixing trays | *Assessment,* pp. 43–44 *Reading and Writing Test Preparation,* pp. 40–41 *Flash Cards* 9, 11, 14–15 | *Transparency 18 Artist Profiles,* pp. 52, 73 *Large Prints 53* and *54 Art Around the World Collection* | *From the Mixed-Up Files of Mrs. Basil E. Frankweiler* by E. L. Konigsburg |
| *The Boy Who Wanted to Talk to Whales,* glass bottles, water in buckets | | | |

## Unit Overview

# 3 Color and Value

**Lesson 1:** The **color wheel** is used to organize colors and to understand how they work together.

**Lesson 2: Neutral colors** are black, white, and gray. They are often used to lighten or darken a color.

**Lesson 3: Complementary colors** are opposite each other on the color wheel.

**Lesson 4: Low-intensity colors** are dull colors.

**Lesson 5: Tints and Shades** are the light and dark values of a color.

**Lesson 6: Color Moods** are created with color schemes.

## Introduce Unit Concepts

"Artists use color to help communicate their ideas and feelings and as a way of bringing together the various parts of a work of art."

"Los artistas usan el color para ayudar a comunicar sus ideas y sentimientos y es una manera de poner juntas las varias partes de una obra de arte."

### Color
- Have each student list on a sheet of paper as many colors as he or she can think of. Ask them to categorize the colors into groups they think go together.

- Ask students to look at their lists and find examples of works of art in this book that best match their categories.

### Cross-Curricular Projects
- See the *Language Arts and Reading, Mathematics, Science,* and *Social Studies Art Connections* books for activities that further develop color and value concepts.

# Color and Value

**Color is used by artists in paintings, drawings, and sculptures.**

*A pas de deux* is a ballet dance for two. *Pas de Deux is* a combination of acrylic paints, fabric, and canvas. Miriam Shapiro often uses a variety of fabrics in her work to remind us of the traditional household arts created by women.

▲ **Miriam Shapiro.** (Canadian). *Pas de Deux.* 1986.
Acrylic and fabric on canvas. 90 × 96 inches (258.6 × 143.84 cm). Steinbaum Krauss Ga New York, New York.

**94** Unit 3

## Fine Art Prints

Display **Large Prints 53** *Red Orchestra* and **54** *The Stampede.* Refer to the prints throughout the unit as students learn about color and value.

**Large Print 53**

**Large Print 54**

Artists use **color** to create different moods and patterns.

▶ What colors do you see in *Pas de Deux?*

▶ What type of mood was created in this collage?

▶ Where are the neutral colors? Where are the complementary colors on the woman's head and in the background?

▶ Which shapes do you think are made from fabric?

**In This Unit** you will learn and practice techniques using color. Here are the topics you will study:
▶ The color wheel
▶ Neutral colors
▶ Complementary colors
▶ Low-intensity colors
▶ Tints and shades
▶ Color moods

## Miriam Schapiro
(1923– )

Miriam Schapiro was a leader in the 1970s feminist movement, a movement which led to increased recognition of women artists. In her paintings, she includes fabrics created by women from the past. She calls these works *femmages.* When she travels, she hunts for unique fabrics to include in her works of art. She is also one of the first artists to use the computer as a tool to produce paintings.

Unit 3   **95**

# Examine the Artwork

"Let's look closely at the painting." "Vamos a observen detalladamente a la pintura."

■ Have students closely examine the painting. Ask them to describe what they see.

■ Have students answer the questions about color and value on page 95.

▶ Shapiro uses all 12 colors of the spectrum.

▶ The colors are all bright and cheerful, creating a happy, energetic feeling.

▶ Neutral colors: The man's tie is black, and his face is white, while the woman's arms and face are yellow and beige. Complementary colors: The yellow face is given purple hair, and the pant legs of both figures are complementary to the colors of the torsos.

# Unit Pretest

Display *Transparency 45* as a pretest. Answers: 1. C, 2. C, 3. B, 4. A, 5. B

# Home Connection

■ See *Home and After-School Connections* for family newsletters and activities for this unit.

---

 ## Art History and Culture

## Miriam Schapiro

Miriam Schapiro (mir´ ē əm shə pir´ o) (1923– ) is considered to be a contemporary feminist artist. Most feminist artists use their work as a means of exploring the various situations of women in modern society. Although the feminist movement in art began at the end of the nineteenth century, it was not until the 1970s that women began to be widely recognized as artists. Schapiro often uses a variety of fabrics in her work to remind us of the traditional household tasks performed by women. The French term *Pas de Deux* means a ballet dance for two. This is a symbolic painting.

See pages 24–25 and 16–21 for more about art history and the subject matter.

**Artist Profiles, p. 60**

*Artist Profile*
**Miriam Schapiro**
b. 1923
Miriam Schapiro (mir´ ē əm shə pir´ ō) is an American artist who was born in Toronto, Canada. She grew up in the Flatbush section of Brooklyn, New York. Her parents encouraged her pursuit of a career in art and sent her to art classes at the Museum of Modern Art. She met her husband, artist Paul Brach, while attending college. They married in 1946 and have a son who is a writer. Schapiro organizes her home life so that art is woven into it. She can move from baking in the kitchen to painting in her studio and back to the kitchen without feeling interrupted. Her husband says that she has learned to live a "seamless life."

UNIT 3 • Color and Value   **95**

## ILLUSTRATOR PROFILE

# John Steptoe
(1950–1989)

As a child, people considered John Steptoe unusual because he liked to stay home and draw. In 1970 he published his first picture book, *Stevie,* which he wrote when he was in his late teens. *Stevie* appeared in its entirety in *Life* magazine. For this book he earned his first award, a Gold Medal from the Society of Illustrators.

Many of Steptoe's works have been praised for both realistically portraying African American life and containing universal themes that appeal to children of all races. During his 20 year career, Steptoe illustrated 16 books, ten of which he wrote. *The Story of Jumping Mouse* and *Mufaro's Beautiful Daughters* were named Caldecott Honor books. In 1989 he was the winner of the Milner Award, voted by schoolchildren from Atlanta, Georgia, for their favorite author.

Today there is an award for illustration named in his honor. The Coretta Scott King/John Steptoe Award for New Talent was presented for the first time in 1995. This award is given to an African American author and to an African American illustrator for an outstanding book and is designed to bring visibility to a writer or artist at the beginning of his or her career as a published book creator. Steptoe's son, Javaka Steptoe, followed in his father's footsteps and became a children's book illustrator.

Throughout Unit 3, share Steptoe's illustrations with the class and discuss the use of color and value. Where does he use tints and shades? What kind of mood do the color schemes create? What kinds of colors does Steptoe use if he wants an object to stand out from others?

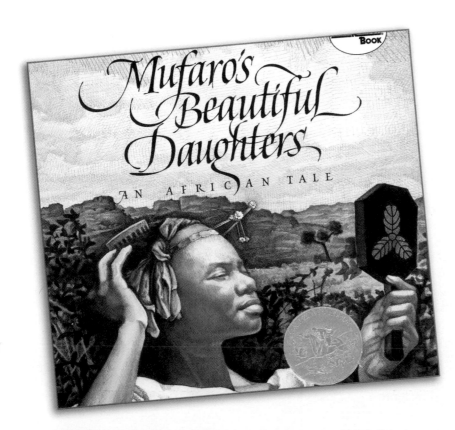

## Music

Color in music refers to the distinctive tone qualities, or timbre, of different instruments and voices. Value, while not a musical term, has a parallel in music: the ability of performers to create subtle differences in tone that are sometimes characterized as "warm" or "cool." Higher pitches are often called "bright" and lower pitches "dull."

## Literature

Use the video or DVD *Hiawatha's Childhood* to introduce the unit concepts. Students can recognize neutral and complementary colors in the visuals, as well as different color values.

**Literature and Art**

## Performing Arts

 Play *The Boy Who Wanted to Talk to Whales.* Have students try to identify the instruments.

**Artsource®**

# The Color Wheel

**Lesson 1** introduces the color wheel. The **color wheel** is made of the three primary, three secondary, and six intermediate colors.

## Objectives

### Art History and Culture

To demonstrate knowledge of the lives and work of David Hockney and Stuart Davis

### Creative Expression

To use a computer program to illustrate six colors on the color wheel

### Aesthetic Perception

To identify how colors are organized on the color wheel

### Art Criticism

To evaluate own work using the four steps of art criticism

## Vocabulary ⭐ Vocabulary

Review the following vocabulary words with students.

**color spectrum** **espectro cromático**—red, orange, yellow, green, blue, and violet, in that order

**color wheel** **círculo cromático**—a circular chart containing the three primary, three secondary, and six intermediate colors organized in the order of the spectrum

See page 119B for additional vocabulary and Spanish vocabulary resources.

### Art Journal: Vocabulary

Have students add these words to the Vocabulary section of their Art Journals.

## Lesson Materials

- 12″ × 12″ white drawing paper
- thick black felt-tip markers
- crayons
- computer with draw and paint applications
- color printer

**Alternate Materials:**
- color pencils
- black-and-white printer
- markers
- watercolor paints

## Program Resources

- *Reading and Writing Test Prep.,* pp. 30–31
- *Transparency 13*
- *Flash Cards* 7, 8
- *Artist Profiles,* pp. 16, 30
- *Animals Through History Time Line*
- *Assessment,* pp. 33–34
- *Large Prints 53* Red Orchestra and *54* The Stampede

### Concept Trace
The Color Wheel
**Introduced:** Level 3, Unit 3, Lesson 3

**Reinforced:** Level 5, Unit 3, Lesson 1

---

## Lesson 1 Arts Integration

### Theatre

Complete Unit 3, Lesson 1, on pages 54–55 of *Theatre Arts Connections.*

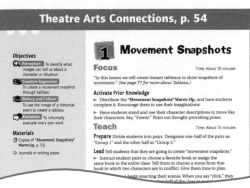

### Music

Musical instruments can be divided into three groups. String instruments make sounds when their strings are vibrated by striking, plucking, or bowing. Percussion instruments make sounds when they are shaken or struck. Wind instruments use vibrating air to make their sound. Listen to "The Grasshopper's Wedding" by Bela Bartok. Can students list on the board the instruments they hear, using the three classifications?

### Movement & Dance

Create a color wheel. Assign 12 people a color from the color wheel: three primary colors, three secondary colors, and six intermediate colors. Once in place, have students from each category (primary, secondary, and intermediate) select an action (swing, stretch, turn, jump) to distinguish each group of colors. When you name each category aloud, that group should use four to eight counts to move in the center or in place, showing their relationship to each other.

# ocus

**Time:** About 10 minutes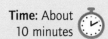

## Activate Prior Knowledge

"What would it be like if all colors were to vanish and everything was only black, white, gray, and brown?" "¿Cómo sería si todos los colores desaparecieran y todo fuera negro, blanco, gris y marrón?"

■ Discuss the answers given by the students. Black, white, gray, and brown are cold colors. The world would not be bright, warm, and exciting.

### Using Literature ⭐ Reading

■ Have students look at the cover of *Sleds on Boston Common: A Story of the American Revolution* by Louise Borden. Have them identify objects that have primary or secondary colors.

### Thematic Connection ⭐ Science

■ **Colors:** Discuss the use of bright colors in the paintings.

## Introduce the Art

## Look

"Study the paintings on these pages carefully." "Estudien cuidadosamente las pinturas en estas páginas."

### Main Idea and Details ⭐ Reading

■ Have students identify the main idea in each painting and the details that support the main idea. *Large Interior Los Angeles* is a symbolic painting of an interior in Los Angeles. The furniture and the walls were created using bright colors. *Report from Rockport* is a painting of a town. The image includes a garage and a gas pump.

## 🏺 Art History and Culture

The time periods reflected in the pictures are modern. The furniture in *Large Interior Los Angeles* appears to be modern, and the gas pump also indicates modern times.

### 💻 Web Connection

To view works of art by David Hockney search **www.nga.gov/gemini/search.htm**, the online catalog of the National Gallery of Art.

---

# The Color Wheel

▲ **David Hockney.** (British). *Large Interior Los Angeles.* 1988.
..................
Oil and ink on cut and pasted paper on canvas. 28 × 42 inches (71.12 × 106.68 cm.). The Metropolitan Museum of Art, New York, New York.

**Look** at the works of art on these pages. Both paintings have a wide range of color. David Hockney used a combination of bright primary colors and neutral colors in his painting. Stuart Davis used a mix of bright colors and unusual shapes. Notice how color is the most important element in both paintings.

## 🏺 Art History and Culture

Use clues such as the furniture design and the gas pump to decide whether the time period reflected in the artwork is modern (done recently) or is from the past.

---

## 🏺 Art History and Culture

### David Hockney

David Hockney (dā´ vəd häk´ nē) (1937– ) is a British artist who has spent many years in the United States. Many of Hockney's drawings and paintings illustrate his fascination with the southern California landscape, lifestyles, light, and colors. Hockney's first California-inspired painting was created in 1964. Currently, he lives mainly in southern California. His work often alternates between abstraction and realism. *Large Interior Los Angeles* is a symbolic painting of an interior.

See pages 24–25 and 16–21 for more about art history and subject matter.

**Artist Profiles, p. 30**

◆ Artist Profile ◆
### David Hockney
b. 1937

David Hockney (dā´ vəd häk´ nē) was born in 1937 into a working class family in the northern industrial section of Bradford, England. By the time he was 11, he had decided to become an artist. At 16, he attended the Bradford School of Art, and went on to study at the Royal College of Art. In 1961, he made his first trip to the United States. The brightness and light of California was a sharp contrast from the rain and fog of England. He was impressed by the sense of space in the sprawling city of Los Angeles, and moved permanently to the United States in 1978 to become part of the California art scene.

▲ **Stuart Davis.** (American).
*Report from Rockport.*
1940.
••••••••••••••••••••••••••••••
Oil on canvas. 24 × 30 inches
(60.96 × 76.2 cm.). The Metropolitan
Museum of Art, New York, New York

**Study** both works of art to find different colors.

▶ What colors did the artists use in their paintings?

▶ How did they separate colors in their paintings?

▶ Do the colors in each piece of art create the same feeling?

▶ If both paintings had been done only in browns, blacks, and whites, would they communicate the same feelings and moods as they do now? Explain your answer.

### Aesthetic Perception

**Seeing Like an Artist** Notice the colors of the spectrum in everyday life. Name things and places where you will find the colors that are on the color wheel.

### Art History and Culture

#### Stuart Davis

Stuart Davis (sto͞o´ ərt dā´ vəs ) (1894–1964) sometimes reworked the same picture several times to explore different ways of arranging and coloring the shapes. *Report from Rockport* was based on an artwork called *Town Square,* which was created in 1925–26. Davis included images in *Report from Rockport* that are also visible in *Town Square.* The images include the garage in the background and the gas pump on the right. He also added circles, stars, and squiggles to the scene. His paintings often contained vibrant colors and shapes that floated across the surface. *Report from Rockport* is an abstract inspired by jazz.

See pages 24–25 and 16–21 for more about art history and subject matter.

**Artist Profiles, p. 16**

Artist Profile
**Stuart Davis**
1894–1964

Stuart Davis (stū´ art dā´ vəs) was born in Philadelphia. He left high school when he was only 16 years old and went to New York City to study art. His long career began when he showed some paintings in the Armory Show in New York City in 1913. This large and important show introduced modern art to many Americans. Afterward Davis's career took off. By the 1920s, he was studying cubism. Through the 1940s, many of his paintings showed his love of jazz music. He even gave some of his paintings musical titles.

## Study

▶ Hockney: red, yellow, orange, blue, green, violet, brown, black. Davis: red, yellow, orange, green, blue, violet, black

▶ Both Hockney and Davis used shapes and lines to seperate color.

▶ Both paintings create a feeling of energy.

▶ The colors would not create the same feeling of energy. They would give the paintings a sense of coldness.

■ For more examples of art from Europe, see the *Art Around the World Collection.*

### Art Journal: Writing

Encourage students to define and illustrate the primary, secondary, and intermediate colors in the Concepts section of their Art Journals. What else do they want to know about the color wheel?

### Aesthetic Perception

**Seeing Like an Artist** Discuss places where colors can be found: flowers in a garden, the produce section of a grocery store, the local paint store, cars, clothes, and so on. Encourage students to become more aware of the colors that they encounter every day.

**Developing Visual Literacy** Discuss the main idea of each artwork. What was the artist trying to convey? Explain to students that the colors and objects in a painting, and the name of a painting, are all clues to what the artist was trying to say. Invite students to examine the painting *Large Interior Los Angeles* and find clues that indicate what it is about.

### Web Connection

Search the Smithsonian American Art Museum Web site **nmaa-ryder.si.edu** to find works of art by Stuart Davis.

# Teach

"Let's make a geometric design using the color spectrum." *"Vamos a hacer un diseño geométrico usando el espectro cromático."*

- Read and discuss the term *color wheel* on page 98.

## Practice

**Materials:** 12" × 12" white drawing paper, thick black felt-tip markers, crayons

**Alternate Materials:** colored pencils

- Distribute the materials and have students follow the directions on page 98.

## Creative Expression

**Materials:** computer with draw and paint applications, color printer

**Alternate Materials:** black-and-white printer, markers, watercolor paints

- Distribute the materials and have students follow the directions on page 99.
- Review the Activity Tips on page 234 for visual examples of techniques, if needed.

### Art Journal: Brainstorming

Have students brainstorm and sketch designs they could use to illustrate the spectral colors in the Ideas section of their Art Journals. Then have students select one design and plan how they will use a computer program for the Creative Expression activity.

# The Color Spectrum

The colors in the **color spectrum**—red, orange, yellow, green, blue, and violet—appear in the same order in natural light. A rainbow is nature's color spectrum.

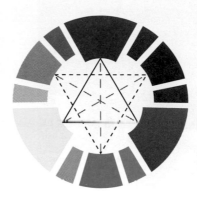

Red, yellow, and blue are the **primary colors.** You cannot create them by mixing other colors.

**Secondary colors**—orange, green, and violet—are created when two primary colors are mixed together. Primary and secondary colors are called **hues.**

**Intermediate colors** are made by blending a primary color with a secondary color. Red-orange is an example of one of the six intermediate colors.

The **color wheel** is made up of the three primary, three secondary, and six intermediate colors. Notice how the colors are organized so that you can easily understand how to mix a color. Artists use the color wheel to organize colors and to understand how colors work together.

## Practice

Create a geometric design.

1. Use a black marker to draw one large geometric shape touching at least two edges of a sheet of paper. Draw a second geometric shape inside your first shape, and then a third shape inside your second shape. Inside each section create geometric patterns.

2. Fill your design with color. In the center shape, use primary colors. In the middle shape, use secondary colors. In the outside shape, use intermediate colors.

## Differentiated Instruction

### Reteach

Have each student use crayons to create a rainbow in the order of the color spectrum. Demonstrate, starting with yellow, and then partially overlap the orange on the yellow to create yellow-orange. Continue with the next color, partially overlapping primary and secondary colors to create intermediate colors.

### Special Needs

Students with learning disabilities may benefit from having a chart of colors displayed near the computer as they choose colors for their project.

### ELL

To help students remember names and kinds of colors, you might ask them to make their own color columns and label them for reference.

◀ **Alexis Lee.**
Age 9.

**Think** about how the student artist created the color wheel design.

 **Creative Expression**

Using a color wheel, create a background for a scene on a computer.

1. Select the line tool on the tool bar. Draw two diagonal lines that touch the edges of the picture plane. It should look like an *X*.

2. At the center of the *X*, draw a horizontal line straight across until it touches one side of the picture plane. Repeat this on the other side. The white drawing area should now be divided into six areas.

3. Usc thc fill tool to pour the colors of the color wheel into each area.

4. Use the computer drawing and painting tools to insert objects into the color wheel.

5. Save and print your work.

**Art Criticism**

**Describe** Which tools did you use to make the lines and colors in your design? Why?

**Analyze** Where did you insert the objects? Why?

**Interpret** What mood does your design express? How do you think the lines and colors help to express that mood?

**Decide** Were you successful in selecting the six colors? Explain.

Unit 3 • Lesson 1 **99**

### Review and Assess

"Let's review what we've learned about color."
"Vamos a revisar lo que hemos aprendido sobre el color."

## Think

The student used the line tool to create the sections of the color wheel, the fill tool to place color in the sections, and the paintbrush tool to draw the plants and animals.

■ Use *Large Prints 53 Red Orchestra* and *54 The Stampede* to have students identify the types of colors each artist used.

### Informal Assessment

■ For standardized-format test practice using this lesson's art content, see pages 30–31 in *Reading and Writing Test Preparation*.

### Art Journal: Critical Thinking

Have students answer the four art criticism questions—Describe, Analyze, Interpret, and Decide—in their Art Journals. In small groups, have students discuss how the colors were arranged in the computer designs that they made in the Creative Expression activity.

## Art Across the Curriculum

Use these simple ideas to reinforce art concepts across the curriculum.

★ **Descriptive Writing** Have students use words to create a description of their classroom as David Hockney used paint to create a description of a room in Los Angeles.

★ **Math** Use the color wheel to review fractions. Green, for example, is $\frac{1}{12}$ of the color wheel.

★ **Science** Discuss how different colors are associated with different seasons.

★ **Social Studies** Discuss how colors are used in maps to clarify information.

★ **Technology** Have students use a computer's paint program to illustrate the primary colors. Visit **SRAonline.com** to print detailed instructions for this activity.
NSAE 6.b

## Lesson 1 Wrap-Up

# The Color Wheel

---

## Extra! For the Art Specialist

**Time:** About 45 minutes

### Focus

Study **Large Print 53** *Red Orchestra* to have students discuss the color spectrum. Where do they see the primary colors, secondary colors, and intermediate colors?

### Teach

Look at the color wheel example in the book and discuss how the colors are arranged. A color wheel is a tool. Explain to students that they will create a unique color wheel, using any shape they choose. Demonstrate mixing two colors together, and compare it to the color on the color wheel. Have students "dry" their brushes each time they rinse them in water so that their paint does not become runny. Have the students complete the alternate activity.

### Reflect

Have students use the four steps of art criticism to evaluate their work. Did they effectively create a color wheel?

### Alternate Activity

**Materials:**
- sketchbook
- 2" × 3" tagboard
- scissors
- 9" × 12" white drawing paper
- pencils, erasers
- tempera paint in primary colors and green
- mixing tray
- paintbrushes
- water container
- paper towels

1. Have students create several quick sketches of shapes they would like to use for their color wheel. Have them choose one and transfer it onto tagboard and cut the shape.

2. On drawing paper, have students lightly trace the shape twelve times.

3. Have students label with pencil the shapes in the order of the color wheel.

4. Students should begin painting the primary colors first. Have students erase the color labels in the shapes as they paint. To complete, students should mix and paint the secondary colors and then the intermediate colors.

### Research in Art Education

Research has shown that "learning happens best when kids have fun, and the arts are fun for kids." It is important to remember that while the arts can act "as catalysts for learning other subject areas across the curriculum," they are also valuable in their own right ("Arts Literacy for Business" in *The Vision for Arts Education in the 21st Century*). As students learn about the color wheel, they may enjoy creating new colors to add to the color wheel.

---

## Assessment

Use the following rubric to evaluate the artwork students make in the Creative Expression activity and to assess students' understanding of the color wheel.

Have students complete page 33 or 34 in their *Assessment* books.

| | Art History and Culture | Aesthetic Perception | Creative Expression | Art Criticism |
|---|---|---|---|---|
| **3 POINTS** | The student demonstrates knowledge of the lives and work of David Hockney and Stuart Davis. | The student accurately identifies how colors are organized on the color wheel. | The student's computer design includes six colors of the color wheel. | The student thoughtfully and honestly evaluates own work using the four steps of art criticism. |
| **2 POINTS** | The student's knowledge of David Hockney and Stuart Davis is weak or incomplete. | The student shows emerging awareness of how colors are organized on the color wheel. | The student's computer design shows some attempt to incorporate six colors of the color wheel. | The student attempts to evaluate own work but shows an incomplete understanding of evaluation criteria. |
| **1 POINT** | The student cannot demonstrate knowledge of David Hockney and Stuart Davis. | The student cannot identify how colors are organized on the color wheel. | The student's computer design does not incorporate six colors of the color wheel. | The student makes no attempt to evaluate own artwork. |

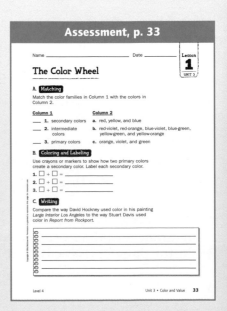

**Assessment, p. 33**

Name _____ Date _____ Lesson 1 UNIT 3

**The Color Wheel**

A. Matching
Match the color families in Column 1 with the colors in Column 2.

Column 1
___ 1. secondary colors
___ 2. intermediate colors
___ 3. primary colors

Column 2
a. red, yellow, and blue
b. red-violet, red-orange, blue-violet, blue-green, yellow-green, and yellow-orange
c. orange, violet, and green

B. Coloring and Labeling
Use crayons or markers to show how two primary colors create a secondary color. Label each secondary color.
1. ☐ + ☐ = _____
2. ☐ + ☐ = _____
3. ☐ + ☐ = _____

C. Writing
Compare the way David Hockney used color in his painting *Large Interior Los Angeles* to the way Stuart Davis used color in *Report from Rockport*.

Level 4      Unit 3 • Color and Value   **33**

---

# Lesson 2 Neutral Colors

**Overview**

Lesson 2 introduces the neutral colors. Black, white, and gray are neutral colors.

## ObjectivesObjective

 **Art History and Culture**

To demonstrate knowledge of the lives and work of Milton Avery and Z. Vanessa Helder

 **Creative Expression**

To use neutral colors to create a calm feeling in an outdoor scene

**Aesthetic Perception**

To recognize neutral colors in a work of art

 **Art Criticism**

To evaluate own work using the four steps of art criticism

### Vocabulary  Vocabulary

Review the following vocabulary words with students before beginning the lesson.

**neutral colors** colores neutros—black, white, and gray

**value** valor—the lightness or darkness of a color

See page 119B for additional vocabulary and Spanish vocabulary resources.

 **Art Journal: Vocabulary**

Have students add these words to the Vocabulary section of their Art Journals.

## Lesson Materials

- 9″ × 12″ white drawing paper
- pencils, crayons
- sandpaper
- chalk in various colors
- sketch paper

**Alternate Materials:**
- color pencils
- 12″ × 18″ black, white, and gray construction paper
- scissors, glue
- oil pastels in neutral colors

## Program Resources

- *Reading and Writing Test Prep.*, pp. 32–33
- *Transparency 14*
- *Flash Card* 11
- *Artist Profiles*, pp. 4, 27
- *Animals Through History Time Line*
- *Assessment*, pp. 35–36
- *Large Prints 53* Red Orchestra and *54 The Stampede*

### Concept Trace

**Neutral Colors**

**Introduced:** Level 4, Unit 3, Lesson 2

**Reinforced:** Level 6, Unit 2, Lesson 2

---

## Lesson 2 Arts Integration

### Theatre

Complete Unit 3, Lesson 2, on pages 56–57 of *Theatre Arts Connections.*

### Music

Any instrumental color can be used in a neutral way through dynamics and rhythm. A melody played by one musical tone color stands out from a quiet background played by another tone color. Listen to "Flute and Drum" by Gunild Keetman. Can students hear the drum occasionally in a pronounced way and occasionally in a neutral way?

### Movement & Dance

Have students walk freely in space. As you name various colors, students will perform the following actions. Neutral colors, walking; red, jumping; yellow, melting; blue, wide low turns. Students should take eight counts for each idea. Ask them to always return to neutral before exploring the next color.

# Focus

**Time: About 10 minutes**

## Activate Prior Knowledge

"Where do you see neutral colors? Are they in manufactured objects or are they found in nature?" "¿Dónde se ven colores neutros? ¿Se encuentran en objetos fabricados o en la naturaleza?"

- Discuss students' responses. Make a list of objects with neutral colors on the board.

**Using Literature** ⭐ Reading

- Have students look at the cover of *Pasteur's Fight Against Microbes* by Beverley Birch and Christian Birmingham. Have them describe the objects that have neutral colors.

**Thematic Connection** ⭐ Social Studies

- **Environment** Discuss the environmental conditions implied in the paintings that are conditions required for a wave to occur or a dam to be built.

## Introduce the Art

# Look

"Look closely at how neutral colors are used in both works of art." "Observen detalladamente cómo se usan los colores neutros en ambas obras de arte."

**Fact and Opinion** ⭐ Reading

- Have students list facts and opinions about the different works of art. Fact: *The White Wave* is a painting of a single wave. Opinion: I think the artist was attempting to create a wave (a moving ridge of water on the surface of a body of water).

### 🏺 Art History and Culture

Understanding the artist's purpose for creating a work of art is an important clue to interpreting it. A piece of art may be the only historical record of an event.

### 💻 Web Connection

Search the collections of the National Gallery of Art at www.nga.gov to find works of art by Milton Avery.

---

 Lesson **2** # Neutral Colors

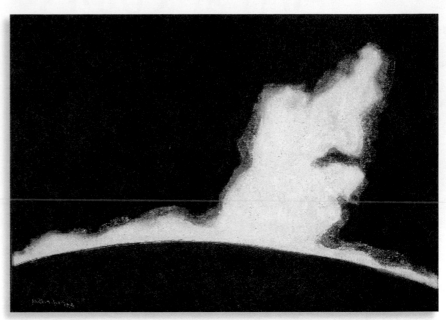

▲ **Milton Avery.** (American). *The White Wave.* 1956.
...........................
Oil on canvas. 30 × 42 inches (76.2 × 106.68 cm.). Herbert F. Johnson Museum of Art. Cornell University, Ithaca, New York.

**Look**  at the artwork on these pages. *The White Wave* is an abstract painting that represents an ocean wave. *Rocks and Concrete* is a landscape painting. It was created as part of a series of paintings used to document the building of the Grand Coulee Dam in eastern Washington. Both artists used neutral colors in their paintings. Neutral colors are often used to create a quiet mood in a work of art.

### 🏺 Art History and Culture

Both Avery and Helder painted landscapes. What other artists are known for painting landscapes?

---

### 🏺 Art History and Culture

#### Milton Avery

Milton Avery (mĭl´ tən ā´ və rē) (1893–1965) was known for his landscape paintings and his use of bold colors. Avery's favorite landscape design included seashores with or without figures. During the 1940s color was the main focus of Avery's paintings. About this time Avery chose to eliminate narrative detail from his paintings. Although Avery was a talented artist, he did not receive recognition as an American master artist until 17 years after his death. In 1982 the Whitney Museum mounted an extensive Avery exhibition that earned him recognition as a master artist.

See pages 24–25 and 16–21 for more about art history and subject matter.

**Artist Profiles, p. 4**

◆ Artist Profile ◆
**Milton Avery**
1893-1964

Milton Avery (mĭl´ tən ā´ və rē) was born in New York but grew up in Connecticut. He loved to paint and travel, and he also loved nature, landscapes, and color. Around 1905, Avery attended both the Connecticut League of Art Students in Hartford, Connecticut, and later the School of the Art Society in Hartford. Often he would paint all day long in his New York studio, sometimes creating five or six paintings or studies in a day. He established himself as a dedicated color field painter. He spent 50 years of his life painting, and created thousands of works of art.

**Study** both works of art to find examples of neutral colors.

▶ What neutral colors are used in each of these paintings?

▶ Which neutral color dominates in each painting?

▶ How does this color affect the overall mood of each painting?

▶ Describe the types of lines used in each painting.

▲ **Z. Vanessa Helder.** (American).
*Rocks and Concrete.* c. 1940.
••••••••••••••••••••••••••••••••••••
Watercolor on paper. 19 ×15⅞ inches (48.26 × 40.34 cm.).
Cheney Cowles Museum, Spokane, Washington.

### Aesthetic Perception

**Design Awareness** Notice images that were created using only neutral colors. The images could come from books, magazines, or television. What mood or feeling do these images create?

### Art History and Culture

#### Z. Vanessa Helder

Z. Vanessa Helder (va nes´ ə held´ ər) (1904–1968) depicted images of architecture and landscapes in many of her paintings. A native of Washington State, Helder created several works of art chronicling the construction of the Grand Coulee Dam in eastern Washington. She was granted permission to visit areas of the construction site where the public was not allowed. *Rocks and Concrete* was created in 1940, seven years after the first stake of the dam was driven into place. Helder married John S. Patterson, an architectural engineer, in 1943. The Grand Coulee Dam, completed in 1975, is one of the modern engineering wonders of the world.

See pages 24–25 and 16–21 for more about art history and subject matter.

**Artist Profiles, p. 27**

◀ Artist Profile ▶
**Z. Vanessa Helder**
1904–1968
Z. Vanessa Helder (va nes´ ə held´ ər) was born in Lynden, Washington, where she began painting when she was only nine years old. She went to school at the University of Washington and the Art Students League in New York, and her artistic talent was so developed that she was widely known for her many exhibitions in New York's art galleries. From 1939 to 1942, Helder taught watercolor and oil painting at the Works Progress Administration's Art Center in Spokane, Washington, and was very interested in documenting the construction of the contested Grand Coulee Dam project.

## Study

▶ Avery: black, white, and gray. Helder: black, white, and gray

▶ Avery: black. Helder: white

▶ Answers may vary. Students may mention a calm or peaceful feeling.

▶ Avery: curved lines. Helder: curved, diagonal, vertical, horizontal, and zigzag lines

■ For more examples of art from North America, see the *Art Around the World Collection.*

### Art Journal: Writing

Encourage students to define and illustrate neutral colors in the Concepts section of their Art Journals. What else do they want to know about neutral colors?

### Aesthetic Perception

**Design Awareness** Discuss neutral colors. Neutral colors often imply calmness, sadness, and serenity. Neutral colors are not bright, so they are not used to express emotions such as joy and anger.

**Developing Visual Literacy** Discuss reasons works of art are created. What are possible reasons an artist would create a work of art? Invite students to share the intent of personal artwork that is used to document an important event, as Helder did when she painted *Rocks and Concrete,* which documents the building of the Grand Coulee Dam.
NSAE 5.a

 **Web Connection**
Visit **www.zvanessahelder.com** to view works of art by Z. Vanessa Helder.

 **each**

Time: About 45 minutes

"Can you use neutral colors to create a design?" "¿Pueden usar colores neutros para crear un diseño?"

- Read and discuss neutral colors on page 102.

- Make sure students choose appropriate vocabulary to discuss color concepts, including neutral colors.
  NSAE 2.a; 2.b

## Practice

**Materials:** 9″ × 12″ white drawing paper, pencils, crayons

**Alternate Materials:** color pencils

- Distribute the materials and have students follow the directions on page 102.

## Creative Expression

**Materials:** sandpaper, chalk in various colors, pencils; sketch paper

**Alternate Materials:** 12″ ×18″ black, white, and gray construction paper; scissors; glue; oil pastels in neutral colors

- Distribute the materials and have students follow the directions on page 103.

- See page 234 in the Activity Tips for visual examples of techniques.

### Art Journal: Brainstorming

Have students brainstorm a list of objects found in an outdoor scene and list them in the Ideas section of their Art Journals. Students should also make rough sketches of their outdoor scenes for the Create activity in the Plans/Sketches section of their Art Journals.

# Using Neutral Colors

Black, white, and gray are **neutral colors.** They are often used to lighten or darken a color—to make it less bright—and to create a mood or feeling.

When you **mix a neutral color** with other hues, or colors, you change its **value.** This means that you change the lightness or darkness of the color. Notice how the color below has been changed by adding neutral colors to it.

## Practice

Draw a calm landscape using only neutral colors.

1. Create a landscape that looks peaceful and calm. On a sheet of paper, lightly sketch a simple landscape. Focus on simple shapes, and do not worry about including details in your sketch.

2. Use crayons to color your landscape. Make sure that you use only neutral colors.

## Differentiated Instruction

### Reteach
Ask students to look around the classroom for examples of objects that are in neutral colors.

### Special Needs
Many students learn best when the content is relevant to their life experience. As an introduction to the lesson activity, if possible, provide students with pictures from their own city that show neutral colors.

### ELL
Share some examples of neutral and bright colors with students who have not been exposed to these terms before asking them to identify the colors. You also might explore the kinds of feelings or moods that are expressed with colors and value changes, pantomiming and describing to reinforce meaning as you go.

◀ **Claire Tucker.**
Age 9.

**Think** about how the student artist used neutral colors.

 **Creative Expression**

What colors are used to create a happy mood? What colors seem to set a quiet or sad mood? Select one color to mix with neutral colors to create a mood for an outdoor scene.

1. Create several very simple sketches of a landscape or seascape. Select one of the sketches for your drawing.

2. Use white chalk to transfer your sketch onto a piece of sandpaper.

3. Choose a color of chalk that will blend with neutral colors.

4. Complete your drawings by blending the colors directly onto the sandpaper.

 **Art Criticism**

**Describe** List the objects you included in your landscape or seascape.

**Analyze** What neutral colors did you use in your drawing?

**Interpret** What mood did you create in your drawing?

**Decide** Do you feel that your drawing is successful? Explain.

  **Time:** About 5 minutes

## Review and Assess

"How can you use neutral colors to create a special mood?" "¿Cómo pueden usar colores neutros para crear un ánimo especial?"

## Think

The student artist used neutral colors to create a calm feeling.

■ Use *Large Prints 53 Red Orchestra* and *54 The Stampede* to have students identify the neutral colors.

## Informal Assessment

■ For standardized-format test practice using this lesson's art content, see pages 32–33 in *Reading and Writing Test Preparation.*

### Art Journal: Critical Thinking

Have students answer the four art criticism questions—Describe, Analyze, Interpret, and Decide—in their Art Journals. In small groups, have students discuss the use of neutral colors in the outdoor scenes that they made in the Creative Expression activity.

## Art Across the Curriculum

Use these simple ideas to reinforce art concepts across the curriculum.

★ **Personal Writing** Have students write a thank-you note to an artist thanking him or her for creating a piece of art.

★ **Math** Use the painting *Rocks and Concrete* to discuss the importance of measurements when building something.

★ **Science** Use the painting *Rocks and Concrete* to discuss geology, the science that deals with the structure of Earth.

★ **Social Studies** Discuss the word *neutral* as it relates to conflicts: "not belonging to either side." Give students examples of countries that remained neutral during major conflicts.

★ **Technology** Have students use a paint or draw program to illustrate neutral colors. Visit **SRAonline.com** to print detailed instructions for this activity.
NSAE 6.b

# Lesson 2 Neutral Colors

**Wrap-Up**

---

## Extra! For the Art Specialist

**Time:** About 45 minutes

### Focus

Study **Large Print 54** *The Stampede* to have students discuss how neutral colors are used. Have students explain how they think the artist mixed the color values they see. What type of mood is created by the use of neutral colors?

### Teach

Explain to students that they will create a landscape or seascape, using tempera paint on a textured surface. Demonstrate blending black and white to create a range of neutral-colored values. Then have students complete the alternate activity.

Note: Sand can be mixed into the tempera paint to give added texture to the painted surface.

### Reflect

Have students use the four steps of art criticism to evaluate their work. Did they effectively create a landscape or seascape using neutral colors? Have them describe the mood they created.

### Alternate Activity

**Materials:**
- sketchbook
- pencils, erasers
- images of land- and seascapes
- tempera paint in black and white only
- mixing tray
- paintbrushes
- water container
- paper towels
- 9" × 12" or larger textured papers
- playground sand

1. Have students look through land and sea images and select one or two to create a sketch. Have them select a textured paper to transfer their sketches.

2. Students should lightly draw the shapes with white paint. Once the composition is completely transferred onto the textured paper, students can begin painting.

3. Have students mix and blend a range of values, using black and white, to paint the entire scene. Sand can be added to the paint to create rougher textures. A small brush should be used to add any important details.

### Research in Art Education

Collaboration is an important benefit of the arts. In the visual arts, students may engage in "enterprises such as painting murals and scenery, producing books, and organizing exhibitions." They also often have the opportunity to learn to appropriately critique the work of others ("Learning in and Through the Arts: Curriculum Implications" in *Champions of Change*, p. 40). Encourage students to collaborate with others as they create works with neutral colors.

---

## Assessment

Use the following rubric to evaluate the artwork students make in the Creative Expression activity and to assess students' understanding of neutral colors.

Have students complete page 35 or 36 in their *Assessment* books.

| | Art History and Culture | Aesthetic Perception | Creative Expression | Art Criticism |
|---|---|---|---|---|
| **3 POINTS** | The student demonstrates knowledge of the lives and work of Milton Avery and Z. Vanessa Helder. | The student accurately identifies neutral colors in a work of art. | The student's outdoor scene clearly illustrates neutral colors. | The student thoughtfully and honestly evaluates own work using the four steps of art criticism. |
| **2 POINTS** | The student's knowledge of Milton Avery and Z. Vanessa Helder is weak or incomplete. | The student shows emerging awareness of neutral colors but cannot consistently identify them in a work of art. | The student's outdoor scene shows some awareness of neutral colors. | The student attempts to evaluate own work but shows an incomplete understanding of evaluation criteria. |
| **1 POINT** | The student cannot demonstrate knowledge of Milton Avery and Z. Vanessa Helder. | The student cannot identify neutral colors in a work of art. | The student's outdoor scene shows no understanding of neutral colors. | The student makes no attempt to evaluate own artwork. |

### Assessment, p. 35

Name _____ Date _____

**Lesson 2 UNIT 3**

**Neutral Colors**

**A. Short Answer**
List the three neutral colors.
1. _____
2. _____
3. _____

**B. Coloring**
Use any color from the color spectrum. Change the value of the color by mixing it with a different neutral color in each of the boxes below.

| 1 | 2 | 3 |
|---|---|---|

**C. Writing**
Write a paragraph describing how Z. Vanessa Helder used neutral colors in Rocks and Concrete. Which neutral colors did she use? How do the neutral colors affect the mood of her painting?

_____
_____
_____

Level 4                    Unit 3 • Color and Value  **35**

# Complementary Colors

Lesson 3 introduces complementary colors. Colors that are opposite each other on the color wheel are complementary colors.

## Objectives

### Art History and Culture

To demonstrate knowledge of Tlingit and folk art

### Creative Expression

To use complementary colors to create a quilt design

### Aesthetic Perception

To define and identify complementary colors in a work of art

### Art Criticism

To evaluate own work using the four steps of art criticism

## Vocabulary  Vocabulary

Review the following vocabulary words with students before beginning the lesson.

**complementary colors** colores complementarios—colors that are opposite each other on the color wheel. There are three sets: red and green, yellow and violet, and blue and orange.

**contrast** contraste—a large difference created when elements are placed next to each other in an artwork

See page 119B for additional vocabulary and Spanish vocabulary resources.

### Art Journal: Vocabulary

Have students add these words to the Vocabulary section of their Art Journals.

## Lesson Materials

- 9" × 9" primary-color paper
- 3" squares of complementary-colored paper
- pencils
- scissors, glue
- 9" × 12" white drawing paper
- color markers
- crayons

**Alternate Materials:**
- white construction paper
- color pencils

## Program Resources

- *Reading and Writing Test Prep.,* pp. 34–35
- *Transparency 15*
- *Flash Cards* 12–14
- *Artist Profiles,* pp. 75, 81
- *Animals Through History Time Line*
- *Assessment,* pp. 37–38
- *Large Prints 53* Red Orchestra and *54 The Stampede*

## Concept Trace
Complementary Colors
**Introduced:** Level 4, Unit 3, Lesson 3

**Reinforced:** Level 5, Unit 3, Lesson 3

---

# Lesson 3 Arts Integration

## Theatre

Complete Unit 3, Lesson 3, on page 58–59 of *Theatre Arts Connections.*

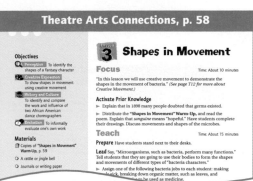

## Music

All types of musical instruments complement the color of the human singing voice. Have students listen to Cantata No. 1, BWV 1 "Wie schon leuchtet der Morgenstern" by Johann Sebastian Bach. How does Bach use the orchestra to complement the voices in chorus?

## Movement & Dance

Complementary colors can be explored by putting students into two lines. Have students wear colored stickers or cards. One line will contain the primary colors. The other line will contain their complementary colors. Name a primary color, like red. All the reds and the complementary color of red (green) should run to the center, find a partner, take hands, spin around once or twice, and then return to place.

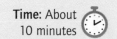# Focus

## Activate Prior Knowledge

"Think about contrasting colors used by a sports team or to celebrate a holiday. Did the colors appear to almost vibrate when you looked at them?" "Piensen acerca de los colores que se usan en un equipo deportivo o para celebrar una festividad. Cuando observan los colores, ¿parecen como si vibraran?"

■ Discuss the answers given by students about various contrasting colors and their symbolism.

### Using Literature ★ Reading

■ Have students look at the cover of *Island of the Blue Dolphins* by Scott O'Dell. Have them identify the complementary colors.

### Thematic Connection ★ Social Studies

■ **Our Country and Its People:** Discuss the significance of works of art such as *Raven Screen* and *Canister* in documenting the history of a group of people.

## Introduce the Art

# Look

"Closely examine the artworks on the pages." "Observen detalladamente las obras de arte en las páginas."

### Environment and Society ★ Social Studies

■ Have students use the functional artwork to discuss the importance of using art as a way to document the history of a group of people. Folk art is often produced by those who work outside the accepted traditions of a particular culture. Students should speculate about whether the designs on *Raven Screen* and *Canister* represent something.

 **Art History and Culture**

Functional works of art can be used for some purpose other than decoration.

 **Web Connection**

Visit **www.moifa.org** (the Museum of International Folk Art) to view examples of folk art.

---

 **Lesson 3** Complementary Colors

**Look** at the artwork on these pages. *Yeihl Nax'in Raven Screen* was made by a family or clan from the Tlingit society. This partition was used to block off a special room at the rear of the house. The most valued clan possessions were kept behind it. The tin canister was used to hold a variety of everyday items. The artists both used complementary colors to decorate these functional works of art.

▲ **Artist unknown.**
(Tlingit, United States).
*Yeihl Nax'in Raven Screen.*
c. 1830.
••••••••••••••••••••••
Spruce and paint. $8\frac{13}{16} \times 10\frac{3}{4}$ feet (2.69 × 3.28 meters). The Seattle Art Museum, Seattle, Washington.

 **Art History and Culture**

What are some other examples of utilitarian art?

---

 **Art History and Culture**

## Tlingit Society

The Tlingit society is thousands of years old. *Raven Screen* was built in the early 1800s, when more than one family often lived together in one house. Today many Tlingit families live in individual modern houses, but their clans often retain one traditional home for ceremonies. These homes are often painted with the traditional Tlingit designs, like those seen in *Raven Screen*.

See pages 24–25 and 16–21 for more about art history and subject matter.

**Artist Profiles, p. 81**

> Artist Profile
>
> ### Yeihl Nax'in Raven Screen
>
> The Tlingit live in the heavily forested and damp coastal islands of southeastern Alaska. They live in large, cedar-planked communal houses filled with carvings and paintings that express the power and prestige of the inhabitants. These symbols are displayed at great feasts called *potlatches*. In Tlingit society, shamans used carvings and paintings as part of their rituals. Shamans were buried with such ritual objects.
>
> ▲ **Artist unknown (Tlingit).** (United States).
> *Yeihl Nax'in Raven Screen.* c. 1830.

**Study** both works of art to identify the complementary colors.

► What are the main colors used in each artwork?

► How did the artists arrange these colors to create designs?

► What similarities and differences in the use of color do you see in these pieces of art?

► How do you feel when you look at each of these works of art?

► What colors seem to show the greatest contrast in each work of art?

▲ **Artist unknown.** (United States). *Canister.* 1825.
............................................
Tin. American Folk Art Museum, New York, New York.

**◑ Aesthetic Perception**

**Design Awareness** Look around your classroom. Identify warm and cool colors. Make a list of the warm colors and their complements.

**🏺 Art History and Culture**

### Folk Art

Folk art consists of paintings, carvings, sculptures, textiles, furniture, functional items such as the *Canister,* and other objects that are produced using traditional techniques handed down from one generation to the next. Most folk artists learn a particular art form either by becoming an apprentice or from an elder. *Canister* is a functional artwork. This means it can be used for some purpose other than for decoration. It is made of tin and most likely painted with enamel.

See pages 24–25 and 16–21 for more about art history and subject matter.

**Artist Profiles, p. 75**

⟨ Artist Profile ⟩

**Canister**

This canister was made by a Pennsylvania Dutch artisan. In 1683 the first German-speaking colonists arrived in the New World to settle William Penn's colony of Pennsylvania. Many of them, such as the Quakers, the Mennonites, the Amish, and the Moravians, were escaping religious persecution. Pennsylvania offered religious freedom for settlers from various levels of society. They included university graduates, highly skilled craftspeople, and farmers.

**rtist unknown.** (United States). *Canister.* 1825.

# Study

► *Raven Screen:* red, blue, black. *Canister:* red, yellow, blue, black

► *Raven Screen* and *Canister:* The contrasting colors are placed next to each other for emphasis.

► Similarities: Both use a red background with added shapes of black and gray. Differences: The colors in *Raven Screen* are not as bright as those in *Canister,* so they have less of a contrast.

► *Raven Screen:* calm and peaceful. *Canister:* lively.

► The complementary colors create the greatest contrast in each piece.

■ For more examples of utilitarian art, see **The National Museum of Women in the Arts Collection.**

**📓 Art Journal: Writing**

Encourage students to define and illustrate complementary colors in the Concepts section of their Art Journals. What else do they want to know about complementary colors?

**◑ Aesthetic Perception**

**Design Awareness** Yellow, orange, and red are warm colors. Warm colors often represent warm things, such as fire and sunshine. Green, blue, and violet are cool colors. Purple is the complement of yellow, blue is the complement of orange, and green is the complement of red.

**Developing Visual Literacy** Discuss reasons why artwork is created. What are possible reasons why an artist would create a work of art? Invite students to interpret ideas and moods of functional artwork by professionals they may have seen in exhibitions or on the Internet.
NSAE 5.a

**💻 Web Connection**
Visit **www.folkartmuseum.org** (American Folk Art Museum) to view examples of folk art.

 **each**

**Time:** About 45 minutes

"Can you use complementary colors to create a design?" "¿Pueden usar colores complementarios para crear un diseño?"

- Read and discuss complementary colors on page 106.

- Make sure students choose appropriate vocabulary to discuss color concepts, including complementary colors.
  NSAE 2.a; 2.b

 **Practice**

**Materials:** 9″ × 12″ white drawing paper, color markers, or crayons

**Alternate Materials:** white construction paper and color pencils

- Distribute the materials and have students follow the directions on page 106.

## Creative Expression

**Materials:** 9″ × 9″ primary color paper, 3″ squares of its complementary color, pencil, scissors, glue

**Alternate Materials:** white construction paper and color pencils

- Distribute the materials and have students follow the directions on page 107.

- See page 235 in the Activity Tips for visual examples of techniques.

### Art Journal: Brainstorming

Have students brainstorm and illustrate possible motif designs in the Ideas section of their Art Journals. Then have them select a design for their quilt in the Creative Expression activity.

---

# Using Complementary Colors

Colors that are opposite each other on the color wheel are **complementary colors.** For example, red is opposite green, so green is the complement of red. Complementary colors create **contrast,** or differences, in artwork. When complementary colors are used together, they make each other look very bright.

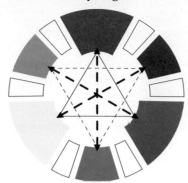

Notice that the complement of each primary color is a secondary color. What is the complement of blue? Of yellow?

Look at the three **sets of complementary colors.** When used together, they can create exciting designs.

### Practice

Create a design by experimenting with complementary colors. Use colored markers or crayons.

1. Sketch several simple designs on a sheet of paper. Choose one design and draw it three times on a second sheet of paper.

2. Color each design with one of the three sets of complementary colors. Use the color wheel as a guide.

---

## Differentiated Instruction

**Reteach**

Give each student a primary- or secondary-color square of paper. Have them hold up the squares and silently find a partner who is holding their complementary color. Make sure to have equal numbers of sets.

**Special Needs**

Students with low motor control may benefit from using shape templates that the teacher stabilizes by holding or taping down to the paper.

**ELL**

Modify the discussions illustrating the meaning of *contrast* and asking students to point to the places where colors contrast the most and by restating questions in simpler terms.

**Think** about how the student artist used complementary colors.

 **Creative Expression**

How would you make a nine-patch design for a quilt? Use complementary colors to make an interesting design.

1. Draw a simple shape inside one of the squares of complementary-colored paper.

2. Cut out the shape carefully in one piece. Cut from one edge, but cut out the center shape in one piece. The square should be in one piece also. Repeat this step four times.

3. Glue the squares to the primary-colored paper. Create an alternating pattern. Then glue the shapes between the squares.

 **Art Criticism**

**Describe** What is the subject of your quilt design?

**Analyze** Which complementary colors and shapes did you use?

**Interpret** How did your complementary colors create contrast and visual excitement?

**Decide** Would your quilt design be better if you used a different shape?

Unit 3 • Lesson 3 **107**

eflect    Time: About 5 minutes

**Review and Assess**

"How can you use complementary colors to create contrast?" "¿Cómo pueden usar los colores complementarios para crear un contraste?"

## Think

The student artist reversed the complementary colors in each square.

■ Use *Large Prints 53 Red Orchestra* and *54 The Stampede* to have students identify the complementary colors that each artist used.

### Informal Assessment

■ For standardized-format test practice using this lesson's art content, see pages 34–35 in *Reading and Writing Test Preparation.*

**Art Journal: Critical Thinking**

Have students answer the four art criticism questions—Describe, Analyze, Interpret, and Decide—in their Art Journals. In small groups, have students discuss the use of complementary colors in the quilt designs that they made in the Creative Expression activity.

● **Art Across the Curriculum** ●

Use these simple ideas to reinforce art concepts across the curriculum.

★ **Persuasive Writing** Have students write a persuasive paragraph to convince a museum curator to visit your art class.

★ **Math** Discuss number lines, noting the placement of positive and negative numbers on opposite ends. Point out that complementary colors on a color wheel are also opposite each other.

★ **Science** Explain that there are special chemicals used to preserve and clean works of art created long ago. Note that *Raven Screen* was created in 1830.

★ **Social Studies** Use the artwork *Canister* to discuss folk art.

★ **Technology** Have students use a paint or draw program to create a complementary color wheel. Visit **SRAonline.com** to print detailed instructions for this activity.
NSAE 6.b

# Complementary Colors

## Extra! For the Art Specialist

**Time:** About 45 minutes

### Focus

Study **Large Print 53** *Red Orchestra* to have students discuss how complementary colors are often used to create contrast in an artwork. Ask students how the main colors are used. Ask them to close their eyes and to open them quickly to identify which color they see first.

### Teach

Explain to students that complementary colors are across from one another on the color wheel. One is a cool color; the other is warm. Explain that they will be using a set of complementary colors to create a symmetrical design. Have the students complete the alternate activity.

### Reflect

Have students use the four steps of art criticism to evaluate their work. Did they effectively create a design that contains complementary colors? Have them describe the colors that they used.

### Alternate Activity

**Materials:**
- 9" × 9" white paper
- pencils, erasers
- ruler
- color markers or color pencils

1. Have students fold their paper in half and in half again so there are four equal sections.

2. Students should draw one simple shape in the center of one section and add three lines that touch two edges of that section.

3. Have students fold the paper in half and transfer the image to the opposite side by tracing the lines. They should transfer one half of the design onto the opposite side of the paper in the same manner.

4. Using either color pencils or markers, have students color their designs using one set of complementary colors. Each of the four sections should be identical.

## Research in Art Education

"Children respond to art in a holistic manner; their reactions are immediate, subjective, and rarely go beyond the 'like/don't like' stage . . . It takes a sensitive teacher to help educate the vision of the child so that appreciation may occur." (Hurwitz, Al, and Stanley Madeja. *The Joyous Vision*. New Jersey: Prentice Hall, 1997.)

## Assessment

Use the following rubric to evaluate the artwork students make in the Creative Expression activity and to assess students' understanding of complementary colors.

Have students complete page 37 or 38 in their *Assessment* books.

| | Art History and Culture | Aesthetic Perception | Creative Expression | Art Criticism |
|---|---|---|---|---|
| **3 POINTS** | The student demonstrates knowledge of Tlingit and folk art. | The student accurately defines and identifies complementary colors in a work of art. | The student's quilt design illustrates complementary colors. | The student thoughtfully and honestly evaluates own work using the four steps of art criticism. |
| **2 POINTS** | The student's knowledge of Tlingit and folk art is weak or incomplete. | The student shows emerging awareness of complementary colors but cannot consistently identify them. | The student's quilt design shows some attempt to illustrate complementary colors. | The student attempts to evaluate own work, but shows an incomplete understanding of evaluation criteria. |
| **1 POINT** | The student cannot demonstrate knowledge of Tlingit and folk art. | The student cannot identify complementary colors in a work of art. | The student's quilt design does not illustrate complementary colors. | The student makes no attempt to evaluate own artwork. |

### Assessment, p. 37

Name _____ Date _____

**Lesson 3** UNIT 3

**Complementary Colors**

**A** Short Answer
Write the answers to the questions.
1. What are complementary colors?

2. Why do artists use complementary colors?

**B** Coloring
In the boxes below, use crayons or markers to create three designs using three different sets of complementary colors.

| 1 | 2 | 3 |
|---|---|---|

**C** Writing
Write a paragraph explaining how complementary colors are used in Yeihl Nax'in Raven Screen.

Level 4

Unit 3 • Color and Value 37

## Lesson 4 Overview

# Low-Intensity Colors

**Lesson 4** introduces low-intensity colors. The brightness or dullness of a color is its intensity.

### Objectives

#### Art History and Culture
To demonstrate knowledge of *Ceremonial Shield* and Paul Klee

#### Creative Expression
To use complementary colors to create a low-intensity desert landscape

#### Aesthetic Perception
To discover how artists use complementary colors to lower the intensity of a color

#### Art Criticism
To evaluate own work using the four steps of art criticism

### Vocabulary  Vocabulary

Review the following vocabulary word with students before beginning the lesson.

**intensity** intensidad—the brightness or dullness of a color

See page 119B for additional vocabulary and Spanish vocabulary resources.

### Art Journal: Vocabulary
Have students add this word to the Vocabulary section of their Art Journals.

### Lesson Materials
- 6" × 6" white construction paper
- crayons, pencils
- 9" × 12" newsprint for sketches
- 12" × 18" heavy white drawing paper
- liquid tempera paints
- paintbrushes, water containers

**Alternate Materials:**
- color pencils
- watercolor paints

### Program Resources
- *Reading and Writing Test Prep.,* pp. 36–37
- *Transparency 16*
- *Flash Card* 20
- *Artist Profiles,* pp. 37, 76
- *Animals Through History Time Line*
- *Assessment,* pp. 39–40
- *Large Prints 53* Red Orchestra and *54 The Stampede*

### Concept Trace
Low-Intensity Colors
**Introduced:** Level 4, Unit 3, Lesson 4

**Reinforced:** Level 6, Unit 2, Lesson 3

## Lesson 4 Arts Integration

### Theatre
Complete Unit 3, Lesson 4, on page 60–61 of the *Theatre Arts Connections.*

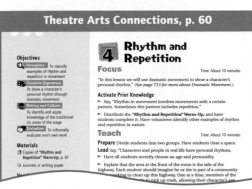

### Music
Any instrumental color can by used in a low intensity way through dynamics and rhythm. Listen to "Humming Chorus" from *Madame Butterfly* by Giacomo Puccini. The tone color does not change in intensity throughout the composition. This music was used in the opera when Madame Butterfly was waiting for a loved one. Ask students how this lack of intensity portray her confidence her loved one will arrive?

### Movement & Dance
High and low intensity can be explored in movement by interpreting words that reflect the three principle elements of dance: space, time, and force/energy. Have students explore slow, low, pressing movements for eight counts. Then have them explore fast, high, darting movements for eight counts.

# Focus

## Activate Prior Knowledge

"Have you ever noticed how the sky becomes less bright or loses some of its intensity as the sun sets?" "¿Alguna vez han notado cómo el cielo se hace menos brillante o pierde algo de intensidad a medida que el sol se oculta?"

- Discuss the answers given by students. Have them communicate ideas about themselves, using sensory knowledge and life experiences.

### Using Literature  Reading

- Have students look at the cover of *Brainstorm!: The Stories of Twenty American Kid Inventors* by Tom Tucker. Have them identify the low-intensity colors.

### Thematic Connection  Language Arts

- **Sharing:** Discuss how artists use their work to share their impressions or emotions with the viewer.

## Introduce the Art

# Look

"Look closely at the works of art on these two pages." "Observen detalladamente las obras de arte de estas dos páginas."

### Comparing and Contrasting  Reading

- Have students list the similarities and differences in the two works of art. Both pieces are examples of dull, low-intensity color. *Ceremonial Shield* is an example of art that is useful. *Mask of Fear* is an abstract painting of a mask.
  NSAE 4.a; 4.b

## Art History and Culture

Possible reasons why we do not know the name of a person who created an artwork are that the person wanted to remain anonymous, or the work was created a long time ago.

 **Web Connection**

Visit www.gksoft.com/govt/en/sb.html to learn more about the Solomon Islands.

---

# Low-Intensity Colors

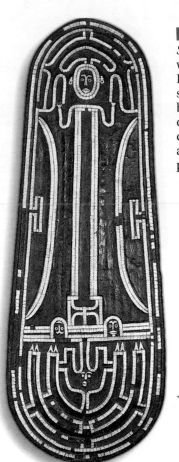

**Look** at the artwork on these pages. *Ceremonial Shield* was woven on the island of Guadalcanal. It was sold to people elsewhere in the Solomon Islands, who decorated it with small pieces of shells. Paul Klee enjoyed the artwork of children because of what he called "the raw energy of the child artist." He often painted and drew like a child in order to capture that raw energy. He was also interested in the masks and costumes that people wore to disguise themselves.

◄ **Artist unknown.** (Melanesia).
*Ceremonial Shield.* c. 1852.
......................................
Basketry, nautilus shell inlay on resin base.
$32\frac{5}{8} \times 9\frac{1}{4}$ inches (82.86 × 23.5 cm.). The Brooklyn Museum, Brooklyn, New York.

##  Art History and Culture

List possible reasons why we might not know the name of a person who created a work of art.

---

## Art History and Culture

### Ceremonial Shield

The Solomon Islands, a volcanic group of islands in the South Pacific, are 1,500 miles north of Sydney, Australia. The inhabitants are Melanesian and Polynesian. Their art usually serves to uphold spiritual power, called "mana." Standard war shields from the Solomon Islands were oval in shape and were plain, although some were painted with a few designs. These shields were not really used in battle but were probably a status symbol for men of high rank. The features of the human figure on the shield are stylized and symbolic. The *Ceremonial Shield* is made of basketry and nautilus shell inlay on a resin base.

See pages 24–25 and 16–21 for more about art history and subject matter.

**Artist Profiles, p. 76**

Artist Profile

**Ceremonial Shield**

The Solomon Islands are a group of volcanic islands in the South Pacific located 1,500 miles north of Sydney, Australia. The inhabitants are Melanesian and Polynesian, and they speak a Malayo-Polynesian language. Polynesian society is based on a political organization headed by chiefs. The art usually serves to uphold spiritual power, or *mana.*

Artist unknown. (Melanesia)

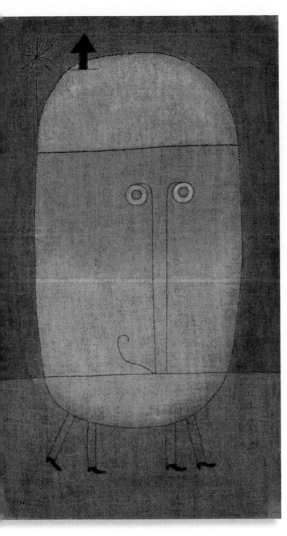

**Study** both works of art to explain how colors are used.

▶ Name the colors you see in these works of art.

▶ What kind of colors are they?

▶ How does color affect the mood of each work?

◀ **Paul Klee.** (Swiss)
*Mask of Fear.* 1932.
· · · · · · · · · · · · · · · · · · · · · · · · ·
Oil on burlap. 39½ × 22½ inches
(100.3 × 57.2 cm.). Museum of
Modern Art, New York, New York.

 **Aesthetic Perception**

**Design Awareness** Notice the color of objects you see every day. Name an object that contains a bright shade and another object that contains a dull shade of each primary color (red, yellow, and blue).

## Art History and Culture

### Paul Klee

Paul Klee (paul klā) (1879–1940) was born into a musical Swiss family. His family hoped he would become a musician. At age five his grandmother gave him his first box of pencils. He thought of himself as an artist from then on, but he kept an interest in music. Klee played his violin for an hour nearly every morning of his life. He married a pianist. As an adult, Klee still drew in a childlike way. Klee believed that childlike drawings were the most creative and original. He was not trying to share his ideas through his work; he just wanted to explore his imagination. Klee could use either hand proficiently for painting.

See pages 24–25 and 16–21 for more about art history and subject matter.

**Artist Profiles, p. 37**

*Artist Profile*
**Paul Klee**
1879–1940

Paul Klee (paul klā) was born into a musical Swiss family. His family hoped he also would become a musician. At age five his grandmother gave him his first box of pencils. He thought of himself as an artist from then on, but he continued to have an interest in music. Klee played his violin for an hour nearly every morning of his life. He married a pianist. As an adult Klee still drew in a childlike way. Klee believed that childlike drawings were the most creative and original. He just wanted to explore his imagination. Klee could use either hand proficiently when painting.

# Study

▶ *Ceremonial Shield*: red, black, and white. *Mask of Fear*: blue-green, brown, black, white.

▶ They are dull, low-intensity colors.

▶ *Ceremonial Shield:* The dominant figure in the middle and the arrowlike points at the end of the curved lines give the feeling of power. *Mask of Fear:* The partial smile on the mask gives the feeling of playfulness.

■ For more examples of abstract art, see *The National Museum of Women in the Arts Collection.*

**Art Journal: Writing**
Encourage students to define and illustrate low-intensity colors in the Concepts section of their Art Journals. What else do they want to know about low-intensity colors?

**Aesthetic Perception**

**Design Awareness** A fire engine may be a bright shade of red, whereas a sunset may be a light shade of red. The sky may be a light shade of blue, whereas a police officer's uniform may be a dark shade of blue. The color of butter may be a light shade of yellow, whereas the color of the yolk of an egg may be a dark shade of yellow.

**Developing Visual Literacy** Discuss the cultural significance of some of the works of art. Invite students to share any personal experiences that contribute to their identification of the simple main ideas expressed in the works or art. For example, do students have objects in their cultures that are part of a particular ceremony?
NSAE 4.a; 4.b

**Web Connection**
Visit **www.artchive.com/artchive/K/klee.html** for more information about Paul Klee. Note: This site is for teacher use only.

 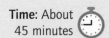

# Teach

**Time:** About 45 minutes

"Let's experiment with intensity by mixing complementary colors." "Vamos a experimentar con la intensidad al mezclar colores complementarios."

- Read and discuss the definition of intensity on page 110.

## Practice

**Materials:** 6" × 6" white construction paper, crayons

**Alternate Materials:** color pencils

- Distribute the materials and have students follow the directions on page 110.

 **Creative Expression**

**Materials:** 9" × 12" newsprint for sketches, 12" × 18" heavy white drawing paper, pencils, liquid tempera paints, paintbrushes, and water containers

**Alternate Materials:** watercolor paints

- Distribute the materials and have students follow the directions on page 111.
- See page 235 in the Activity Tips for visual examples of techniques.

### Art Journal: Brainstorming

Have students brainstorm things that might be found in a desert and list them in the Ideas section of their Art Journals. Then have students draw a few sketches of their desert landscapes for the Creative Expression activity.

---

# Intensity

The brightness or dullness of a color is its **intensity.** For example, because the yellow of a lemon is bright, it has high intensity. The yellow of mustard has a lower intensity because it is a duller yellow.

When you mix a color with its complement, you lower its intensity; it becomes less bright. The more of the complementary color you add, the duller the color becomes. When you add equal amounts of complementary colors, you create a brown or gray color.

## Practice

Experiment with intensity by mixing complementary colors. Use crayons.

1. Use one primary color, such as red, and color a light layer on a sheet of paper.
2. Color over the first color with its complement.
3. Do this again, using other sets of complementary colors.

---

## Differentiated Instruction

**Reteach**

Give each student a piece of window screen or nylon, a piece of clear acetate or a glass jar, and squares of colored construction paper. Have students take turns placing the various items on top of the colored construction paper and observing how the intensity changes.

**Special Needs**

Some students may have difficulty associating low-intensity colors with the bright sun of a desert landscape. After a discussion and demonstration of low-intensity colors, ask students to create a landscape that includes these colors.

**ELL**

Use magazine pictures, posters, and books to familiarize students with the desert before they begin planning their sketches for the Creative Expression activity. Offer examples of high- and low-intensity color contrast.

◀ **Cody Ellison.**
Age 9.

**Think** about what complementary colors this student artist could use if he added animals to his landscape.

 **Creative Expression**

What scenes come to mind when you think of a dull-colored or low-intensity landscape? Use complementary colors to create a low-intensity desert landscape.

1. Use your imagination to identify things you might find in a desert. What colors would they be?

2. Plan a desert landscape by making a few sketches. Include a variety of lines in your sketches.

3. Lightly draw your favorite sketch on a large piece of white paper. Begin by painting your background. Use complementary colors to create low-intensity colors for your desert landscape.

 **Art Criticism**

**Describe** How did you create low-intensity colors? What problems did you have while painting, and how did you solve them?

**Analyze** Which set of complementary colors did you choose?

**Interpret** What mood do the colors in your painting create?

**Decide** Do you feel your painting is successful?

 **Reflect**    Time: About 5 minutes

### Review and Assess

"What have you learned about low-intensity colors?" "¿Qué han aprendido acerca de los colores de baja intensidad?"

## Think

The student artist could have made the animals different tints and shades of blue.

■ Use *Large Prints 53* Red Orchestra and *54 The Stampede* to have students identify the low-intensity colors that each artist used.

### Informal Assessment

■ For standardized-format test practice using this lesson's art content, see pages 36–37 in *Reading and Writing Test Preparation.*

**Art Journal: Critical Thinking**

Have students answer the four art criticism questions—Describe, Analyze, Interpret, and Decide—in their Art Journals. In small groups, have students discuss the use of low-intensity colors in the desert landscapes that they created in the Creative Expression activity.

### ● Art Across the Curriculum ●

Use these simple ideas to reinforce art concepts across the curriculum.

★ **Expository Writing** Have students write an explanation of how they created their landscape scenes in the Creative Expression activity.

★ **Math** Discuss estimation as it relates to measurement, noting that artists may use estimation to determine the amount of color needed to create a dull or bright color.

★ **Science** The Solomon Islands, where the *Ceremonial Shield* was decorated, are a volcanic group of islands. Discuss the effects of a volcano eruption on a community.

★ **Social Studies** Discuss possible reasons why people of the Solomon Islands made the *Ceremonial Shield.*

★ **Technology** Have students edit the colors in a computer's paint program to create an intensity scale. Use one set of complementary colors. Visit **SRAonline.com** to print detailed instructions for this activity.
NSAE 6.b

# Lesson 4 Wrap-Up

# Low-Intensity Colors

## Extra! For the Art Specialist

**Time: About 45 minutes**

### Focus

Study **Large Print 54** *The Stampede* and discuss how artists sometimes mix complementary colors to create areas of low intensity or dull color in their art.

### Teach

Review the complementary color sets that were learned in the previous lesson. Demonstrate how to mix sets of complementary colors to lower the intensity. Ask the students to bring in images of landscapes for their project. Explain that their use of color will help set the mood or feel of the region they choose to paint. Have the students complete the alternate activity.

### Reflect

Have students use the four steps of art criticism to evaluate their work. Did they effectively create a landscape with low-intensity colors? Have students describe how the low-intensity colors contribute to the mood of their landscapes.

## Alternate Activity

**Materials:**
- student-collected landscape images
- sketchbook
- heavy white drawing paper
- pencils, erasers
- tempera or acrylic paints, all colors
- brushes in a variety of sizes
- mixing plate
- water containers
- newspaper

1. Have students look closely at their collected images. Have them make a composite drawing of their images in a sketchbook. A composite drawing is several images, combined to create one image or drawing.

2. Students should transfer their drawings onto paper and select a set of complementary colors that represents the region in their drawings. The colors do not need to be realistic but should create the feel of the specific region.

3. Have students paint the background first. They can create low-intensity colors by mixing complementary colors.

## Research in Art Education

One study showed that when students study art forms from minority cultures (in the case of this particular study, Native American music), this instruction seems to be "effective in diminishing students' stereotypical attitudes and perceptions toward a minority culture." The arts can help teachers become "catalysts for cultural understanding and respect" ("North American Indian Music Instruction: Influences upon Attitudes, Cultural Perceptions, and Achievement" in *Schools, Communities, and the Arts: A Research Compendium*). As students examine *Ceremonial Shield,* encourage them to discuss how they can use art to learn about other cultures.

## Assessment

Use the following rubric to evaluate the artwork students make in the Creative Expression activity and to assess students' understanding of low-intensity colors.

Have students complete page 39 or 40 in their **Assessment** books.

| | Art History and Culture | Aesthetic Perception | Creative Expression | Art Criticism |
|---|---|---|---|---|
| **3 POINTS** | The student demonstrates knowledge of *Ceremonial Shield* and Paul Klee. | The student shows some understanding of how artists use complementary colors to lower the intensity of a color. | The student's desert landscape incorporates low-intensity colors. | The student thoughtfully and honestly evaluates own work using the four steps of art criticism. |
| **2 POINTS** | The student's knowledge of *Ceremonial Shield* and Paul Klee is weak or incomplete. | The student shows emerging awareness of how complementary colors lower intensity but cannot consistently identify it. | The student's desert landscape shows some attempt to incorporate low-intensity colors. | The student attempts to evaluate own work, but shows an incomplete understanding of evaluation criteria. |
| **1 POINT** | The student cannot demonstrate knowledge of *Ceremonial Shield* and Paul Klee. | The student cannot identify the use of complementary colors to lower the intensity of a color. | The student's desert landscape shows no attempt to incorporate low-intensity colors. | The student makes no attempt to evaluate own artwork. |

### Assessment, p. 39

Name _____ Date _____

**Lesson 4 UNIT 3**

**Low-Intensity Colors**

**A. Short Answer**
Write answers to the questions.
1. What happens when complementary colors are mixed together? _____
2. What is meant by the word *intensity* when talking about color? _____

**B. Drawing**
In the box below, use color pencils to illustrate how complementary colors change each other.

**C. Writing**
Look closely at *Ceremonial Shield*. Briefly describe how the intensity of the colors focuses our attention on certain parts of the work.

Level 4

Unit 3 • Color and Value **39**

 **Lesson 5**
**Overview**

# Tints and Shades

**Lesson 5** introduces tints and shades. The value of a color is the darkness or lightness of that color. Light values are called *tints*. Dark values are called *shades*.

## Objectives

 **Art History and Culture**

To demonstrate knowledge of the lives and work of Wayne Thiebaud and Clara Peeters

 **Creative Expression**

To use tints and shades to create a direct-observation drawing of a plant

 **Aesthetic Perception**

To identify how artists use tints and shades to change the value of a color in a work of art

 **Art Criticism**

To evaluate own work using the four steps of art criticism

### Vocabulary  Vocabulary

Review the following vocabulary words with students before beginning the lesson.

**value** valor—the darkness or lightness of a color

**tint** tinte—a light value that is created when white is added to a color

**shade** sombra—a color having a dark value when black is added to it

See page 119B for additional vocabulary and Spanish vocabulary resources.

 **Art Journal: Vocabulary**

Have students add these words to the Vocabulary section of their Art Journals.

## Lesson Materials

- 12″ × 18″ white drawing paper
- pencils, rulers
- liquid tempera paints
- brushes, water containers
- sponges, mixing trays
- oil pastel paints, paper towels
- newspaper, construction paper
- plants

**Alternate Materials:**
- crayons
- color pencils

## Program Resources

- *Reading and Writing Test Prep.,* pp. 38–39
- *Transparency 17*
- *Flash Cards* 9–10
- *Artist Profiles,* pp. 53, 65
- *Animals Through History Time Line*
- *Assessment,* pp. 41–42
- *Large Prints 53 Red Orchestra* and *54 The Stampede*

### Concept Trace
**Tints and Shades**
**Introduced:** Level 2, Unit 3, Lessons 5–6

**Reinforced:** Level 5, Unit 3, Lesson 1

## Lesson 5 Arts Integration

### Theatre

Complete Unit 3, Lesson 5, on pages 62–63 of the *Theatre Arts Connections.*

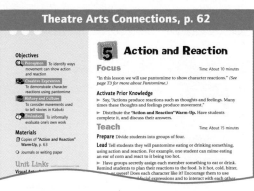

### Music

 A professional singer is said to use "shading" to portray expression in his or her performance. Have students listen to "I Am the Very Model of a Modern Major General" from *The Pirates of Penzance* by Gilbert and Sullivan. What does the singer do with his voice to change expression?

### Movement & Dance

Have students march in place at the same time. Give one student a white scarf and another student a black scarf. Have them run (separately) through the other students, weaving in and around them. As the white scarf passes them, the marchers should change their marching by making it softer and lighter. When the black scarf passes, their movements becomes stronger and heavier.

# Focus

## Activate Prior Knowledge

"Look around the classroom for colors found in shadows and in highlighted areas of objects. Describe these colors." "Busquen alrededor del salón de clase colores que se encuentran en sombras y en áreas de objetos destacados. Describan estos colores."

■ Discuss the answers given by the students and list the colors on the board.

### Using Literature ⭐ Reading

■ Have students look at the cover of *Frozen Fire: A Tale of Courage* by James Houston. Have them identify the tints and shades.

### Thematic Connection ⭐ Science

■ **Food/Nutrition:** Discuss the theme of food in the paintings. Ask students if their families have traditional foods that they like to eat.

## Introduce the Art

# Look

"Study the paintings on these pages carefully." "Estudien cuidadosamente las pinturas de estas páginas."

### Cause and Effect ⭐ Reading

■ Have students identify the tints and shades and the effect they have on the paintings. The shade on the cake and cake slices in *Around the Cake* creates an impression of the sun shining on the cake or a light glowing over the cake. The shades underneath the seafood containers in *Still Life of Fish and Cat* give the impression that there is a light shining down. The artist used tints and shades on the fish and the cat.

## 🏺 Art History and Culture

A still life is a collection of objects that do not move.

### 💻 Web Connection

Search www.famsf.org to find works of art by Wayne Thiebaud.

---

# Tints and Shades

**Look** at the artwork on these pages. *Around the Cake* was painted in 1962. *Still Life of Fish and Cat* was painted during the seventeenth century. Thiebaud used light values in his painting. Peeters used dark values in her painting. Both paintings are still lifes. Compare the use of tints and shades in the two paintings.

▲ **Wayne Thiebaud.** (American). *Around the Cake.* 1962.
.............................
Oil on canvas. 22 1/8 × 28 1/16 inches (56.19 × 71.27 cm.). Spencer Museum of Art, University of Kansas. Lawrence, Kansas.

## 🏺 Art History and Culture

What does the term *still life* mean?

---

## 🏺 Art History and Culture

### Wayne Thiebaud

Wayne Thiebaud (wān tē´ bō) (1920– ) created several paintings of bakeshop goodies during the 1960s and '70s. *Four Cupcakes; Window Cakes; French Pastries; Pies, Pies, Pies;* and *Around the Cake* were all created by Thiebaud during that period. In some of these works of art, Thiebaud isolated the subjects, placing them in rows in a vacant setting and making them three-dimensional. Most of the paintings Thiebaud created from that period were done from memory. He has also created works of art with various other subjects.

See pages 24–25 and 16–21 for more about art history and subject matter.

**Artist Profiles, p. 65**

◆ Artist Profile ◆

### Wayne Thiebaud
b. 1920

Wayne Thiebaud (wān tē´ bō), one of California's most famous contemporary painters, has earned as many awards for excellence in teaching as he has for his painting and printmaking. He became interested in drawing in high school and later worked as a freelance cartoonist and illustrator. He continued his artwork during his military service in the U.S. Air Force during World War II. He drew cartoons for the military base newspaper. In 1949 Thiebaud decided to become a painter. His first one-person show in New York City was praised by the critics. At that time his subjects were mass-produced consumer goods, particularly junk food, and he was mistakenly classified with the pop artists

▲ **Clara Peeters.** (Flemish). *Still Life of Fish and Cat.* After 1620.

••••••••••••••••••••••••••••••

Oil on panel. 13½ × 18½ inches (34.29 × 46.99 cm.). National Museum of Women in the Arts, Washington, D.C.

**S**tudy both paintings to see how tints and shades are used.

▶ What are some of the colors used in both paintings?

▶ Which colors are darker or lighter than others? How did the artists create these colors?

▶ What are some similarities and differences in these paintings?

▶ How does the use of color help in creating a mood in each painting?

### ⚒ Aesthetic Perception

**Design Awareness** Look through images in this book, or think of other images that contain tints and shades. What emotions or moods do tinted and shaded colors create?

## 🏺 Art History and Culture

### Clara Peeters

Clara Peeters (klä´ ra pē´ tərz) (1594–1657) was one of the first women known to paint still lifes. Very little is known about her life. Her earliest dated oil paintings were created during 1607 or 1608, when she was a teenager. *Still Life of Fish and Cat* was created during the early part of the seventeenth century, when still life was a new subject matter in northern Europe. This painting was the first artwork by a woman that Wallace and Wilhelmina Halliday collected. Their collection of works of art by women was the founding collection of the National Museum of Women in the Arts.

See pages 24–25 and 16–21 for more about art history and subject matter.

**Artist Profiles, p. 53**

◆ Artist Profile ◆

### Clara Peeters
1594-1657

Clara Peeters (klä´ ra pē´ tərz), who lived in Antwerp, Flanders (Belgium), was one of the originators of still-life painting in the seventeenth century. She produced, signed, and dated paintings while she was a teenager. Very little is known about her education, her life, and her career.

◀ **Clara Peeters.** (Belgian). *Portrait of a lady believed to be Clara Peeters* (detail). 17ᵗʰ century.

••••••••••••••••••••••••••••••

Oil on panel. Phillips' Fine Art Auctioneers, London England.

## Study

▶ *Around the Cake:* light yellow and white. *Still Life of Fish and Cat:* tints and shades of brown.

▶ These are created by adding white or black to a color.

▶ Similarities: Both contain shades and/or tints, both are oil paintings, both are still lifes, and the subject matter in both paintings is food. Differences: *Around the Cake* has a light value. *Still Life of Fish and Cat* has a dark value.

▶ Answers will vary. Make sure students' answers are reasonable.

■ For more examples of still lifes, see *The National Museum of Women in the Arts Collection.*

### 📓 Art Journal: Writing

Encourage students to define and illustrate tints and shades in the Concepts section of their Art Journals. What else do they want to know about tints and shades?

### 🔍 Aesthetic Perception

**Design Awareness** Discuss tints and shades. Artists generally use tints to represent sunny days or a feeling of happiness and joy. Shades are generally used to represent dark, gloomy days and nighttime or a feeling of mystery and danger.

**Developing Visual Literacy** Discuss with students how various pictures make them feel. Invite students to share any personal experiences that contribute to their understanding of the works of art. For example, how does viewing the cake in the painting *Around the Cake* make them feel?

### 💻 Web Connection

Search **worldart.sjsu.edu** to find works of art by Clara Peeters.

# Teach

**Time: About 45 minutes**

"Today we will experiment with creating value scales using tints and shades." "Hoy, vamos a experimentar creando escalas de valores usando tintes y sombras."

- Read and discuss the definitions of *value, tint,* and *shade* on page 114.

- Make sure students choose appropriate vocabulary to discuss value.
  NSAE 2.a; 2.b

## Practice

**Materials:** 12" × 18" white drawing paper, pencils, rulers, liquid tempera paints, brushes, water containers, sponges

**Alternate Materials:** crayons or color pencils

- Distribute the materials and have students follow the directions on page 114.
  NSAE 2.a; 2.b

## Creative Expression

**Materials:** plants, oil pastel paints, brushes, water containers, and mixing trays, paper towels, newspaper, construction paper

**Alternate Materials:** color pencils, color paper

- Distribute the materials and have students follow the directions on page 115.

- See page 236 in the Activity Tips for visual examples of techniques.

- If time permits, encourage students to invent additional ways to produce the Creative Expression activity, using a variety of art media and materials.
  NSAE 1.b; 1.c

### Art Journal: Brainstorming

Have students brainstorm possible colors for their observation drawings in the Ideas section of their Art Journals. Students should also create practice sketches of their plants for the Creative Expression activity.

# Value of a Color

The **value** of a color is the darkness or lightness of that color. Light values are called **tints.** Dark values are called **shades.**

To create a **tint,** mix a color with white. Tints are usually used to show areas where light touches the surface of an object drawn or painted. Tints are also used to show a sunny day and to create a feeling of happiness and joy.

To create a **shade,** add black to a color. Shades are used to show shadows and give the feeling of gloom and mystery to a work of art. Most artists do not use solid black for shadows; they use shades of color instead.

## Practice

Create value scales by experimenting with tints and shades. Use tempera paints.

1. Fold a sheet of paper horizontally and open it up. Label the top half "Tints" and the bottom half "Shades." Draw a long rectangle on each half and divide it into five sections.

2. Select a color for your tint. Add a drop or two of the color to white paint, and paint the first section on your paper. Add a drop or two more of color each time you paint another section so that you have a gradual change from a very light tint to the pure color.

3. Use the same color for creating shades. Add black to your color to create shades of that color.

## Differentiated Instruction

### Reteach
Have students collect several samples of one color from magazines, fabric samples, and paint samples. Ask them to arrange these samples in order of darkest to lightest.

### Special Needs
Visual and written reminders of instructional steps are often helpful to students with special needs. For this activity, create and display a chart of the tints and shades of one color as well as directions for how to create tints and shades.

### ELL
Pair students with more fluent English-speaking peers to look through magazines to find tints and shades of colors. Use this as an opportunity for the students to acquire new vocabulary in a low-risk situation.

◀ **Jessica Flakes.**
Age 9.

**Think** about what kind of tints and shades the student artist used.

 **Creative Expression**

What are some objects in nature that are one color with many different tints and shades? Use tints and shades to create a direct-observation painting.

1. Look at a plant. Notice its basic shape and contours. Lightly sketch the plant. Make sure your drawing touches three edges of your paper.

2. Select a set of complementary colors. Use one color to paint the plant. Add black and white to create tints and shades of that color. Observe the shadows and highlights in the plant.

3. Paint the background with tints and shades of the second color.

**Art Criticism**

**Describe** Describe the shapes and lines in your painting. Describe your complementary-color scheme.

**Analyze** What did you notice when you were limited to using only two colors plus black and white?

**Interpret** How do the value changes affect the mood of your painting?

**Decide** Were you able to successfully produce a painting using tints and shades of one color?

Unit 3 • Lesson 5 **115**

---

◉ **Art Across the Curriculum** ◉

Use these simple ideas to reinforce art concepts across the curriculum.

★ **Poetry Writing** Have students write a poem about colors.

★ **Math** Distinguish between *greater than* and *less than*, using value in art.

★ **Science** Use the painting *Still Life of Fish and Cat* to discuss different types of fish.

★ **Social Studies** Use the painting *Around the Cake* to discuss birthday celebrations, noting that different cultures have different ways of celebrating birthdays.

★ **Technology** Have students edit the colors in a paint or draw program to illustrate tints and shades of a color. Visit **SRAonline.com** to print detailed instructions for this activity.
NSAE 6.b

---

 **Reflect**  Time: About 5 minutes

**Review and Assess**

"How can you use tints and shades to create shadows and highlights?" "¿Cómo pueden usar tintes y sombras para hacer sombreados y claros?"

# Think

The student artist added white to create tints of her colors, and black to create shades.

■ Use *Large Prints 53 Red Orchestra* and *54 The Stampede* to have students identify different tints and shades.

## Informal Assessment

■ For standardized-format test practice using this lesson's art content, see pages 38–39 in *Reading and Writing Test Preparation*.

**Art Journal: Critical Thinking**

Have students answer the four art criticism questions—Describe, Analyze, Interpret, and Decide—in their Art Journals. In small groups, have students discuss how they created the tints and shades in the paintings that they made in the Creative Expression activity.

# Tints and Shades

**Extra!** For the Art Specialist

**Time:** About 45 minutes

## Focus

Have students study *Large Print 54 The Stampede.* Ask students how the use of dark and light value affects the artwork.

## Teach

Explain to students that they will be painting an area of a still life. They will be using tints and shades of a set of complementary colors to complete their work. Demonstrate mixing white and black with a color. Emphasize to the students that when painting they should show a wide range of values. Have the students complete the alternate activity.

## Reflect

Have students use the four steps of art criticism to evaluate their work. Did they effectively use a variety of tints and shades in their still lifes?

### Alternate Activity

**Materials:**

- sketchbook
- viewfinder
- pencils, erasers
- tempera paints
- brushes in a variety of sizes
- water container
- mixing plates
- newspapers to cover work areas

1. Have students collect objects from around the room and arrange a still life. There should be objects of varying sizes and drapery for the arrangement.

2. Have students use a viewfinder to study various areas of their still lifes. Have them sketch two different viewpoints.

3. Have students select their best sketch and lightly transfer it onto paper. Then have them select one set of complementary colors.

4. Students should mix and paint objects, first using tints and shades of one of their colors. Then they should use a second complementary color in a range of values to complete the background.

## Research in Art Education

"Art is a biological phenomenon that has been present as a characteristic of the human race ever since Homo sapiens emerged from prehistory. Since art is the skill man uses to give meaningful form to his intuitions and perceptions, art was one of the chief agencies of man's emergence." (Herbert Read, *Education Through Art.* Random House, 1974.)

## Assessment

Use the following rubric to evaluate the artwork students make in the Creative Expression activity and to assess students' understanding of tints and shades.

Have students complete page 41 or 42 in their *Assessment* books.

| | Art History and Culture | Aesthetic Perception | Creative Expression | Art Criticism |
|---|---|---|---|---|
| **3 POINTS** | The student demonstrates knowledge of the lives and work of Wayne Thiebaud and Clara Peeters. | The student can identify the use of tints and shades to change the value in a work of art. | The student's drawing illustrates tints and shades. | The student thoughtfully and honestly evaluates own work using the four steps of art criticism. |
| **2 POINTS** | The student's knowledge of Wayne Thiebaud and Clara Peeters is weak or incomplete. | The student shows emerging awareness of tints and shades but cannot consistently identify when they are used to change a value. | The student's drawing shows some awareness of tints and shades. | The student attempts to evaluate own work, but shows an incomplete understanding of evaluation criteria. |
| **1 POINT** | The student cannot demonstrate knowledge of Wayne Thiebaud and Clara Peeters. | The student cannot identify tints and shades in a work of art. | The student's drawing shows no understanding of tints and shades. | The student makes no attempt to evaluate own artwork. |

**Assessment, p. 41**

Name _____ Date _____

**Lesson 5** UNIT 3

### Tints and Shades

**A** Coloring
Use crayons or color pencils to create a dark value scale.

**B** Vocabulary
Complete the sentences.
1. A _____ is created when you add white to a color. It has a light value.
2. When you add black to a color, you create a _____

**C** Writing
Look closely at *Around the Cake* and *Still Life of Cat and Fish.* Describe how both artists used values and tints to portray light and shadows in their paintings.

Level 4

Unit 3 • Color and Value **41**

# Color Moods

Lesson 6 introduces color moods. Artists use color schemes to create moods.

## Objectives

 **Art History and Culture**

To demonstrate knowledge of the lives and work of Georgia O'Keeffe and Malcah Zeldis

 **Creative Expression**

To use a color scheme to create an imaginary scene

 **Aesthetic Perception**

To identify and compare different color schemes

 **Art Criticism**

To evaluate own work using the four steps of art criticism

### Vocabulary  Vocabulary

Review the following vocabulary words with students before beginning the lesson.

**monochromatic** monocromático—having only one color

See page 119B for additional vocabulary and Spanish vocabulary resources.

### Art Journal: Vocabulary

Have students add this word to the Vocabulary section of their Art Journals.

## Lesson Materials

- white drawing paper
- crayons, color pencils
- pencils
- sketch paper
- paper towels, newspaper
- tempera paints
- brushes
- water containers, mixing trays

**Alternate Materials:**
- oil pastels

## Program Resources

- *Reading and Writing Test Prep.,* pp. 40–41
- *Transparency 18*
- *Flash Cards* 9, 11, 14–15
- *Artist Profiles,* pp. 52, 73
- *Animals Through History Time Line*
- *Assessment,* pp. 43–44
- *Large Prints 53* Red Orchestra and *54 The Stampede*

### Concept Trace
Color Moods
**Introduced:** Level 4, Unit 3, Lesson 6

**Reinforced:** Level 5, Unit 3, Lesson 2

---

## Lesson 6 Arts Integration

### Theatre

Complete Unit 3, Lesson 6, on pages 64–69 of *Theatre Arts Connections.*

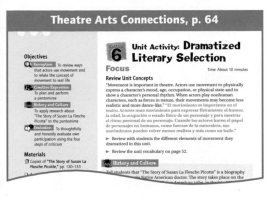

Theatre Arts Connections, p. 64

### Music

 Music from the movies often portrays the mood of a scene before anyone speaks. In the movie *Fantasia,* Mickey Mouse takes on too much work. Have students listen to "Sorcerer's Apprentice" by Paul Dukas. Ask students how the mood changes through the music?

### Movement & Dance

Music gives mood to a dance, as color gives mood to a painting. Play two different pieces of music. Select from popular music, classical music, jazz, opera, country, and hip hop. Ask students to sway to each piece of music as it is played, paying attention to the mood it creates, its tempo, and its overall feeling.

# Focus

**Time: About 10 minutes**

## Activate Prior Knowledge

"Have you ever seen a work of art, a piece of fabric, or a room decorated in different values of only one color? Describe how it looked." "¿Han visto alguna vez una obra de arte, un pedazo de tela o una habitación decorados en diferentes valores de un solo color? Describan cómo era."

- Discuss the answers given by students.

### Using Literature ⭐ Reading

- Have students look at the cover of *From the Mixed-Up Files of Mrs. Basil E. Frankweiler* by E. L. Konigsburg. Have them explain what kind of mood the colors created.

### Thematic Connection ⭐ Language Arts

- **Imagination:** Discuss how imagination was used by O'Keeffe to transfer music to visual art and by Zeldis to create a scene that never existed.

## Introduce the Art

## Look

"Study the paintings on these pages closely." "Estudien detalladamente las pinturas de estas páginas."

### Drawing Conclusions ⭐ Science

- Have students use clues such as the name of the painting and objects included in each to determine the message in the painting. O'Keeffe: The title includes the word *music,* and the lines and colors appear to illustrate some type of rhythm, so O'Keeffe could have been using colors and lines to represent music.

### 🏺 Art History and Culture

In places where resources are scarce, most artwork created in that region are created using similar media. In places such as the United States, where resources are plentiful, artwork from the same region often is created using completely different media.

### 🖥 Web Connection

Visit **www.okeeffemuseum.org** to view works of art by Georgia O'Keeffe.

---

# Color Moods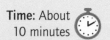

**Look** at the artwork on these pages. Georgia O'Keeffe created *Blue and Green Music* in 1919. The title of the artwork implies music. Malcah Zeldis painted *Miss Liberty Celebration* in 1987. This painting includes notable historical figures such as Elvis Presley, Albert Einstein, and Marilyn Monroe. Both artists used colors to create moods.

▲ **Georgia O'Keeffe.** (American).
*Blue and Green Music.* 1919.
Oil on canvas. 23 × 19 inches (58.4 × 48.3 cm.).
The Art Institute of Chicago, Chicago, Illinois.

### 🏺 Art History and Culture

Could artwork from a particular region be created using similar media? Note that both paintings were created by American artists.

---

### 🏺 Art History and Culture

## Georgia O'Keeffe

Georgia O'Keeffe (jor´ jə ō´ kēf´) (1887–1986) was a remarkable artist who created artwork for more than 60 years. O'Keeffe, who was known to have painted many of her works in series, gained inspiration for many of her paintings from places she visited and subjects that intrigued her. In 1919 she created the "Music—Pink and Blue" series. This series of paintings attempted to translate musical and rhythmic movement to visual arts. When she was about 70 years old, O'Keeffe took a three-and-a-half-month trip around the world by air. The places she visited on this trip inspired a series of paintings.

See pages 24–25 and 16–21 for more about art history and subject matter.

**Artist Profiles, p. 52**

### Artist Profile

## Georgia O'Keeffe
**1887–1986**

Georgia O'Keeffe (jôr´ jə ō kēf´) was born in Sun Prairie, Wisconsin. At the age of ten she began taking private art lessons, but the thing she liked most was experimenting with art at home. By 13, she had decided to become an artist. She trained under experts and won many prizes for her art. For years she challenged the art world with her unique vision. She eventually became famous for her spectacular, larger-than-life paintings of natural objects, including flowers, animal skulls, and shells. She loved nature, especially the desert of New Mexico, where she spent the last half of her life. O'Keeffe was married to the famous American photographer Alfred Stieglitz and appears in many of his photographs.

**Study** both paintings and notice the similarities and differences in the color schemes.

▶ What types of lines, shapes, and colors do you see? Are any of these elements repeated?

▶ How do you think the artists created the colors they used?

▶ Why do you think the artists chose the colors they used in their paintings?

▶ What feelings or moods are created by the paintings?

▲ **Malcah Zeldis.** (American).
*Miss Liberty Celebration.* 1987.
Oil on corrugated cardboard. 54½ × 36½ inches
(138.43 × 92.71 cm.). Smithsonian American
Art Museum, Washington, D.C.

 **Aesthetic Perception**

**Design Awareness** Notice the different color schemes you see each day. Give examples of how different color schemes can be used for specific purposes.

## Art History and Culture

### Malcah Zeldis

Malcah Zeldis (mal´ kə zel´ dəs) (1931– ) is a self-taught artist who creates colorful images of her culture. Zeldis was born in New York, raised in Detroit, and spent some of her adult life living in Israel. Her paintings are kept in several important museums, such as the Smithsonian Institution. Zeldis has received recognition by folk-art critics. She is also a noted children's book illustrator. *Miss Liberty Celebration* is narrative. It was created to commemorate the artist's recovery from cancer. Abraham Lincoln, Elvis Presley, Albert Einstein, and Marilyn Monroe are among the noted figures depicted in this painting. Zeldis also included herself on the lower right.

See pages 24–25 and 16–21 for more about art history and subject matter.

**Artist Profiles, p. 73**

*Artist Profile*
**Malcah Zeldis**
b. 1931
Folk painter Malcah Zeldis (mal´ kə zel´ dəs) was born in New York and grew up in Detroit. Her family was originally from Russia, and at the age of 17 she went to live in Israel for ten years, where she taught herself to paint. She uses her artwork to express admiration for her Jewish heritage and people of all faiths and ethnicities. Zeldis has illustrated a number of children's books and fills her paintings with an optimistic view of life that celebrates the diversity of America.

# Study

▶ O'Keeffe: Repeated curved, zigzag, and diagonal lines, with primarily green, blue, and white. Zeldis: Repeated shapes and horizontal and vertical lines, with primarily blue, yellow, and red.

▶ By mixing colors

▶ To create a mood

▶ The analogous color scheme in O'Keeffe's painting creates a calm, peaceful mood. The complementary color scheme in Zeldis's painting captures the excitement of her celebratory feelings.

■ For more examples of art from North America, see the ***Art Around the World Collection.***

### Art Journal: Writing
Encourage students to define and illustrate a neutral color scheme and complementary color schemes in the Concepts section of their Art Journals. What else do they want to know about color schemes?

## Aesthetic Perception

**Design Awareness** Encourage students to list examples of how different color schemes are used to represent different things. For example, students would use different colors to represent a scene of a beach party, a battle scene, or a snowy day.

**Developing Visual Literacy** Discuss the significance of each artwork. Invite students to produce visuals to complement the meaning of an artwork. For example, have students create pictures of important figures in American history who could be a part of the painting *Miss Liberty Celebration.*

### Web Connection
Visit **www.edlingallery.com/gallery.htm** to view works of art by Malcah Zeldis.

 each **Time:** About 45 minutes

"Let's design a watch, using monochromatic colors." *"Vamos a diseñar un reloj usando colores monocromáticos."*

- Read and discuss the information about color schemes on page 118.

## Practice

**Materials:** white drawing paper, crayons, or color pencils

**Alternate Materials:** pencils

- Distribute the materials and have students follow the directions on page 118.

**Materials:** white drawing paper, pencils, sketch paper, paper towels, liquid tempera paints, newspaper, brushes, water containers, mixing trays

**Alternate Materials:** color pencils

- Distribute the materials and have students follow the directions on page 119.
- See page 236 in the Activity Tips for visual examples of techniques.
- Have students integrate a variety of ideas about community in their paintings.
  NSAE 5.b

### Art Journal: Brainstorming

Have students brainstorm landscapes and list them in the Ideas section of their Art Journals. Then have each student select a landscape to portray in the Creative Expression activity.

# Using Color Schemes

Artists use color schemes to create moods. A color scheme is a plan for organizing colors. Different color schemes create different moods.

 **Monochromatic** means "having one color." A monochromatic color scheme uses only one hue, or color, and the values of that color. For example, red, light red, and dark red, if used together without any other colors, would be a **monochromatic color scheme.**

 A **spectral color scheme** uses all the colors of the rainbow: red, orange, yellow, green, blue, and violet.

 A **neutral color scheme** uses black, white, and a variety of grays.

 A **complementary color scheme** uses one set of complementary colors; for example, red and green, blue and orange, and yellow and violet.

 An **analogous color scheme** uses colors that are side by side on the color wheel and have a common hue.

## Practice

Create a nonobjective design using monochromatic colors. Use color pencils.

1. Think of a mood. Using one color pencil, along with black and white, create a nonobjective design.
2. Use monochromatic colors to tie the design together.

## Differentiated Instruction

**Reteach**
Ask students to look through this book for examples of monochromatic colors in artwork.

**Special Needs**
To increase students' memory recall of color schemes, create a chart of nonobjective designs that use each color scheme.

**ELL**
Provide students with contextual information about landscapes before asking them to design and paint one. Magazines, art posters, and storybooks can help students visualize their scenes.

◀ **Kelsey Mei-Lin Fuller.**
Age 9.

**Think** about how the feel of this artwork would change if the student artist had used warm colors.

### Creative Expression

What is your favorite color scheme? Select a color scheme to paint an imaginary scene that includes land, vegetation, buildings, and transportation.

1. Think about the way colors affect the look of a scene.
2. Make several sketches of an imaginary scene. Choose your best one.
3. Choose a color scheme that fits your scene. Fill your scene with color.

### Art Criticism

**Describe** Describe the things in your painting.

**Analyze** What color scheme did you use?

**Interpret** Was there a particular mood you wanted to create? If so, did you achieve it? Give your painting a poetic name.

**Decide** Do you feel that using a specific color scheme was helpful for creating a mood in your painting?

Unit 3 • Lesson 6 **119**

## Review and Assess

"How can you use monochromatic colors to create an imaginary scene?" "¿Cómo pueden usar colores monocromáticos para crear una escena imaginaria?"

## Think

If the student artist used warm colors, they would have created a warmer, more peaceful feeling.

- Use *Large Prints 53* Red Orchestra and *54 The Stampede* to have students identify the color schemes each artist used.

## Informal Assessment

- Have students create an exhibition of their paintings. Students should evaluate the exhibition to interpret their peers' ideas. NSAE 5.c
- For standardized-format test practice using this lesson's art content, see pages 40–41 in *Reading and Writing Test Preparation.*

### Art Journal: Critical Thinking

Have students answer the four art criticism questions—Describe, Analyze, Interpret, and Decide—in their Art Journals. Have small groups of students discuss the use of monochromatic colors in the paintings that they made in the Creative Expression activity.

### Art Across the Curriculum

Use these simple ideas to reinforce art concepts across the curriculum.

★ **Narrative Writing** Have students write realistic stories about a celebration for the Statue of Liberty.

★ **Math** Have students compare how numbers in a multiplication table form families and how colors in a color scheme also form families.

★ **Science** Discuss rainbows, noting that a spectral color scheme uses all six rainbow colors.

★ **Social Studies** Discuss the significance of the Statue of Liberty.

★ **Technology** Have students edit the colors in a paint or draw program to produce an analogous color scheme. Visit **SRAonline.com** to print detailed instructions for this activity. NSAE 6.b

## Lesson 6 Wrap-Up

# Color Moods

 **For the Art Specialist**

**Time:** About 45 minutes

## Focus

Study **Large Print 54** *The Stampede* to have students discuss how monochromatic colors are often used to create a mood in an artwork. *How does looking at this artwork affect the way you feel?*

## Teach

Explain to students that when tints and shades of one color are used the color scheme is called monochromatic. Explain to students that they will be creating a cityscape, using tints and shades of one color. Have the students complete the alternate activity.

## Reflect

Have students use the four steps of art criticism to evaluate their work. Have students describe the colors they used in their cityscapes.

### Alternate Activity

**Materials:**

- sketchbook
- images of buildings and cities
- pencils, erasers
- tempera paints
- brushes in a variety of sizes
- water container
- mixing plates
- newspapers to cover work areas

1. Have students study their collected images and create two quick sketches of cityscapes.

2. Have students select their best sketch and lightly transfer it onto paper. Then they should select one color that will work best with their drawing.

3. Students should mix and paint building shapes first, using tints and shades of a color. Then students should paint the background.

4. Have students use a fine-line paintbrush to add details to complete their cityscape painting.

## Research in Art Education

Schools with rich in-school art programs tend to have a more positive atmosphere—children at these schools are "more likely than children in low-arts schools to have a good rapport with their teachers." This holds true across socioeconomic lines ("Learning in and Through the Arts: Curriculum Implications" in *Champions of Change*, p. 41). As students learn about color moods, encourage them to think about how colors are used to illustrate different atmospheres or environments.

## Assessment

Use the following rubric to evaluate the artwork students make in the Creative Expression activity and to assess students' understanding of color moods.

Have students complete page 43 or 44 in their *Assessment* books.

| | Art History and Culture | Aesthetic Perception | Creative Expression | Art Criticism |
|---|---|---|---|---|
| **3 POINTS** | The student demonstrates knowledge of the lives and work of Georgia O'Keeffe and Malcah Zeldis. | The student can identify and compare different color schemes. | The student's imaginary scene shows one color scheme. | The student thoughtfully and honestly evaluates own work using the four steps of art criticism. |
| **2 POINTS** | The student's knowledge of Georgia O'Keeffe and Malcah Zeldis is weak or incomplete. | The student's identification and comparison is weak and incomplete. | The student's imaginary scene shows an attempt to use one color scheme. | The student attempts to evaluate own work, but shows an incomplete understanding of evaluation criteria. |
| **1 POINT** | The student cannot demonstrate knowledge of Georgia O'Keeffe and Malcah Zeldis. | The student cannot identify or compare different color schemes. | The student's imaginary scene shows no attempt to use a color scheme. | The student makes no attempt to evaluate own artwork. |

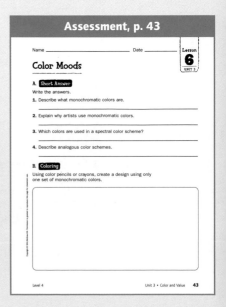

**Assessment, p. 43**

Name _____ Date _____

**Color Moods** — Lesson 6 UNIT 3

**A. Short Answer**
Write the answers.
1. Describe what monochromatic colors are.

2. Explain why artists use monochromatic colors.

3. Which colors are used in a spectral color scheme?

4. Describe analogous color schemes.

**B. Coloring**
Using color pencils or crayons, create a design using only one set of monochromatic colors.

Level 4     Unit 3 • Color and Value   **43**

# Unit 3 Vocabulary Review

**analogous color scheme**—uses colors that are side by side on the color wheel and have a common color **esquema de colores análogos**—usa colores que están adyacente en el círculo cromático y tienen un color en común

**color scheme**—a plan for organizing the colors used in an artwork **esquema de colores**—un plan para organizar los colores usados en una obra de arte

**color spectrum**—band of colors in the order of red, orange, yellow, green, blue, and violet **espectro cromático**—cinta de colores en el orden de rojo, anaranjado, amarillo, verde, azul y violeta

**color wheel**—made of the three primary, three secondary, and six intermediate colors **círculo cromático**—hecho de los tres colores primarios, tres secundarios y seis intermediarios

**complementary color scheme**—uses one set of complementary colors, for example, red and green, blue and orange, and yellow and violet **esquema de colores complementarios**—usa un grupo de colores complementarios, por ejemplo, rojo y verde, azul y anaranjado, y amarillo y violeta

**complementary colors**—colors that are opposite each other on the color wheel **colores complementarios**—colores que están opuesto uno al otro en el círculo cromático

**contrast**—differences **contraste**—diferencias

**hues**—another name for colors **matices**—otro nombre para colores

**intensity**—the brightness or dullness of a color **intensidad**—la brillantez o matidez de un color

**intermediate colors**—yellow-green, red-orange, blue-green; made by combining a primary color with either of the secondary colors that are adjacent on the color wheel **colores intermediantes**—amarillo-verde, rojo-anaranjado, azul-verde; hecho por la mezcla de un color primario con cualquier de los colores secundarios que están adyacente en el círculo cromático.

**intermediate colors**—made by blending a primary color with a secondary color **colores intermediantes**—hecho mezclando un color primario con un color secundario

**mix a neutral color**—mix a neutral color with another color to change its value **mezclar un color neutro**—mezclar un color neutro con otro color para cambiar su valor.

**monochromatic**—a color scheme that is made of one hue and the tints and shade of that hue **monocromático**—esquema de colores que está hecho de un color y los tintes y sombra de ese color

**monochromatic color scheme**—uses only one color and the values of that color **esquema de colores monocromáticos**—usa solamente un color y los valores de ese color

**neutral color scheme**—uses black, white, and a variety of grays **esquema de colores neutros**—negro, blanco, y gris

**neutral colors**—black, white, and gray **colores neutros**—negro, blanco y gris

**set of complementary colors**—there are three sets on the color wheel: red and green, blue and orange, and yellow and violet. **grupo de colores complementarios**—Hay tres grupos en el círculo cromático: rojo y verde, azul y anaranjado, y amarillo y violeta

**shade**—any color blended with black **sombra**—cualquier color mezclado con negro

**secondary colors**—orange, green, and violet; the result of mixing two primary colors **colores secundarios**—anaranjado, verde, y violeta; el resultado de la mezcla de dos colores primarios

**primary colors**—red, yellow, and blue; used to mix the other colors on the color wheel **colores primarios**—rojo, amarillo, y azul; usados para mezclar los otros colores en el círculo cromático.

**spectral color scheme**—uses all the colors of the rainbow: red, orange, yellow, green, blue, and violet **esquema de colores del espectro**—usa todos los colores del arco de iris: rojo, anaranjado, amarillo, verde, azul, y violeta.

**tint**—any color blended with white **tinte** cualquier color mezclado con el blanco

**value**—the lightness or darkness of a color **valor**—la claridad u oscuridad de un color

# Wrapping Up Unit 3
# Color and Value

Wrapping Up Unit 3
Color and Value

 ## Art Criticism

**Critical Thinking** Art criticism is an organized system for looking at and talking about art. Anyone can criticize art without being an expert. The purpose of art criticism is to get the viewer involved in a perception process that delays judgment until all aspects of an artwork have been studied.

■ See pages 28–29 for more about art criticism.

## Describe

▶ Closest part: There is a woman sitting in a wooden rocking chair. She is wearing a long red dress. Her feet are bare, and she holds a handkerchief. She is wearing a ring on her left hand. She has long black hair. Her head is tilted to one side. Her head almost touches the top of the canvas, and her skirt touches the bottom. Farthest part: A landscape painting in a plain wooden frame hangs on a blue wall. The floor is a variety of browns.

## Analyze

▶ Primary colors are visible in the red dress and the blue wall. The green of the grass, the violet collar on her dress, and her dull orange skin—these are secondary colors. The yellow-green in the picture on the wall is an intermediate color.

▶ Black has been mixed with brown to create dark shadows on the rocking chair. Black has been mixed with green to make the shadows on the grass in the picture on the wall. The woman's dress is a variety of light values of red. Gray has been mixed with white to show shadows on the woman's handkerchief.

▶ Yellow and brown have a light value. Blue, green, and red have a dark value.

▶ There are low-intensity colors in the rocking chair, the floor, and the woman's skin.

▲ **Paul Gauguin.** (French).
*Faaturuma (Melancholic).* 1891.
Oil on canvas. 37 × 26¾ inches (93.98 × 67.95 cm.).
The Nelson Atkins Museum of Art, Kansas City, Missouri.

**120** Unit 3

## Art History and Culture

### Paul Gauguin

Paul Gauguin (pôl gō gan´) (1848–1903) was known for his sensuous use of pure colors. Gauguin's mother was of Spanish-Peruvian origin, and he spent some of his childhood in Peru. Gauguin's interest in art began after the death of his mother in 1867, when Gustave Arosa, an art collector, was appointed his guardian. Gauguin lived in Tahiti from 1891 to 1893. He painted *Faaturuma* while living in Tahiti. He often painted subjects that reflected his interest in other cultures. He settled permanently in the South Pacific in 1895 after having created many paintings in Paris and later experiencing a succession of failures.

See pages 24–25 and 16–21 for more about art history and subject matter.

**Artist Profiles, p. 22**

◆ Artist Profile ◆
**Paul Gauguin**
1848–1903

As one of France's leading postimpressionist painters, the artistic career of Paul Gauguin (pôl gō gan´) did not begin until he was a 25-year-old stockbroker. He decided to become a painter when he saw the first impressionist exhibit in Paris, France, in 1874, and throughout the next 30 years he developed his own style independent from impressionism and full of influences and experiences from his life. He was not content or fulfilled in Europe, however, and in 1891 he left his family and job to move to Tahiti and various other destinations in the South Pacific. With the exception of a two-year absence, Gauguin remained in Tahiti for the rest of his life, painting until his death in 1903.

 **Art Criticism** Critical Thinking

**Describe** **What do you see?**
During this step you will collect information about the subject of the work.
▶ What do you see in the closest and farthest parts of the painting?

**Analyze** **How is this work organized?**
Think about how the artist has used the elements and principles of art.
▶ Which primary, secondary, and intermediate colors do you see in the painting?
▶ Do you see any neutral colors? Where are they?
▶ Which colors have a light or a dark value?
▶ Where do you see low intensity colors?

**Interpret** **What is the artist trying to say?**
Use the clues you discovered during your analysis to find the message the artist is trying to show.
▶ What is the mood of this painting?
▶ What do you think the woman is thinking about?
▶ Do you have a place you like to go sit and think?

**Decide** **What do you think about the work?**
Use all the information you have gathered to decide whether this is a successful work of art.
▶ Is the work successful because it is realistic, because it is well organized, or because it has a strong message? Explain.

# Interpret

▶ Answers will vary. Students may say the painting has a quiet or thoughtful mood because of the woman's facial expression. The contrast between the dress and the background is not very strong because the wall is a grayish blue, and the dress is a light value of red.

▶ Answers will vary. The answers should include reference to her facial expression, her drooping posture, the handkerchief in her hand, the ring on her finger, and possibly her long red dress, her bare feet, the rocking chair, and the bare room.

▶ Answers will vary. Students may have a tree house, a place in their yard, or a corner of their room that they like to go for a quiet moment.

# Decide

▶ Answers will vary. Most will say a strong message, but realism and composition may be cited.

### Art Journal: Writing
Have students write answers to Aesthetic Perception in their Art Journals. Have them discuss their answers in small groups.

 ## Aesthetic Perception

**Seeing Like an Artist** Have students think about a friend or family member or bring in a picture of a friend or family member to display. Ask students to describe how the picture compares to *Faaturuma*.
NSAE 3.a

**Describe** ▶ List and describe everything you see in the picture.

**Analyze** ▶ What colors do you see in the picture?
▶ How do the colors contribute to the look of the person?

**Interpret** ▶ How does the picture make you feel?
▶ What name would you give the person? Why?

**Decide** ▶ Do you have strong feelings when you look at the picture?

"Color is often used by artists to communicate an emotion or set a mood in a work of art." "El color es usado frecuentemente por los artistas para comunicar emoción o crear ánimo en una obra de arte."

 **T** Review unit vocabulary with students, using *Transparency 29.*

 ## Art Journal: Writing

Have students answer the questions on page 122 in their Art Journals or on a separate sheet of paper. Answers: 1. B, 2. A, 3. B, 4. C, 5. A

**T** For further assessment, have students complete the unit test on *Transparency 45.*

### VISIT A MUSEUM
## The San Francisco Museum of Modern Art

► Have students plan and create a mini art museum in the classroom, media center, or other area within the school where people may view the exhibit.

"There is a logic of colors, and it is with this alone, and not with the logic of the brain, that the painter should conform."

—Paul Cézanne

---

Color and Value, continued

## Show What You Know

Answer these questions on a separate sheet of paper.

❶ Red, orange, yellow, green, blue, and violet are the colors in the _____.
   A. primary spectrum
   B. color spectrum
   C. secondary spectrum

❷ Red, yellow, and blue are _____ colors.
   A. primary
   B. spectrum
   C. secondary

❸ Orange, green, and violet are _____ colors.
   A. primary
   B. secondary
   C. spectrum

❹ _____ colors are made by blending a primary color with a secondary color.
   A. Spectrum
   B. Hue
   C. Intermediate

❺ The _____ is made up of the three primary, three secondary, and six intermediate colors.
   A. color wheel
   B. spectrum wheel
   C. intermediate wheel

---

### VISIT A MUSEUM
## The San Francisco Museum of Modern Art

The San Francisco Museum of Modern Art in California was the first museum on the West Coast built to hold only twentieth-century art. The museum has more than 15,000 works of art in its collection. The collection consists of modern and contemporary art, including paintings, sculptures, photographs, architectural drawings, and models. The museum is also known for its wide collection of art by California artists. In addition to the exhibits, the museum offers lectures, special events, and many activities for seniors and children.

---

## Unit Assessment Options

### Aesthetic Perception

**Practice** Have students select one of concepts in the Show What You Know section on page 122 then find examples of each concept in the classroom.

### Creative Expression

**Student Portfolio** Have students review all the artwork they have created during this unit and select the pieces they wish to keep in their portfolios.

### Art Criticism

**Activity** Have students select an artwork from this unit and study it using the four steps of art criticism. (See pages 28–29 for more information about art criticism.) Have students work alone or in pairs and present their findings aloud or in writing.

# Color and Value in Music

"The Boy Who Wanted to Talk to Whales" is a musical created with very unusual instruments. The color of an instrument is the kind of sound it makes. Flutes and marimbas are different colors in an ensemble. Robert Minden uses ordinary objects such as a carpenter's saw, tin cans, and vacuum cleaner hoses as musical instruments.

**What to Do** Create a bottle orchestra with a monochromatic color scheme.

Collect empty glass bottles of different sizes and shapes. Experiment by blowing over the mouth of a bottle to hear the sound it makes. The biggest bottle will make the lowest note. Leave this bottle empty; fill others with increasingly more water to raise the sound of the note.

1. Working in groups of six, create the first six notes of a scale (do, re, mi, fa, so, la); each bottle has a different note. Experiment with putting the right amount of water in each bottle to make each note.

2. Sit in a circle in the right sequence of notes. Play the scale from low to high; reverse.

3. With your six notes, play the tune, "Twinkle, Twinkle, Little Star."

4. Pick a conductor to count "one, two, ready, begin" and have all the groups play together.

5. Add two more notes (ti, do) to complete the scale.

▲ The Robert Minden Ensemble. "The Boy Who Wanted to Talk to Whales" excerpts.

 **Art Criticism**

**Describe** What color do you think of when you hear the sound of blown bottles?

**Analyze** How did you use water to create the notes of a scale?

**Interpret** What feelings or moods are created by the sound color of blown bottles?

**Decide** Were you successful in creating the notes and in playing "Twinkle, Twinkle, Little Star"?

---

 **Art History and Culture**

## Music, Storytelling, and Color

Just as an artist uses color to give vibrancy and intensity to a painting, musicians use different amounts of energy as they produce the notes they play. This comes from the emotion, attitude, and skill that musicians bring to their interpretations. By using a variety of traditional instruments and found objects, the Robert Minden Ensemble creates moods and soundscapes, as well as giving voices and emotions to different characters in their stories.

---

# Color and Value in Music

**Objective:** To create a bottle orchestra with a monochromatic color scheme

**Materials:** *The Boy Who Wanted to Talk to Whales*, performed by the Robert Minden Ensemble. Running time: video: 2:50/audio: 6:00. Glass bottles and water in buckets.

## Focus
**Time:** About 5 minutes

- Discuss the information on page 123.

**Art History and Culture**

- Have students discuss how music has changed over the years.

## Teach
**Time:** About 30 minutes

**Aesthetic Perception**

- Have students experiment with blowing across the mouth of empty bottles, then filling them with different amounts of water to make different musical notes.

**Creative Expression**

- Divide students into groups of six, with six bottles and water. Have students create the fist six notes of a scale, using different levels of water. Have them learn to play this tune by blowing across the right bottles.

- **Informal Assessment** When the students perform the song, comment positively on their interpretations.

## Reflect
**Time:** About 10 minutes

**Art Criticism**

- Have students answer the four art criticism question on page 123 aloud or in writing.

- Did students correctly create six notes of a scale and cooperatively play "Twinkle, Twinkle, Little Star?"

# Unit 4 Planning Guide

| | Lesson Title | Suggested Pacing | Creative Expression Activity |
|---|---|---|---|
| Lesson 1 | Forms | 1 hour | Design a sculptured form. |
| Lesson 2 | Additive Sculpture | 1 hour | Create an additive sculpture. |
| Lesson 3 | Subtractive Sculpture | 1 hour | Make an animal form. |
| Lesson 4 | Visual Texture | 1 hour | Create a narrative picture using visual textures. |
| Lesson 5 | Tactile Texture | 1 hour | Create a weaving with a variety of textures. |
| Lesson 6 | Emphasis | 1 hour | Distort a photograph using the computer. |
| ART SOURCE ARTSOURCE | Form and Texture in Dance | 35 minutes | Bring a toy to life using body movements. |

| Materials | Program Resources | Fine Art Resources | Literature Resources |
|---|---|---|---|
| clay, masking tape, squares of burlap or muslin, clay tools, water, paper towels | *Assessment,* pp. 45–46 *Reading and Writing Test Preparation,* pp. 42–43 *Home and After-School Connections* | *Transparency 19* *Artist Profiles,* pp. 41, 47 *Large Prints 55* and *56* *The National Museum of Women in the Arts Collection* | *Chimpanzee Family Book* by Jane Goodall |
| cardboard tubes, clay, found objects, fabric scraps | *Assessment,* pp. 47–48 *Reading and Writing Test Preparation,* pp. 44–45 | *Transparency 20* *Artist Profiles,* pp. 8, 80 *Large Prints 55* and *56* *Art Around the World Collection* | *Look-Alikes: The More You Look, the More You See!* by Joan Steiner |
| plaster, mixing bowl, water, clean milk cartons, carving tools, forks, paper clips | *Assessment,* pp. 49–50 *Reading and Writing Test Preparation,* pp. 46–47 *Flash Card* 20 | *Transparency 21* *Artist Profiles,* pp. 77, 79 *Large Print 55* *Art Around the World Collection* | *The Secret Garden* by Frances Hodgson Burnett |
| pencils, color pencils, large sheets of white paper, glue, old magazines, scissors | *Assessment,* pp. 51–52 *Reading and Writing Test Preparation,* pp. 48–49 *Flash Cards* 18–19 | *Transparency 22* *Artist Profiles,* pp. 6, 38 *Large Print 55* *The National Museum of Women in the Arts Collection* | *Slinky Scaly Slithery Snakes* by Dorothy Hinshaw Patent |
| cardboard, found materials, pencils, acrylic paint, glue | *Assessment,* pp. 53–54 *Reading and Writing Test Preparation,* pp. 50–51 | *Transparency 23* *Artist Profiles,* pp. 13, 63 *Large Prints 55* and *56* *The National Museum of Women in the Arts Collection* | *Casey at the Bat* by Earnest Lawrence Thayer, illustrated by Christopher Bing |
| computer, paint or draw program, printer, photo-editing program, scanner | *Assessment,* pp. 55–56 *Reading and Writing Test Preparation,* pp. 52–53 *Flash Card* 15 | *Transparency 24* *Artist Profiles,* pp. 57, 68 *Large Prints 55* and *56* *The National Museum of Women in the Arts Collection* | *A Mouse Called Wolf* by Dick King-Smith |
| *The Nutcracker,* "The Waltz of the Flowers," a variety of toys or pictures of toys | | | |

# Unit Overview

## 4 Form, Texture, and Emphasis

**Lesson 1:** A **form** is an object with three dimensions: height, width, and depth.

**Lesson 2: Additive sculpture** is created by adding materials to a form.

**Lesson 3: Subtractive sculpture** is created by removing material by carving until a sculpture is complete.

**Lesson 4: Visual texture** is the illusion of a three-dimensional surface based on the memory of how something feels.

**Lesson 5: Tactile texture** is how something actually feels on its surface.

**Lesson 6: Emphasis** is used to control the order in which parts of a work are noticed.

## Introduce Unit Concepts

"Artists use form, texture, and emphasis to communicate how things look and feel." "Los artistas usan la forma, la textura y el énfasis para comunicar cómo son y cómo se sienten las cosas."

### Form and Texture

- Tell students the definition of *form* and discuss how forms are part of their daily lives.

- On the board, make a list of words used to describe texture. Have students name objects that correspond to the words.

### Emphasis

- Ask students to describe how they draw attention to, or emphasize, the main points in a report or a speech.

### Cross-Curricular Projects

- See the *Language Arts and Reading, Mathematics, Science,* and *Social Studies Art Connections* books for activities that further develop the concepts of form, texture, and emphasis.

# Form, Texture, and Emphasis

◀ **Michelangelo.** (Italian). *Pietà.* c. 1500.

Marble. $68\frac{1}{2} \times 76\frac{3}{4}$ inches (174 × 195 cm.). St. Peter's Basilica, Rome, Italy.

**Artists use form, texture, and emphasis to create different types of artwork.**

*Pietà* was created by Michelangelo around 1500. Michelangelo carved many sculptures of people from marble. He created *Pietà* when he was twenty-five years old. To make the adult son look natural on his mother's lap, Michelangelo made her robes very large.

**124** Unit 4

## Fine Art Prints

Display *Large Prints 55 Floating City* and *56 Wrapped Reichstag Building*. Refer to the prints throughout the unit as students learn about form, texture, and emphasis.

**Large Print 55**

**Large Print 56**

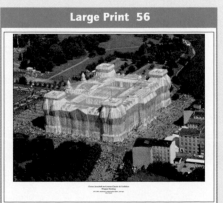

Artists use **form** to create three-dimensional works of art.

► From how many sides could you view this sculpture?

Artists create **texture** in their work to show how things look and feel.

► How would you describe the texture of the sculpture?

Artists use **emphasis** to control the order in which parts of a work are noticed.

► What is the first thing you see when you view this sculpture?

**In This Unit** you will learn about different ways that artists create forms. You also will learn about texture and emphasis.

Here are the topics you will study:

► Forms
► Additive sculpture
► Subtractive sculpture
► Visual texture
► Tactile texture
► Emphasis

# Michelangelo
(1475–1564)

Michelangelo was an Italian painter, sculptor, poet, architect, and engineer. *Pietà* was Michelangelo's major early work. His most famous sculpture, however, is *David,* which was created from 1501 to 1504. The choice of stone for his sculptures was very important because he believed the statue already existed within the marble. Although he loved sculpting, he is probably most famous for his huge painting on the ceiling of the Sistine Chapel in Rome, Italy.

# Examine the Artwork

"Let's look closely at the sculpture." "Vamos a mirar detalladamente la escultura."

■ Have students examine the sculpture. Ask them to describe what they see.

■ Have students answer the questions about form, texture, and emphasis on page 125.

  ► You can walk completely around this sculpture and observe the unity from all angles.

  ► The sculpture has a smooth texture in some areas, such as the man's legs, and a rough texture in other areas, such as the folds in the skirt.

  ► The woman's face is the first thing the viewer sees when he or she looks at the sculpture.

# Unit Pretest

T Display *Transparency 46* as a pretest. Answers: 1. C, 2. A, 3. A, 4. B, 5. C

# Home Connection

■ See *Home and After-School Connections* for family newsletters and activities for this unit.

## Art History and Culture

### Michelangelo

Michelangelo (mī, kə lan´ jə lō) (1475–1564) was 25 years old when he completed *Pietà*. The sculpture is signed on the diagonal strap across the woman's chest. Michelangelo began creating *David,* his most famous sculpture, a year after completing *Pietà.* It took him four years to finish *David.* Michelangelo was considered the greatest sculptor in Italy when he created these monumental works of art. He lived and worked during the Renaissance. Michelangelo also demonstrated talents in painting, poetry, architecture, and engineering.

See pages 24–25 and 16–21 for more about art history and subject matter.

**Artist Profiles, p. 45**

Artist Profile

**Michelangelo**
1475–1564

Michelangelo (mi kə lan´ jə lō) Buonarroti was born in the mountain village of Caprese, Italy. Even at an early age, his talent for drawing was obvious. His father, a Florentine official who was connected to the ruling Medici family, apprenticed his son to the master painter Ghirlandaio. After two years Michelangelo attended the sculpture school sponsored by the Medici family. He was introduced to the leaders of France by Lorenzo de´ Medici. When Lorenzo died, Michelangelo fled to Rome, where he examined many newly unearthed classical statues. In 1505, he was given two commissions: a tomb for Julius II, and the painting of the ceiling of the Sistine Chapel. It took him four years to cover the ceiling.

# Unit 4 Arts Integration

### ILLUSTRATOR PROFILE
## Lynne Cherry
(1952– )

When she was growing up in Philadelphia, Pennsylvania, Lynne Cherry loved to draw. Cherry's mother, Helen Cogancherry, an illustrator of children's books, always encouraged her daughter to write and draw. Cherry would go on to earn a bachelor of fine arts degree from Philadelphia's Tyler School of Art and a master's degree in history from Yale University.

Cherry is the author and/or illustrator of more than 30 children's books, including the classic *The Great Kapok Tree.* A consistent theme in Cherry's work is respect for nature, a message she also brings directly to children in many school presentations each year. Her tireless efforts to integrate environmental studies with core curriculum prompted Cherry to found the Center for Children's Environmental Literature (CCEL) in 1992.

Cherry's depth of feeling for her natural subjects is evident in her detailed, expressive illustrations. The cross-hatching technique used in her ink drawings gives the illustrations amazing vibrancy.

Throughout Unit 4, share Cherry's illustrations with the class and discuss the use of form, texture, and emphasis in her illustrations. What kind of geometric and free-form forms can students identify? How does Cherry create visual texture?

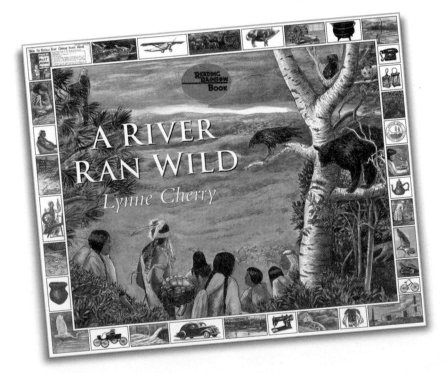

## Music

Form in music relates to the way a composition is organized. Students can identify the ABA form in short orchestra compositions, such as "Eine Kleine Nacht Musik" by Mozart. Texture in music generally refers to combining melody and harmony to create layers of sound. It can also be used in describing the effect of layering together several different rhythm patterns. Emphasis in music is used when the composer wants to stress a special part in some way.

## Literature

Show *Eskimo Art* on video or DVD to introduce the unit concepts. Have students identify the forms they see. Students should also notice the textures of objects and find examples of emphasis.

**Literature and Art**

## Performing Arts

Show *The Nutcracker.* Point out various forms and textures.

**Artsource®**

# Forms

**Lesson 1** introduces **forms.** Sculptors communicate their feelings, ideas, and views of the world through form.

## Objectives

###  Art History and Culture

To demonstrate knowledge of the lives and work of Henry Moore and Jacques Lipchitz

### Creative Expression

To use clay to create a three-dimensional sculptured form

###  Aesthetic Perception

To identify and compare two-dimensional shapes and three-dimensional forms

###  Art Criticism

To evaluate own work using the four steps of art criticism

## Vocabulary ⭐ Vocabulary

Review the following vocabulary words with students before beginning the lesson.

**two-dimensional** bidimensional—a shape that can be measured in two ways: by height and width

**three-dimensional** tridimensional—a form that can be measured by height, width, and depth

See page 149B for additional vocabulary and Spanish vocabulary resources.

###  Art Journal: Vocabulary

Have students add these words to the Vocabulary section of their Art Journals.

## Lesson Materials

- white drawing paper
- pencils, color pencils
- clay, clay tools
- masking tape
- squares of burlap or muslin
- craft sticks
- plastic utensils
- water dishes
- paper towels

**Alternate Materials:**

- crayons
- salt dough or plasticine

## Program Resources

- *Reading and Writing Test Prep.,* pp. 42–43
- *Transparency 19*
- *Artist Profiles,* pp. 41, 47
- *Animals Through History Time Line*
- *Assessment,* pp. 45–46
- *Large Prints 55* Floating City and *56* Wrapped Reichstag Building
- *The National Museum of Women in the Arts Collection*

### Concept Trace

**Forms**

**Introduced:** Level 3, Unit 2, Lesson 4

**Reinforced:** Level 5, Unit 2, Lesson 5

---

## Lesson 1  Arts Integration

### Theatre

Complete Unit 4, Lesson 1, on pages 72–73 of *Theatre Arts Connection.*

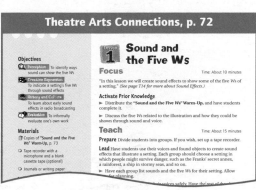

### Music

 Form in music relates to the way a composition is organized. A letter of the alphabet is assigned to each section. A is the first section, B is a contrasting section, C is a third section, and so on. Examples are: AA, "This Land is Your Land;" AB, "La Raspa;" ABA, "Eine Kleine Nacht Musik." Have students listen to "Los Mariachis" and note the return of A.

### Movement & Dance

Have students find an object that has an interesting form. Then have them create a way to translate it into the body, looking at its mass, weight, and shape. Have students explore four ways to move with the free-form object and organize the movements into a sequence. Students should take four counts for each idea and four counts to transition.

# Focus

Time: About 10 minutes

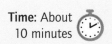

## Activate Prior Knowledge

"Can you name some objects that are three-dimensional? "¿Pueden nombrar algunos objetos que son tridimensionales?

■ Discuss and list students' answers on the board.

**Using Literature**  Reading

■ Have students read *The Chimpanzee Family Book* by Jane Goodall. Point out different forms and explain to students how forms differ from shapes.

**Thematic Connection** ⭐ Science

■ **Environment:** Sculptors should use materials that are appropriate for the environment in which their sculpture will be displayed. Discuss materials that are appropriate for different environments.

## Introduce the Art

# Look

"Let's take a close look at the two works of art." "Vamos a observar detalladamente las dos obras de arte."

**Measurement** ⭐ Mathematics

■ Discuss various units of measurement, such as inches, feet, and centimeters. Point out that shapes can be measured two ways—by height and width—and forms can be measured three ways—by height, width, and depth, for example.

## 🏺 Art History and Culture

Students' answers will vary. Some may comment that the sculptures are simplistic; therefore, modern technology was not needed to create them.

 **Web Connection**

Visit **www.henry-moore-fdn.co.uk/site/thesite/ blackboard.html** to discover new aspects of Henry Moore and his work.

---

# Forms

▲ **Henry Moore.** (English). *Oval with Points.* 1968–1970.
. . . . . . . . . . . . . . . . . . . . . . .
Bronze. 130$\frac{1}{8}$ inches (332 cm.).
The Henry Moore Foundation,
Perry Green, England.

**Look**  at the works of art on these pages. Moore used rounded forms to create his bronze sculpture. His sculpture looks like the figure 8. Lipchitz used black marble to create his sculpture. He used simple, flat forms to create *Reclining Figure with Guitar*. This sculpture represents a person.

## 🏺 Art History and Culture

These sculptures were created in the twentieth century. Do they look like they could have been created in an earlier century? Explain.

## 🏺 Art History and Culture

### Henry Moore

Henry Moore (hen´ rē mor) (1898–1986) created monumental sculptures that were primarily intended for open-air settings. In addition to creating bronze casts and carvings, Moore, who is one of the twentieth-century's best-known sculptors, also created drawings and watercolors. *Oval with Points* is part of a theme of sculptures that includes at least two other sculptures, *Pointed Forms and Three Points.* Moore created many other sculptures representing the human form in various situations and interactions.

See pages 24–25 and 16–21 for more about art history and the subject matter.

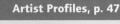

**Artist Profiles, p. 47**

 **Artist Profile**

**Henry Moore**
1898–1986

Henry Moore (hen´ rē mor) was born in Castleford, England. When he was ten, he told his father he wanted to become a sculptor. At 18, he left home to join the army during World War I. He began studying art after the war. By age 23, he was a serious sculptor.

▲ **Jacques Lipchitz.**
(Lithuanian). *Reclining Figure with Guitar.*

Black marble. $16\frac{3}{8} \times 27\frac{5}{8} \times 13\frac{1}{2}$ inches
($41.61 \times 70.16 \times 34.29$ cm.).
The Museum of Modern Art, New York,
New York.

**S**tudy the two sculptures to see how the artists worked with form.

▶ What kinds of forms do you see in each sculpture?

▶ List the similarities and differences in the look of each work.

▶ Why do you think the artists chose to make their sculptures abstract rather than realistic?

### Aesthetic Perception

**Design Awareness** Look around you. Do you notice the many objects that have three or more surfaces?

## Study

▶ Moore: rounded form. Lipchitz: simple, flat forms.

▶ Similarities: Both pieces make use of free-form forms. Differences: Moore used a rounded form, while Lipchitz's figure is flat and very abstract. Moore used bronze to create his sculpture; Lipchitz used black marble to create his sculpture.

▶ Both artists chose to make their sculptures abstract, perhaps to focus on the shapes and forms created by figures and their interactions.

■ For more examples of abstract and nonobjective art, see *The National Museum of Women in the Arts Collection.*

### Art Journal: Writing

Encourage students to define and illustrate forms in the Concepts section of their Art Journals. What else do they want to know about forms?

### Aesthetic Perception

**Design Awareness** Discuss objects with three or more surfaces. Students may mention a desk, pencil, book, or chair. Explain to students that objects with three or more surfaces are three-dimensional because they can be measured in height, width, and depth.

**Developing Visual Literacy** Invite students to carefully observe each artwork to find shapes or forms that represent objects, letters, numbers, words, and people. The figure 8 appears in the center of *Ovals with Points.* *Reclining Figure with Guitar* is a sculpture of a human figure.

## Art History and Culture

### Jacques Lipchitz

Jacques Lipchitz (zhäk lēp shēts) (1891–1973) was born Chaim Jacop Lipchitz. In 1909 he moved to Paris, where he studied sculpting at the École des Beaux-Arts. Lipchitz was influenced by the early twentieth-century cubist painters Pablo Picasso and Georges Braque. His sculptures reflect geometric shapes found in cubist paintings. When Lipchitz moved to New York City in 1941, he didn't know a word of English, nor did he have any money. Although he had already attained international recognition for his sculptures, he earned his living by accepting commissions for portraits. Lipchitz later returned to creating sculptures.

See pages 24–25 and 16–21 for more about art history and the subject matter.

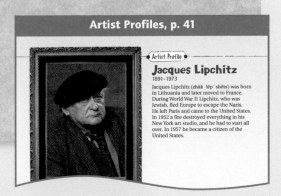

**Artist Profiles, p. 41**

◆ Artist Profile ◆
**Jacques Lipchitz**
1891-1973
Jacques Lipchitz (zhäk lēp' shēts) was born in Lithuania and later moved to France. During World War II Lipchitz, who was Jewish, fled Europe to escape the Nazis. He left Paris and came to the United States. In 1952 a fire destroyed everything in his New York art studio, and he had to start all over. In 1957 he became a citizen of the United States.

 **Web Connection**
Visit **www.marlboroughgallery.com/artists.html** to view other works by Jacques Lipchitz.

**Time:** About 45 minutes

"Can you change a shape into a form?"
"¿Pueden cambiar una figura en una forma?"

- Read and discuss shape and form on page 128.

## Practice

**Materials:** white drawing paper, pencils, colored pencils

**Alternate Materials:** crayons

- Distribute the materials and have students follow the directions on page 128.

## Creative Expression

**Materials:** clay; masking tape; squares of burlap or muslin; clay tools, such as craft sticks, plastic utensils or sharpened pencils; water dishes; paper towels

**Alternate Materials:** salt dough or plasticine

- Review procedures for working with clay on pages 226–227.
- Distribute the materials and have students follow the directions on page 129.
- Review the Activity Tips on page 237 for visual examples of techniques if needed.

### Art Journal: Brainstorming

Have students brainstorm ideas for forms in the Ideas section of their Art Journals. Then have students create sketches of their forms for the Creative Expression activity.

---

# Using Forms and Shapes

A shape, such as a square, is two-dimensional. It is flat and can be measured in only two ways: by height and by width.

A **form,** such as a cube, is three-dimensional. It can be measured in three ways: by height, width, and depth. Think of a form as a solid object that has thickness. The following illustrations show how shapes and forms are related.

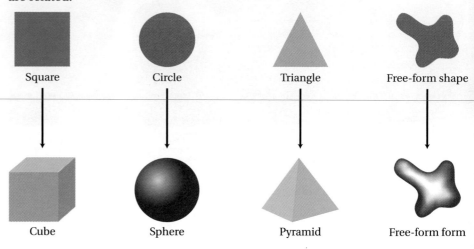

Square          Circle          Triangle          Free-form shape

Cube          Sphere          Pyramid          Free-form form

## Practice

Change shapes into forms. Use color pencils.

1. Draw the same shape two times. Color each shape a solid color.
2. Change the second shape into a form, creating the illusion of three dimensions by adding more lines and shading. Blend complementary colors for shadows.

---

## Differentiated Instruction

**Reteach**
Ask students to list several objects that can be measured in three ways: height, width, and depth. Ask them to share the names of a few of them with the class.

**Special Needs**
The use of turntables used in ceramic painting or household serving turntables may assist students in looking at the form from all angles.

**ELL**
Students may hesitate to share their observations aloud in a large group. As an alternative or a precursor to a large-group discussion, have students share their ideas with partners or in small groups. Encourage them to answer the four questions at the end of the lesson by rephrasing the questions.

◀ **Aaron Ragans.**
Age 7.

**Think** about the kinds of forms the student artist used.

## Creative Expression

What forms would you choose to create? Use clay to create a three-dimensional sculptured form that is interesting from every point of view.

1. Think about the different forms you see every day. Some are natural organic forms, and some are made by people.

2. Make a large potato form out of clay. Keep turning your form, making sure to work on all surfaces. Use your fingers to press into some surfaces and to pull up other surfaces. Create at least one curved hole that goes completely through the clay.

## Art Criticism

**Describe** Explain how you made your sculpture.

**Analyze** How did you turn a basic shape into a form? Did you use free-form style or geometric forms?

**Interpret** Give your work a descriptive title.

**Decide** Is your form interesting from every point of view?

# Reflect

## Review and Assess

"Let's review what we have learned about shapes and forms." "Vamos a revisar lo que hemos aprendido sobre figuras y formas."

## Think

The artists used circular forms and free-form forms to create a non-objective sculpture.

- Use *Large Prints 55 Floating City* and *56 Wrapped Reichstag Building* to have students identify forms.

## Informal Assessment

- Invite a local sculptor to the class, so the artist can share his or her portfolio, if possible. Students can interpret ideas and moods in the artist's portfolio.
  NSAE 5.b; 5.c
- For standardized-format test practice using this lesson's art content, see pages 42–43 in *Reading and Writing Test Preparation.*

## Art Journal: Critical Thinking

Have students answer the four art criticism questions—Describe, Analyze, Interpret, and Decide—in their Art Journals. In small groups, have students discuss the use of forms in their sculptures.

## Art Across the Curriculum

Use these simple ideas to reinforce art concepts across the curriculum.

★ **Expository Writing** Have students write expository paragraphs to explain two- and three-dimensional shapes.

★ **Math** Have students learn more about weight, an element you could use to compare sculptures.

★ **Science** Discuss more about alloys, such as bronze, used in Moore's sculpture.

★ **Social Studies** Discuss the meaning of the word *century,* noting that both sculptures were created during the twentieth century and that we are now in the twenty-first century.

★ **Technology** Have students use a paint or draw program to create three-dimensional shapes. Visit **SRAonline.com** to print detailed instructions for this activity.
NSAE 6.b

## Extra! For the Art Specialist

**Time:** About 45 minutes

### Focus

Study **Large Print 56** *Wrapped Reichstag Building* and ask the students to explain the difference between a two-dimensional object and a three-dimensional form. Even though the print or image is flat, how can they tell that the artwork is really a form?

### Teach

Tell the students that they will be creating a three-dimensional form similar to the work of Henry Moore. Explain that Moore abstracted his figures by simplifying the body forms and eliminating details such as features. Have the students follow the directions to complete the alternate activity.

### Reflect

Have students use the four steps of art criticism to evaluate their work. Have them describe their figures.

### Alternate Activity

**Materials:**
- sketchbook
- pencils, erasers
- clay
- clay tools or plastic knife
- clay mat such as textured wallpaper, burlap or cotton fabric
- slip containers

1. Have students sketch several images of reclining or sitting figures. Then have them choose the sketch they like best.

2. Have students form a piece of clay into a potato shape. Students should look at their sketches and begin by pinching and pulling out the clay to form the head.

3. Tap the clay lightly to flatten the body slightly. Have students make three cuts into the clay with a clay tool or plastic knife to create arms and legs.

4. Have students bend and mold the figure into position. The form should be simple with minimal details. Refer to Henry Moore's work to see how he created the face.

## Research in Art Education

"Only through a multifaceted education program that develops divergent as well as convergent thinking—that encourages intuitive as well as rational thought processes—can today's young learner begin to be prepared to cope with the rapidly changing aspects of a technology-oriented world." (Herberholz, Barbara, and Lee Hanson. *Early Childhood Art.* New York: McGraw-Hill, 1994.)

## Assessment

Use the following rubric to evaluate the artwork students make in the Creative Expression activity and to assess students' understanding of forms.

Have students complete page 45 or 46 in their *Assessment* books.

| | Art History and Culture | Aesthetic Perception | Creative Expression | Art Criticis |
|---|---|---|---|---|
| **3 POINTS** | The student demonstrates knowledge of the lives and work of Moore and Lipchitz. | The student accurately identifies and compares two-dimensional shapes and three-dimensional forms. | The student's artwork is clearly three-dimensional. | The student thoughtfully and honestly evaluates own work using the four steps of art criticism. |
| **2 POINTS** | The student's knowledge of the lives and work of Moore and Lipchitz is weak or incomplete. | The student shows emerging awareness of two-dimensional shapes and three-dimensional forms but cannot consistently identify them. | The student's artwork shows some attempt to create a three-dimensional form. | The student attempts to evaluate own work but shows an incomplete understanding of evaluation criteria. |
| **1 POINT** | The student cannot demonstrate knowledge of the lives and work of Moore and Lipchitz. | The student cannot identify two-dimensional shapes or three-dimensional forms. | The student's artwork is not three-dimensional. | The student makes no attempt to evaluate own work. |

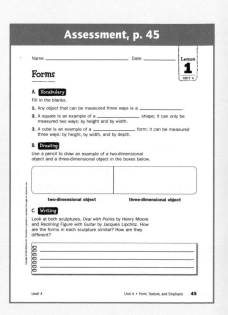

**Assessment, p. 45**

Name _____ Date _____ Lesson **1** UNIT 4

**Forms**

**A. Vocabulary**
Fill in the blanks.
1. Any object that can be measured three ways is a _____.
2. A square is an example of a _____ shape; it can only be measured two ways: by height and by width.
3. A cube is an example of a _____ form; it can be measured three ways: by height, by width, and by depth.

**B. Drawing**
Use a pencil to draw an example of a two-dimensional object and a three-dimensional object in the boxes below.

two-dimensional object          three-dimensional object

**C. Writing**
Look at both sculptures, *Oval with Points* by Henry Moore and *Reclining Figure with Guitar* by Jacques Lipchitz. How are the forms in each sculpture similar? How are they different?

Level 4          Unit 4 • Form, Texture, and Emphasis **45**

# Lesson 2 Additive Sculpture

**Lesson 2** introduces additive sculpture. Adding something to a sculpture is one technique for changing a form.

## Objectives

### Art History and Culture
To demonstrate knowledge of Mayan culture and the life and art of Teodora Blanco

### Creative Expression
To use clay to create an additive sculpture of a person

### Aesthetic Perception
To define and identify additive sculpture

### Art Criticism
To evaluate own work using the four steps of art criticism

### Vocabulary ⭐ Vocabulary

Review the following vocabulary words with students before beginning the lesson.

**relief sculpture** escultura en relieve—a type of sculpture in which forms project into space

**freestanding sculpture** escultura autoestable—a type of sculpture that is surrounded by space on all sides

See page 149B for additional vocabulary and Spanish vocabulary resources.

### Art Journal: Vocabulary
Have students add these words to the Vocabulary section of their Art Journals.

## Lesson Materials
- cardboard tube
- clay
- found objects such as buttons, feathers, fabric scraps

**Alternate Materials:**
- cone-form posterboard
- self-hardening clay

## Program Resources
- *Reading and Writing Test Prep.*, pp. 44–45
- *Transparency 20*
- *Artist Profiles,* pp. 8, 80
- *Animals Through History Time Line*
- *Assessment,* pp. 47–48
- *Large Prints 55* Floating City and *56* Wrapped Reichstag Building
- *Art Around the World Collection*

### Concept Trace
Additive Sculpture
**Introduced:** Level 3, Unit 2, Lesson 5
**Reinforced:** Level 4, Unit 4, Lesson 2

---

## Lesson 2 Arts Integration

### Theatre
Complete Unit 4, Lesson 2, on pages 74–75 of *Theatre Arts Connections.*

**Theatre Arts Connections, p. 74**

**Objectives**
- **Perception** To identify ways sound can show setting
- **Creative Expression** To create sound effects to show setting in a theatre game
- **History and Culture** To learn about the history of radio in California
- **Evaluation** To informally evaluate one's own work

**Materials**
- Copies of "Sound Shows Setting" Warm-Up, p. 75
- Journals or writing paper

#### Lesson 2 Sound Shows Setting

**Focus** Time: About 10 minutes
"In this lesson we will play a theatre game in which sound effects show setting." *(See page 75 for more about Theatre Games.)*

**Activate Prior Knowledge**
▶ Hand out the "Sound Shows Setting" Warm-Up. Read the poem aloud, and then have students answer the questions.
▶ Discuss how the nonsense words evoke sounds that illustrate a knight's battle in the "tulgey wood" with the imaginary monster.

**Teach** Time: About 15 minutes
**Prepare** Divide students into groups of four.
**Lead** Say, "We are going to play a theatre game in which each group will improvise the battle between the knight and the Jabberwock. Two of you in each group will improvise the battle's actions while the other two use their voices to create sound effects." Have the entire class work together on improvising environmental sound effects that could show the setting. Remind students that although they are going to improvise a battle, they

### Music
Adding more layers of musical melodies in a composition is called creating thicker texture. Listen to "Canon in D Major" by Pachelbel. A canon is a form where an extended melody is imitated in its entirety in additional voices entering one at a time. Pachelbel's canon has three voices over a bass line. Have students listen for the complexity of the harmony when all voices are playing together.

### Movement & Dance
Divide students into groups of four. The first student should make a free-form sculpture in four counts, then freeze. Have the remaining students in the group each take a turn and find a way to connect the sculpture through touch. Encourage students to explore different levels and parts of the body that connect.

 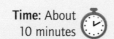

# Focus

## Activate Prior Knowledge

"Think about sculptural forms you have seen. Did they have decorations and details added to them?" "Piensen en formas esculpidas que hayan visto. ¿Se les agregó adornos y detalles a las esculturas?"

- Have students compare the sculptures they have seen to objects in the room that are either continuous forms or forms with added details.

### Using Literature ⭐ Reading

- Have students look at the illustration in *Look-Alikes: The More You Look, the More You See!* by Joan Steiner. Have them discuss how objects were added to the sculptures.

### Thematic Connection ⭐ Social Studies

- **Neighborhoods/Communities:** Discuss how certain communities are known for the type of art they produce. For example, the Mayans produced many ceramic sculptures.

## Introduce the Art

# Look

"Let's study the artwork on both pages." "Vamos a estudiar la obra de arte en ambas páginas."

### Ancient History ⭐ Social Studies

- Have students discuss the significance of when these works of art were created. Ancient artifacts educate us about people and cultures that created them. Students should note that *Standing Ruler* was created by the Mayans from A.D. 600 to 800. Much of what we know today about the Mayans comes from ancient artifacts.

 **Art History and Culture**

Have students examine the dates the sculptures were created. *Standing Ruler* was created by members of an ancient civilization.

## 🖥 Web Connection

Search the pre-Colombian art selection at **www.kimbellart.org/database/index.cfm** to view examples of Mayan art.

---

# Additive Sculpture

**Look** at the artwork on these pages. *Standing Ruler* is a Mayan sculpture created between A.D. 600 and A.D. 800. *Woman* by Teodora Blanco was created in 1965. These clay sculptures were created hundreds of years apart. Notice how both forms look more interesting because of decorations.

◄ **Artist unknown.** (Mayan).
*Standing Ruler.* c. A.D. 600–800.
••••••••••••••••••••••••••••••••••
Ceramic with traces of paint. 9½ inches high (24.13 cm.).
Kimbell Art Museum, Fort Worth, Texas.

 **Art History and Culture**

Which of these sculptures was created by a member of an ancient civilization?

---

**Art History and Culture**

## Mayan Sculptures

*Standing Ruler* is a Mayan sculpture created with ceramic and traces of paint. This artifact was recovered in Guatemala. It represents a Mayan lord dressed to impersonate a dynastic ancestor. Decorations on the costume have been found in other portrayals of Mayan rulers. The decorations appear to define the rank of the Mayan lord. The role of Mayan sculptures in belief and ritual is not clear.

See pages 24–25 and 16–21 for more about art history and the subject matter.

**Artist Profiles, p. 80**

*Artist Profile*

### Standing Ruler

The kingdom of the Mayan people covered a large geographic area of what today is called Central America and southern Mexico. Historians can date evidence of the Mayan culture back to 700 B.C. The ancient Maya had a complex written language, many unique forms of art and architecture, sophisticated methods of producing crops, accurate calendars and other methods of keeping time, and an impressive knowledge of astronomy and other sciences. The Maya were spiritual people who believed in a supernatural world and worshipped gods that appeared to be part human and part animal.

Artist unknown. (Mayan) *Standing Ruler*

Study both sculptures to see how the artists used decorative techniques.

▶ What kinds of forms were used to create each sculpture?

▶ Describe the forms that were added to each sculpture.

▶ Which sculpture has the most forms added to it?

◀ **Teodora Blanco.** (Mexican). *Woman.* 1965.
. . . . . . . . . . . . . . . . . . . . . . . . . . . . . . . .
Earthenware. 27¼ inches tall (69.22 cm.). Museum of International Folk Art, Museum of New Mexico, Santa Fe, New Mexico.

 **Aesthetic Perception**

**Design Awareness** Think about the buildings in your neighborhood. Which buildings have decorative forms added to their surfaces to make them interesting?

## Art History and Culture

### Teodora Blanco

Teodora Blanco (tā ō dor´ ä bläng´ kō) (1928–1980) created sculptures in the village of Atzompa, Mexico. Sculptures produced in this village were usually decorated with flowers, and they usually represented women's physical and spiritual link with nature. Although Blanco had no formal art training, she is considered one of Mexico's great ceramic artists. She won many prizes, medals, and awards for her extraordinary sculptures. Her sculptures were collected by important people such as Nelson Rockefeller, who traveled to Mexico to meet her. Blanco's legacy has continued through the work of family members, including her son and daughter, who are also sculptors.

See pages 24–25 and 16–21 for more about art history and the subject matter.

**Artist Profiles, p. 8**

*Artist Profile*
**Teodora Blanco**
1928-1980
Teodora Blanco (tā´ ō dōr ä  blän´ kō) was born in a poor village in Mexico where little girls were required to learn to make pots. Their plain but useful pots were sold to help support the family. Unlike many of her playmates, Blanco loved to work with clay. When she went to the market to sell her pots, she also stopped at the museum to study the artwork there. In time, she began to decorate her pots with figures. Blanco's unique pots sold well, so she was encouraged to experiment with her figures.

As she became a recognized artist, Blanco took an active role in her community, helping families in need as well as encouraging young potters. Now three

---

# Study

▶ *Standing Ruler:* Rectangular and square forms were used to make the geometric figure form used to create the basic sculpture. *Woman:* A rounded, free-form figure was used to create the basic sculpture.

▶ *Standing Ruler:* There is a rectangular device over his mouth, a shield in his left hand, and a wide belt around his waist, and he is wearing a headdress. *Woman:* Two rectangular forms were added onto both sides of the figure to create arms, a cherub face and flower decorations. The hat was also an added form.

▶ *Standing Ruler:* This sculpture is composed of a combination of geometric and free-form forms. *Woman:* This sculpture is an example of free-form form.

■ For more examples of art from North America, see the **Art Around the World Collection.**

**Art Journal: Writing**
Encourage students to define and illustrate *additive sculpture* in the Concepts section of their Art Journals. What else do they want to know about additive sculpture?

## Aesthetic Perception

**Design Awareness** Most buildings have decorative forms added to them. Windows, doors, porches, flowers, and arches are all examples of decorative forms that can be added to buildings.

**Developing Visual Literacy** Have students discuss the significance of the sculptures. The Mayan sculpture represents a ruler. Blanco's sculpture may represent women's link with nature. Have students select, organize, or produce visuals to complement and extend the meanings of the sculptures.

**Web Connection**
Visit **hirshhorn.si.edu/index.asp** to view the collection of sculptures at the Hirshhorn Museum and Sculpture Garden. This site is for teacher use only.

# Teach

**Time:** About 45 minutes

"Can you build a sculpture using only items that you find on and around your desk?"
"¿Pueden construir una escultura usando solo artículos que encuentren en su pupitre o alrededor de éste?"

- Read and discuss additive sculpture on page 132.

## Practice

**Materials:** found objects

**Alternate Materials:** clay

- Distribute the materials and have students follow the directions on page 132.

## Creative Expression

**Materials:** cardboard tube, clay, found objects, such as buttons, feathers, fabric scraps

**Alternate Materials:** cone-form posterboard, self-hardening clay

- Distribute the materials and have students follow the directions on page 133.

- Review the Activity Tips on page 237 for visual examples of techniques if needed.

### Art Journal: Brainstorming

Have students brainstorm people they could portray in their additive sculpture in the Ideas section of their Art Journals. Then have students create a sketch of the person they will portray in the Creative Expression activity.

---

# Creating Additive Sculpture

Sculpture includes all three-dimensional pieces of art. One type of sculpture, **relief sculpture,** has objects that stick out from a flat surface. Another type, **freestanding sculpture,** is surrounded by space on all sides.

When something is added to either a relief or freestanding sculpture, it becomes an **additive sculpture.** Materials such as paper, cardboard, metal, and wood can be used to create additive sculpture.

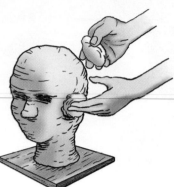

## Practice

Build a temporary additive relief sculpture. Use items found in your desk.

1. Create an additive relief sculpture on your desk using only items found in and around your desk. Use a variety of shapes and sizes.

2. Arrange items such as erasers, rulers, and books carefully to make your sculpture interesting.

---

## Differentiated Instruction

**Reteach**

Have students use the additive technique and modeling clay to make faces. They can roll out balls of clay and use the techniques of scoring and joining to create several expressive faces.

**Special Needs**

Some students may have difficulty combining the clay slab and the posterboard base. Students can still gain an understanding of additive sculpture if the base is omitted.

**ELL**

Begin the Creative Expression activity by showing students pictures of people they could portray in their additive sculptures. Each student can share his or her ideas with a partner, then quickly draw the ideas, labeling the additions while describing them.

◄ **Jasmine Krasle.**
Age 9.

**Think** about how the student artist created the additive sculpture.

 **Creative Expression**

How would you create a portrait of a person using additive sculpture?

1. Brainstorm ideas of people you could portray in your sculpture (soldier, soccer player, football player, police officer, firefighter, doctor, character from a story).

2. Use a cardboard tube or a cone made from poster board as a support. Place a slab of clay around the support. This can be a background support or part of a seated body (even a chair).

3. Create body parts and connect them to the support.

4. Add clothing and tools using thin slabs, coils, and other forms.

 **Art Criticism**

**Describe** Describe the person you portrayed in your sculpture.

**Analyze** Is your figure a geometric or free-form form?

**Interpret** Give your sculpture a title.

**Decide** What would you do differently the next time you create a sculpture?

 **eflect**  Time: About 5 minutes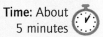

## Review and Assess

"Let's discuss what we have learned about additive sculpture." "Vamos a hablar de lo que hemos aprendido sobre la escultura aditiva."

## Think

The artists added coils of clay to the sculpture to create clothes.

■ Use *Large Prints 55 Floating City* and *56 Wrapped Reichstag Building* to have students identify how artists create additive sculpture.

## Informal Assessment

■ Have students place their completed sculptures in one area of the room. Students should interpret ideas and moods in the exhibition created by their peers.
NSAE 5.a; 5.b

■ For standardized-format test practice using this lesson's art content, see pages 44–45 in *Reading and Writing Test Preparation.*

### Art Journal: Critical Thinking

Have students answer the four art criticism questions—Describe, Analyze, Interpret, and Decide—in their Art Journals. In small groups, have students discuss how they created their additive sculptures.

## Art Across the Curriculum

Use these simple ideas to reinforce art concepts across the curriculum.

★ **Descriptive Writing** Have students write a paragraph describing a sculpture.

★ **Math** Review multidigit addition.

★ **Science** Discuss recycling, noting that recycled materials can be added to clay to create additive sculptures.

★ **Social Studies** Discuss Spanish influences in the United States such as food, fashion, and architecture.

★ **Technology** Have students use the computer's paint or draw program to create an additive sculpture. Visit **SRAonline.com** to print detailed instructions for this activity.
NSAE 6.b

# Additive Sculpture

## Extra! For the Art Specialist

**Time:** About 45 minutes

### Focus

Study **Large Print 55** *Floating City* and discuss with students various techniques used to decorate three-dimensional forms. Have students explain why this is considered an example of additive sculpture.

### Teach

Explain to the students that they will work with clay to create a three-dimensional wall hanging of a fish in which the scales and details are added. Demonstrate rolling out a clay slab and joining techniques. Have the students follow the directions to complete the alternate activity.

### Reflect

Have students use the four steps of art criticism to evaluate their work. Have them describe the fish they created.

### Alternate Activity

**Materials:**

- sketchbook
- pencils, erasers
- fish images
- clay, clay tools
- rolling pin, kiln
- clay mat
- slip in containers
- brushes
- glaze in various colors

1. Have students sketch several images of fish. Have them add details and choose their best sketch.

2. Have students use a roller and flatten a piece of clay into a slab. Then have them draw their fish shape on the slab. Once the fish is the correct shape and size, students should retrace the drawing with a pencil to cut out the shape.

3. Students should roll out coils or small balls of clay to attach as scales. They can add fins or eyes using the score and slip method.

4. Have students use clay tools to add details and textures. When the clay is dry, glaze can be added.

## Research in Art Education

There are several possible reasons for the academic achievement associated with student involvement in arts organizations. Arts organizations tend to place high expectations for achievement on participating students; they give students a chance to perform school-related tasks (such as reading, calculating, and planning), and these organizations value and encourage risk taking ("Living the Arts Through Language and Learning" in *Critical Links*, p. 78). As students complete this lesson, point out that features such as Using Literature give them a chance to integrate school-related tasks such as reading.

## Assessment

Use the following rubric to evaluate the artwork students make in the Creative Expression activity and to assess students' understanding of additive sculpture.

Have students complete page 47 or 48 in their *Assessment* books.

| | Art History and Culture | Aesthetic Perception | Creative Expression | Art Criticism |
|---|---|---|---|---|
| **3 POINTS** | The student demonstrates knowledge of Mayan culture and the life and art of Teodora Blanco. | The student accurately defines and identifies additive sculpture. | The student's artwork is clearly an additive sculpture. | The student thoughtfully and honestly evaluates own work using the four steps of art criticism. |
| **2 POINTS** | The student's knowledge of Mayan culture and the life and art of Teodora Blanco is weak or incomplete. | The student shows emerging awareness of additive sculpture but cannot consistently identify it. | The student's artwork shows some attempt to create an additive sculpture. | The student attempts to evaluate own work but shows an incomplete understanding of evaluation criteria. |
| **1 POINT** | The student demonstrates no knowledge of Mayan culture or the life and art of Teodora Blanco. | The student cannot define or identify additive sculpture. | The student's artwork shows no understanding of additive sculpture. | The student makes no attempt to evaluate own work. |

**Assessment, p. 47**

Name _____ Date _____

Lesson 2 UNIT 4

### Additive Sculpture

**A. Short Answer**
Write the answers.
1. What is additive sculpture?

2. List three different materials that can be used to create additive sculpture.
a. _____
b. _____
c. _____

**B. Drawing**
In the space below, use a pencil to create a design for an additive sculpture that would be made out of clay.

**C. Writing**
Write a paragraph describing the techniques used to create *Woman* by Teodora Blanco.

Level 4      Unit 4 • Form, Texture, and Emphasis   47

# Subtractive Sculpture

**Lesson 3** introduces subtractive sculpture. An artist creates a subtractive sculpture by carving into a form to alter its appearance.

## Objectives

 **Art History and Culture**

To demonstrate knowledge of Egyptian and Aztec cultures

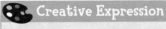 **Creative Expression**

To create a subtractive free-form sculpture

 **Aesthetic Perception**

To learn how subtractive sculptures are created

**Art Criticism**

To evaluate own work using the four steps of art criticism

## Vocabulary ⭐ Vocabulary

Review the following vocabulary words with students before beginning the lesson.

**positive space** espacio positivo—the area in a work of art that shapes and objects fill

**negative space** espacio negativo—the empty spaces surrounding shapes and forms

See page 149B for additional vocabulary and Spanish vocabulary resources.

 **Art Journal: Vocabulary**

Have students add these words to the Vocabulary section of their Art Journals.

## Lesson Materials

- white drawing paper
- pencils, erasers
- plaster
- mixing bowl
- water
- clean milk cartons
- carving tools such as plastic utensils and paper clips

**Alternate Materials:**
- white construction or copier paper
- clay
- clay carving tools

## Program Resources
- *Reading and Writing Test Prep.*, pp. 46–47
- *Transparency 21*
- *Flash Card* 20
- *Artist Profiles*, pp. 77, 79
- *Animals Through History Time Line*
- *Assessment*, pp. 49–50
- *Large Print 55* Floating City
- *Art Around the World Collection*

## Concept Trace
**Subtractive Sculpture**

Introduced: Level 3, Unit 2, Lesson 1

Reinforced: Level 5, Unit 2, Lesson 1

---

# Lesson 3 Arts Integration

## Theatre

Complete Unit 4, Lesson 3, on pages 76–77 of the *Theatre Arts Connections*.

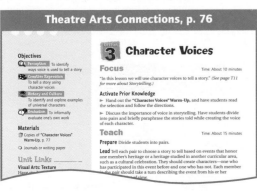

Theatre Arts Connections, p. 76

## Music

Taking layers of melodies out of a composition until there is only one instrument playing is called creating a thinner texture. Contemporary composers use new combinations of instruments and even nontraditional sounds in order to create new sound combinations. Have students listen to "Miniwanka," or "The Moments of Water," by Murray Schafer. Have them think about texture changes.

## Movement & Dance

Have students form groups of five; each student will represent the numbers one through five. Each group will have eight counts to create an instant shape that shows three levels and is connected through touch. Slowly subtract each student by calling out a number. Students must leave the shape without disturbing it or changing the position of anyone else.

**Time:** About 10 minutes

## Activate Prior Knowledge

"Think about a sculpture you have seen. Did it have open areas around and between its forms?" "Piensen acerca de una escultura que hayan visto. ¿Tenía áreas abiertas alrededor de y entre sus formas?"

- Discuss students' answers and how open areas in sculptures help create forms.

**Using Literature** ⭐ Reading

- Have students look at the illustrations of the garden sculptures in *The Secret Garden* by Frances Hodgson Burnett. Have them describe how they think the sculptures were created.

**Thematic Connection** ⭐ Science

- **Animals:** Discuss the differences between wild and domestic animals. For example, a jaguar is a wild animal, while domestic cats are usually smaller and tamed.

## Introduce the Art

# Look

"Let's take a close look at the two works of art." "Vamos a observar detalladamente las dos obras de arte."

**Animals** ⭐ Science

- How did the artists show the unique characteristics of these animals? *Jaguar:* The artist focused on the claws and the jaw of the animal to portray its strength and power. *Egyptian Cat:* The smooth, slender features of this cat are part of the basic form, with the only details being the carved lines of the facial features. The front limbs and ears are the only features that stand out, due to the space between them.

 **Art History and Culture**

Cats were valued in both cultures. Egyptians had laws protecting their cats. The jaguar represented an important figure in Aztec culture.

🖥 **Web Connection**

Visit **www.nmai.si.edu/exhibits/ancient/** to learn more about ancient Mexican art.

---

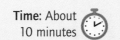 **Lesson 3** Subtractive Sculpture

▲ **Artist unknown.** (Aztec/Mexico). *Jaguar.* c. 1440–1521.
Stone. $4\frac{15}{16} \times 5\frac{11}{16} \times 11\frac{1}{16}$ inches (12.5 × 14.5 × 28 cm). The Brooklyn Museum, New York, New York.

**Look** at the artwork on these pages. Both forms are simple and have no additive detail. The Aztec jaguar was carved from stone more than 400 years ago. *Egyptian Cat* was made between 950 and 300 B.C. Notice that although both pieces are carved cat sculptures, they look very different.

 **Art History and Culture**

Do you think cats were important animals in the Egyptian and Aztec cultures? Explain.

---

 **Art History and Culture**

## Aztec Culture

*Jaguar* was carved by an Aztec artist sometime during the fifteenth or sixteenth century. The Aztecs lived during the fifteenth and early sixteenth centuries and ruled a large empire in what is now central and southern Mexico. The Aztec capital was Tenochtitlán. Elaborate systems of agriculture and irrigation are among the remarkable accomplishments of the Aztec empire. The appearance of Spanish explorers in 1519 halted the expansion and progress of the Aztec empire. The Jaguar represented Tezcatlipoca, who was the god of night and a major figure in Aztec history.

See pages 24–25 and 16–21 for more about art history and the subject matter.

**Artist Profiles, p. 79**

◇ Artist Profile ◇

**Jaguar**

The Aztecs believed in supernatural forces. Their artists were in charge of creating the mythical and religious images used in rituals and daily life. The artists held some power because it was believed that they could materialize gods and spirits in stone. Judging from the style of this jaguar, it was likely carved in a major city by an Aztec carver who worked in a workshop of carvers.

**Study** both works of art to find similarities and differences in the forms.

► What kinds of forms did the artists use?

► What are some similarities and differences in these sculptures?

► Which sculpture has open areas? How does this affect its look?

◄ **Artist unknown.** (Egypt). *Egyptian Cat.* Late Dynasty.

Bronze. 4¾ × 3 inches (12 × 7.6 cm.). The Metropolitan Museum of Art, New York, New York.

 **Aesthetic Perception**

**Seeing Like an Artist** What is your favorite animal? Think about all the qualities that make that animal unique.

## Art History and Culture

### Egyptian Culture

The ancient Egyptians produced amazing architectural monuments, sculptures, and paintings. The Egyptians achieved a high stage of civilization long before most other cultures. Today travelers visit Egypt to view the many monuments that represent the achievements of ancient Egyptians. Cats were considered members of the Egyptian household thousands of years ago. The Egyptians had laws to protect their cats, which were used by Egyptians to hunt fish and mice.

See pages 24–25 and 16–21 for more about art history and the subject matter.

**Artist Profiles, p. 77**

**Artist Profile**

**Egyptian Cat**
Ancient Egypt was ruled by pharaohs, and every pharaoh had hundreds of servants. Many artists in Egypt were servants of the pharaohs. This cat sculpture probably was made by one of these royal artisans.

◄ **Artist unknown.** (Egypt). *Egyptian Cat.* Late Dynasty.

## Study

► Both sculptures are made of simple rounded forms.

► Similarities: Both *Jaguar* and *Egyptian Cat* are sculptures representing cats made without additive details. Differences: *Jaguar* is carved from a hard, dense stone, and it appears to be heavier and more solid than *Egyptian Cat. Egyptian Cat* is a bronze cast and appears to be lighter and sleeker than *Jaguar.* NSAE 4.a; 4.c

► *Egyptian Cat* has open areas between the ears and front legs, making it seem much lighter and more graceful than the compact density of *Jaguar.*

■ For more examples of art from Africa, see the **Art Around the World Collection.**

**Art Journal: Writing**
Encourage students to define and illustrate subtractive sculpture in the Concepts section of their Art Journals. What else do they want to know about subtractive sculpture?

**Aesthetic Perception**

**Seeing Like an Artist** Discuss characteristics that make an animal unique. These could include features such as size, facial features, and the pace at which it moves.

**Developing Visual Literacy** Discuss what each artwork conveys. What meaning was each artist trying to convey? Invite students to share any personal experiences that contribute to their understanding of the artwork. For example, have students seen different types of cats at a zoo?

**Web Connection**
Visit www.metmuseum.org/collections/ to learn more about Egyptian art.

 each

**Time:** About 45 minutes

"Can you use positive and negative space to create a sculpture?" "¿Pueden usar espacio positivo y negativo para crear una escultura?"

- Read and discuss positive and negative space on page 136.

### Practice

**Materials:** white drawing paper, pencils, erasers

**Alternate Materials:** white construction or copier paper

- Distribute the materials and have students follow the directions on page 136.

### Creative Expression

**Materials:** plaster; mixing bowl; water; clean milk cartons; carving tools, such as plastic utensils, butter knives, spoons; forks for textures; paper clips for details

**Alternate Materials:** clay carving tools, clay

- Distribute the materials and have students follow the directions on page 137.
- Review the Activity Tips on page 238 for visual examples of techniques if needed.

### Art Journal: Brainstorming

Have students brainstorm ideas for animals in the Ideas section of their Art Journals. Then have students create a sketch of the animal they will carve in the Creative Expression activity.

---

# Using Positive and Negative Space

Artists can change a form by carving. When an artist carves pieces away from a form, it is called a **subtractive sculpture.** This is because part of the original material is being taken away, or subtracted.

A figure, shape, or object is the positive space. It takes up room and is usually the first thing we notice when looking at a work of art.

Some forms are created so that we can move around them and see them from all sides. The area around, under, above, and between an object is the negative space. It is the area, or air, around the object.

 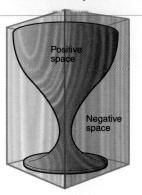

Positive space

Negative space

### Practice

Experiment with using positive and negative space in a sculpture design. Use pencil.

1. Draw a square or rectangle. Using the side of the pencil point, color the shape evenly. Do not bear down with the point.

2. Think of a design you would like to create. Using an eraser, carefully subtract the negative spaces and watch your sculpture design appear.

**136**    Unit 4 • Lesson 3

---

### Differentiated Instruction

**Reteach**

Give each student an egg-sized piece of modeling clay or another type of clay that is easy to manipulate. Ask students to form a cube by shaping and turning the clay to create six surfaces. Using the point of a pencil, show students how a house can be carved out of the cube.

**Special Needs**

Some students may work best with tools that fit in the palm of the hand, such as steel wool or sandpaper. If students have difficulty holding tools with thin handles, the surface area of the handle can be built up using tape and foam rubber.

**ELL**

Students may hesitate to discuss the abstract concepts involved in this lesson. Make the language concrete for them by pantomiming meanings that describe characteristics. Then, write the appropriate word on the board under a sketch of an animal that exhibits that characteristic.

◄ **Nadia Panskey.**
Age 9.

**Think** about how the student artist created the subtractive sculpture.

### Creative Expression

Design a simple animal or free-form sculpture from plaster.

1. Sketch a simple animal form, such as a fish, or a free-form form. Use at least one curve in the design.

2. Tear the cup off the plaster your teacher prepared. Use a pencil to draw your design into the plaster. Draw on all sides.

3. Use a spoon to scrape away the plaster surrounding your design. The design will slowly appear as you carve.

4. Use a paperclip to carve out small areas. Add texture and details. Turn your sculpture as you carve. When you finish carving, lightly sand the areas you want smooth.

### Art Criticism

**Describe** Describe the animal you created.

**Analyze** What kind of form did you carve? Did you include negative space?

**Interpret** Give your sculpture a title that includes two expressive adjectives.

**Decide** Were you successful in creating a three-dimensional form that is interesting from all points of view?

# Reflect
Time: About 5 minutes

## Review and Assess

"Let's review what we have learned about subtractive sculpture." "Vamos a repasar lo que aprendimos sobre la escultura sustractiva."

## Think

The artists used carving tools to remove some of the plaster surface.

■ Use **Large Print 55** *Floating City* to have students identify how artists create subtractive sculpture.

## Informal Assessment

■ For standardized-format test practice using this lesson's art content, see pages 46–47 in **Reading and Writing Test Preparation.**

### Art Journal: Critical Thinking

Have students answer the four art criticism questions—Describe, Analyze, Interpret, and Decide—in their Art Journals. In small groups, have students discuss the different animals modeled in their subtractive sculptures in the Creative Expression activity.

## Art Across the Curriculum

Use these simple ideas to reinforce art concepts across the curriculum.

★ **Poetry Writing** Have students write poems about cats or another animal.

★ **Math** Review multidigit subtraction.

★ **Science** Use both sculptures to discuss characteristics of the cat family. Give examples of the different members of the cat family, such as jaguars, tigers, lions, and leopards.

★ **Social Studies** Use both pieces of ancient art to talk about how archaeologists use findings such as these to learn about the lives of ancient people.

★ **Technology** students use a draw or paint program to create a drawing of the animal they carved in the Creative Expression activity. Visit **SRAonline.com** to print detailed instructions for this activity.
NSAE 6.b

**Lesson 3 Wrap-Up**

# Subtractive Sculpture

## Extra! For the Art Specialist

**Time:** About 45 minutes

### Focus

Study *Large Print 55* *Floating City* and discuss with students various techniques used in subtractive sculpture. Ask students if this could be considered an example of subtractive sculpture.

### Teach

Prepare cups or containers of plaster prior to the lesson. As a class, select a theme, such as the zoo or the ocean. Explain to students that they will carve simple shapes based on the class theme. Demonstrate drawing on all sides and carving into the plaster with a spoon as an introduction to this lesson. Have the students complete the alternate activity.

### Reflect

Have students use the four steps of art criticism to evaluate their work. Have them explain how their sculptures fit the class theme.

### Alternate Activity

**Materials:**
- sketchbook
- pencils, erasers
- collected images
- modeling plaster
- plastic bowl or bucket, cold water
- mixing stick
- paper cup or container
- assorted carving tools
- newspapers
- paper towels

1. Have students select an image and sketch a simple animal form such as a fish or reptile. The design should be simple.

2. Have students tear the mold from the plaster form. Have them use a pencil to draw their sketches into the plaster.

3. Students should use a spoon to scrape away the plaster surrounding the design. They can use a nail or a paper clip to carve out small areas or add texture and details. When students finish carving, they should sand lightly the areas they want smooth.

4. Create a class display. Have students document interesting facts about the species they carved.

## Research in Art Education

"Talk about art, or art criticism, is probably one of the ways we share the contents of our inner lives without embarrassment. Art criticism is very much like teaching: it is the sharing of discoveries about art, or in some cases about life, where art has its ultimate source." (Hurwitz, Al, and Stanley Madeja. *The Joyous Vision.* New Jersey: Prentice Hall, 1997.)

## Assessment
Use the following rubric to evaluate the artwork students make in the Creative Expression activity and to assess students' understanding of subtractive sculpture.

Have students complete page 49 or 50 in their *Assessment* books.

| | Art History and Culture | Aesthetic Perception | Creative Expression | Art Criticism |
|---|---|---|---|---|
| **3 POINTS** | The student demonstrates knowledge of Egyptian and Aztec cultures. | The student can explain how subtractive sculptures are created. | The student's sculpture is clearly a subtractive sculpture. | The student thoughtfully and honestly evaluates own work using the four steps of art criticism. |
| **2 POINTS** | The student shows some knowledge of Egyptian and Aztec cultures. | The student shows emerging awareness of how subtractive sculptures are created. | The student's sculpture shows some attempt to create a subtractive sculpture. | The student attempts to evaluate own work but shows an incomplete understanding of evaluation criteria. |
| **1 POINT** | The student cannot demonstrate knowledge of Egyptian or Aztec cultures. | The student cannot explain how subtractive sculptures are created. | The student's sculpture is not a subtractive sculpture. | The student makes no attempt to evaluate own work. |

### Assessment, p. 49

Name _____ Date _____

**Lesson 3 UNIT 4**

**Subtractive Sculpture**

**A. Short Answer**
Write the answer to the question.
What type of sculpture is created when an artist carves away from a form?
_____

**B. Coloring**
Use crayons or markers to draw a shape in each of the two boxes below. Color in only the positive space in the first box, and color in only the negative space in the second box.

|  |  |
|---|---|
| positive space | negative space |

**C. Writing**
Look at the sculptures *Aztec Jaguar* and *Egyptian Cat*. Write a paragraph describing the positive and negative spaces you see.

Level 4                    Unit 4 • Form, Texture, and Emphasis  **49**

# Visual Texture

**Lesson 4** introduces visual texture. Visual texture creates the illusion of texture in a work of art to show how something feels.

## Objectives

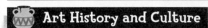 **Art History and Culture**

To demonstrate knowledge of the lives and art of Romare Bearden and Lee Krasner

 **Creative Expression**

To use visual textures in magazine photos to create a picture that tells a story

 **Aesthetic Perception**

To define and identify visual texture

**Art Criticism**

To evaluate own work using the four steps of art criticism

## Lesson Materials

- old magazines
- scissors
- large white paper
- pencils, colored pencils,
- glue

**Alternate Materials:**
- construction paper
- crayons

## Program Resources

- *Reading and Writing Test Prep.*, pp. 48–49
- *Transparency 22*
- *Flash Cards* 18–19
- *Artist Profiles*, pp. 6, 38
- *Animals Through History Time Line*
- *Assessment*, pp. 51–52
- *Large Print 55* Floating City

---

**Concept Trace**

Visual Texture

**Introduced:** Level 3, Unit 5, Lesson 3

**Reinforced:** Level 5, Unit 5, Lesson 1

---

## Vocabulary ⭐ Vocabulary

Review the following vocabulary words with students before beginning the lesson.

**invented texture** *textura inventada*—visual texture in which an artist uses lines or other elements to create a textural look without any specific texture in mind

**simulated texture** *textura simulada*—visual texture in which the texture created imitates the look of a real texture

See page 149B for additional vocabulary and Spanish vocabulary resources.

 **Art Journal: Vocabulary**

Have students add these words to the Vocabulary section of their Art Journals.

---

# Lesson 4 Arts Integration

## Theatre

Complete Unit 4, Lesson 4, on pages 78–79 of the *Theatre Arts Connections.*

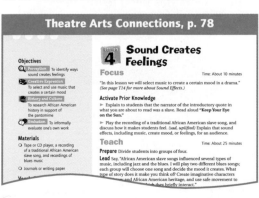

## Music

Texture in music describes whether one melody is alone or with other contrasting melodies (polyphony), or with harmonic accompaniment. Listen to "The Moldau" by Bedrich Smetana. The Moldau is a river in his native Czechoslovakia. The piece starts with a small flow of melody from two flutes depicting two streams coming out of the mountains. Have students listen for how the texture changes as it continues and instruments are added.

## Movement & Dance

Discuss objects that have hard or soft textural images and create words to describe them, for example, smooth silk, crashing waves, rolling hills, and feathery pillows. Have students explore each of these ideas in movement with a partner. Then working together, have them select three and organize them into a sequence, ending with a held position.

# Focus

Time: About 10 minutes

## Activate Prior Knowledge

"Can you describe how the textures of objects around you look, how they might feel, and how they actually feel?" "¿Pueden describir cómo son las texturas de los objetos a tu alrededor, cómo se sentirían y cómo se sienten de verdad?"

■ Discuss the answers given by students. List the objects they name on the chalkboard.

### Using Literature  Reading

■ Have students read *Slinky Scaly Slithery Snakes* by Dorothy Hinshaw Patent. Have students describe the textures that they see.

### Thematic Connection  Science

■ **Cooperation and Competition:** Discuss with students how artists sometimes create works in which the materials cooperate to create a smooth texture or compete to create a rough texture.

## Introduce the Art

# Look

"Let's take a close look at the two works of art." "Vamos a observar detalladamente las dos obras de arte."

### Compare and Contrast  Reading

■ Have students list similarities and differences in the collages. Differences: Bearden used blue, purple, green, and white. Krasner used black, yellow, and green. Bearden: Invented texture. Krasner: Simulated texture. Bearden: Collage acrylic on board. Krasner: Oil and collage on canvas. Similarities: Both are smooth and matte textures.

 **Art History and Culture**

Discuss student responses. Some modern American artists who create collages are: Jaune Quick-to-See Smith, Robert Rauschernberg, and Miriam Schapiro.

 **Web Connection**

Visit **www.artic.edu/artaccess/AA_AfAm/** to view works of art by African Americans.

---

# Visual Texture

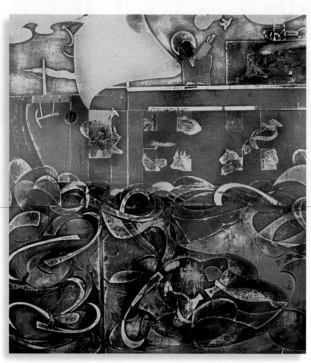

▲ **Romare Bearden.** (American).
*Noah, Third Day.* 1972.
. . . . . . . . . . . . . . . . . . . . . . . . . . .
Collage, acrylic on board. 40½ × 35½ inches (102.87 × 90.17 cm.). High Museum of Art, Atlanta, Georgia.

**Look** at the works of art on these pages. Romare Bearden is best known for his collages made from pieces of old photographs, scraps of paper, and painted paper. During the 1950s Krasner began cutting apart her works and recombining them into collages. Notice the texture of the collages.

 **Art History and Culture**

Both collages were created by modern American artists. Can you name any other modern American artists?

 **Art History and Culture**

## Romare Bearden

Romare Bearden (rō mâr bēr´ dən) (1911–1988) was an African American painter and collage maker who incorporated subject matter derived from the life of African Americans into many of his works. Bearden often incorporated images of the rural South, Harlem, and St. Maarten into his work. Bearden was an influential artist in America. During the 1960s he was a member of a group of artists called the Spiral Group, who were concerned with the struggle for social equality. Bearden's work has been featured in many important publications and on the covers of *Fortune, Time,* and *The New York Times* magazines.

See pages 24–25 and 16–21 for more about art history and the subject matter.

**Artist Profiles, p. 6**

Artist Profile ●
**Romare Bearden**
1911–1988
Romare Bearden (rō mar´ bēr dən) was born in North Carolina. His family moved to Harlem in New York City when he was three years old. His family's home became a meeting place for artists, writers, and musicians during the Harlem Renaissance. Bearden studied math, not the arts, in college, but he worked as a cartoonist and illustrator to pay for it. When he was 21, he decided to become a professional artist. Over the years, Bearden studied art in New York City and Paris, France. He also worked as a social worker, served in the army, and wrote several songs and books. Bearden was known as a warmhearted, friendly man.

▲ **Lee Krasner.** (American).
*Milkweed.* 1955.
·······························
Oil and collage on canvas. 85⅜ × 57¾
inches (216.87 × 146.67 cm.). Albright
Knox Art Gallery, Buffalo, New York.

**Study** both works of
art for visual texture.

▶ Does the texture of
each collage appear
to be real, as in a
photograph, or
created to imitate
texture?

▶ Select two categories
of texture that fit each
collage, for example,
rough or smooth, and
shiny or matte.

▶ How could the artists
have created different
textures? If the
artwork is rough, how
could the artist have
made it smooth? If it
is smooth, how could
the artist have made
it rough?

## Aesthetic Perception

**Design Awareness** Use examples to illustrate the difference
between real and visual texture.

## Study

▶ *Noah, Third Day:* It appears to imitate
texture. It looks like the artist used lines
and other elements to create a textured
look. It is invented texture. *Milkweed:* The
texture appears to be real as in a
photograph. It is simulated texture.

▶ Both are smooth and matte.

▶ The artists could have added materials to
the surface of the work to make it rough or
omitted materials from the surface to
make it smooth.

■ For more examples of abstract and
nonobjective art, see *The National
Museum of Women in the Arts Collection.*

### Art Journal: Writing

Encourage students to define visual
texture in the Concepts section of their Art
Journals. What else do they want to know
about visual texture?

## Aesthetic Perception

**Design Awareness** Real texture is the opposite
of visual texture. With real texture you can tell
what the object feels like (for example, rough
or smooth) by touching it. You can feel the
texture of the fabric your clothes are made of.
Visual texture appears in a picture. With
visual texture you can look at the picture and
imagine what the texture feels like.

**Developing Visual Literacy** Have students
speculate on what meaning each image
conveys. Invite students to use clues such as
the title of the work or similar works they have
seen to determine the messages of the collages.

## Art History and Culture

### Lee Krasner

Lee Krasner (lē krazˊnər) (1908–1984) was born Lenore Krassner in
Brooklyn New York. Krasner was married to Jackson Pollock, a well-
known artist, for eleven years. Many believe her work was often
undervalued because she was known as Pollock's wife and because
of sexist biases. Krasner first exhibited her paintings during the
1940s. During the 1950s she began to cut pieces from her existing
paintings and glue the pieces of canvas and paper onto raw canvas
to create collage paintings. *Milkweed* was created during this
period. In the 1960s and
1970s, Krasner finally
received recognition for her
work.

See pages 24–25 and 16–21
for more about art history
and the subject matter.

**Artist Profiles, p. 38**

◆ Artist Profile ◆
**Lee Krasner**
1908-1984
Lee Krasner (lē krazˊnər) was a major
figure in the first generation of American
artists. She developed a new style of
abstract painting in the late 1940s and
early 1950s. As the wife of Jackson Pollock,
the acknowledged leader of abstract
expressionism, Krasner participated
in the style's evolution. She was known
for bringing color back into the all-over
technique that she and Pollock shared.
During much of her lifetime Krasner's
reputation was obscured by her
husband's accomplishments.

### Web Connection
Visit **naples.cc.sunysb.edu/CAS/pkhouse.nsf** to
learn more about the life and art of Lee Krasner.

# Teach

Time: About 45 minutes

"Can you identify simulated and invented texture?" "¿Pueden identificar texturas simuladas e inventadas?"

- Read and discuss visual texture on page 140.

## Practice

**Materials:** old magazines, scissors, pencil, paper

- Distribute the materials and have students follow the directions on page 140.

- Give students examples of a rough visual texture, such as pictures of a cake, tree bark, and grass.

## Creative Expression

**Materials:** pencils, colored pencils, large sheets of white paper, glue, old magazines, scissors

**Alternate Materials:** construction paper, crayons

- Distribute the materials and have students follow the directions on page 141.

- Have students integrate a variety of ideas about life events and family into their visual texture pictures, if possible.
NSAE 3.a; 3.b

- Challenge students to invent ways to explore photographic imagery in their work using a variety of art media and materials.
NSAE 1.c; 1.d

- Review the Activity Tips on page 238 for visual examples of techniques if needed.

### Art Journal: Brainstorming

Have students brainstorm story ideas in the Ideas section of their Art Journals. Then have students plan how they will use pictures to tell their stories in the Creative Expression activity.

## Using Visual Texture

Visual texture can be created in two ways. **Simulated texture** is texture that imitates the look of real texture. Artwork that incorporates simulated texture looks realistic. **Invented texture** is created when the artist uses lines or other elements to make a textural look without any specific texture in mind.

The four kinds of visual texture are **rough,** **smooth,** **shiny,** and **matte.** Textures can be divided into two sets: rough or smooth and shiny or matte. They also can be combined as:

Rough and shiny

Rough and matte

Smooth and shiny

Smooth and matte

## Practice

Look for pictures in magazines that illustrate the four kinds of visual texture.

1. Cut pictures from magazines that show visual texture.

2. Divide the pictures into four categories: rough and shiny, rough and matte, smooth and shiny, and smooth and matte.

3. Label each category.

## Differentiated Instruction

**Reteach**
Have the students look through their textbooks for examples of visual textures. Students should note whether the textures are smooth or rough.

**Special Needs**
If students have difficulty beginning this activity, direct them to Bearden's or Krasner's artwork and ask them to describe what is happening and the mood of the work. Then have them identify textures that helped to create that mood.

**ELL**
To help students, you might simplify the definitions of invented and simulated texture offered in the text. Explore the room, looking for examples of simulated textures and offer examples of invented textures as well. Check for students' understanding before moving to individual work.

◀ **Caroline Flynn.**
Age 8.

**Think** about how the student artist created visual texture in the artwork.

 **Creative Expression**

How could you use visual textures from magazines to create a picture that tells a story?

1. Decide on your illustration, and make some sketches.

2. What kinds of things do the textures you collected remind you of? Study them. What can you use them for in your picture? Draw the shapes for your picture on the images and cut them out of the magazine.

3. Arrange the visual texture shapes on your paper and glue them down. Draw the rest of your scene to fill the entire page and color it with color pencils.

**? Art Criticism**

**Describe** Describe the story you told.

**Analyze** What kinds of visual texture did you use?

**Interpret** How do the visual textures that you used affect the look of your work?

**Decide** Were you able to use visual textures you found to make new shapes successfully?

 **Reflect** Time: About 5 minutes

**Review and Assess**

"Let's review what we have learned about visual texture." "Vamos a revisar lo que hemos aprendido acerca de la textura visual."

## Think

The artist used various pictures from magazines that look like they have textures. Then she cut the pictures into shapes that represented the objects in her picture.

■ Use **Large Prints 55** *Floating City* and **56** *Wrapped Reichstag Building* to have students identify visual textures.

## Informal Assessment

■ Have students create portfolios of their artwork. Have students exchange their portfolios to interpret ideas and moods in original artwork by their peers.
NSAE 5.a; 5.b

■ For standardized-format test practice using this lesson's art content, see pages 48–49 in *Reading and Writing Test Preparation.*

**Art Journal: Critical Thinking**
Have students answer the four art criticism questions—Describe, Analyze, Interpret, and Decide—in their Art Journals. In small groups, have students discuss the use of visual texture in their Creative Expression activity.

**◉ Art Across the Curriculum ◉**

Use these simple ideas to reinforce art concepts across the curriculum.

★ **Persuasive Writing** Have students create visual texture in advertisements by combining words and pictures.

★ **Math** Discuss organizing data as it relates to math (graphing) and art. Note that an artist creating a collage may organize the materials to reflect a theme in the collage.

★ **Science** Have students make a list of objects found in nature and discuss the texture of the objects on the list.

★ **Social Studies** Discuss what life was like in the rural South for African Americans, a theme reflected in works by Romare Bearden.

★ **Technology** Have students use the pattern feature in a word processing program to create visual texture on a page. Visit **SRAonline.com** to print detailed instructions for this activity.
NSAE 6.b

## Lesson 4 Wrap-Up

# Visual Texture

**Time:** About 45 minutes

## Focus

Study **Large Print 56** *Wrapped Reichstag Building* and discuss how artists use a variety of textures in both two- and three-dimensional works of art. Have students explain the difference between visual and tactile textures.

## Teach

Discuss how artists use texture to create interest and to appeal to our sense of touch. Explain to the students that they will use pencils to create an animal drawing that imitates different textures. Then have the students complete the alternate activity.

## Reflect

Have students use the four steps of art criticism to evaluate their work. Have them describe how they created visual texture in their drawings.

### Alternate Activity

**Materials:**
- sketchbook
- pencils, erasers
- 9" × 12" or larger white drawing paper
- qraphite pencil or a Number 2 pencil
- magazine images and books on animals

1. Have students select an image of an animal. Have them practice drawing or imitating the textures needed for their animal. Students should create several sketches of their animal.

2. Students should use pencil to draw the sketch they like best. Have them sketch a background with minimal detail.

3. Have students imitate the animal textures, using a graphite pencil. Have them use hatching, gradation, and stippling in the drawing. Have students use a wide range of values from very light to almost dark.

4. Students may choose to leave the background without color in order to focus on the animal.

## Research in Art Education

Research has shown that "the correlation in the United States between choosing to study the arts and achieving well academically is not a function of SES [socioeconomic status]." Although there may still be questions about the relationship between the arts and academic achievement, it is important that we provide opportunities for students of all SES levels to learn about the arts ("Involvement in the Arts and Human Development: Extending an Analysis of General Associations and Introducing the Special Cases of Intensive Involvement in Music and Theatre Arts" in *Critical Links*, p. 70).

## Assessment

Use the following rubric to evaluate the artwork students make in the Creative Expression activity and to assess students' understanding of visual texture.

Have students complete page 51 or 52 in their **Assessment** books.

| | Art History and Culture | Aesthetic Perception | Creative Expression | Art Criticism |
|---|---|---|---|---|
| **3 POINTS** | The student demonstrates knowledge of the lives and art of both artists. | The student accurately defines and identifies visual texture in a work of art. | The student's picture clearly shows visual textures. | The student thoughtfully and honestly evaluates own work using the four steps of art criticism. |
| **2 POINTS** | The student shows some knowledge of the lives and art of both artists. | The student shows emerging awareness of visual texture but cannot consistently identify it. | The student's picture shows some attempt to create visual textures. | The student attempts to evaluate own work but shows an incomplete understanding of evaluation criteria. |
| **1 POINT** | The student demonstrates no knowledge of the lives and art of either artist. | The student cannot define or identify visual texture in a work of art. | The student's picture does not show visual textures. | The student makes no attempt to evaluate own work. |

### Assessment, p. 51

Name _____ Date _____

**Lesson 4 UNIT 4**

**Visual Texture**

**A. Short Answer**
Write the answers below.
What are two ways of creating visual texture?
1. _____
2. _____

What are the four kinds of visual texture?
1. _____
2. _____
3. _____
4. _____

The four kinds of visual texture can be combined as:
1. _____
2. _____
3. _____
4. _____

**B. Writing**
Look closely at *Noah, Third Day* by Romare Bearden and *Milkweed* by Lee Krasner. Compare the ways both artists used visual texture in their works of art.

_____

Level 4                    Unit 4 • Form, Texture, and Emphasis   **51**

# Tactile Texture

**Lesson 5** introduces tactile texture. **Tactile texture** is an element of art that refers to how something feels.

## Objectives

 **Art History and Culture**

To demonstrate knowledge of the lives and art of Chryssa and Sandy Skoglund

 **Creative Expression**

To create a tactile-texture weaving

**Aesthetic Perception**

To identify tactile texture in a work of art and the environment

**Art Criticism**

To evaluate own work using the four steps of art criticism

## Lesson Materials
- paper, pencils
- glue
- found materials
- cardboard
- acrylic paint

**Alternate Materials:**
- vinyl tile
- felt-tip pens

## Program Resources
- *Reading and Writing Test Prep.,* pp. 50–51
- *Transparency 23*
- *Artist Profiles,* pp. 13, 63
- *Animals Through History Time Line*
- *Assessment,* pp. 53–54
- *Large Prints 55* Floating City and *56* Wrapped Reichstag Building
- *The National Museum of Women in the Arts Collection*

### Concept Trace
Tactile Texture
**Introduced:** Level 3, Unit 5, Lesson 2

**Reinforced:** Level 5, Unit 5, Lesson 1

## Vocabulary  Vocabulary

Review the following vocabulary word with students before beginning the lesson.

**tactile texture** textura táctil—how something actually feels on the surface

See page 149B for additional vocabulary and Spanish vocabulary resources.

### Art Journal: Vocabulary

Have students add this word to the Vocabulary section of their Art Journals.

## Lesson 5 Arts Integration

### Theatre

Complete Unit 4, Lesson 5, on pages 80–81 of *Theatre Arts Connections.*

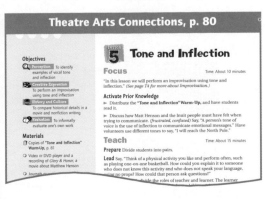

### Music

Have students listen to "Variations on Simple Gifts" from *Appalachian Spring* by Aaron Copeland. Copeland created the ballet *Appalachian Spring* for the dancer Martha Graham in 1944. His textures are open and transparent. One of the ways he created this open sound was grouping few instruments together, sometimes very high instruments with low pitched instruments.

### Movement & Dance

Place six natural objects of different textures in a bag. Have groups explore the objects through touch. Have them think of words to describe each of the objects. Have students explore moving like descriptive words associated with each object for eight counts. Have each group select three ideas and create a short sequence with a clear beginning, middle, and ending.

 **ocus**

Time: About 10 minutes

## Activate Prior Knowledge

"Use one word to describe some of the tactile textures you come across every day." "Usa una palabra para describir algunas de las texturas táctiles que se encuentran todos los días."

■ Discuss the answers given by the students and list on the board the words used to describe the tactile textures. (rough, smooth)

**Using Literature** ⭐ Reading

■ Look at the scanned images in *Casey at the Bat* by Ernest Lawrence Thayer, illustrated by Christopher Bing. Have students describe how the images might feel if touched.

■ **Look Again:** Discuss the importance of closely examining the artwork several times to find visual clues that explain the message in the artwork.

## Introduce the Art

## Look

"Let's take a close look at the two works of art." "Vamos a observar detalladamente las dos obras de arte."

**Fact and Opinion** ⭐ Reading

■ Have students use both works of art to differentiate between fact and opinion. For example, it is a fact that *Americanoom* is a relief sculpture; it is an opinion that the metal markings on the sculpture are beautiful.

 **Art History and Culture**

Answers will vary and may include amateur and professional artists. Make sure students' answers are reasonable.

💻 **Web Connection**

Visit www.sandyskoglund.com/ to view works of art by this artist. Note that site is for teacher use only.

**142** UNIT 4 • Form, Texture, and Emphasis

---

  # Tactile Texture

▲ **Sandy Skoglund.** (American). *The Cocktail Party.* 1992.
..................................
Cibachrome print. 48 × 65 inches (121.92 × 165.1 cm.). Private collection.

**Look** at the works of art on these pages. Skoglund used hot-glue guns to attach puffed cheese to mannequins and furniture. She also dressed live models in clothes covered with puffed cheese. Chryssa used steel forms and neon tubing to represent letters in her relief sculpture. The signs in New York City's Times Square inspired her to create sculptures that use letters.

 **Art History and Culture**

Skoglund's installation includes live models. Chryssa experimented with light. Do you know of any other artists who use unique media?

**142** Unit 4 • Lesson 5

---

🏺 **Art History and Culture**

### Sandy Skoglund

Sandy Skoglund (san´ dē skōg lund´) (1946– ) is a sculptor and a photographer. Skoglund builds installations that are made of sculpted forms, everyday objects, and people. She first creates the sculpted forms, then assembles the installation, and then she photographs her creation. When she is finished, she sells pieces of her work, such as the sculptures. Photographs of her installations have been included in many exhibitions. Human interaction in the natural world is a recurring theme in Skoglund's work.

See pages 24–25 and 16–21 for more about art history and the subject matter.

**Artist Profiles, p. 63**

*Artist Profile*
**Sandy Skoglund**
b. 1946

Sandy Skoglund (san´ dē skōg lund´) spent the first part of her childhood near Boston and then moved around the United States with her family. She had polio when she was young, and the time she spent indoors cultivated her passion for drawing. Her drawings often depicted fantasy lands and environments. These early imaginations have filtered into her work today with installations that create entirely new environments with fantastic elements, such as walls of jam and floors of eggshells. Skoglund has been an undergraduate professor at Rutgers University and credits her students with keeping her in touch with the world outside the New York art scene.

Study both works of art to find the tactile textures.

▶ Describe the materials used to create both sculptures.

▶ Locate a rough-textured surface in each artwork.

▶ Locate a smooth-textured surface in both works of art.

▲ **Chryssa.** (Greek).
***Americanoom.*** 1963.

Aluminum, welded steel, stainless
steel, and neon. 90 × 108 inches
(228.6 × 274.32 cm.).
Lowe Art Museum, University of
Miami, Coral Gables, Florida.

### Aesthetic Perception

**Design Awareness** Think about decisions you make every day,
such as what to eat and what to wear. How does texture affect
how you make these decisions?

### Art History and Culture

#### Chryssa

Chryssa (kris´ ə) (1933– ) is a Greek-born American sculptor. She
was born Chryssa Vardea, the youngest of three children, in Athens,
Greece. She moved to the United States during the early 1950s. Her
fascination with the flashing signs and brilliant nighttime sky of
Times Square led her to work creatively with neon lights while
producing sculptures. *Americanoom* is a product of her efforts in
working with neon lights. Chryssa often includes metal letters and
symbols in her sculptures. She has been known to use newspapers
also when creating
sculptures.

See pages 24–25 and 16–21
for more about art history
and the subject matter.

**Artist Profiles, p. 13**

◆ Artist Profile ◆

**Chryssa**
b. 1933

Born and educated in Greece, Chryssa
(kris´ ə) first studied social work but
redirected her career path, because she felt
that many relief funds ignored people in
need. She studied in Athens, Paris, and
California, and began her artistic career as
a sculptor in New York during the 1950s. Her
exploration of neon light and commercial
signs was a new combination of materials to
the art scene and opened up many avenues
for her public installations. Chryssa does
her own metalwork and the physical labor
required by her art. She is regarded as highly
motivating by her coworkers.

## Study

▶ Skoglund: Puffed cheese, people,
mannequins, humans. Chryssa: Metal and
neon lights.

▶ Skoglund: The entire installation has a
rough texture. Chryssa: The relief
sculpture is rough except for the lower
right panel.

▶ The lower right panel has a smooth texture.

■ For more examples of abstract and
nonobjective art, see *The National
Museum of Women in the Arts Collection.*

### Art Journal: Writing

Encourage students to define tactile
texture in the Concepts section of their Art
Journals. What else do they want to know
about tactile texture?

### Aesthetic Perception

**Design Awareness** Discuss decisions that may
require us to consider texture. For example,
would students rather wear a shirt that is
made from a smooth-textured material such
as silk or a rough-textured material such
as tweed?

**Developing Visual Literacy** Discuss the media
used to create the sculptures. Have students
suggest a list of alternate materials the artists
could have used to create their sculptures.
How would the sculptures be different if the
artists had used the suggested materials?

### Web Connection

Browse the Decorative Arts & Sculpture section of
**www.clevelandart.org/Explore/** to view different
types of sculptures.

# Teach

**Time:** About 45 minutes

"How can you collect and make tactile textures?" "¿Cómo pueden reunir y hacer texturas táctiles?"

- Read and discuss tactile texture on page 144.

## Practice

**Materials:** paper, glue, classroom materials such as pencil sharpener shavings and bits of paper

- Distribute the materials and have students follow the directions on page 144.

## Creative Expression

**Materials:** cardboard, found materials, pencils, acrylic paint, glue

**Alternate Materials:** vinyl tile, felt-tip pens

- Distribute the materials and have students follow the directions on page 145.

- Review the Activity Tips on page 239 for visual examples of techniques if needed.

### Art Journal: Brainstorming

Have students brainstorm a list of materials they could use to create their tactile-texture compositions in the Ideas section of their Art Journals. Then have students plan the designs of their tactile-texture compositions.

---

# Using Tactile Texture

**Tactile texture** is an element of art that refers to how things feel. Texture is perceived by touch and sight. The two basic categories of tactile textures are rough and smooth. Many adjectives describe the different variations of rough and smooth surfaces, such as *velvety, fluffy, slick,* or *bumpy.*

The textures of objects reflect light differently. The way a surface looks depends on how it reflects light.

Rough-textured surfaces reflect light unevenly.

Smooth-textured surfaces reflect light evenly.

## Practice

Create a design using tactile texture.

1. Use paper and classroom materials such as pencil sharpener shavings, eraser shavings, and bits of paper to illustrate tactile texture.

2. Create designs on the paper using a pencil, then glue your materials onto the designs.

---

## Differentiated Instruction

### Reteach
Have the students close their eyes, feel an object, and describe the object they are holding or touching. Explain that if they can feel it, it has tactile texture.

### Special Needs
Increase student's descriptive language skills by creating a chart on which texture words are recorded. As an extension to this activity, students could find an example of each texture word and glue it onto the chart.

### ELL
Use real objects to make textures "come alive" for students. You can pass around examples of various textures and then brainstorm what else might fit into those groups.

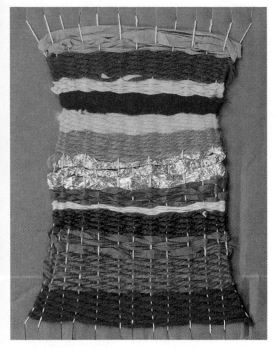

◀ **Brittany Bennett.**
Age 9.

**Think** about what kind of tactile texture the student artist used.

 **Creative Expression**

What could you use to make a weaving with texture? Use tactile textures to create a weaving.

1. Think about materials you could use for a texture weaving. Collect a variety of materials with a variety of textures, such as yarn, ribbon, leather, and wire.

2. Prepare a piece of cardboard for weaving by notching and stringing the warp threads.

3. Use a variety of textures in your weaving. Think about color variation as you weave.

 **Art Criticism**

**Describe** List the steps you followed to make your weaving.

**Analyze** What textures did you use to create your weaving? Are their surfaces smooth, rough, shiny, or dull?

**Interpret** How can you use your weaving?

**Decide** Did you include a variety of textures in your weaving?

 **Reflect**  **Time:** About 5 minutes

### Review and Assess

"Let's review what we've learned about tactile texture." *"Vamos a repasar lo que hemos aprendido sobre la textura táctil."*

## Think

The artist used string that has a smooth texture and wrinkled raffia and aluminum foil that have a rough texture.

- Use *Large Prints 55 Floating City* and *56 Wrapped Reichstag Building* to have students identify tactile textures.

### Informal Assessment

- For standardized-format test practice using this lesson's art content, see pages 50–51 in *Reading and Writing Test Preparation.*

**Art Journal: Critical Thinking**

Have students answer the four art criticism questions—Describe, Analyze, Interpret, and Decide—in their Art Journals. In small groups, have students discuss their use of found materials and form conclusions about their weavings.
NSAE 1.b

---

**Art Across the Curriculum**

Use these simple ideas to reinforce art concepts across the curriculum.

★ **Narrative Writing** Have students use Sandy Skoglund's installation as a setting to write a narrative paragraph.

★ **Math** Use the Skoglund installation to discuss proportion.

★ **Science** Discuss sources of light, both natural and artificial, noting that Chryssa used neon lights in her relief sculpture.

★ **Social Studies** Chryssa is a Greek-born American sculptor. Discuss the differences between a naturalized and a regular citizen.

★ **Technology** Have students create at least two shapes and fill them with programmed texture from a computer. Visit **SRAonline.com** to print detailed instructions for this activity.
NSAE 6.b

**Lesson 5** Wrap-Up

# Tactile Texture

 **For the Art Specialist** **Time:** About 45 minutes

## Focus

Study **Large Print 55** *Floating City* and discuss various materials used in the artwork. Do they all look like they would feel the same?

## Teach

Prior to starting this lesson, have students collect ribbon, lace, fabric scraps, buttons, beads, discarded costume jewelry, and other objects that can be attached to a wall hanging. Also have students select two landscape pictures and create sketches. Explain to the students that they will create a fabric wall hanging using a variety of textures. Have the students complete the alternate activity by following the directions.

## Reflect

Have students use the four steps of art criticism to evaluate their work. Have them describe the objects they used in their wall hanging.

### Alternate Activity

**Materials:**

- sketchbook
- pencils, erasers
- landscape images
- 12" × 12" or larger felt panels in a variety of colors
- variety of fabric scraps 9" or larger
- thread, needles
- scissors, craft glue
- collected objects

1. Have students select their best sketch.

2. Have students choose a felt background for their landscape. Have them select three different textured fabrics.

3. Students should cut the objects that are in the background from the fabric. Next they should cut the objects in the middle ground and foreground.

4. Materials such as ribbon or buttons can be used for trees and bushes. Have students glue their objects in place.

5. Have students use thread to embellish their wall hanging. Have them attach tabs to the top for hanging purposes.

## Research in Art Education

"Just as culture shapes art, art shapes culture. Our convictions, our technology, and our imagination shape our images, and our images, in turn, shape our perception of the world." Eisner, Elliot. (*The Role of Disciplined-Based Art Education in America's Schools.* The Getty Center for Arts Education in the Arts, 1987.)

## Assessment

Use the following rubric to evaluate the artwork students make in the Creative Expression activity and to assess students' understanding of tactile texture.

Have students complete page 53 or 54 in their *Assessment* books.

| | Art History and Culture | Aesthetic Perception | Creative Expression | Art Criticism |
|---|---|---|---|---|
| **3 POINTS** | The student accurately demonstrates knowledge of the lives and art of both Skoglund and Chryssa. | The student accurately identifies tactile texture in a work of art and the environment. | The student's weaving clearly illustrates tactile texture. | The student thoughtfully and honestly evaluates own work using the four steps of art criticism. |
| **2 POINTS** | The student shows some awareness of the lives and art of both Skoglund and Chryssa. | The student shows some awareness of tactile texture in a work of art and the environment. | The student's weaving shows some attempt to illustrate tactile texture. | The student attempts to evaluate own work but shows an incomplete understanding of evaluation criteria. |
| **1 POINT** | The student cannot demonstrate knowledge of the lives or art of either Skoglund and Chryssa. | The student does not understand tactile texture in a work of art and the environment. | The student's weaving does not illustrate tactile texture. | The student makes no attempt to evaluate own work. |

**Assessment, p. 53**

Name _____ Date _____ Lesson **5** UNIT 4

**Tactile Texture**

**A. Short Answer**
Write the answer to the question.
What are the two categories of tactile texture?
1. _____
2. _____

**B. Writing**
Describe what texture is. Give an example of tactile texture.
_____
_____

**C. Writing**
*The Cocktail Party* is made of tactile textures. Write a descriptive paragraph about the tactile textures that were used.
_____
_____

Level 4    Unit 4 • Form, Texture, and Emphasis   **53**

**Lesson 6 Overview**

# Emphasis

Lesson 6 introduces emphasis. Emphasis is the principle of art that makes one part of an artwork stand out more than other parts.

## Objectives

 **Art History and Culture**

To demonstrate knowledge of the lives and art of Rembrandt van Rijn and Peter Paul Rubens

**Creative Expression**

To create a focal point in a photograph of an athlete

**Aesthetic Perception**

To identify emphasis in a work of art

**Art Criticism**

To evaluate own work using the four steps of art criticism

### Vocabulary ⭐ Vocabulary

Review the following vocabulary words with students before beginning the lesson.

**emphasis** énfasis—the principle of art that makes one part of an artwork stand out more than any other parts

**focal point** punto focal—the area of an artwork that is emphasized

See page 149B for additional vocabulary and Spanish vocabulary resources.

 **Art Journal: Vocabulary**

Have students add these words to the Vocabulary section of their Art Journals.

### Lesson Materials
- computer
- printer
- paint or draw program
- scanner
- photo-editing program

**Alternate Materials:**
- photographs
- digital camera
- color pencils
- word-processing program

### Program Resources
- *Reading and Writing Test Prep.,* pp. 52–53
- *Transparency 24*
- *Flash Card 15*
- *Artist Profiles,* pp. 57, 68
- *Animals Through History Time Line*
- *Assessment,* pp. 55–56
- *Large Prints 55* Floating City and *56* Wrapped Reichstag Building
- *The National Museum of Women in the Arts Collection*

### Concept Trace
**Emphasis**
**Introduced:** Level 3, Unit 6, Lesson 3
**Reinforced:** Level 5 Unit 6, Lesson 3

## Lesson 6 Arts Integration

### Theatre

Complete Unit 4, Lesson 6, on pages 82–87 of *Theatre Arts Connections.*

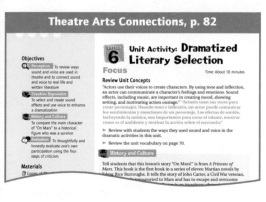

### Music

There are various musical devices for creating emphasis in music. To create meter in music, a strong beat is combined with weak beats to create duple or triple meter, as in boom-chick boom-chick or boom-chick-chick boom-chick-chick. Have students sing or listen to "Turn the World Around" by Robert M. Freedman and Harry Belafonte. Have them clap the rhythm of the refrain while you count 1-2-3-1-2. Have students put the emphasis on beat one.

### Movement & Dance

Mark off a canvas on the floor, outlining it with string or tape. Have one student enter the canvas and find a place to stand so that attention is drawn to a certain area. Add students one at a time, until there are ten students standing on the canvas. On a signal, have the group move to different areas.

# Focus

## Activate Prior Knowledge

"Can you think of ways you emphasize certain ideas or feelings over others?"

"¿Pueden pensar en maneras de enfatizar ciertas ideas o sentimientos sobre otros?"

■ Discuss student responses. Students may mention underlining a word in a sentence or raising their voices to make sure someone hears them.

### Using Literature ★ Reading

■ Read *A Mouse Called Wolf* by Dick King-Smith. Have students look at the cover illustrated and describe how the illustrator created emphasis.

### Thematic Connection ★ Social Studies

■ **Friendship:** Discuss the theme of friendship in the paintings. Do the people in both paintings appear to be friends or trying to make friends?

## Introduce the Art

# Look

"Let's take a close look at the two works of art." "Vamos a observar detalladamente las dos obras de arte."

### Summarizing ★ Reading Skill

■ Have students summarize the subject matter in each painting. Rembrandt's painting is a narrative picture of the meeting of two important women. Rubens's painting is a meeting of two groups: the leader of the group on the left is a woman who is attempting to appease the leader of the soldiers on the right.

 **Art History and Culture**

Both paintings were created during the 1600s. Students should mention that the paintings were created in the past.

 **Web Connection**

Visit **www.rembrandthuis.nl/bedankt_en.html**, the Rembrandt House Museum, to learn more about the artist.

---

# 6 Emphasis

◀ **Rembrandt van Rijn.** (Dutch). *The Visitation.* 1640.
................................................
Oil on oak panel. $22\frac{1}{4} \times 18\frac{7}{8}$ inches (56.52 × 47.96 cm.). The Detroit Institute of Arts, Detroit, Michigan.

**Look** at the works of art on these pages. Notice the people in the spotlight of Rembrandt's painting. Rembrandt is famous for using light like a spotlight to emphasize the important area, or focal point, of a painting. In *The Meeting of David and Abigail,* Rubens emphasized the two main characters and made them the focal point of the work by placing them near the center and by having the other people in the work look at them.

 **Art History and Culture**

Look at the clothing and the settings of the paintings. Do the pictures represent modern times or the past?

---

 **Art History and Culture**

## Rembrandt van Rijn

Rembrandt van Rijn (rem´ brandt vän rīn´) (1606–1669) painted, drew, and etched portraits, landscapes, figures, and animals. He was a very popular portrait painter during the late 1620s and early 1630s. In 1642 Rembrandt produced his most famous portrait, *The Nightwatch,* which was of a military company. His financial situation declined, and he lived in poverty for the next 25 years. Rembrandt produced about 400 paintings, more than 1000 drawings, and about 300 etchings. He is often referred to as the greatest Dutch painter of his era. Rembrandt also taught art for most of his life.

See pages 24–25 and 16–21 for more about art history and the subject matter.

**Artist Profiles, p. 68**

◆ Artist Profile ◆

**Rembrandt van Rijn**
1606-1669

Rembrandt van Rijn (rem´ brandt vän rin´) was the most influential Dutch artist of the seventeenth century. The seventh of nine children born to a miller and his wife, Rembrandt showed talent early in life. His parents took great interest in providing him with an education despite their modest income. Rembrandt studied a short time at the Leiden Latin School in the Netherlands to prepare for a profession as a city administrator. His parents eventually removed him from school and placed him in apprenticeships with painters. After moving to Amsterdam in 1631, he gained the commissions of several wealthy patrons and achieved great success. Rembrandt ____ a large portion of the money he

**Study** these works of art to see which areas the artists emphasized.

▶ How did each artist create a focal point in his painting?

▶ Do you see any contrasting colors?

▶ How are the paintings similar and different?

▲ **Peter Paul Rubens.** (Flemish).
***The Meeting of David and Abigail.*** c. 1625–1628.

Oil on canvas. 70¼ × 98 inches
(178.44 × 248.92 cm). The Detroit
Institute of Arts, Detroit, Michigan.

**Aesthetic Perception**

**Design Awareness** Think of billboards and commercials. Why are some images bigger or brighter in billboards and commercials?

Unit 4 • Lesson 6 **147**

## Art History and Culture

### Peter Paul Rubens

Peter Paul Rubens (pē´ tər pôl rōō´ bənz) (1577–1640) was an influential Baroque artist in northern Europe during the seventeenth century. Baroque is an artistic style that emphasizes movement, strong value contrasts, and variety. Rubens, who created many landscape and portrait paintings, also designed tapestries, book illustrations, and his own house. Because of a high demand for his work, Rubens's compositions were sometimes created by assistants and pupils, who worked from sketches created by Rubens. Rubens would then add the finishing touches to the compositions.

See pages 24–25 and 16–21 for more about art history and the subject matter.

**Artist Profiles, p. 57**

◆ Artist Profile ◆

**Peter Paul Rubens**
1577–1640

Peter Paul Rubens (pē´ tər pôl rōō´ bənz) grew up in Antwerp, Flanders (now Belgium). He began to study painting at a young age and continued creating and overseeing the production of an enormous quantity of work. Rubens was actively involved in the politics of seventeenth-century Europe, and at times helped conduct negotiations and peace treaties. His successful diplomatic efforts were recognized by Charles I of England, and the King was so impressed that he knighted the artist. Regarded as a master painter, humanist, courtier,

## Study

▶ Rembrandt highlighted two women with a supernatural glow of light to show that they are the most important people in the painting. Rubens emphasized the two main characters and made them the focal point of the work by placing them near the center.

▶ Rubens: The woman's dark robe contrasts against the light dresses of her servants and the light ground, and the man is contrasted against the light sky.

▶ Similarities: Both paintings are narratives. Both were created during the 1600s. Both paintings feature people. The colors used to create the paintings are similar. Differences: The setting of the Rembrandt painting is a castle. The setting of the Rubens painting is a forest.

■ For more examples of genre paintings, see ***The National Museum of Women in the Arts Collection.***

### Art Journal: Writing

Encourage students to define emphasis in the Concepts section of their Art Journals. What else do they want to know about emphasis?

### Aesthetic Perception

**Design Awareness** Images of products are often emphasized in billboards and commercials because advertisers want the image of the product to be the first part or the most memorable part of the advertisement.

**Developing Visual Literacy** Discuss what each artwork "says." For example, in the Rubens painting the woman in the center appears to be offering the man bread, or attempting to appease the leader of the band of soldiers. Invite students to speculate about the emotion(s) the artist was trying to convey. Students may mention fear or sadness.

**Web Connection**
Visit www.mcs.csuhayward.edu/~malek/Rubens .html to view works of art by Peter Paul Rubens.

LESSON 6 • Emphasis **147**

 # Teach

**Time:** About 45 minutes

"How can you show emphasis in a self-portrait?" "¿Cómo pueden mostrar énfasis en un autorretrato?"

- Read and discuss emphasis on page 148.

- Have students choose appropriate vocabulary to discuss the use of emphasis. NSAE 2.a

## Practice

**Materials:** white drawing paper, pencils

**Alternate Materials:** crayons

- Distribute the materials and have students follow the directions on page 148.

## Creative Expression

**Materials:** computer, printer, paint or draw program, photo editing program, scanner

**Alternate Materials:** digital camera, word-processing program, photographs, color pencils

- Distribute the materials and have students follow the directions on page 149.

- Have students invent ways to explore photographic imagery, using a variety of art media and materials. NSAE 1.c; 1.d

- Review the Activity Tips on page 239 for visual examples of techniques if needed.

### Art Journal: Brainstorming

Have students brainstorm a list of events in the Ideas section of their Art Journals. Then have students select an event to paint in the Creative Expression activity and plan how they will show emphasis in their paintings.

---

# Using Emphasis

**Emphasis** is the principle of art that makes one part of an artwork stand out more than any other part. The element or area that is noticed first is the dominant element or area. The dominant area is also called the **focal point.**

When emphasizing an element such as line, shape, form, space, color, value, or texture, make one element more important than others.

When emphasizing an area in a work of art, make that area stand out more than all the other areas in the work.

## Practice

Create a drawing of your face.

1. Using a pencil, draw your face.
2. Emphasize an area of the drawing that you want your viewers to focus on.

---

## Differentiated Instruction

**Reteach**

Have students look through their textbooks and try to find works with strong areas of emphasis, or focal points.

**Special Needs**

Draw an event showing a focal point. Provide visual prompts that students can refer to as they begin this activity. The prompts should illustrate some of the techniques artists use to create a focal point, including placement, size, and color.

**ELL**

Students may benefit from hearing the questions in Describe, Analyze, Interpret, and Decide phrased in language that is easy for them to understand. For example, "Describe the people in your painting" is more easily understood than "Describe the subject matter of your painting."

◄ **Olajawan Thompkins.**
Age 10.

**Think** about what the student artist emphasized in this artwork.

 **Creative Expression**

Create a composition that emphasizes an athlete. Choose a sport where the focal point would be on a single athlete in a group of people.

1. Find a picture of an athlete that can be imported into a blank paint or draw file, or scan a picture into a file.
2. Save the picture as a line drawing.
3. Use the paint tool to color in the athlete in bold bright colors.
4. Color in the rest of the picture, including the crowd, in neutral colors.

**Art Criticism**

**Describe** Describe the subject matter in your painting.

**Analyze** What is the focal point of your painting?

**Interpret** Give your work a title that expresses the mood.

**Decide** Were you successful in using contrast of value to create a focal point?

**Reflect**  Time: About 5 minutes

### Review and Assess

"Let's review what we've learned about emphasis." *"Vamos a repasar lo que hemos aprendido sobre el énfasis."*

## Think

The artist emphasized the quarterback's helmet by making it red and yellow, which stands out from the black and white images.

■ Use *Large Prints 55 Floating City* and *56 Wrapped Reichstag Building* to have students identify the focal point in each artwork.

## Informal Assessment

■ Have students visit a local art gallery or museum, if possible. Have them interpret moods and ideas in exhibitions by professional artists. NSAE 4.c; 5.c

■ For standardized-format test practice using this lesson's art content, see pages 52–53 in *Reading and Writing Test Preparation.*

**Art Journal: Critical Thinking**

Have students answer the four art criticism questions—Describe, Analyze, Interpret, and Decide—in their Art Journals. In small groups, have students discuss the use of emphasis in their Creative Expression paintings.

---

**Art Across the Curriculum**

Use these simple ideas to reinforce art concepts across the curriculum.

★ **Personal Writing** Have students write a letter to a parent or guardian emphasizing something that is important to them.

★ **Math** Discuss ways of emphasizing numbers. For example, in a report, a graph is a great way to illustrate the relationship between numbers.

★ **Science** Discuss colors that could be emphasized in pictures of different environmental scenes. For example, green would be emphasized in a picture of a forest.

★ **Social Studies** Discuss the culture of European countries, noting that both artists featured in this lesson were European.

★ **Technology** Have students use a paint or draw program to create a design showing emphasis. Visit **SRAonline.com** to print detailed instructions for this activity.
NSAE 6.b

## Lesson 6 Wrap-Up

# Emphasis

## Extra! For the Art Specialist

**Time:** About 45 minutes

### Focus

Have students study *Large Print 56 Wrapped Reichstag Building* to understand how artists sometimes emphasize an area of an artwork through the use of one of the art elements.

### Teach

Discuss how color contrast or a different shape, line, or texture will draw the viewer's attention and emphasizes an area of an artwork. Explain to students that they will create a painting of an object found in nature. By using contrasting colors and making the object large, they will be able to emphasize the object. Have students complete the alternate activity.

### Reflect

Have students use the four steps of art criticism to evaluate their work. Have them explain how they created emphasis in their paintings.

### Alternate Activity

**Materials:**
- sketchbooks
- pencils, erasers
- images of objects found in nature: magazines, photographs, postcards, and so on
- 12" × 12" white drawing paper
- color wheel
- tempera paints
- various brushes
- water containers
- newspapers, paper towels

1. Have students look through the collected images and select one. Then have them create several sketches of the object, keeping the sketch simple.

2. Students should transfer the drawing to paper using a pencil. Have them center the drawing so it touches three edges.

3. Have students paint the object. Have them look at the color wheel and decide which color would best contrast with the main color of the object.

4. Have students paint the background with the contrasting color they chose.

## Research in Art Education

Not only do arts-involved students tend to have positive academic development, but "the comparative gains for arts-involved youngsters generally become more pronounced over time" ("Involvement in the Arts and Human Development: General Involvement and Intensive Involvement in Music and Theatre Arts" in *Champions of Change*, pp. 2–7). The longer students pursue the arts, the greater the benefit.

## Assessment

Use the following rubric to evaluate the artwork students make in the Creative Expression activity and to assess students' understanding of tactile texture.

Have students complete page 55 or 56 in their *Assessment* books.

| | Art History and Culture | Aesthetic Perception | Creative Expression | Art Criticism |
|---|---|---|---|---|
| **3 POINTS** | The student demonstrates knowledge of the lives and art of Rembrandt and Rubens. | The student accurately identifies emphasis in a work of art. | The student's photograph of an athlete clearly has a focal point. | The student thoughtfully and honestly evaluates own work using the four steps of art criticism. |
| **2 POINTS** | The student shows some awareness of the lives and art of Rembrandt and Rubens. | The student shows emerging awareness of emphasis but cannot consistently identify it. | The student's photograph of an athlete shows some attempt to create a focal point. | The student attempts to evaluate own work but shows an incomplete understanding of evaluation criteria. |
| **1 POINT** | The student cannot demonstrate knowledge of the lives or art of either Rembrandt and Rubens. | The student cannot identify emphasis in a work of art. | The student's photograph of an athlete does not have a focal point. | The student makes no attempt to evaluate own work. |

**Assessment, p. 55**

Name _____ Date _____

**Emphasis** Lesson 6 UNIT 4

**A.** Short Answer
Write the answers to the questions.
What is emphasis?

What are the two types of emphasis?
1.
2.
What are the seven elements of art?
1. ___ 5. ___
2. ___ 6. ___
3. ___ 7. ___
4. ___

**B.** Drawing
Draw a picture of your favorite animal. Emphasize an area of your drawing.

Level 4    Unit 4 • Form, Texture, and Emphasis    55

# Unit 4 Vocabulary Review

**additive sculpture**—when something is added to either relief or freestanding sculpture **escultura aditiva**—cuando se agrega algo a una escultura de relieve o a una escultura autoestable

**dominant element**—the element in a work of art that is noticed first **elemento dominante**—el elemento en una obra de arte que se observa primero

**emphasis**—the principle of design that stresses one area in an art work over another area **énfasis**—el principio de diseño que destaca un área en una obra de arte sobre otra área

**focal point**—the point at which the receding lines meet. It is the first part of a composition to attract the viewer's attention **punto focal**—el punto en el cual se encuentran las líneas alejadas. Es la primera parte de una composición que atrae la atención del espectador

**form**—a three-dimensional object that is measured by height, width, and depth **forma**—un objeto tridimensional que se mide según su altura, ancho y profundidad

**invented texture**—created when an artist uses lines or other elements to make a textural look without any specific texture in mind **textura inventada**—creada cuando un artista usa líneas u otros elementos para crear una apariencia de textura sin pensar en ninguna textura en particular

**isolation**—an object is emphasized by its placement apart from other objects **aislamiento**—un objeto se enfatiza o resalta según su colocación alejado de otros objetos

**matte**—a dull, sometimes rough finish **mate**—un acabado opaco, a veces áspero

**relief sculpture**—a type of sculpture that has objects that stick out from a flat surface **escultura de relieve**—un tipo de escultura que tiene objetos que sobresalen de una superficie plana

**rough**—a surface that has ridges; not smooth **áspero**—una superficie que tiene surcos y no es lisa

**shiny**—bright from reflected light **radiante**—que brilla por la reflexión de la luz

**simulated texture**—imitates real textures; see also visual texture **textura simulada**—imita las texturas reales, ver también textura visual

**smooth**—a surface free from roughness; even **suave**—una superficie libre de asperezas y que es lisa

**subtractive sculpture**—when an artist carves pieces away from a form **escultura sustractiva**—cuando un artista corta o talla pedazos de una forma

**tactile texture**—actual texture, texture that can really be felt **textura táctil**—textura real, textura que se puede sentir o palpar de verdad

**texture**—the art element that refers to the way something feels **textura**—el elemento artístico que se refiere a la manera en que se siente algo

**visual texture**—or simulated texture, imitates real texture. It is texture if we can see how it feels. **textura visual**—o textura simulada, imita la textura real. Es textura si podemos ver cómo se siente.

**visual weight**—cannot be measured on a scale; it is measured by which objects the viewer's eyes see first **peso visual**—no puede medirse en un peso; se mide según los objetos que vea primero la vista del espectador

---

## Vocabulary Practice

**T** Display *Transparency 40* to review unit vocabulary words.

**Syllabication** ⭐ Vocabulary
Have students separate into syllables the word *isolation*. Repeat the process for other unit vocabulary words.

**Venn Diagrams** ⭐ Vocabulary
Have students create a Venn diagram to show how some of the unit vocabulary words are related.

**Context Clues** ⭐ Vocabulary
Have students write a sentence using context clues for the word *texture*. Repeat the process for other unit vocabulary words.

# Wrapping Up Unit 4

# Form, Texture, and Emphasis

## Art Criticism

**Critical Thinking** Art criticism is an organized system for looking at and talking about art. You can criticize art without being an expert. The purpose of art criticism is to get the viewer involved in a perception process that delays judgment until all aspects of an artwork have been studied.

■ See pages 28–29 for more about art criticism.

## Describe

▶ The sculpture is made of small found objects of plastic, metal, and wood. Some objects we can recognize are a guitar upside down on the stegosaurus's upper back, just below the sixth plate; a red bowl at the top of its left front leg; and a metal "S" above its left front leg, below the fourth plate.

▶ The stegosaurus is 14 feet high, so students could probably reach its stomach.

## Analyze

▶ The whole piece is a free-form form, but parts of it are geometric forms. The plates on its back are polygons. The legs are cylinders. The points on its tail are cones.

▶ This is an additive sculpture because found objects have been joined together to create a freestanding assembled sculpture.

▶ The overall tactile texture is rough because it is made of many smaller items that create an irregular surface; but it contains many objects that have all the different textures.

▶ Answers will vary. Some might say the head because it stands out in front. Others might say the tail with its sharp spikes. Some might say the spikes on the back because they are different.

▲ **Leo Sewell.** (American). *Stegosaurus.* 1984.
. . . . . . . . . . . . . . . . . . . . . . . .
Mixed media. 14 × 7 × 20 feet (4.3 × 2.1 × 6.1 meters). Location unknown.

## Art History and Culture

### Leo Sewell

Leo Sewell (lē´ō soō´əl) (1945– ) has earned a reputation nationally and internationally for his sculptures created from recycled items. His sculptures are often created from found objects such as plastic, metal, and wood. Sewell uses nails, bolts, and screws to assemble the found objects. Sewell, who holds a master's degree in art history from the University of Delaware, has created sculptures of zoo animals, dinosaurs, and human figures.

See pages 24–25 and 16–21 for more about art history and the subject matter.

**Artist Profiles, p. 62**

Artist Profile

**Leo Sewell**
b. 1945

Leo Sewell (lē´ō soō´al) grew up in Annapolis, Maryland, near a dump. His parents always challenged him to be creative, so he began making art with a few simple tools and the things he collected from the junkyard. His early, simple pieces eventually progressed into elaborate, decorative sculptures that have been exhibited throughout the world. His artwork can be found in children's museums and large corporations, and he also creates commissioned work. Sewell's studio is in Philadelphia, Pennsylvania.

 **Art Criticism** Critical Thinking

**Describe** **What do you see?**

During this step you will collect information about the subject of the work.

▶ What does the sculpture seem to be made of? Describe the objects.

▶ If you were to stand next to the stegosaurus's leg, how high could you reach?

**Analyze** **How is this work organized?**

Think about how the artist used the elements and principles of art.

▶ Is this sculpture geometric or freeform? Explain.

▶ Is this is an additive sculpture or a subtractive sculpture? How do you know?

▶ Would you say the overall tactile texture of the sculpture is rough, smooth, shiny, or matte? Why?

▶ What is the area of emphasis on this sculpture? Explain your answer.

**Interpret** **What is the artist trying to say?**

Use the clues you discovered during your analysis to find the message the artist is trying to show.

▶ Why do you think the artist used found materials for his sculptures?

▶ Do you think this is what a stegosaurus really looked like? Why or why not?

**Decide** **What do you think about the work?**

Use all the information you have gathered to decide whether or not this is a successful work of art.

▶ Is the work successful because it is realistic, because it is well organized, or because it has a strong message?

## Interpret

■ Answers will vary. Students might say he wanted to recycle trash, he wanted materials that were abundant, or he did not want to spend much money on materials. Others might say he liked the look of the old objects.

■ Answers will vary. Students might say that the stegosaurus may have had plates and a spiked tail, but that there were no bowls, guitars, or other manufactured materials. Therefore, the stegosaurus would have had some other type of skin.

## Decide

▶ Answers will vary. Many will choose a message because the artist has recycled trash, but composition may be mentioned. Most will not choose realism because of the materials used to create the work even though it does look like a stegosaurus.

**Art Journal: Writing**

Have students write answers to Aesthetic Perception in their Art Journals.

## Aesthetic Perception

**Seeing Like An Artist** Have students think about a dinosaur or bring in a picture of a dinosaur. How does the picture compare with *Stegosaurus?* Discuss the dinosaur on display.

**Describe** ▶ List and describe everything you see in the picture.

**Analyze** ▶ Discuss the form, texture, and emphasis.

▶ How do the form, texture, and emphasis contribute to the look of the dinosaur?

**Interpret** ▶ How does the picture make you feel?

▶ What name would you give the dinosaur? Why?

**Decide** ▶ Do you have strong feelings when you look at the picture?

"Artists use form, texture, and emphasis to communicate how things look and feel."

"Los artistas usan la forma, la textura y el énfasis para comunicar cómo son y cómo se sienten las cosas."

**T** Review unit vocabulary with students using *Transparency 40.*

### Art Journal: Writing

Have students answer the questions on page 152 in their Art Journals or on a separate sheet of paper. Answers: 1. B, 2. B, 3. A, 4. C, 5. A

**T** For further assessment, have students complete the unit test on *Transparency 46.*

### CAREERS IN ART
## Technology

► Encourage students to discuss their school Web page or their favorite Web page. What does it look like? Is it easy to follow the layout of the page? Are the graphics the right size?

"Nature contains the
elements, in color and
form, of all pictures, as
the keyboard contains the
notes of all music. But
the artist is born to...
bring forth from chaos
glorious harmony."

—James McNeill Whistler

---

Form, Texture, and Emphasis, continued

## Show What You Know

Answer these questions on a separate sheet of paper.

**1** In a _____ sculpture, objects stick out from the surface.
A. subtractive
B. relief
C. freestanding

**2** A(n) _____ sculpture is created when an artist carves pieces away from a form.
A. additive
B. subtractive
C. relief

**3** An artist uses (a) _____ to make one part of an artwork stand out more than other parts.
A. emphasis
B. relief sculpture
C. free-standing sculpture

**4** _____ texture refers to how things feel.
A. Invented
B. Visual
C. Tactile

**5** Two ways of creating visual texture include using _____ texures.
A. simulated and invented
B. shiny and matte
C. rough and smooth

**152** Unit 4

---

### CAREERS IN ART
## Technology

Technology touches all aspects of our lives, including art. Artists use technology to create your favorite games, Web pages, and illustrations.

**Computer graphics designers** use a computer to create and arrange illustrations, and the layout of a page. They must think about how to arrange shapes and colors on a page.

**Digital filmmakers** create short films for the Internet. They must think about how to make the film visually appealing to the audience.

**Computer-game developers** have a variety of roles when creating computer games, including designing the music and sound effects, developing the game, and drawing the characters and scenery.

▲ **Computer graphics designers**

---

## Unit Assessment Options

### Aesthetic Perception

**Practice** Have students select one of the concepts in the Show What You Know section on page 152, then find examples of each concept in the classroom.

### Creative Expression

**Student Portfolio** Have students review all the artwork they have created during this unit and select the pieces they wish to keep in their portfolios.

### Art Criticism

**Activity** Have students select an artwork from this unit and study it using the four steps of art criticism. (See pages 28–29 for more information about art criticism.) Have students work alone or in pairs and present their findings aloud or in writing.

# Form and Texture in Dance

"The Nutcracker" is a traditional holiday ballet. A girl named Clara receives a nutcracker for a present. This leads to a dream where she and the Nutcracker Prince visit "The Land of Sweets," where dolls and flowers come to life wearing colorful, beautifully textured costumes.

**What to Do** Create mime or dances based on toy forms and actions.

In the "Land of Sweets" a variety of dolls come to life and dance. Think about some of the following toys and how you might bring them to life through mime or dance:

jack-in-the-box    ball    spring coils
yo-yo           dolls    computer games

1. Talk about toys with your classmates. Describe their form and think of words that explain how they move.

2. Select one toy that you like. Create a mime or use creative dance to capture the form of the toy, as well its actions. Find variety in the form and movements. Use rhythm. Have a clear beginning, middle, and end.

3. In small groups, perform your "toys" together.

▲ The Joffrey Ballet of Chicago. "The Nutcracker, 'Waltz of the Flowers'" excerpt and "The Story of the Nutcracker."

 **Art Criticism**

**Describe** Describe the form and actions of the toy you selected.

**Analyze** What choices did you make in miming or moving your toy? Why?

**Interpret** What feelings or ideas came to mind as you brought your toy to life?

**Decide** How well do you think you did in portraying the form and actions of your toy?

Unit 4    **153**

---

 **Art History and Culture**

### The Nutcracker

*The Nutcracker* was first performed in 1892 in St. Petersburg, Russia. It is a traditional holiday ballet based on a story by E.T.A. Hoffmann, called *The Nutcracker and the King of the Mice.* The story was published in 1819 and was later simplified in 1890 by the Russian choreographer Marius Petipa, who presented it to Peter Ilyich Tchaikovsky, who wrote the inspiring score. This production of *The Nutcracker* is conceived by Gerald Arpino and presented by the Joffrey Ballet, whose purpose is to revive major historical ballets and to present new choreography that draws from American life.

---

 # Form and Texture in Dance

**Objective:** To bring a toy to life using mime or creative dance

**Materials:** *The Nutcracker,* "*Waltz of the Flowers,*" performed by the Joffrey Ballet. Running time: 5:12. A variety of toys or pictures of toys.

## Focus

Time: About 5 minutes

- Discuss the information on page 153.

 **Art History and Culture**

- Have students discuss how toys have changed. Have students create a list of toys they used to play with but are no longer being made.

## Teach

Time: About 20 minutes

 **Aesthetic Perception**

- Show a variety of toys. Ask students to describe how the toys are put together.

**Creative Expression**

- Have students interact with their selected toys to see how they can or cannot move.

- **Informal Assessment** When students perform their mime or movement study, comment positively on their efforts.

## Reflect

Time: About 10 minutes

 **Art Criticism**

- Have students answer the four art criticism questions on page 153 aloud or in writing.

- Were students able to successfully show the form and actions of a toy?

# Unit 5 Planning Guide

| | Lesson Title | Suggested Pacing | Creative Expression Activity |
|---|---|---|---|
| **Lesson 1** | Foreground, Middle Ground, and Background | 1 hour | Create a perspective drawing. |
| **Lesson 2** | Perspective Techniques | 1 hour | Make a landscape drawing. |
| **Lesson 3** | Point of View | 1 hour | Photograph an object from different points of view. |
| **Lesson 4** | Face Proportion | 1 hour | Create a self-portrait. |
| **Lesson 5** | Body Proportions | 1 hour | Draw a portrait. |
| **Lesson 6** | Distortion | 1 hour | Use a computer to distort a photograph. |
| **ARTSOURCE** | Space and Proportion in Music | 40 minutes | Create a simple stringed instrument. |

| Materials | Program Resources | Fine Art Resources | Literature Resources |
|---|---|---|---|
| paper for sketches, white paper, pencils, soft erasers, viewing frames | *Assessment,* pp. 57–58 *Reading and Writing Test Preparation,* pp. 54–55 *Home and After-School Connections* | *Transparency 25* *Artist Profiles,* pp. 49, 54 *Large Prints 57* and *58* *The National Museum of Women in the Arts Collection* | *A Day's Work* by Eve Bunting |
| white paper, pencils, erasers, dustless chalk, tempera paints, paper plates for palettes, paintbrushes, containers for water | *Assessment,* pp. 59–60 *Reading and Writing Test Preparation,* pp. 56–57 | *Transparency 26* *Artist Profiles,* pp. 58, 72 *Large Prints 57* and *58* *Art Around the World Collection* | *Tuesday* by David Wiesner |
| camera, film, three-dimensional objects | *Assessment,* pp. 61–62 *Reading and Writing Test Preparation,* pp. 58–59 | *Transparency 27* *Artist Profile,* p. 51 *Large Prints 57* and *58* *The National Museum of Women in the Arts Collection* | *The Gardener* by Sarah Stewart |
| white paper, pencil, eraser, soft and hard pastels, mirrors | *Assessment,* pp. 63–64 *Reading and Writing Test Preparation,* pp. 60–61 *Flash Card* 18 | *Transparency 28* *Artist Profiles,* pp. 28, 56 *Large Prints 57* and *58* *Art Around the World Collection* | *Dear Mr. Henshaw* by Beverly Cleary |
| pencils, white drawing paper, crayons, magazines | *Assessment,* pp. 65–66 *Reading and Writing Test Preparation,* pp. 62–63 *Flash Card* 18 | *Transparency 29* *Artist Profiles,* pp. 25, 70 *Large Prints 57* and *58* *The National Museum of Women in the Arts Collection* | *Grandfather's Journey* by Allen Say |
| digital camera, computer, draw or paint software, printer, paper | *Assessment,* pp. 67–68 *Reading and Writing Test Preparation,* pp. 64–65 | *Transparency 30* *Artist Profiles,* pp. 11, 15 *Large Prints 57* and *58* *Art Around the World Collection* | *Zathura* by Chris Van Allsburg |
| *Jaropo Azul,* small cardboard boxes, rubber bands of different lengths and widths | | | |

# Unit Overview

## 5 Space, Proportion, and Distortion

**Lesson 1:** There are three terms used to describe the placement of objects on a **picture plane**—foreground, middle ground, and background.

**Lesson 2: Perspective** is the technique used to create the feeling of **depth** on a flat surface.

**Lesson 3: Point of view** is the angle from which the viewer sees an object.

**Lesson 4: Face proportions** help artists place features correctly on the human face.

**Lesson 5:** Artists use the length of the head, from the chin to the top of the skull, to help them in measuring **body proportions**.

**Lesson 6:** Artists use **distortion** to change the sizes of objects from their normal proportions.

# Introduce Unit Concepts

"Artists use proportion and distortion to draw human faces and bodies. Space gives the appearance of depth in a flat surface." "Los artistas usan proporción y distorsión para dibujar caras y cuerpos humanos. Espacio da la apariencia de profundidad en una superficie plana."

## Space and Proportion
- Have students work as a class in defining the term *space*.

- Have students look up the meanings of *pro-* and *portion* in the dictionary. What do they think the word *proportion* means based on the meanings of these word parts?

## Distortion
- Have students heard the phrase "the story was distorted"? Discuss what the term means as applied to this phrase.

## Cross-Curricular Projects
- See the *Language Arts and Reading, Mathematics, Science,* and *Social Studies Art Connections* books for activities that further develop space, proportion, and distortion concepts.

# Space, Proportion, and Distortion

▲ **John Singleton Copley.** (American). *Sir William Pepperrell and His Family.* 1778.

Oil on canvas. 90 × 108 inches (228.6 × 274.32 cm.). North Carolina Museum of Art, Raleigh, North Carolina.

## Artists use accurate proportions to realistically depict people and objects.

Copley painted this realistic portrait of the Pepperrell family in 1778. The Pepperrell family lived in New England until about the time of the American Revolution, when they moved to England. At about the same time, Sir William Pepperrell lost most of his wealth. Notice that Copley used correct proportions to make the painting realistic.

**154** Unit 5

## Fine Art Prints

Display *Large Prints 57 Nighthawks* and *58 Chance Meeting.* Refer to the prints throughout the unit as students learn about space, proportion, and distortion.

**Large Print 57**

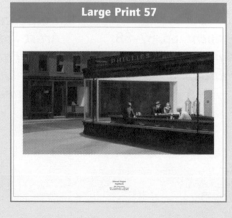

**Large Print 58**

Artists use space in paintings to give the appearance of depth on a flat surface.

▶ How do you think John Singleton Copley created space in *Sir William Pepperrell and His Family*?

▶ Which objects in the painting look closer to you? Which objects look farther away?

Artists use accurate **proportions** to show people or things realistically.

▶ Do you think the people in Copley's painting look like they have been painted with accurate proportions? Explain.

**In This Unit** you will learn about different ways that artists show size and placement. Here are the topics you will study:
▶ Foreground, middle ground, and background
▶ Perspective techniques
▶ Point of view
▶ Face proportion
▶ Body proportions
▶ Distortion

# John Singleton Copley

(1738-1815)

John Singleton Copley was a popular portrait painter during the eighteenth century. When he was seventeen years old he created a portrait of George Washington. In his attempt to capture details and to make his subjects appear natural, Copley sometimes required fifteen or sixteen sittings for a single portrait. Copley moved to England during the American Revolution and did not return to America.

Unit 5  **155**

# Art History and Culture

## John Singleton Copley

John Singleton Copley (jän sing´ gəl tən kä´ plē) (1738–1815) is considered one of the finest painters of colonial America. His straightforward and realistic style produced portraits of great strength. Copley wanted to see how his art would be received overseas, so he sent *Henry Pelham, Boy with Squirrel* to England. His work was praised, and he decided to move to England in 1774. Although he remained in England for the rest of his life and was moderately successful, his historical paintings never had the vitality or realism of his Boston portraits.

See pages 24–25 and 16–21 for more about art history and subject matter.

**Artist Profiles, p. 14**

# Examine the Artwork

"Let's study this portrait by John Singleton Copley." "Vamos a estudiar este retrato de John Singleton Copley."

■ Have students examine Copley's portrait and ask them to describe how the principles of space and proportion are used. Distortion is not used in this painting. Ask them why they think Copley chose not to use distortion.

■ Have students answer the questions about space, proportion, and distortion on page 155.

▶ Students answers will vary, but make sure their answers are reasonable. Point to examples of how Copley used the six perspective techniques.

▶ The brown-and-white dog in the lower left corner looks the closest. The trees seem to appear the farthest away, especially the trees that appear in the middle ground.

▶ Students' answers will vary, but most will say they are comparing the height of the children in the painting to that of the adults.

# Unit Pretest

**T** Display *Transparency 47* as a pretest. Answers: 1. B, 2. A, 3. A, 4. C, 5. B

# Home Connection

■ See *Home and After-School Connections* for family newsletters and activities for this unit.

# Unit 5 Arts Integration

## ILLUSTRATOR PROFILE
# Maurice Sendak
(1928– )

Maurice Sendak was born in Brooklyn, New York. He was often sick as a child, and his mother worried about his health. Most of Sendak's books have a moon somewhere in the scene; the moon represents his mother watching over him to make sure he was well.

Sendak loved to read and draw as a child and got his first job as an illustrator while he was still in high school. His childhood experiences influenced many of his later works, including his most famous book, *Where the Wild Things Are*. Sendak has said that the wild things were inspired by his aunts and uncles, who would smother him with attention as a boy.

Sendak has written more than a dozen books and has illustrated more than 70 books for other authors.

Throughout this unit, share Sendak's illustrations with the class and discuss the use of space in his works of art. Which parts of the illustrations are behind other parts? Which parts are positive space? Which parts are negative space?

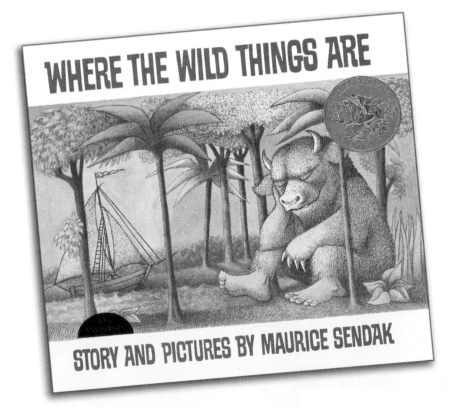

## Music
Spaces in music are called rests. Spaces of silence before and after a song can set it off from nonmusical sounds. Distortion is sometimes used in music for dramatic effect. Tone colors are sometimes distorted also. In "Tubby the Tuba," the tuba's sound is distorted when Tubby accidentally "sits" on the tune. Have students find the rests in this song.

## Literature
Show the DVD or video *At the Crossroads* to introduce the concepts of space, distortion, and proportion. Pause the DVD or video and have students identify these concepts.

Literature and Art

## Performing Arts
 Play *Joropo Azul.* Have students listen carefully to the music.

Artsource®

# Foreground, Middle Ground, and Background

**Lesson 1** introduces perspective and the terms *foreground, middle ground,* and *background.* **Perspective** is the technique used for creating the illusion of depth on a flat surface.

## Objectives

 **Art History and Culture**

To demonstrates knowledge of the lives and work of Camille Pissarro and Berthe Morisot

 **Creative Expression**

To create a drawing with the illusion of depth, using foreground, middle ground, and background

 **Aesthetic Perception**

To identify how artists use foreground, middle ground, and background to create the illusion of depth

 **Art Criticism**

To evaluate own work using the four steps of art criticism

## Vocabulary  Vocabulary

Review the following vocabulary words with students before beginning the lesson.

**depth** profundidad—the appearance of deep space or distance in a two-dimensional work of art

**picture plane** plano del retrato—the name used to describe the surface of a drawing or painting

See page 179B for additional vocabulary and Spanish vocabulary resources.

 **Art Journal: Vocabulary**

Have students add this word to the Vocabulary section of their Art Journals.

## Lesson Materials

- 9" × 12" paper for sketches
- landscape pictures
- 12" × 18" white drawing paper
- pencils
- soft erasers
- viewing frames

**Alternate Materials:**
- charcoal

## Program Resources

- *Reading and Writing Test Prep.,* pp. 54–55
- *Transparency 25*
- *Artist Profiles,* pp. 49, 54
- *Animals Through History Time Line*
- *Assessment,* pp. 57–58
- *Large Prints 57* Nighthawks and *58* Chance Meeting
- *The National Museum of Women in the Arts Collection*

### Concept Trace
Foreground, Middle Ground, and Background
**Introduced:** Level 3, Unit 2, Lesson 2

**Reinforced:** Level 5, Unit 2, Lesson 3

---

## Lesson 1 Arts Integration

### Theatre

Complete Unit 5, Lesson 1, on pages 90–91 of *Theatre Arts Connections.*

**Theatre Arts Connections, p. 90**

### Music

When a soloist is featured in a composition, the accompaniment is the background. If the composer wants the accompaniment to be as important as the solo, the part will be composed to relate equally with the soloist. Listen to "Dance for Clarinet and Piano" by Aaron Marx. Have students identify when the clarinet is in the foreground.

### Movement & Dance

The farthest point from the audience is upstage (background); the closest point is downstage (foreground). The space in the middle is called center stage. Select six students and place each student in a different part of the stage. Have some students stand and others sit. Ask students which people appear closer and farther away.

# Focus

Time: About 10 minutes

## Activate Prior Knowledge

"Think about standing on a street. How do the buildings appear to change in size as you look down the street?" "Piensen que están parados en una calle. ¿Cómo parecen cambiar de tamaño los edificios cuando ves hacia la calle?"

■ As a class, discuss the student responses and compare them to placement in works of art. Explain to students that buildings appear smaller the farther away they are.

### Using Literature ★ Reading

■ Look at the illustrations in *A Day's Work* by Eve Bunting. Discuss how the illustrator Ronald Himler created depth in the pictures. Have students name objects that appear in the foreground, middle ground, and background of various illustrations.

### Thematic Connection ★ Social Studies

■ **Country Life:** Have students look at the two paintings in this lesson and name places they have visited or seen that look similar. Have them explain how living in the country is different from living in a city.

## Introduce the Art

# Look

"Look closely at both works of art and find objects located in the foreground, middle ground, and background." "Vamos a observar detalladamente a las dos obras de arte y encontrar objetos en el frente, medio fondo, y fondo."

### Animal Classification ★ Science

■ Have students identify whether a goose is an herbivore or a carnivore.

### 🏺 Art History and Culture

In *Art Connections,* students have already studied the work of French artists Henri Matisse and Paul Gauguin.

 **Web Connection**
Search www.nga.gov to find works of art by Camille Pissarro.

---

# Foreground, Middle Ground, and Background

▲ Camille Pissarro. (French). *The Hermitage at Pontoise.* 1867.
..........................
Oil on canvas. 59⅝ × 79 inches (151.44 × 200.66 cm.). Solomon R. Guggenheim Museum, New York, New York.

**Look** at the artwork on these pages. *The Hermitage at Pontoise* is a landscape painting. It shows a village path at the bottom of a collection of houses in Pontoise, France, known as The Hermitage. *Girl in a Boat with Geese* is also a landscape painting. How do you think the artists created the appearance of deep space or distance in the paintings?

### 🏺 Art History and Culture

Pissarro and Morisot were French. What other French artists have you studied?

---

### 🏺 Art History and Culture

## Camille Pissarro

Camille Pissarro (kä mēl´ pə sär´ ō) (1830–1903) has been considered the leader of the original impressionists and was the only one who exhibited at all eight of the impressionist exhibitions between 1874 and 1886. Pissarro influenced many artists, including Mary Cassatt, Paul Cézanne, and Paul Gauguin. Although his talents have always been acknowledged, Pissarro did not receive the same universal acclaim as other impressionist painters. *The Hermitage at Pontoise* was painted in the realist style, before he adopted the impressionist style.

See pages 24–25 and 16–21 for more about art history and the subject matter.

**Artist Profiles, p. 54**

● Artist Profile ●
## Camille Pissarro
1830–1903

Camille Pissarro (kä mēl´ pə sär´ ō) was born in the Virgin Islands. As a young boy, he attended boarding school near Paris. Although his father was a prosperous merchant, Pissarro was not interested in following the family business, so at the age of 25 he went to live and paint in Paris. He was regarded by his contemporaries as a virtuous man—loyal, patient, honest, and wise with his friends and his family. He was revered by younger painters such as Degas and Cézanne, and was considered the unofficial moderator among the earlier group of impressionists. Although he endured financial hardship throughout his career, by the age of 62 he finally established a sound reputation and

▲ **Berthe Morisot.** (French).
*Girl in a Boat with Geese.* 1889.
Oil on canvas. 25¾ × 21½ inches (65.405 × 54.61 cm.).
National Gallery of Art, Washington, D.C.

**Study** these works of art and notice the placement of the objects.

▶ Which part of each painting appears to be closest to the viewer?

▶ Which part of each painting appears to be farthest from the viewer?

▶ Which part of each painting appears to be in the middle?

## Study

▶ Pissarro: The road and the people appear to be closest to the viewer because they are in the foreground. Morisot: The grassy area seems to be closest to the viewer because it is in the foreground.

▶ Pissarro: The clouds and the sky seem to be farthest away because they are in the background. Morisot: The trees and the sky on the far bank of the river seem farthest away because they are in the background.

▶ Pissarro: The houses and some of the country landscape appear in the middle ground. Morisot: Three of the geese, the girl, the boat, the river, and some of the landscape appear in the middle ground.

■ For more examples of landscapes, see *The National Museum of Women in the Arts Collection.*

### Art Journal: Writing

Have students explain what *perspective* means to them in the Concepts section of their Art Journals. What else do they want to know about perspective?

## Aesthetic Perception

**Seeing Like an Artist** Look down at your shoe and then look at the shoe of a classmate who is far away. Which shoe seems to be larger?

## Aesthetic Perception

**Design Awareness** Have students discuss their findings. Have them explain why one of the shoes appears larger. Make sure that students are examining a shoe that is far away so they can discuss that objects in the distance appear smaller than objects that are close to the viewer.

**Developing Visual Literacy** Have students describe how each painting makes them feel. Does the weather depicted in each painting have anything to do with the way they are feeling? Invite students to share their personal experiences that remind them of these paintings. NSAE 1.a

## Art History and Culture

### Berthe Morisot

Berthe Morisot (bârt môr´ē s ō) (1841–1895) was a member of the French upper middle class during the nineteenth century, and many of her works deal with the leisure pursuits of this social class. Morisot often used family as models in her artwork. Morisot was one of the founding members of impressionism. Impressionism captured everyday subjects and emphasized the momentary effects of sunlight. Even though she was recognized as a notable impressionist artist in France, she did not receive recognition in British and American historical accounts of that period until the mid 1970s.

See pages 24–25 and 16–21 for more about art history and the subject matter.

**Artist Profiles, p. 49**

◆ Artist Profile ◆
**Berthe Morisot**
1841–1865
Berthe Morisot (bârt môr´ē´s ō) was born in France. She was the granddaughter of the painter Fragonard. Taught by her father, she learned how to draw when she was very young. Later she took painting lessons with her sister. She began selling her paintings when she was 23, but she never felt that she was treated as an equal of male painters. When she was 33, she married Eugene Manet, the brother of Édouard Manet. They had one daughter, Julie.

🖥 **Web Connection**
Search www.the-athenaeum.org/artworks (find the artist by name) to view works of art by Berthe Morisot.

 each

"We will use perspective techniques to draw pictures of our environment." "Usaremos técnicas perspectivas para dibujar pinturas de nuestro ambiente."

- Read and discuss the location of the foreground, the middle ground, and the background in the artwork on page 158.

## Practice

**Materials:** landscape pictures

- Distribute the materials and have students follow the directions on page 158.

 **Creative Expression**

**Materials:** 9" × 12" paper for sketches, 12" × 18" white drawing paper, pencils, soft erasers, viewing frames

**Alternate Materials:** charcoal

- Distribute the materials and have students follow the directions on page 159.
- Review the Activity Tips on page 240 for visual examples of techniques if needed.

### Art Journal: Brainstorming

Ask students to create a list of places in their environment that might make an interesting perspective drawing and to place this list in their Art Journals. Students will need to select one of these places for their Creative Expression activity.

---

# Using Perspective

A **picture plane** is the surface of a drawing or painting. There are three terms used to describe the high and low placement of objects on a picture plane: foreground, middle ground, and background.

The **foreground** is the part of the picture plane that appears closest to the viewer. The foreground is usually at the bottom of the picture plane.

The **background** is the part of the picture plane that seems to be farthest from the viewer. It is usually located at the top of the picture plane.

The **middle ground** is the area in a picture between the foreground and background.

## Practice

Play a perspective game. Use landscape pictures.

1. Work in small groups. Have a person name an object in one of the landscapes.
2. Another person in the group then says whether the object is in the foreground, middle ground, or background.
3. Have everyone in the group take turns naming objects.

---

## Differentiated Instruction

**Reteach**

Ask students to sit at one end of a long hallway or an outside area that shows depth. Have two students of different heights stand away from the group to illustrate size change and to explain foreground, middle ground, and background.

**Special Needs**

To reinforce student understanding of size relationships in the picture plane, choose three objects of the same size and color. Choose an area of the classroom for the picture plane. Place the objects so students can note the differences.

**ELL**

Students may find it helpful to have other students augment their responses when explaining techniques to others. Try designating partners and allowing them to practice together before presenting to the group.

◄ **Max Murphy.**
Age 9.

**Think** about how the student artist created space in this drawing.

 **Creative Expression**

What in your environment could you use to make an interesting perspective drawing? Use perspective techniques.

1. Think about details in your environment that you might include in your drawing.

2. Look through a viewing frame, and do two quick sketches of different areas. Choose one to make into a finished drawing.

3. Divide the picture plane on your paper into foreground, middle ground, and background. Begin by drawing the larger shapes of the foreground. Fill in the middle ground and background. Finish by adding details to the foreground.

 **Art Criticism**

**Describe** Describe the scene you drew. List the things you included.

**Analyze** Explain how you used the foreground, background, and middle ground. How did you create the illusion of depth?

**Interpret** Give your work a creative title.

**Decide** Do you feel you were successful in creating the illusion of depth? Explain.

 Time: About 5 minutes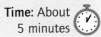

## Review and Assess

"Let's review what we have learned about creating the illusion of depth." "Revisemos lo que hemos aprendido para crear una ilusión de profundidad."

# Think

The artist placed flowers and a close-up of a tree in the foreground. A medium-sized tree and animal are in the middle ground, and a smaller animal and smaller trees are in the background. A stream runs through the middle of the drawing and gets thinner as it moves farther back.

■ Use *Large Prints 57* Nighthawks and *58 Chance Meeting* and ask students to compare how each artist created the illusion of depth.

## Informal Assessment

■ For standardized-format test practice using this lesson's art content, see pages 54–55 in *Reading and Writing Test Preparation.*

### Art Journal: Critical Thinking

Have students answer the four art criticism questions—Describe, Analyze, Interpret, and Decide—in their Art Journals. Have students discuss within table groups how they created the illusion of depth in their drawings. Have them explain what items they placed in the foreground, the middle ground, and the background.

## Art Across the Curriculum

Use these simple ideas to reinforce art concepts across the curriculum.

★ **Descriptive Writing** Have students write a paragraph about the landscape in *The Hermitage at Pontoise.*

★ **Math** Have students explain what a multiple number is.

★ **Science** Have students discuss animals that are similar to geese.

★ **Social Studies** Have students make a list of places they have visited that look like the two paintings in the lesson.

★ **Technology** Using a paint or draw program, have students create a simple landscape, making sure to include at least one object in the foreground, middle ground, and background. Visit **SRAonline.com** to print detailed instructions for this activity.
NSAE 6.b

# Foreground, Middle Ground, and Background

## Extra! For the Art Specialist

Time: About 45 minutes

### Focus

Have students study **Large Print 57** *Nighthawks* and discuss how the feeling of depth was created in the artwork. What do students notice about the details and the size of the objects?

### Teach

Explain to students that they will create a landscape based on a real place, using collected images from photographs or magazines. Have them begin collecting photographs and magazine images prior to the lesson. Demonstrate blending and mixing oil pastels. Then have students complete the alternate activity.

### Reflect

Have students use the four steps of art criticism to evaluate their work. Have students describe the objects they included in the foreground, middle ground, and background.

### Alternate Activity

**Materials:**
- sketchbooks
- pencils, erasers
- 12" × 18" black drawing or construction paper
- collected landscape images
- oil pastels

1. Choose a place you want to depict, and collect images of that place.

2. Create sketches of the landscapes. Be sure to place objects in the background, middle ground, and foreground.

3. Transfer the selected sketches to paper. Use oil pastels to color in the sky area first. Overlap and blend the colors.

4. Continue coloring the middle ground and then the foreground. Add any shadows, highlights, and textures last.

## Research in Art Education

Students in after-school arts-based programs gain practice in working with adults to plan, develop, and execute ideas and to assess "next steps from a current situation" that they rarely receive in any other context ("Imaginative Actuality" in *Champions of Change*, p. 27). These are valuable workplace skills.

## Assessment

Use the following rubric to evaluate the artwork students make in the Creative Expression activity and to assess students' understanding of how perspective is used in drawing.

| | Art History and Culture | Aesthetic Perception | Creative Expression | Art Criticism |
|---|---|---|---|---|
| **3 POINTS** | The student demonstrates knowledge of the lives and work of Pissarro and Morisot. | The student accurately identifies how artists create the illusion of depth. | The student's drawing demonstrates how to create the illusion of depth using the foreground, middle ground, and background. | The student thoughtfully and honestly evaluates own work using the four steps of art criticism. |
| **2 POINTS** | The student's knowledge of the lives and work of Pissarro and Morisot is weak or incomplete. | The student shows an emerging awareness of how artists create the illusion of depth but cannot consistently identify it. | The student's drawing shows some awareness of how to create the illusion of depth using the foreground, middle ground, and background. | The student attempts to evaluate own work but shows an incomplete understanding of evaluation criteria. |
| **1 POINT** | The student cannot demonstrate knowledge of the lives and work of Pissarro or Morisot. | The student cannot identify how artists create the illusion of depth. | The student's drawing shows no understanding of how to create the illusion of depth using the foreground, middle ground, and background. | The student makes no attempt to evaluate own work. |

Have students complete page 57 or 58 in their *Assessment* books.

### Assessment, p. 57

Name _____  Date _____

Lesson 1 UNIT 5

**Foreground, Middle Ground, and Background**

**A. Drawing**
Using a pencil, draw an outdoor scene with a background, middle ground, and foreground. Label each section.

**B. Short Answer**
Write the answer to the question.
What is a picture plane?

**C. Writing**
Look at *The Hermitage at Pontoise* by Camille Pissarro. Describe how Pissarro used perspective in this painting.

Level 4                Unit 5 • Space, Proportion, and Distortion  **57**

# Perspective Techniques

**Lesson 2** introduces how perspective techniques are used to create space in two-dimensional works of art. Artists use perspective techniques in paintings to make things seem close or far away.

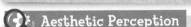
## Objectives

 **Art History and Culture**

To demonstrates knowledge of the lives and work of Grant Wood and Antonio Ruíz

 **Creative Expression**

To create a landscape drawing using the six perspective techniques

 **Aesthetic Perception**

To identify the use of the six perspective techniques in two-dimensional art

 **Art Criticism**

To evaluate own work using the four steps of art criticism

## Vocabulary ⭐ Vocabulary

Review the following vocabulary word with students before beginning the lesson.

**perspective techniques** técnicas perspectivas—the six techniques an artist uses to create the illusion of depth in two-dimensional art: overlapping, size, placement, detail, color, converging lines

See page 179B for additional vocabulary and Spanish vocabulary resources.

 **Art Journal: Vocabulary**

Have students add this word to the Vocabulary section of their Art Journals.

## Lesson Materials

- 12" × 18" white paper
- pencils, erasers, dustless chalk
- tempera paints in dispenser bottles
- paper plates for palettes
- paintbrushes of various sizes
- containers for water

**Alternate Materials:**

- markers
- crayons

## Program Resources

- *Reading and Writing Test Prep.,* pp. 56–57
- *Transparency 26*
- *Artist Profiles,* pp. 58, 72
- *Animals Through History Time Line*
- *Assessment,* pp. 59–60
- *Large Prints 57* Nighthawks and *58 Chance Meeting*
- *Art Around the World Collection*

### Concept Trace
Perspective Techniques
**Introduced:** Level 3, Unit 2, Lesson 3

**Reinforced:** Level 5, Unit 2, Lesson 2

---

## Lesson 2 Arts Integration

### Theatre

Complete Unit 5, Lesson 2, on pages 92–93 of *Theatre Arts Connections.*

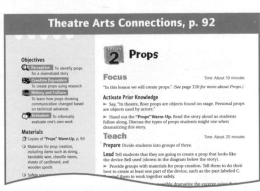

### Music

 Listen to the use of dynamics in "Beadle" from *Pictures at an Exhibition,* by Modest Mussorgsky. This music depicts a lumbering hand cart coming toward the listener and passing by. The aural perception of the advancing cart is played louder as it approaches. The texture also changes when strings are added to the melody. Ask students if the strings add to the effect of the cart coming closer.

### Movement & Dance

Create two lines of people across the classroom. The lines should start wide apart and then gradually converge. Have students travel along these lines using movements, such as sliding, jogging, and leaping.

# Focus

**Time: About 10 minutes**

## Activate Prior Knowledge

"Think about riding in a car. Why does the road ahead look like it is getting smaller?"

"Piensen en un paseo en un automóvil. ¿Por qué la carretera en frente parece achicarse?"

■ Discuss students' answers to the question and what makes things in the distance look smaller even though we know they are full size. Ask students if they have ever been in an airplane and looked out the window. This experience is similar to riding in a car, except the viewer is looking down.

### Using Literature ⭐ Reading

■ Have students read *Tuesday* by David Wiesner. Have them identify the perspective techniques he used to create depth.

### Thematic Connection ⭐ Science

■ **Seasons:** Have students explain what happens to the environment during the four seasons. What colors do they associate with each season?

## Introduce the Art

# Look

Let's look closely at the two landscape paintings." "Vamos a observar detalladamente a las dos pinturas de paisaje."

### Places and Regions ⭐ Social Studies

Have students discuss whether the two paintings look like any place they have visited. Students might say that Wood's painting looks like a small country town in the United States. Ruíz's painting might remind students of Mexico or Spain.

 **Art History and Culture**

Explain to students that American regionalism refers to artists, mostly from the Midwest, who became popular in the 1930s.
NSAE 4.a

 **Web Connection**

Visit xroads.virginia.edu/~MA98/haven/wood/home.html for more information about Grant Wood.
**Note:** This Web site is for teacher use only.

---

 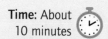 # Perspective Techniques

▲ **Grant Wood.** (American). *The Birthplace of Herbert Hoover, West Branch, Iowa.* 1931.
.................................
Oil on composition board. 29⅝ × 39¾ inches (75.24 × 100.97 cm.). The Minneapolis Institute of Arts, Minneapolis, Minnesota.

**Look** at the artwork on these pages. *The Birthplace of Herbert Hoover, West Branch, Iowa* was painted by Grant Wood in the Midwest region of the United States. *The Bicycle Race* was painted by Antonio Ruíz at about the same time in Mexico. Both artists used perspective techniques to create the illusion of depth in their paintings.

 **Art History and Culture**

Grant Wood was an American regionalist. He painted scenes from his region of the United States.

---

 **Art History and Culture**

## Grant Wood

Grant Wood (grant wo͞od) (1892–1942) was born in Iowa and was considered a regionalist painter. Regionalists painted idealistic scenes and events that were typical of their personal regions of the United States. Wood's landscapes were looked upon as idealized visions of America's heartland, but in the 1930s they were not contemporary. The United States at this time was in the middle of the machine age, and machines did not enter into Wood's landscapes. Many in Iowa thought Wood was a political radical. His painting of President Hoover's quiet, peaceful birthplace at a time when many were losing their farms was a statement about Hoover's insensitivity in dealing with America's economic situation.

See pages 24–25 and 16–21 for more about art history and the subject matter.

**Artist Profiles, p. 72**

◆ Artist Profile ◆

**Grant Wood**
1892–1942

Grant Wood (grant wo͞od) was born in Iowa and lived there most of his life. His father died when Wood was ten years old. When he was 14 he won third prize in a national Crayola contest by coloring a leaf. He studied drawing and design after high school. As a soldier in World War I, he designed artillery camouflage. After the war, Wood taught art in several high schools and studied art during multiple trips to Europe. In 1927, he retired from teaching high school to paint full-time. Later he served as the Iowa director of the Public Works Art Project. He taught at the University of Iowa and lectured across the nation.

▲ **Antonio Ruíz.** (Mexican).
*The Bicycle Race.* 1938.

Oil on canvas. 14½ × 16½ inches
(36.83 × 41.91 cm.). Philadelphia
Museum of Art, Philadelphia,
Pennsylvania.

**S**tudy both paintings to find examples of perspective techniques.

▶ Find an object that overlaps and covers part of a second object.

▶ Find an object that seems to be close to you. Find an object that seems to be far away.

▶ Find an object with very clear details. Find an object with few details.

▶ Find an object that is painted with bright colors. Find an object that is painted with dull colors.

▶ Find lines that seem to be getting closer together as they move away from you.

### Aesthetic Perception

**Seeing Like an Artist** Look around your classroom. Find objects and lines like the ones you found in the paintings.

Unit 5 • Lesson 2    **161**

## Art History and Culture

### Antonio Ruíz

Antonio Ruíz (an tōn´ yō rōō ēs´) (1897–1964) was a Mexican painter and stage designer. He first designed sets for the cinema and later for children's theater. He was nicknamed *El Corcito* because of his resemblance to a famous bullfighter of his time. His small paintings were known for their rich color and sense of humor. He created two murals in Mexico and four in San Francisco, California. He lived in the United States at different times in his life and was a painting teacher and founder of the School of Painting and Sculpture known as "La Esmeralda." Ruíz did not produce a large amount of works; he created about 50 oils and the same number of drawings.

See pages 24–25 and 16–21 for more about art history and the subject matter.

**Artist Profiles, p. 58**

♦ Artist Profile ♦

**Antonio Ruíz**
1897–1964

Antonio Ruíz (an tōn´ yō rōō ēs´) was born in Mexico City. He grew up in an educated family that also appreciated the arts. His grandfather was a painter, his mother a concert pianist, and his father a physician. As a child, Ruíz loved to play with construction sets. After studying art in Mexico, he moved to California, where he designed movie sets. After two years he returned to Mexico to paint and to direct children's theatre. In time, he became the director of Mexico's School of Painting and Sculpture. Ruíz also taught scenery design at the University of Mexico.

## Study

▶ Ruíz: The figures in the lower left overlap the viewing stands, which overlap the trees. Wood: There are trees that overlap each other.

▶ Wood: Individual leaves on the tree in the lower left corner are larger than the houses in the distance. Ruíz: The figures at the bottom seem closer than the soldiers in the middle ground.

▶ The trees in the distance do not have as much detail as the oak tree in the lower left corner.

▶ The colors on the clothes near the viewer seem brighter than those in the distance.

▶ Ruíz and Wood: The lines that define the edges of the roads seem to grow closer as they get farther from the viewer.

■ For more examples of art from North America, see the *Art Around the World Collection.*

### Art Journal: Writing

Have students create their own definitions for the six perspective techniques and place them in the Concepts section of their Art Journals. What else do they want to know about the six perspective techniques?

### Aesthetic Perception

**Seeing Like An Artist** Discuss which objects in the classroom look like images found in the paintings. Have students look out the classroom window, if possible, to expand their comparison. Items like bicycles and trees will most likely be located outside.

**Developing Visual Literacy** Have students speculate on what each painting says about the communities being depicted. How are these communities similar to their own? If they are different, have students describe their communities.

### Web Connection

Visit **www.asombrarte.net/artistas/ latinoamericanos/ruiz_antonio/ruiz.htm** to view more works of art by Antonio Ruíz. **Note:** This Web site is in Spanish and for teacher's use only. Use a search engine to translate the page, if needed.

LESSON 2 • Perspective Techniques **161**

# Teach

"How could you illustrate the six perspective techniques?" "¿Cómo pueden ilustrar las seis técnicas perspectivas?"

- Read and discuss the information about how to use the six perspective techniques on page 162.

## Practice

**Materials:** 12" × 18" white paper, pencils, erasers

**Alternate Materials:** dustless chalk

- Distribute the materials and have students follow the directions on page 162.

 ## Creative Expression

**Materials:** 12" × 18" white paper, pencils, erasers, dustless chalk, tempera paints in dispenser bottles, paper plates for palettes, paintbrushes of various sizes, containers for water

**Alternate Materials:** markers, crayons

- Distribute the materials and have students follow the directions on page 163.
- Have students integrate a variety of ideas about their families and communities in their landscape drawings.
  NSAE 2.a
- Review the Activity Tips on page 240 for visual examples of techniques if needed.

### Art Journal: Brainstorming

Have students brainstorm ideas to illustrate depth in a landscape and place their ideas in their Art Journals. Students should refer to these ideas for their Creative Expression activity.

# Using Perspective

**Perspective** is the technique used to create the feeling of depth on a flat surface. **Depth** is the appearance of distance on a flat surface. You saw examples of the following six perspective techniques in the two paintings on the previous pages.

 **Overlapping** When one object covers part of a second object, the first seems to be closer to the viewer.

 **Size** Large objects seem to be closer to the viewer than small objects.

 **Placement** Objects placed near the bottom of a picture seem to be closer to the viewer than objects placed higher on the picture.

 **Detail** Objects with clear, sharp edges and many details seem to be closer to the viewer. Objects that lack detail and have fuzzy outlines seem to be farther away.

 **Lines** Parallel lines seem to move toward the same point as they move farther away from the viewer.

 **Color** Brightly colored objects seem closer to the viewer. Objects with pale, dull colors seem to be farther away.

### Practice

Illustrate each of the six perspective techniques. Use a pencil.

1. Fold your paper into six equal boxes. Print the name of one perspective technique in each of the six boxes.

2. Draw designs to illustrate each perspective technique.

## Differentiated Instruction

**Reteach**
Have students look through this book to find five works of art that create the illusion of depth. Ask them to list the title of each work and describe the perspective techniques the artist used.

**Special Needs**
Sequence instruction for students with learning disabilities by having them include one perspective technique at a time and checking for understanding as each technique is incorporated.

**ELL**
Allow students to point to the perspective technique and use appropriate vocabulary as you or other students describe it so you can check for understanding.

◀ **Bill Keith.**
Age 9.

**Think** about the perspective techniques the student artist used in this landscape.

### Creative Expression

How can a landscape show perspective? Use perspective techniques in a landscape scene.

1. Think about the things you see in your environment every day.
2. Sketch several scenes you would like to draw. Include all six perspective techniques in your sketches.
3. Select your best sketch. Use chalk to draw the scene, and fill it with color. Remember to use all six perspective techniques to create the feeling of depth.

### Art Criticism

**Describe** Describe the subject matter of your painting.

**Analyze** How did you use perspective techniques to create the illusion of depth in your painting?

**Interpret** What kind of mood did you create in your painting? Which element do you think affects this mood most?

**Decide** If you could redo this painting, what would you do to improve it?

Unit 5 • Lesson 2   **163**

## Art Across the Curriculum

Use these simple ideas to reinforce art concepts across the curriculum.

★ **Narrative Writing** Have students write a story from the perspective of one of the cyclists in *The Bicycle Race.*

★ **Math** Explain to students that *circumference* is the outside measurement of a circle.

★ **Science** Have students discuss why the leaves of some trees change colors.

★ **Social Studies** Have students compare the idea of neighborhood in American and Hispanic societies.

★ **Technology** Using a paint or draw program, have students illustrate one of the six perspective techniques and label it. Visit **SRAonline.com** to print detailed instructions for this activity.
NSAE 6.b

 **R**eflect   Time: About 5 minutes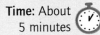

### Review and Assess

"Let's review the perspective techniques that artists use to show depth." "Revisemos las técnicas perspectivas que los artistas usan para demostrar profundidad."

## Think

The artist used all six perspective techniques. For example, overlapping can be seen in the tree branches; larger objects are placed in the foreground; and brighter-colored objects appear to be closer to the viewer.

■ Use *Large Prints 57 Nighthawks* and *58 Chance Meeting* to have students identify the perspective techniques that each artist used.

### Informal Assessment

■ Have students display their landscapes in an area of the room to create an exhibition. Invite other classes to visit the exhibition, but have those students who created the display interpret ideas in works of art presented by their peers.

■ For standardized-format test practice using this lesson's art content, see pages 56–57 in *Reading and Writing Test Preparation.*

### Art Journal: Critical Thinking

Have students answer the four art criticism questions—Describe, Analyze, Interpret, and Decide—in their Art Journals. Discuss the use of perspective in their paintings. Have students evaluate their classmates' paintings to see how they created the illusion of depth.

# Perspective Techniques

## Extra! For the Art Specialist

### Focus

Have students study **Large Print 57** *Nighthawks* and discuss how the feeling of depth was created in the artwork. How do the objects in the foreground differ from those in the middle ground and background?

### Teach

Review the six perspective techniques. Explain to students that they will create a cityscape, using the six perspective techniques. Then have them complete the alternate activity.

### Reflect

Have students use the four steps of art criticism to evaluate their work. Were students able to incorporate all six perspective techniques?

### Alternate Activity

**Materials:**
- sketchbooks
- 12" × 18" heavy white drawing paper
- pencils, erasers
- fine-line permanent marker
- watercolors
- brushes
- water containers
- newspapers
- color pencils
- city images

1. Look at images of cities and create a sketch of a real or imaginary city. Be sure to include the six perspective techniques.

2. Transfer their drawings onto paper. Paint the sky first. The other objects will then overlap this area of the painting. Continue painting their scene.

3. Use fine-line markers to outline the objects in the foreground and important objects in the middle ground. Objects in the background should not be outlined.

4. Use color pencils and markers to add details. Add any shadows, highlights, and textures last.

## Research in Art Education

Learning in the arts may help students develop a positive self-concept. Many studies have shown that the arts seem to "promote learning, interpersonal communication, and the establishment of positive identity." A positive self-concept is important, as it has been shown to "aid the development of necessary values and skills" ("The Effects of Arts and Music Education on Students' Self-Concept" in *Schools, Communities, and the Arts: A Research Compendium*).

## Assessment

Use the following rubric to evaluate the painting students make in the Creative Expression activity and to assess students' understanding of how perspective techniques are used in two-dimensional art.

Have students complete page 59 or 60 in their *Assessment* books.

| | Art History and Culture | Aesthetic Perception | Creative Expression | Art Criticism |
|---|---|---|---|---|
| **3 POINTS** | The student demonstrates knowledge of the lives and work of Wood and Ruíz. | The student accurately identifies the use of the six perspective techniques in two-dimensional art. | The student's landscape demonstrates the use of the six perspective techniques. | The student thoughtfully and honestly evaluates own work using the four steps of art criticism. |
| **2 POINTS** | The student's knowledge of the lives and work of Wood and Ruíz is weak or incomplete. | The student shows an emerging awareness of perspective techniques in two-dimensional art, but cannot consistently identify them. | The student's landscape shows some awareness of the six perspective techniques. | The student attempts to evaluate own work but shows an incomplete understanding of evaluation criteria. |
| **1 POINT** | The student cannot demonstrate knowledge of the lives and work of Wood or Ruíz. | The student cannot identify the six perspective techniques in two-dimensional art. | The student's landscape shows no understanding of the use of the six perspective techniques. | The student makes no attempt to evaluate own work. |

### Assessment, p. 59

Name _____ Date _____

**Lesson 2** UNIT 5

**Perspective Techniques**

**A. Matching**
Match each term in Column 1 with its description in Column 2.

**Column 1**
___ 1. parallel lines
___ 2. overlapping
___ 3. placement
___ 4. color

**Column 2**
a. Objects near the bottom of a picture seem to be closer than objects higher in the picture.
b. Objects that are pale seem to be farther away, while brightly colored objects seem closer.
c. Straight lines that seem to move toward the same point as they appear to move farther away.
d. One object partially covers another object.

**B. Drawing**
Draw three examples of perspective techniques. Label each technique.

**C. Writing**
Look at *The Bicycle Race* by Antonio Ruíz. Describe three different perspective techniques he used.

Level 4    Unit 5 • Space, Proportion, and Distortion    **59**

 **Lesson** **3** **Overview**

# Point of View

Lesson 3 introduces the concept of point of view. Artists often study an object or scene from different points of view and observe the space around it.

## Objectives

 **Art History and Culture**

To demonstrate knowledge about the life, culture, and art of Michael Naranjo

 **Creative Expression**

To take a photograph of a three-dimensional object from different points of view

 **Aesthetic Perception**

To identify how artists study an object from different points of view

 **Art Criticism**

To evaluate own work using the four steps of art criticism

### Vocabulary  Vocabulary

Review the following vocabulary word with students before beginning the lesson.

**point of view** **punto de vista**—the angle from which you see an object or scene

See page 179B for additional vocabulary and Spanish vocabulary resources.

 **Art Journal: Vocabulary**

Have students add this word to the Vocabulary section of their Art Journals.

## Lesson Materials
- white paper
- pencils, erasers
- camera and film
- three-dimensional objects

**Alternate Materials:**
- crayons
- markers
- digital camera
- computer
- printer
- scanner

## Program Resources
- *Reading and Writing Test Prep.,* pp. 58–59
- *Transparency 27*
- *Artist Profiles,* pp. 51
- *Animals Through History Time Line*
- *Assessment,* pp. 61–62
- *Large Prints 57* Nighthawks and *58* Chance Meeting
- *The National Museum of Women in the Arts Collection*

### Concept Trace
Point of View
**Introduced:** Level 4, Unit 1, Lesson 3
**Reinforced:** Level 4, Unit 5, Lesson 3

---

## Lesson 3 Arts Integration

### Theatre

Complete Unit 5, Lesson 3, on pages 94–95 of *Theatre Arts Connections.*

### Music

**SPOTLIGHT on MUSIC** Listen to "Promenade" from *Pictures at an Exhibition,* by Modest Mussorgsky. Each musical piece in *Pictures at an Exhibition* portrays one painting that Mussorgsky saw at an exhibit. He used variety in elements of tone color, tempo, melody, texture, beat, and rhythm to express his feelings, or point of view, of each of the paintings.

### Movement & Dance

Have students study an outdoor three-dimensional object, such as a tree, fence, or climbing bars. Have them look at the object in a variety of ways. How does their positioning affect their point of view?

# Focus

**Time:** About 10 minutes

## Activate Prior Knowledge

"Think about an object that you own and like very much. What happens to that object as you turn it and view it from different angles?"

"Piensen de un objeto que tienen y les gustan mucho. ¿Qué le pasa a ese objeto cuando lo viran y lo ven en angulos diferentes?"

■ Discuss students' responses. Explain that objects do not appear the same from different angles. For example, when you turn a bottle upside-down and just focus on the shape in front of you, the image will not look like a bottle at all. It will look like a circle if it is a tapered cylindrical shape.

### Using Literature ★ Reading

■ Read *The Gardener* by Sarah Stewart. Have students examine the illustrations in the book and explain a character's point of view.

### Thematic Connection ★ Science

■ **Balance:** Have students decide whether a real person could stand like the figure in *Eagle's Song*. Then have them create a list of words that they associate with the word *balance*.

## Introduce the Art

# Look

"Study the photos on these pages closely."

"Estudien detalladamente las fotografías en estas páginas."

### Cultural Symbolism ★ Social Studies

■ Have students discuss how different cultures symbolize the eagle. What does it mean in their community? Most students will say that the eagle symbolizes freedom and power to many cultures.

 ## Art History and Culture

Using only this book, students have studied these bronze sculptures: *Coming of Age* by Allan Houser; *Oval with Points* by Henry Moore; and *Egyptian Cat* by an unknown artist.

 **Web Connection**

Visit **www.acbvi.org/albums/hm/museum.html** for more information about Michael Naranjo and the visually impaired.

---

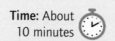  ## Point of View

▲ **Michael Naranjo.** (American). *Eagle's Song.* 1992.
Bronze. 12 × 22 × 10½ inches (30.48 × 55.88 × 26.67 cm.). Private collection.

**Look** at the sculpture on these pages. The images on these two pages show the same artwork from three different views. Michael Naranjo was blinded in the Vietnam War, so his ideas often come from things he saw in his past. The views of *Eagle's Song* from three different angles show his ability to create a three-dimensional piece of art from memory.

 ## Art History and Culture

What other bronze sculptures have you studied?

---

## Art History and Culture

### Michael Naranjo

Michael Naranjo (mī´ kəl nä rän´ hō) (1944– ) is a Tewa Native American of the Santa Clara Pueblo group. He is a sculptor and works mainly in wax and stone. As a child, Naranjo helped his mother, who was a potter, mix white clay with brown clay by stepping on it. Mixing the clay was like a dance, a rhythmic stepping. He was blinded by a grenade in 1968 while serving in the army in Vietnam. While in the hospital in Japan, he began modeling with clay. Naranjo gets his ideas for his sculptures from the past. He visualizes the image and, working carefully, feels his way around a piece of wax or stone as he first carves the image in his mind.

See pages 24–25 and 16–21 for more about art history and the subject matter.

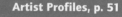

**Artist Profiles, p. 51**

**♦ Artist Profile ♦**

**Michael Naranjo**
b. 1944

Michael Naranjo (mī´ kəl nä rän´ hō) was born into a family of artists in the Tewa Indian pueblo in Santa Clara, New Mexico. His mother and three of his nine brothers and sisters are artists or writers. Naranjo's mother, a ceramic artist, taught all of her children to sculpt in clay. As a child Naranjo liked to make models of animals and people using his mother's clay.

In 1967 Naranjo was drafted into the army and sent to fight in the Vietnam War. When he was only 22 years old, a grenade exploded near his face, and he lost his eyesight. His right hand was also severely injured. Despite these disabilities, he used his skills to create figures in wax, and

Study the different views of the sculpture.

▶ What part of the sculpture do you notice first in each view?

▶ How do the shapes change in the different views?

▶ How do the shadows and highlights change?

 **Aesthetic Perception**

**Seeing Like an Artist** Slowly turn your hand while holding a pencil. Look at them from different angles. How does the pencil change as you turn it? How does your hand change as you turn it?

▲ **Michael Naranjo.** (American). *Eagle's Song.* 1992.
........................................
Bronze. 12 × 22 × 10½ inches (30.48 × 55.88 × 26.67 cm). Private collection.

## Art History and Culture

### Michael Naranjo

Naranjo finds wax easier to work with because if he makes a mistake, he can easily fix it by adding more wax to the form. Once he has completed his wax sculptures, they are then sent to a foundry, where they are cast in bronze. Naranjo prefers not to use tools when he sculpts with wax because he cannot feel what the tip of the metal piece is touching. Naranjo said this about his art: "My art comes from an emotion which is stimulated by external forms. I like the soft, gentle lines of life."

See pages 24–25 and 16–21 for more about art history and the subject matter.

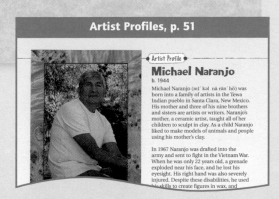

**Artist Profiles, p. 51**

*Artist Profile*
**Michael Naranjo**
b. 1944

Michael Naranjo (mīʹ kəl nä ränʹ hō) was born into a family of artists in the Tewa Indian pueblo in Santa Clara, New Mexico. His mother and three of his nine brothers and sisters are artists or writers. Naranjo's mother, a ceramic artist, taught all of her children to sculpt in clay. As a child Naranjo liked to make models of animals and people using his mother's clay.

In 1967 Naranjo was drafted into the army and sent to fight in the Vietnam War. When he was only 22 years old, a grenade exploded near his face, and he lost his eyesight. His right hand was also severely injured. Despite these disabilities, he used his skills to create figures in wax, and

## Study

▶ In each view of the sculpture, the wingspan is the most noticeable at first glance.

▶ In the first view, the shape of the wings is narrow, and the frontal shapes of the arms and legs bend forward. The view from above shows the broad shape of the head and the flat, wide wings. The back angle view organizes the sculpture into more defined shapes of the head, wings, torso, and legs.

▶ Highlights are picked up on the head, arms, and legs of the figure and also the tips of the wings in the first view. The second view highlights the arms and knee but uses more shadows to define the wing. The third view balances shadows of the back, head, and lower leg with highlights on the neck area, wing, and tail area.

■ For more examples of portraits, see *The National Museum of Women in the Arts Collection.*

**Art Journal: Writing**
Encourage students to explain what *point of view* means in the Concepts section of their Art Journals. What else do they want to know about point of view?

 **Aesthetic Perception**

**Seeing Like An Artist** Discuss students' responses. Make sure students notice how the shadows change on the hand and the pencil. Also they should notice that they see more or less of the pencil depending on their point of view. Ask students how they could create more dramatic shadows on their hands.

**Developing Visual Literacy** Discuss Naranjo's use of bronze as a medium. Ask students how a bronze sculpture would feel. Then ask them if the meaning behind the sculpture would change if it were made from a different medium.

**Web Connection**
Visit www.veteransadvantage.com/herovets/MichaelNaranjo.html for more information about Michael Naranjo. **Note:** This Web site is for teacher use only.

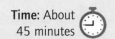

# Teach

**Time:** About 45 minutes

"How can you photograph an object from three points of view?" "¿Cómo pueden fotografiar un objeto desde tres puntos de vista?"

- Read and discuss using point of view on page 166.

## Practice

**Materials:** white paper, pencils, erasers

**Alternate Materials:** crayons, markers

- Explain that students will be drawing two different points of view and that their drawings will be line, or contour drawings. Review the definition of *contour drawing*.

- Distribute the materials and have students follow the directions on page 166.

## Creative Expression

**Materials:** camera, film, three-dimensional objects

**Alternate Materials:** pencil, paper, digital camera, computer, printer, scanner

- Distribute the materials and have students follow the directions on page 167.

- Have students integrate a variety of ideas about life events in their photographs.

- Have students invent ways to explore photographic imagery, using a variety of art media and materials.
  NSAE 1.a; 1.b; 1d

- Review the Activity Tips on page 241 for visual examples of techniques if needed.

### Art Journal: Planning

Have students create a list of objects they think look interesting from different points of view. Have them place their list in their Art Journals. Have students refer to their lists when they begin the Creative Expression activity.

# Using Point of View

A **point of view** is the angle from which the viewer sees an object. The shapes and forms a viewer sees depend on his or her point of view. There are four common points of view: front view, back view, side view, and overhead view.

Notice how your perception changes as you look at the same object from different points of view.

Front View

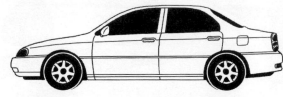
Side View

Back View

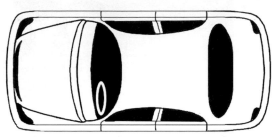
Overhead View

## Practice

Describe an object from two different points of view. Use a pencil.

1. Fold a sheet of paper in half. Label each half with the point of view you will be using. Select an object from your desk and study it carefully from two different points of view.

2. Write down the parts of the object you see from each point of view.

## Differentiated Instruction

**Reteach**

Have students look through a professional artist's portfolio or Web site and identify the points of view of five works of art.

**Special Needs**

To reinforce artists' use of point of view and to help students make connections to real life, include comic strips that utilize different points of view.

**ELL**

When discussing points of view, provide students with several visual images so they can see the difference between each view. Then show the images again, and have students practice using the correct vocabulary.

◀ **Madeline Jobrack.**
Age 9.

**Think** about the different points of view of the photographs.

### Creative Expression

What object would make an interesting subject to photograph from three different points of view? Photograph a three-dimensional object from three points of view.

1. Think about three-dimensional objects you would like to photograph. Select one.

2. Look carefully at the object you have chosen. Place it in front of you. Walk around it, stand above it, and lie on the ground and look at it. Choose and photograph the object from your three favorite points of view.

### Art Criticism

**Describe** What objects did you select to photograph?

**Analyze** Describe the shapes in your three photographs and how they changed with each different point of view.

**Interpret** What point of view is most interesting? Explain.

**Decide** What could make your photographs more interesting?

**eflect**

### Review and Assess

"What have we learned about point of view?"
"¿Qué hemos aprendido sobre el punto de vista?"

## Think

The artist photographed the wheelbarrow from the back, front and side.

■ Use *Large Prints 57 Nighthawks* and *58 Chance Meeting* and ask students to compare and contrast the points of view in each artwork.

### Informal Assessment

■ Have students create a separate photography portfolio. Have them exchange their portfolios with a partner and interpret moods and ideas in their peer's portfolio.
NSAE 5.a; 5.c

■ For standardized-format test practice using this lesson's art content, see pages 58–59 in *Reading and Writing Test Preparation.*

### Art Journal: Critical Thinking

Have students answer the four art criticism questions—Describe, Analyze, Interpret, and Decide—in their Art Journals. Have students discuss why they chose the photographs they did. If time permits, have the class create a photography exhibit to display the photographs so students can evaluate each other's work.

## Art Across the Curriculum

Use these simple ideas to reinforce art concepts across the curriculum.

★ **Poetry Writing** Have students write a poem about an eagle using similes.

★ **Math** Explain to students that a protractor is used to measure the size of an angle.

★ **Science** Have students list the characteristics of an eagle.

★ **Social Studies** Have students describe what their community has done to help the visually impaired.

★ **Technology** Using a paint or draw program, have students draw a computer from two different points of view. Visit **SRAonline.com** to print detailed instructions for this activity.
NSAE 6.b

# Extra! For the Art Specialist

**Time:** About 45 minutes

## Focus

Have students study **Large Print 58** *Chance Meeting* and discuss how artists study objects from different viewpoints to learn more about the object. Have them describe the objects they see in the poster.

## Teach

Review the four most common points of view with students. Have them handle different objects and look at them carefully from different points of view, describing how the shapes change as the point of view changes. Then have students complete the alternate activity.

## Reflect

Have students use the four steps of art criticism to evaluate their work. Have students describe the point of view they selected.

## Alternate Activity

**Materials:**
- sketchbooks
- pencils, erasers
- 9" × 12" white drawing paper
- charcoal
- kneaded erasers
- textbooks

1. Select three books to arrange. All three books must touch each other. Look at the books. Lay your head down or stand up to look at the arrangement. Select two points of view and make quick sketches.

2. Transfer one of their sketches onto paper. The drawing should almost touch the edges of the paper.

3. Begin by lightly working with the charcoal to color the drawing. Use a tissue to blend the charcoal to create medium values.

4. Use more pressure with the charcoal to create darker values. Knead the erasers and pick up the charcoal in areas that are the lightest. Try to create a range of values from very light to very dark in the artwork.

## Research in Art Education

"At a time when the development of thinking skills is particularly important . . . the presence of a program that fosters flexibility, promotes a tolerance for ambiguity, encourages risk taking and depends upon the exercise of judgment outside the sphere of rules is an especially valuable resource." (Eisner, Elliot W. *The Arts and the Creation of Mind.* New Haven: Yale Univ. Press, 2002.)

## Assessment

Use the following rubric to evaluate the artwork students make in the Creative Expression activity and to assess students' understanding of how artists use point of view.

Have students complete page 61 or 62 in their *Assessment* books.

| | Art History and Culture | Aesthetic Perception | Creative Expression | Art Criticism |
|---|---|---|---|---|
| **3 POINTS** | The student accurately demonstrates knowledge of the life, art, and culture of Naranjo. | The student accurately identifies how artists use different points of view in works of art. | The student's photograph shows how to use different points of view. | The student thoughtfully and honestly evaluates own work using the four steps of art criticism. |
| **2 POINTS** | The student shows an emerging awareness of the life, art, and culture of Naranjo but cannot consistently identify them. | The student shows an emerging awareness of how artists use different points of view, but cannot use it consistently. | The student's photograph shows some awareness of how to use different points of view. | The student attempts to evaluate own work but shows an incomplete understanding of evaluation criteria. |
| **1 POINT** | The student cannot demonstrate information about the life, art, or culture of Naranjo. | The student cannot identify how artists use different points of view in works of art. | The student's photograph shows no understanding of how to use different points of view. | The student makes no attempt to evaluate own work. |

### Assessment, p. 61

Name _____ Date _____ Lesson **3** UNIT 5

**Point of View**

**A. Drawing**
Draw a house using the four different points of view.

Back View — Overhead View

Front View — Side View

**B. Writing**
Describe how the shapes used in your four drawings changed with each perspective.

**C. Writing**
Look carefully at *Eagle's Song* by Michael Naranjo. Explain which point of view you like best.

Level 4 — Unit 5 • Space, Proportion, and Distortion **61**

 **Lesson 4 Overview**

# Face Proportion Measurements

Lesson 4 introduces the principle of proportion. **Proportion** is the principle of art concerned with the size relationship of one part to another. **Face proportions** are the relationship of one feature of a face to other features.

## Objectives

 **Art History and Culture**

To demonstrates knowledge of the lives and work of Auguste Renoir and Robert Henri

 **Aesthetic Perception**

To identify how accurate face proportion is used in two-dimensional portraits

 **Creative Expression**

To create a self-portrait, using correct face proportions

 **Art Criticism**

To evaluate own work using the four steps of art criticism

### Vocabulary  Vocabulary

Review the following vocabulary words with students before beginning the lesson.

**central axis** eje central—a real or imaginary line that is down the center of an object

**profile** perfil—a side view of a person or animal

See page 179B for additional vocabulary and Spanish vocabulary resources.

 **Art Journal: Vocabulary**

Have students add this word to the Vocabulary section of their Art Journals.

## Lesson Materials

- 12″ × 18″ white paper
- pencil, eraser
- soft and hard pastels
- mirrors

**Alternate Materials:**
- color pencils
- markers
- photographs

## Program Resources

- *Reading and Writing Test Prep.,* pp. 60–61
- *Transparency 28*
- *Flash Card* 18
- *Artist Profiles,* pp. 28, 56
- *Animals Through History Time Line*
- *Assessment,* pp. 63–64
- *Large Prints 57* Nighthawks and *58* Chance Meeting
- *Art Around the World Collection*

### Concept Trace
Face Proportions
**Introduced:** Level 4, Unit 5, Lesson 4

**Reinforced:** Level 5, Unit 4, Lesson 3

---

## Lesson 4 Arts Integration

### Theatre

Complete Unit 5, Lesson 4, on pages 96–97 of *Theatre Arts Connections.*

**Theatre Arts Connections, p. 96**

### Music

Faces have symmetry. In music, the form that has symmetry is ABA. In ABA form, the outer two sections are the same with a contrasting section in the middle. Have students sing or listen to "Cumber del Sol." The form is refrain, verse, refrain. Ask students if this the same form of "Shoo Fly."

### Movement & Dance

Have students explore a variety of facial expressions. Have them warm up their faces, using the following actions: chewing movements, open yawns, stretching and contracting the face. Then have students explore different facial expressions, such as sad, happy, confused, and anxious. Have students look at other students and note how the eyebrows, cheeks, and mouth effect expressions.

# Focus

**Time: About 10 minutes**

## Activate Prior Knowledge

"Have you seen a painted portrait before? "¿Han visto antes un retrato pintado?"

■ As a class, discuss student responses. Ask students how they think artists create portraits. Explain that sometimes artists have the subject pose for them each day that they work, and other times artists work from photographs. Have students compare and contrast a painted portrait and a photograph of a person.

### Using Literature [★] Reading

■ Look at the cover illustration of *Dear Mr. Henshaw* by Beverly Cleary. Discuss how face proportions are used on the cover.

### Thematic Connection [★] Science

■ **Feelings:** Have students examine the portraits of the children in this lesson and determine how they are feeling. What facial expressions led them to believe that the child was feeling this way?

## Introduce the Art

# Look

"Look closely at how face proportions are used in these two portraits." "Observen detalladamente cómo se usaron las proporciones faciales en estos dos retratos."

### Family [★] Social Studies

Have students communicate their ideas about what role children play in a family. Have them draw from their own life experiences and their sensory knowledge.

## Art History and Culture

Some contemporaries of Renoir and Henri were Camille Pissarro, Paul Gauguin, and Berthe Morisot. They were artists who lived and worked during the same period.

### Web Connection

Visit **www.expo-renoir.com** for more information about Renoir. **Note:** This Web site is for teacher use only.

## Lesson 4 — Face Proportion Measurements

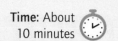

**Look** at the artwork on these pages. Renoir and Henri created many portraits. *Portrait of a Young Boy (Andre Berard)* was painted in 1879. *Bernadita* was painted in 1922. Notice the direction in which each subject is facing. Do the portraits appear to be real?

◀ **Auguste Renoir.** (French). *Portrait of a Young Boy (Andre Berard).* 1879.

Pastel on paper. $16\frac{1}{2} \times 11\frac{3}{4}$ inches (41.91 × 29.85 cm.). Norton Museum of Art, West Palm Beach, Florida.

 **Art History and Culture**

Renoir and Henri were contemporaries. What are contemporaries?

 **Art History and Culture**

### Auguste Renoir

At the age of 13, Auguste Renoir (o gūst´ ren´ war) (1841–1919) began painting on porcelain. Renoir, along with Claude Monet, was one of the founding members of the impressionist movement. The impressionists were the first to take their canvasses outdoors to paint in natural sunlight. Their goal was to give objects a shimmering, sunlit quality. At first, critics scorned the work of the impressionists. Today they are among the most admired painters in the history of art.

See pages 24–25 and 16–21 for more about art history and the subject matter.

**Artist Profiles, p. 56**

Artist Profile ◆

**Pierre-Auguste Renoir**
1841–1919

Pierre-Auguste Renoir (pyär´ ō gōst´ ren wär´) was one of the most widely known and best-loved European painters. The sixth of seven children, Renoir was born into a poor family in Limoges, France. His father was a tailor, and the family had to live in a slum, with few luxuries or comforts. Renoir showed signs of talent at an early age in many artistic fields. Although he was a talented singer, he became an apprentice at a porcelain factory, where for five years he copied French masterpieces onto plates and soup tureens. During this apprenticeship Renoir developed his brushwork and his passion for the eighteenth century French

◀ **Robert Henri.** (American). *Bernadita.* 1922.
••••••••••••••••••••••••••••
Oil on canvas. 24⅛ × 20⅛ inches
(61.27 × 51.11 cm.). San Diego
Museum of Art, San Diego, California.

**Study** the works of art to see how each artist used face proportions.

▶ What is the difference in the position of each face?

▶ Compare the placement of the mouth and the eyes in both paintings.

▶ Where are the ears in relation to the eyes and nose?

 **Aesthetic Perception**

**Design Awareness** Look at pictures in magazines. Are the faces in proportion?

# Art History and Culture

## Robert Henri

Although his name sounds French, Robert Henri (rob´ ərt hen´ rē) (1865–1929) was an American painter, born in Ohio. He was an advocate of realism, and he established a group known as *The Eight.* The group protested the ideal conservatism of the National Academy of Design. Henri painted mainly portraits and landscapes, using a thick application of paint and depicting light and shade by contrasting them boldly. After 1909, his paintings became more colorful as he experimented with the techniques of artist Hardesty Maratta.

See pages 24–25 and 16–21 for more about art history and the subject matter.

**Artist Profiles, p. 28**

**Artist Profile**
**Robert Henri**
1865–1929

Robert Henri (rob´ art hen´ rē) was born Robert Henry Cozad in Cincinnati, Ohio. He changed his name when his father was accused of murder. Henri showed great artistic talent at a young age and was encouraged by his parents to pursue painting at the Pennsylvania Academy of Fine Arts, and later the Academie Julian and École des Beaux-Arts in Paris, France. When he returned from Paris, he became a widely known and respected teacher, emphasizing the importance of his students' creative freedom. He also stressed his own artistic freedom and founded The Eight, a group of American artists who joined his rebellion against the strict confines of academic art.

# Study

▶ Renoir: The boy's head is tilted slightly to the right. Henri: The girl's face is tilted to the left.

▶ The boy's eyes are closer together than the girl's eyes. Both children have similar mouths, but the girl's lips are fuller.

▶ Renoir: The top of the ear lines up with the middle of the eyebrow, and the bottom of the ear lines up with the bottom of the nose. Henri: The top of the ear is hidden under the girl's hair, and the bottom of the ear lines up with the bottom of the nose.

■ For more examples of art from Europe, see *Art Around the World Collection.*

**Art Journal: Writing**
Have students explain what *proportion* means to them in the Concepts section of their Art Journals. What else do they want to know about face proportions?

**Aesthetic Perception**

**Design Awareness** Discuss how most of the faces have similar head shapes, which are oval; the eyes are spaced evenly on either side of the noses; and the ears seem to be in-line with the noses.

**Developing Visual Literacy** Have students look closely at the backgrounds of the two portraits. Do they think the backgrounds add anything to the portrait? What do they think about the color schemes? Have students explain what would happen if objects were added to the backgrounds.

**Web Connection**
Visit www.askart.com/Biography.asp for more information about Robert Henri. **Note:** This Web site is for teacher use only.

 **each**

Time: About 45 minutes

"How will you use face proportions in your self-portrait?" "¿Cómo usarían proporciones de la cara en su autorretrato?"

- Read and discuss using face proportions on page 170.

## Practice

**Materials:** 12″ × 18″ white paper, pencil, eraser

**Alternate Materials:** color pencils

- Distribute the materials and have students follow the directions on page 170.

## 🎨 Creative Expression

**Materials:** 12″ × 18″ white paper, pencil, eraser, soft and hard pastels, mirrors

**Alternate Materials:** color pencils, markers, photographs

- Distribute the materials and have students follow the directions on page 171.
- Review the Activity Tips on page 241 for visual examples of techniques if needed.

### 📓 Art Journal: Brainstorming

Ask students to look at themselves in a mirror. What makes them unique from the other students in their class? Have students write the things that make them unique in their Art Journals. Have them refer to this before they begin their Creative Expression activity.

**170** UNIT 5 • Space, Proportion, and Distortion

---

# Using Face Proportions

**Proportion** is the principle of art related to the size relationships of one part to another, such as a hand to a wrist. Artists use several techniques to draw things in proportion.

Artists use **face proportions** to help place features correctly on a human face. Artists use guidelines, which are lightly drawn lines, which are to more accurately draw both full-face and profile portraits.

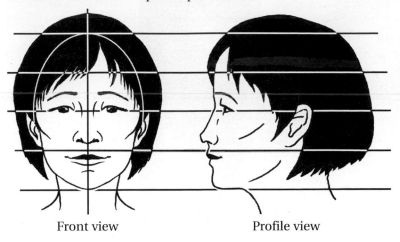

Front view          Profile view

## Practice

Practice drawing a profile. Use a pencil.

1. Draw the shape of the head in profile. Add guidelines, using the second drawing shown above as a reference.
2. Add the eye, nose, mouth, chin, ear, hair, and neck.

**170**   Unit 5 • Lesson 4

---

### ✦ Differentiated Instruction ✦

**Reteach**

Have students find an example of a face in a magazine. Ask them to draw a line down the center, the central axis, and the three guidelines showing the eyes, bottom of the nose, and hairline.

**Special Needs**

Sequence instruction for students by allowing time for guided practice of portrait techniques. Students can practice techniques, using a predrawn face template with light guidelines.

**ELL**

When explaining face proportions to students, point to where the central axis and the three guidelines would be on your face. Then have students demonstrate on their own faces.

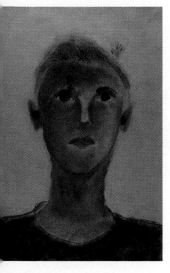

◀ **Taylor Bontz.**
Age 9.

**Think** about how the student artist created this self-portrait.

###  Creative Expression

Spend a few minutes examining your face in a mirror. Draw a self-portrait with accurate face proportions.

1. Draw an egg shape for your head.

2. Draw a guideline from the top of the oval to the bottom. Draw a horizontal line across the center. Divide each half one more time with light guidelines.

3. Sketch your eyes so that the center line goes through the center of each eye. Be sure you have a space between the eyes about the width of one eye. Follow the diagram on page 170. Draw your nose, ears, hair, and neck.

4. Use pastels to add color. Color the background with a contrasting color.

### Art Criticism

**Describe** List the steps you followed to draw your self-portrait.

**Analyze** Describe the shapes and lines you used to draw the features in your self-portrait.

**Interpret** What kind of emotion is represented in your self-portrait?

**Decide** What could you do to the background to make it more interesting?

Unit 5 • Lesson 4    **171**

### Review and Assess

"What have you learned about face proportions in self-portraits?" "¿Qué han aprendido acerca de proporciones de cara en autorretratos?"

## Think

The artist created a front view of the subject's face. The eyes are evenly spaced, with the nose in between them.

■ Use **Large Prints 57** *Nighthawks* and **58** *Chance Meeting* and ask students to compare how the two images use face proportions. How are they similar? How are they different?

### Informal Assessment

■ Invite a local artist to the class, who specializes in portraits, if possible. Have students interpret ideas and moods in the artist's portfolio. NSAE 5.a

■ For standardized-format test practice using this lesson's art content, see pages 60–61 in **Reading and Writing Test Preparation.**

### Art Journal: Critical Thinking

Have students answer the four art criticism questions—Describe, Analyze, Interpret, and Decide—in their Art Journals. Have students discuss within table groups how they used face proportion. Ask them to notice the similarities and differences. Have the groups share their findings with the class.

## Art Across the Curriculum

Use these simple ideas to reinforce art concepts across the curriculum.

★ **Personal Writing** Have students create a list of things they would like to wear in their next school picture.

★ **Math** Explain to students that symmetry occurs when an object can be divided into two identical halves.

★ **Science** Explain to students that each half of a person's face is slightly different, even though each half seems to be the same.

★ **Social Studies** Have students explain the role school plays in children's lives.

★ **Technology** In a word-processing program, have students insert two examples of clip art that demonstrate correct face proportions and two that do not. Have them label each example. Visit **SRAonline.com** to print detailed instructions for this activity. NSAE 6.b

# Face Proportion Measurements

## Extra! For the Art Specialist

**Time:** About 45 minutes

### Focus

Have students study **Large Print 57** *Nighthawks* to learn how artists depict face proportions in their artwork. Have them describe how the artist arranged the facial features.

### Teach

Demonstrate drawing a face in proportion for students. Explain to students that they will draw a face in proportion, using either a magazine image or a personal photograph. Then have them follow the steps for the alternate activity.

### Reflect

Have students use the four steps of art criticism to evaluate their work. Have students describe the image they selected and how they drew correct face proportions.

### Alternate Activity

**Materials:**
- sketchbooks
- pencils, erasers
- 12" × 18" white or black paper
- personal photographs or magazine images
- tempera paints
- paintbrushes
- mixing trays
- water containers
- cotton swab
- newspaper

1. Find an image of a face showing a frontal view. Practice drawing the face in proportion.

2. Select white or black paper. Use a light piece of chalk to sketch the face.

3. Paint the skin first. Next paint the whites of the eyes, the iris, and the clothing. Use a cotton swab to paint the pupil. Layer colors to create textures.

4. Create a background that best complements the portrait.

## Research in Art Education

"The arts help students develop their abilities to appreciate and interpret art of other cultures and to learn about people of the past through exposure to reproductions, to art works in museums and galleries, or through discussions about contemporary artists and art works." (Andra Nyman, "Cultural Content, Identity, and Program Development: Approaches to Art Education for Elementary Educators," in *Contemporary Issues in Art Education*, edited by Y. Gaudelius and P. Speirs, 61–69. New Jersey: Prentice Hall, 2002.)

## Assessment

Use the following rubric to evaluate the artwork students make in the Creative Expression activity and to assess students' understanding of how face proportion is used in creating portraits.

Have students complete page 63 or 64 in their *Assessment* books.

| | Art History and Culture | Aesthetic Perception | Creative Expression | Art Criticism |
|---|---|---|---|---|
| **3 POINTS** | The student demonstrates knowledge of the lives and work of Renoir and Henri. | The student accurately identifies the use of accurate face proportions in a variety of works of art. | The student's artwork demonstrates how to use correct face proportions. | The student thoughtfully and honestly evaluates own work using the four steps of art criticism. |
| **2 POINTS** | The student's knowledge of the lives and work of Renoir and Henri is weak or incomplete. | The student shows an emerging awareness of accurate face proportions in a variety of works of art but cannot consistently identify them. | The student's artwork shows some awareness of how to use correct face proportions. | The student attempts to evaluate own work but shows an incomplete understanding of evaluation criteria. |
| **1 POINT** | The student cannot demonstrate knowledge of the lives and work of Renoir or Henri. | The student cannot identify how accurate face proportions are used in an artwork. | The student's artwork shows no understanding of how to use correct face proportions. | The student makes no attempt to evaluate own work. |

**Assessment, p. 63**

Name _____ Date _____

**Face Proportion Measurements**

Lesson 4 UNIT 5

**A. Matching**
Match each word in Column 1 to its definition in Column 2.

Column 1
___ 1. portrait
___ 2. self-portrait
___ 3. proportion

Column 2
a. an image of a person, especially the face and upper body
b. the relationship of one part to another or to the whole
c. the image of a person's face painted by that person

**B. Drawing**
Draw a face using correct face proportions.

**C. Writing**
Look at *Portrait of a Young Boy* and *Bernadita*. Write a paragraph comparing each of the portraits.

Level 4          Unit 5 • Space, Proportion, and Distortion    **63**

## Lesson 5 Overview

# Body Proportions

Lesson 5 continues with the concept of proportion and discusses how body proportions are used. **Body proportions** are based on the average size of the human figure, which is $7\frac{1}{2}$ heads tall.

## Objectives

 **Art History and Culture**

To demonstrate knowledge of the lives and works of Andrea del Verrochio and Duane Hanson

 **Creative Expression**

To create a drawing of a model, using correct body proportions

 **Aesthetic Perception**

To understand how body proportions are used to convey real-life human forms in three-dimensional works of art

 **Art Criticism**

To evaluate own work using the four steps of art criticism

### Vocabulary  Vocabulary

Review the following vocabulary word with students before beginning the lesson.

**proportion** proporción—refers to the relationship of one part to another part

See page 179B for additional vocabulary and Spanish vocabulary resources.

 **Art Journal: Vocabulary**

Have students add this word to the Vocabulary section of their Art Journals.

### Lesson Materials

- magazines
- pencil, eraser
- scissors
- ruler
- 9" × 12" white drawing paper
- crayons

**Alternate Materials:**

- photographs from home
- color pencils

### Program Resources

- *Reading and Writing Test Prep.*, pp. 62-63
- *Transparency 29*
- *Flash Card* 18
- *Artist Profiles*, pp. 25, 70
- *Animals Through History Time Line*
- *Assessment*, pp. 65-66
- *Large Prints 57* Nighthawks and *58* Chance Meeting
- *The National Museum of Women in the Arts Collection*

### Concept Trace

**Body Proportions**

**Introduced:** Level 4, Unit 5, Lesson 5

**Reinforced:** Level 5, Unit 4, Lesson 1

---

## Lesson 5 Arts Integration

### Theatre

Complete Unit 5, Lesson 5, on pages 98–99 of *Theatre Arts Connections.*

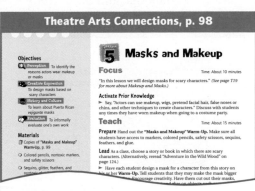

### Music

 In a large form of music that has movements, acts, or stand alone compositions, the composer takes care to balance the size of each to create unity within the whole. Have students listen to "Nessun Dorma" from *Turandot* by Giacomo Puccini. The format of an opera is so large that all the action can stop for the singing of an aria. An aria can also stand on its own in vocal performances.

### Movement & Dance

Have students explore a variety of expressive body gestures. Have students perform the following warm-up exercises: roll their shoulders, circle their arms, rock their hips, and lift their knees. Have them create a series of gestures using different parts of the body that show they are surprised, angry, or curious.

# Focus

## Activate Prior Knowledge

"Have you ever seen a realistic statue of a person?" "¿Han visto alguna vez una estatua realista de una persona?"

- As a class, discuss student responses. Explain that in many statues, artists go to great lengths to get the right proportions. The Greeks created sculptures based on what they believed were ideal beauty and proportions. Contemporary sculptures are based on what real people look like, not of the "ideal" figure, as in ancient Greece.

### Using Literature 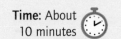 Reading

- Read *Grandfather's Journey* by Allen Say. Have students evaluate the images of people to see if they have correct body proportions.

### Thematic Connection 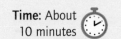 Science

- **Human Body:** Explain to students that skin protects the human body and helps keep out germs and other harmful materials. What other facts do students know about the human body?

## Introduce the Art

# Look

"Look closely at how the works of art are based on body proportions." "Miren de cerca cómo las obras de arte son basadas en proporciones del cuerpo."

### Mood 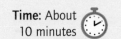 Reading

Have students interpret the mood the artists created in each statue. Some might say that Verrocchio created a powerful and determined mood, and Hanson created a thoughtful, and possibly a sad, mood.

 **Art History and Culture**

The bronze that was used to make *David* is visible. Hanson used bronze for the interior structure for *High School Student*.

 **Web Connection**

Visit **www.kfki.hu/~arthp/bio/v/verocchi/ biograph.html** for more information about Verrocchio.
**Note:** This Web site is for teacher use only.

---

 **Lesson 5** Body Proportions

**Look** at the artwork on these pages. Andrea del Verrocchio was an Italian painter and sculptor. *David* is probably his most popular sculpture. Duane Hanson created many life-size sculptures of human figures. His sculptures are so realistic that they are often mistaken for live people.

◀ **Andrea del Verrocchio.** (Italian). *David.* 1473–1475.
••••••••••••••••••••••••••••••••••
Bronze with traces of gold leaf. $49\frac{3}{16}$ inches tall (125 cm.). Museo Nazionale del Bargello, Florence, Italy.

 **Art History and Culture**

Both *David* and *High School Student* are made of bronze. Why do they look different?

 **Art History and Culture**

## Andrea del Verrocchio

Andrea del Verrocchio (än drā´ ə del və rô´ kē ō) (1435-1488) was born in Florence, Italy, and operated a successful artists' workshop. He is best known as the master of Leonardo da Vinci, and his work is often overshadowed by his famous student. Verrocchio was a goldsmith, sculptor, draftsman, and painter, but not much of his work survives today. The inspiration for his work came from the contemporary interest in the past and in the study of nature. He approached each of his projects as a new challenge and often went against traditional aesthetics and conventional techniques.

See pages 24–25 and 16–21 for more about art history and the subject matter.

**Artist Profiles, p. 70**

**Artist Profile**

**Andrea del Verrocchio**
1435-1488

Andrea del Verrocchio (än drā´ ə del və rô´ kē ō) was a Florentine sculptor during the early Italian Renaissance. He was born Andrea di Cione, and he took the name Verrocchio from the master in his first apprenticeship, Giuliano Verrocchi. Originally a goldsmith, the artist eventually became a sculptor, and also did some painting. His family was rarely financially secure, so he supported several of his brothers and sisters through the sale of his artwork. Later he provided the funds for the education of his younger brother's children. Verrocchio never married. Instead he immersed himself in the creation of his

**Study** the body proportions of these sculptures.

► Which artist's work looks more realistic? Explain.

► Can you figure out which objects in *High School Student* were not created by Hanson, but were added?

► How are the sculptures similar and how are they different?

◄ **Duane Hanson.** (American). *High School Student.* 1990.
Mixed media with accessories. Collection of Mrs. Duane Hanson.

## Aesthetic Perception

**Design Awareness** Think about when you shop for clothes. How are the clothes arranged?

## Art History and Culture

### Duane Hanson

As a boy, Duane Hanson (dwān han[t]´ sən) (1925–1996) carved figures out of logs. As an adult, he became a high school art teacher. He experimented with many styles and mediums in the 1950s, but he could not find the right mixture to communicate his feelings. During the 1960s, he discovered how he wanted to use art to communicate to people. After he saw the work of George Segal, he began to develop his "expressionist realism." He first created macabre sculptures to make political statements, but then he turned to social statements. Hanson said this about his later work: "My art is not about fooling people. It's the human attitudes I am after… My work is a re-creation, not a facsimile."

See pages 24–25 and 16–21 for more about art history and the subject matter.

**Artist Profiles, p. 25**

**Artist Profile**

**Duane Hanson**
1925-1996
Duane Hanson (dwān han´ sən) carved little figures out of logs using kitchen knives as a boy in his native Minnesota. Later he attended art school and taught art in Atlanta, Georgia and Miami, Florida. The same art dealer who discovered Andy Warhol arranged for Hanson's first solo exhibition. His life-size sculptures of ordinary people were an immediate success with the public. People could identify with his work. Hanson married and had five children. He continued to plan and create sculpture until the end of his life.

## Study

► Hanson's work looks more realistic because he placed real clothes on the student. Also his skin color and hair look real.

► The clothes, shoes, and book were added to the statue. The hair is probably a wig, which was also added.

► Both sculptures are of men, and they are standing. Both have one arm straight and one arm bent. Hanson's student looks lifelike and is actually wearing clothes. Verrocchio's man is one color, and his clothes are part of the sculpture.

■ For more examples of portraits, see *The National Museum of Women in the Arts Collection.*

### Art Journal: Writing

Encourage students to write about what they know about statues in the Concepts section of their Art Journals. What else do they want to know about statues and body proportion?

## Aesthetic Perception

**Design Awareness** Stores usually arrange clothes by department (men, women, boys, and girls). Then, within each department the clothes are grouped by designer or size. Explain to students that this system assists customers when they need to find clothes that are proportionate to their bodies.

**Developing Visual Literacy** Have students speculate if the mood that each artist intended would change if the statues in this lesson were placed in a different environment. For example, if David were placed in a garden with many bright flowers, he might not look as powerful or strong. What would happen if David were placed next to a warrior that was taller?
NSAE 4.c; 5.a

## Web Connection

Visit **www.artmolds.com/ali/halloffame/duane_hanson.htm** for more information about Duane Hanson. **Note:** This Web site is for teacher use only.

 **each** **Time:** About 45 minutes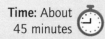

"How can you use body proportions in a drawing?" "¿Cómo pueden usar proporciones del cuerpo en una pintura?"

- Read and discuss using body proportions on page 174.

## Practice

**Materials:** magazines, scissors, ruler

**Alternate Materials:** photographs from home

- Distribute the materials and have students follow the directions on page 174.

##  Creative Expression

**Materials:** pencils, 9" × 12" white drawing paper, magazines, crayons

**Alternate Materials:** color pencils

- Distribute the materials and have students follow the directions on page 175.

- Review the Activity Tips on page 242 for visual examples of techniques if needed.

### Art Journal: Planning

Ask students to work with a partner, listing questions and observations based on body proportions in their Art Journals. Have them refer to these lists when in preparation for the Creative Expression activity.

# Using Body Proportions

Although people vary in size and shape, most people have the same proportions.

Artists use the length of the head, from the chin to the top of the skull, to help them in measuring proportion. The average adult is seven and one-half heads tall. A child may be five heads tall, while an infant might be only three heads tall.

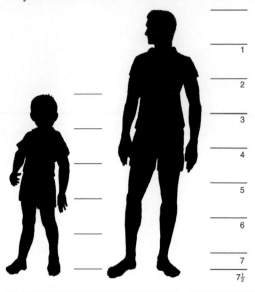

### Practice

Compare body proportions.

1. Look through a magazine and cut out pictures of an adult, a child, and an infant. Make sure that the pictures you find are complete images of each person, standing or walking.

2. Measure the head in each photo. Use that measurement to see how many "head" lengths the body is.

## Differentiated Instruction

**Reteach**

Have students look through their **Art Connections** textbook for examples of body proportion.

**Special Needs**

Drawing correct body proportions can be a challenge for many students. Because of this, be sure to provide ample time for guided practice with students during this lesson activity.

**ELL**

Have students practice the "heads tall" concept by figuring out how many "heads tall" they are. Then have them figure out how many "heads tall" you are.

◀ **Sarah Bowie.**
Age 9.

**Think** about how this student artist used body proportion.

 **Creative Expression**

How would you draw a figure with correct body proportions? Use sighting to help you get correct proportions.

1. Study the model and setting. Use sighting to determine how the different parts relate to each other.
2. Place the lines for seven and one-half "heads." Fill the paper from top to bottom.
3. Sketch the figure; use a light color crayon such as yellow.
4. After the sketch is complete, fill your composition with color, texture, and value.

 **Art Criticism**

**Describe** Describe the pose of the model and the setting.

**Analyze** What details did you add to your drawing?

**Interpret** What type of mood does your drawing communicate?

**Decide** Do you feel you were able to use body proportions successfully in your drawing? Explain.

**eflect** 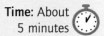 Time: About 5 minutes

### Review and Assess
"How did you use correct body proportions in your final drawing?" "¿Cómo usaron correctamente las proporciones del cuerpo en su dibujo final?"

## Think
The artist used correct body proportions in the portrait. The objects in the background do not look larger or smaller than necessary.

■ Use *Large Prints 57 Nighthawks* and *58 Chance Meeting* and ask students to compare how the artists each used body proportions in their works of art. How are they different? How are they similar?

### Informal Assessment
■ Have students interpret ideas in their peer's portraits. Have them examine the portraits to see if there is any type of message being communicated.
NSAE 5.a; 5.b
■ For standardized-format test practice using this lesson's art content, see pages 62–63 in *Reading and Writing Test Preparation.*

**Art Journal: Critical Thinking**
Have students answer the four art criticism questions—Describe, Analyze, Interpret, and Decide—in their Art Journals. Have students discuss as a class how they used body proportions in their drawings. Before they learned about body proportions, how did they create drawings of people?

### Art Across the Curriculum

Use these simple ideas to reinforce art concepts across the curriculum.

★ **Persuasive Writing** Have students write a letter persuading an artist to use them as his or her next model of a student.

★ **Math** Have students convert the height of *David* to feet and meters.

★ **Science** Explain to students the difference between mass and weight.

★ **Social Studies** Have students discuss ancient Greece and Rome.

★ **Technology** Using a paint or draw program, have students draw a simple figure with correct body proportions. Visit **SRAonline.com** to print detailed instructions for this activity.
NSAE 6.b

**Lesson 5**

 **Wrap-Up**

# Body Proportions

---

## Extra! For the Art Specialist

**Time:** About 45 minutes

### Focus

Study **Large Print 58** *Chance Meeting* and discuss how body proportion was used. How are the body parts arranged? Are the people in the right proportion?

### Teach

Explain to students that they will create a series of quick studies of their classmates, concentrating on their gestures and body proportions. They will select one of their studies to make a final pen-and-watercolor-wash painting. Have students complete the alternate activity.

### Reflect

Have students use the four steps of art criticism to evaluate their work. Have students describe how they used correct body proportions.

### Alternate Activity

**Materials:**

- sketchbooks
- pencils, erasers
- 9" × 12" white drawing paper
- medium-point pen or permanent marker
- watercolor paints
- large wash brushes
- water containers
- paper towels, newspaper

1. Take turns posing for one another, making several quick drawings.

2. Use a pen or marker to transfer one of their sketches onto paper. Be sure to keep the figure in the correct proportions. Shading techniques such as hatching and cross-hatching can be added.

3. Use watercolors to create washes over their drawings. You may choose to use only two colors, cool or warm colors, or just a light wash of one color.

### Research in Art Education

Arts competencies can be beneficial when problems need to be solved in other disciplines—for example, "when a theory in science could be understood more fully through the construction of a three-dimensional mobile; or when a mathematical problem could be approached more easily through a closely observed drawing of a shell" ("Learning in and Through the Arts: Curriculum Implications" in *Champions of Change*, p. 42).

---

## Assessment

Use the following rubric to evaluate the artwork students make in the Creative Expression activity and to assess students' understanding of how body proportions are used in two-dimensional works of art.

Have students complete page 65 or 66 in their *Assessment* books.

| | Art History and Culture | Aesthetic Perception | Creative Expression | Art Criticism |
|---|---|---|---|---|
| **3 POINTS** | The student demonstrates knowledge of the lives and work of Verrocchio and Hanson. | The student accurately identifies the use of body proportions in three-dimensional works of art. | The student's drawing demonstrates how to use correct body proportions. | The student thoughtfully and honestly evaluates own work using the four steps of art criticism. |
| **2 POINTS** | The student's knowledge of the lives and work of Verrocchio and Hanson is weak or incomplete. | The student shows an emerging awareness of body proportions in three-dimensional works of art but cannot consistently identify them. | The student's drawing shows some awareness of how to use correct body proportions. | The student attempts to evaluate own work but shows an incomplete understanding of evaluation criteria. |
| **1 POINT** | The student cannot demonstrate knowledge of the lives and work of Verrocchio or Hanson. | The student cannot identify body proportions in three-dimensional works of art. | The student's drawing shows no understanding of how to use correct body proportions. | The student makes no attempt to evaluate own work. |

**Assessment, p. 65**

Name _____ Date _____

**Lesson 5** UNIT 5

**Body Proportions**

**A.** Short Answer
Write the answer to the question.
What are body proportions?

**B.** Drawing
Draw the human body in proportion.

**C.** Writing
Look at *High School Student* by Duane Hanson. Write a paragraph describing the sculpture and its proportions.

Level 4    Unit 5 • Space, Proportion, and Distortion **65**

## Lesson 6 — Distortion
### Overview

Lesson 6 introduces another type of proportion known as distortion. **Distortion** is when the objects are stretched, bent, or twisted from their normal proportions.

### Objectives

 **Art History and Culture**

To demonstrate knowledge of the lives and work of Salvador Dalí and Marc Chagall

 **Creative Expression**

To create a distorted computer image

 **Aesthetic Perception**

To identify and better understand how distortion is used in both two-dimensional works of art

 **Art Criticism**

To evaluate own work using the four steps of art criticism

---

## Vocabulary ⭐ Vocabulary

Review the following vocabulary words with students before beginning the lesson.

**distortion** distorsión—a deviation from normal or expected proportions

**exaggeration** exageración—an increase or enlargement beyond what is expected or normal

See page 179B for additional vocabulary and Spanish vocabulary resources.

 **Art Journal: Vocabulary**

Have students add these words to the Vocabulary section of their Art Journals.

---

### Lesson Materials

- envelopes
- scrap paper
- pencil
- digital camera
- computer
- draw or paint software
- printer, paper

**Alternate Materials:**

- photographs from home
- word-processing program
- scanner

### Program Resources

- *Reading and Writing Test Prep.*, pp. 64–65
- *Transparency 30*
- *Artist Profiles*, pp. 11, 15
- *Animals Through History Time Line*
- *Assessment*, pp. 67–68
- *Large Prints 57* Nighthawks and *58* Chance Meeting
- *Art Around the World Collection*

### Concept Trace

Distortion

**Introduced:** Level 4, Unit 5, Lesson 6

**Reinforced:** Level 5, Unit 4, Lessons 4–5

---

## Lesson 6 Arts Integration

### Theatre

Complete Unit 5, Lesson 6, on pages 100–105 of *Theatre Arts Connections.*

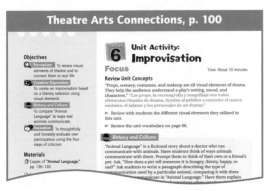

Theatre Arts Connections, p. 100

### Music

 Distortion is not a term used in music; however, if you lengthen out a melody by making it twice as slow, it is called augmentation. Have students sing or listen to "Mongolian Sheep Herding Song." The melodic pattern is sung in quarter notes until the last phrase. Ask students what note value is used to create augmentation.

### Movement & Dance

Have students form a large circle. While they hold hands, have students explore ways that the circle can be distorted. Have some students high and some low, or have half of the circle move with one type of energy and the other half move with another type.

# Focus

Time: About 10 minutes

## Activate Prior Knowledge

"Have you ever seen a cartoon character with a strange face?" "¿Han visto alguna vez un carácter de muñe quitos con una cara extraña?"

- As a class, discuss students' responses. Explain that many cartoon characters have a distorted feature on their faces. Sometimes people can tell if the character is good, bad, smart, or silly just by looking at the distorted features. Ask students what kind of facial distortions would give a clue to how a character is feeling.

### Using Literature ⭐ Reading

- Read *Zathura* by Chris Van Allsburg. Have students discuss how reality has been distorted in the story. Then have students identify any illustrations that have been distorted.

### Thematic Connection ⭐ Social Studies

- **Taking a Stand:** Have students discuss why Dalí's and Chagall's art might not be appreciated by many people. They both took a stand and created the type of art they wanted to.

## Introduce the Art

# Look

"Study the two works of art on these pages. Why don't these images look real?" "Estudien las dos obras de arte en estas páginas. ¿Por qué estas imágines no lucen real?"

### Predicting Outcomes ⭐ Math

Have students predict if the elephants in Dalí's painting could physically walk.

## Art History and Culture

Abstract and nonobjective art are similar, but there are no recognizable objects in a nonobjective work of art.

### 🖥 Web Connection

Visit **www.salvadordalimuseum.org/** for more information about Salvador Dalí. **Note:** This Web site is for teacher use only.

---

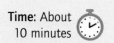

# Distortion

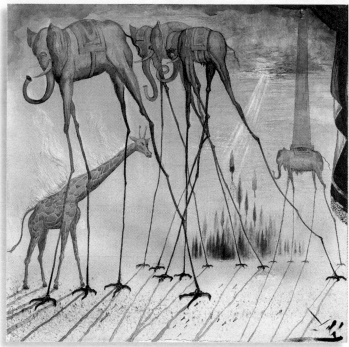

**Look** at the artwork on these pages. Both of these paintings include people and animals that do not look normal. The elephants in Dalí's painting have stretched legs and bird-like feet. In Chagall's painting, the cat has a human face, and the man has two faces. Both works of art look like they belong in a dream.

▲ **Salvador Dalí.** (Spanish). *The Elephants* (Design from the Opera la Dona Spagnola il Cavaliere Romana). 1961.
..........................
Pencil, watercolor, gouache. 27.5 × 27.5 inches (69.9 × 69.9 cm.). Indianapolis Museum of Art, Indianapolis, Indiana.

## Art History and Culture

Both of these paintings are abstract. What is the difference between abstract and nonobjective art?

---

## Art History and Culture

### Salvador Dalí

Salvador Dalí's (sal´ və dor dä´ lē) (1904–1989) talent was recognized early, after his first one-man show in Barcelona in 1925. His painting *Persistence of Memory* is still one of the best-known surrealist works. By 1940 Dalí was moving into a new style that eventually became known as his classic period, which focused on science and religion. As an artist, Dalí was not limited to a particular style or media. The body of his work, from early impressionist paintings through his transitional surrealist works, and into his classical period, reveals an evolving artist.

Dalí worked in all media, including oils, watercolors, drawings, graphics, sculptures, and jewelry.

See pages 24–25 and 16–21 for more about art history and the subject matter.

**Artist Profiles, p. 15**

**Artist Profile**
**Salvador Dalí**
1904–1989

Salvador Dalí (sal´ və dor dä lē´) was born in Spain and grew up in a prosperous family. During his childhood he spent summers in a small coastal village in Spain, where his parents built his first studio, and many of his paintings portray his love of that area. Dalí earned fame and recognition early in his career with exhibitions in both Europe and the United States, and he continued to receive attention throughout his career, which spanned many styles and artistic experiments. Dalí was a surrealist, and he considered his paintings to be "dream photographs." He explored many different techniques and materials which influenced the surrealist movement everywhere. He ...ved to America and then Spain, where he

**Study** how each artist used distortion.

▶ Which painting has more noticeable distortion?

▶ In each artwork, which images look strange but are not distorted?

▶ What feelings do you experience when you look at these paintings?

▲ **Marc Chagall.** (Russian/French). *Paris Through the Window.* 1913.

Oil on canvas. $53\frac{1}{2} \times 55\frac{3}{4}$ inches (135.89 × 141.61 cm.). Solomon R. Guggenheim Museum, New York, New York.

### 🔍 Aesthetic Perception

**Seeing Like an Artist** Think about how a person's face changes when he or she hears good or bad news. What happens to his or her face?

### 🏺 Art History and Culture

#### Marc Chagall

Marc Chagall (märk shə gäl′) (1887–1985) was born in Vitsyebsk, a small town in Russia. He studied art in Saint Petersburg and then in Paris. After the Russian Revolution he returned to his hometown to become the director of the Art Academy of Vitsyebsk. In 1919 Chagall became art director of the Moscow Jewish State Theater, where he painted murals in the lobby and created sets for the shows. In 1923 he returned to France, where he lived most of the remainder of his life. Chagall was influenced by French cubism and Russian expressionism.

See pages 24–25 and 16–21 for more about art history and the subject matter.

**Artist Profiles, p. 11**

◆ Artist Profile ◆

**Marc Chagall**
1887–1985

Marc Chagall (mark sha gäl′) was born in a small town in Russia, Vitebsk, which is now part of Belarus. He studied art in Saint Petersburg and then in Paris, France. After the Russian revolution he served as the director of the art academy in his hometown. From 1919 to 1922, Chagall was the art director of the Moscow Jewish State Theater. He painted murals in the theater lobby and created sets for the shows. In 1923, he moved to France. He spent most of the rest of his life there, except for a brief period of residence in the United States from 1941 to 1948.

## Study

▶ The distortion of the elephants' legs in Dalí's painting is more noticeable.

▶ Dalí: There are floating trees, and a giraffe has flames on its back. Chagall: There is a person floating next to the Eiffel Tower, and two other people are turned sideways below the Eiffel Tower.

▶ Students will answer this question differently based on their personal experiences. There is no one right answer, but make sure that the student's explanation is reasonable.

■ For more examples of art from Europe, see the *Art Around the World Collection.*

### 📓 Art Journal: Writing

Encourage students to write about what the word *distortion* means to them in the Concepts section of their Art Journals. What else do they want to know about distortion?

### 🔍 Aesthetic Perception

**Seeing Like An Artist** Explain to students that when a person hears good news, he or she might smile and their eyes might get larger. However, when a person hears bad news, his or her eyes get smaller, and a frown may appear. Have students explain what happens if someone yells when they hear bad news.

**Developing Visual Literacy** Have students examine the paintings. Ask them to think of songs or types of music that would go along with each artwork. For example, a song with a slow, loud beat might represent the elephants walking in Dalí's work. Have students also think of music that would not go along with each work of art.

### 💻 Web Connection

Visit **www.guggenheim.org/new_york_index.html** for more information about the Solomon R. Guggenheim Musuem.

# Teach

**Time:** About 45 minutes

"How will you use distortion in your computer image?" "¿Cómo usarían distorsión en su imagen de computadora?"

- Read and discuss using distortion on page 178.

## Practice

**Materials:** envelopes, scrap paper, pencil

- Prepare the envelopes before the class arrives.

- Distribute the materials and have students follow the directions on page 178.

## Creative Expression

**Materials:** digital camera, computer, draw or paint software, printer, paper

**Alternate Materials:** photographs from home, word-processing program, scanner

- Distribute the materials and have students follow the directions on page 179.

- Review the Activity Tips page 242 for visual examples of techniques if needed.

### Art Journal: Brainstorming

Ask students to think of people that they know who have many facial expressions. Have them place the names, along with a description of the expressions, in their Art Journals. Have them also note if they have pictures of these people.

---

# Using Distortion

Artists sometimes use **distortion** to exaggerate an object or feature. Distortion involves stretching, bending, twisting, or changing the sizes of objects from their normal proportions. Distortion is often used to communicate an idea or strong emotion. Enlarged eyes, for example, could suggest fear or wonder. Artists use distortion in paintings, drawings, and sculptures.

Which features have been distorted in the above images?

## Practice

Work in groups to act out an emotion using facial expressions.

1. Work in small groups. Your teacher will select the name of an emotion or expression from an envelope for your group to act out.

2. Look at the emotion or expression that was assigned to your group. As a group, practice exaggerating the facial expression assigned.

3. Take turns with the other groups in your class performing expressions. Can you correctly guess the emotions expressed by your classmates?

---

## Differentiated Instruction

**Reteach**

Have students look through the large prints for examples of face distortion. Have them compare the face distortions in each example they find.

**Special Needs**

Successful use of technology such as computers and art software programs can build confidence in all students. Give students with disabilities the opportunity to use and experiment with technology and to share their competence with others.

**ELL**

When explaining facial distortion to students, show them several pictures of the same face with a different feature distorted each time. Have them explain what is different from the previous picture.

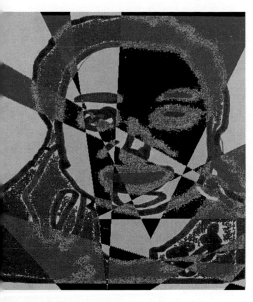

◀ **Shelby Neesmith.**
Age 9.

**Think** about how the student artist used distortion in this image.

###  Creative Expression

Create a distorted self-portrait using the computer.

1. Insert a picture of yourself onto a blank photo-editing file.

2. Convert the picture to a line drawing. Save your work.

3. Choose different areas of your face to stretch and distort. Try moving some features around. Save your work and print a copy.

4. Use a marker to divide the areas of your face into different sections.

5. Color each section using a different color pencil.

### Art Criticism

**Describe** What tools did you use to distort your image?

**Analyze** Describe the textures and color schemes you used to alter your image. What type of distortion did you use?

**Interpret** How does distortion affect the mood of your work? Explain.

**Decide** Do you think you were successful in creating distortion in your artwork? Explain.

Unit 5 • Lesson 6 **179**

## Review and Assess

"What have you learned about using distortion?" "¿Qué han aprendido sobre el uso de distorsión?"

# Think

The artist used a variety of shapes and colors to distort the image

- Use *Large Prints 57 Nighthawks* and *58 Chance Meeting* and ask students to compare how the artists each used distortion in their works of art. How are they different? How are they similar? What objects are not distorted?

## Informal Assessment

- For standardized-format test practice using this lesson's art content, see pages 64–65 in *Reading and Writing Test Preparation.*

### Art Journal: Critical Thinking

Have students answer the four art criticism questions—Describe, Analyze, Interpret, and Decide—in their Art Journals. Have students discuss within groups how they distorted their computer images. Ask them to discuss similarities and differences and to share their work with the class.

---

## Art Across the Curriculum

Use these simple ideas to reinforce art concepts across the curriculum.

★ **Expository Writing** Have students write the steps involved in distorting a photograph.

★ **Math** Have students approximate the size of the cat in Chagall's painting compared to the Eiffel Tower.

★ **Science** Have students compare the size of real elephants to Dalí's elephants.

★ **Social Studies** Have students share what they know about Paris, France.

★ **Technology** Using a word-processing program, have students find clip art of images with distorted faces. Use the distorted images to make a collage. Visit **SRAonline.com** to print detailed instructions for this activity.
NSAE 6.b

# Lesson 6 Wrap-Up

# Distortion

## Focus

Have students examine the artwork in this lesson and discuss how distortion is used to draw attention to a certain area in an artwork. What effect does the distortion have on the artwork?

## Teach

Explain to students that they will create a collage self-portrait. They will use images from magazines and will distort the facial features by gluing a different mouth, nose, or eyes onto a face shape. Demonstrate how to cut excess paper from a magazine image so that only the wanted shape exists. Then have students complete the alternate activity.

## Reflect

Have students use the four steps of art criticism to evaluate their work. Have students describe how they created their self-portaits.

### Alternate Activity

**Materials:**
- sketchbooks
- pencils, erasers
- magazines
- 12" × 18" construction paper in any color
- glue, scissors
- paper towels, newspaper

1. Begin by thinking about your features. Then look through magazines to collect images. Find a large face shape that is similar to your face as well as similar eyes, nose, and mouth.

2. Cut excess paper from around the features before laying it on your face. If there is room on the paper, add a neck, shoulders, or a full body.

3. Once the images have been arranged, glue the shapes into place

4. Display the self-portrait, along with the rest of the class, and have classmates identify it.

## Research in Art Education

Students are challenged by the comprehensive nature of big art projects, and "in doing so, [they] master an enormous number of artistic skills, direct a myriad of aesthetic and expressive qualities toward given ends, and symbolize human behaviors and emotions in a great variety of ways." Art projects can also provide students with the opportunity to learn time management skills *(Gaining the Arts Advantage: Lessons from School Districts that Value Arts Education)*.

## Assessment

Use the following rubric to evaluate the artwork students make in the Creative Expression activity and to assess students' understanding of how distortion is used in two-dimensional works of art.

Have students complete page 66 or 67 in their *Assessment* books.

|  | Art History and Culture | Aesthetic Perception | Creative Expression | Art Criticism |
|---|---|---|---|---|
| **3 POINTS** | The student demonstrates knowledge of the lives and work of Dalí and Chagall. | The student accurately identifies the use of distortion in a variety of works of art. | The student's computer image demonstrates the use of distortion. | The student thoughtfully and honestly evaluates own work using the four steps of art criticism. |
| **2 POINTS** | The student's knowledge of the lives and work of Dalí and Chagall is weak or incomplete. | The student shows an emerging awareness of distortion in a variety of works of art but cannot consistently identify it. | The student's computer image shows some awareness of how to use distortion. | The student attempts to evaluate own work but shows an incomplete understanding of evaluation criteria. |
| **1 POINT** | The student cannot demonstrate knowledge of the lives and work of Dalí or Chagall. | The student cannot identify how distortion is used in an artwork. | The student's computer image shows no understanding of how to use distortion. | The student makes no attempt to evaluate own work. |

### Assessment, p. 67

Name _____ Date _____

Lesson 6 UNIT 5

**Distortion**

**A.** Short Answer
Answer each question.
1. What is distortion?
_____
_____

2. What is an example of distortion?
_____
_____

**B.** Drawing
Draw a distorted expression.

**C.** Writing
Look at the painting by Dalí from this lesson, and write a paragraph explaining how he used distortion.

Level 4　　　Unit 5 • Space, Proportion, and Distortion　**67**

**central axis**—a real or imaginary line that is down the center of an object **eje central**—una línea real o imaginaria que está debajo del centro de un objeto.

**distortion**—a deviation from normal or expected proportions **distorsión**—una desviación de proporciones normales o esperadas

**exaggeration**—an increase or enlargement beyond what is expected or normal **exageración**—un aumento o engrandecimiento más de lo esperado o normal

**perspective**—the technique for creating the illusion of depth on a flat surface **perspectiva**—la técnica de crear la ilusión de profundidad en una superficie plana

**depth**—the appearance of deep space or distance in a two-dimensional work of art **profundidad**—la apariencia de un espacio profundo o distancia en una obra de arte bidimensional.

**perspective techniques**—the six techniques an artist uses to create the illusion of depth in two-dimensional art: overlapping, size, placement, detail, color, converging lines **técnicas perspectivas**—la seis técnicas que un artista usa para crear la ilusión de profundidad en arte bidimensional: superponer, tamaño, lugar, detalle, color y líneas convergentes.

**picture plane**—the name used to describe the surface of a drawing or painting **plano de la pintura**—el nombre usado para describir la superficie de una pintura o dibujo.

**point of view**—the angle from which you see an object or scene **punto de vista**—el ángulo en que uno puede ver el objeto o escena

**space**—the art element that refers to the areas above, below, between, within, and around an object **espacio**—el elemento artístico que refiere a áreas hacia arriba, debajo, entre, adentro, y alrededor de un objeto

**profile**—a side view of a person or animal **perfil**—una vista lateral de una persona o animal

**self-portrait**—a two- or three-dimensional artwork that an artist makes of him- or herself **autorretrato**—obra de arte bi o tridimensional que un artista hace de sí mismo

**proportion**—refers to the relationship of one part to another part **proporción**—se refiere a la relación de una parte a la otra

## Vocabulary Practice

**T** Display *Transparency 41* to review unit vocabulary words.

**Word Parts** ⭐ Vocabulary
Have students identify the prefixes, root words, and/or suffixes of the vocabulary words. Ask the students if breaking the words into their parts helps them better understand the meaning of each word.

**Compare and Contrast Meanings** ⭐ Vocabulary
Have volunteers select a vocabulary word, such as *space*, and compare and contrast the various meanings of the word. Make sure students take into account if a vocabulary word has more than one part of speech. Repeat the process for other unit vocabulary words.

**Examples** ⭐ Vocabulary
Without using the term *positive space*, describe an area of positive space in the classroom. Invite a volunteer to identify what you have described. Repeat the process for other unit vocabulary words.

## Art Criticism

**Critical Thinking** Art criticism is an organized system for looking at and talking about art. You can criticize art without being an expert. The purpose of art criticism is to get the viewer involved in a perception process that delays judgment until all aspects of the artwork have been studied. Push the students to expand beyond the art criticism questions.

■ See pages 28–29 for more about art criticism.

## Describe

▶ There are five people who are running in a race. They are wearing running shorts, tank tops, and running shoes with spikes. They carry red, yellow, white, and black batons.

▶ The setting is a track field. The people are on a curved track. There is a straight track that has four poles for vaulting on it.

## Analyze

▶ The end of the running track and the three runners are in the foreground. The two smaller runners are in the middle ground. The straight running track with the poles is in the background.

▶ Lawrence used some of the following perspective techniques. Overlapping: The leg of the runner with the red shoes covers the leg of the runner with the blue shoes. Placement: The runners near the bottom of the page seem to be closer to the viewer than the two who are higher up on the page. Lines: The white outlines of the track seem to get closer as they move farther back into the picture.

▶ The viewer is looking down on the track.

▶ The legs of the runners are longer than normal, some of the arms look smaller than normal, and some of the torsos and necks look short.

▲ **Jacob Lawrence.** (American). *Study for the Munich Olympic Games Poster.* 1971.

Gouache on paper. 35½ × 27 inches (90.17 × 68.58 cm.). Seattle Art Museum, Seattle, Washington.

## Art History and Culture

### Jacob Lawrence

Jacob Lawrence (jā´ kəb lär´ ənz) (1917–2000) was born in Atlantic City, New Jersey, but his family moved to Harlem in 1930, at the end of the Harlem Renaissance. Lawrence's most famous work is a series of paintings called *The Migration of the Negro.* Most of Lawrence's work portrays the lives of African Americans. Lawrence also made paintings about his personal experiences, including his service in the Coast Guard during World War II. Lawrence later became an art professor.

See pages 24–25 and 16–21 for more about art history and the subject matter.

**Artist Profiles, p. 39**

Artist Profile
**Jacob Lawrence**
1917–2000

Jacob Lawrence (jā´ kəb lär´ ənz) had parents who met on their migration to the North. His father was born in South Carolina, and his mother in Virginia. Lawrence was born in Atlantic City, New Jersey, in 1917. The family finally settled in Harlem in 1929 at the end of the Harlem Renaissance. Because his mother worked all day, she enrolled Lawrence in the Harlem Art Workshop after school to keep him out of trouble. He had many excellent teachers there, including Charles Alston. Lawrence won a scholarship to the American Artists School. He taught at New York's Pratt Institute from 1958 to 1965. From 1970, he taught at the University of Washington in Seattle, where he also served as head of the

## Art Criticism | Critical Thinking

**Describe** **What do you see?**

During this step you will collect information about the subject of the work.

▶ How many people do you see? What kinds of facial expressions do they have?

▶ What are the people doing? What are they wearing?

▶ What is the setting?

**Analyze** **How is this work organized?**

Think about how the artist used the elements and principles of art.

▶ Which people or objects look closest to you? Which look farthest away?

▶ What is in the foreground, the middle ground, and the background?

▶ Where do you see a part of someone's body that overlaps and covers part of another person or object?

▶ What is the point of view of this painting?

▶ Where do you see distortion?

**Interpret** **What is the artist trying to say?**

Use the clues you discovered during your analysis to find the message the artist is trying to show.

▶ Which runner do you think will win the race? Why?

▶ What is the mood of this painting?

▶ What sounds would you hear if you could go into the painting?

**Decide** **What do you think about the work?**

Use all the information you have gathered to decide whether this is a successful work of art.

▶ Is the work successful because it is realistic, because it is well-organized, or because it has a strong message?

Unit 5 **181**

## Interpret

▶ The elongated legs and the smaller torsos and arms emphasize the stretch and tension of the runners' legs.

▶ Answers will vary. Some may notice how the leg of the runner on the left is overlapping the next runner's leg and say that these two will get their legs twisted and fall. Some may think the man on the right will leap ahead to win the race.

## Decide

▶ Students' answers will vary based on individual experiences. They may use more than one aesthetic theory to explain the success of this work.

**Art Journal: Writing**

Have students write answers to Aesthetic Perception in their Art Journals. Have them discuss their answers in small groups.

## Aesthetic Perception

**Seeing Like an Artist** Have students recall times they were in relay races or times when they watched a race. How do their memories compare to Jacob Lawrence's artwork?

**Describe** ▶ Describe everything you remember about the race.

**Analyze** ▶ When did you notice any distorted images?

▶ What do you remember about the spacing of the participants?

**Interpret** ▶ If you were a viewer, how did the race make you feel?

▶ If you were a participant, what were the other participants feeling?

**Decide** ▶ Next time you participate in or watch a relay race, what are you going to pay attention to?

"Artists use proportion and distortion to draw human faces and bodies. Space gives the appearance of depth in a flat surface." "Los artistas usan proporción y distorsión para dibujar caras y cuerpos humanos. Espacio da la apariencia de profundidad en una superficie plana."

**T** Review the unit vocabulary with students using *Transparency 41.*

### Art Journal: Writing
Have students answer the questions on page 182 in their Art Journals or on a separate sheet of paper. Answers: 1. A, 2. B, 3. A, 4. C, 5. B

**T** For further assessment, have students complete the unit test on *Transparency 47.*

## VISIT A MUSEUM
# Smithsonian Institution

► Have students explore Smithsonian Institution's Web site for students at **smithsonianeducation.org/students/index.html.** Then have them discuss what they viewed online with others.

"My belief is that it is most important for an artist to develop an approach and philosophy about life–if he has developed this philosophy, he does not put paint on canvas, he puts himself on canvas."

–Jacob Lawrence

---

Space, Proportion, and Distortion, continued
## Show What You Know
Answer these questions on a separate sheet of paper.

**1** _____ is the principle of art concerned with the size relationships of one part to other parts.
A. Proportion
B. Distortion
C. Perspective

**2** _____ is the angle from which the viewer sees an object.
A. Placement
B. Overlapping
C. Point of view

**3** The _____ is the part of the picture plane that appears closest to the viewer.
A. middle ground
B. background
C. foreground

**4** Artists sometimes use _____ to exaggerate an object.
A. proportion
B. distortion
C. point of view

**5** _____ is the technique used to create the feeling of depth on a flat surface.
A. Texture
B. Perspective
C. Emphasis

**182** Unit 5

## VISIT A MUSEUM
# The Smithsonian Institution

The Smithsonian Institution was established in 1846 with money given by English scientist James Smithson. Today there are more than 142 million artifacts and works of art at the Smithsonian. It is also a center for research in the arts, sciences, and history. It consists of fourteen museums, the National Zoo in Washington, D.C., and two museums in New York City. Nine of the museums are located on the National Mall in Washington D.C., between the United States Capitol and the Washington Monument.

▲ The Smithsonian's first building, known as the castle.

## Unit Assessment Options

### Aesthetic Perception
**Practice** Have students select one of the concepts in the Show What You Know section on page 182, then find examples of each concept in the classroom.

### Creative Expression
**Student Portfolio** Have students review all the artwork they have created during this unit and select the pieces they wish to keep in their portfolios.

### Art Criticism
**Activity** Have students select an artwork from this unit and study it using the four steps of art criticism. (See pages 28–29 for more information about art criticism.) Have students work small groups and present their findings aloud or in writing.

## Space and Proportion in Music

Alfredo Rolando Ortiz was born in Cuba. When he was eleven years old he moved to Venezuela, where he first heard harp music. He began to learn the harp from his friend Fernando, and then from a master harpist. Ortiz later became a doctor, but eventually gave that up to devote his life to the harp.

**What to Do** With a partner, make a simple stringed instrument.

Vibration is the basis of sound. Vibration is movement. Sound is the sensation caused in your ear by the movement of air. You can hear vibrations when you stretch a string tightly between two points and pluck the string.

1. Take a small box without a lid and stretch rubber bands around the box. Make sure that rubber bands have different thicknesses.

2. Pluck the "strings" to see if you get different tones, or sounds. The thickness, tension, and length of the strings will change the sound.

3. Decide which lengths or thicknesses of rubber bands produce higher or lower tones or pitches.

▲ Alfredo Rolando Ortiz *Joropo Azul.*

 ### Art Criticism

**Describe** Describe how you made your instrument.

**Analyze** What did you do to get a higher or lower tone or pitch?

**Interpret** What did you feel as you created an instrument and heard the sounds it made?

**Decide** Were you able to get a satisfying musical sound from your simple instrument?

Unit 5 **183**

 ## Art History and Culture

### Harp Music

The harp may have been inspired by the sound of a hunter's bow, and a hollow sound box was added to amplify the sound. There were harps in ancient Egypt, Medieval Arabia, and Persia. Framed harps started in Ireland and Scotland during the ninth century and are the ancestors of the folk harps of Latin America. Many types of harps are found throughout the world, but there were no harps in the pre-Colombian Americas. The first harps were brought to the Americas by the Spanish missionaries.

 ## Space and Proportion in Music

**Objective:** To create a simple string instrument with a partner

**Materials:** *Joropo Azul* performed by Alfredo Rolando Ortiz. Running time: 1:45.

## Focus
Time: About 10 minutes

- Discuss the information on page 183.

### Art History and Culture

- Have students discuss different types of stringed instruments from a variety of cultures.

## Teach
Time: About 25 minutes

### Aesthetic Perception

- Have students think of words or images that they associate with harp music.

### Creative Expression

- Have students experiment with creating different tones or pitches.

- **Informal Assessment** Provide positive feedback and encourage refinement.

## Reflect
Time: About 5 minutes

### Art Criticism

- Have students answer the four art criticism questions on page 183 aloud or in writing.

- Did students successfully create a simple string instrument?

UNIT 5 • Space, Proportion, and Distortion **183**

# Unit 6 Planning Guide

| | Lesson Title | Suggested Pacing | Creative Expression Activity |
|---|---|---|---|
| Lesson 1 | Formal Balance | 1 hour | Make a relief sculpture that resembles a post. |
| Lesson 2 | Informal Balance | 1 hour | Create a family portrait. |
| Lesson 3 | Radial Balance | 1 hour | Make a wall hanging with radial balance. |
| Lesson 4 | Harmony | 1 hour | Create a model of a sculpture. |
| Lesson 5 | Variety and Emphasis | 1 hour | Create an animal drawing. |
| Lesson 6 | Unity | 1 hour | Make a wrapped coil basket. |
| ART SOURCE ARTSOURCE | Balance, Harmony, Variety, and Unity in Dance | 35 minutes | Create a dance using work movements. |

| Materials | Program Resources | Fine Art Resources | Literature Resources |
|---|---|---|---|
| foam sheets in a variety of colors, craft glue, paper clips, scissors | *Assessment*, pp. 69–70 <br> *Reading and Writing Test Preparation*, pp. 66–67 <br> *Home and After-School Connections* <br> *Flash Card* 12 | *Transparency 31* <br> *Artist Profiles*, pp. 17, 78 <br> *Large Print 59* <br> *The National Museum of Women in the Arts Collection* | *The Wright Brothers for Kids: How They Invented the Airplane with 21 Activities Exploring the Science and History of Flight* by Mary Kay Carson, Laura D'Argo |
| white paper, watercolor crayons, pencils, erasers, paintbrushes, water containers, paper towels | *Assessment*, pp. 71–72 <br> *Reading and Writing Test Preparation*, pp. 68–69 <br> *Flash Card* 13 | *Transparency 32* <br> *Artist Profiles*, pp. 34, 59 <br> *Large Print 60* <br> *The National Museum of Women in the Arts Collection* | *Littlejim's Dreams* by Thomas B. Allen |
| wooden craft sticks, yarn in a variety of colors, glue | *Assessment*, pp. 73–74 <br> *Reading and Writing Test Preparation*, pp. 70–71 <br> *Flash Card* 14 | *Transparency 33* <br> *Artist Profile*, pp. 35, 61 <br> *Large Prints 59* and *60* <br> *Art Around the World Collection* | *Fair Weather* by Richard Peck |
| white paper, scissors, glue, pencil, erasers, mixing palettes, cardboard, found objects, tempera paint, paintbrushes, water containers, newspaper, paper towels | *Assessment*, pp. 75–76 <br> *Reading and Writing Test Preparation*, pp. 72–73 <br> *Flash Cards* 17–18 | *Transparency 34* <br> *Artist Profiles*, pp. 5, 29 <br> *Large Prints 59* and *60* <br> *The National Museum of Women in the Arts Collection* | *Body Parts in Rebellion* by Regan Dunnick |
| white drawing paper, pencils, crayons, watercolors, paintbrushes, black permanent markers, newspapers, images of animals, water containers, paper towels | *Assessment*, pp. 77–78 <br> *Reading and Writing Test Preparation*, pp. 74–75 <br> *Flash Cards* 16, 18 | *Transparency 35* <br> *Artist Profiles*, pp. 26, 52 <br> *Large Prints 59* and *60* <br> *The National Museum of Women in the Arts Collection* | *The Circuit* by Francisco Jimenez |
| cotton coils $\frac{1}{4}''$ or $\frac{1}{2}''$ (12' per student); fabric scraps cut or torn into one inch strips; plastic 3-inch tapestry needles | *Assessment*, pp. 79–80 <br> *Reading and Writing Test Preparation*, pp. 76–77 <br> *Flash Card* 18 | *Transparency 36* <br> *Artist Profiles*, pp. 33, 74 <br> *Large Prints 59* and *60* <br> *The National Museum of Women in the Arts Collection* | *A Wrinkle in Time* by Madeleine L'Engle |
| *Danza de Reata* and *Jarabe del Amor Ranchero,* props to accompany the student dances | | | |

# Unit Overview

## Balance, Harmony, Variety, and Unity

**Lesson 1: Symmetry** occurs when two halves of a balanced artwork are identical.

**Lesson 2: Informal balance** is a way of organizing parts of a design so that unlike objects have equal visual weight.

**Lesson 3: Radial balance** occurs when the art elements radiate from a central point.

**Lesson 4: Harmony** is the principle of art that creates unity by stressing similarities of separate but related parts.

**Lesson 5: Variety** is the principle of art which is concerned with difference or contrast.

**Lesson 6: Unity** is the oneness achieved by properly using the elements and principles in art.

# Introduce Unit Concepts

"Artists use balance, variety, harmony, and unity in two- and three-dimensional works of art." "Los artistas usan equilibrio, variedad, armonía y unidad en las obras de arte bi y tridimensionales."

## Balance and Variety

■ Ask students to find examples of balance in the classroom or in the school.

■ Ask student what the word *variety* means to them. Have students discuss their interpretations.

## Harmony and Unity

■ Have students think about harmony in music. What do they think *harmony* means in art?

■ Have students come up with expressions in which the words *united* and *unity* are used.

## Cross-Curricular Projects

■ See the *Language Arts and Reading, Mathematics, Science,* and *Social Studies Art Connections* books for activities that further develop balance, harmony, variety, and unity concepts.

**184** UNIT 6 • Balance, Harmony, Variety, and Unity

---

**Unit 6**

# Balance, Harmony, Variety, and Unity

▲ **Judith Leyster.** (Dutch). *The Concert.* c. 1661.
............................
Oil on canvas. 24 × 34¼ inches (61 × 87 cm.). National Museum of Women in the Arts, Washington, D.C.

## Artists use balance, variety, harmony, and unity to organize works of art.

Judith Leyster enjoyed painting musical scenes. Based on people in Leyster's other works, the singer has been tentatively identified as the artist herself, the violinist as her husband, and the lute player as a family friend. The figures in the painting have to work together as a unit, "in concert," which has led some people to believe that this scene symbolizes the value of harmony.

**184**   Unit 6

## Fine Art Prints

Display *Large Prints 59 Dla'el (Interior House Post)* and *60 Snowstorm: Steamboat off a Harbour's Mouth.* Refer to the prints throughout this unit as students learn about variety, harmony, and unity.

**Large Print 59**

**Large Print 60**

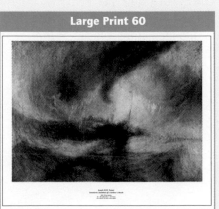

Artists use different types of **balance** in all types of artwork.

▶ Pretend there is an imaginary line down the center of the painting. Describe how each half is arranged.

Artists use **variety** to show differences or contrasts in works of art.

▶ Describe the different people you see in the painting.

Artists can stress the similarities of separate but related parts in works of art by using **harmony.**

▶ Which parts of this work look similar?

**Unity** is the feeling of oneness that artists use in their art.

▶ What about this work makes all the pieces look like they belong?

**In This Unit** you will learn how artists use balance. You will create personal works of art using a variety of media based on formal, informal, and radial balance. You will learn how artists use variety, harmony, and unity to bring together art elements.

Here are the topics you will study:
▶ Formal balance
▶ Informal balance
▶ Radial balance
▶ Harmony
▶ Variety
▶ Unity

## Judith Leyster
(1609–1660)

Judith Leyster was successful as a portrait and genre specialist. She became one of two female members of the Haarlem painters' guild and had students of her own. She was a wife and a mother as well as an artist. It is believed that Leyster may have managed the family's business and properties.

## Art History and Culture

### Judith Leyster

Judith Leyster (jo͞o´ dəth  lā´ stər) (1609–1660) was an artist who excelled at painting the familiar—scenes of ordinary people pursuing daily activities. Leyster was licensed in 1633 as a painter in the Guild of St. Luke of Haarlem. Most of her signed and dated paintings were made before her 1636 marriage to another genre painter, Jan Miense Molenaer. Leyster often signed her work with a distinctive monogram: her initials intertwined with a star. This signature was intended as a pun on the artist's name, which means "leading star."

See pages 24–25 and 16–21 for more about art history and the subject matter.

**Artist Profiles, p. 40**

● Artist Profile ●
**Judith Leyster**
1609–1660
Judith Leyster (jo͞o´ dəth  lā´ stər) was an artist who excelled at painting the familiar—ordinary people pursuing daily activities. Leyster was licensed in 1633 as a painter in the Guild of St. Luke of Haarlem in the Netherlands. Most of her signed and dated paintings were made before her 1636 marriage to another genre painter, Jan Miense Molenaer. It seems she stopped painting after she married. Leyster often signed her work with a distinctive monogram, her initials intertwined with a star. This signature was intended as a pun on the artist's name that means "leading star."

# Examine the Artwork

"Let's examine this painting by Judith Leyster." *"Vamos a examinar esta pintura de Judith Leyster."*

■ Have students study Judith Leyster's painting *The Concert*. Then have them communicate ideas about concerts in their school and community using life experiences or sensory knowledge. NSAE 3.a

■ Have students answer the questions about variety, harmony, and unity on page 155.

▶ On the left side there is a man. On the right side there are a man and woman.

▶ The man on the left is playing a violin and looking to his right. The woman looks like she is singing; she is looking upward. The man on the right is playing a guitarlike instrument and is looking to his left.

▶ All three people have their heads tilted, and they are looking to the side. They are wearing some type of head covering and lacy collars.

▶ Student responses will vary. Some will say it is the similar facial expressions; others will say it is the way they are dressed.

# Unit Pretest

T  Display **Transparency 48** as a pretest. Have students write their answers on a separate piece of paper. Answers: 1. A, 2. C, 3. B. 4. B, 5. A

# Home Connection

■ See **Home and After School Connections** for family newsletters and activities for this unit.

# Unit 6 Arts Integration

ILLUSTRATOR PROFILE
## Patricia Polacco
(1944– )

Patricia Polacco was born in Lansing, Michigan. As a child, Polacco was very close to both sets of grandparents. These relationships influenced her later work; many of her books include interactions between young people and elderly people.

Polacco did not learn to read until she was 14 years old, when she was diagnosed with dyslexia. She had always enjoyed art, however, and used to make small books "like thick greeting cards" for friends and family members. As an adult she studied art in Australia, France, England, and Russia and worked as a museum restorer.

Polacco published her first book, *Meteor!,* when she was 41 years old. She has since written and illustrated over 30 picture books. Her books are often based on childhood memories, family stories, and folktales. Her illustrations mix bright colors, patterned backgrounds, and white space.

Throughout Unit 6, share Polacco's illustrations with the class and discuss the use of balance, harmony, variety, and unity in her works of art. How does Polacco create unified illustrations? What type of balance does she use most often?

## Music

Balance in music is usually associated with symmetrical forms. Harmony in music refers to different pitches played or sung at the same time, producing chords. Unity and variety give compositions identity and character. Have students sing or listen to a song and have them identify the sections of the piece that create unity and variety.

## Literature

Show the video or DVD *King Bidgoods in the Bathtub* to introduce the concepts of balance, harmony, variety, and unity. Pause the video or DVD and have students describe the balance, harmony, variety, or unity of the scene.

Literature and Art

## Performing Arts

 Show *Danza de Reata* and *Jarabe del Amor Ranchero.* Point out balance and unity.

Artsource®

# Lesson 1 Overview

# Formal Balance
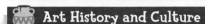

**Lesson 1** introduces the art principle of balance and symmetry. **Balance** is the principle of design that deals with visual weight in an artwork. **Symmetry** is a type of formal balance in which two halves of a balanced artwork are mirror images of each other.

## Objectives

### Art History and Culture
To demonstrate knowledge of the Maori people and Charles Edenshaw

### Creative Expression
To design a house post using symmetrical balance

### Aesthetic Perception
To identify how formal balance is used in art and the environment

### Art Criticism
To evaluate own work using the four steps of art criticism

## Vocabulary  Vocabulary

Review the following vocabulary words with students.

**central axis** eje central—a real or imaginary dividing line that can run in two directions: vertically and horizontally

**symmetry** simetría—a type of formal balance in which two halves of a balanced artwork are identical, mirror images of each other

See page 209B for additional vocabulary and Spanish vocabulary resources.

### Art Journal: Vocabulary
Have students add these words to the Vocabulary section of their Art Journals.

## Lesson Materials
- foam sheets in a variety of colors
- craft glue
- paper clips
- scissors
- textbooks

**Alternate Materials:**
- color construction paper
- markers
- found objects
- magazines

## Program Resources
- *Reading and Writing Test Prep.,* pp. 66–67
- *Transparency 31*
- *Flash Card* 12
- *Artist Profiles,* pp. 17, 78
- *Animals Through History Time Line*
- *Assessment,* pp. 69–70
- *Large Print 59* Dla'ehl (Interior House Post)
- *The National Museum of Women in the Arts Collection*

## Concept Trace
Formal Balance
**Introduced:** Level 3, Unit 4, Lesson 1
**Reinforced:** Level 5, Unit 5, Lesson 4

---

## Lesson 1 Arts Integration

### Theatre
Complete Unit 6, Lesson 1, on pages 108–109 of *Theatre Arts Connections.*

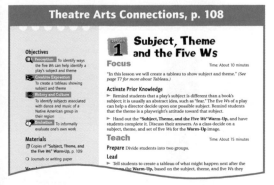

### Music
 Have students sing or listen to "This Land is Your Land." This song is verse and refrain, but it is in AA form. Ask students what this form says about the music in the verse as compared to the refrain.

### Movement & Dance
Symmetrical balance is secure and stable. Have students balance so both sides of the body are equal. For example, have them balance on two hands and two legs. Have students create smooth transitions that go from one symmetrical balance to another.

# Focus

## Activate Prior Knowledge

"Have you ever seen a building that, if divided down the center, was identical on each half?" "¿Alguna vez han visto un edificio que, si se dividiera por el medio, sería idéntico en cada mitad?"

■ As a class discuss the student responses. Explain that in many public buildings, such as town or city halls, each half of the building is identical. This type of balance is derived from the Greeks and Romans.

### Using Literature ★ Reading

■ Have students read some passages from *The Wright Brothers for Kids: How They Invented the Airplane with 21 Activities Exploring the Science and History of Flight.* Then identify objects that are symmetrically balanced.

### Thematic Connection ★ Social Studies

■ **Architecture** Have students describe different types of buildings they think are interesting. Make sure students include buildings that they might not have liked but thought there was something unique about them.

## Introduce the Art

# Look

"Look closely at the two halves of these works of art." "Miren detalladamente a las dos mitades de estas obras de arte."

### Summarizing ★ Reading

■ Have students locate a historical document that discusses either the totem poles or house posts. Then have them summarize their findings.

## Art History and Culture

Possible answers: knives, hammers, sandpaper, mallets, and chisels.

### Web Connection
Visit **www.maori.org.nz** for more information about the Maori culture.

---

# Formal Balance

**Look** at the works of art on these pages. *Figure from House Post* was carved by a Maori artist of New Zealand. The Maori have many legends to explain their history and the elements of nature. *Model Totem Pole* was carved from argillite, which is a very soft shale. The images on the totem pole, starting from the top, are a bear, two watchmen, a sea bear, a seal, a bearlike figure, and another bear holding a fish.

◄ **Artist unknown.** (Maori/New Zealand). *Figure from House Post.* Nineteenth century.
.....................................
Wood. 43 inches tall (109.2 cm.). The Metropolitan Museum of Art, New York, New York.

## Art History and Culture

What kind of tools might the artists have used to create these two works of art?

---

## Art History and Culture

### Figure from House Post

The Maori people settled in New Zealand during the Neolithic Stone Age. The importance of individuals in Maori society was determined by birth order and gender. Firstborn sons inherited leadership roles. Land, canoes, and houses were communal property. Personal possessions were limited to clothes, weapons, and a few other items. The Great God of the Maori people was the forest god, Tane.

See pages 24–25 and 16–21 for more about art history and the subject matter.

**Artist Profiles, p. 78**

Artist Profile ◊

**Figure from House Post**

The Maori people settled in New Zealand during the neolithic stone age. The importance of individuals in Maori society was determined by birth order and gender. Firstborn sons inherited leadership roles. Land, canoes, and houses were communal property. Personal possessions were limited to clothes, weapons, and a few other items.

◄ **Artist Unknown.** (Maori, New Zealand). *Figure from House Post.* Nineteenth century.

**Study** both works of art to find examples of formal balance.

▶ Where do you see repeated lines, shapes, forms, and colors?

▶ What similarities do you see in the two works of art?

▶ If you could draw a line down the center of each work, dividing it in half, how would one half relate to the other?

◀ **Charles Edenshaw.** (Canadian/Haida). *Model Totem Pole.* c. 1885.
.................................................
Argillate. 19 × 3 × 2¾ inches tall (48.3 × 7.6 × 7 cm.). Seattle Museum of Art, Seattle, Washington.

 **Aesthetic Perception**

**Design Awareness** Think about objects you see every day that would look the same on both sides if they were divided in half.

## Art History and Culture

### Charles Edenshaw

Charles Edenshaw (chärlz ē´dən shô)(1839–1924) was born on Prince of Wales Island. For more than 200 years, Haida artists, such as Edenshaw, have been carving argillite sculptures. Edenshaw married Isabella K'woiyang, and they had seven children. When his two young sons died, Edenshaw sought comfort by teaching young carvers Haida myths and numerous carving techniques. Edenshaw earned a reputation as an artist and was noticed by anthropologists and museum collectors who were determined to record and collect Haida art.

See pages 24–25 and 16–21 for more about art history and the subject matter.

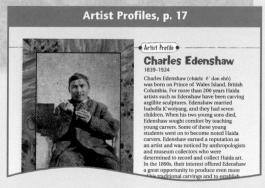

**Artist Profiles, p. 17**

◆ Artist Profile ◆
**Charles Edenshaw**
1839–1924

Charles Edenshaw (chärlz ē´dan shô) was born on Prince of Wales Island, British Columbia. For more than 200 years Haida artists such as Edenshaw have been carving argillite sculptures. Edenshaw married Isabella K'woiyang, and they had seven children. When his two young sons died, Edenshaw sought comfort by teaching young carvers. Some of these young students went on to become noted Haida carvers. Edenshaw earned a reputation as an artist and was noticed by anthropologists and museum collectors who were determined to record and collect Haida art. In the 1890s, their interest offered Edenshaw a great opportunity to produce even more traditional carvings and to establish

## Study

▶ There are repeated curved lines and circular shapes in *Figure from House Post.* There are repeated dots, curved and diagonal lines, and animal forms in *Model Totem Pole.*

▶ The sculptures appear to be animal-like. The figures look more imaginary than real.

▶ *Figure from House Post* is symmetrical in the head region, but the lower portion has subtle differences on each half. Each half of *Model Totem Pole* is identical.

■ For more examples of utilitarian art, see *The National Museum of Women in the Arts Collection.*

### Art Journal: Writing

Have students explain in the Concepts section of their Art Journals what it means to say that something is symmetrical. What else do they want to know about symmetry?

 **Aesthetic Perception**

**Design Awareness** Have students communicate ideas about themselves and their families using life experiences and sensory knowledge. Explain that public structures are often arranged symmetrically. One half is a mirror image of the other half. This is a calming and predictable arrangement that people feel comfortable with because it is reliable and stable.
NSAE 3.a
**Developing Visual Literacy** Discuss the use of repeated shapes and objects in each structure. Look closely at how the two structures were arranged. Why do they think these posts were designed this way?

**Web Connection**
www.nativepubs.com/nativepubs/Apps/bios/03 56EdenshawCharles.asp for more information about Charles Edenshaw.

 **Teach**

 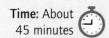

"What type of house post will you design?"
"¿Qué tipo de columna van a diseñar?"

- Read and discuss using formal balance on page 188.

## Practice

**Materials:** textbooks

**Alternate Materials:** magazines

- Distribute the materials and have students follow the directions on page 188.

## Creative Expression

**Materials:** foam sheets in a variety of colors, craft glue, paper clips, scissors

**Alternate Materials:** color construction paper, markers, found objects

- Distribute the materials and have students follow the directions on page 189.
- Review the Activity Tips on page 243 for visual examples of techniques if needed.

### Art Journal: Planning

Have students think about whom they would like to choose as the subject of their house posts. Once students have decided, have them create a list in their Art Journals of adjectives that describe the persons. Students should refer to this during the Creative Expression activity.

# Using Formal Balance

**Formal balance** is a way of organizing parts of a design so that equal, or very similar, elements are placed on opposite sides of a central line. The central line may be part of the design or an imaginary line.

**Symmetry** is a type of formal balance in which two halves of an object or work of art are mirror images of each other.

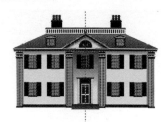

### Practice

Look for examples of formal balance.

1. Look through your textbook or books that include works of art and find examples of formal balance.

2. Discuss how each artist used formal balance. Examine each image and see if the artist used exaggeration.

## Differentiated Instruction

**Reteach**
Have students find an example of symmetry in the classroom. Ask them to create a sketch of the object and describe how they drew it.

**Special Needs**
Give students an opportunity to demonstrate their learning in this project by having them verbally share how their sculpture shows formal balance.

**ELL**
Demonstrate the concept of symmetry, using a volunteer and classroom objects. Have students pass items to the volunteer to create different examples of symmetry.

◄ **Dee Scott.**
Age 9.

**Think** about whether the student artist used formal balance in this sculpture.

## Creative Expression

Create a relief sculpture with formal balance that represents you or a member of your family.

1. Curve a foam sheet and make a cylinder form that is twelve inches tall. Glue the cylinder and secure it with paper clips at the top and bottom.

2. Cut geometric or free-form shapes to represent yourself or a member of your family.

3. Add shapes to represent the eyes, nose, mouth, and hair. Use sizes, shapes, and colors to create exaggeration in the face.

4. Attach the face to your post. Use more shapes to create arms, legs, and other patterns on the post.

## Art Criticism

**Describe** Who is the subject of your sculpture?

**Analyze** What types of shapes and colors did you use?

**Interpret** What kind of mood does your sculpture create?

**Decide** Do you like the way your sculpture turned out? Explain.

 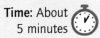

# Reflect
Time: About 5 minutes

## Review and Assess

"How did you create a house post?" "¿Cómo crearon una comumna de casa?"

## Think

The artist created formal balance by placing the objects on a cylinder. The design on both halves of the sculpture is similar.

■ Use **Large Print 59** Dla'ehl (*Interior House Post*) to ask students to describe the artist's use of formal balance.

## Informal Assessment

■ For standardized-format test practice using this lesson's art content, see pages 66–67 in **Reading and Writing Test Preparation.**

### Art Journal: Critical Thinking

Have students answer the four art criticism questions—Describe, Analyze, Interpret, and Decide—in their Art Journals. Have students discuss within groups how they used formal balance. Ask them to notice the similarities and differences. Have the groups share their findings with the class.

---

## Art Across the Curriculum

Use these simple ideas to reinforce art concepts across the curriculum.

★ **Personal Writing** Have students write a letter to Charles Edenshaw, asking him about his artwork.

★ **Math** Have students estimate the weight of the works of art in the lesson.

★ **Science** Have students describe items in nature that are symmetrical.

★ **Social Studies** Explain to students that for approximately 200 years, Haida artists have carved argillite sculptures.

★ **Technology** Using a paint or draw program, create a design that is symmetrical. Visit **SRAonline.com** to print detailed instructions for this activity.
NSAE 6.b

## Extra! For the Art Specialist

**Time: About 45 minutes**

### Focus

Have students study **Large Print 59** *Dla'ehl (Interior House Post)* and learn how some artists use formal balance to organize an artwork so that opposite sides are the same or very similar.

### Teach

Explain to students that they will create a plastic foam print self-portrait. This type of printing technique is known as a relief because the surface area holds the ink and is printed. The incised lines or drawing remains the paper color. Demonstrate pressing into the plastic foam to make the lines needed to create a printing plate. Have the students complete the alternate activity.

### Reflect

Have students use the four steps of art criticism to evaluate their work. Have them describe their self-portraits.

### Alternate Activity

**Materials:**
- sketchbooks
- mirrors
- plastic foam
- white drawing paper
- pencils, erasers
- printing ink
- brayer
- inking tray
- newspaper

1. Have students sketch a self-portrait. Have them concentrate on using simple lines when drawing their features

2. Have students draw their faces on the plastic foam. Next have them use pressure to trace over the lines so they are indented into the plate.

3. Students should number their papers 1, 2, and 3. Have them squirt a tablespoon of ink into the center of the tray. Students can use a brayer to roll a layer of ink onto the plate.

4. Have students place paper 1 on top of the inked image. With their palms flat, have them rub the back of the paper. They should carefully remove the paper and make two more prints.

### Research in Art Education

It has been shown that "elementary [art] programs establish a foundation in the arts for all students, not just for those in specialized programs or those who choose an arts course of study in high school." Providing consistent, quality instruction in the arts in elementary school also ensures that students have the time to foster skills in the arts. Many of these skills take time to develop. *(Gaining the Arts Advantage: Lessons from School Districts that Value Arts Education)*

### Assessment

Use the following rubric to evaluate the artwork students make in the Creative Expression activity and to assess students' understanding of how symmetry is used in architecture.

Have students complete page 69 or 70 in their **Assessment** books.

| | Art History and Culture | Aesthetic Perception | Creative Expression | Art Criticism |
|---|---|---|---|---|
| **3 POINTS** | The student demonstrates knowledge of the Maori people and Charles Edenshaw. | The student accurately identifies the use of formal balance in art and the environment. | The student's house post demonstrates how to use formal balance. | The student thoughtfully and honestly evaluates own work using the four steps of art criticism. |
| **2 POINTS** | The student's knowledge of the Maori people and Charles Edenshaw is weak or incomplete. | The student shows an emerging awareness of formal balance, but cannot consistently identify it. | The student's house post shows some awareness of how to use formal balance. | The student attempts to evaluate own work but shows an incomplete understanding of evaluation criteria. |
| **1 POINT** | The student cannot demonstrate knowledge of the Maori people or Charles Edenshaw. | The student cannot identify how formal balance is used in art and the environment. | The student's house post shows no understanding of how to use formal balance. | The student makes no attempt to evaluate own work. |

### Assessment, p. 69

Name _____ Date _____
Lesson 1 UNIT 6

**Formal Balance**

**A. Drawing**
Using a pencil and a crayon or marker, draw a symmetrical design. Make sure that when you add colors to your design you add them symmetrically.

**B. Vocabulary**
Fill in each blank with the word that correctly completes each sentence.
1. Symmetry is one type of _____ balance.
2. Balance occurs when the visual elements (lines, shapes, colors) are _____.

**C. Writing**
Write a paragraph explaining how formal balance is used in *Figure from House Post*.

Level 4     Unit 6 • Balance, Variety, Harmony, and Unity     **69**

# Informal Balance

Lesson 2 introduces another type of balance known as informal balance. **Informal balance** is a way of organizing parts of a design so that unlike objects have equal visual weight. **Asymmetry** is another name for informal balance.

## Objectives

### Art History and Culture
To demonstrate knowledge of the lives and work of Joshua Johnson and John Singer Sargent

### Creative Expression
To create a family portrait using informal balance

### Aesthetic Perception
To identify how informal balance is used in two-dimensional works of art

### Art Criticism
To evaluate own work using the four steps of art criticism

## Vocabulary ⭐ Vocabulary

Review the following vocabulary words with students before beginning the lesson.

**asymmetrical balance** equilibrio asimétrico—another name for informal balance

**informal balance** equilibrio informal—a way of organizing parts of a design so that unlike objects have equal visual weight

See page 209B for additional vocabulary and Spanish vocabulary resources.

### Art Journal: Vocabulary
Have students add these words to the Vocabulary section of their Art Journals.

## Lesson Materials
- white paper
- watercolor crayons
- pencils, erasers
- assorted brushes
- water container
- paper towels
- scale
- classroom objects

Alternate Materials:
- crayons
- watercolor paints

## Program Resources
- *Reading and Writing Test Prep.,* pp. 68–69
- *Transparency 32*
- *Flash Card* 13
- *Artist Profiles,* pp. 34, 59
- *Animals Through History Time Line*
- *Assessment,* pp. 71–72
- *Large Print 60* Snowstorm: Steamboat off a Harbour's Mouth
- *The National Museum of Women in the Arts Collection*

## Concept Trace
**Informal Balance**
Introduced:  Level 4, Unit 6, Lesson 2

Reinforced:  Level 5, Unit 5, Lesson 5

## Lesson 2  Arts Integration

### Theatre
Complete Unit 6, Lesson 2, on pages 110–111 of *Theatre Arts Connections.*

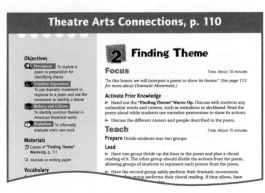

### Music
**SPOTLIGHT on MUSIC** Balance in music can describe how evenly different parts are performed at the same time to make the desired blend. Have students listen to "Akinla," from *African Suite* by Fela Sowande. Discuss whether all parts are equal in dynamics at all times.

### Movement & Dance
Asymmetrical balance is daring. Have students balance using opposites in the body. For example, have them balance on one hand and one leg or balance on two hands and one leg. Ask students how it feels to be in a pose that is daring and less stable?

# Focus

## Activate Prior Knowledge

"Have you seen a photograph before in which more people or objects were on one side more than the other?" "¿Alguna vez han visto una fotografía donde había más gente u objetos en un lado que en el otro?"

■ As a class, discuss the student responses. Explain that in many photographs and images people and objects are not arranged symmetrically.

### Using Literature ⭐ Reading

■ Look at the cover illustration of *Littlejim's Dreams* by Thomas B. Allen. Discuss how informal balance is used in the cover illustration.

### Thematic Connection ⭐ Science

■ **Imbalance:** Have students give examples of things that can be imbalanced. Once students offer an example, have them explain whether the imbalance can be easily corrected.

## Introduce the Art

# Look

"Look closely at how the children are arranged in these two works of art." "Miren detalladamente la manera en que los niños están ordenados en estas dos obras de arte."

### Compare and Contrast ⭐ Reading

Have students describe and compare a variety of individual responses to the works of art in this lesson. Answers will vary. Make sure answers include comments about other portraits they have seen or learned about in school.

 **Art History and Culture**

Explain to students that artists who create portraits are actually taking on the role of historians because they are recording what people and places look like during the times in which they lived.

 **Web Connection**

Visit **www.marylandartsource.org/artists/ detail_00000091.html** for more information about Joshua Johnson.

---

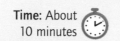 ## Informal Balance

▲ **Joshua Johnson.** (American). *The Westwood Children.* c. 1807.
.........................................
Oil on canvas. 41⅛ × 46 inches (104.5 × 116.8 cm.). National Gallery of Art, Washington, D.C.

**Look** at the two works of art on these pages. Both of these works show the children arranged in informal balance. *The Westwood Children* shows the sons of John and Margaret Lorman Westwood. Westwood was able to commission the portrait from Joshua Johnson at the height of his popularity. Johnson was one of the first African Americans to become a professional artist in the United States. John Sargent created *The Daughters of Edward Darley Boit* for his friend, artist Edward Darley Boit. Each girl is unique, to express her age and personality.

 **Art History and Culture**

Portraits from the past show us what people looked like and how they dressed.

---

 **Art History and Culture**

### Joshua Johnson

Born into slavery in Baltimore, Maryland, Joshua Johnson (jäsh´ wə jän´ sən) (1763–1824) received his freedom in 1782 and advertised himself as a portrait painter in Baltimore, becoming the first successful and free African-American portraitist. Johnson moved around Baltimore frequently, and it is thought that he may have supplemented his career by painting furniture.

See pages 24–25 and 16–21 for more about art history and the subject matter.

**Artist Profiles, p. 34**

**◆ Artist Profile ◆**

**Joshua Johnson**
active 1796–1824

Born into slavery in Baltimore, Maryland, Joshua Johnson (jäsh´ wə jän´ sən) received his freedom in 1782 and advertised himself as a portrait painter in Baltimore, becoming the first successful African American portraitist. Johnson moved around Baltimore frequently, and it is thought that he may have supplemented his career by painting furniture. Little is known of his later life and activities, and no recorded information exists concerning his whereabouts or career after 1824.

▲ **Joshua Johnson.** (American). *The Westwood...*

**Study** the way informal balance is used to organize these paintings.

▶ If you could draw a line down the center of each work of art, what differences would you see in the two halves?

▶ Which side of each artwork has more people?

▶ What appears to be closest to the viewer in each artwork?

▲ **John Singer Sargent.** (American). *The Daughters of Edward Darley Boit.* 1882.

Oil on canvas. 87 × 87 inches (221 × 221 cm.). Boston Museum of Fine Arts, Boston, Massachusetts.

### Aesthetic Perception

**Design Awareness** Look at your teacher's desk. Do you see formal or informal balance?

### Art History and Culture

#### John Singer Sargent

Though John Singer Sargent (jän  sing´ ər  sär´ jənt) (1856–1925) usually never stayed in one location for very long, he eventually spent a long period of his career in England. Regarded as one of the most successful international society portrait artists at the turn of the century, Sargent influenced European and American artists with his technical skills and techniques. He was such a determined artist that he painted more than 900 oils and more than 2,000 watercolors between 1877 and 1925.

See pages 24–25 and 16–21 for more about art history and the subject matter.

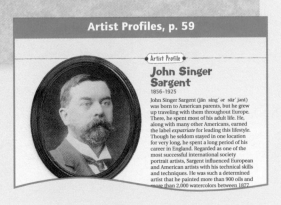

**Artist Profiles, p. 59**

*Artist Profile*

**John Singer Sargent**
1856–1925

John Singer Sargent (jän  sing´ ər  sär´ jənt) was born to American parents, but he grew up traveling with them throughout Europe. There, he spent most of his adult life. He, along with many other Americans, earned the label *expatriate* for leading this lifestyle. Though he seldom stayed in one location for very long, he spent a long period of his career in England. Regarded as one of the most successful international society portrait artists, Sargent influenced European and American artists with his technical skills and techniques. He was such a determined artist that he painted more than 900 oils and more than 2,000 watercolors between 1877

# Study

▶ *The Daughters of Edward Darly Boit:* There are more objects on the left side of the painting. *The Westwood Children:* Two of the children are on the left side, while the tallest child appears in both halves of the painting.

▶ *The Daughters of Edward Darly Boit:* There are two girls in each half of the painting. *The Westwood Children:* The left side of the painting technically has two and a half boys.

▶ *The Daughters of Edward Darly Boit:* the girl playing with her doll on the floor; *The Westwood Children:* the dog that is carrying the bird

■ For more examples of portraits, see ***The National Museum of Women in the Arts Collection.***

### Art Journal: Writing

Have students explain what informal balance means in the Concepts section of their Art Journals. What else do they want to know about informal balance and asymmetry?

### Aesthetic Perception

**Design Awareness** Have students imagine a line drawn through the center of your desk. Explain to students that artists often use informal balance in their paintings to create an interesting composition.

**Developing Visual Literacy** Discuss the arrangement of objects in each work of art. Where are these objects placed in relation to the central axis? Ask students to share personal experiences that contribute to their interpretations. For example, have they ever had to pose for a portrait before?

**Web Connection**
Visit **www.mfa.org** for more information about the Museum of Fine Arts, Boston.

 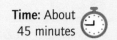

# Teach

"How will you use informal balance to arrange your portrait?" "¿Cómo van a usar el equilibrio informal para ordenar su retrato?"

- Read and discuss using informal balance on page 192.

- Have students choose appropriate vocabulary to discuss the use of art principles, such as balance.
  NSAE 2.a

## Practice

**Materials:** balance scale, classroom objects

- Distribute the materials and have students follow the directions on page 192.

 ## Creative Expression

**Materials:** white paper, watercolor crayons, pencils, erasers, assorted brushes, water containers, paper towels

**Alternate Materials:** crayons, watercolor paints

- Distribute the materials and have students follow the directions on page 193.

- Review the Activity Tips on page 243 for visual examples of techniques if needed.

### Art Journal: Discussing

After discussing how artists use informal balance, ask students to come up with one question for each of the ways in which informal balance is created. There should be one question each for size, color, texture, and position. Have students write their questions in their Art Journals.

---

# Using Informal Balance

**Informal balance,** or **asymmetry,** can be seen but not measured. Artists use informal balance to organize parts of a design so that objects have equal visual weight.

**Visual weight** is not measured on a scale. It is measured by which object the viewer's eyes see first. Differences in color, shape, and contour affect visual weight.

Bright colors have more visual weight than dull colors.

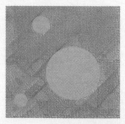

Large shapes have more visual weight than small shapes.

A busy contour, or border, has more visual weight than a smooth contour.

Position, or placement, can be used to create informal balance.

## Practice

Use a balance scale to create informal balance.

1. Gather various objects from around the classroom.

2. Create informal balance by adding different combinations of objects on the scale.

---

## Differentiated Instruction

**Reteach**

Have students identify free-form shapes in the classroom. Then have them explain why the shapes are asymmetrical.

**Special Needs**

Encourage students to make connections between the lesson activity and the art history exemplars by asking them to show the personalities of each family member in their portraits.

**ELL**

Have students look at photographs of activities around the school. View the images in the classroom, and discuss how balance was created.

◀ **Carma Scott.**
Age 9.

**Think** about how the student artist created informal balance in this portrait.

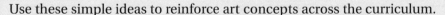

### Creative Expression

Create a family portrait with informal balance.

1. Think of the members of your family. Imagine a time when you are relaxing together. Where are the people sitting?
2. Use a pencil to lightly sketch the scene.
3. With watercolor crayons, fill in the large areas of your drawing.
4. Use water and a watercolor brush to blend the watercolor crayon.
5. After the painting dries, use markers to add hair, eyes, eyebrows, lips, and other details.

### Art Criticism

**Describe** Describe the setting and the people in the portrait.

**Analyze** How did you organize the portrait to create informal balance?

**Interpret** What mood does your portrait create?

**Decide** Would this portrait have the same mood if it had formal balance? Explain.

Unit 6 • Lesson 2 **193**

Time: About 5 minutes

### Review and Assess

"Were you able to create a portrait using informal balance?" "¿Pudieron crear un retrato usando equilibrio informal?"

## Think

The artist created informal balance by placing the people in a setting where they would normally be relaxed. The people and objects are not equal on both sides, but they have the same visual weight.

■ Use **Large Print 60** *Snowstorm: Steamboat off a Harbour's Mouth* to have students discuss informal balance. Compare the use of informal balance to the works of art in the lesson.

### Informal Assessment

■ For standardized-format test practice using this lesson's art content, see pages 68–69 in **Reading and Writing Test Preparation.**

### Art Journal: Critical Thinking

Have students answer the four art criticism questions—Describe, Analyze, Interpret, and Decide—in their Art Journals. Have students display their work and discuss how they used informal balance. Ask the students to discuss their selection of objects and how they chose to arrange them.

## Art Across the Curriculum

Use these simple ideas to reinforce art concepts across the curriculum.

★ **Narrative Writing** Have students write a dialogue for the Westwood children.

★ **Math** Have students understand how fractions and decimals can look different but are equal, similar to the concept of visual weight.

★ **Science** Have students discuss the density of the objects used for the Practice activity.

★ **Social Studies** Have students compare the way children dress today to the children's dress depicted in the lesson.

★ **Technology** Using a paint or draw program, have students create a landscape that shows informal balance. Visit **SRAonline.com** to print detailed instructions for this activity.
NSAE 6.b

## Lesson 2 — Wrap-Up
# Informal Balance

---

### Extra! For the Art Specialist

**Time:** About 45 minutes

## Focus

Study *Large Print 60* Snowstorm: *Steamboat off a Harbour's Mouth* and discuss how some artists use informal balance in an artwork to give equal visual weight to both halves even though they are not the same or similar.

## Teach

Ask students to collect a variety of objects for a still life. As a class, arrange the objects, and view the still life from all sides. Give each of the students a viewfinder to look at the still life. Demonstrate using a viewfinder to help compose an arrangement. Show students how to close one eye when looking through the viewfinder. Have students complete the alternate activity.

## Reflect

Have students use the four steps of art criticism to evaluate their work. Have them describe how they arranged their still lifes.

### Alternate Activity

**Materials:**
- sketchbooks
- viewfinders
- pencils, erasers
- 12" × 18" drawing paper
- fine-line markers
- watercolor paints
- paintbrushes
- water containers

1. Using a viewfinder, have students create several sketches of their still lifes. Have them draw at least two different views.

2. Have students select their best sketches and transfer them onto paper. Their drawings should touch at least three edges of the paper, and two of the objects must overlap. Have students use a fine-line marker to trace over the lines. They can add hatching or cross-hatching to show shadows.

3. Have students use paint to add color to their drawings. Have them overlap and blend the colors.

## Research in Art Education

"If perception is basic to all learning, if selective viewing is a desirable kind of behavior, and if conceptualization comes after sensory experiences, then it becomes imperative that teachers provide paths for numerous visual and tactile explorations so as to keep all of the child's senses alive and active." (Herberholz, Barbara, and Lee Hanson. *Early Childhood Art*. New York: McGraw-Hill, 1994.)

---

## Assessment

Use the following rubric to evaluate the artwork students make in the Creative Expression activity and to assess students' understanding of how informal balance is used in two-dimensional works of art.

Have students complete page 71 or 72 in their *Assessment* books.

| | Art History and Culture | Aesthetic Perception | Creative Expression | Art Criticism |
|---|---|---|---|---|
| **3 POINTS** | The student demonstrates knowledge of the lives and work of Johnson and Sargent. | The student accurately identifies the use of informal balance in two-dimensional works of art. | The student's portrait demonstrates how to use informal balance. | The student thoughtfully and honestly evaluates own work using the four steps of art criticism. |
| **2 POINTS** | The student's knowledge of the lives and work of Johnson and Sargent is weak or incomplete. | The student shows an emerging awareness of informal balance in two-dimensional works of art, but cannot consistently identify it. | The student's portrait shows some awareness of how to use informal balance. | The student attempts to evaluate own work but shows an incomplete understanding of evaluation criteria. |
| **1 POINT** | The student cannot demonstrate knowledge of the life and work of Johnson or Sargent. | The student cannot identify how informal balance is used in two-dimensional works of art. | The student's portrait shows no understanding of how to use informal balance. | The student makes no attempt to evaluate own work. |

### Assessment, p. 71

Name _____ Date _____

**Informal Balance** — Lesson 2, UNIT 6

**A.** Drawing
Using a pencil, design a mask that shows informal balance.

**B.** Vocabulary
Circle the correct answer to each question.
1. What is one type of informal balance?
symmetry    negative space    asymmetry    positive space
2. What is an example of something that has informal balance?
face    square    ball    chair    hand

**C.** Writing
Look at *The Westwood Children* by Joshua Johnson. Describe how he used informal balance in this portrait.

Level 4    Unit 6 • Balance, Variety, Harmony, and Unity    71

# Radial Balance

**Lesson 3** introduces another type of balance called radial balance. **Radial balance** is a type of balance that occurs when the art elements come out, or radiate, from a central point. The **focal point** is the area of an artwork that is emphasized.

## Objectives

 **Art History and Culture**

To demonstrate knowledge of American folk artists

 **Creative Expression**

To design a wall hanging with a radial design

**Aesthetic Perception**

To identify how radial balance is used in a variety of works of art

**Art Criticism**

To evaluate own work using the four steps of art criticism

### Lesson Materials
- wooden craft sticks
- yarn in a variety of colors
- glue
- white paper
- pencils

**Alternate Materials:**
- color string
- notebook paper

### Program Resources
- *Reading and Writing Test Prep.*, pp. 70–71
- *Transparency 33*
- *Flash Card* 14
- *Artist Profiles,* pp. 35, 61
- *Animals Through History Time Line*
- *Assessment,* pp. 73–74
- *Large Print 59* Dla'ehl (Interior House Post) and *Print 60* Snowstorm: Steamboat off a Harbour's Mouth
- *Art Around the World Collection*

### Concept Trace
Radial Balance
**Introduced:** Level 4, Unit 6, Lesson 3
**Reinforced:** Level 5, Unit 5, Lesson 6

## Vocabulary  Vocabulary

Review the following vocabulary words with students before beginning the lesson.

**focal point** punto focal—the area of an artwork that is emphasized

**radiate** radiar—to come out from a central point

See page 209B for additional vocabulary and Spanish vocabulary resources.

 **Art Journal: Vocabulary**

Have students add these words to the Vocabulary section of their Art Journals.

# Lesson 3 Arts Integration

## Theatre

Complete Unit 6, Lesson 3, on pages 112–113 of *Theatre Arts Connections.*

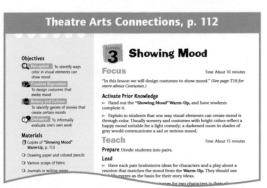
Theatre Arts Connections, p. 112

## Music

 Musical forms have balance. Music in the Western tradition also has forms that create balance. Rondo form is one main musical idea over and over again with contrasting sections between. Have students listen to the rondo from "Rage over a Lost Penny" by Ludwig van Beethoven. How many times do students hear the A section?

## Movement & Dance

Radial balance comes out from the center. Divide students into groups of six. Each group should make a circle by holding hands. Have students move their feet together and make their bodies long. Have everyone move their arms in the same direction out from the circle, forming rays.

# Focus

**Time:** About 10 minutes

## Activate Prior Knowledge

"Have you ever looked at a design in a kaleidoscope?" "¿Alguna vez han visto un diseño en un kaleidoscopio?"

■ Discuss students' responses. Explain that radial designs, like those seen in a kaleidoscope, are often created for decorative purposes.

### Using Literature ★ Reading

■ Look at the cover illustration of *Fair Weather* by Richard Peck. Discuss how radial balance is used in the cover illustration. The radial balance in a Ferris wheel is not only decorative but functional.

### Thematic Connection ★ Math

■ **Circular Shapes:** Have students think of everyday objects that are circular. Then have them explain why they think the object is not another geometric shape, such as a triangle or square. For example, if a wheel on a bike is a shape other than a circle, the rider would not have a smooth ride.

## Introduce the Art

# Look

"Look closely at how repeated lines, shapes, and colors are arranged in the works of art." "Miren detalladamente la manera en que las líneas repetidas, las figuras y los colores están ordenados en las obras de arte."

### Rounding ★ Math

Have students look at the dimensions of the works of art in this lesson. Then have them round the dimensions to the nearest tens place. *Sunburst:* 70 × 40 × 20; *Lovebird Token:* 20 × 20.

 **Art History and Culture**

Explain to students that radial designs in many cultures are symbolic or used for meditative purposes.

💻 **Web Connection**

Visit **www.graphics.cornell.edu/online/mandala** for more information about mandalas. Note: This Web site is for teacher use only.

---

Lesson **3** # Radial Balance

**Look** at the two works of art on these pages. They are both examples of radial balance. Both pieces were made by folk artists. Folk art is usually made by people who have had little or no formal schooling in art. Folk artists usually make works of art with traditional techniques and content. The styles have been handed down through many generations, and they come from particular regions. Notice how the design in each work of art radiates out from the center in a circular design.

◄ **John Scholl.** (American). *Sunburst.* 1907–1916.
Paint on wood with wire on metal. 71 × 38 × 24½ inches (180.3 × 96.5 × 62.2 cm.). American Folk Art Museum, New York, New York.

 **Art History and Culture**

A painting within a circle is often called a *tondo* in Western tradition and a *mandala* in Eastern tradition.

---

 **Art History and Culture**

## John Scholl

John Scholl (jän shōl) (1827–1916) was born in Württemberg, Germany, and immigrated to the United States. He settled in the forested region of Germania, Pennsylvania, and worked as a builder. Some of his constructions included his own house, the village church, and the general store. Scholl received no artistic training, but when he retired at the age of 80, he began to create hand-carved, decorative wooden objects. He did not carve for commercial reasons, and he never sold any of his work.

See pages 24–25 and 16–21 for more about art history and the subject matter.

**Artist Profiles, p. 61**

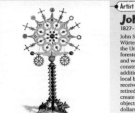

◆ Artist Profile ◆
### John Scholl
1827-1916

John Scholl (jän shōl) was born in Württemburg, Germany, and immigrated to the United States in 1853. He settled in the forested region of Germania, Pennsylvania, and worked as a builder. Some of his constructions included his own house and additional houses, the village church, the local brewery, and the general store. Scholl received no artistic training, but when he retired at the age of eighty, he began to create hand-carved, decorative wooden objects that now sell for thousands of dollars at folk art auctions. He did not carve for commercial reasons, and he never sold any of his work. Until 1967, his entire collection remained together and in the possession of his children and

▲ **William Johnson.** (American).
*Lovebird Token.* Early nineteenth century.

Watercolor and ink on cut paper. $16\frac{1}{8} \times 16$ inches
($41 \times 40.6$ cm.). American Folk Art Museum, New York,
New York.

**Study** the radial design in each work of art.

▶ Where do the designs begin?

▶ If you turn your textbook, do the designs change? Do they stay the same?

▶ What are the differences in the types of forms and shapes each artist used?

 **Aesthetic Perception**

**Seeing Like an Artist** What are some objects in nature that are circular in shape, such as a flower?

## Art History and Culture

### Lovebird Token

Little is known about the artist who created this watercolor love token aside from his name. It is assumed that William Johnson (c. nineteenth century) made this piece while living in Pennsylvania. *Lovebird Token* features a geometric design made of concentric rings and a detailed center illustration. Each of the rings displays lines of a poem dedicated to the recipient of the love token, an unnamed young woman.

See pages 24–25 and 16–21 for more about art history and the subject matter.

**Artist Profiles, p. 35**

● Artist Profile ●
**William Johnson**
Little is known about the artist who created this watercolor love token aside from his name. It is assumed that William Johnson made this piece while living in Pennsylvania, and that he may have been of German or English heritage. The style of the artwork as well as the location where its owner lived suggests that it was made by a member of the extensive Pennsylvania German community during the early nineteenth century.

◄ **William Johnson.** (American).
*Lovebird Token.* Early nineteenth century.

Watercolor and ink on cut paper. $16\frac{1}{8} \times 16$ inches ($41 \times 40.6$ cm.).
American Folk Art Museum, New York, New York.

## Study

▶ Both designs begin in the middle.

▶ *Sunburst:* The design changes because the stand appears in different places. *Lovebird Token:* The overall design does not change, but the words written on the token are not in the same places.

▶ *Sunburst:* There are mostly circular forms with a few free-form forms. *Lovebird Token:* There are two types of bird shapes and one free-form shape that is repeated in the center.

■ For more examples of art from North America, see the *Art Around the World Collection.*

### Art Journal: Writing

Have students explain what the word *radial* means in the Concepts section of their Art Journals. What else do they want to know about radial balance?

### Aesthetic Perception

**Design Awareness** Have the students discuss the various types of radial designs they have noticed in nature. Some examples are the rings on a tree, a spider web, a snowflake, and ripples of water in a pond.

**Developing Visual Literacy** Discuss the use of repeated shapes and lines in each artwork. Have students look closely at how the two pieces are arranged. Can they find the central axis? Why do they think these objects were designed this way? Ask students to explain their answers.

### Web Connection

Visit **www.folkartmuseum.org** for more information about the American Folk Art Museum in New York.

# Teach

**Time:** About 45 minutes

"How will you create your radial design?"
"¿Cómo van a crear su diseño radial?"

- Read and discuss using radial balance on page 196.

## Practice

**Materials:** white paper, pencils

**Alternate Materials:** notebook paper

- Distribute the materials and have students follow the directions on page 196.

## Creative Expression

**Materials:** wooden craft sticks, yarn in a variety of colors, glue

**Alternate Materials:** color string

- Distribute the materials and have students follow the directions on page 197.

- Review the Activity Tips on page 244 for visual examples of techniques if needed.

### Art Journal: Drawing

Have students sketch a variety of radial designs in the Idea section of their Art Journals. Students can refer to these sketches for ideas when they create a radial design.

---

# Using Radial Balance

**Radial balance** occurs when the elements in a design (line, shape, color, and/or form) radiate, or come out, from one central point. Radial balance is an example of symmetry because both sides of the design are mirror images of each other.

You can find radial balance both in nature and in objects made by people. If you look closely at a flower, you will see that the petals are often arranged around a central point. The top of an umbrella also has radial balance.

## Practice

Find examples of radial balance in your classroom.

1. Divide a sheet of paper into two columns.
2. Label the first column *Nature* and the second column *Humanmade*.
3. List examples of radial balance in the correct columns.

---

## Differentiated Instruction

**Reteach**

Using pieces of yarn, have students demonstrate radial balance.

**Special Needs**

Foster student competence in art making by challenging them to use more than two sticks, add different colors, or use material other than yarn for the weaving.

**ELL**

Present the information on radial balance, using a visual example like a flower. Point to the petals, and show that they move out from the center.

◀ **Peter George.**
Age 8.

**Think** about how the student artist created radial balance.

Use radial balance to create a wall hanging.

1. Cross wooden craft sticks and glue them together. Glue the end of a piece of yarn behind the center of the sticks.

2. Hold the sticks so they look like an *X*. With the yarn hanging from the bottom, wrap it diagonally over the middle and then over the top right arm of the *X*.

3. Turn the *X* one clockwise turn to wrap each stick. As you wrap the yarn, make sure the rows of yarn lie side by side.

4. Change the color of yarn. Tie the next color to the end of the first piece and continue to wrap. Tie the end of the last piece of yarn and tuck it under. Tie a loop on top as a hanger.

**Art Criticism**

**Describe** Describe the design of your wall hanging.

**Analyze** How did you use radial balance in your design?

**Interpret** Where could you place your wall hanging?

**Decide** What changes would you make to improve your design?

# Art Across the Curriculum

Use these simple ideas to reinforce art concepts across the curriculum.

★ **Expository Writing** Have students write a paragraph explaining in what type of setting *Sunburst* should be displayed.

★ **Math** Have students measure the diameter of the circle images in the works of art.

★ **Science** Explain to students that sea anemones and sea stars have radial balance.

★ **Social Studies** Have students compare different types of folk art they have seen from around the world.

★ **Technology** Using the shape tools in a paint or draw program, have students create a design that demonstrates radial balance. Visit **SRAonline.com** to print detailed instructions for this activity.
NSAE 6.b

 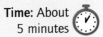

# Reflect

**Time:** About 5 minutes

## Review and Assess

"How did you create radial balance in your wall hanging?" ¿Cómo crearon equilibrio radial en su muralla?

## Think

The artist created radial balance by wrapping the yarn around the middle of the craft sticks and working outward.

■ Use *Large Prints 59 Dla'el (Interior House Post)* and *60 Snowstorm: Steamboat off a Harbour's Mouth* and ask students to explain why these are not examples of radial balance.

## Informal Assessment

■ For standardized-format test practice using this lesson's art content, see pages 70–71 in *Reading and Writing Test Preparation.*

### Art Journal: Critical Thinking

Have students answer the four art criticism questions—Describe, Analyze, Interpret, and Decide—in their Art Journals. Have students discuss within groups the intent of their wall hangings. Then have them form conclusions about their personal artwork in their Art Journals.
NSAE 5.a; 5.c

# Radial Balance

## Extra! For the Art Specialist

Time: About 45 minutes

### Focus

Have students look at the works of art in this lesson and discuss how some artists use radial balance in an artwork to enhance a shape or form. Have them describe how the elements are arranged.

### Teach

Discuss how radial designs occur in nature. Explain to students that they will make a clay radial design based on natural objects. Have students collect a variety of natural objects such as feathers, leaves, nuts, twigs, or shells, and have them create several simple sketches. Then have students complete the alternate activity.

### Reflect

Have students use the four steps of art criticism to evaluate their work. What objects in nature influenced their designs?

## Alternate Activity

**Materials:**
- sketchbooks
- pencils, erasers
- 8" circle pattern
- clay
- clay mat or textured wallpaper
- rolling pin
- clay tools

1. Have students use a ball of clay to roll out a slab. Have them trace a circle and cut it. Students should select one sketch and roll out another slab. Students should draw their image into the clay and cut it. Then have them trace the shape three times and cut them.

2. Have students arrange the four clay shapes in the center of the circle so they radiate outward. Have them attach the shapes using the score and slip method. Have students cut another shape from the clay and follow the same steps to create four more shapes. These should be attached between the first set of shapes. Students can use clay tools to add details.

3. Once the radial designs have air-dried, fire them.

## Research in Art Education

"The elementary classroom offers an environment that can foster creativity, independence, self-awareness, self-expression, and an understanding of the visual world. Education through art can provide opportunities for exploring one's creativity, for communicating ideas, and enabling students to express themselves through the use of materials, processes, and tools." (Andra Nyman, "Cultural Content, Identity, and Program Development: Approaches to Art Education for Elementary Educators," in *Contemporary Issues in Art Education*, edited by Y. Gaudelius and P. Speirs, 61–69. New Jersey: Prentice Hall, 2002.)

## Assessment

Use the following rubric to evaluate the artwork students made in the Creative Expression activity and to assess students' understanding of how radial balance is used in works of art.

Have students complete page 73 or 74 in their *Assessment* books.

|  | Art History and Culture | Aesthetic Perception | Creative Expression | Art Criticism |
|---|---|---|---|---|
| **3 POINTS** | The student demonstrates knowledge of American folk artists. | The student accurately identifies the use of radial balance in a variety of works of art. | The student's wall hanging demonstrates how to use radial balance. | The student thoughtfully and honestly evaluates own work using the four steps of art criticism. |
| **2 POINTS** | The student's knowledge of American folk artists is weak or incomplete. | The student shows an emerging awareness of radial balance in a variety of works of art, but cannot consistently identify it. | The student's wall hanging shows some awareness of how to use radial balance. | The student attempts to evaluate own work but shows an incomplete understanding of evaluation criteria. |
| **1 POINT** | The student cannot demonstrate knowledge of American folk artists. | The student cannot identify how radial balance is used in an artwork. | The student's wall hanging shows no understanding of how to use radial balance. | The student makes no attempt to evaluate own work. |

### Assessment, p. 73

Name _____ Date _____ Lesson **3** UNIT 6

**Radial Balance**

A. Drawing
Use a marker or a crayon to draw a design showing radial balance.

B. Short Answer
What are the two places in which you can find radial balance?
1. _____
2. _____

C. Writing
Study *Sunburst* by John Scholl. What did he do to create radial balance in the sculpture?

Level 4      Unit 6 • Balance, Variety, Harmony, and Unity  **73**

# Harmony

**Lesson 4** is about how the art principle of harmony is used in three-dimensional works of art. **Harmony** is the principle of art that creates unity by stressing similarities of separate but related parts.

## Objectives

 **Art History and Culture**

To demonstrate knowledge of the lives and work of Vladimir Baranoff-Rossine and Barbara Hepworth

 **Creative Expression**

To create a model for a sculpture using harmony

**Aesthetic Perception**

To understand how harmony is used in three-dimensional works of art

 **Art Criticism**

To evaluate own work using the four steps of art criticism

### Vocabulary  Vocabulary

Review the following vocabulary words with students before beginning the lesson.

**harmony armonía**—the principle of art that creates unity by stressing similarities of separate but related parts

**assemblage montaje**—a technique in which an artist collects found materials and assembles them into a three-dimensional work of art

See page 209B for additional vocabulary and Spanish vocabulary resources.

### Art Journal: Vocabulary

Have students add these words to the Vocabulary section of their Art Journals.

## Lesson Materials

- objects from desks
- white paper
- scissors, glue
- pencil, erasers
- mixing palettes
- cardboard
- found objects
- tempera paint
- paintbrushes
- water containers
- newspaper
- paper towels

**Alternate Materials:**
- markers
- oil pastels

## Program Resources

- *Reading and Writing Test Prep.*, pp. 72–73
- *Transparency 34*
- *Flash Cards* 17, 18
- *Artist Profiles*, pp. 5, 29
- *Animals Through History Time Line*
- *Assessment*, pp. 75–76
- *Large Print 59 Dla'ehl (Interior House Post)* and *Print 60 Snowstorm: Steamboat off a Harbour's Mouth*
- *The National Museum of Women in the Arts Collection*

### Concept Trace
Harmony
**Introduced:** Level 3, Unit 6, Lesson 1

**Reinforced:** Level 5, Unit 6, Lesson 1

---

## Lesson 4 Arts Integration

### Theatre

Complete Unit 6, Lesson 4, on pages 114–115 of *Theatre Arts Connections.*

**Theatre Arts Connections, p. 114**

Objectives

**A Director Shows Theme**

**Focus**                Time: About 10 minutes

"In this lesson we will direct improvisations to show theme." *(See page T4 for more about Improvisation.)*

**Activate Prior Knowledge**
▶ Discuss how a director uses theme. He or she first identifies it (often with the help of others), and then works with designers and actors to communicate this theme.

**Teach**                Time: About 15 minutes

**Prepare** Divide students into groups of three.
**Lead** Read aloud "The Mystery of Roanoke Island." Say, "We are going to improvise what might have happened to the Lost Colony. Decide what you think might have happened to them. Choose a subject, theme, and mood based on your idea."
▶ Have each group assign roles, such as Eleanor Dare (mother of Virginia) or Chief Manteo of the Croatoans, and choose a director. Explain that the director and actors must work together on the dramatization; the director should only make changes to better

### Music

The life work of Johann Sebastian Bach set down the harmonies that Western music is built upon. Have students listen to the last movement of "Brandenburg Concerto No. 5." He wrote six of these concertos, named after the Margrave of Brandenburg who commissioned them.

### Movement & Dance

Put students into lines of seven. Each line should have a leader. Have the leader create a pathway on which his or her line will travel, controlling the speed, the level, and the direction. Have all the lines work simultaneously, with a sense of harmony, but they should not have contact or cross into each other's paths.

 **ocus**  Time: About 10 minutes

## Activate Prior Knowledge

"Have you ever created or seen a sculpture in which different materials were used?"

"¿Alguna vez han creado o visto una escultura donde se usaron diferentes materiales?"

■ As a class, discuss students' responses. Explain that sometimes artists use materials that are not normally thought of as an art material. They will use harmony to bring these unusual materials together.

### Using Literature ⭐ Reading

■ Look at the cover illustration of *Body Parts in Rebellion* by Regan Dunnick. Discuss how the image on the cover uses harmony through color and subject. Each object is part of a body. Although each section is separated, we naturally associate them together. The color yellow harmonizes the scattered parts.

### Thematic Connection ⭐ Social Studies

■ **Cooperation:** Have students discuss how working together in a group can create harmony. How do people feel if there is harmony in a group?

## Introduce the Art

# Look

"Look closely at both sculptures to compare how Baranoff-Rossine and Hepworth used harmony in their works." "Miren detalladamente ambas esculturas para comparar cómo Baranoff-Rossine y Hepworth usaron armonía en sus obras."

### Probability ⭐ Math

Have students examine the works of art in this lesson and determine what other shapes each sculpture could have taken, such as a square.

### 🏺 Art History and Culture

Explain to students that when artists become famous their other work sometimes gets overshadowed. Students should not assume that artists create only one type of art.

### 💻 Web Connection

Visit **www.moma.org** for more information about the Museum of Modern Art.

---

 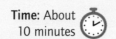

# Harmony

**Look** at the works of art on these pages. *Symphony Number 1* is made of different kinds of wood shapes and forms and a variety of textures. The repetition of curved lines on the sculpture and on the edges of the shapes and the predominantly warm color scheme give the sculpture harmony. *Three Forms* is a pure white marble sculpture. It consists of only three geometric forms on a block of marble. Hepworth harmonized this sculpture by selecting one color—white.

◀ **Vladimir Baranoff-Rossine.** (Russian/Ukranian). *Symphony Number 1.* 1913.

Polychrome wood, cardboard, and crushed eggshells. $63\frac{1}{4} \times 28\frac{1}{2} \times 25$ inches (160.7 × 72.4 × 63.5 cm.). Museum of Modern Art, New York, New York.

### 🏺 Art History and Culture

Baranoff-Rossine and Hepworth created paintings as well as sculpture.

---

### 🏺 Art History and Culture

## Vladimir Baranoff-Rossine

Vladimir Baranoff-Rossine (vlə dē´ mir bə rä´ nəf rōs ēn´) (1888–1944) began his studies at Odessa and then attended the imperial Academie des Beaux Arts of St. Petersburg, Russia. When he was 22, Baranoff-Rossine relocated to Paris, France, where he began to exhibit his works professionally. During his time in Paris, his work evolved and became more geometric, a reflection of the creative impact of his friendship with French cubist artists.

See pages 24–25 and 16–21 for more about art history and the subject matter.

**Artist Profiles, p. 5**

⬥ Artist Profile ⬥

### Vladimir Baranoff-Rossine
1888-1944

Vladimir Baranoff-Rossine (vlə dē´ mir bə rä´ naf  rōs ēn´) was born in 1888 in Ukraine. He began his studies at Odessa and then attended the imperial Academie des Beaux Arts of St. Petersburg, Russia. When he was 22, Baranoff-Rossine relocated to Paris, France, where he began to exhibit his works professionally. During his time in Paris, his work evolved and became more geometric, a reflection of the creative impact of his friendship with other French cubist artists. After returning to St. Petersburg in 1917, he spent several years teaching art to pupils in his studio, married, and started a family. After returning to

**Study** both sculptures to see how the artists created harmony.

▶ What shapes and forms are repeated in each sculpture?

▶ What does *Symphony Number 1* look like?

▶ What kinds of textures can you see on each sculpture?

▲ **Barbara Hepworth.** (English). *Three Forms.* 1935.
.........................................
Serravezza marble. 7⁷⁄₈ × 21 × 13½ inches (20 × 53.3 × 34.3 cm.). Tate Gallery, London, England.

### Aesthetic Perception

**Design Awareness** Look through your textbook for other sculptures. Compare the two sculptures in this lesson with others you find.

### Art History and Culture

#### Barbara Hepworth

Barbara Hepworth (bärb´ ə rə hep´ wûrth) (1903–1975) was an English sculptor known for her abstract works in wood, stone, and metal. As a child, she took trips through the countryside with her father. The beauty of rural areas impressed her, and the land became a theme in her art. After studying art and sculpture in England, Hepworth moved to Rome and then returned to England. In 1965 she was named a dame of the British Empire.

See pages 24–25 and 16–21 for more about art history and the subject matter.

**Artist Profiles, p. 29**

◀ Artist Profile ▶
**Barbara Hepworth**
1903–1975
Barbara Hepworth (bärb´ ə rə hep´ wûrth) was an English sculptor known for her abstract works in wood, stone, and metal. As a child in Yorkshire, she took car trips through the countryside with her father. She was impressed by the contrast between the beauty of rural areas and the grime of industrial towns. The land became a theme she returned to again and again in her art. After studying art and sculpture in England, Hepworth moved to Rome and then returned to England. She married twice, once to a sculptor and once to a painter. She had a son and a set of triplets. Her relationship with her children also became an important theme of her work. In 1965, she was honored by being named a dame.

## Study

▶ *Symphony Number 1:* There is a variety of rectangular and triangular forms and three circular forms. *Three Forms:* There are two oval forms.

▶ In both pieces, the negative space is limited, creating a heavy appearance to the objects in the positive space.

▶ *Symphony Number 1:* There are rough, matte, and smooth textures. *Three Forms:* The forms are smooth and the light that shines on them gives them a shiny appearance.

■ For more examples of abstract and nonobjective art, see *The National Museum of Women in the Arts Collection.*

### Art Journal: Writing

Have students explain what *assemblage* means to them in the Concepts section of their Art Journals. What else do they want to know about harmony in three-dimensional art?

### Aesthetic Perception

**Design Awareness** While students search for other sculptures, remind them that they should not only find works of art with many similarities but with differences as well. Have them look at the shapes, colors, and lines each artist used.

**Developing Visual Literacy** Discuss the use of lines, shapes, and color in each artwork. Ask the students if the various parts look familiar. Explain that artists often are inspired by the environment in which they live and work. Ask students to share personal experiences that contribute to their interpretations.

### Web Connection
Visit **www.sculpturesite.com** for more information about contemporary sculpture. **Note:** This Web site is for teacher use only.

**each**   Time: About 45 minutes

"Can you harmonize a variety of objects in a group sculpture?" "¿Pueden armonizar una variedad de objetos en una escultura de grupo?"

- Read and discuss using harmony on page 200.

## Practice

**Materials:** objects from desks

**Alternate Materials:** found objects

- Distribute the materials and have students follow the directions on page 200.

 ### Creative Expression

**Materials:** white paper, scissors, glue, pencils, erasers, mixing palettes, cardboard, found objects, tempera paint, paintbrushes, water containers, newspaper, paper towels

**Alternate Materials:** markers, oil pastels

- Distribute the materials and have students follow the directions on page 201.
- Have students integrate a variety of ideas about community in their sculptures.
  NSAE 3.a; 3.b
- Review the Activity Tips on page 244 for visual examples of techniques if needed.

### Art Journal: Brainstorming

Ask students to think about their school environment and brainstorm locations for their sculptures. Then have them place a list in their Art Journals of objects they could use for the Creative Expression activity.

# Using Harmony

**Harmony** is the principle of art that creates unity by stressing similarities of separate but related parts. You can create harmony by repeating a shape or color or by using closely related or similar elements.

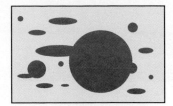

Analogous colors create harmony. They are colors that sit next to each other on the color wheel and share a common color on the color wheel.

An **assemblage** is a three-dimensional work of art made of many pieces put together. An artist can make a harmonious assemblage by using related shapes and colors.

### Practice

Build a temporary sculpture on your desk that shows harmony. Use objects from your desk.

1. Create a harmonious sculpture using several objects.
2. Take apart your sculpture and build it another way.

## Differentiated Instruction

**Reteach**
Ask students to look at the architecture in their neighborhoods for examples of harmony.

**Special Needs**
Public art often has a social purpose. Use this lesson as an opportunity for students to explore the ways that the elements of art can be used as symbols to represent and express ideas such as harmony or unity among people.

**ELL**
Have students group together different objects in the classroom to create harmony.

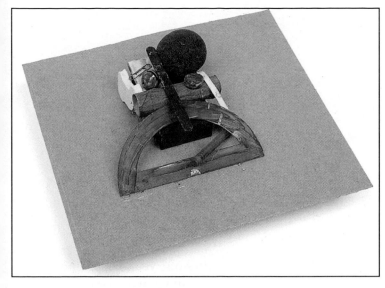

◄ **Cecelia Bonilla.**
Age 9.

**Think** about how the student artist created harmony.

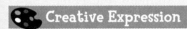
### Creative Expression

What type of sculpture would fit your school setting? Create a model of a sculpture using harmony.

1. Think of the type of sculpture that would fit the environment of your school. Choose an appropriate site for your sculpture.

2. Draw several sketches of how you want your sculpture to look. Select one sketch as your plan.

3. Using cardboard and found objects, build a model of your sculpture. Use analogous colors to create harmony in your design.

### Art Criticism

**Describe** Describe the materials you used to create your model and the site you chose for it.

**Analyze** How did you create harmony in your sculpture?

**Interpret** Give your sculpture a title.

**Decide** Do you think your model is a success? Explain.

# Reflect
**Time:** About 5 minutes

## Review and Assess

"Explain how you created harmony in your sculpture. Which art element ties your work together?" *"Expliquen cómo crearon armonía en su escultura. ¿Qué elemento artístico unifica su obra?"*

## Think

The artist created harmony through the repetition of rounded shapes and analogous colors.

- Use *Large Prints 59 Dla'ehl (Interior House Post)* and *60 Snowstorm: Steamboat Off a Harbour's Mouth* to have students identify how harmony was used. Describe the lines, shapes, colors, and objects in each work.

## Informal Assessment

- For standardized-format test practice using this lesson's art content, see pages 72–73 in *Reading and Writing Test Preparation.*

### Art Journal: Critical Thinking

Have students answer the four art criticism questions—Describe, Analyze, Interpret, and Decide—in their Art Journals. In small groups, haves students describe the harmony in their completed sculptures. Have students interpret ideas and moods in their peers' original artwork. Do the student artists agree with their peers?
NSAE 5.a; 5.c

---

## Art Across the Curriculum

Use these simple ideas to reinforce art concepts across the curriculum.

★ **Persuasive Writing** Write a paragraph persuading a museum to include *Three Forms* in its modern sculpture collection.

★ **Math** Have students identify different geometric shapes in each work of art.

★ **Science** Explain to students that large wooden sculptures may appear heavier than they actually are. It depends on the density of the wood.

★ **Social Studies** Have students discuss how a person's job can influence the type of art he or she creates.

★ **Technology** Using a paint or draw program, have students create a design for an abstract sculpture that shows harmony. Visit **SRAonline.com** to print detailed instructions for this activity.
NSAE 6.b

## Lesson 4 Wrap-Up

# Harmony

 **Extra!** ## For the Art Specialist

 **Time:** About 45 minutes

## Focus

Have students study **Large Print 59** *Dla'ehl (Interior House Post)* and discuss how some artists use harmony to bring together various parts of an artwork based on the similarities. Have them identify which element is repeated most often.

## Teach

Cover a bulletin board with newspaper and then a layer of bulletin board paper. This will ensure that paint does not bleed through. Explain to students that they will make a group mural based on a class theme. Their work will be harmonized based on color. Have the students complete the alternate activity.

## Reflect

Have students use the four steps of art criticism to evaluate their work. Did they effectively use harmony in the mural?

### Alternate Activity

**Materials:**
- sketchbooks
- pencils, erasers
- permanent markers
- water-based paints
- brushes in various sizes
- paint trays
- water containers
- sponges
- drop cloth for the floor

1. As a class, decide on a theme for the mural. Once the theme has been selected, have students look for ideas in books, magazines, and photographs. When an artist works on a mural, a drawing, called a cartoon, is transferred onto the wall. It is called a cartoon because it is a simple line drawing.

2. Have students create a cartoon on the prepared area for the final class drawing. Have them paint the background first, using only one color or tints and shades of that color. This will help harmonize the mural when it is completed.

3. Have students paint the other objects. They can add details with smaller brushes.

## Research in Art Education

One study showed that students on average gained eight percentile points on a standardized language arts test after one year of learning in an arts-integrated classroom and gained sixteen percentile points after two years. After three years, students "outscored non-program students on the writing and drawing assessments of social studies content learning" ("Different Ways of Knowing: 1991–94 National Longitudinal Study Final Report" in *Schools, Communities, and the Arts: A Research Compendium*).

## Assessment

Use the following rubric to evaluate the artwork students make in the Creative Expression activity and to assess students' understanding of how harmony is used in sculpture.

Have students complete page 75 or 76 in their *Assessment* books.

|  | Art History and Culture | Aesthetic Perception | Creative Expression | Art Criticism |
|---|---|---|---|---|
| **3 POINTS** | The student demonstrates knowledge of the lives and work of Baranoff-Rossine and Hepworth. | The student accurately identifies the use of harmony in sculpture. | The student's model demonstrates how to use harmony in sculpture. | The student thoughtfully and honestly evaluates own work using the four steps of art criticism. |
| **2 POINTS** | The student's knowledge of the lives and work of Baranoff-Rossine and Hepworth is weak or incomplete. | The student shows an emerging awareness of harmony in sculpture, but cannot consistently identify it. | The student's model shows some awareness of how to use harmony. | The student attempts to evaluate own work but shows an incomplete understanding of evaluation criteria. |
| **1 POINT** | The student cannot demonstrate knowledge of the life and work of Baranoff-Rossine or Hepworth. | The student cannot identify how harmony is used in an artwork. | The student's model shows no understanding of how to use harmony. | The student makes no attempt to evaluate own work. |

### Assessment, p. 75

Name _____ Date _____

**Lesson 4** UNIT 6

**Harmony**

**A. Matching**
Match the words in Column 1 with their definitions in Column 2.

**Column 1**
___ 1. analogous colors
___ 2. assemblage
___ 3. harmony

**Column 2**
a. things that go together because they have similarities
b. colors that create harmony
c. a three-dimensional work of art made of many pieces put together

**B. Drawing**
Use markers or crayons to draw a picture that has analogous colors. Write the names of the analogous colors you used.

I used _____

**C. Writing**
Look at *Three Forms* by Barbara Hepworth and write a brief description about how she created harmony in the sculpture.

Level 4     Unit 6 • Balance, Variety, Harmony, and Unity   **75**

# Lesson 5 Overview

# Variety and Emphasis

**Lesson 5** introduces the art principle of variety. **Variety** is the principle of art that is concerned with difference or contrast. It can be created through the use of the art elements of line, shape, and color.

## Objectives

 **Art History and Culture**

To demonstrate knowledge of the lives and work of Georgia O'Keeffe and Martin Johnson Heade

### Creative Expression

To use variety to create an animal crayon resist painting

 **Aesthetic Perception**

To identify how variety and emphasis are used in two-dimensional works of art

### Art Criticism

To evaluate own work using the four steps of art criticism

## Vocabulary  Vocabulary

Review the following vocabulary words with students before beginning the lesson.

**contrast** contraste—a technique for creating a focal point or area of interest in a work of art using differences in elements

**variety** variedad—the principle of art that is concerned with difference or contrast

See page 209B for additional vocabulary and Spanish vocabulary resources.

### Art Journal: Writing

Have students add these words to the Vocabulary section of their Art Journals.

## Lesson Materials

- white drawing paper
- pencils, crayons
- watercolors
- paintbrushes
- black permanent markers
- newspapers
- images of animals
- water containers
- paper towels

**Alternate Materials:**

- white and color construction paper
- color markers or pencils
- oil pastels

## Program Resources

- *Reading and Writing Test Prep.*, pp. 74–75
- *Transparency 35*
- *Flash Cards* 16, 18
- *Artist Profiles*, pp. 26, 52
- *Animals Through History Time Line*
- *Assessment*, pp. 77–78
- *Large Print 59* Dla'ehl (Interior House Post) and *Print 60* Snowstorm: Steamboat off a Harbour's Mouth
- *The National Museum of Women in the Arts Collection*

### Concept Trace

Variety

**Introduced:** Level 3, Unit 6, Lesson 2

**Reinforced:** Level 5, Unit 6, Lesson 2

---

# Lesson 5 Arts Integration

## Theatre

Complete Unit 6, Lesson 5, on pages 116–117 of *Theatre Arts Connections*.

Theatre Arts Connections, p. 116

## Music

 Have students listen to the melody "change color" as it moves around the band in "East St. Louis Toddle-o" by Duke Ellington. Ellington worked with superb artists that could improvise on a melody to the point that a listener might not know it is still there.

## Movement & Dance

Have students move freely in the room, weaving around each other. Students can choose to walk, skip, slide or use any combination of these movements. Students may freeze and begin to walk again at any point. Have half of the class observe this activity. What action is being emphasized? How is it being emphasized?

 **ocus**

Time: About 10 minutes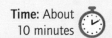

## Activate Prior Knowledge

"Have you ever seen a quilt made with various pieces of fabric?" "¿Alguna vez han visto una colcha con varios retazos de tela?"

- As a class, discuss students' responses. Explain that a lot of designers use lines, shapes, and colors to create patterns and designs that are interesting to see. Variety is so intriguing that the viewer often looks at the work for a long length of time.

### Using Literature ⭐ Reading

- Study the cover illustration of *The Circuit* by Francisco Jimenez. Discuss how variety is used to create interest in the illustration. Have the students form groups and discuss what they believe the book may be about based only on the information they see on the cover.

### Thematic Connection ⭐ Science

- **Plants:** Have students communicate ideas about plants they have seen in their community, using sensory knowledge and life experiences.
NSAE 3.a

## Introduce the Art

## Look

"Look closely at how variety is used in the two works of art on these pages." "Miren detalladamente cómo se usó la variedad en las dos obras de arte de estas páginas."

### Looking at Details ⭐ Reading

Have students look at both works of art and list the details in each. Ask students if one artwork has more details than the other. Heade's painting has more details.

### 🏺 Art History and Culture

Students answers will vary, but provide some of the following as examples. The rose, an ancient symbol of joy, is now associated with love. Irises are symbols of friendship, help, and faith. They are associated with French nobility as is the Fleur-de-lis.

 **Web Connection**
Visit **www.okeeffemuseum.org** for more information about Georgia O'Keeffe.

---

 **Variety and Emphasis**

▲ **Georgia O'Keeffe.** (American). *Yellow Hickory Leaves with Daisy.* 1928.
.......................
Oil on canvas. 30 × 40 inches (76.2 × 101.6 cm.). The Art Institute of Chicago, Chicago, Illinois.

**Look** at the two paintings. O'Keeffe introduced variety into her painting of yellow leaves by placing the white daisy at the bottom. The small, busy white petals of the daisy contrast with the large yellow hickory leaves and create an area of emphasis. In Heade's painting, which is full of variety, the focal point is the orchid. The pale lavender color and the silky texture of the orchid's petals make it different from everything else in the work.

### 🏺 Art History and Culture

What do flowers symbolize in different cultures?

### 🏺 Art History and Culture

#### Georgia O'Keeffe

Georgia O'Keeffe (jôr´ jə ō kēf´) (1887–1986) trained under experts and won many prizes for her art. For years she challenged the art world with her unique vision. She eventually became famous for her spectacular, larger-than-life paintings of natural objects including flowers, animal skulls, and shells. She loved nature, especially the desert of New Mexico where she spent the last half of her life.

See pages 24–25 and 16–21 for more about art history and the subject matter.

**Artist Profiles, p. 52**

**Artist Profile**
**Georgia O'Keeffe**
1887–1986
Georgia O'Keeffe (jôr´ jə ō kēf´) was born in Sun Prairie, Wisconsin. At the age of ten she began taking private art lessons, but the thing she liked most was experimenting with art at home. By 13, she had decided to become an artist. She trained under experts and won many prizes for her art. For years she challenged the art world with her unique vision. She eventually became famous for her spectacular, larger-than-life paintings of natural objects, including flowers, animal skulls, and shells. She loved nature, especially the desert of New Mexico, where she spent the last half of her life. O'Keeffe was married to the famous American photographer Alfred Stieglitz and appears in many of his photographs.

**Study** the works of art to see how the artists created variety.

▶ What do you notice about each artist's use of color?

▶ Describe the focal point in each painting.

▶ What are the similarities and differences of the two works of art?

▲ **Martin Johnson Heade.** (American). *Cattleya Orchid and Three Brazilian Hummingbirds.* 1871.

Oil on wood. 13¾ × 18 inches (34.8 × 45.6 cm.). National Gallery of Art, Washington, D.C.

### Aesthetic Perception

**Seeing Like an Artist** Think of a flower or vegetable garden. What kind of variety is possible there?

### Art History and Culture

#### Martin Johnson Heade

Martin Johnson Heade (mär´ tən jän[t]´ sən hed) (1819–1904) was born in rural Pennsylvania and led a long and varied artistic career. His early career in portraits gave way to landscapes in the mid-nineteenth century and established him as a leading luminist painter. He was well traveled, moving from city to city in search of subject matter and finally found inspiration in the constantly changing forms of landscape painting.

See pages 24–25 and 16–21 for more about art history and the subject matter.

**Artist Profiles, p. 26**

*Artist Profile*
**Martin Johnson Heade**
1819-1904

Martin Johnson Heade (mär´ tan jän´ san hed) was born in rural Pennsylvania, and led a long and varied artistic career. His early career in portraits gave way to landscapes in the mid-nineteenth century and established him as a leading luminist painter. He was well-traveled, moving from city to city in search of subject matter. He finally found inspiration in the constantly changing forms of landscape painting.

## Study

▶ Both artists used bright colors to catch the viewer's eye.

▶ O'Keeffe: The focal point is a white daisy with a yellow center. It is placed in the center of the foreground. Heade: The focal point is the bud of the cattleya orchid, which is made of tints and shades of red. It is located in the middle ground on the left side of the painting.

▶ Similarities: They both deal with nature. There are flowers and leaves in each, and each artist worked with two basic colors. Differences: There are only two objects in O'Keeffe's painting as compared to numerous objects in Heade's painting. O'Keeffe used high intensity colors, and Heade used a mixture of high and low intensities.

■ For more examples of still lifes, see *The National Museum of Women in the Arts Collection.*

### Art Journal: Writing

Have students explain what *variety* means to them in the Concepts section of their Art Journals. What else do they want to know about variety?

### Aesthetic Perception

**Design Awareness** Have students discuss the different types of vegetables in a garden. Some vegetables grow underground, while others grow above the ground. Some vegetables like a lot of sun and others prefer shade.

**Developing Visual Literacy** Discuss the use of variety to make works of art more interesting. Ask students to compare how O'Keeffe and Heade created variety. Have students interpret the mood of each artwork. Do they think the artists' use of variety influenced their interpretation of the mood?
NSAE 5.a; 5.c

### Web Connection

Visit **http://www.smithsonianmag.si.edu/smithsonian/issues00/jan00/heade.html** for more information about Martin Johnson Heade.

# Teach

"How is variety used in two-dimensional art? How can you use it in your work?" "¿Cómo se usa la variedad en el arte bidimensional? ¿Cómo la pueden usar en su trabajo?"

■ Read and discuss using variety and emphasis on page 204.

## Practice

**Materials:** white drawing paper, crayons

**Alternate Materials:** color construction paper, color markers or pencils

■ Distribute the materials and have students follow the directions on page 204.

■ Make sure that the students leave some of the paper above and below the cut shape.

## Creative Expression

**Materials:** white drawing paper, pencils, crayons, watercolors, paintbrushes, black permanent markers, newspapers, images of animals, water containers, paper towels

**Alternate Materials:** color markers, oil pastels

■ Distribute the materials and have students follow the directions on page 205.

■ Review the Activity Tips on page 245 for visual examples of techniques if needed.

## Art Journal: Ideas/Sketches

Have students generate a list of animals to use for their drawings. Students can also collect images of animals. Have them place their lists and any collected images in their Art Journals. They can refer to them during the Creative Expression activity.

---

# Using Variety and Emphasis

**Variety** is created in art through differences and contrasts. Artists can create variety by adding something different to a design to give a break in the repetition.

**Emphasis** is a principle of design that makes one part of an artwork stand out more than the other parts. The element that is noticed first is the **dominant element.**

## Practice

Use your initials to show variety.

1. Fold a sheet of white paper into two sections. In the first section, draw one design of your initials and color with one color.

2. In the second box, draw an initial design that shows variety. You might draw different patterns or use contrasting colors.

---

## Differentiated Instruction

**Reteach**

Have students look through this textbook and the *Large Prints* for examples of variety and emphasis.

**Special Needs**

Help students make responsible choices in art making by teaching them the importance of planning and sketching ideas before starting on the final draft. For this activity, have students try out several different contrasting colors in their journals before selecting one.

**ELL**

When explaining variety to students, use visuals such as a group of different types of fruit and a group of oranges.

◄ **Juliette Simmons.**
Age 8.

**Think** about how the student artist used variety and emphasis.

 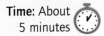
## Review and Assess

"Did you create emphasis in your drawing?"
"¿Crearon énfasis en su dibujo?"

# Think

The artist used several different plants and a tiger to create variety. The focal point of the painting is placed in the center and is a different color from the background.

■ Use *Large Prints 59 Dla'ehl (Interior House Post)* and *60 Snowstorm: Steamboat Off a Harbour's Mouth* and ask students to compare how both artists used variety in their works of art. Have students identify if there is a focal point in each.

## Informal Assessment

■ For standardized-format test practice using this lesson's art content, see pages 74–75 in *Reading and Writing Test Preparation.*

---

### Creative Expression

Create an animal drawing that demonstrates variety and emphasis.

1. Select an animal image or images and develop a sketch. Add a background to the sketch.

2. Transfer the sketch to a large sheet of drawing paper and trace it with a black marker.

3. Color in the animal or animals using crayons to create textures.

4. Using watercolors, paint the entire background in a color that contrasts with the color of the animal, to create variety.

### Art Criticism

**Describe** Describe the animal in your drawing.

**Analyze** What is the area of emphasis in your drawing? How did you create it?

**Interpret** Give your drawing a title.

**Decide** Were you successful in using variety to create an area of emphasis in your drawing? Explain.

---

### Art Journal: Critical Thinking

Have students answer the four art criticism questions—Describe, Analyze, Interpret, and Decide—in their Art Journals. Have students discuss within groups how they created variety and emphasis in their drawings. Ask students to invent ways to produce drawings that demonstrate variety and emphasis, using a variety of art media and materials.
NSAE 1.a; 1.b

---

## Art Across the Curriculum

Use these simple ideas to reinforce art concepts across the curriculum.

★ **Descriptive Writing** Have students write a paragraph about his or her favorite flower or plant.

★ **Math** Have students examine the leaves and flowers in *Yellow Hickory Leaves with Daisy* to see whether they are symmetrical.

★ **Science** Explain to students the concept of photosynthesis.

★ **Social Studies** Explain to students that the growth of flowers and plants is based on the climate of a location.

★ **Technology** Have students use a paint or draw program to create a collage of a flower. Visit **SRAonline.com** to print detailed instructions for this activity.
NSAE 6.b

# Variety and Emphasis

## Extra! For the Art Specialist

**Time:** About 45 minutes

### Focus

Have students study **Large Print 59** *Dla'ehl (Interior House Post)* and discuss how some artists will use variety and emphasis in an artwork. Have them describe the lines, shapes, and colors they see. Do they think any one shape, color, line, or area is emphasized?

### Teach

Discuss how artists will sometimes alter one element in an artwork to emphasize that area. Explain to students that they will create a mobile. By keeping the center shape simple with little details, emphasis will be created. Have students complete the alternate activity.

### Reflect

Have students use the four steps of art criticism to evaluate their work. Have them describe how they constructed their mobiles.

### Alternate Activity

**Materials:**
- 4"x 4" tagboard
- pencils, erasers
- scissors
- rulers
- string or thread
- hole punch
- hangers
- over-writing markers

1. Have students draw a different free-form shape on four pieces of tagboard. On the fifth piece, have students draw an oval or circle.

2. Have students color each of the four free-form shapes with different colors and patterns. They can use over-writing markers to create the patterns. The geometric shape should be a solid color.

3. Have students cut the shapes. They can create patterns on the back of the free-form shapes, but the back of the geometric shape should remain solid.

4. Have students punch a hole at the top of each shape and attach varying lengths of thread. Students should arrange their shapes on the hanger so that the solid shape is in the center.

## Research in Art Education

Research has shown that artistically talented at-risk students make greater gains in reading scores on standardized tests when the arts are integrated into the curriculum ("Using Art Processes to Enhance Academic Self-Regulation" in *Critical Links*, p. 64). The amount of training in arts-integration that their teachers had received predicted how great these gains were.

## Assessment
Use the following rubric to evaluate the artwork students made in the Creative Expression activity and to assess students' understanding of how variety and emphasis is used in two-dimensional works of art.

Have students complete page 77 or 78 in their *Assessment* books.

| | Art History and Culture | Aesthetic Perception | Creative Expression | Art Criticism |
|---|---|---|---|---|
| **3 POINTS** | The student demonstrates knowledge of the lives and work of O'Keeffe and Heade. | The student accurately identifies the use of variety and emphasis in two-dimensional works of art. | The student's crayon resist painting demonstrates how to use variety and emphasis. | The student thoughtfully and honestly evaluates own work using the four steps of art criticism. |
| **2 POINTS** | The student's knowledge of the lives and work of O'Keeffe and Heade is weak or incomplete. | The student shows an emerging awareness of variety and emphasis in two-dimensional works of art but cannot consistently identify them. | The student's crayon resist painting shows some awareness of how to use variety and emphasis. | The student attempts to evaluate own work but shows an incomplete understanding of evaluation criteria. |
| **1 POINT** | The student cannot demonstrate knowledge of the life and work of O'Keeffe or Heade. | The student cannot identify how variety and emphasis are used in an artwork. | The student's crayon resist painting shows no understanding of how to use variety and emphasis. | The student makes no attempt to evaluate own work. |

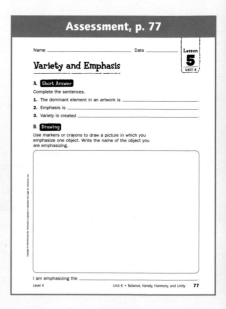

Assessment, p. 77

Name _____ Date _____ Lesson 5 UNIT 6

**Variety and Emphasis**

**A. Short Answer**
Complete the sentences.
1. The dominant element in an artwork is _____
2. Emphasis is _____
3. Variety is created _____

**B. Drawing**
Use markers or crayons to draw a picture in which you emphasize one object. Write the name of the object you are emphasizing.

I am emphasizing the _____
Level 4            Unit 6 • Balance, Variety, Harmony, and Unity   **77**

   **Unity**

Overview

**Lesson 6** The art principle of unity as used in three-dimensional form is explored. **Unity** is the oneness that is achieved by properly using the elements and principles in art. Unity is created when the art principles of variety and harmony work together.

### Objectives

 **Art History and Culture**

To demonstrate knowledge of lives and work of Mary A. Jackson and Western Apache basket weavers

**Creative Expression**

To create a unified coil basket

**Aesthetic Perception**

To identify how unity is used in three-dimensional forms

**Art Criticism**

To evaluate own work using the four steps of art criticism

**Vocabulary** ⭐ Vocabulary

Review the following vocabulary word with students before beginning the lesson.

**unity** unidad—the feeling of wholeness or oneness that is achieved by properly using the elements and principles in art

See page 209B for additional vocabulary and Spanish vocabulary resources.

 **Art Journal: Writing**

Have students add this word to the Vocabulary section of their Art Journals

## Lesson Materials

- magazines
- glue, scissors
- white paper
- pencils
- cotton coils $\frac{1}{4}''$ or $\frac{1}{2}''$ (12' per student)
- fabric scraps cut or torn into 1-inch strips
- plastic 3-inch tapestry needles

**Alternate Materials:**
- white construction paper
- heavy twine

## Program Resources
- *Reading and Writing Test Prep.*, pp. 76–77
- *Transparency 36*
- *Flash Card* 18
- *Artist Profiles*, pp. 33, 74
- *Animals Through History Time Line*
- *Assessment*, pp. 79, 80
- *Large Print 59 Dla'ehl (Interior House Post)* and *Print 60 Snowstorm: Steamboat off a Harbour's Mouth*
- *The National Museum of Women in the Arts Collection*

### Concept Trace
Unity
**Introduced:** Level 3, Unit 6, Lesson 4
**Reinforced:** Level 5, Unit 6, Lesson 5

## Lesson 6 Arts Integration

### Theatre

Complete Unit 6, Lesson 6, on pages 118–119 of *Theatre Arts Connections.*

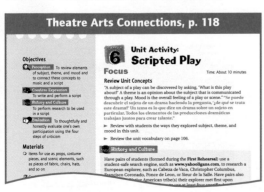

### Music

 Listen to "Canon in D Major" by Pachelbel. The three high melodies start at different times, creating a "canon." (Singing a round has the effect of a canon, except in a canon every part finishes at the same time.) The bass line has a very simple job to create unity. Ask students what happens to the bass line. Students should reply it creates unity.

### Movement & Dance

In small groups, and working with the dance structure called *A B A form,* have students create dynamic shapes together. The first shape should show unity (A). The second shape should show contrast (B). The third shape should show unity again (A). Also include level variation by putting the *A* shapes on one level and the *B* shape on another.

ocus

**Time:** About
10 minutes

## Activate Prior Knowledge

"What kind of baskets have you seen?" "¿Qué tipo de cestas han visto?"

- Discuss students' responses. Explain that baskets used to be handwoven. But with advancements in technology, machines can make baskets quicker than a person can. Ask students if they have ever made a basket.

**Using Literature**  Reading

- Look at the cover illustration of *A Wrinkle in Time* by Madeleine L'Engle. Discuss how the various objects are unified by the harmonious use of blue.

**Thematic Connection**  Social Studies

- **American Society:** Have students identify the roles of art, such as basket weaving, in American society. Make sure students discuss Native American society as well.
NSAE 4.a; 4.b

## Introduce the Art

# Look

"Let's compare how unity was created in these baskets." "Vamos a comparar cómo fue creada la unidad en estas cestas."

**Create a Model**  Science

Have students invent a new piece of machinery. Ask them to combine two or three objects and create a drawing of a new machine that would help save time performing a task.

### Art History and Culture

Explain to students that there are two broad categories of basket construction: plaited and coiled. Interlacing warp and weft threads makes plaited baskets. Sewing a spiral snakelike foundation together in a flat or ascending coil makes coil baskets.

**Web Connection**
Visit www.craftsreport.com/november01/mary.html
for more information about Mary A. Jackson.

**206** UNIT 6 • Balance, Harmony, Variety, and Unity

---

**Lesson**
# 6 Unity

**Look** at the baskets on these pages. Mary Jackson was first taught to make sweetgrass baskets by her mother and grandmother. Along with passing down their techniques through the generations, they also passed down an oral history of their family. The Western Apache basket was used for storage, as a serving dish, for transporting items, and for ceremonial purposes. Both baskets were made using the coil technique. Coiling is a stitching technique in which the coils of the core material are stitched together with a binding material.

▲ **Mary A. Jackson.** (American).
*Low Basket with Handle.* 1999.

Sweetgrass, pine needles, and palmetto. 16 × 17 inches (40.6 × 43.2 cm.). Smithsonian American Art Museum, Washington, D.C.

### Art History and Culture

The oldest known baskets were found in Faiyûm, in Upper Egypt. Tests have shown that they are between 10,000 and 12,000 years old.

**206** Unit 6 • Lesson 6

### Art History and Culture

#### Mary A. Jackson

Mary A. Jackson (1945– ) was born in South Carolina and learned how to make baskets from her mother when she was only four years old. This basket-making tradition has been part of her family for many generations. When Jackson left her secretarial job to be at home with her son, she began making baskets full-time. She believes this art form puts her in touch with her ancestors and history.

See pages 24–25 and 16–21 for more about art history and the subject matter.

**Artist Profiles, p. 33**

**Artist Profile**
**Mary Jackson**
b. 1945

Mary Jackson (má´ rē jak´ sən) was born in South Carolina and learned how to make baskets from her mother when she was four years old. After graduating from high school, Jackson stopped making baskets and moved to New York. She resumed making baskets in her spare time when she moved back to the south in 1972. When Jackson left her secretarial job to be at home with her son she began making baskets full time. She believes this art form puts her in touch with her ancestors and history. Jackson travels across the country to present lectures on her cultural heritage at museums, galleries, and conventions. She also leads workshops in schools and arts organizations throughout the United States.

**Study** how the artists created unity in the work of art.

▶ What similarities do you see in the baskets? What differences do you see?

▶ What shapes and forms do you see on the Apache basket?

▶ What colors did each artist use?

▲ **Artist unknown.**
(Western Apache/North America).
*Basket.* c. 1900.
Willow, devils claw, wood. 28 inches (71.1 cm.).
Detroit Art Institute, Detroit, Michigan.

 **Aesthetic Perception**

**Design Awareness** Have you ever seen a basket that is similar to either work of art in this lesson?

## Art History and Culture

### Basket

This basket (c. 1900) was made by an unidentified Western Apache artist. Many Apache artisans of this time made baskets specifically to sell to tourists. They did not sign their work or indicate their identity on these baskets, so it is impossible to know exactly who made any particular piece. It is believed that this basket was made by a member of the Western Apache Tonto group of the southwestern United States.

See pages 24–25 and 16–21 for more about art history and the subject matter.

**Artist Profiles, p. 74**

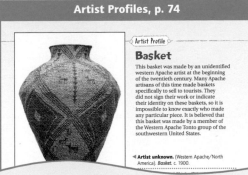

⊳ Artist Profile ⊲
**Basket**
This basket was made by an unidentified western Apache artist at the beginning of the twentieth century. Many Apache artisans of this time made baskets specifically to sell to tourists. They did not sign their work or indicate their identity on these baskets, so it is impossible to know exactly who made any particular piece. It is believed that this basket was made by a member of the Western Apache Tonto group of the southwestern United States.

◄ **Artist unknown.** (Western Apache/North America) *Basket.* c. 1900.

## Study

▶ Similarities: The woven patterns look very tight because there are no gaps. They look like they could be used to carry objects. Differences: Jackson's basket has a handle and is shallow. The Western Apache basket is deep and has animals interwoven into the design.

▶ There are diamond and triangle shapes, as well as animal shapes.

▶ The color schemes are similar in each piece. *Basket* has a darker color scheme that includes the color black.

■ For more examples of utilitarian art, see *The National Museum of Women in the Arts Collection.*

### Art Journal: Writing

Have students explain what *unity* means to them in the Concepts section of their Art Journals. What else do they want to know about unity in weaving?

 **Aesthetic Perception**

**Design Awareness** Have students describe baskets they have seen that look similar to the baskets in the lesson. Explain that in unity in three-dimensional form all the different parts usually do not work as well alone as they do together.

**Developing Visual Literacy** Have students look closely at both works of art. Make sure they choose appropriate vocabulary to discuss the use of unity. Point out to the students that both baskets were handwoven. Have students explain how they think each was created.
NSAE 2.a; 2.b

💻 **Web Connection**
Visit **www.indianterritory.com/pages/ aboutapachebaskets.htm** for more information about Apache baskets. **Note:** This Web site is for teacher use only.

# Teach

**Time:** About 45 minutes

"How can you use unity in your coiled basket?" "¿Cómo pueden usar la unidad en su cesta?"

■ Read and discuss using unity on page 208.

## Practice

**Materials:** magazines, glue, scissors, white paper, pencils

**Alternate Materials:** white construction paper

■ Distribute the materials and have students follow the directions on page 208.

## Creative Expression

**Materials:** cotton coils $\frac{1}{4}''$ or $\frac{1}{2}''$ (12′ per student); fabric scraps cut or torn into 1-inch strips; 3-inch plastic tapestry needles

**Alternate Materials:** heavy twine

■ Distribute the materials and have students follow the directions on page 209.

■ Review the Activity Tips on page 245 for visual examples of techniques if needed.

### Art Journal: Planning

Demonstrate how to start a coil basket. Have students take notes and place them in their Art Journals. Have them refer to their notes and the Coil Basket Technique Tips during the Creative Expression activity.

# Using Unity

**Unity** is oneness. It brings order to the world. It helps the viewer focus on a work of art as a whole instead of on its individual parts. Unity helps the viewer see what different parts of a design have in common and how they belong together. When an artist uses unity, he or she harmonizes the variety, or different elements or objects, by making them relate to one another.

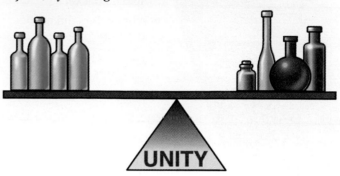

## Practice

Look through magazines and find examples of harmony, unity, and variety.

1. On a sheet of white paper, write the headings *Harmony, Unity,* and *Variety.*

2. Find an example of each one in a magazine and glue it under the correct heading.

**208** Unit 6 • Lesson 6

## Differentiated Instruction

**Reteach**
Have students look around the room for things that are made of different parts but go together, for example, the computer system and printer or table and chairs.

**Special Needs**
Assess student's understanding of unity by asking them to verbally share the ways that their coil basket illustrates the principle of unity.

**ELL**
When discussing unity, draw unified images on the board, and show how the different parts make the whole.

◀ **Drew Matthews.**
Age 9.

**Think** about how the student artist used unity in this basket.

 **Creative Expression**

Create unity in a wrapped coil basket.

1. Your teacher will give you a coil that has one end cut at an angle. Refer to page 225 to begin.

2. Continue wrapping the coil with fabric and making stitches on the first row about every five inches apart.

3. To make the sides of your coil basket, place one row of coiling on top of the previous row and stitch tightly. Continue adding rows of coiling.

4. To finish the basket, taper the end of the coil and lay it flat against the last row. Wrap your fabric tightly three times around the coil and cut the remaining fabric.

**Art Criticism**

**Describe** Describe the fabric you used in your basket.

**Analyze** How did you unify your basket?

**Interpret** If you could enlarge your basket, what size would you make it? What would it be used for?

**Decide** Were you successful in creating unity in your basket? Explain.

 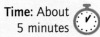

## Review and Assess

"Were variety and harmony used to create unity in your basket?" "¿Se usaron la variedad y la armonía para crear unidad en su cesta?"

# Think

The artist used unity by layering the unwrapped coils on top of each other to form the basket.

■ Use **Large Print 59** Dla'ehl (Interior House Post) and **60** Snowstorm: Steamboat Off a Harbour's Mouth to ask students to compare how the artists each used unity in their works of art.

## Informal Assessment

■ For standardized-format test practice using this lesson's art content, see pages 76–77 in **Reading and Writing Test Preparation.**

### Art Journal: Critical Thinking

Have students answer the four art criticism questions—Describe, Analyze, Interpret, and Decide—in their Art Journals. Have students place their baskets in one area of the classroom to create an exhibit. Have classmates view the exhibit and the moods of their peers' baskets. Also have them identify the overall mood of the exhibition.
NSAE 5.a; 5.c

## ● Art Across the Curriculum ●

Use these simple ideas to reinforce art concepts across the curriculum.

★ **Narrative Writing** Have students write a short story about the history of Basket.

★ **Math** Have students make a pie graph that shows the makeup of the class.

★ **Science** Have students discuss the different parts of a computer system.

★ **Social Studies** Have students discuss the Western Apache culture.

★ **Technology** Have students use a paint or draw program to design a woven blanket. Visit **SRAonline.com** to print detailed instructions for this activity..
NSAE 6.b

# Unity

## Extra! For the Art Specialist

**Time:** About 45 minutes

### Focus

Have students study **Large Print 60** *Snowstorm: Steamboat Off a Harbour's Mouth* to understand how artists use unity to bring together different objects or art elements so that everything fits together in a work of art.

### Teach

Explain to students that they will create a fabric painting of a person they admire. They will embellish it with various collected objects. Color will be used to unify the various parts. Ask students to collect a variety of materials prior to beginning this lesson. They may choose to attach some personal items to their painting. Have students complete the alternate activity.

### Reflect

Have students use the four steps of art criticism to evaluate their work. Have each student describe the person they chose to depict.

### Alternate Activity

**Materials:**
- sketchbooks
- pencil, eraser
- fabric pieces
- cardboard
- masking tape
- fabric paints
- paintbrushes
- water containers
- mixing trays
- newspaper
- found objects
- embroidery thread and needles
- scissors

1. Have students choose a subject for their portraits. Have them sketch the person from the waist or shoulders up.

2. Have students tape the fabric to cardboard and transfer their drawings.

3. Have students use fabric paint to paint their portraits. Students should choose one color or family of colors to paint the background. Have them lift the tape and let the fabric dry flat.

4. Students can use thread to embellish their portraits. Have them add found objects or personal items.

## Research in Art Education

"All the evidence points to a relationship between the arts and the other academic disciplines that is clear and compelling, indicating to both fields that one cannot really flourish without the influence of the other" (Letter from Jerrold Ross to Milton Goldberg, May 22, 1992). Strive to make as many cross-curricular connections as you can while teaching the elements and principles of art to students

## Assessment

Use the following rubric to evaluate the artwork students made in the Creative Expression activity and to assess students' understanding of how unity is used in three-dimensional forms.

Have students complete page 79 or 80 in their *Assessment* books.

| | Art History and Culture | Aesthetic Perception | Creative Expression | Art Criticism |
|---|---|---|---|---|
| **3 POINTS** | The student demonstrates knowledge of the lives and work of Mary A. Jackson and Western Apache basket weavers. | The student accurately identifies the use of unity in three-dimensional art. | The student's coil basket demonstrates how to use unity. | The student thoughtfully and honestly evaluates own work using the four steps of art criticism. |
| **2 POINTS** | The student's knowledge of the lives and work of Mary A. Jackson and Western Apache basket weavers is weak or incomplete. | The student shows an emerging awareness of unity in three-dimensional art, but cannot consistently identify it. | The student's coil basket shows some awareness of how to use unity. | The student attempts to evaluate own work but shows an incomplete understanding of evaluation criteria. |
| **1 POINT** | The student cannot demonstrate knowledge of the life and work of Mary A. Jackson or Western Apache basket weavers. | The student cannot identify how unity is used in three-dimensional art. | The student's coil basket shows no understanding of how to use unity. | The student makes no attempt to evaluate own work. |

### Assessment, p. 79

Name _____ Date _____

**Lesson 6** UNIT 6

**Unity**

**A** Short Answer
Write the answer to the question.
What is unity in art?

**B** Drawing
Design a basket showing unity.

**C** Writing
Write a paragraph describing how Mary Jackson created unity in *Low Basket with Handle*.

Level 4      Unit 6 • Balance, Variety, Harmony, and Unity   **79**

# Unit 6 Vocabulary Review

**assemblage**—a technique in which an artist collects found materials and assembles them into a three-dimensional work of art **montaje**—una técnica en que un artista recoge materiales que encuentra y los agrupa en una obra de arte tridimensional

**asymmetrical balance**—another name for informal balance **equilibrio asimétrico**—una técnica para crear un punto focal o área de interés en una obra de arte mediante las diferencias en los elementos

**central axis**—a real or imaginary dividing line that can run in two directions: vertically and horizontally **eje central**—una línea divisora real o imaginaria que puede extenderse en dos direcciones: vertical y horizontal

**contrast**—a technique for creating a focal point or area of interest in a work of art using differences in elements **contraste**—una técnica para crear un punto focal o área de interés en una obra de arte usando diferencias en los elementos

**focal point**—the area of an artwork that is emphasized **punto focal**—el área de una obra de arte que se le da énfasis

**harmony**—the principle of art that creates unity by stressing similarities of separate but related parts **armonía**—el principio artístico que crea unidad al destacar las semejanzas de las partes separadas pero relacionadas

**informal balance**—a way of organizing parts of a design so that unlike objects have equal visual weight **equilibrio informal**—una manera de organizar partes de un diseño para que objetos diferentes tengan el mismo peso visual

**radiate**—to come out from a central point **radiar**—sobresale de un punto central

**symmetry**—a type of formal balance in which two halves of a balanced artwork are identical, mirror images of each other **simetría**—un tipo de equilibrio formal en el cual dos mitades de una obra de arte equilibrada son imágenes idénticas de cada una

**two-dimensional decoration**—flat decoration produced on the surface of a work of art **decoración bidimensional**—decoración plana producida en la superficie de una obra de arte

**unity**—the feeling of wholeness or oneness that is achieved by properly using the elements and principles in art **unidad**—la sensación de integridad que se logra al usar adecuadamente los elementos y principios artísticos

**variety**—the principle of art that is concerned with difference or contrast **variedad**—el principio artístico que trata de la diferencia o el contraste

---

## Vocabulary Practice

**T** Display *Transparency 42* to review unit vocabulary words.

**Reference** ⭐ Vocabulary
Have students look up *variety* in a dictionary of quotations. Do any of the quotations refer to art? Explain.

**Multiple Meanings** ⭐ Vocabulary
Have volunteers select a vocabulary word, such as *harmony*, and look it up in a dictionary to determine if the word has multiple meanings. Repeat for other unit vocabulary words.

**Related Words** ⭐ Vocabulary
Have students create a list of related words for the word *unity*. Have students refer to a dictionary, if necessary. Repeat the process for other unit vocabulary words.

# Wrapping Up Unit 6

## Balance, Harmony, Variety, and Unity

▲ **Viola Frey.** (American). *Family Portrait.* 1995.
Glazed ceramic. 84 × 79 × 29½ inches (213.4 × 200.7 × 74.9 cm.).
Hirshhorn Museum and Sculpture Garden, Washington, D.C.

## Art Criticism

**Critical Thinking** Art criticism is an organized system for looking at and talking about art. You can criticize art without being an expert. The purpose of art criticism is to get the viewer involved in a perception process that delays judgment until all aspects of the artwork have been studied. Push students to expand beyond the art criticism questions.

■ See pages 28–29 for more about art criticism.

### Describe

► Possible answers include the following: The large head and shoulders of a man are in the center. A woman's head is on top of the man's large head. The men are wearing suits and ties, except a small figure with a baseball bat. The women are wearing different dresses.

► There is a rectangular base that seems to be divided into five pieces.

### Analyze

► This work is organized using formal balance. This is not perfect symmetry, but both sides are almost the same.

► The large man's head has the most visual weight because it is larger.

► Colors are repeated. All the men wear blue suits. The women wear yellow. There are touches of red on their clothes.

► Variety is created by the size differences in the figures.

► The man's large head in the center is the area of emphasis.

► The wide-open eyes and noses are similar. The figures share the same colors.

## Art History and Culture

### Viola Frey

Viola Frey (vī ō´ lə frī) (1933– ) was born in Lodi, California, on a farm and vineyard. She grew up with strong female role models and became a collector of found objects. She especially likes collecting little figurines from flea markets. She creates cast molds of the figurines, making them in her own style and binding them together in appropriate forms. Frey's large ceramic human figures also reference or critique the modern world and are often covered with symbols and textures that give them an appearance similar to assemblage as well.

See pages 24–25 and 16–21 for more about art history and the subject matter.

**Artist Profiles, p. 21**

*Artist Profile*
**Viola Frey**
b. 1933

Viola Frey (vī ō´ lə frī) was born in Lodi, California, on a farm and vineyard. She grew up with strong female role models and became a collector of found objects. She especially likes collecting little figurines from flea markets, and she inserts these objects into ceramic assemblage artwork. These sculptures represent the way the modern world has come to depend on material goods. Frey's large ceramic human figures also reference or critique the modern world and are often covered with symbols and textures that give them an appearance similar to assemblage.

 **Art Criticism** Critical Thinking

**Describe** **What do you see?**
During this step you will collect information about the subject of the work.
- ▶ What do you see in this sculpture?
- ▶ What is at the bottom?

**Analyze** **How is this work organized?**
Think about how the artist used the elements and principles of art.
- ▶ What kind of balance do you see in this work?
- ▶ Which form seems to have the most visual weight?
- ▶ Where do you see harmony?
- ▶ Where do you see variety?
- ▶ What is the area of emphasis in this work?
- ▶ What similarities bring unity to the sculpture?

**Interpret** **What does the artwork say?**
Combine clues you collected during description and analysis with your personal experiences to find out what this painting is about.
- ▶ Why do you think the man in the center is so big?
- ▶ Who are the other people?

**Decide** **What do you think about the work?**
Use all the information you have gathered to decide why this is a successful work of art.
- ▶ Is the work successful because it is realistic, because it is well organized, or because it has a strong message?

## Interpret

- ▶ Answers will vary. Students may say it is because he is the father or is the oldest. Some may say he is the most important member of the family.

- ▶ Answers will vary. Students may say the woman's head in the center is the mother of the family. The two large couples on the sides may be the children and their spouses. The little figures may be the grandchildren.

## Decide

- ▶ Answers will vary. Most will say this has a strong message because of the composition. Some may like the story they see in the work.

> **Art Journal: Writing**
> Have students write answers to Aesthetic Perception in their Art Journals. Have them discuss their answers in small groups.

 **Aesthetic Perception**

**Seeing Like an Artist** Have students think about family or group portraits they may have seen. Then have them compare the scenes to *Family Portrait*.

**Describe** ▶ Describe the people in the portrait.

**Analyze** ▶ What kind of variety is in the portrait?
▶ Does the portrait seem unified?
▶ Is the portrait balanced?

**Interpret** ▶ What feelings do you have when you think of the portrait? Why?

**Decide** ▶ If you could have created the portrait, what would you change?

"Artists use balance, harmony, variety, and unity in two- and three-dimensional works of art." "Los artistas usan equilibrio, armonía, variedad y unidad en las obras de arte bi y tridimensionales."

**T** Review the unit vocabulary with students using *Transparency 42.*

### Art Journal: Writing
Have students answer the questions on page 212 in their Art Journals or on a separate sheet of paper. Answers: 1. A, 2. C, 3. C, 4. C, 5. A

**T** For further assessment, have students complete the unit test on *Transparency 48.*

## CAREERS IN ART
## Illustrators

▶ Explain to students that medical illustrations appear in medical textbooks, medical advertisements, professional journals, instructional films, computer-assisted learning programs, magazines, and television programs. Although the majority of medical illustrations are for print media, medical illustrators also work in three dimensions, creating anatomical teaching models, models for simulated medical procedures, and prosthetic parts for patients.

> "...you have to know your craft. You have to know it in painting. You have to know it in any area you're in."
>
> —Viola Frey

---

Balance, Harmony, Variety, and Unity, continued

## Show What You Know

Answer these questions on a separate sheet of paper.

**1** _____ occurs when the elements in a design come out from a central point.
A. Radial balance
B. Formal balance
C. Informal balance

**2** _____ is the principle of art that creates unity by stressing similarities of separate but related parts.
A. Variety
B. Unity
C. Harmony

**3** _____ is created in art through differences and contrasts.
A. Unity
B. Harmony
C. Variety

**4** _____ helps the focus on a work of art to be on the whole instead of on its individual parts.
A. Variety
B. Harmony
C. Unity

**5** _____ is a type of formal balance in which two halves of an object or work of art are mirror images of each other.
A. Symmetry
B. Variety
C. Emphasis

## Unit Assessment Options

###  Aesthetic Perception

**Practice** Have students select one of the concepts in the Show What You Know section on page 212 then find examples of each concept in the classroom.

### Creative Expression

**Student Portfolio** Have students review all the artwork they have created during this unit and select the pieces they wish to keep in their portfolios.

###  Art Criticism

**Activity** Have students select an artwork from this unit and study it using the four steps of art criticism. (See pages 28–29 for more information about art criticism.) Have students work small groups and present their findings aloud or in writing.

---

## CAREERS IN ART
## Illustrators

Illustrators have traditionally drawn pictures on paper to help explain things or make them attractive. Now many illustrators have begun to use computers.

**Medical illustrators** are professional artists with training in medicine and science who create visual material to help record and distribute medical, biological, and related knowledge.

**Technical illustrators** collect and prepare information required for the creation of graphics to be used in technical publications.

**Marine illustrators** are artists with training in biology and science who create visual material to help explain sea animals and their environments.

▲ Medical illustrator

# Balance, Harmony, Variety, and Unity in Dance

The dance in the picture is based on ranch life in Mexico. The male dancer twirls a lariat that is used to rope cattle. At first he dances alone with the rope, stepping in and out of the twirling circle. Later a female dancer joins him and they dance together in the circle.

**What to Do** Choose a type of work and create a dance about it, using a prop.

1. List different types of work. What actions are done and what objects are used? Choose an action and a prop to use.

2. Explore the actions involved in the work. For example, practice the action of sweeping with an imaginary broom. Create emphasis by making one part of your action or dance dominant. Use dance elements such as size, direction, and energy to turn ordinary work into dance motion.

3. Share your ideas with a partner. Put four of your best ideas together in a way that creates unity.

4. Perform your dance.

▲ Ballet Folklorico de Mexico. "Danza de Reata" and "Jarabe del Amor Ranchero," excerpts from *Zacatecas*.

 **Art Criticism**

**Describe** What elements did you and your partner use to give your dance harmony and unity?

**Analyze** Explain how you used emphasis to change a work movement into a dance movement.

**Interpret** What moods did you create with your four work movements?

**Decide** Do you think you succeeded in changing work motions into dance motion?

Unit 6    **213**

 **Art History and Culture**

## Traditional Dance and Music

The dance and music of a people of common cultural, racial, and/or religious heritage is called either ethnic or folk. Folk dance and music are usually the more recreational forms, which are for fun, group participation, and identity. They express the style and traditions of the culture and also show the influences from outside cultures. This dance reflects the influence of the Spanish and European cultures on Mexico. It is a distinctive Mexican style called *Mestizo*. When horses were brought to Mexico, ranches were built and people took on a new way of life and work. This dance portrays the Mestizo life of the caballero and ranchero, or rancher.

# Balance, Harmony, Variety, and Unity in Dance

**Objective:** To create dance using work movements.

**Materials:** *Danza de Reata* and *Jarabe del Amor Ranchero*, performed by Ballet Folklorico de Mexico. Running time: 7:55. Props to accompany the student dances.

## **F**ocus

Time: About 5 minutes

### **Art History and Culture**

■ Have students discuss what they know about Mexico. Have a volunteer locate Mexico on a map.

## **T**each

Time: About 20 minutes

### **Aesthetic Perception**

■ Have students brainstorm types of work and the actions of each to use in their work dances.

### **Creative Expression**

■ Coach students to work at different levels; change the size; give it a rhythm; change speeds; vary the energy; and use different body parts.

## **R**eflect

Time: About 10 minutes

### **Art Criticism**

■ Did students effectively create work dances with a partner?

# Drawing

It is important to allow the students to experiment with the drawing media. Use gentle guidance to show them how to properly hold the drawing media. Prior to use, demonstrate the techniques as they are illustrated here. Proper handling and use will increase success and establish good habits for the future. It will also make the media last longer.

## Pencil

**Blending** is a technique of shading in which the student holds the pencil on its side, between the thumb and other fingers, and shades with the side of the lead.

- Primary grade pencils with a medium-soft lead are ideal for all shading techniques.

- To create darker values, students should use the side of the pencil lead, press harder, and shade over areas more than once.

- To create lighter values, students should press lightly and shade over the area less.

- Gradations from dark to light can be created by smearing a shaded area into an area not yet shaded with a paper stump made of a tightly rolled paper towel.

**Hatching** is a pattern of parallel lines. How closely together the lines are drawn determines the value of that part of the drawing.

In **Crosshatching,** the parallel lines overlap each other. Like with hatching, the distance of the lines from each other determines the value.

**Stippling** is a series of dots that create value and value change. Careful control of the placement of all shading is important, especially stipple dots. Be sure that students are carefully drawing these dots rather than simply dotting their paper with them.

---

## Technique Tips
# Drawing
### Pencil

With a pencil, you can add form to your objects with shading. With the side of your pencil lead, press and shade over areas more than once for darker values. You can also use lines or dots for shading. When lines or dots are drawn close together, darker values are created. When dots or lines are drawn farther apart, lighter values are created.

Blending

Cross-hatching

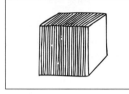

Hatching

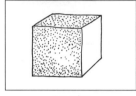

Stippling

# Technique Tips

## Color Pencil

You can blend colors with color pencils. Color with the lighter color first. Gently color over it with the darker color until you have the effect you want.

With color pencils, you can use the four shading techniques.

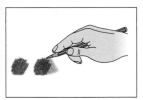

Shadows can be created by blending complementary colors.

## Color Pencils

- When blending colors with color pencils, it is important to color the lighter color before the darker one. A color can be darkened easily, but it is almost impossible to lighten a color.

- To create shadows, blend complementary colors. This will create browns and darker colors.

## Felt-Tip Pen

Felt-tip pens are a practical substitute for pen and ink. Their narrow points make them ideal for drawing details and contour line drawings.

- They can be used to draw over lightly sketched pencil drawings.

- They can be used to draw a picture which can then be painted with watercolors. (The ink is water-soluble and may run when touched by wet paint.)

- Students should avoid pressing too hard when drawing so as not to damage the tip; this is especially true when stippling.

- After use, the cap should always be replaced.

## Technique Tips

### Fine-Point Felt-Tip Pen

Fine-point felt-tip pens can be used to make either sketches or finished drawings. They are ideal for contour drawings.

Use the point of a fine-point felt-tip pen to make details.

Fine-point felt-tip pens can be used for hatching, cross-hatching, and stippling.

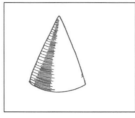 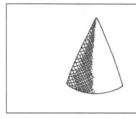 

| Hatching | Cross-hatching | Stippling |

Always replace the cap so the fine-point felt-tip pen does not dry out.

# Technique Tips

## Marker

Markers can be used to make sketches or finished drawings.

Use the point of the marker to make thin lines and small dots.

Use the side of the tip for coloring in areas and for making thick lines.

Always replace the cap so the marker does not dry out.

## Marker

- To avoid damage and to achieve better control, students should not press hard on the marker tip.

- For thin lines and dots, a conical-tipped marker can be used.

- The side of the tip can be used to make wider lines and color in areas.

- Remind students to replace the cap to prevent drying.

## Color Chalk

- Color chalks are used to make colorful, soft designs. The use of dustless chalk is recommended for elementary classrooms. The tip of the chalk is used much like an oil pastel to make lines. To fill a space or shape with solid color, use gentle force and color over an area more than once.

- Colors can be mixed or blended by smearing them together with a paper towel wrapped around a finger.

- Like oil pastels, color chalks break easily. Reassure students that these pieces can still be used like new ones.

- Color chalks become dirty from use. Instruct students to mark on a paper towel until the colors are clean.

## Oil Pastels

- Oil pastels are pigments that are mixed with oil and compressed into sticks. They are used like crayons. By pressing with gentle force and coloring over an area several times, students can create the effect of paint.

- Students can create lines by drawing with the tip. Large spaces can be colored with the tip or the side.

- Textures can be created by making marks such as dots and lines. Textures can also be made by layering colors and scratching through with a paper clip straightened out at one end.

- Colors can be mixed or blended by smearing them with a paper towel wrapped around a finger.

- Oil pastels break easily. Reassure the students that these pieces can still be used like new ones.

- If the oil pastels become dirty from use, instruct the students to mark on a paper towel until the colors are clean again.

# Technique Tips

### Color Chalk

Color chalks can be used to make colorful, soft designs.

You can use the tip of the color chalk to create lines and shapes and to fill spaces. As with pencil, you can also use them for blending to create shadows.

Color chalk is soft and can break easily. Broken pieces are still usable. Colors can be mixed or blended by smearing them together with your finger or a tissue.

### Oil Pastels

Oil pastels are colors that are mixed with oil and pressed into sticks. When you press down hard with them, your pictures will look painted.

Oil pastels are soft with strong colors. You can use oil pastels to color over other media, such as tempera or crayon. Then you can scratch through this covering to create a design.

# Technique Tips

## Painting

### Tempera

1. Fill water containers halfway. Dip your brush in the water. Wipe your brush on the inside edge of the container. Then blot it on a paper towel to get rid of extra water. Stir the paints. Add a little water if a color is too thick or dry. Remember to clean your brush before using a new color.

2. Always mix colors on the palette. Put some of each color that you want to mix on the palette. Then add the darker color a little at a time to the lighter color. Change your water when it gets too cloudy.

3. To create lighter values, add white. To darken a value, add a tiny amount of black. If you have painted something too thickly, add water and blot it with a clean paper towel.

4. Use a thin pointed brush to paint thin lines and details. For thick lines or large areas, press firmly on the tip or use a wide brush.

5. Wash your brush when you are finished. Reshape the bristles. Store brushed with bristles up.

# Painting

## Tempera

- For best results, it is recommended that quality liquid tempera paint is used.

- To remove excess water from the brush, gently wipe the end of the brush on the inside edge of the container. This will allow the water to run back into the container. Discourage students from tapping their brushes on the rim of the container. This will prevent paint splatters.

- When mixing paints on a palette, always mix the darker color into the lighter color a little at a time until the desired color is reached. This reduces wasted paint. Paper plates work well as palettes and reduce cleanup.

- Use a thin brush for details.

- Use a wide brush for large spaces.

## Watercolors

- School watercolors come in semimoist cakes. Moisten each cake that is going to be used by dripping a little water from the brush onto the cake and gently stirring the water on the surface of the paint.

- Create thick lines by gently pressing down on the brush.

- Create thin lines by lightly touching the surface of the paper with the tip of the brush.

- To create textures such as stipple (dots) or lines, demonstrate these techniques:

  1. Wet a round, soft-bristled watercolor brush.
  2. Carefully squeeze excess water from the bristles.
  3. Gently divide the bristles into spikes.
  4. Carefully touch the moistened paint cake with the bristle tips so that some paint is absorbed by the bristles.
  5. Lightly touch the paper with the separated bristles. Gentle taps create irregular dots. Gentle, upward strokes create irregular lines.
  6. When finished, rinse, clean, and reshape the brush.

- To create lighter values, the hue should be thinned with water using these steps:

  1. Use a watery brush.
  2. Thin the hue on the palette with water.
  3. Brush water over an already painted area.
  4. Blot the wet, painted area with a paper towel.

- To create darker values, add drops of black to the hue on the palette, *one at a time*, until the desired value is achieved.

## Wash

Painting or sponging water onto the paper prior to painting will create soft lines, soft-edged shapes, and softer colors. The water should be allowed to soak into the paper before painting.

- To create sharp, clear lines and shapes, students should paint on dry paper with a damp brush.

- To create a fuzzy look, students should paint on dry paper with a dry brush and very little paint.

## Technique Tips

### Watercolor

1. Fill water containers halfway. Dip your brush in the water. Wipe your brush on the inside edge of the container. Then blot it on a paper towel to get rid of extra water. With your brush, add a drop of water to each watercolor cake and stir. Remember to clean your brush whenever you change colors.

2. Always mix colors on a palette. Put some of each color that you want to mix on the palette. Then add the darker color a little at a time to the lighter color. Change your water when it gets too dark.

3. To create lighter values, add more water. To darken a value, add a tiny amount of black. If you have painted something too quickly, add water to the paint on the paper and blot it with a clean paper towel.

4. Use a thin pointed brush to paint thin lines and details. For thick lines or large areas, press firmly on the tip or use a wide brush.

5. For a softer look, tape your paper to the table with masking tape. Use a wide brush to add water to the paper, working in rows from top to bottom. This is a wash. Let the water soak in a little. Painting on wet paper will create a soft or fuzzy look. For sharper forms or edges, paint on dry paper, using only a little water on your brush.

6. Wash your brushes when you are finished. Reshape the bristles. Store brushes with the bristles up.

# Technique Tips

## Chinese Painting

To hold the brush properly, first place the brush horizontally between the thumb and the index and middle fingers. Then move the ring finger behind the brush and in turn move the little finger up to rest against the ring finger.

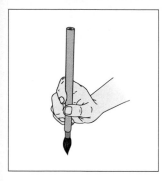 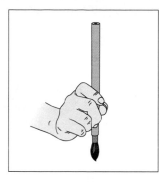

To paint the vertical stroke, rest the wrist lightly on the table. Then lift your elbow about three inches. When moving the brush, move not only the fingers but your whole arm. This allows a wider range of movement and a more accurate motion of the brush.

 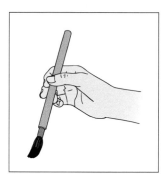

To paint the slanting stroke, place your fingers higher on the handle than you do with the vertical stroke. As you hold the brush, let the handle of the brush slant to one side.

# Printmaking

## Making Stamps

- If students wish to cut a sponge into a specific shape, use thin sponges. Draw the shape on the sponge with a marker and use scissors to cut it out.

- Oil-based modeling clay can also be used to make a stamp. This is done by drawing or sculpting a design on a flat piece of modeling clay. There are a variety of tools manufactured for carving clay. Some classroom items that will work just as well include plastic eating utensils, craft sticks, and paper clips. The straightened end of a paper clip can be used to draw in the clay. The rounded end can be used as a gouge to carve clay away. To create a raised stamp, simply add pieces of clay to the bottom of the clay stamp.

## Printing a Sponge Print

- Dispense colors onto individual palettes, or spread out on a surface large enough to avoid mixing. Lightly press the sponge into the paint, being careful not to get too much paint on it. Lift the sponge and lightly press it into place on the paper. The sponge should be thoroughly rinsed between colors.

## Technique Tips

## Printmaking

### Making Stamps

Three methods for making stamps are listed below. You can cut either a positive or negative shape into most of these objects. Be sure to talk with your teacher or another adult about what kinds of tools you can safely use.

Cut sponges into shapes.

Using a pencil, clay tool, tip of a paper clip, or another object, draw or sculpt a design on a flat piece of modeling clay.

Using a pencil, tip of a paper clip, or another object, draw or sculpt a design on a flat piece of plastic foam.

# Technique Tips

## Printing Stamps

1. Put a small amount of water-based printing ink or some paint onto a hard, flat surface. Roll a softer roller, called a brayer, back and forth in the ink until there is an even coating of paint on both the surface and the brayer.

2. Roll the brayer filled with ink over the printing. stamp. Thc ink should cover the stamp evenly without going into the grooves of your design.

3. You can also use a brush to coat the stamp evenly with paint. Whichever method you use, be careful not to use too much ink or paint.

4. Gently press your stamp onto your paper. Then peel the paper and stamp apart and check your print. If you wish to make several prints of your design, you should ink your stamp again as needed.

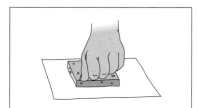

5. When you have finished, wash the brayer, the surface, and the stamp.

## Making Prints

- Below is the procedure for using a brayer, which is a soft roller, to make prints.

    1. Pour a small amount of water-based printing ink or paint onto a flat, solid surface. Roll the brayer in the ink or paint until there is an even coating on the surface and brayer.

    2. Roll the brayer over the top of the stamp. The ink should cover the stamp evenly without getting into the grooves of the design.

    3. Apply the stamp carefully to the paper, rubbing the back of the stamp with the side of the fist.

    4. Peel the paper and stamp apart.

    5. Reink the stamp as needed if you wish to make more than one print.

    6. When finished, wash the brayer, surface, and stamp.

- Another method for making prints calls for a paintbrush to apply the ink or paint. This method works better than the brayer with a raised stamp that the brayer would flatten out. Brush the ink or paint onto the stamping surface. Then follow the steps above, ending with thoroughly cleaning the brush.

# Collage

## Scissors

■ It is important to teach students safety when they use scissors. They should always cut away from their bodies. Of course they should never point their scissors at others, spin them on the table, or walk around the room with them.

■ There are scissors specially made to spring open for students who are physically challenged, or who are not yet developmentally ready to use standard school scissors. Many scissors on the market today can be used with the right or left hand. If these are not available, keep a supply of "lefty" scissors for students who need them.

■ To cut thick yarn or fabric, encourage students to work in pairs. While one cuts, the other can stretch the yarn or fabric. This makes cutting easier and encourages cooperation.

## Arranging a Design

A collage is a work of art in which bits and pieces of paper, fabric, and other materials are glued onto a surface to create a **composition.**

■ Provide a variety of textured and colored papers, yarns, fabrics, and found objects for students to use. Hard-to-cut materials should be precut for students.

■ When using paper, students may choose to tear and/or cut their shapes.

■ Encourage students to arrange the design first. They should pay as much attention to the negative spaces as the positive ones.

■ Glue only after the final colors, shapes, and textures have been chosen and arranged. White glue will attach most porous items to the background surface.

## Glue

■ To attach two pieces of fabric or paper, use only a few drops of glue and smooth them with the tip of the bottle.

■ When finished, students should wipe the bottle clean with a paper towel, close the top, and store upright.

## Technique Tips

### Collage

In a collage, objects or pieces of paper, fabric, or other materials are pasted onto a surface to create a work of art. When planning your collage, consider such things as:

■ Size of shapes and spaces

■ Placement of shapes and spaces

■ Color schemes

■ Textures

Remember that the empty (negative) spaces are also part of your design. Plan a collage as you would plan a painting or a drawing. After deciding what shapes and objects you want to use, arrange them on the paper. When you have made an arrangement you like, glue your shapes and objects to the paper.

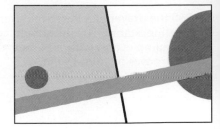

### Weaving

1. Measure and cut notches one-quarter inch apart and one-half inch deep on opposite sides of the cardboard.
2. Tape the warp thread to the back and string from top to bottom. Continue to wrap the thread through each notch until you reach the end. Tape the end of the thread to the cardboard.
3. Start to weave horizontally at the bottom of the loom in an over-one-under-one motion.
4. Do not pull the weft threads too tight.

# Technique Tips

## Coiled Basket

1. Bend the tapered end against itself and begin wrapping with your first strip of fabric.

2. Once the tapered end is secure, begin wrapping a single coil until about five inches of coil is covered.
3. Secure the first row by wrapping a stitch into the center opening.

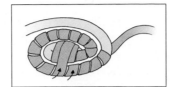

4. Continue wrapping the coil with fabric. About every five inches, attach a stitch onto the last row. The holding stitch goes over one row only.

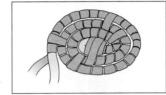

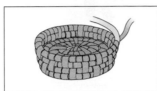

5. To make the side of the coil basket, place one row of coiling on top of the previous row and stitch tightly.

6. To finish the basket, taper the end and lay it flat against the last row. Wrap your fabric tightly three times and cut the remaining fabric.

# Sculpting

## Working with Clay

- Always protect the work area with a cloth or newspaper. Clay dust is messy. Always wash the tables after working with clay.

- To help prevent earth clay from drying and cracking, students should not overhandle the clay. Keep damp paper towels nearby for students to keep their hands moist.

- The following steps are for modeling a person or animal from clay:

  1. Roll the piece of clay into an oval-shaped form. Describe this to the students as a "potato" shape.
  2. Pinch a head shape on one end.
  3. Pinch and pull out arms and legs.
  4. Leave some, but not too much, clay for the body.
  5. Squeeze the head, arms, legs, and body into the desired shapes.

- Clay is often sold in 25 pound bags. The bags are usually strong enough to keep the clay damp, but be sure to close the bag tightly with a twist tie or some other devise to keep it sealed. It is a good idea to place the bag inside a second bag, like a heavy duty garbage bag, for long-term storage.

## Carving Clay

There are a variety of tools manufactured for carving clay. Some classroom items that will work just as well are plastic eating utensils, craft sticks, and paper clips. The straightened end of a paper clip can be used to draw in the clay. The rounded end can be used as a gouge to carve clay away.

## Sculpting

### Clay

Pinch and pull clay into the desired shape.

### Joining two pieces of clay

*Score*, or scratch, both pieces so they will stick together.

Attach the pieces with some *slip*, which is watery clay.

*Squeeze* the two pieces together. *Smooth* the edges.

# Technique Tips

## Clay Slab Construction

To roll a slab of clay, press a ball of clay into a flat shape on a cloth-covered board. Place one one-quarter-inch slat on each side of the clay. Use a roller to press the slab into an even thickness. With a straightened paper clip, trim the slab into the desired shape.

Wrap unfinished sculptures in plastic to keep them moist until finished.

When you are constructing a form such as a container or a house with slabs of clay, it may be necessary to stuff the form with wads of newspaper to support the walls. The newspaper will burn out in the kiln.

## Soap and Plaster Sculpture

You can carve sculptures from clay, soap, or plaster forms. Draw the basic shape of your idea onto all sides of the form. Keep your design simple. Carve a little bit at a time, using a spoon, a paper clip, or a plastic knife, while constantly turning your form.

## Joining Clay

- Clay is joined by using **slip,** a creamy mixture of clay and water. Slip can be made by putting a few dry pieces of clay in a container and covering them with water. When the clay dissolves, stir to achieve a creamy consistency.

- Joining clay also requires a scoring tool such as a straightened paper clip. The steps below are called the four *Ss*—score, slip, smooth, and squeeze.

  1. **Score** the two pieces to be joined.
  2. Apply **slip** to one of the surfaces.
  3. **Smooth** the seam.
  4. **Squeeze** the two surfaces together.

## Painting Clay

- Once clay has been properly fired in a kiln it can be painted with tempera or acrylic paints. It can be glazed and refired.

- The biggest problem with firing student work is that the clay must be thoroughly dried before firing. This can be achieved in an old kiln by stacking everything that is ready to be fired in the kiln and then leaving the lid cracked open. Turn on only one heating coil to dry out the ware for a few hours before closing the lid and firing it up to the desired temperature.

## Plaster Sculpture

- Make plaster carving blocks well ahead of time. Below is a procedure you can use to prepare plaster blocks:

  1. Fill one third of a flexible rubber bucket with water.
  2. Wearing a dust mask, scoop plaster into the water until an "island" peaks and stays above the surface of the water.
  3. Add a couple handfuls of vermiculite on top of the plaster. (This is added for softness and can be purchased at garden centers.)
  4. Wear rubber gloves and mix with your hands, squeezing out any lumps. Do not add more plaster. The mixture will thicken.
  5. Working quickly, pour the plaster into clean, opened half-pint milk cartons, filling them. Plaster will set up in 20–30 minutes.
  6. Leave the excess plaster in the bucket to harden. **Do not pour into the sink.**
  7. Remove each carton by tearing it away from the plaster block.
  8. For carving it is best to let the plaster dry completely. Depending on the humidity, this may take a week.

# Activity Tips

**Types of Lines**

### Creative Expression

1. Think about a cause that concerns you, such as pollution. Write a short slogan or message that expresses your concerns.

2. Design a poster about your cause. Use the different kinds of lines and line variations that you saw in the artwork. Plan a way to work your slogan into a design, like Jaune Quick-to-See Smith did.

Unit 1 · Lesson 2 **Gesture Drawings**

### Creative Expression

1. Think about how action is captured in a drawing. Use quick, sketchy lines.

2. Take turns with classmates freezing in a movement. Hold poses for 30 seconds. Each time you draw someone new, change the crayon color.

3. Repeat lines and shapes and let your figures overlap to fill the entire page.

# Activity Tips

**Observation Drawings**

### 🎨 Creative Expression

1. Think about repeating lines and shapes to draw gestures.
2. Go to the school playground and watch all the action that is taking place.
3. Sketch a variety of gestures from a specific point of view. Show the gestures from a specific point of view. Show the gestures of the children and some of their environment. Fill the entire page. Be sure to overlap your objects and use a variety of lines.

**Contour Lines**

### 🎨 Creative Expression

1. Observe the edges and ridges of objects and of people around you.
2. Create a blind contour drawing of the model. Do not lift the chalk from the construction paper as you work.
3. On a new sheet of construction paper, make a slower, regular contour drawing of the model. You may look at your paper, but do not pick up the chalk. The line must be one continuous line.
4. Add several objects to your drawing.

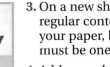

## Observation Drawing

- If students are unable to go to the school playground, have them observe a gym class or some other activity.

## Contour Lines

- Before students complete the Creative Expression activity, demonstrate the difference between a contour and a blind contour drawing.

## Flowing Lines

■ Before students complete the Creative Expression activity, demonstrate the different Chinese brush-painting hand positions. Refer to page 221 of the Technique Tips for more details.

## Shading Techniques

■ If you need a light source to set up the still lifes, ask other school staff members. If there is a stage in the school, a spotlight might be located there.

# Activity Tips

Unit 1 · Lesson 5 **Flowing Lines**

**Creative Expression**

1. Examine a piece of bamboo. Notice how it grows.
2. Watch your teacher demonstrate two Chinese brush-painting hand positions. Practice these positions. Then practice the brushstrokes on newsprint using watered-down black ink.
3. Using the same black ink, paint several pieces of bamboo on white paper. Sit straight and hold your breath while making each brushstroke. Remember to breathe before the next stroke.

Unit 1 · Lesson 6 **Shading Techniques**

**Creative Expression**

1. Think about ways to portray the value (lightness or darkness) of objects in your classroom.
2. Arrange a still life. Use five or more objects. Set up a lamp or spotlight so the light is coming from one side.
3. Using a pencil, lightly sketch the shapes of the objects. Use a variety of hatching techniques to represent the light and dark areas of your composition.

# Activity Tips

## Geometric Shapes

 **Creative Expression**

1. Think about a theme for your collage. Make some quick sketches. Use mostly geometric shapes.

2. Draw your best sketch. Add collected materials to make your collage.

3. Before you glue the materials to the paper, arrange your collage until you find a design you like. Use as many geometric shapes as you can. Fill the background with color.

## Free-Form Shapes

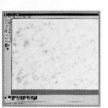

**Creative Expression**

1. Use the computer airbrush tool to create an ocean-like background of blues and greens, with a sand-colored bottom.

2. Use the paintbrush tool to create free-form shapes that look like seaweed and shells.

3. Color the free-form drawings with bright colors, using the paintbrush tool.

4. Save and print a copy of your undersea fantasy painting.

Activity Tips **231**

## Free-Form Shapes

 As an alternative to using the computer, students can create a drawing.

## Pattern

- Before students complete the Creative Expression activity, demonstrate how to use a brayer. Make sure students do not use too much ink.

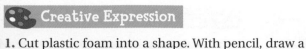

# Activity Tips

### Creative Expression

1. Cut plastic foam into a shape. With pencil, draw a design on the foam.
2. Choose where you will place the print on the construction paper.
3. Roll a thin layer of ink onto the foam.
4. Lay the foam on the construction paper. Gently rub to transfer the design.
5. Repeat the design as many times as you want.
6. Let the paper dry, then draw and color geometric shapes in the background.

Unit 2 · Lesson 4 — **Visual Rhythm**

### Creative Expression

1. Think about an activity that has rhythmic movement. The event or activity should involve people, for example, a parade, a sports activity, or a dance performance.
2. Make sketches of people participating in the event. Place the people in uniforms.
3. Plan a composition that will have visual beats (the people) and rests (negative spaces).
4. Draw your figures with chalk on the paper. Finish with oil pastel colors.

# Activity Tips

- The beats in students' works of art may move in a straight line or may wander around the paper.

- Students may use more than one color to paint the background, but they should not leave any white paper.

## Unit 2 · Lesson 5    Rhythm and Movement

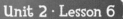

**Creative Expression**

1. Listen to music and imagine the shape and placement of the beats. Visualize the line movement to represent the melody.

2. Select related oil pastel colors to represent the beat and the melody. Select dark watercolors to use in the background.

3. Listen again and draw the beats using one color. Press heavily.

4. Listen again, and using a second color, draw the melody lines. Again, press hard.

5. Paint the background using the watercolors that you selected.

## Unit 2 · Lesson 6    Flowing Rhythm

**Creative Expression**

1. Think about how lines can show rhythm. Cut a variety of curving lines and long, flowing free-form shapes from paper.

2. Arrange the cut shapes on the paper until you get a flowing-rhythm design you like. Then glue down the shapes.

## The Color Wheel

- In order to make straight lines, show students how to hold down the shift key and draw at the same time.

## Neutral Colors

- Before students complete the Creative Expression activity, demonstrate how to blend neutral colors of chalk with another color of chalk.

# Activity Tips

**Unit 3 · Lesson 1**  **The Color Wheel**

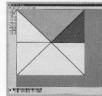
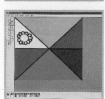

### Creative Expression

1. Select the line tool on the tool bar. Draw two diagonal lines that touch the edges of the picture plane. It should look like an *X*.

2. At the center of the *X*, draw a horizontal line straight across until it touches one side of the picture plane. Repeat this on the other side. The white drawing area should now be divided into six areas.

3. Use the fill tool to pour the colors of the color wheel into each area.

4. Use the drawing and painting tools to insert objects into the color wheel. Save and print the file.

**Unit 3 · Lesson 2**  **Neutral Colors**

### Creative Expression

1. Create several very simple sketches of a landscape or seascape. Select one of the sketches for your drawing.

2. Use white chalk to transfer your sketch onto a piece of sandpaper.

3. Choose a color of chalk that will blend with neutral colors.

4. Complete your drawings by blending the colors directly onto the sandpaper.

# Activity Tips

**Complementary Colors**

■ Before students complete the Creative Expression activity, demonstrate how to cut out a shape in one piece.

**Unit 3 · Lesson 3**   Complementary Colors

 Creative Expression

1. Draw a simple shape inside one of the squares of complementary-colored paper.
2. Cut out the shape carefully in one piece. Cut from one edge, but cut out the center shape in one piece. The square should be in one piece also. Repeat this step four times.
3. Glue the squares to the primary-colored paper. Create an alternating pattern. Then glue the shapes between the squares.

**Unit 3 · Lesson 4**   Low-Intensity Colors

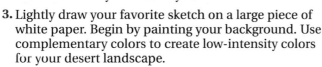

Creative Expression

1. Use your imagination to identify things you might find in a desert. What colors would they be?
2. Plan a desert landscape by making a few sketches. Include a variety of lines in your sketches.
3. Lightly draw your favorite sketch on a large piece of white paper. Begin by painting your background. Use complementary colors to create low-intensity colors for your desert landscape.

Activity Tips **235**

## Tints and Shades

■ Pre-mixed green tempera paint can be used to mix intermediate colors because it is very hard to get a true green when mixing yellow and blue tempera.

# Activity Tips

**Unit 3 · Lesson 5**   **Tints and Shades**

**Creative Expression**

1. Look at a plant. Notice its basic shape and contours. Lightly sketch the plant. Make sure your drawing touches three edges of your paper.

2. Select a set of complementary colors. Use one color to paint the plant. Add black and white to create tints and shades of that color. Observe the shadows and highlights in the plant.

3. Paint the background with tints and shades of the second color.

**Unit 3 · Lesson 6**   **Color Moods**

**Creative Expression**

1. Think about the way colors affect the look of a scene.

2. Make several sketches of an imaginary scene. Choose your best one.

3. Choose a color scheme that fits your scene. Fill your scene with color.

# Activity Tips

**Forms**

### 🎨 Creative Expression

1. Think about the different forms you see every day. Some are natural organic forms, and some are made by people.

2. Make a large potato form out of clay. Keep turning your form, making sure to work on all surfaces. Use your fingers to press into some surfaces and to pull up other surfaces. Create at least one curved hole that goes complctcly through the clay.

. . . . . . . . . . . . . . . . . . . . . . . . . . . . . . . . . . . . . . . . . . . . . . .

**Additive Sculpture**

### 🎨 Creative Expression

1. Brainstorm ideas of people you could portray in your sculpture (soldier, soccer player, football player, police officer, firefighter, doctor, character from a story).

2. Use a cardboard tube or a cone made from poster board as a support. Place a slab of clay around the support. This can be a background support or part of a seated body (even a chair).

3. Create body parts and connect them to the support.

4. Add clothing and tools using thin slabs, coils, and other forms.

Activity Tips **237**

## Additive Sculpture

- In order to save time, have the tubes or cones made from posterboard ready for students before they begin the Creative Expression activity.

- Before students complete the Creative Expression activity, demonstrate how to attach pieces of clay using the slip and score method.

## Subtractive Sculpture

- Collect plastic utensils before students begin the Creative Expression activity. Ask the school cafeteria if they have any extra utensils.

## Visual Texture

- Cake texture could be tree bark or rough rocks, grass could be hair, cotton ball pictures could be clouds, cloud pictures could be animal fur, a flowered dress could be used for a bush of flowers or a flower bed, and water surfaces could be used for clothes or drapes.

# Activity Tips

**Unit 4 · Lesson 3** | **Subtractive Sculpture**

**Creative Expression**

1. Sketch a simple animal form, such as a fish, or a free-form form. Use at least one curve in the design.
2. Tear the cup off the plaster your teacher prepared. Use a pencil to draw your design into the plaster. Draw on all sides.
3. Use a spoon to scrape away the plaster surrounding your design. The design will slowly appear as you carve.
4. Use a paperclip to carve out small areas. Add texture and detail. Turn your sculpture as you carve. When you finish carving, lightly sand the areas you want smooth.

**Unit 4 · Lesson 4** | **Visual Texture**

**Creative Expression**

1. Decide on your illustration, and make some sketches.
2. What kinds of things do the textures you collected remind you of? Study them. What can you use them for in your picture? Draw the shapes for your picture on the images and cut them out of the magazine.
3. Arrange the visual texture shapes on your paper and glue them down. Draw the rest of your scene to fill the entire page and color it with color pencils.

# Activity Tips

**Tactile Texture**

### 🎨 Creative Expression

1. Think about materials you could use for a texture weaving. Collect a variety of materials with a variety of textures, such as yarn, ribbon, leather, and wire.

2. Prepare a piece of cardboard for weaving by notching and stringing the warp threads.

3. Use a variety of textures in your weaving. Think about color variation as you weave.

**Emphasis**

### 🎨 Creative Expression

1. Find a picture of an athlete that can be imported into a blank paint or draw file, or scan a picture into a file.

2. Save the picture as a line drawing.

3. Use the paint tool to color in the athlete in bold, bright colors.

4. Color the rest of the picture, including the crowd, in neutral colors.

## Tactile Texture

- Have students begin to collect various objects to incorporate into their weavings prior to starting this lesson.

- Another alternative to cardboard boxes is the back of paper pads. Tear the back off and clean off the top so there is no left-over glue.

- Demonstrate the following weaving technique: **Tabby:** This is the basic weave and is also called a basket weave. The pattern is over-under-over-under.

## Emphasis

- If available, have students use a photo-editing program for this activity.

# Activity Tips

**Foreground, Middle Ground, and Background**

### Creative Expression

1. Think about details in your environment that you might include in your drawing.

2. Look through a viewing frame, and do two quick sketches of different areas. Choose one to make into a finished drawing.

3. Divide the picture plane on your paper into foreground, middle ground, and background. Begin by drawing the larger shapes of the foreground. Then fill in the middle ground and next the background. Finish by adding details to your foreground.

**Unit 5 · Lesson 2** **Perspective Techniques**

### Creative Expression

1. Think about the things you see in your environment every day.

2. Sketch several scenes you would like to draw. Include all six perspective techniques in your sketches.

3. Select your best sketch. Use chalk to draw the scene, and fill it with color. Remember to use all six perspective techniques to create the feeling of depth.

# Activity Tips

**Point of View**

### 🎨 Creative Expression

1. Think about three-dimensional objects you would like to photograph. Select one.
2. Look carefully at the object you have chosen. Place it in front of you. Walk around it, stand above it, or lie on the ground and look at it. Choose and photograph your three favorite points of view.

.................................................

**Face Proportion Measurements**

### 🎨 Creative Expression

1. Use a pencil to draw an egg shape for your head.
2. Draw a guideline from the top of the oval to the bottom. Find the center of the oval. Draw a horizontal line across the center. Divide each half one more time with light guidelines.
3. Sketch your eyes so that the center line goes through the center of your eyes. Be sure you have a space the width of one eye between the eyes. Follow the diagram on page 170 and continue looking in the mirror. Draw your nose, ears and hair, and neck.
4. Complete the drawing by using pastels to add color. Add interest to the background with a contrasting color.

Activity Tips **241**

## Point of View

- Give students these three tips for taking a good picture: (1) get close to the subject; (2) keep the background interesting but not busy; and (3) take several photographs of the subject.

## Face Proportion Measurements

- Show students that by wrapping a piece of paper towel around their index finger they can blend oil pastels together. This technique can also be used to make a gradual value change.

## Distortion

- If available, have students use a photo-editing program for this activity.

- Students can choose to complete the entire activity on the computer, but this may require using a variety of programs.

# Activity Tips

**Unit 5 · Lesson 5**  **Body Proportions**

**Creative Expression**

1. Study the model and setting using sighting to determine how the different parts relate to each other.
2. Place your seven and a half head lines so that your figure will fill the paper from top to bottom.
3. Sketch the figure using a light color crayon, such as yellow.
4. After the sketch is complete, fill the composition with color, texture, and value.

**Unit 5 · Lesson 6**  **Distortion**

**Creative Expression**

1. Insert a picture of yourself onto a blank photo editing file.
2. Convert the picture to a line drawing. Save your work.
3. Choose different areas of the face to stretch and distort. Try moving some features around. Save your work and print a copy.
4. Use a marker to divide the areas of the face into sections.
5. Color each section using a different color pencil.

# Activity Tips

**Formal Balance**

### 🎨 Creative Expression

1. Curve a foam sheet and make a cylinder form twelve inches tall. Glue the cylinder and secure it with paper clips at the top and bottom.

2. Cut geometric or free-form shapes to represent yourself or a member of your family.

3. Add shapes to represent the eyes, nose, mouth, and hair. Use sizes, shapes, and colors to create exaggeration in the face.

4. Attach the face to your post. Use more shapes to create arms, legs, and other patterns on the post.

---

**Informal Balance**

### 🎨 Creative Expression

1. Think of the members of your family. Imagine a time when you are relaxing together. Where are the people sitting?

2. Use a pencil to lightly sketch the scene.

3. With watercolor crayons, fill in the large areas of your drawing.

4. Use water and a watercolor brush to blend the watercolor crayon.

5. After the painting dries, use markers to add the hair, eyes, eyebrows, lips and other details.

## Formal Balance

- The teacher may need a hot-glue gun and glue sticks to attach some objects.

## Informal Balance

- Before students complete the Creative Expression activity, demonstrate how to use watercolor crayons and a brush to blend the colors.

## Radial Balance

▪ To save time, have the craft sticks glued together before students begin the Creative Expression activity.

## Harmony

▪ Send a letter home reminding students to begin collecting small objects for their sculptures, such as buttons, fabric scraps, wire, and beads.

# Activity Tips

## Radial Balance

### Creative Expression

1. Cross wooden craft sticks and glue them together. Glue the end of a piece of yarn behind the center of the sticks.

2. Hold the sticks so they look like an *X*. With the yarn hanging from the bottom, wrap it diagonally over the middle and then over the top right arm of the *X*.

3. Turn the *X* one clockwise turn to wrap each stick. As you wrap the yarn, make sure the rows of the yarn lie side by side. Continue to wrap until you see an "eye" forming at the center.

4. Tie the end of the last piece of yarn and tuck it under. Tie a loop of yarn on top for hanging your design.

## Harmony

### Creative Expression

1. Think of the type of sculpture that would fit the environment of your school. Choose an appropriate site for your sculpture.

2. Draw several sketches of how you want your sculpture to look. Select one sketch as your plan.

3. Using cardboard and found objects, build a model of your sculpture. Use analogous colors to create harmony in your design.

# Activity Tips

Unit 6 · Lesson 5 **Variety and Emphasis**

### Creative Expression

1. Select an animal image or images and develop a sketch. Add a background to the sketch.

2. Transfer the sketch to a large sheet of drawing paper and trace it with a black marker.

3. After your teacher demonstrates, color in the animal or animals using crayons to create textures.

4. Paint the entire background using watercolors in a color that contrasts with the color of the animal to create variety.

Unit 6 · Lesson 6 **Unity**

### Creative Expression

1. Your teacher will give you a coil that has one end cut at an angle. Refer to the Coiled Basket Technique Tips to start wrapping the first row.

2. Continue wrapping the coil with fabric and making stitches on the first row about every five inches apart.

3. To make the sides of your coil basket, place one row of coiling on top of the previous row and stitch tightly. Continue adding rows of coiling.

4. To finish the basket, taper the end of the coil and lay it flat against the last row. Wrap your fabric tightly three times around the coil and cut the remaining fabric.

Activity Tips **245**

## Variety and Emphasis

- Before students complete the Creative Expression activity, demonstrate how to use crayons to create texture. Explain to students that the background objects should not have as much visual texture as the animal they are emphasizing.

## Unity

- Before students complete the Creative Expression activity, prepare a coil with a tapered end for each student. The coils should be approximately twelve feet per student. This will make a basket approximately five inches tall.

- Demonstrate how to wrap and fasten a coil.

# Visual Index

**Artist Unknown**
*Egyptian Cat*
716–332 B.C. (page 135)

**Artist Unknown**
*Standing Ruler*
c. A.D. 600–800. (page 130)

**Artist Unknown**
*Jaguar*
c. 1440–1521.
(page 134)

**Andrea del Verrocchio**
*David*
1473–1475. (page 172)

**Michelangelo**
*Pietà*
c. 1500. (page 124)

**Pieter Bruegel
(the Elder)**
*Children's Games*
1560. (page 44)

**Paolo Veronese**
*Sheet of Studies for "The
Martyrdom of Saint George"*
1566. (page 41)

**Clara Peeters**
*Still Life of Fish and Cat*
after 1620. (page 113)

**Peter Paul Rubens**
*The Meeting of David and
Abigail*
1625–1628. (page 147)

**Judith Leyster**
*The Concert*
c. 1631–1633. (page 184)

**Rembrandt van Rijn**
*The Visitation*
1640. (page 146)

**Gu Mei**
*Orchids and Rocks*
1644. (page 52)

**John Singleton Copley**
*Sir William Pepperrell and His Family*
1778. (page 154)

**Katsushika Hokusai**
*Boy with a Flute*
early 19th century.
(page 53)

**William Johnson**
*Lovebird Token*
early 19th century.
(page 195)

**Artist Unknown**
*Figure from House Post*
19th century. (page 186)

**Joshua Johnson**
*The Westwood Children*
c. 1807. (page 190)

**Artist Unknown**
*Canister*
1825. (page 105)

**Artist Unknown**
*Yeihl Nax'in Raven Screen*
c. 1830. (page 104)

**Katsushlka Hokusal**
*Winter Loneliness,* from
*One Hundred Poems*
*Explained by the Nurse*
1839. (page 87)

**Artist Unknown**
*Ceremonial Shield*
c. 1852. (page 108)

**James McNeill Whistler**
*Drouet*
1859. (page 56)

**Camille Pissarro**
*The Hermitage at Pontoise*
1867. (page 156)

**Martin Johnson Heade**
*Cattleya Orchid and Three*
*Brazilian Hummingbirds*
1871. (page 203)

**Pierre-Auguste Renoir**
*Portrait of a Young Boy*
*(Andre Berard)*
1879. (page 168)

**Chief Black Hawk**
*Crow Men in Ceremonial Dress*
1880–1881. (page 78)

**John Singer Sargent**
*The Daughters of Edward*
*Darley Boit*
1882. (page 191)

**Charles Edenshaw**
*Model Totem Pole*
c. 1885. (page 187)

**Berthe Morisot**
*Girl in a Boat with Geese*
c. 1889. (page 157)

**Paul Gauguin**
*Faaturuma (Melancholic)*
1891. (page 120)

**Artist Unknown**
*Basket*
c. 1900. (page 207)

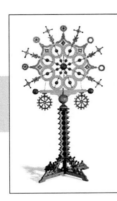

**John Scholl**
*Sunburst*
1907–1916. (page 194)

**Vladimir Baranoff-Rossine**
*Symphony Number 1*
1913. (page 198)

**Marc Chagall**
*Paris Through the Window*
1913. (page 177)

**Natalya Goncharova**
*Maquillage*
1913. (page 34)

**Wassily Kandinsky**
*Little Painting with Yellow (Improvisation)*
1914. (page 37)

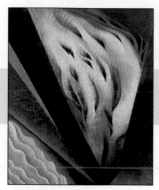

**Georgia O'Keeffe**
*Blue and Green
Music*
1919. (page 116)

**Robert Henri**
*Bernadita*
1922. (page 169)

**Jacques Lipchitz**
*Reclining Figure with Guitar*
1928. (page 127)

**Georgia O'Keeffe**
*Yellow Hickory
Leaves with Daisy*
1928. (page 202)

**Grant Wood**
*The Birthplace of Herbert
Hoover, West Branch, Iowa*
1931. (page 160)

**Paul Klee**
*Mask of Fear*
1932. (page 109)

**Giorgio Morandi**
*Still Life with Coffee Pot*
1933. (page 57)

**Stuart Davis**
*Composition*
1935. (page 64)

**Barbara Hepworth**
*Three Forms*
1935. (page 199)

**Antonio Ruíz**
*The Bicycle Race*
1938. (page 161)

**Emily Carr**
*Self Portrait*
1939. (page 60)

**Henri Matisse**
*Portrait of a Woman
with a Hood*
1939. (page 49)

**Stuart Davis**
*Report from Rockport*
1940. (page 97)

**Z. Vanessa Helder**
*Rocks and Concrete*
c. 1940. (page 101)

**Joan Miró**
*Symbols and Love
Constellations of a Woman*
1941. (page 79)

**Richard Pousette-Dart**
*Within the Room*
1942. (page 83)

**Joaquín Torres-García**
*Abstract Art in Five Tones and Complementaries*
1943. (page 67)

**Lee Krasner**
*Milkweed*
1955. (page 139)

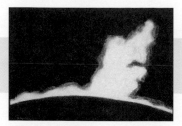

**Milton Avery**
*The White Wave*
1956. (page 100)

**Audrey Flack**
*Self Portrait (the Memory)*
1958. (page 40)

**Salvador Dalí**
*The Elephants (Design from the Opera la Dona Spagnola il Cavaliere Romanoa)*
1961. (page 176)

**Wayne Thiebaud**
*Around the Cake*
1962. (page 112)

**Chryssa**
*Americanoom*
1963. (page 142)

**Teodora Blanco**
*Woman*
1965. (page 131)

**Minnie Evans**
*Design Made at
Airlie Gardens*
1967. (page 70)

**Henry Moore**
*Oval with Points*
1968–1970. (page 126)

**Eliot Elisofon**
*Asante Paramount Chief
Nana Akyanfuo Akowuah
Dateh II, Akwamuhene of
Kumase*
1970. (page 75)

**Paul Goodnight**
*Endangered Species*
c. 1970. (page 45)

**Jacob Lawrence**
*Study for the Munich Olympic
Games Poster*
1971. (page 180)

**Romare Bearden**
*Noah, Third Day*
1972. (page 138)

**Allan Houser**
*Coming of Age*
1977. (page 86)

**Leo Sewell**
*Stegosaurus*
1984. (page 150)

**Miriam Schapiro**
*Pas de Deux*
1986. (page 94)

**John Biggers**
*Shotguns, Fourth Ward*
1987. (page 66)

**John Biggers**
*Starry Crown*
1987. (page 90)

**Malcah Zeldis**
*Miss Liberty Celebration*
1987. (page 117)

**David Hockney**
*Large Interior Los Angeles*
1988. (page 96)

**Jaune Quick-to-See Smith**
*Rainbow*
1989. (page 36)

**Duane Hanson**
*High School Student*
1990. (page 173)

**Benny Andrews**
*Patriots*
1991. (page 48)

**Michael Naranjo**
*Eagle's Song*
1992. (page 164)

**Michael Naranjo**
*Eagle's Song*
1992. (page 165)

**Sandy Skoglund**
*The Cocktail Party*
1992. (page 142)

**Patssi Valdez**
*The Magic Room*
1994. (page 82)

**Viola Frey**
*Family Portrait*
1995. (page 210)

**Elizabeth Murray**
*Riverbank*
1997. (page 71)

**Carolyn Mazloomi**
*Mask Communion*
1998. (page 74)

**Mary A. Jackson**
*Low Basket with Handle*
1999. (page 206)

# Glossary

## A

**additive sculpture** (ad' i tiv skulp' chər), *noun*  When something is added to either relief or freestanding sculpture

**alternating pattern** (ôl' tər nāt ing pat' ərn), *noun*  Can repeat a motif, but change position; alter spacing between motifs or add a second motif

**analogous color scheme** (ə nal' ə gəs kul' ər skēm'), *noun* Uses colors that are side by side on the color wheel and have a common color

**ant's view** (ants' vu'), *noun* Viewers feel they are looking up, toward an object or figure.

**assemblage** (ä säm bläzh'), *noun* A sculpture technique in which a variety of objects is assembled to create one complete piece

**asymmetry** (ā sim' i trē), *noun* Another name for informal balance

## B

**background** (bak' ground'), *noun* The area of the picture plane farthest from the viewer

## B

**balance** (bal' əns), *noun*  The principle of design that deals with visual weight in an artwork

**bird's-eye view** (bûrdz ī vu'), *noun* Or aerial view; viewers feel they are looking down on a scene.

**blending** (blen ding), *noun* A shading technique that creates a gradual change from light to dark or dark to light

**blind contour drawing** (blīnd' kon' tūr drô' ing), *noun*  A drawing that is made by looking at the object being drawn, not at the paper.

**body proportions** (bod' ē prə pôr shənz), *noun*  The size relationship of one part of the body to another

## C

**central axis** (sen' trəl ak' sis), *noun* A real or imaginary dividing line which can run in two directions, vertically and horizontally

**close-up view** (klos' up vu'), *noun* Viewers feel they are right next to an object, or are a part of the action in a picture.

**collage** (kō läzh), *noun*   A two-dimensional work of art made up of pieces of paper and/or fabric to create the image.

**color** (kul' ər), *noun*   1. The art element that is created from reflected light; 2. In balance: a brighter color has more visual weight than a dull color; 3. In perspective: bright-colored objects seem closer, while dull or pale objects appear farther away.

**color scheme** (kul' ər skēm'), *noun*   A plan for organizing the colors used in an artwork

**color spectrum** (kul' ər spek' trum), *noun*   A band of colors in the order of red, orange, yellow, green, blue, and violet

**color wheel** (kul' ər 'wēl), *noun*   Shows the color spectrum bent into a circle

**complementary color scheme** (kom' plə men tə rē kul' ər skēm'), *noun*   Uses one set of complementary colors; for example, red and green, blue and orange, and yellow and violet

**complementary colors** (kom' plə men tə rē kul' ərz), *noun*   Colors that are opposite each other on the color wheel

**contour** (kon' tür), *noun*   The edges and surface ridges of an object

**contour hatching** (kon' tür hach' ing), *noun*   A shading technique that follows the form of an object

**contour line** (kon' tür līn), *noun*   Defines the edges and surface ridges of an object

**contrast** (kon' trast), *noun*   1. Difference; 2. A technique for creating a focal point or area of interest in a work of art using differences in elements; 3. In emphasis: contrast occurs when one element stands out from the rest of the work.

**cool colors** (kül kul' erz), *noun*   Green, violet, and blue. They suggest coolness and move away from the viewer.

**cross-hatching** (krôs hach' ing), *noun*   A shading technique created when sets of parallel lines cross or intersect

**curved** (kûrvd), *adj.*   A line that bends and changes gradually or turns inward to form spirals

# D

**dark lines** (dark līnz), *noun*   Created by using less water for watercolor paints

**detail** (dē tāl), *noun*   One of the six perspective techniques. Objects with fuzzy, blurred edges appear farther away than those with clear sharp edges.

**diagonal** (dī ag' ə nəl), *noun (adj)*   A line that moves on a slant

**distortion** (di stôr shən), *noun*   A deviation from normal or expected proportions

**dominant element** (dom' ə nənt el' ə mənt), *noun*   The element in a work of art that is noticed first.

# E

**emphasis** (em' fə sis), *noun* The principle of design that stresses one area in an art work over another area

**exaggeration** (eg zaj' ə rā' shən), *noun* To increase or enlarge beyond what is expected or normal

# F

**face proportions** (fas' prə pôr shənz), *noun* The relationship of one feature of a face to another feature

**faraway view** (fär' ə wa' vu'), *noun* Or eye-level view; viewers feel they are standing far away from the scene.

**flowing lines** (flō ing līnz), *noun* Create a feeling of calm and gracefulness. Flowing lines are fluid; they change direction and size.

**flowing rhythm** (flō ing rith' əm), *noun* Created when curved lines or shapes are repeated

**focal point** (fo' kəl point'), *noun* The point which the receding lines meet. It is the first part of a composition to attract the viewer's attention.

**foreground** (fôr' ground'), *noun* The area of the picture plane that is closest to the viewer

**form** (form), *noun* A three-dimensional object that is measured by height, width, and depth

**formal balance** (fôr' mel bal' əns), *noun* Occurs when equal or similar elements are placed on opposite sides of a central axis

**free-form forms** (frē' fôrm' fôrmz), *noun* Three-dimensional forms with irregular edges often found in nature

**free-form shapes** (frē' fôrm' shāps), *noun* Two-dimensional images made of straight or curved lines or a combination of both

**freestanding sculpture** (frē stan' ding skulp chər), *noun* A type of sculpture that is surrounded by space on all sides.

# G

**geometric forms** (je' ə met' rik fôrmz), *noun* Mathematically precise forms based on geometric shapes

**geometric shapes** (je' ə met' rik shāps), *noun* Mathematically precise shapes: circle, square, and triangle

**gesture** (jes' chər), *noun* An expressive movement

**gesture lines** (jes' chər līnz), *noun* Lines drawn to capture the movement of a person, an animal, or an object in a painting or drawing

**gesture sketch** (jes' chər skech), *noun* Quick drawings used to capture the position or pose of the body

# H

**harmony** (här' mə nē), *noun* The principle of art which creates unity by stressing similarities of separate but related parts

**hatching** (hach' ing), *noun* A shading technique that looks like a series of parallel lines

**horizontal** (hôr' ə zon təl), *noun* Lines that move from side to side

**hue** (hū), *noun* Another name for color

# I

**informal balance** (in fôr'məl bal' əns), *noun* A way of organizing parts of a design so that unlike objects have equal visual weight

**intensity** (in ten' si te), *noun* The brightness or dullness of a color

**intermediate colors** (in' tər m' de it kul' ərs), *noun* Yellow-green, red-orange, blue-green; made by combining a primary with either of the secondary colors that are adjacent on the color wheel

**invented texture** (in ven' təd teks' chər), *noun* Created when an artist uses lines or other elements to make a textural look without any specific texture in mind

**isolation** (ī' sə lā' shən), *noun* An object is emphasized by its placement apart from other objects.

# L

**light lines** (līt līnz), *noun* Created by adding more water to watercolor paints

**line** (līn), *noun* A mark drawn by a tool such as a pencil, pen, or paintbrush as it moves across a surface

**lines** (līnz), *noun* One of the six perspective techniques. Parallel lines seem to converge or move toward the same point as they move away from you.

**location** (lō cā' shən), *noun* Artists can emphasize an object by placing it closer to the center of the piece.

# M

**matte** (mat), *noun* A dull, sometimes rough finish

**middle ground** (mid' əl ground'), *noun* The area of the picture plane that is usually toward the center

**minimal details** (min ə məl dē tāl), *noun* Used in gesture sketches to complete the drawing

**mix a neutral color** (miks ā nü trəl kul' ər), *noun* Mix a neutral color with another color to change its value

**mixed-media** (mikst mē dē' ə), *noun* An art object that has been created from an assortment of media or materials

**monochromatic** (mon' ə kro mat' ik), *adj.* A color scheme that is made up of one color and the tints and shade of that color

**monochromatic color scheme**
(mon' ə kro mat' ik kul' ər skēm'),
*noun*   Uses only one color and the
values of that color

**motif** (mō tēf), *noun*   A unit that is
made up of objects or art elements
which is repeated

# N

**negative space** (neg' ə tiv spas'),
*noun*   The empty space that surrounds objects, shapes, and forms

**neutral color scheme** (nü trəl kul'
ər skēm'), *noun*   Uses black, white,
and a variety of grays

**neutral colors** (nü trəl kul' ərz),
*noun*   Black, white, and gray

**nonobjective** (non' əb jek' tiv), *adj.*
Art that has no recognizable subject
matter

# O

**overlapping** (o' vər lap ing), *noun*
1. One object covers a portion of
another object. 2. In perspective:
one of the six perspective techniques; the object covering another
will appear closer to the viewer, creating a feeling of depth.

# P

**parallel lines** (per ə lel līnz), *noun*
Lines that move in the same direction and always stay the same
distance apart

**pattern** (pat' ərn), *noun*
A repeated surface decoration

**perspective techniques** (pər spek'
tiv tek neks'), *noun*   The six techniques an artist uses to create the
illusion of depth in two-dimensional
art: overlapping, size, placement,
detail, color, converging lines

**picture plane** (pik' chər plān'),
*noun*   The surface of a drawing or
painting

**placement** (plās ment), *noun*   One
of the six perspective techniques.
Objects placed lower in the picture
plane appear to be closer than those
placed near eye level. There are
three areas on a picture plane: foreground, middle ground, and background.

**point of view** (point' əv vū), *noun*
The angle at which the viewer sees
an object

**portrait** (por trət), *noun*   A two or
three-dimensional artwork created
in the image of a person or animal

**position** (pə zish' ən), *noun*   In
balance: a larger, positive shape and
a small, negative space can be balanced by a small, positive shape and
a large, negative space.

**positive space** (poz' i tiv spas'),
*noun*   Refers to any object, shape,
or form in two- and three-
dimensional art

**primary colors** (pri' mer ē kul' ərs),
*noun*   Red, yellow, and blue, used
to mix the other colors on the color
wheel

**profile** (prō fīl), *noun*   A side view
of a person or animal

**proportion** (prə pôr' shən), *noun*
The principle of art that is concerned with the size relationship of one part to another

# R

**radial balance** (rā' dē əl bal' əns), *noun*   A type of balance that occurs when the art elements come out, or radiate, from a central point

**random pattern** (ran' dəm pat' ərn), *noun*   Occurs when the motif is repeated in no apparent order

**regular pattern** (reg' yə lər pat' ərn), *noun*   Occurs when identical motifs are repeated with an equal amount of space between them

**relief sculpture** (ri lēf skulp chər), *noun*   A type of sculpture that has objects that stick out from a flat surface.

**repeated lines** (rē pē təd līnz), *noun*   Used to give the feeling of movement or motion in a gesture drawing

**repeated shapes** (rē pē təd shāps), *noun*   Used to give the feeling of movement or motion in a gesture drawing; the more times a shape is repeated, the faster the motion looks.

**rough** (rəf), *noun*   A surface that has ridges; not smooth

# S

**secondary colors** (sek' ən der' ē kul' ərs), *noun*   Oorange, green and violet; the result of mixing two primary colors

**self-portrait** (self por trət), *noun*
A two or three-dimensional artwork that an artist makes of him or herself

**sets of complementary colors** (set əf kom' plə men tə rē kul' ərz), *noun*   There are three sets on the color wheel: red and green, blue and orange, and yellow and violet.

**shade** (shād), *noun*   Any color blended with black

**shading** (shā ding), *noun*   A technique for creating dark values or darkening an area by repeating marks such as lines or dots

**shape** (shāp) *noun*   A two-dimensional area that is measured by height and width

**silhouette** (sil' ü et') *noun*   The shape of a shadow

**shiny** (shī nē), *noun*   Bright from reflected light

**simulated texture** (sim' u la' təd teks chər), *noun*   Imitates real textures, see also visual texture

**size** (sīz), *noun*   1. In perspective: objects that are closer look larger than objects that are farther away; 2. In balance: a large shape or form will appear to be heavier than a small shape, and several small shapes can balance one large shape.

**space** (spās), *noun* The art element that refers to the areas above, below, between, within, and around an object

**spectral color scheme** (spek trəl kul' ər skēm'), *noun* Uses all the colors of the rainbow: red, orange, yellow, green, blue, and violet

**smooth** (smüth), *noun* A surface free from roughness; even

**still life** (stil' līf'), *noun* The arrangement of common inanimate objects from which artists draw or paint

**subtractive sculpture** (sub trak tiv skulp chər), *noun* When an artist carves pieces away from a form

**symmetry** (sim' i trē), *noun* A type of formal balance in which two halves of a balanced artwork are identical, mirror images of each other

# T

**tactile texture** (tak' təl teks' chər), *noun* Actual texture, texture that can really be felt

**texture** (teks' chər), *noun* 1. The art element that refers to the way something feels; 2. In balance: a rough texture has an uneven pattern of highlights and shadows. For this reason, a rough surface attracts the viewer's eyes more easily than a smooth, even surface.

**thick line** (thik līn), *noun* Created by beginning with a thin line and gradually pressing the brush down

**thin line** (thin līn), *noun* Created when a brush is held vertically to paper and touched lightly with the tip of the brush

**tint** (tint), *noun* any color blended with white

**two-dimensional** (tü' di men' shən nəl ), *adj.* Flat; can only be measured by height and length

# U

**unity** (ū' ni tē), *noun* The feeling of wholeness or oneness that is achieved by properly using the elements and principles in art

# V

**value** (val' ū), *noun* The lightness or darkness of a color

**variety** (və ri' ə tē), *noun* The principle of art which is concerned with difference or contrast

**vertical** (vür' tə kəl), *noun* A line that moves from top to bottom

**visual movement** (vizh' ü əl müv' mənt), *noun* Occurs when the eye is pulled through a work of art by of rhythm of beats and rests

**visual rhythm** (vizh' ü əl rith' əm), *noun* The principle of design that organizes the elements in a work of art by repeating elements and/or objects

**visual texture** (vizh' ü əl teks' chər), *noun* Or simulated texture, imitates real texture. It is the illusion of a three-dimensional surface.

**visual weight** (vizh' ü əl wāt), *noun* cannot be measured on a scale; it is measured by which objects the viewer's eyes see first.

# W

**warm colors** (wōrm' kul' ərz), *noun* Red, yellow, and orange. They suggest warmth and come forward toward the viewer.

# Z

**zigzag** (zig' zag) *noun (adj.)* A line that is made by joining diagonal lines

# Index

# Acknowledgments

Grateful acknowledgment is given to the following publishers and copyright owners for permissions granted to reprint selections from their publications. All possible care has been taken to trace ownership and secure permission for each selection included. In case of any errors or omissions, the Publisher will be pleased to make suitable acknowledgments in future editions.

NOT ONE DAMSEL IN DISTRESS by Jane Yolen. Jacket used with permission of Harcourt, Inc. All Rights Reserved.

MUFARO'S BEAUTIFUL DAUGHTERS by JOHN STEPTOE. COVER ART COPYRIGHT © 1987 BY JOHN STEPTOE. PERMISSION GRANTED BY THE ESTATE OF JOHN STEPTOE AND THE JOHN STEPTOE LITERARY TRUST. ALL RIGHTS RESERVED.

From ONE MORNING IN MAINE by Robert McCloskey, Copyright 1952, renewed © 1980 by Robert McCloskey. Used by permission of Viking Penguin, A Division of Penguin Young Readers Group, A Member of Penguin Group (USA) Inc., 345 Hudson Street, New York, NY 10014. All rights reserved.

A RIVER RAN WILD by Lynne Cherry. Jacket used with permission of Harcourt, Inc. All Rights Reserved.

From PINK AND SAY by Patricia Polacco, copyright © 1994 by Patricia Polacco. Used by permission of Philomel Books, A Division of Penguin Young Readers Group, A Member of Penguin Group (USA) Inc., 345 Hudson Street, New York, NY 10014. All rights reserved.

WHERE THE WILD THINGS ARE by MAURICE SENDAK. COPYRIGHT ©1963, 1991 MAURICE SENDAK. Used by permission of HarperCollins Publishers.

# Photo Credits

Cover Alfred Stieglitz Collection, gift of Georgia O'Keeffe, 1969.835. Image © The Art Institute of Chicago. © 2004 The Georgia O'Keeffe Foundation/Artists Rights Society (ARS), New York; 5 Dallas Museum of Art, Dallas, Texas; 6 Smithsonian American Art Museum/Art Resource, NY. © Estate of Stuart Davis/Licensed by VAGA, New York, New York; 7 Steinbaum Krauss Gallery, New York; 8 © Scala/Art Resource, NY/ St. Peter's Basilica, Vatican State; 9 North Carolina Museum of Art. Purchased with funds from the State of North Carolina; 10 National Museum of Women in the Arts. Washington, DC; 12 (tl) Museum of Fine Arts, Boston, (tr) Hirshhorn Museum and Sculpture Garden, Smithsonian Institution, Gift of Joseph H. Hirshhorn, 1966, (bl) Dallas Museum of Art, Dallas, Texas, (br) © Philip Hayson/Photo Researchers Inc; 13 (tl) Honolulu Academy of Art. Honolulu, Hawaii. Gift of James A. Michener, 1955 (13,694), (tr) Purchased with funds provided by the Smithsonian Collections Acquisition Program. Photograph by Frank Khoury. National Museum of African Art, Smithsonian Institution, Washington D.C., (bl) Image no.EEPA 1474. Eliot Elisofon Photographic Archives, National Museum of African Art, Smithsonian Institution, Washington, D.C., (br) Royal British Columbia Museum, Victoria, Canada; 15 (tl) The Ogden Museum of Southern Art, University of New Orleans, Gift of the Benny Andrews Foundation, (tr) Amon Carter Museum, Fort Worth, Texas. 1999.33.E, (bl) From the Girard Foundation Collection, in the Museum of International Folk Art, a unit of the Museum of New Mexico, Santa Fe, New Mexico. Photographer: Michel Monteaux, (br) © Carl & Ann Purcell/Corbis; 16 Helen Birch Bartlett Memorial Collection, 1926.252. Photograph © 2001, The Art Institute of Chicago, All Rights Reserved; 17 © Northwest Museum of Arts & Culture. Photo by David Anderson; 18 Wadsworth Atheneum, Hartford. The Ella Gallup Sumner and Mary Catlin Sumner Collection Fund; 19 (t) Dallas Museum of Art, Dallas, Texas, (b) Smithsonian American Art Museum, Washington, DC/Art Resource, NY. © Elizabeth Catlett/Licensed By VAGA, New York, New York; 20 National Gallery, London/Art Resource, NY. Erich Lessing, photographer; 21 Frank Fortune; 22 (t, tcl, tcr, br, bcr) © Photodisc/Getty Images, Inc, (bcl, bl) © Digital Vision/Getty Images, Inc; 23 (t) © Corbis, (tcl, tcr, bl, bcl, bc)© Photodisc/Getty Images, Inc, (br) © Index Stock; 24, 26, 28, 30 San Francisco Museum of Modern Art. © Banco de Mexico Diego Rivera & Frida Kahlo Museum Trust. Av. Cinco de Mayo No.2, Col. Centro, Del. Cuauhtemoc 06059, Mexico, D.F; 32-33 © Aaron Haupt; 34 Dallas Museum of Art, Dallas, Texas. © 2004 Artists Rights Society (ARS), New York/ADAGP, Paris; 35 © Tretyakov Gallery, Moscow, Russia/Bridgeman Art Library; 36 Steinbaum Krauss Gallery; 37 Philadelphia Museum of Art: The Louis and Walter Arensberg Collection. 1950-134-103. © 2004 Artists Rights Society (ARS), New York/ADAGP, Paris; 38 © Eclipse Studios; 39 Frank Fortune; 40 Miami University Art Museum, Oxford, Ohio; 41 Courtesy of the J. Paul Getty Museum; 42 © Eclipse Studios; 43 Randy Ellett; 44 Photograph © Erich Lessing/Art Resource, NY; 45 Courtesy of Bing Davis; 46 © Eclipse Studios; 47 Randy Ellett; 48 Cumberland Gallery, Nashville, TN; 49 The Bridgeman Art Library; 50 © Eclipse Studios; 51 Randy Ellett; 52 Arthur M. Sackler Gallery, Smithsonian Institution; 53 Freer Gallery, Smithsonian Institution; 54 © Eclipse Studios; 55 Randy Ellett; 56 Los Angeles County Museum of Art, The Julius L. and Anita Zelman Collection. Photo © 2003 Museum Associates/LACMA; 57 © Bettmann/Corbis, © 2004 Artists Rights Society (ARS), New York/SIAE, Rome; 58 © Eclipse Studios; 59 Randy Ellett; 60 © National Gallery of Canada, Ottawa. Gift of Peter Bronfman, 1990; 62 Courtesy of the Wadsworth Atheneum, Hartford, CN; 63 Craig Schwartz; 64 Smithsonian American Art Museum/Art Resource, NY. © Estate of Stuart Davis/Licensed by VAGA, New York, New York; 65 © Ralph Morse/Getty Images; 66 Hampton University Museum; 67 Collection Albright-Knox Art Gallery, Buffalo, New York. Gift of Mr. and Mrs. Armand J. Castellani, 1979. © 2004 Artists Rights Society (ARS), New York/VEGAP, Madrid; 68 © Eclipse Studios; 69 Frank Fortune; 70 Smithsonian American Art Museum/Art Resource, NY; 71 Collection Albright-Knox Art Gallery Buffalo, New York. Sarah Norton Goodyear Fund, 1997; 72 © Eclipse Studios; 73 Randy Ellett; 74 Frank Fortune; 75 Image no.EEPA 1474. Eliot Elisofon Photographic Archives, National Museum of African Art, Smithsonian Institution, Washington, D.C; 76 Eclipse Studios; 77 Randy Ellett; 78 Thaw Collection Fenimore House Museum/NYSHA, Cooperstown, New York. Photo © 1998 by; 79 The Art Institute of Chicago. Gift of Gilbert W. Chapman. © 2004 Succession Miro/Artists Rights Society (ARS), New York/ADAGP, Paris; 80 Eclipse Studio; 81 Randy Ellett; 82 © Smithsonian American Art Museum, Washington, DC/Art Resource, NY; 83 Collection of the Whitney Museum of American Art, New York. Promised 50th Anniversary Gift of the Artist; 84 © Eclipse Studios; 85 Frank Fortune; 86 Denver Art Museum; 87 Honolulu Academy of Art. Honolulu, Hawaii. Gift of James A. Michener, 1955 (13,694); 88 © Eclipse Studios; 89 Frank Fortune; 90 Dallas Museum of Art, Dallas, Texas; 92 The Image Bank/Getty Images, Inc; 93 Allen Nomura; 94 Steinbaum Krauss Gallery, New York; 95 © Suzanne Opton/Courtesy Steinbaum Krauss Gallery; 96 The Metropolitan Museum of Art, Purchase, Natasha Gelman Gift, in honor of William S. Lieberman, 1989. (1989.279) Photograph © 1990 The Metropolitan Museum of Art. © David Hockney; 97 The Metropolitan Museum of Art, Edith and Milton Lowenthal Collection, Bequest of Edith Abrahamson Lowenthal, 1991. (1992.24.1) Photograph © 1992 The Metropolitan Museum of Art. © Estate of Stuart Davis/Licensed by VAGA, New York, New York; 98 © Eclipse Studios; 99 Alexis Lee; 100 Gift of Helen Hooker Roelofs in memory of her father, Elon Huntington Hooker, Class of 1896. Courtesy of the Herbert F. Johnson Museum of Art, Cornell University. © 2004 Milton Avery Trust/Artists Rights Society (ARS), New York; 101 © Northwest Museum of Arts & Culture. Photo by David Anderson; 102 © Eclipse Studios; 103 Randy Ellett; 104 The Seattle Art Museum, Gift of John H. Haulberg. Photo by Paul Macapia; 105 Collection of the American Folk Art Museum, New York; Gift of the Historical Society of Early American Decoration; 106 © Eclipse Studios; 107 Randy Ellett; 108 The Brooklyn Museum, Brooklyn, New York. Frank L. Babbott and Carl H. DeSilver Funds; 109 © Digital image The Museum of Modern Art/Licensed by Scala/Art Resource, NY. © 2004 Artists Rights Society (ARS), New York/ADAGP, Paris; 110 © Eclipse Studios; 111 Frank Fortune; 112 © Wayne Thiebaud/Licensed by VAGA, New York, New York; 113 National Museum of Women in the Arts, Washington D.C; 114 © Eclipse Studios; 115 Frank Fortune; 116 Alfred Stieglitz Collection, Gift of Georgia O'Keeffe, 1969.835. Image © The Art Institute of Chicago. © 2004 The Georgia

# Notes

# Notes

# Table of Contents

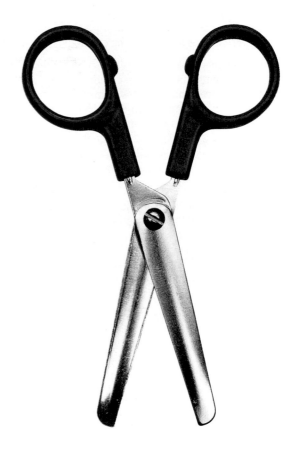

# The Elementary Art Curriculum

Rosalind Ragans, Ph.D., Associate Professor Emerita, Georgia Southern University

Art education is for all students. It provides learning opportunities for the artistically talented few, as well as the many students who may never produce art outside the classroom.

A strong elementary visual arts curriculum teaches students that they can communicate a variety of ideas and emotions in many different ways. Students learn that some problems have many different solutions, and they will not be afraid to use divergent-thinking strategies. They will learn concepts and techniques that will give them control of the visual images they produce.

A strong elementary art curriculum also enables students to expand their perceptive, interpretive, and analytical abilities. They learn to find meaning in visual images, and they learn to identify aesthetic qualities in a variety of works of art and in the environment. They begin to develop the ability to make aesthetic judgments.

The visual arts have always been an integral component in the history of humanity, and through the study of art history, students will develop a better understanding of beliefs and ideas that are different from their own.

The four components of a quality art program are Aesthetic Perception, Art Criticism, Art History and Culture, and Art Production and Creative Expression.

##  Aesthetic Perception

Aesthetics is a branch of philosophy. In visual art, aesthetics becomes the study of the nature of beauty and art. Aesthetics is concerned with the question "What is art?" In the past, aesthetics was defined as the study of beauty because the creation of beauty was thought to be the purpose of art. Today, some aestheticians still believe that the purpose of art is to create beauty or beautifully organized arrangements of the elements of art. Some believe that art must imitate reality. Others think of art as a strong means to communicate ideas and emotions.

Aesthetic concepts are the core of the *Art Connections* curriculum. They are the framework upon which all aspects of art learning are constructed. The **About Aesthetic Perception** section in the *Student Edition* and *Teacher Edition* offers concrete methods for introducing students to aesthetics.

## Art Criticism

Works of art are the focus of every lesson. Art criticism is the sequential process used in this textbook to guide students through the procedures needed to learn from these works of art. Art criticism enables students to learn from works of art that have been created by artists from many cultures and time periods. Art criticism also provides a procedure that students can use to objectively study their own art products.

The four-step process of art criticism will help students expand their perceptive, analytical, interpretive, and aesthetic valuing abilities. The sequential steps of art criticism are similar to those used in the scientific method. During the first two steps, **Describe** and **Analyze,** students are asked to collect data objectively. During the third step, **Interpret,** students speculate about the meaning of the work based on the data collected: they make a hypothesis abut the idea, emotion, or mood expressed by the artist. During the fourth step, **Decide,** or aesthetic judgment, the students offer their conclusions about the work of art.

Art criticism helps students study a work of art before making an aesthetic judgment. Too often, beginners look at a work of art briefly and immediately make a value judgment. The sequential procedures in art criticism force the students to postpone judgment while becoming immersed in the image.

In this program art criticism is used as a higher-level method of thinking about the concepts taught in each unit. One work of art has been selected that emphasizes the elements or principles that were the focus of the lesson. Art criticism is also used to help students make a personal assessment of the artwork produced during the Creative Expression activities. The questions offered are neutral and avoid judgments involving likes and dislikes. This avoids embarrassing moments when discussing works in front of peers.

## Art History and Culture

*Art Connections* is not an art history text, but any study of art should begin with learning something about the history of world art and the people who created it. Information about art history related to the featured work of art in each lesson is provided for the students throughout the text. The **About Art History and Culture** section provides an overview of how to include art history information in classroom instruction. Additional information is provided for the teacher in each lesson and in ancillary materials such as the *Artist Profiles* books and on the backs of the *Large Prints.* The *Art Around the World* collection and *The National Museum of Women in the Arts Collection* contain works of art from many countries and provide additional historical and cultural information.

## Art Production and 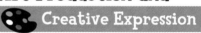 Creative Expression

Each lesson includes an art production activity identified as **Practice** and **Creative Expression** in the *Student Edition.* This is the place for each student to creatively explore the lesson concept. Hands-on activities are often the most enjoyable aspect of art learning. The student integrates and internalizes the verbal and visual concepts of the lesson during the creative manipulation of art materials. While every component in the art program is equally important, every component does not need equal time. Art production requires the longest amount of time.

Do not skip the self-assessment section of the lesson. Most students would be embarrassed to offer subjective statements about their own work or the work of classmates. The four steps of art criticism offer an objective procedure for thinking about the concepts and technical procedures used during the creation of art.

## Art Magazine Resources for Teachers

| | | |
|---|---|---|
| *American Artist* | *ARTnews* | *Crayola Kids* |
| *Art Education* | *Arts and Activities* | *Scholastic Art* |
| *Art to Zoo* | *Arts Education Policy Review* | *School Arts* |

# About Aesthetic Perception

Richard W. Burrows , Executive Director, Institute for Arts Education, San Diego, California

*The Association of Institutes for Aesthetic Education promotes and fosters aesthetic education principles and practices through professional and institutional development. The Association provides policy and program leadership to the arts and education field at the national, state, and local levels.*

*Aesthetics* has been defined as the branch of philosophy that focuses on the nature of beauty, the nature and value of art, and the inquiry processes and human responses associated with those topics.

Aesthetic perception can be most simply defined as an educational approach designed to enhance understanding of artistic expression. Aesthetic perception requires two primary elements to exist: a work of art and a viewer to perceive it. An aesthetic perception approach to viewing works of art is predicated on the belief that the arts can be studied in an active, experiential way. The focus is on developing skills of perception by using works of art as a "textbook" or a focus for study. The instruction delivered by teachers is in partnership with the work of art.

Aesthetic perception provides opportunities to heighten perception and understanding through direct encounters with a broad spectrum of works of art. Students and teachers become actively involved with the artwork—observing, listening to and discussing works of art, and exploring their perceptions of these works through participatory activities. The focus is on developing skills of perception through greater understanding of art forms, of how artists make aesthetic choices, and of how these understandings relate to other aspects of life.

## Misconceptions About Aesthetic Perception

As aesthetic perception approaches have become more widely used, a number of misconceptions have developed about the purpose of aesthetic perception education in the understanding of works of art.

### Multidisciplinary Versus Interdisciplinary

The purpose of aesthetic perception is not to explore the commonalities among works of art. Each work of art must be studied separately first; connections should be made after an in-depth understanding of that particular work. Every work of art has a separate intention and

different meaning. If aesthetic perception is to develop a thinking- or meaning-based understanding of the work of art, then activities must reflect that point of view.

### You Cannot Teach What You Do Not Like

A strong "personal" negative reaction to a work of art does not invalidate it as an object of study for students.

### Arts Integration

While arts experiences must integrate with all other areas of the curriculum, it is important to understand the separate language that the arts have and acknowledge the connections with other cross-curricular areas as they arise.

### The Therapeutic Value of Aesthetic Perception

Very often students and teachers will comment on the therapeutic value of aesthetic perception—it seems separate from the actual art-making processes. This is often a side effect of active engagement in artistic creation and perception. This is not the purpose of aesthetic perception, which should be seen as an alternative way of viewing the work of art and the world in which it is created.

## Using Aesthetic Perception

Below are some guidelines for using an aesthetic-perception approach to education.

### Deciding What to Teach

It would not be appropriate to teach the same elements over and over in connection with each work of art. Instead, knowledge of all of the elements within a given art discipline should provide the background knowledge for making a decision about what aesthetic perception experiences to design. These decisions should be based on the most predominant elements in the work of art—the responses and the backgrounds of the students.

### Creating a Safe Space and Adopting a Critical Stance

It is important to create a working and learning environment with both students and teachers in which they feel comfortable taking risks and trying out new ideas. This does not mean, however, that everything that occurs in aesthetic perception has to be met with uncritical approval. Instead, experiences can be structured so that participants receive feedback on their aesthetic choices and are given an opportunity to revise and improve their solutions to problems.

### Documenting the Experience

Various types of documentation serve as a way of recording the aesthetic perception events as they occur or are revisited. This documentation should include written observations, interviews, journals, and student projects. It is important in any case to record this work in order to be able to see the "habits of mind" that reveal themselves in this complex and rich way of thinking and knowing.

Aesthetic perception is a long-term undertaking and requires a patient conviction that the arts and aesthetic perception should be a part of the learning experience of young people. It requires flexibility, stamina, ingenuity, and perseverance. The rewards are astronomical in terms of student response, content understanding, and classroom relationships.

# Introduction to Art History

Gene A. Mittler, Ph.D., Professor Emeritus, Texas Tech University

> "The art of the Greeks, of the Egyptians, of the great painters who lived in other times, is not an art of the past; perhaps it is more alive today than it ever was. Art does not evolve by itself; the ideas of people change and with them their mode of expression."   —Pablo Picasso

One of the primary goals of education in the visual arts is to prepare students to make and support intelligent and sensitive decisions about works of art. In order to make those kinds of decisions students can employ two ways of examining and responding knowledgeably to visual art forms. One of these ways, art criticism, involves them in learning *from* works of art. Another approach is art history, which enables students to learn *about* works of art and the artists who created them.

## The Art History Approach to Learning about Art and Artists

Art historians contend that no work of art can be fully understood unless it is viewed in relation to the circumstances in which it was created. Every artwork is created in a particular place at a particular time in history and to some degree is bound to reflect the prevailing conditions of that time and place. For example, an art history approach to the study of a painting by Rembrandt would include an examination of seventeenth century Holland— the time and place in which that particular artist lived and worked. Adhering to this approach would require that students focus attention on the social, religious, and economic conditions that existed in the republic at that time in history before focusing attention on the painter and his work. All these conditions would have impacted Rembrandt's choice of subject matter, medium, his way of handling materials, and the visual language he chose to use in expressing his ideas and feelings.

Art history, then, involves a study of the visual arts in relation to the times and places from which they sprang. This study will provide students with a richer, broader, and deeper understanding of the specific art objects selected for study and the world as it existed when those art objects were created. However, to determine the significance of the place of a particular work, such as a picture by Rembrandt, involves more than just an examination of the world conditions at the time that artist lived. It also requires a study of what went on in the world *before* and *after* Rembrandt painted his picture. A study of this kind will show students that Rembrandt, like all artists, took into account the works of other artists, selecting some ideas and techniques to use in his own painting while rejecting other ideas and techniques. This is a valuable lesson that students can apply to their own efforts to create art.

Consequently, a historical examination of a painting by Rembrandt would include the identification of any artists who may have influenced his style of painting. The most important of these artists was the Italian painter Caravaggio, whose paintings Rembrandt never saw, but without which his own work would not have taken on certain stylistic innovations. However, to understand Caravaggio, students would have to become acquainted with the artists *he* admired as well as the ones he rejected while arriving at his own revolutionary painting style. Thus, students adhering to an art history approach will find themselves involved in a fascinating learning process not unlike a game of dominoes, in which an entire row of game pieces is seen to collapse by upsetting the first domino in that row. The very last "domino" to fall in this comparison of art history to dominoes would be the very first visual image ever created—perhaps an image scratched on the rough wall of a cave by the very first prehistoric artist.

## The Use of Historical Periods

For convenience, art historians divide the history of art into more or less artificial periods such as Medieval, Renaissance, Baroque, and Rococo. Doing so does no harm as long as students are reminded that the changes in art history identified by these labels, like changes of the seasons, are gradual. Each historical period passes into the next as smoothly as spring passes into summer.

If it can be assumed that an understanding of the present can be illuminated by a study of the past, then a chronological ordering of art history periods can be most helpful. By beginning at the beginning and observing the changes in art created from one year, decade, or century to the next, students will find it easier to understand how the art produced today has its roots in the art produced in the past. If students are to gain an understanding of art history, they should be afforded opportunities to see and learn about art examples from every corner of the world representing every historical period, not just those created by Western artists.

In every art history period students will encounter artists whose works preserve the traditional values of earlier artists, artists who chose to build upon current art trends, and still other artists who opted to explore revolutionary ways of expressing themselves through their art. Art history is filled with the stories of artists who accepted or rejected, endorsed or protested, conformed or reformed, contrasted or destroyed, dreamed of the past or conjured up visions of the future—but every one of those artists did so from the springboard of his or her own time and place, be that tenth-century China or twentieth-century America.

## Art History as a Means of Understanding Each Other

Through art history students learn that a painting, a statue, or a temple is a consequence of how imaginative, sensitive members of any given society viewed and responded to the world around them. Art history also encourages students to regard works of art as more than objects that are pleasing to the eye, more than splendid and original products of human skill and inventiveness. Works of art also represent springboards for learning, revealing how differently people thought and acted at different times and in different geographical locations throughout the long history of humankind. A work of art reveals not only the customs, social habits, architecture, and technical achievements of its time and place; it also reflects the prevailing fears, beliefs, superstitions, desires, and values of people living in different ages at different geographic locations. Art history, then, is a vital part of the history of the human race.

# Art History and Changing Tastes

As they study art history, students will discover that, over time, works of art do not always look the same to the people viewing them. This happens because people from different times and places look at art from different points of view. Cultures vary and change and so do tastes. Take any great artist or any great work of art from a bygone era and note how there have been periods in which that artist or work has been highly regarded, treated with indifference, or even ridiculed. For example, few today would venture a negative judgment of a painting created by Rembrandt, who is universally regarded as one of the greatest artists of all time. Yet, over the years, this Dutch master has not always been understood or appreciated. Indeed, when Italian artists first viewed a painting by Rembrandt they were puzzled and disappointed. They failed to understand why this artist was so highly regarded. His style, they concluded, was most peculiar because it made use of large areas of dark values and made no use of outlines favored by Italian artists.

Students must learn that art is a two-way process involving *both* artist and viewer. If students are to grasp more than the superficial appearance of a work of art, they must be prepared to learn its purpose, its *contemporary* meaning within the society in which it was produced, and its place in the historical process. No work of art is created in a vacuum. If students are to share in the ideas and feelings that contributed to the creation of a work of art, they must recognize the concepts, desires, and expectations of the person expressing those ideas and feelings at a particular point in time. This will result in a richer, broader, deeper understanding of both the artwork and the culture that witnessed its creation.

# The Art History Operations

The study of art history is made easier for students if a plan of action is offered. One such plan makes use of four steps, or operations, that bear the same labels used to describe the four steps used in art criticism. These operations are description, analysis, interpretation, and decision. However, while these operations enable students to gain information from works of art during art criticism, they also are used to help students gather information about those works during art history. Briefly, the four art history operations are:

**Description** During this first operation, students seek to discover when, where, and by whom the work was created. In other words, they determine the period in which the work was created, the place where the artist lived, and, assuming it is known, the name of the artist.

**Analysis** This operation requires students to identify the unique features in a work of art that determine its artistic style. In the visual arts, style has come to mean the personal and unique way in which the artist uses the elements and principles of art to express ideas and feelings. For example, one artist may choose to delineate shapes in his painting by surrounding them with a heavy dark outline. Another painter might ignore the use of an outline and suggest shapes by creating areas of bright hues that contrast with the dull hues surrounding them.

> "Art historians contend that no work of art can be fully understood unless it is viewed in relation to the circumstances in which it was created."

**Interpretation** When interpreting a work of art, students take into account the impact of time and place upon the artist. It is during this operation that they learn that pictures of the same subject painted at the same time but in different geographic locations typically differ in appearance because they reflect different traditions and values. A landscape painted in fifteenth-century Italy will differ dramatically from a landscape painted at the same time in Japan. Moreover, a work of art created in the same country but at different times may also bear few stylistic similarities. A landscape painted by a French artist living and working in the late nineteenth century would have little in common with a landscape done by a French artist living and working at the beginning of the same century.

In an effort to express themselves in visual terms, artists make use of the materials and processes placed in their hands by the circumstances of time and place. Thus, a nineteenth-century African artist might have carved a figure from a piece of wood to serve as a dwelling place for a departed spirit, while a seventeenth-century artist applied his brush to canvas to paint a lifelike portrait of his king. In the spotlight of history, the efforts of both artists are magnified or diminished, honored or dismissed by forces that neither could predict or control but that had little to do with the values the artists sought to express in their work. It is the desire to discover those values that motivates students when interpreting artists' works.

**Decision** The final art history operation requires that students make a decision about the historical importance of a work of art. They will discover that some works are more important than others because they were the first examples of a new, revolutionary style. Others are found to be significant because they are the most accomplished and successful examples of a particular style. As their knowledge and understanding of art grows, students will find themselves liking a great many more works of art than they thought possible at the start. Gradually they will gain confidence in their historical judgments and exercise skill in defending those judgments.

Art history is a fascinating, provocative learning experience affording students the opportunity to travel through time and space. It provides them with access to the inner lives of many kinds of people and offers clues to where we come from and who we are. Finally, art history reveals that artists and their art have succeeded in helping people communicate with each other in a manner we cannot express in any other way.

# Art Criticism

Rosalind Ragans, Ph.D., Associate Professor Emerita, Georgia Southern University

Art criticism is organized discussion about art. The art criticism procedures used in this program were developed by Edmund B. Feldman based on his analysis of the writings of professional art critics. He organized the elaborate procedures followed by critics and summarized them into four steps. The purpose of these four steps is to delay impulse judgments of visual images and to involve the viewer in a complex interaction with the image that can result in a truly aesthetic experience.

Art criticism involves the use of high-level thinking skills. The viewer translates the visual language of the image created by an artist into everyday words. To have a truly aesthetic experience the viewer must go beyond simple identification and recognition to the types of thinking required to analyze, interpret, and judge visual clues.

Anyone can do art criticism. All that is needed are eyes to see the image and a brain to think about what is seen. Art criticism gives a viewer of any age the confidence to discuss a work of art without worrying about what other people have said about it. One does not need to know anything about the artist, the style, or the time when the work was made to get involved with the work. After the steps of art criticism have been followed in a school setting, students are usually so interested in the art that they want to know more about the who, what, where, when, and how of the work. In other words, the students are ready to learn about art history and culture.

## Description

The first step of art criticism is a clue-collecting step. The purpose of this step is to get to know the work as intimately and deeply as one can. All the information from the credit line should be noted. It is important for the viewer to know whether the artwork is 20 × 30 inches or 20 × 30 feet. The medium with which the work is made is also important. Whether a piece of sculpture is modeled with clay or carved from stone affects the viewer's impression. Then the observer names everything that is seen in the image. During description the observer must remain objective. All the descriptive terms must be neutral, value-free words.

## Analysis

This is an advanced form of description. It is also an objective, clue-collecting step. During this stage the viewer studies the elements of art and the principles that have been used to organize those elements. It is during this step that the viewer begins to discover how the artist has organized the formal qualities of the work to create the content or meaning. In this program you will see how the art criticism lesson at the end of each unit is used to reinforce the concepts taught during each unit. Works of art have been selected that will help the student comprehend the artist's use of the specific elements or principles that were introduced in that unit.

## Interpretation

This is the most important part of art criticism. It is during this step that the viewer pulls together all the descriptive and analytical observations to make sense of the work. The viewer makes inferences about the mood, meaning, or message being conveyed by the work. This step goes beyond narration to a generalization about life. The viewer makes guesses, but these ideas must be supported by the clues collected during the first two steps. This can be the most difficult step because it requires imagination and courage. Every interpretation can be different because each is based on the feelings and life experiences of the viewer. No one individual has done or seen exactly the same things as the next person. The viewer may see ideas in a work of art that were never dreamed of by the artist. That is not wrong. It simply means that the work is so powerful that it carries special meanings for everyone.

A good interpretation goes beyond answering "What is happening?" to answering "What does it mean?"

## Decision (Judgment)

This is the step where a professional critic will decide the quality of a work. Is this as good as the rest of the works by this artist? How does it measure up to the works of other artists in the same group? The students who are using this program do not have enough experience to make that level of decision, so the works of art in *Art Connections* have been selected because they have already been judged to be outstanding examples of art.

The students are asked to make personal decisions. There are two levels of judgment to be made. The first is "Do you like the work?" This opinion may be embarrassing for students to share in front of classmates, and it is best left unspoken. No one can ever tell someone else what they should like or dislike.

The second level of judgment is also subjective. We ask the student to decide why the work is successful, and we use aesthetic theories to help each individual make decisions about the work. The three aesthetic theories that we employ are the most common theories: imitationalism/realism, formalism/composition, and emotionalism/expressionism. More than one theory can be used to judge a work of art.

- Some critics think the most important thing about a work of art is the realistic presentations of the subject matter. People with this point of view think that an artwork should imitate life. This theory, called **imitationalism** or **realism,** focuses on realistic representation.
- Other critics think that composition is the most important factor in a work of art. This aesthetic theory, called **formalism** or **composition,** places emphasis on the design qualities, the arrangement of the elements of art using the principles of art.
- **Emotionalism** or **expressionism** is the theory concerned with the content or meaning of the work. This theory requires that a work of art convey a message. It must arouse a response of feelings, moods, or emotions in the viewer.

In this program we provide leading questions to help the teacher and student delve into a work of art by using the steps of art criticism. These are not all the questions that can be addressed in viewing a work, and teachers are encouraged to go beyond what is presented on the pages of these books.

# Meeting National and State Standards for Art Education

Nan Yoshida

*Art Connections* has been carefully designed to help educators meet the standards of state and national art curriculum guidelines.

The *National Standards for Arts Education* are part of Goals 2000, the overarching plan for improving American education. Approved by the United States Congress in 1994, the standards describe what every young American student should know and be able to do in the arts.

In addition to the national standards, individual states have curriculum documents that set forth guidelines and requirements in subject areas. For example, both the *Texas Essential Knowledge and Skills for Art* and the *Visual and Performing Arts Framework for California Public Schools, Kindergarten through Grade Twelve* discuss four components of visual arts education common to most other state guidelines.

Placing the national standards side by side with the Texas and California standards, one can readily see that the documents match in their expectations of what students should know and be able to do in the visual arts.

*Art Connections* has been developed with these national and state expectations in mind. Every lesson in the program was designed to address the components of art education in Aesthetic Perception, Art History and Culture, Creative Expression, and Art Criticism.

## Aesthetic Perception

### (Artistic Perception)

Each lesson begins with Activate Prior Knowledge, which asks students to recall and visualize an image from personal experience that will help them take a purposeful look at the artwork.

Introduce the Art focuses students' attention on specific attributes of the artwork, design elements and principles, underlying structures, and functions. As students answer the questions about the work of art, they develop critical *observation* skills.

Aesthetic Perception directs students to extend their artistic perception to their environment and objects in the environment. The transition is made to use keen visual and tactile perception of formal art objects in everyday life (lifelong learning).

> "In **Art Connections** students are exposed to a variety of types and styles of art from many cultures and historical periods."

## Art History and Culture

### (Cultural Context)

In *Art Connections* students are exposed to a variety of types and styles of art from many cultures and historical periods. Students study art from Africa; Asia; Australia; Europe; and North, Central, and South America. They learn about the role of the artist in societies. They develop appreciation for paintings, drawings, prints, photographs, sculptures, textiles, and architecture. They relate to folk, decorative, functional, and formal arts.

While information about the works of art and the artist is necessarily brief in the *Student Edition,* teachers are encouraged to use the Art History and Culture feature of the *Teacher Edition* and the *Artist Profiles* books to provide students with enriching information about the artists, the periods of art history, and cultural perspectives.

## Creative Expression

### (Art Production)

Creative expression is fundamental to every art lesson. The Practice activity provides a structure for students to apply lesson concepts in meaningful practice. In the Creative Expression activity, students refine their new knowledge and skills by producing original artwork based on their personal visions. The lessons throughout the program introduce a variety of art media and techniques.

## Art Criticism

### (Aesthetic Valuing)

Reflection and self-assessment are inherent in the art-making process. Upon completion of the Creative Expression activity, students

evaluate their own work using the four steps of art criticism: Describe, Analyze, Interpret, and Decide. These four steps of art criticism are a method for making an informed critique of others' artwork as well.

## Arts Integration

In addition to the high priority placed on teaching the visual arts as a unique discipline, both national and state standards recommend the appropriate integration or interrelation of the visual arts with the other arts disciplines of music, dance, and theatre. Toward this goal, every unit in *Art Connections* culminates with a lesson integrating one of these performing arts. In addition, connections are made to music and movement/dance in every lesson of the *Teacher Edition.*

## Curriculum Integration

The *Teacher Edition* has an Art Across the Curriculum section that ties art concepts to other curriculum areas. Every lesson has a connection to Reading/Language Arts, Math, Science, Social Studies, and Technology.

### National Standards for Arts Education © 1994

1. Understand and apply media, techniques, and processes.
2. Use knowledge of structures and functions.
3. Choose and evaluate a range of subject matter, symbols, and ideas.
4. Understand the visual arts in relation to history and cultures.
5. Reflect upon and assess the characteristics and merits of their work and the work of others.
6. Make connections between the visual arts and other disciplines.

# The Development of Children's Art

Rosalind Ragans, Ph.D.

A child's ability to make and understand art develops along with his or her cognitive, social, emotional, and physical development. In 1947 Victor Lowenfeld was the first to identify and label the sequential stages that students move through as they create images. Since then many others have continued to study the development of children's visual images.

Understanding these stages will help you recognize what your students are doing; however, you must also understand that these stages describe untutored progression through the making of images. There are many outside influences on students, and these will show in their work. A well-meaning adult might teach a child to make stick figures, and because they are so easy to make, the child adopts this symbol.

Just as reading levels vary widely within one class, so do art abilities. Just as you teach students to appreciate differences in ability in other subject areas, you must help them understand that not everyone will have the same art abilities at the same time.

There are many different versions of the developmental stages; here we present a three-step version of art development. The stages of artistic development are useful norms that can help you, but they are **not** rules that must be followed.

## The Manipulative Stage

### Ages 2–5 (Grade K)

This has been called the scribble stage, and it is usually seen in children from two to five years old. During the early part of this stage, the child makes random, disordered scribbles. Making art at this stage is such a sensory experience that the child may hold crayons in both hands. Children who have opportunities to scribble produce a wide variety of lines, marks, dots, and shapes. The child who develops a variety of graphic marks during the scribble years will use them to produce complex symbolic drawings as he or she matures. Children who rarely scribble will have a more limited range of expression, and they will need a great deal of encouragement to continue drawing.

As the random scribbles become more controlled, the child starts to pull the marks into circular patterns until a mandala, or rough circle, is created. Rhoda Kellogg, who

studied thousands of children's drawings from all over the world, found that the mandala appears as the final stage between random scribbling and representation. This controlled scribble becomes a named scribble. Expressive concepts develop as children recognize the relationship between their marks and the visual outcome.

## The Symbol-Making Stage

### Ages 4–9 (Grades 1–4)

When a child makes the connection between images and an idea, a shape becomes a symbol. During this stage children develop a series of distinct images that stand for objects in their experiences. These symbols are eventually related to an environment within the drawing. The first representation of a person is a mandala. This can represent anyone the child wants it to be. Although this shape appears to be just a head, it represents the entire person. Soon the child adds a line and two marks, which represent a person with a mouth and two eyes. Then two lines are added to the shape to represent legs, two lines for arms, and a scribble for hair. The child is drawing what he or she knows, not what he or she sees. As children develop from the early symbolic stage into the symbol-making stage, they start to add more details and develop a symbol that includes all the body parts.

At first, space is not a consideration, and the size of symbols in a work is related to importance. Objects and people seem to float. Eventually the child wants to make people and objects stand up and will line things up on the bottom of the paper or on a baseline. Along with a baseline, the child starts to represent the sky with a strip of color across the top of the paper that includes a round symbol with radiating lines for the sun. As far as the child is concerned, the space between the sky and the baseline is air. The sky will not touch the earth until the child develops a more mature sense of perception, usually the result of sensitive art instruction.

Another spatial problem is overlap. Children realize that two objects cannot occupy the same space at the same time, and they avoid overlapping. As the environments they depict become more complex, children may use a bird's-eye view, a foldover view, or multiple views to represent space.

Children in this stage develop their own schema, or image, that resembles an actual object. Once a schema has been invented it will be used over and over. As the child continues to make art, the schema will become more detailed and sophisticated.

Giving a child this age coloring books may lead to self-doubt because of the conflict between the child's schema and the adult image. After coloring a seated dog in a coloring book, the child may become frustrated when his or her own drawing of a dog does not measure up to his or her memory of the adult image. Because children are exposed to so many adult images, many of which have low artistic quality, it is helpful for the teacher to expose children to the many high-quality works of art available in this program.

## The Preadolescent Stage

### Ages 8–13 (Grades 3–8)

Preadolescent children are still naturally inquisitive and creative, but they have learned to be more cautious. They have become very sensitive to peer opinion. They have reached a "crisis of confidence" regarding the images they make. If a work doesn't look exactly the way they think it should, or if it looks childlike, they reject the art product. This is the time when many children become frustrated and stop making art.

This is a critical time in students' visual development. They need to be taught to work slowly and with patience. They need to be taught drawing skills such as perspective and human proportions. They need to master the language of art and the use of design principles. They need the technical skills to master the various media such as painting, printmaking, ceramics, and sculpture.

Students need to see how different artists in the past have solved problems, and to observe what contemporary artists are doing today. Artists solve problems differently, and young people need to be exposed to many different ideas as they try to create their own solutions to visual problems.

The strong art teacher will lead students over this perilous bridge of doubt by gently stretching their minds to help them see more so that they can do more. At every stage in the child's visual development, a strong, understanding teacher can help the child move forward.

# Brain-Based Learning

Jamye Ivey, K–12 Art Supervisor, Dougherty County School System, Georgia

At the end of the school day, teachers often face many unanswered questions concerning the young people whose education is their responsibility. Educators cannot help but wonder why students fail to respond to instructional strategies that were successful in their own experiences. Why is today's student so different?

## Brain Research

Neuroscientists are now able to supply some of the answers that have plagued educators for years. The amazing, constantly changing world of technology has unlocked for researchers a new realm of understanding of the human brain. With the aid of advanced medical techniques and strategies using equipment such as MRI, FMRI, CAT, and PET scans, the working brain can be observed. Translating these new and often startling medical findings into the educational arena has provided the classroom teacher with practical methodologies and a better understanding of how, why, and when students learn best.

The brain is the most powerful organ in the body. Researchers have discovered that today's brains grow better in the real world than in artificial learning environments. Students must be able to connect their learning to previous experience in order for new learning to occur. For years teachers have designed and taught units with the activities culminating in field trips. When we consider these recent findings, we realize this procedure should be reversed. The field trip provides the student relevance that would facilitate learning. Without a related experience in the memory bank of past experiences, the learner finds no significance in the new material.

It is also important to note that synapses in the brain are formed, strengthened, and maintained by interaction with experience. The stronger the synapses, the faster the messaging travels and the greater the number of neural pathways that are created in the brain. This enables a person to be capable of creating more flexible thought processing and better memory.

Research confirms that environments shape brains. Teachers should create an environment that provides the best opportunities for this generation of young people to learn. Students of today need to move, talk, and touch more than previous learners did. Eric Jensen explains that the part of the brain that processes movement is the same part that processes learning. Thus, there needs to be movement in the classroom.

Today, we know that lecturing is the poorest way to present new learning. Only about fifty percent of the audience is actively listening in any given oral presentation. Students learn the most at the beginning of a presentation, the second-most at the end, and the least in the middle. Learners need breaks during teacher talk sessions. The attention span of a preadolescent is ten to twelve minutes.

This generation of children has more trouble organizing thoughts and learns on a more global scale. Expect students to want to understand the big picture before dealing with the details. One way to accomplish this is to let the class spend a few minutes looking through the whole chapter before focusing on the first page.

We know now that students cannot learn if they feel threatened or stressed. If a teacher shouts at a student, it takes fifteen minutes for the adrenaline levels to subside in all the students in the class. The glucose needed for cognitive functioning is redirected to combat stress, so all learning is governed to some extent by emotions. The constant threat of failure needs to be removed and recognition should be placed on individual performance, experience, and interest. Pressure, tension, and stress slow down or eliminate learning.

## Brain-Based Learning and the Arts

Art teachers are known for using creative methods to capture the imaginations of their students. Need, novelty, meaning, and emotion are four ways to gain a student's attention, and using humor during instruction increases attention by fifty percent. A happy classroom is a more brain-compatible classroom.

The arts are an important part of effective teaching and an essential component of brain-compatible instruction. There is evidence that art-making has been around for over one million years. Brain research documents the arts as basic to the brain. Every culture in human history has one common thread: all had the arts. Stable art, music, and dance experiences not only enhance the aesthetic life of the learner, but they also provide important activity for the growing neurological system.

For both teacher and student, the most encouraging summation from recent research is that we continue to grow brain cells regardless of our age. Noted neuroscientist

Marion Diamond explains that it is best to keep the brain curious and active. In her opinion the most significant finding of her career has been that the brain can learn at any age. Be a lifelong learner and engage in physical activities, which also helps build brain cells. Stay curious and stay active. How affirming this is for art educators because the successful teaching of art daily demands both creative curiosity and physical endurance.

## References

Sousa, David A. (2002). *How the Brain Learns, Second Edition.* Corwin Press.

Sylwester, Robert (1995). *A Celebration of Neurons, an Educator's Guide to the Brain.* Alexandria, VA: Association for Supervision and Curriculum Development.

Eric Jensen (2001). *Arts With the Brain in Mind.* Alexandria, VA: Association for Supervision and Curriculum Development.

Sprenger, Marilee (1999). *Learning & Memory-The Brain in Action.* Alexandria, VA: Association for Supervision and Curriculum Development.

Armstrong, Thomas (1987). *In Their Own Way.* G.P. Putnam's Sons.

Armstrong, Thomas (1991). *Awakening Your Child's Natural Genius.* G.P. Putnam's Sons.

# Classroom Management and Motivation Strategies for Teaching Elementary Art

Bunyan Morris, Art Teacher, Effingham County School System, Georgia

While motivating students to express themselves visually through creative means, the elementary art teacher is challenged with the task of maintaining proper classroom management. The purpose of this article is to provide some practical methods of motivating creative thought and action under the guidance of successful classroom management. Combine these methods with your own to give students the best learning experience possible.

**Be Prepared.** Begin the lesson excited and ready. Students will pick up on your mood the moment they walk into the room. If you set the tone at the beginning and grasp immediate control, it will be much easier to keep it throughout the lesson. It is important to have art prints and demonstration materials ready and in place for the initial focus. Practice an activity before demonstrating it if it is the first time that it has been taught. Something might happen that could not be foreseen; prepare for the best and the worst. Also, it might be a good idea to practice a concept or an activity that has not been taught in a long time. Even classroom veterans forget things.

**Focus.** For the initial focus of the lesson, gather the students into a group on the floor, in chairs, or on benches in an area of the room that is ready for discussion and demonstration. By gathering the students into a compact group, it is easier to make eye contact and to keep the attention of all learners. If there is no room for a separate demonstration and discussion spot, gather the tables or desks into a closer group so that no one is "out of reach."

**Introduce the Art.** Always introduce a lesson with a work of art that relates to what the students will be learning. Students get excited playing detective. Finding clues and ideas in a painting or sculpture allows them to make their own interpretations and assessments about art. They will in turn learn to apply this to their own work. The students don't have to know that this activity has a lofty term called *art criticism* to gain from its purpose. Encouraging them to ask questions and share ideas about a master work will give the students motivation and fresh ideas to take into the Creative Expression portion of the lesson.

**Moving to Art Production.** Always control the manner in which students move to the Creative Expression area from the Demonstration/Discussion center. Release students in a manner that will keep order but not quell their enthusiasm about the lesson. Use positive reinforcement by complimenting those who are sitting quietly, and send them first. It will not take long for the others to catch on. After time most of the students will become conditioned to this expectation. Even if they've been involved in a lively discussion, they will automatically become settled as this transitional period approaches.

**Classroom Design.** Not only should the students be orderly, but the classroom must also be organized and conducive to the movement of the teacher and students. The Creative Expression stations should have enough space between them for the teacher to reach every student. There should be enough space in traffic areas for student movement. Children need easy access to supply shelves and sinks, and should be able to move from one Creative Expression station to another unencumbered. The supplies should be organized on leveled shelves so that the students will return them to their proper places. If the teacher keeps the room and supplies organized, hopefully the students will too.

As well as keeping the room and supplies organized, the rest of the room should be visually pleasing. Display student art with master prints. This builds self-esteem. When possible, display every child's work. Make learning centers organized and interesting. Keep interesting objects around the room for visual reference. These objects might include plants, pottery, old bottles, discarded sports equipment, old toys, or anything that might capture the attention and interest of your students. Use these objects in still lifes and as objects of visual reference for lines, shapes, and other elements and principles of art.

When moving about the room assisting students, it is important to keep the senses alive and be aware of what is happening with the other students. See and hear what they think you can't.

**Closing the Lesson.** Normally one should try to close the class with a review of the lesson's objectives. This should be short and interesting. This is also the time to reward the students for good behavior. The art teacher must set the criteria for earning the award. Do not give the award if it is not earned. Of course, the students must be aware of the opportunity to earn an award ahead of time.

One method that works is to award the students with a "Super Behavior Card." This is simply a colorful card that can be given to the class to take back to their classroom teacher for having good behavior during art. This requires the cooperation of the classroom teacher to award the students in some manner for collecting a certain number of Super Behavior Cards. Awards might include a popcorn party or extra time at recess. If the classroom teacher is unwilling, you will have to provide the award in your class. Awarding of the Super Behavior Card can be coordinated with cleanup at the end of the period. Choose one student at the table who cleans up most thoroughly and quietly to carry the Super Behavior Card back to the classroom teacher. The students at each table will work together to earn the Super Behavior Card.

Hopefully these ideas and suggestions will reduce the challenge of maintaining classroom control and motivating students. The individual teacher must decide what works best for each situation. All of the motivation and management techniques suggested here have been tried and have been proven to work. Combined with each teacher's individual strategies, they will increase the probability of success in the art classroom.

## A Sampling of Art Games for Home or School

*Art Lotto: National Gallery of Art.* Safari Limited, Miami, Florida.

*ARTDECK.* Aristoplay, Ann Arbor, Michigan.

*The Fine Art Game.* Piatnik, Wiener Spielkartenfabrik, Ferd. PIATNIK & Söhne.

*Where Art Thou?* WJ Fantasy, Inc., Bridgeport, Connecticut.

# Art Instruction for Students with Disabilities

Mandy Yeager, Art Educator, Ph.D. Student, The University of North Texas, Denton, Texas

Art education empowers all students to look at, respond to, create, and enjoy works of art. Students who are disabled are no exception to this privilege. The arts have often been understood as an equalizing force in the education of students with disabilities; often these students experience discrimination from peers and adults because of their disability. This discrimination often manifests itself in avoidance of or lowered expectations for these students. Stereotypes of persons with disabilities cast them as helpless, unintelligent, dangerous, or contemptible. These stereotypes are maintained by a lack of knowledge or personal experiences with persons who are disabled.

The visual arts, because they use images to express ideas about the human experience, play a vital role in challenging and eliminating many of these stereotypes. The current emphasis of art education upon visual literacy allows students to examine and transform stereotypes that exist in the media regarding all types of differences (including age, race, class, gender, and ability). Artists throughout time have engaged in this process of recording and seeking to transform societal injustices through visual imagery.

The benefits of art for students with disabilities cannot be underestimated. The skills gained in visual arts often result in increased confidence and ability in other academic subjects. Arts-based learning is often effective because of the ways it engages the multiple senses and abilities of students.

The arts also give students opportunities to explore, express, and celebrate their identities. Teachers who include the work of artists with disabilities in their art curriculum help all students realize that disability is a part of the human experience and does not prevent anyone from being a creator of art.

## Resources to Assist Art Educators

The first step to developing competence is to develop an understanding of the child's disability. There are a number of resources to assist the art teacher in this regard.

### Resources at the School Level

Resources at the school level include special-education staff and related service providers who have contact with the child such as occupational and physical therapists. All of these staff members can provide the art teacher with insight into the child's learning strengths and needs and his or her physical and emotional development. They can also provide helpful suggestions for how a particular art medium or tool can be made accessible to a particular student.

Another valuable resource for the art teacher is the student's Individualized Education Plan (IEP). This plan exists for every student receiving special education services and provides information about learning styles, needs, and modifications. The *Individuals with Disabilities Education Act* (IDEA) requires that all regular education teachers of students with disabilities have access to the child's IEP and are provided support in implementing modifications to the general curriculum.

Art educators can design their art curricula to meet students' annual IEP goals. For instance, art criticism activities have the potential to enhance students' expressive language skills. Cooperative learning activities such as mural painting can foster social skills. Art production often produces self-efficacy in students with disabilities as they learn to trust their ability to achieve success. Art teachers who engage in this process of reviewing a child's IEP and delineating the ways that art curricula can address annual goals become more confident in their abilities to successfully instruct students with disabilities.

## Art Education and Disability Organizations

VSA arts has been designated by the U.S. Congress as the National Coordinating Agency of Arts in Learning for Persons with Disabilities. The agency fulfills this role through a vast network of state affiliates. VSA arts produces art and disability awareness curricula and showcases the work of students with disabilities by regularly sponsoring national calls for art. It also provides access to the work of artists with disabilities.

The Special Needs Interest Group of the National Art Education Association (NAEA) meets annually at the NAEA convention to discuss best practices in art education and disability. This group publishes a column in the bimonthly publication *NAEA News*.

## Adapting the Art Experience for Students with Disabilities

It is often necessary to adapt some aspect of the art experience for students with disabilities. Adaptations ensure that learning is accessible to every child; as such, adaptation is a principle of good instruction.

Adapting the art experience is essentially a creative activity, as many different combinations of students, media, and processes coalesce in one semester of art instruction. Accordingly, effective adaptations are individualized and begin with knowledge of a particular student's learning strengths and needs. Teachers may choose to adapt art media, instructional strategies, and/or physical space, depending upon the situation. This process of adaptation often begins by observation of students in an introductory art-making experience. If a student is having difficulty with an art task, try to determine the source of the difficulty. Consult with other school staff and use some of the resources listed below to determine what is most appropriate for the student and situation.

The adaptations accompanying every lesson in this text are provided as suggestions only, because learning needs and strengths vary with each child, medium, and project. It is hoped that art educators, upon reading this article, will feel equipped to utilize available resources to design and implement empowering learning experiences for all students.

### Resources

**Disability Education Organizations**

National Dissemination Center for Children with Disabilities (NICHCY), www.nichy.org/index.html

The Council for Exceptional Children, www.cec.sped.org/

ERIC Clearinghouse on Disability and Gifted Education, http://ericec.org

**Art and Disability Organizations and Resources**

VSA arts, www.vsarts.org

Art, Disability and Expression Online Exhibit, www.vsarts.org/showcase/exhibits/disability/index.html

The National Art Education Association Special Needs Interest Group

EDGE: Education for Disability and Gender Equity, www.disabilityhistory.org/dwa/edge/curriculum/index-netscape.htm

National Arts and Disability Center (NADC), http://nadc.ucla.edu/

# Safe Use of Art Materials

Mary Ann Boykin, Director, The Art School for Children and Young Adults
University of Houston—Clear Lake, Texas

Elementary art teachers need to be aware of safety issues that can affect the well-being of the children they teach, as well as themselves. Follow the guidelines established by the Center for Safety in the Arts to assure that neither students nor teachers are injured by the unsafe use of art materials.

Elementary teachers should do two things to prevent problems. The first is to keep all toxic and hazardous substances out of the classroom. The second is to know how to use the materials safely, because any materials can become hazardous when used inappropriately.

## Toxic Substances

A toxic substance is defined by the Center for Occupational Hazards as "a poison which can damage your body's organ systems when you are overexposed to it." This harm can be immediate or can be the result of repeated exposure over time. Toxic substances can enter the body in three ways:

1. absorption through the skin
2. inhalation through the nose or mouth
3. ingestion through eating or drinking in the area where toxic materials are being used

It is up to the teacher to make sure toxic substances do not enter the classroom and that all materials are used safely to avoid problems.

Pregnant women and those who are nursing must be especially careful to prevent exposure to toxic substances. Fumes, sprays, dusts, and powders present a real hazard to the fetus, can be transferred to the infant through the mother's milk, and can be carried home to the infant or young child through dusts and residue picked up by clothing and hair. The safe path is to completely avoid exposure to any toxin by carefully reading labels and applying common sense to the situation. For example, if you plan to mix powdered tempera paint or work with chalks or clay, the safe method would include use of a respirator mask, which would prevent inhalation of these substances.

## Children and Safe Art Materials

Preschool and elementary children are particularly vulnerable to unsafe art materials for a variety of reasons. Their lower body weight allows a toxic substance to become more concentrated in their bodies. Because children have a more rapid metabolism than adults, toxic substances are more quickly absorbed into their bodies. Children also tend to have more hand-to-mouth contact than adults, which allows ingestion of toxic materials. Furthermore, children are easily distracted from safety warnings regarding materials as they become involved in the art process. The tendency of children to have cuts and scratches also allows for ready entry of toxins into their bodies.

## What the Labels Mean

Since 1990 our government has required the labeling of all hazardous materials. Any product labeled as hazardous is totally inappropriate for the elementary school. Safe art materials carry the statement that the material "Conforms to ASTMD-4236." A simple "nontoxic" statement on a product is not adequate.

The Arts and Crafts Materials Institute developed a voluntary program to provide a safe standard for materials used by children. Products bearing the labels AP (Approved Product) or CP (Certified Product) have been tested by toxicologists in major universities and have been deemed safe for children to use. The HL (Health Label) on art products indicates that these products are appropriate to use with children 12 years old or older under the supervision of an art teacher. Products with HL labels are not safe for elementary children.

## Safe Art Materials

The following are guidelines for choosing and using basic art materials in a safe manner.

### Drawing Materials

- Use only water-soluble AP- or CP-designated markers. Permanent markers are extremely dangerous and can cause lung and liver damage if inhaled. Never use permanent markers in the elementary classroom.
- Do not use scented markers. This teaches children to sniff or smell materials.
- Use only dustless chalk. The amount of dust created in a classroom by twenty children wiping and blowing chalk can be irritating to those who suffer from allergies, asthma, and other respiratory problems.
- Use oil pastels; the colors are richer than crayons and the satisfaction is greater! Crayons should also bear the AP or CP label to ensure that no lead is present in these materials.

### Painting Materials

- Use only liquid tempera and/or watercolor paints. If you must use powdered tempera paints, mix these outside and have the paints ready before children enter the classroom. Avoid inhaling the powders of tempera paints.
- Do not use any spray paints or fixatives. These are extremely dangerous.

### Printmaking Materials

- Use only water-soluble printers' inks. Do not use any solvent-based inks.
- Use pencils to carve into unused foam trays for printing blocks. Do not use mat knives or other sharp instruments.

### Collage Materials

- Sharp scissors should not be used by young children; blunt points are safe. Fourth- and fifth-graders may use rounded points with teacher supervision.
- Use only school paste or white glue for adhering papers. Do not use rubber cement unless it bears the AP or CP label. Do not use any solvent-based glues.

### Sculpture and Three-Dimensional Materials

- Use premixed, moist clay for sculpture and pottery. Do not allow students to take home any unfired clay.
- Remind students to wash their hands thoroughly after using clay. The residual dust can be harmful and irritating if inhaled.
- Paint clay pieces with tempera or watercolor paints. Do not use glazes. Some have the approved labels, but they are not recommended for elementary use.
- Use pencils, craft sticks, or other blunt tools to carve clay. Soapstone should not be used for carving in a closed environment.
- Read labels carefully on pastes used for papier-mâché, because some pastes contain pesticides or preservatives that are extremely harmful.

### Stitchery, Weaving, and Fiber Materials

- Use blunt plastic needles and loosely woven fabrics such as burlap for stitchery. Blunt metal tapestry needles are safe if their use is supervised.
- Young children will have trouble cutting fabric and yarn with their scissors. Precut lengths of fabric and yarn prior to introducing a task.

# The Community as a Resource for Art Materials

**Willis "Bing" Davis, Associate Professor Emeritus, Central State University, Ohio**
**President and Founder of SHANGO: The Center for the Study of African American Art & Culture**

Ingenuity, resourcefulness, and creative survival have always been important to most successful art and classroom teachers when it comes to providing meaningful arts experiences for students. We are known as collectors who almost never throw anything away. Some art and classroom teachers will need to acquire the skill of always being on the lookout for resources, materials, and supplies that can supplement art materials in the classroom. It can be fun; plus, it stimulates the imagination and creative impulse. This is also a great way to build bridges and advocates for arts education.

Think of all the things you use in the art room. How many can be found locally? Safe, usable materials or supplies that can be found free or reduced in price leave more of the art budget to buy the things that have to be purchased. There are different forms of searching for inexpensive and free materials for art activities. The following are a few tried and proven ways to acquire materials, supplies, and resources that can be used for art and other educational activities.

## Materials in the School Building

- Leftover wood or metal from a shop class
- Clean, empty food containers from the food-service area
- Cardboard tubes from the food-service area or copy machine
- Scrap paper from copy machines

## Annual Open-House Night Resources

Open house is a great time to post a small list of hand tools needed for the art program. You would be surprised by how many extra hammers, pliers, screwdrivers, bent forks, and so on are in garages and basements. Many parents or caregivers also work at places that have by-products that could supplement the art materials in the art program.

## Local Business Material Sources

- *Wood* Lumberyards are usually willing to let teachers collect boxes of scrap wood for art production. Some lumberyards will even let you leave a box with your school's name on it.
- *Wallpaper* Ask for discontinued wallpaper design sample books from paint stores.
- *Paper* Large quantities of damaged paper may be available from local paper or paper distribution companies.

> "Many local service organizations have an interest and commitment to youth and the arts."

## Community Resources

- Many communities participate in the popular "Take a Child to Work" programs that allow children to see and experience where their parents or caregivers work. Almost every school also has a career day when many professional individuals visit schools to talk to students about potential careers. Both programs put schools, students, and teachers into direct contact with local businesses.
- Teachers may find that companies with national headquarters in their communities often have a strong commitment to those communities and their educational systems. Teachers can assist these companies in reaching their community commitment goals by suggesting ways to assist the school art program. Local businesses may want to sponsor the visit of a local artist or donate materials.
- Many local service organizations have an interest and commitment to youth and the arts. They often look for art and cultural events and activities to which they can

contribute. Find out how they want to contribute and help them reach their goal. These events could be funding an exhibit, hosting an art reception, donating materials and supplies, framing student artwork for display in the hallways, sponsoring a local or major art field trip, and so on.

## Artist Resources

- Local and regional emerging artists live in every community and can make meaningful contributions to the school art program. Artists from the community or region offer a "realness" to the program from knowing and living in the area.
- Some artists do a good job at demonstrating, some do a good slide lecture, some are more effective in large or small groups, some do great critique sessions, and some may be better mentoring one-on-one. Each individual teacher or school district can develop an annotated artist directory listing the artists' strong points for reference.
- Most communities also have one or more local arts groups or arts organizations that can assist schools in identifying and securing the services of local artists. A local arts group may be willing to do a series of Member Art Demos over the course of the year in your school.
- Another great source of local and regional artists can be found in the colleges and universities in your area. The college or university art program can show your students some of the quality art teachers students might be working with in the future. This is a great source of judges for student competitions.

## Art Agencies at Local and State Levels

While everyone is aware of the existence of the National Endowment for the Arts in Washington, D.C., many may not be aware that there are state arts agencies and many community-based arts councils that can be an important resource for your art program. Find ways to let everyone in the community help your art program to be the best it can be.

# Displaying Students' Art

Jackie Ellett

"My picture is hanging in the hall!" exclaims an excited second-grader. Yes, having one's work displayed is exciting. When you display a child's artwork, you are communicating two things to that child: you value what he or she has created *and* you value the child.

## Why Display Students' Art?

Students are intrigued by the work their peers produce and are eager to join in any discussion that arises from the shared experiences of the work. They often compare what they have created to the work made by their peers. A natural aesthetic experience occurs, and questions and comparisons arise. These are either verbalized or internalized, depending on the circumstance of the viewing. "Why did Erin paint that flower large and the others small?" "I like the details of the seeds that Galvin added to his painting; I'll do more details next time." These are examples of questions, comments, or thoughts that may arise when students are viewing a display. Not only do displays allow students to appreciate their completed projects, but they also allow students to aspire to better art endeavors.

A class display allows students the opportunity to stand back and critique their work. A teacher-led critique is best. Students are able to evaluate their work, gain insight into things they may not have thought about, and may learn a new solution to a problem they have encountered. Discussing their works as you would a fine-art print validates the importance of what they have created. Art is so personal that a discussion can become quite insightful.

Preschool and early elementary-aged students are eager to take their works of art home to show their parents what they have created. You should ask permission of all students to display their work. By asking permission you are showing respect for their work, and for those students as individuals.

Displays are also a good way to show administrators, parents, and the community what students are learning.

## Where to Display Students' Art

Many art educators believe that the farther away from the classroom the display, the more selective the images need to be. In the classroom, every student's art may be displayed.

This area can be controlled by the teacher, students, or both. Students can be allowed to change their own work when they decide to.

Outside of the classroom there is usually an assigned area for each class to display its work. Bulletin boards made of composition board are the most desirable of all surfaces for two-dimensional art. Artwork is easily attached using staples, and the walls are protected from any damage.

Setting up a school gallery of permanent or rotating student art is wonderful for promoting the art program within a school. This should be housed in a high-traffic area where parents, administrators, and visitors can view students' art. In "Leadership and the Elementary Art Specialist: Twenty Ways to Improve Your Program's Position in the Educational System," Phillip Dunn recommends establishing a "Principal's Permanent Art Collection." Having a gallery within the school with professionally matted and framed student art communicates that students' works and the art program are valued. In an era where budget cuts are customary, promoting the work of students is very important to the survival of art programs.

Displays in local businesses, civic centers, or art centers help educate the public about the work being done within their schools. These exhibits contain a mix of student art that has gone through a selection process. Depending on the guidelines and formality of the display, the works can be mounted, matted, or framed, with three-dimensional works displayed in sculpture cases or on sculpture stands.

## How to Display Students' Art

Student art can be displayed in a variety of ways. Some teachers take digital photos of their students in the process of creating a work of art and critiquing their work, and then take a photo of the finished art itself. These images can be posted on a school Web site with descriptions of the activity. Digital images are sometimes used as screen savers on the school's computer system and highlighted on closed-circuit TVs in the classrooms. The most common method of display, however, is the bulletin board. These have evolved from simple displays to elaborate descriptions of the process and documentation of student learning. Teacher-focused bulletin boards have given way to student-focused displays that often include student reflections

and interpretations. Including descriptions of the process and background information adds to better understanding of the learning that has taken place.

Two-dimensional works of art should be mounted on larger contrasting or neutral-toned paper. The top and sides are usually of equal width with the bottom larger, unless the work is square, in which case all four sides are equal in width. When matting art, a two- to three-inch mat is standard, with the bottom being an inch wider than the top and sides. The mat acts as a resting place, so when arranging mounted or matted art, the works should not overlap.

A sheet of butcher paper or bulletin-board paper can be attached to a wall to define a display area and unify the works of art. Poster board or construction paper cut wider on all sides than the largest paper used by a class can be attached to the wall as an area for mounting individual students' work. Glue a clothespin to the top of the mounted paper so students can easily change their artwork. The background papers are usually in neutral colors, although primary colors may be used in classrooms for younger children. Each background paper is individually identified by placing the child's name in large print on a label.

Three-dimensional works look best in sculpture cases or on sculpture stands. Not every school can afford these. Arranging sturdy boxes of varying heights and covering them with complementary cloths allow sculptures to be equally viewed. If sculptures are of varying sizes, the largest should always be placed toward the back and the small works in front. Arranging works in odd numbers creates interest as well.

Mobiles and kites are best displayed from the ceiling. Make certain that all materials are well attached and that the items hung from the ceiling are secure so they do not fall or set off sensor alarms. As with all displays, it is important to know your school's policies about the types of adhesives allowed. Hot glue has a tendency to peel paint, low-temperature glue guns may not work on some surfaces, and double-sided tape can leave a residue. Humidity and the wall's surface both affect what will and will not work. Reusable tacky putty sticks to most surfaces and leaves few marks.

Displays do much to enhance and rejuvenate students' spirits and allow students to communicate in a way that is neither mathematical nor verbal. The art that students make is very personal and deserves careful attention when being displayed.

# Art Assessments

Assessment in art can be problematic for a variety of reasons. Many educators are reluctant to evaluate a student's creative expression as good or bad. Because there are often no right or wrong answers, students and their parents could challenge a teacher's subjective opinion of a work if it is reflected in a letter grade. Furthermore, many teachers without a strong art background do not feel qualified to grade student artwork. In addition, teachers do not want to discourage creative expression by giving a low grade or an undeserved grade. Many people also often feel that talented students have the advantage in art class and that students should not be evaluated on how talented they are, but rather on how much effort they put into their work and how much progress they make.

All of these assessment difficulties stem from the focus on art production in the art classroom, rather than a reflection of art history and culture, aesthetics, or art criticism. A broader focus in the art classroom and a variety of assessment options may help in more effective art assessment.

## Assessment of Lesson Objectives

Instead of subjective opinions of whether or not one likes a student's artwork, students can be evaluated on whether or not they meet the art lesson objectives or demonstrate the knowledge and skills introduced in the lesson. In a quality art program, there are objectives for aesthetic perception, art history, and art criticism, as well as for demonstrating understanding of the elements and principles of art in art production.

In *Art Connections,* every lesson has four clear, measurable objectives. At the end of each lesson, a rubric provides evaluation criteria for each objective.

## Art Production: Evaluating Student Artwork

Art teachers frequently evaluate student artwork on the basis of how well it reflects the elements and principles of art that are being stressed in the lesson and how well the student meets the criteria for the artwork. Some teachers can construct rubrics or standards for the artwork beforehand and tell students how their work will be evaluated at the time it is assigned. Other teachers use written or mental checklists of their standards as they look at student artwork. Teachers may use this form of evaluation as an opportunity to discuss the work with a student and find out whether the student thought he or she met the objectives for the artwork.

In *Art Connections,* teachers can also use the Assessment Masters in the *Assessment* book to get an idea of whether a student understands the elements or principle of art for a lesson.

## Art Criticism and Aesthetic Perception: Self- and Peer-Assessment

The four-step process of art criticism (Describe, Analyze, Interpret, Decide) provides a procedure that students can use to objectively study their own art products, as well as the works of others. The sequential steps of art criticism are similar to those used in the scientific method. During the first two steps, Describe and Analyze, students are asked to collect data objectively. During the third step, Interpret, students speculate about the meaning of the work based on the data collected: they make a hypothesis about the idea, emotion, or mood expressed by the artist. During the fourth step, Decide, students offer their aesthetic judgment about the work of art. The sequential procedures in art criticism force students to postpone judgment while becoming immersed in the image. It forces them to have a fully funded visual experience before drawing conclusions about a work.

*Art Connections* includes art criticism questions for every Creative Expression activity. Additionally, the Aesthetic Perception feature in every lesson of the *Student Edition* provides students with an opportunity to evaluate their developing aesthetic perception.

## Art History and Culture

Art is a visual record of history and diverse cultures. The goals for elementary art education are that students understand and appreciate different historical periods, cultures, and artistic styles and develop respect for the traditions and contributions of diverse societies.

In *Art Connections* every lesson introduces a work of art from a particular culture, time, and style. In the Introduce the Art strategies, teachers are encouraged to compare, contrast, and share the Art History and Culture information as well as the information provided in *Artist Profiles* to help students develop an understanding of the visual arts in relation to history and cultures. Through discussion and elements in students' own artwork, teachers can evaluate students' awareness in this area.

## Portfolio Assessment

Art educators could claim to have inspired the growing use of portfolio assessment in other subject areas. Many art teachers collect the best examples of a student's work and look at the progress over time. They display it and discuss it with students and parents. Student art journals with ideas, drawings, and sketches also provide an opportunity for portfolio assessment.

In *Art Connections* students are encouraged to keep their best work in a Student Portfolio and to maintain an Art Journal. Reminders of these types of portfolio assessments appear in the *Teacher Edition.*

## Performance Assessment

Unlike other subject areas, art education has a long tradition of performance assessment. In art class students make things to demonstrate what they can do. In quality art programs, teachers use performance descriptions not only for art production, but also for art criticism, art history and culture, and aesthetic perception to aid them in evaluating student demonstrations of their knowledge and skills in art.

In *Art Connections,* every work of art a student produces can be considered for performance assessment of the lesson concept. Performance assessments can also involve discussions about the works of art to introduce the lesson concept and art criticism questions.

Art not only enables teachers to evaluate student knowledge and skills in art each year, but it also provides a wonderful opportunity to assess students' growth and development over time. Students and parents are often reluctant to discard artwork and fondly review it from time to time to see how children's ideas and skills have changed. Schools often keep examples of student artwork in student portfolios from year to year.

A thoughtful and fair art assessment program enables teachers to really see how much their students are capable of accomplishing.

# Art and Cross-Curricular Connections

Tina Farrell

The study and production of artwork enhances learning in all areas of the curriculum. When teachers and students connect art to other subjects, learning occurs in the natural and interrelated way that it exists in the real world. We know from experience that learning is most meaningful when it is interconnected, not isolated. Therefore, making the natural connections that exist within each discipline of study, art including, enhances total understanding and brings meaning to fragmented information.

Below are a few of the ways that art education can impact the study of other subjects.

***Reading/Language Arts*** In the viewing and analysis of a work of art, students develop oral and written communication skills. Teachers can enhance the language process by writing art terms and concepts on the board, having students generate lists of adjectives and adverbs to describe works of art, encouraging reflective inquiry into art, having students read about art and artists, and having students use works of art as stimuli for all forms of writing.

***Mathematics*** Mathematics concepts are enhanced through art. When math concepts are presented or expressed in a visual or manipulative manner, students can more easily grasp them. The comparison and development of shapes and forms, visual-spatial relationships, measurement, proportion, estimation, and grids and graphs, for example, all are best explained through art.

> "We know from experience that learning is most meaningful when it is interconnected—not isolated."

***Science*** In the art-making process, children learn that multiple ways to solve problems exist. They learn to discover, imagine, try new materials and techniques, experiment, develop and test hypotheses, and observe and record visual data. These are many of the skills, objectives, and habits of mind taught in science.

***Social Studies*** The history of the world is reflected in the functional and aesthetic works of art produced by the peoples of the world. Children can gain great insights about near and distant cultures through the study of art, artifacts, and architecture.

***The Arts*** The arts all complement each other in the skills, elements, principles, and beliefs that are emphasized in each one. Each discipline presents a unique way to express ideas and transform emotions into song, dance, interactions, words, or images. Visual artists research, develop rough drafts (sketches), plan, develop ideas, produce completed visual ideas, and sign and title their works. These are the processes that authors, writers, dancers, composers, actors, and poets also employ.

***Life Skills*** In art, children develop craftsmanship, self-discipline, dedication to a task, skills for working both individually and cooperatively, and pride in one's work. These skills are necessary for success in all areas of their lives.

***Critical-Thinking Skills*** Studying the visual arts develops higher-level thinking skills as studenst analyze, compare, interpret, synthesize, and make inferences and judgments about works of art.

Art is a great integrating subject because art, first and foremost, is a form of human communication. Art is one of the first forms of communication for children. Children often express complex ideas through visual symbols that represent their beginning language systems. Art is a vehicle for children to learn about the world around them and to organize the information in a comprehensive format. As young children draw, they take textures, shapes, and colors from a complex world and form them into coherent visual images. This visual cognition, a powerful way for children to process information, is the basis for learning in and through art.

## A Sampling of Art Program Resources for Schools

*The California Arts Project*
(http://www.ucop.edu/tcap/aeol.html)
*Getty Education Institute for the Arts*
(http://www.artsednet.getty.edu)
*The Kennedy Center ArtsEdge*
(http://artsedge.kennedy-center.org)

*The Metropolitan Museum of Art*
(http://www.metmuseum.org/explore/index.asp)
*The Educator's Reference Desk*
(http://www.eduref.org/cgi-bin/res.cgi/Subjects/Arts)

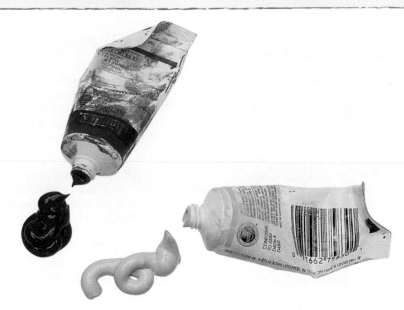

# Integrating the Four Art Forms

**Susan Cambigue-Tracey, Education Division, The Music Center of Los Angeles County**

Albert Einstein said, "Imagination is more important than knowledge." Without exercising the imagination, knowledge is stored in the individual containers of the mind, but connections are not made. When students are taught to use the elements, skills, and content of the visual and performing arts the possibilities for synthesizing and applying what they know are multiplied. Teachers need to ensure that imagination and creativity are always nourishing the roots of learning.

The importance of artistic activity for all students goes beyond the intrinsic value of each art form in itself. Real arts investigation requires the rigor of being able to focus, make decisions, develop discipline, promote originality, and undertake research, study, and practice. Helping students to experience new ways of thinking and seeing allows them to construct personal meaning from what they experience and to build confidence and motivation.

Each art form is a discrete discipline with its own elements, vocabulary, and strategies. However, it is interesting to see connections among them where there are fundamental concepts shared across the arts and other subjects. For example, lines in art are the marks used to create images. Line in dance is the path of gestures and traveling movements, as well as body design. Line in music is a melody and also the lyrics of a song, while lines in theatre are the words that the actors speak.

A common core of knowledge is built through the arts. The principles of visual art, such as emphasis, variety, harmony, unity, and contrast, are the underlying principles used to creating anything—an architectural structure, a musical composition, a piece of literature, a dance, or a play.

It is easy to find ways to integrate one or more of the art forms and still make connections that are viable and authentic. For example, when viewing and discussing a work of art from a particular time period or culture, select music from that same time period or culture. Aztec art will have more relevance when Aztec-inspired music is played or students can view an Aztec dance and see the colors and design of the costumes. A style of music might also inspire art. Matisse did a jazz series that begs for jazz music and dance. Students can then see and hear the structural and improvisational aspects of this style in three different art forms.

When viewing or painting family scenes in art, challenge students to think of family activities that can be portrayed in a tableau, or live,

frozen picture. When viewing or creating sculpture, pair students and have one person become the "clay" and the other the "sculptor" who shapes the clay with respect and cooperation. This can extend into dance by directing the sculpted person (clay) to develop a movement idea lasting eight counts that starts and ends with the sculpted pose or form. Two people in contrasting sculptural poses can have eight counts to slowly transform from one into the other.

Three-dimensional forms in art can inspire counterbalanced (push, pull, leaning) designs made by small groups. A story, such as "The Two Skyscrapers Who Wanted to Have a Child" by Carl Sandburg, could be retold using story theatre or be portrayed in tableaux or as dramatized scenes. Students could also research musical selections to accompany their work.

> "Imagination is more important than knowledge."
> —Albert Einstein

Students will be better able to express emotions in their visual artwork if they first work with them through drama, music, and dance. Students can begin by showing a variety of emotions in the face, hands, and feet and then move toward portraying these emotions in postures such as sitting, standing, and walking. Everyday activities such as cooking or brushing teeth can be done with different emotional motivations. Students can also create short musical pieces depicting an emotion or mood or find music that expresses specific feelings or moods.

All four performing arts can become a powerful component of integrated learning. For example, during a fifth-grade project focused on the Lewis and Clark expedition, students did research in books and on the Internet to collect historical, scientific, geographical, and cultural content. This information served as the basis for group projects in music, dance, theatre, visual arts, technology, and language.

Challenged by well-designed tasks, students discussed what they knew and selected different aspects to explore through dance, music, theatre, and visual art. They learned songs of the times, listened to traditional fiddle music, and learned a rhythmic chant that was used to measure the depth of rivers. In dances, they captured the sense of traveling through "boundless space"; portrayed animals encountered during the expedition; created weather conditions such as storms; and showed the struggles in navigating rivers, waterfalls, and mountains. In theatre, students drew upon the historical characters, interpreted various scenarios, and read journal entries of Lewis and Clark. Visual art classes focused on observation drawings of plants and wild animals.

Students also created journals in which they recorded their feelings, observations, sketches, and discoveries. They were able to make connections between their own journeys and that of the Corps of Discovery. Finally, the students shared what they had learned about this epic journey in a multi-arts culmination.

The arts bring accessibility and vitality to learning, empowering students to construct meaning that has relevance for their lives. When children learn to draw, they learn to see. When children learn to act, they learn how it feels to be in different roles, cultures, and circumstances. When children learn to dance, they learn to feel comfortable in their bodies and to use movement expressively. When children learn to play an instrument, they learn perseverance and the rewards of expression through music. When children learn to sing, they release their voices and are empowered to harmonize. When children learn to write a play, they learn to observe life by thinking, reflecting, and writing. When creativity and imagination are nurtured, children learn how to use all of their resources to solve problems, to dream, and build on the ideas of others.

# The Creative Process and Problem Solving

Bunyan Morris, Art Teacher, Effingham County School System, Georgia

There is great reward in watching the artistic growth of a child. Simply providing the media and the time for creating is not enough. The student's natural curiosity and desire to create must be nurtured, encouraged, and challenged. Even the brightest and most talented students need a teacher's guidance in developing the critical-thinking skills necessary for creative problem solving. The intention of this article is to provide ideas and methods for fostering creativity by developing and encouraging divergent problem solving and critical-thinking skills in elementary school art students.

## Classroom Management

Fostering creativity in the art classroom is possibly an art teacher's most important skill. In order to encourage creativity, a teacher must be able to relate to students at their thinking level and then guide them to a higher level of cognitive reasoning. Classroom and behavior management are essential. There cannot be an atmosphere of creativity in a room with chaos. That is not to say that one must be a firm authoritarian. A good art teacher will learn how to walk the fine line between maintaining order and maximizing creative energy among students. Although some may not admit it, all students prefer an educational environment that is free from annoying distractions created by other students. Therefore, good behavior management is a must for maintaining a creative environment.

## Visual References

Introducing a lesson with a work of art and going through the art criticism process is a tried and true method of encouraging creativity. It is important to discuss works of art that are related to the objectives of the lesson. Working strictly from imagination and memory is usually not effective. Students must have visual references from which to gather ideas.

Picture files, reference books, and the Internet are just a few sources for visual images. Photographs of people and various natural and humanmade objects provide ideas and references for drawing. Images can be collected from magazines and calendars or unwanted photographs. The image file should be organized according to subject matter or theme.

Reference books filled with images related to the lesson should be available to students. They may be checked out of the media center and kept in the room, or they may belong to the classroom. Some media specialists are willing to search for and reserve books that a teacher may need for an upcoming lesson.

An image search on the Internet is one method to help students access a visual reference that may not be available in the classroom's image file, reference books, or the school's media center.

## Art Journals

Students who keep art journals maintain handy reference tools. An art journal is the best way to record ideas through sketching and writing. If art journals and writing tools are kept handy, students can jot down ideas or make sketches to save for future use. Ideas can come to mind any place or any time such as in the cafeteria, on the playground, or at the bus stop. The method or tool doesn't really matter that much. It is just important that students have a way of practicing and recording creative ideas.

## Exercising the Brain

Reading should be encouraged. Students who like to read perform better in all subjects. Descriptive language stimulates the imagination. Reading a passage about the beauty of a tree or the sound of a waterfall creates a visual image in the brain. This visual image can be stored in the sketchbook and later rendered as a sculpture, painting, or drawing. Encouraging reading encourages creativity. Teachers and schools should encourage parents to limit their children's time watching television because this takes away from reading and creative play time.

## Resting the Brain

Teachers should be tolerant of students taking small breaks. Sometimes students need down time to regenerate their mental energy. This down time can take the form of daydreaming or play. Both are important to the creative process. Common sense and good judgment is used to determine when a student is using time for thinking as opposed to just wasting time. Students should be reminded to get a

> "Fostering creativity in the art classroom is possibly an art teacher's most important skill."

good night's sleep every night. This is not something teachers can control, but it should be encouraged. We all know that brains function better after a good night's rest.

## Enriching Observation Skills

Enriched observation skills lead to more focused experimentation in art. Artists are naturally observant, but teachers know that most students are not born with natural talent. Through practice, all students can enrich their observation and critical-thinking skills. It is important to get students to slow down and see what they might not otherwise observe. One way to do this is to play an observation game. With the students' help, the teacher can set up a still life in the room. A fun game similar to "I Spy" can be played once the still life is ready. The students describe textures, lines, shapes, colors, and other elements and principles of art found within the real-life objects. The teacher writes the observations and descriptions on the board. Once the game is over and students move to the project portion of the lesson, they will be better equipped with enriched observation skills and more focused critical-thinking skills as they create.

In order to gain more focused and creative experimentation from students, an important goal of every art teacher should be to encourage creativity and divergent problem solving and critical thinking. Hopefully, teachers will find value in the ideas shared in this article and combine them with their own ideas to encourage creativity in their students.

# Using Writing to Enhance Your Art Curriculum

Mary Lazzari, Ed.S., Elementary Art Teacher, Clarke County School District, Athens, Georgia

In recent decades, art teachers have expanded their area of expertise from art production to lessons that include art criticism, art history, and aesthetics. Art is being used as a vehicle not only for increasing creativity but also for developing thinking skills. One way to broaden the art experience and enhance these skills is through guided, interactive writing techniques. Writing about art is an essential component of a well-rounded art curriculum because it provides students with the opportunity to transform thoughts and feelings into words and images. It can also provide the art teacher a more personalized format for communicating with a large student population and assist art teachers in meeting the increased demand to qualify and quantify their students' learning.

> "Art is being used as a vehicle not only for increasing creativity but also for developing thinking skills."

A visual arts curriculum rich in written language activities can facilitate the development of higher-order thinking skills, such as the ability to analyze, defend, and interpret. The use of written statements can help students slow down and refine their thoughts about their own art and the art of others. Words can become the voice for a shy or inarticulate student. With writing as a means of self-expression, art educators can be more in tune with their students' inner thoughts. Some art teachers may be reluctant to incorporate writing into their curriculum because they fear a less than enthusiastic response from their students. Here are a variety of suggestions that can help motivate elementary students to write about art.

## Journals

Whether it is a few sheets of paper stapled together or a spiral notebook, students enjoy having a place to write their private thoughts and feelings. Journals can be used to record the thought process from the beginning to the end of a project. It can also be a place to brainstorm ideas or vent frustrations. Art teachers can give written feedback and encouragement to each student in his or her journal.

## Titles

**Materials:** *Selected works of art, pencil and paper*

At the completion of a project, students can write descriptive titles for their works of art. A title can inform, challenge, or even surprise a viewer. Younger children or students with a language deficit can dictate the title as the teacher writes. Include the student's title when displaying the artwork. Students can also think of a new title for a famous work of art. Compare it to the artist's original title and discuss the similarities and differences.

## Acrostic Poems

**Materials:** *Selected works of art, pencil and paper (for individual writings), or dry/wipe board (for group writing)*

Select an artist's name or art topic and write the letters vertically. Instruct students to think of words that describe the artist or topic. Students should think of a decriptive word for each letter in the artist's name or art topic. Descriptive words can start, end, or have the letter anywhere in the selected word. Display acrostic poems with the art work that inspired them.

## Venn Diagrams

**Materials:** *Individual sheets of Venn diagrams (or draw a large diagram on the board for a whole group discussion); a set of art postcards*

Place an image in each of the two outer circles of the Venn diagram. Students describe qualities they see in each of the two works of art. Qualities that are unique to each image are written in the circle that contains the image. Qualities that they have in common are written in the center of the diagram where the two circles overlap. Invite individuals or groups to share their observations. Mount and display Venn diagrams with student artwork.

## Artist Statements

**Materials:** *Pencil and paper*

Direct students to write three to five sentences about their artwork. Have the students consider these questions: What did I study? What did I create? What did I learn? Display the artist statements with the completed artwork.

## Writing Buddies

If you have students who are reluctant or unmotivated to write during art class, have them work in groups. Ask for a student

volunteer to be the group secretary. This student is responsible for writing down the group's thoughts and ideas. Students who are not strong in written expression will still feel success in sharing their ideas and opinions.

## Brainstorming Ideas

Incorporate writing at the beginning of a lesson by having students use writing devices such as webs. The main topic is placed on the center of the page and ideas that support or expand it are written on the sides.

## Vocabulary

Incorporate vocabulary into the art room. Post the "Word of the Day" on a chart or bulletin board display. Build a "Word Wall" with art vocabulary that is added throughout the year. Use word labels on art materials and equipment around the room. Create art flash cards with art words or concepts printed on them. Use the flash cards to find elements such as line, shape, and color in works of art or to review these concepts at the beginning or end of a lesson.

## Try writing yourself!

Post statements about projects when displaying your students' works of art. Describe the learning objects and concepts in your statement. Use the display to inform parents, teachers and administrators about the rich and interesting learning that is taking place in your art class. Include articles about lessons, projects, and student achievements in your school or district newsletter.

Writing is an important means of creative expression. It is as valid and essential to the art curriculum as drawing or painting. Using writing to augment the art curriculum not only improves the students' ability to express ideas, it helps the art teacher communicate more effectively with every student. When art teachers integrate art instruction and writing about art, the entire curriculum is enhanced. By pairing art production, a realization of students' thoughts and ideas, with writing, a reflective way to understand and validate their opinions and feelings, art teachers can broaden the scope of the art experience. At the same time, the art teacher will develop a critical means to record and assess student learning.

# The Importance of Cultural Diversity Through Art in the Elementary Classroom

Jane Rhoades Hudak, Ph.D., Professor of Art, Georgia Southern University

Culture is learned. People acquire information about the world and how to deal with it as members of a society. Individuals do not learn about their culture by themselves. Children learn about the art of their own culture and other cultures through family and friends, through the mass media, and through the Internet. The information learned this way is often valuable, but it cannot be relied upon to always give adequate and correct information. Schools are often the most effective place for giving students the opportunity to learn about the art of their culture and other cultures.

Our view of the nature of the world and our place in it is expressed and communicated culturally. Every society has institutions that teach culture—family and school are two of the best examples in our society. All societies have religions, which are bodies of cultural knowledge and practices. We also have rituals for birth and death. All cultures have objects that are used for everyday living. We express our world and views through dance, drama, music, and art. We decorate our world and our bodies. We paint our faces and the walls of our houses. We make music with instruments and our voices. All this activity is shaped by our participation in a cultural tradition.

A quality elementary art program provides a wonderful opportunity for teachers to expose students to a variety of cultures as well as their own and to help them to become culturally aware. Following are several of the areas such a program can enhance.

## Art Promotes Intracultural Understanding

Through a culturally diverse art program, students begin to understand the role and function that art and artists play in society. Through learning about the art of other cultures, they have the opportunity to identify similarities and differences among their culture and others. They learn that art reflects the religion, politics, economics, and other aspects of a culture.

Through a quality art program, students can address issues of ethnocentrism, bias, stereotyping, prejudice, discrimination, and racism. Students can learn that no one racial, cultural, or national group is superior to another and that no one group's art is better than another.

## Art Teaches Self-Esteem Through Diversity

Through a quality art program, students learn to recognize, acknowledge, and celebrate racial and cultural diversity through art within their own society. A good program helps promote the enhancement and affirmation of their self-esteem and encourages pride in their heritage. Personal expression is encouraged, and the result is often a statement in visual form that is both inventive and filled with personal meaning.

## Art Teaches Effective Communication

When a quality art program is implemented, students are encouraged to increase their visual literacy skills. Students begin to understand that artists transmit information that cannot be disclosed through other modes of communication. Students learn visual literacy by looking, understanding, talking, writing, and making images. They learn that each society has its own way of communicating through image. Through a culturally sensitive art program, students will be able to discuss and compare art from other societies.

## Art Teaches about the Past

Through a quality art program, students develop sensitivity and understanding for the history of humankind. For many periods in history, it is only through visual remains or material culture that societies' cultures can be pieced together. Experiences that students have with these art objects from the past teach them respect for others, challenge their minds, and stimulate not only their intellect but also their imagination.

## Art Teaches Critical Thinking

A culturally sensitive art program encourages a variety of critical thinking skills. When students look at art from other cultures, they make critical judgments and develop their own opinions. Students are asked to identify and recall information; to organize selected facts and ideas; to use particular facts, rules, and principles; to figure out component parts or to classify; and to combine ideas and form a new whole.

## Art Teaches Perceptual Sensitivity and Aesthetic Awareness

As a result of a quality art program, students develop a keen sense of awareness and an appreciation for beauty. They learn that each culture has its own criteria for beauty. Art experiences help cultivate an aesthetic sensitivity and respect for the natural and humanmade environment. Art classes are the only place in the school curriculum where students learn about what constitutes quality visual design—about harmony, order, organization, and specific design qualities such as balance, movement, and unity.

## Art Teaches Creativity

When a culturally sensitive art program is implemented, creativity in all students is stimulated and nurtured. Students learn to solve problems creatively. They learn that every society has some form of creative expression. In some societies, no one special person is called an artist—everyone in the culture makes "art" objects.

Teachers can help prevent students from having a simplistic view of other cultures and help them understand the cultural context of how and why works of art are created. *Art Connections* has been carefully constructed so that students will be exposed to works of art that represent a wide variety of cultures. Questions and strategies are designed to help teachers put art in a cultural context for students. The Art History and Culture feature in the *Teacher Edition* and the *Artist Profiles* book provide additional information about the works of art and the artists.

As a teacher, you are a cultural transmitter. A quality art program taught by a culturally sensitive teacher benefits every student. When educators teach in a systematic, meaningful way, students acquire knowledge about art and cultures that will benefit them throughout their lives.

# Museum Education

Marilyn J.S. Goodman, Director of Education, Solomon R. Guggenheim Museum

Museums are truly magnificent places. In recent years, these bastions of culture have taken tremendous strides toward making their collections accessible to a broader audience. Museum educators are usually eager to share new information and ideas and are delighted to assist school educators with programs and materials that can easily be incorporated into the classroom. Museums contain a wealth of treasures that offer extraordinary resources for teachers and students, and which will undoubtedly enrich the overall classroom experience.

Getting acquainted with museums in your region can be a real eye-opener. Museums collect objects that document human achievement, both in our own and in other cultures. A local historical society or farm museum might contain a variety of clothing and tools that can bring history to life. A science museum may offer interactive exhibits about phenomena in the natural or physical sciences, sensory perception, new technologies, or space exploration. A children's museum will offer hands-on displays specially designed to motivate young children to learn by doing. Art museums contain visually stunning works that reflect the diversity of human thought and experience.

Museums do not supplant classroom instruction. They enhance and reinforce what is taught by providing raw materials in the forms of objects, artifacts, and exhibits. Museums give students the chance to see and sometimes handle the real thing. It is one thing to talk about Egypt's role in the history of civilization; it is another thing entirely to see the wrappings on a cat mummy, discover hieroglyphs on a sarcophagus, or be overwhelmed by the power and grandeur of large stone sculptures of kings and queens.

When students have the chance to look at portraits, still lifes, landscapes, genre scenes, furniture, clothing, and artifacts, they learn more than by just seeing a picture of a person, place, or thing. They learn how to "read" a culture. Perhaps more importantly, they learn to develop their own process of investigation and critical inquiry. What was this person's life really like? What can one learn about the class structure of this society? What can we tell about craftspeople, available materials, or the objects this society valued? What does the clothing tell us about the climate of the region? What can we learn about the geography, topography, and vegetation? What did people eat? How did they spend leisure time? What were their religious beliefs? Is there any evidence of trade and communication with other regions? What scientific inventions were present at the time? Can one tell if they communicated through language or by writing? Because children are naturally curious, objects will motivate them to think, research, and learn.

> "A visit to a museum will make the curriculum come alive as students begin to explore objects and learn about their meanings."

A visit to a museum will make the curriculum come alive as students begin to explore objects and learn about their meanings. Museum objects give us information in a way that is very different from reading about the objects. Students must think critically to determine both the questions and answers for themselves. A first-hand, visual investigation of an object's style, material, subject matter, and physical characteristics offers preliminary clues to deciphering its meaning. When the exploration is combined with other knowledge, such as the geography and natural resources of a region; the historical context; the social, political, and economic structure of a culture; or even advances in science and technology, students can be engaged in a type of learning that is truly multidisciplinary and may lead them into other areas of study. Moreover, methods for gathering information go far beyond what people see. Exploring objects and works of art allows students to use all of their senses, combining intellect with intuition. The opportunity for experiential, emotional, and intellectual learning is always present.

Museum objects present different historical and cultural perspectives. Students can gather information about people, culture, belief systems, values, and the ways people lived in the past. Museum visits encourage students to see things from broader global and intellectual points of view, developing respect for the work, lives, and points of view of others. Students are encouraged to respond in a variety of ways and on different levels. Most importantly, students are invited to formulate and express their ideas and then discuss them with others.

To learn about museum resources, teachers can contact the education departments of museums in their region. If teachers explain the level of their students, the subjects they are studying, and the specific aspects of the curriculum they would like to supplement, the museum's education department can help to tailor the resources to the class. In addition to guided tours and workshops, the museum education department may offer materials for loan, including slides, pamphlets, posters, postcards, kits, and other printed materials. Some museums have teacher resource rooms filled with books, films, videos, CD-ROMs, and computer databases geared toward educators. Trained staff is available to answer questions or to help teachers develop a complete learning unit that can integrate museum objects with classroom studies.

Using museums is an excellent way to enrich and enliven the classroom experience. Educators can take the first step by learning all they can about the rich and diverse resources available to them and their students.

# U.S. Museum Resources

## Alabama

**1** Birmingham Museum of Art
*2000 8th Avenue North,
Birmingham*
http://www.ARTSbma.org

**2** Mobile Museum of Art
*4850 Museum Drive, Mobile*
http://www.mobilemuseum
ofart.com

**3** Montgomery Museum
of Fine Arts
*1 Museum Drive, Montgomery*
http://www.mmfa.org

## Alaska

**4** Alaska State Museum
*395 Whittier Street, Juneau*
http://www.museums.
state.ak.us/asmhome.html

**5** Anchorage Heritage Library
Museum
*301 West Northern Lights
Boulevard, Anchorage*
http://www.wellsfargohistory.
com/museums/alaska.ht

**6** Anchorage Museum
of History and Art
*121 West 7th Avenue,
Anchorage*
http://www.anchorage
museum.org

## Arizona

**7** Heard Museum
*2301 N Central Avenue, Phoenix*
http://www.heard.org/

**8** Phoenix Art Museum
*1625 North Central Avenue,
Phoenix*
http://www.phxart.org

**9** Scottsdale Museum
of Contemporary Art - (SMOCA)
*7380 E 2nd St, Scottsdale*
http://www.scottsdalearts.org

## Arkansas

**10** Arkansas State
University Museum
*Jonesboro, AR 72467*
http://museumastate.edu

**11** Historic Arkansas Museum
*200 East 3rd Street,
Little Rock*
http://www.arkansashistory.
com/

**12** Old State House Museum
*300 West Markham Street,
Little Rock*
http://www.oldstatehouse.com

## California

**13** Asian Art Museum
of San Francisco
*Golden Gate Park, San Francisco*
http://www.asianart.org

**14** Berkeley Art Museum
and Pacific Film Archive
*2625 Durant Avenue, Berkeley*
http://www.bampfa.berkeley.
edu

**15** El Museo Mexicano -
Mexican Museum
*Fort Mason Center,
Building D, San Francisco*
http://www.mexican
museum.org

**16** J Paul Getty
Center Museum
*1200 Getty Center Drive,
Los Angeles, CA*
http://www.getty.edu

**17** Japanese American
National Museum
*369 East 1st Street,
Los Angeles*
http://www.janm.org

**18** Korean American Museum
*3780 Wilshire Boulevard
# 220, Los Angeles*
http://www.kamuseum.org

**19** L A County Museum
of Art
*5905 Wilshire Boulevard,
Los Angeles*
http://www.lacma.org

**20** San Francisco Museum
of Modern Art
*151 3rd Street Building A,
San Francisco*
http://www.sfmoma.org/

**21** Santa Barbara
Museum of Art
*1130 State Street, Santa Barbara*
http://www.sbmuseart.org

**22** Southwest Museum
*234 Museum Drive, Los Angeles*
http://www.southwest
museum.org/

## Colorado

**23** Aspen Art Museum
*590 North Mill Street, Aspen*
http://www.aspenart
museum.org

**24** Boulder Museum
of Contemporary Art
*1750 Thirteenth Street, Boulder*
http://www.bmoca.org/

**25** Denver Art Museum
*100 West 14th Avenue, Denver*
http://www.denverart
museum.org

## Connecticut

**26** New Britain Museum
of American Art
*56 Lexington Street,
New Britain*
http://www.nbmaa.org

**27** Norwalk Museum
*41 North Main Street, Norwalk*
http://www.norwalkct.org/
norwalkmuseum/index.htm

**28** Wadsworth Atheneum
Museum of Art
*600 Main Street, Hartford*
http://www.wadsworth
atheneum.org/

## Delaware

**29** Delaware Art Museum
*800 S Madison Street
Suite B, Wilmington*
http://www.delart.org

**30** Sewell C Biggs Museum
of American Art
*406 Federal Street, Dover*
http://www.biggsmuseum.
org

31 Winterthur Museum
*Route 52, Winterthur*
http://www.winterthur.org/

## Florida

**32** Bass Museum of Art
*2121 Park Ave, Miami*
http://www.bassmuseum.org/

**33** Key West Art and
Historical Society
*281 Front Street, Key West*
http://www.kwahs.com

**34** Lowe Art Museum
*1301 Stanford Drive, Miami*
http://www.lowemuseum.
com/

**35** Miami Art Museum
*101 West Flagler Street, Miami*
http://www.miamiart
museum.org/

**36** Museum of Fine Arts,
St Petersburg
*255 Beach Drive Northeast, St
Petersburg*
http://www.fine-arts.org

**37** Salvador Dali Museum
*1000 3rd Street South,
St Petersburg*
http://www.salvadordali
museum.org

## Georgia

**38** Albany Museum of Art
*311 Meadowlark Drive, Albany*
http://www.albany
museum.com/

**39** High Museum of Art
*1280 Peachtree Street
Northeast, Atlanta, GA*
http://www.high.org

**40** Morris Museum of Art
*1 10th Street, Augusta*
http://www.themorris.org

## Hawaii

**41** Contemporary Museum,
Honolulu
*2411 Makiki Heights Drive,
Honolulu*
http://www.tcmhi.org

**42** Kauai Museum
*4428 Rice Street, Lihue*
http://www.kauaimuseum.org

**43** University of Hawaii
at Manoa Art Gallery
*University of Hawaii at Manoa,
Honolulu*
http://www.hawaii.edu/
artgallery

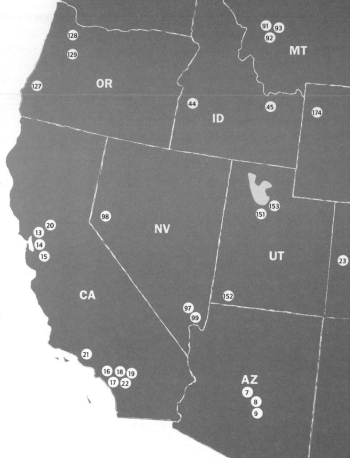

## Idaho

**44** Boise Art Museum
*670 Julia Davis Drive, Boise*
http://www.boiseart
museum.org

**45** Eagle Rock Art Museum
and Education Center, Inc.
*300 S Capital Avenue,
Idaho Falls*
http://www.eaglerockart
museum.org

## Illinois

**46** Art Institute of Chicago
*111 South Michigan Avenue,
Chicago*
http://www.artic.edu/aic/

**47** Krannert Art Museum
*500 East Peabody Drive,
Champaign*
http://www.kam.uiuc.edu

**48** Martin D'Arcy
Museum of Art
*6525 N Sheridan Road,
Chicago*
http://darcy.luc.edu

**49** Mitchell Museum
of the American Indian
*2600 Central Park Ave,
Evanston*
http://www.mitchell
museum.org/

**50** Museum of
Contemporary Art
*220 East Chicago Avenue,
Chicago*
http://www.mcachicago.org

**51** Smart Museum of Art
*5550 South Greenwood Avenue,
Chicago*
http://smartmuseum.
uchicago.edu/

## Indiana

**52** Brauer Museum of Art
*Valparaiso University Center
for the Arts, Valparaiso*
http://wwwstage.valpo.edu/
artmuseum/index.html

**53** Eiteljorg Museum
of American Indian
and Western Art
*500 West Washington Street,
Indianapolis*
http://www.eiteljorg.org

**54** Indianapolis
Museum of Art
*1200 West 38th Street,
Indianapolis*
http://www.ima-art.org

# U.S. Museum Resources (continued)

## Iowa

**55** Cedar Rapids
Museum of Art
*410 3rd Avenue Southeast,
Cedar Rapids*
http://www.crma.org

**56** Davenport Museum of Art
*1737 West 12th Street,
Davenport*
http://www.art-dma.org

**57** Dubuque Museum of Art
*36 East 8th Street, Dubuque*
http://www.dbqart.com

## Kansas

**58** Coutts Memorial Museum
*110 North Main Street,
El Dorado*
http://skyways.lib.ks.us/
kansas/museums/coutts/ind

**59** Spencer Museum of Art
*1301 Mississippi Street,
Lawrence*
http://www.ukans.edu/~sma/

**60** Wichita Art Museum
*West Museum Boulevard,
Wichita*
http://www.wichitaart
museum.org

## Kentucky

**61** Kentucky Museum
of Arts + Design
*609 West Main Street, Louisville*
http://www.kentuckycrafts.org

**62** Speed Art Museum, the
*2035 South Third St., Louisville*
http://www.speedmuseum.org

**63** University of Kentucky
Art Museum
*Rose and Euclid Avenue,
Lexington*
http://www.uky.edu/Art
Museum/

## Louisiana

**64** African-American Museum
*125 New Market Street,
St Martinville*
http://stmartinparish-
la.org/tourism_africanmuseum

**65** Louisiana State Museum
*751 Chartres Street, New Orleans*
http://lsm.crt.state.la.us/

**66** New Orleans
Museum of Art
*City Park 1 Collins Diboll Circle,
New Orleans*
http://www.noma.org

## Maine

**67** Farnsworth Art Museum
*352 Main Street, Box 466,
Rockland*
http://farnsworthmuseum.org/

**68** Ogunquit Museum
of American Art
*Shore Road, Ogunquit*
http://www.ogunquit
museum.org

**69** Portland
Museum of Art
*7 Congress Square, Portland*
http://www.portlandmuseum.
org

## Maryland

**70** African Art
Museum of Maryland
*5430 Vantage Point Road,
Columbia*
http://www.Africanart
museum.org

**71** Baltimore
Museum of Art
*10 Art Museum Drive, Baltimore*
http://www.artbma.org/

**72** Walters Art Museum
*600 North Charles Street,
Baltimore*
http://www.thewalters.org

## Massachusetts

**73** Harvard University
Art Museums
*32 Quincy Street, Cambridge*
http://www.artmuseums.
harvard.edu/

**74** Institute of Contemporary
Art
*955 Boylston Street, Boston*
http://www.icaboston.org

**75** MASS MoCA -
Massachusetts Museum
of Contemporary Art
*87 Marshall Street, North Adams*
http://www.massmoca.org

**76** Mead Art Museum
*Amherst College, PO Box 5000,
Amherst*
http://www.amherst.edu/
~mead/

**77** Museum of Fine Arts
Boston
*465 Huntington Avenue, Boston*
http://www.mfa.org/

**78** Worcester Art Museum
*55 Salisbury Street, Worcester*
http://www.worcesterart.org

## Michigan

**79** Cranbrook Art Museum
*39221 Woodward Avenue,
PO Box 801, Bloomfield Hills*
http://www.cranbrook.
edu/art/museum/

**80** Detroit Institute of Arts
*5200 Woodward Avenue,
Detroit*
http://www.dia.org

**81** Grand Rapids
Art Museum
*55 Division Ave N, Grand Rapids*
http://www.gramonline.org

## Minnesota

**82** Frederick R Weisman
Art Museum
*333 East River Road # 200,
Minneapolis*
http://hudson.acad.umn.edu/

**83** Minnesota Museum
of American Art
*Landmark Center 75 West 5th
Street West, St Paul*
http://www.mmaa.org

**84** Walker Art Center
*725 Vineland Place,
Minneapolis*
http://www.walkerart.org

## Mississippi

**85** Lauren Rogers
Museum of Art
*5th Avenue and 7th Street,
Laurel*
http://www.lrma.org/

**86** Mississippi Museum
of Art
*201 E Pascagoula St
Ste 103, Jackson*
http://www.msmuseumart.
org/

**87** Walter Anderson
Museum of Art
*510 Washington Avenue,
Ocean Springs*
http://www.walteranderson
museum.org/

## Missouri

**88** Albrecht-Kemper Art Museum
*2818 Frederick Avenue, St Joseph*
http://www.albrecht-
kemper.org/

**89** Nelson-Atkins
Museum of Art
*4525 Oak Street, Kansas City*
http://www.nelson-
atkins.org/

**90** St Louis Art Museum
*1 Fine Arts Drive, St Louis*
http://www.slam.org

## Montana

**91** Art Museum of Missoula
*335 North Pattee Street,
Missoula*
http://www.artmissoula.org/

**92** Hockaday Museum
of Art
*2nd Avenue East at
Third Street, Kalispell*
http://www.hockadayart
museum.org/

**93** Montana Museum
of Art and Culture
*University of Montana, Missoula*
http://www.umt.edu/partv/
famus/

## Nebraska

**94** Joslyn Art Museum
*2200 Dodge St., Omaha*
http://www.joslyn.org

**95** Museum of Nebraska Art
(MONA)
*2401 Central Avenue, Kearney*
http://monet.unk.edu/mona/

**96** Sheldon Memorial
Art Gallery and
Sculpture Garden
*University of Nebraska-Lincoln,
12th and R Streets, Lincoln*
http://sheldon.unl.edu/

## Nevada

**97** Las Vegas Art Museum
*9600 West Sahara Avenue,
Las Vegas*
http://www.lvam.com

**98** Nevada Museum of Art
*160 West Liberty Street, Reno*
http://www.nevadaart.org

**99** Walker African-American
Museum and Research Center
*705 W Van Buren Ave,
Las Vegas*
http://members.aol.com/
Bigbrwnsis/

## New Hampshire

**100** Currier Museum of Art
*201 Myrtle Way, Manchester*
http://www.currier.org

**101** Hood Museum of Art
*Wheelock Street, Hanover*
http://web.dartmouth.
edu/~hood/

**102** Mariposa Museum
*26 Main Street, Peterborough*
http://www.mariposa
museum.org

## New Jersey

**103** Jane Voorhees
Zimmerli Art Museum
*71 Hamilton St, Rutgers
University, New Brunswick*
http://www.zimmerlimuseum.
rutgers.edu

**104** Jersey City Museum
*350 Montgomery Street,
Jersey City*
http://www.jerseycity
museum.org/

**105** Princeton University
Art Museum
*Princeton University, Princeton*
http://www.princetonart
museum.org/

## New Mexico

**106** Georgia O'Keeffe Museum
*217 Johnson Street, Santa Fe*
http://www.okeeffe
museum.org

**107** Harwood Museum of Art
*238 Ledoux Street, 4080
NDCBU, Taos*
http://www.harwood
museum.org

**108** Institute of American
Indian Arts Museum
*Cathedral Place, Santa Fe*
http://www.iaiancad.org

## New York

**109** Albright-Knox
Art Gallery
*1285 Elmwood Avenue, Buffalo*
http://www.albrightknox.org

**110** Metropolitan Museum
of Art
*6626 Metropolitan Avenue
FL 2, Flushing*
http://www.Metmuseum.org/

**111** Museum of Modern Art
MoMA
*11 West 53 Street , New York*
http://www.moma.org/

**112** New Museum
of Contemporary Art
*583 Broadway, New York*
http://www.newmuseum.org/

**113** Solomon R Guggenheim
Museum, New York
*1071 5th Ave at 89th, New York*
http://www.guggenheim.org
/new_york_index.html

**114** Whitney Museum
of American Art
*945 Madison Avenue FL 5,
New York*
http://www.whitney.org

## North Carolina

**115** Ackland Art Museum
*Columbia and Franklin Street,
Chapel Hill*
http://www.ackland.org

**116** Duke University
Museum of Art
*Buchanan Blvd-Trinity Avenue,
Durham*
http://www.duke.edu/web/
duma/

**117** North Carolina Museum
of Art
*2110 Blue Ridge Road, Raleigh*
http://www.ncartmuseum.org/

## North Dakota

**118** *North Heritage Center of
the State Historical Society of
North Dakota, Bismarck*
http://www.state.nd.us/hist/
index.html

**119** North Dakota
Museum of Art
*Centennial Drive, Grand Forks*
http://www.ndmoa.com

**120** Plains Art Museum
*219 7th Street South, Fargo*
http://www.plainsart.org/

## Ohio

**121** Cincinnati Art Museum
*953 Eden Park Drive, Cincinnati*
http://www.cincinnatiart
museum.com/

**122** Cleveland Museum of Art
*11150 East Boulevard, Cleveland*
http://www.clemusart.com/

**123** Columbus Museum of Art
*480 East Broad Street, Columbus*
http://www.columbusmuseum.
org

## Oklahoma

**124** Fred Jones Jr
Museum of Art
*410 West Boyd Street,*
*University of Oklahoma, Norman*
http://www.ou.edu/fjjma/

**125** Oklahoma City
Art Museum
*3113 Pershing Boulevard,*
*Oklahoma City*
http://www.okcartmuseum.
com/

**126** Philbrook Museum of Art
*2727 South Rockford Road,*
*Tulsa, OK*
http://www.philbrook.org/

## Oregon

**127** Coos Art Museum
*235 Anderson Avenue, Coos Bay*
http://www.coosart.org

**128** Portland Art Museum
*1219 SW Park Ave., Portland*
http://www.pam.org

**129** University of Oregon
Museum of Art
*1223 University of Oregon,*
*Eugene*
http://uoma.uoregon.edu/

## Pennsylvania

**130** The Andy Warhol
Museum
*117 Sandusky Street, Pittsburgh*
http://www.clpgh.org/warhol/

**131** The Palmer
Museum of Art
*Curtin Rd, The Pennsylvania*
*State University, University Park*
http://www.psu.edu/dept/
palmermuseum/

**132** Philadelphia
Museum of Art
*26th Street and the Benjamin*
*Franklin Parkway, Philadelphia*
http://pma.libertynet.org/

## Rhode Island

**133** Museum of Art,
Rhode Island School of Design
*224 Benefit Street, Providence*
http://www.risd.edu/

**134** Museum Of Primitive
Art & Culture
*1058 Kingstown Road,*
*South Kingstown*

**135** National Museum
of American Illustration
*Vernon Court 492 Bellevue*
*Avenue , Newport*
http://www.american
illustration.org

## South Carolina

**136** Gibbes Museum of Art
*135 Meeting Street, Charleston*
http://www.gibbes.com/

**137** Columbia Museum of Art
*Main and Hampton Streets,*
*Columbia*
http://www.colmusart.org/

**138** The Spartanburg County
Museum of Art
*385 S Spring St., Spartanburg*
http://www.sparklenet.com/
museumofart

## South Dakota

**139** Journey Museum
*222 New York Street, Rapid City*
http://www.journeymuseum.org

**140** Oscar Howe Art Center
and Middle Border Museum
*1300 E University Street P.O*
*Box 1071 Mitchell*
http://www.oscarhowe.com/
index.htm

**141** South Dakota Art Museum
*P.O Box 2250, Brookings*
http://web.sdstate.edu/sites/
artmuseum/

## Tennessee

**142** Hunter Museum of Art
*10 Bluff View, Chattanooga*
http://www.huntermuseum.
org/

**143** Institute of Egyptian
Art and Archaeology
*The University of Memphis,*
*Memphis*
http://www.memst.edu/
egypt/about.html

**144** Knoxville Museum of Art
*1050 Worlds Fair Park Drive,*
*Knoxville*
http://www.knoxart.org

## Texas

**145** Dallas Museum of Art
*1717 North Harwood, Dallas*
http://dm-art.org/

**146** Kimbell Art Museum
*3333 Camp Bowie Blvd.,*
*Fort Worth*
http://kimbellart.org/

**147** Mexic-Arte Museum
*419 Congress Avenue, Austin*
http://www.mexic-arte
museum.org

**148** The Museum of Fine Arts
*1001 Bissonnet, Houston*
http://mfah.org/

**149** Panhandle-Plains
Historical Museum,
West Texas A&M University
*2401 4th Ave., Canyon*
http://www.wtamu.edu/
museum/

**150** San Antonio Museum
of Art
*200 West Jones Avenue,*
*San Antonio*
http://www.sa-museum.org

## Utah

**151** BYU Museum of Art
*Brigham Young University,*
*Provo*
http://www.byu.edu/moa/

**152** St George Art Museum
*175 East 200 North, St George*
http://www.ci.st-george.ut.us/
arts/artmuseum.php

**153** Utah Museum of Fine
Arts, University of Utah
*370 South 1530 East*
*University of Utah , Salt Lake City*
http://www.utah.edu/umfa/

## Vermont

**154** The Bennington Museum
*West Main St., Bennington*
http://www.bennington
museum.com

**155** Robert Hull
Fleming Museum
*Colchester Avenue, Burlington*
http://www.uvm.edu/
~fleming/home/

**156** Shelburne Museum
*US Route 7, PO Box 10,*
*Shelburne*
http://www.shelburne
museum.org

## Virginia

**157** Chrysler Museum of Art
*245 West Olney Rd., Norfolk*
http://www.chrysler.org/

**158** Maier Museum of Art
*2500 Rivermont Avenue,*
*Lynchburg*
http://www.rmwc.edu/
Maier/

**159** Virginia Museum
of Fine Arts
*2800 Grove Ave., Richmond*
http://www.vmfa.state.va.us/

## Washington

**160** Frye Art Museum
*704 Terry Ave., Seattle*
http://fryeart.org/

**161** Jundt Art Museum
*502 East Boone Avenue,*
*Spokane*
http://www.gonzaga.edu/
Campus+Resources/Museums
+an

**162** Seattle Art Museum
*100 University St., Seattle*
http://seattleartmuseum.
org/

## Washington, D.C.

**163** Arthur M Sackler Gallery
and the Freer Gallery of Art
*1050 Independence Avenue, SW*
http://www.asia.si.edu/
default.htm

**164** Corcoran Gallery of Art
*500 17th Street Northwest*
http://www.corcoran.org/

**165** Hirshhorn Museum
and Sculpture Garden
*Independence Avenue*
*and 7th Street Southwest*
http://hirshhorn.si.edu/

**166** National Gallery of Art
http://www.nga.gov/

**167** The National Museum
of Women in the Arts
*1250 New York Ave., NW*
http://www.nmwa.org/

**168** Smithsonian Museums
Smithsonian Institution
http://www.si.edu/

## West Virginia

**169** Huntington Museum
of Art
*2033 McCoy Rd., Huntington*
http://www.hmoa.org/

**170** Oglebay Institute:
Mansion Museum and
Glass Museum
*Burton Center, Wheeling*
http://www.oionline.com/

## Wisconsin

**171** Elvehjem Museum of Art
*800 University Avenue,*
*Madison*
http://www.lvm.wisc.edu

**172** Leigh Yawkey Woodson
Art Museum
*700 North Twelfth St, Wausau*
http://www.lywam.org/

**173** Milwaukee Art Museum
*750 North Lincoln Memorial*
*Dr., Milwaukee*
http://www.mam.org/

## Wyoming

**174** National Museum
of Wildlife Art
*2820 Rungius Road, Jackson*
http://www.wildlifeart.org

**175** University of Wyoming
Art Museum
*2111 Willett Dr., Laramie*
http://uwadmnweb.uwyo.
edu/artmuseum/

# World Museum Resources

## Argentina

**1** Fundacion Federico Klemm
*Buenos Aires, Argentina*
www.fundacionfjklemm.org

## Australia

**2** Art Gallery of New South Wales
*Sydney, Australia*
www.artgallery.nsw.gov.au/

**3** Australian National Art Gallery
*Canberra, Australia*
www.nga.gov.au/Home/index.cfm

**4** Museum of Contemporary Art
*Sydney, Australia*
www.mca.com.au/

## Austria

**5** Kunsthistorisches Museum Wien
*Vienna, Austria*
www.khm.at/

## Bahrain

**6** Al Hayat Museum
*Manama, Bahrain*
www.beitalquran.com/

## Brazil

**7** Museu Historico Nacional
*Rio de Janeiro, Brazil*
www.museuhistoriconacional.com.br/ingles/index.htm

## Canada

**8** Art Gallery of Calgary
*Calgary, Canada*
www.artgallerycalgary.com/

**9** Morris and Helen Belkin Art Gallery, University of British Columbia
*Vancouver, Canada*
www.belkin-gallery.ubc.ca/

**10** Art Gallery of Newfoundland and Labrador
*St. Johns, Canada*
www.mun.ca/agnl/main.html

**11** Art Gallery of Nova Scotia
*Halifax, Canada*
www.agns.gov.ns.ca/

**12** Art Gallery of Ontario
*Toronto, Canada*
www.ago.net/navigation/flash/index.cfm

**13** National Gallery of Canada
*Ottawa, Canada*
www.national.gallery.ca/

**14** The Montreal Museum of Fine Arts
*Quebec, Canada*
www.mmfa.qc.ca/en/index.html

**15** McMichael Canadian Art Collection
*Toronto, Canada*
www.mcmichael.com/

**16** Winnipeg Art Gallery
*Winnipeg, Canada*
www.wag.mb.ca/

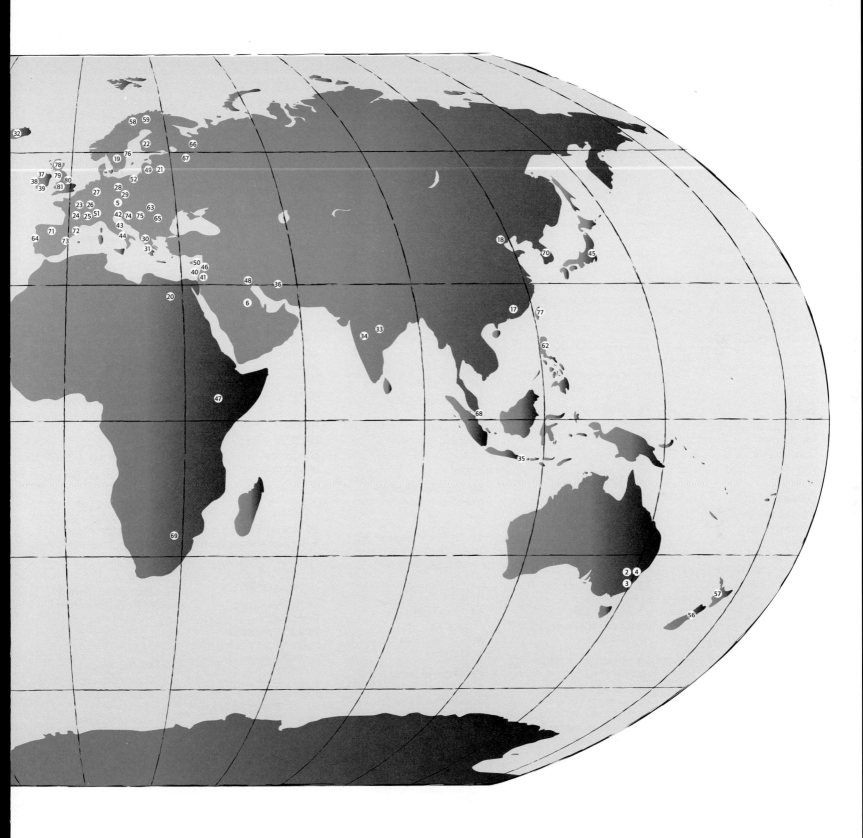

# World Museum Resources

## China

**17** Hong Kong Museum of Art
*Hong Kong, China*
www.lcsd.gov.hk/CE/Museum/Arts/english/intro/eintro.html

**18** Palace Museum
*Beijing, China*
www.dpm.org.cn/

## Denmark

**19** National Museum
*Copenhagen, Denmark*
www.natmus.dk/sw1413.asp

## Egypt

**20** The Egyptian Museum
*Cairo, Egypt*
www.egyptianmuseum.gov.eg/

## Estonia

**21** Estonian National Museum
*Tartu, Estonia*
www.erm.ee/?lang=ENG

## Finland

**22** The Finnish National Gallery
*Helsinki, Finland*
www.fng.fi/fng/rootnew/en/vtm/etusivu.htm

## France

**23** The Louvre
*Paris, France*
www.louvre.fr/louvrea.htm

**24** Musee d'Orsay,
*Paris, France*
www.musee-orsay.fr/

**25** Centre Georges Pompidou
*Paris, France*
www.cnac-gp.fr/Pompidou/Accueil.nsf/tunnel?OpenForm

## Germany

**26** Neues Museum
*Nuremberg, Germany*
www.nmn.de/

**27** Hamburg Kunsthalle
*Hamburg, Germany*
www.hamburger-kunsthalle.de/

**28** Alte National Galerie
*Berlin, Germany*
www.alte-nationalgalerie.de/

**29** Bauhaus Archiv Museum of Design
*Berlin, Germany*
www.bauhaus.de/english/

## Greece

**30** Acropolis Museum
*Athens, Greece*
www.culture.gr/2/21/211/21101m/e211am01.html

**31** Benaki Museum
*Athens, Greece*
www.benaki.gr/index-en.htm

## Iceland

**32** Living Art Museum
*Reykjavik, Iceland*
www.nylo.is/English/index.html

## India

**33** National Museum of India
*New Delhi, India*
www.nationalmuseumindia.org/index.html

**34** Chhatrapati Shivaji Maharaj Vastu Sangrahalaya
(Formerly the Prince of Wales Museum of Western India)
*Mumbai (Bombay), India*
www.bombaymuseum.org/

## Indonesia

**35** Agung Rai Museum of Art
*Ubud, Bali, Indonesia*
www.nusantara.com/arma/

## Iran

**36** National Museum of Iran
*Tehran, Iran*
www.nationalmuseumofiran.com/

## Ireland

**37** Hunt Museum
*Limerick, Ireland*
www.huntmuseum.com/

**38** Irish Museum of Modern Art
*Dublin, Ireland*
www.modernart.ie/

**39** National Gallery of Ireland
*Dublin, Ireland*
www.nationalgallery.ie/

## Israel

**40** The Israel Museum
*Jerusalem, Israel*
www.imj.org.il/

**41** Tel Aviv Museum of Art
*Tel Aviv, Israel*
www.tamuseum.com/

## Italy

**42** Uffizi Gallery
*Florence, Italy*
www.uffizi.firenze.it/welcomeE.html

**43** Museo di Roma
*Rome, Italy*
www.museodiroma.comune.roma.it/PalazzoBraschi/inizio.mostra

**44** Vatican Museum
*Vatican City*
http://mv.vatican.va/3_EN/pages/MV_Home.html

## Japan

**45** Kyoto National Museum
*Tokyo, Japan*
www.kyohaku.go.jp/index e.htm

## Jordan

**46** Darat al Funun Home for the Arts
*Amman, Jordan*
www.daratalfunun.org/

## Kenya

**47** National Museum of Kenya
*Nairobi, Kenya*
www.museums.or.ke/

## Kuwait

**48** Kuwait National Museum
*Kuwait City, Kuwait*
www.kmia.org.kw

## Latvia

**49** State Museum of Art
*Riga, Latvia*
www.vmm.lv/en/muzejs.html

## Lebanon

**50** American University of Beirut Archaeology Museum
*Beirut, Lebanon*

## Liechtenstein

**51** Kunstmuseum Liechtenstein
*Vaduz, Liechtenstein*
www.kunstmuseum.li/web2306e/index.html

## Lithuania

**52** Lithuanian Art Museum
*Vilnius, Lithuania*
www.ldm.lt/ldm_en.htm

## Mexico

**53** Museo de Arte Moderno
*Mexico City, Mexico*
www.arts-history.mx/museos/mam/home2.html

**54** National Museum of Anthropology
*Mexico City, Mexico*
www.mna.inah.gob.mx/

**55** Museo de Arte Contemporaneo de Oaxaca
*Oaxaca, Mexico*
www.arts-history.mx/museos/maco/home.html

## New Zealand

**56** Centre of Contemporary Art
*Christchurch, New Zealand*
www.coca.org.nz/

**57** Auckland Art Gallery
*Auckland, New Zealand*
www.aucklandartgallery.govt.nz/

## Norway

**58** National Gallery of Norway
*Oslo, Norway*
www.museumsnett.no/nasjonalgalleriet/flash_versjon_engelsk/

**59** Lillehammer Art Museum
*Lillehammer, Norway*
www.lillehammerartmuseum.com/

## Panama

**60** Museo de Arte Contemporaneo de Panama
*Panama, Republic of Panama*
www.macpanama.org/

## Peru

**61** Museo Arqueologico Rafael Larco Herrera
*Lima, Peru*
museolarco.perucultural. org.pe/

## Philippines

**62** Philippine National Museum
*Manila, Philippines*
http://nmuseum.tripod. com/

## Poland

**63** Polish National Museum
*Warsaw, Poland*
www.mnw.art.pl/

## Portugal

**64** Museu Calouste Gulbenkian
*Lisbon, Portugal*
www.gulbenkian.pt/

## Romania

**65** The National Museum of Art of Romania
*Bucharest, Romania*
http://art.museum.ro/ museum.html

## Russia

**66** The State Hermitage Museum
*St. Petersburg, Russia*
www.hermitagemuseum. org/

**67** Pushkin Museum of Fine Arts
*Moscow, Russia*
www.museum.ru/gmii/

## Singapore

**68** Singapore Art Museum
*Singapore, Republic of Singapore*
www.nhb.gov.sg/SAM/ sam.shtml

## South Africa

**69** Pretoria Art Museum
*Pretoria, South Africa*
www.pretoriaartmuseum. co.za/

## South Korea

**70** Seoul Metropolitan Museum of Art
*Seoul, South Korea*
www.metro.seoul.kr/ muse/eng/

## Spain

**71** Guggenheim Bilbao Museum
*Bilbao, Spain*
www.guggenheim- bilbao.es/idioma.htm

**72** Museu d'Art Contemporani
*Barcelona, Spain*
www.macba.es/home.php

**73** Valencian Institute of Modern Art
*Valencia, Spain*
www.ivam.es/

## Switzerland

**74** Kunstmuseum Basel
*Basel, Switzerland*
www.kunstmuseumbasel. ch/de/

**75** Kunsthaus
*Zurich, Switzerland*
www.kunsthaus.ch/

## Sweden

**76** National Museum
*Stockholm, Sweden*
www.nationalmuseum.se/

## Taiwan

**77** National Palace Museum
*T'aipei, Taiwan*
www.npm.gov.tw/english/ index-e.htm

## United Kingdom

**78** National Gallery of London
*London, England*
www.nationalgallery. org.uk/

**79** British Museum
*London, England*
www.thebritishmuseum. ac.uk/

**80** Tate Gallery
*London, England*
www.tate.org.uk/home/ default.htm

**81** Victoria and Albert Museum
*London, England*
www.vam.ac.uk/

## Uruguay

**82** Museo Nacianal de Artes Visuales
*Montevideo, Uruguay*
www.mnav.gub.uy/

# Elements and Principles of Art

## Scope and Sequence

| Elements of Art | Level K | | | | | | Level 1 | | | | | | Level 2 | | | | | | Level 3 | | | | | |
|---|---|---|---|---|---|---|---|---|---|---|---|---|---|---|---|---|---|---|---|---|---|---|---|---|
| | U1 | U2 | U3 | U4 | U5 | U6 | U1 | U2 | U3 | U4 | U5 | U6 | U1 | U2 | U3 | U4 | U5 | U6 | U1 | U2 | U3 | U4 | U5 | U6 |
| Line | 1–6 | | | | | | 1–6 | 1 | | | | | 1–4 | | | | | | | 1–2 | | | | |
| Shape | | 1–6 | | | 6 | | | 1–6 | | 1 | | | 5–6 | | | | | | 2, 4 | 3–6 | | | | |
| Color | | | 1–6 | | | | | | 1–6 | | | | | | 1–3 | | 1, 3 | | | 1–6 | | | | |
| Value | | | | | | | | | | | | | | | 4–6 | | | | | | 1 | | | |
| Space | | | | 1, 3 | | | | | | 2, 5, 6 | | | | 5–6 | | | | | | 1–3 | | | | |
| Form | | | 2–6 | 5 | | | | | | 1–4 | | 4 | 1–4 | | | | 2, 4 | | 4–6 | | | | | |
| Texture | | | | | 1–6 | | | | | 1–3 | | | | | | | 5–6 | | | | | 5–6 | | |

| Principles of Art | Level K | | | | | | Level 1 | | | | | | Level 2 | | | | | | Level 3 | | | | | |
|---|---|---|---|---|---|---|---|---|---|---|---|---|---|---|---|---|---|---|---|---|---|---|---|---|
| | U1 | U2 | U3 | U4 | U5 | U6 | U1 | U2 | U3 | U4 | U5 | U6 | U1 | U2 | U3 | U4 | U5 | U6 | U1 | U2 | U3 | U4 | U5 | U6 |
| Pattern | | | | | 1 | | | | | 4–5 | | | | | 1–2 | | | | | | | | 1–3 | |
| Rhythm | | | | | 2 | | | | | | 6 | | | | 3–6 | | | | | | | | 4–6 | |
| Balance | | | | 3–4 | | | | | | | 1–2 | | | | | 1–2 | | | | | | 1–4 | | |
| Proportion | | | | | | | | | | | | | | | | | | | | | | | | |
| Emphasis | | | | | | | | | | 3–4 | | | | | | 3–4 | | | | | | | | 3–4 |
| Variety | | | | | | | | | | | | | | | | | 3–4 | | | | | | | 2 |
| Harmony | | | | | | | | | | | | | | | | | 1–2 | | | | | | | 1 |
| Unity | | | | | 5–6 | | | | | | 5–6 | | | | | | 5–6 | | | | | | | 5–6 |

*Numbers indicate lesson numbers within a given unit.

| Level 4 | | | | | | Level 5 | | | | | | Level 6 | | | | | |
|---|---|---|---|---|---|---|---|---|---|---|---|---|---|---|---|---|---|
| U1 | U2 | U3 | U4 | U5 | U6 | U1 | U2 | U3 | U4 | U5 | U6 | U1 | U2 | U3 | U4 | U5 | U6 |
| 1-6 | | | | | | 1-2 | | | | | | | 1 | | | | |
| | 1-2 | | | | | 3 | 1 | | | | | | 2 | | | | |
| | | 1-4 | | | | | | 1-4 | | | | | | 1-4 | | | |
| | | 5-6 | | | | 4-6 | | | | | | | | 2-3 | | | |
| | | | 1-3 | | | | 1-3 | | | | | | | | 5-6 | | |
| | | 1-3 | | | | | 4-6 | | | | | | | 3-4 | | | |
| | | | 4-5 | | | | | | 1 | | | | | 5-6 | | | |

| Level 7 — Exploring Art | Level 8 — Understanding Art |
|---|---|
| Chapter 2, 6, 7, 8, 9, 10, 11 | Chapter 2, 6, 8, 9, 12, 15, 16 |
| Chapter 2, 6, 8, 9, 10, 11 | Chapter 2, 3, 5, 8, 9, 13, 14, 16, 17 |
| Chapter 2, 4, 8, 9, 11, 13 | Chapter 2, 3, 4, 8, 11, 12, 14–17 |
| Chapter 14 | Chapter 13, 14, 15 |
| Chapter 2, 4, 10, 12 | Chapter 6, 7, 13, 15 |
| Chapter 2, 6, 11, 12, 13 | Chapter 6, 14, 15 |
| Chapter 2, 14 | Chapter 3, 5, 6, 11–16 |

| Level 4 | | | | | | Level 5 | | | | | | Level 6 | | | | | |
|---|---|---|---|---|---|---|---|---|---|---|---|---|---|---|---|---|---|
| U1 | U2 | U3 | U4 | U5 | U6 | U1 | U2 | U3 | U4 | U5 | U6 | U1 | U2 | U3 | U4 | U5 | U6 |
| | 3 | | | | | 5-6 | | | | | | | 1-3 | | | | |
| | 4-6 | | | | | | | 2-3 | | | | | 4-6 | | | | |
| | | | | | 1-3 | | | 4-6 | | | | | | | 1-4 | | |
| | | | | 4-6 | | | 1-6 | | | | | | | | 1-6 | | |
| | | | 6 | | 5 | | | | 3-4 | | | | | 5-6 | | | |
| | | | | | 5 | | | | | 2 | | | | | | | 1-2 |
| | | | | | 4 | | | | | 1 | | | | | | | 3-4 |
| | | | | | 6 | | | | | 5-6 | | | | | | | 5-6 |

| Level 7 — Exploring Art | Level 8 — Understanding Art |
|---|---|
| Chapter 3, 6 | Chapter 7, 8, 10, 15, 17 |
| Chapter 3, 4, 7 | |
| Chapter 3, 11, 12 | Chapter 5, 7, 9, 10, 11, 13 |
| Chapter 3, 11, 14 | Chapter 5, 11, 12 |
| Chapter 3, 11 | Chapter 5, 10, 11, 12, 16 |
| Chapter 3, 6, 13 | Chapter 3, 4, 5, 10, 15 |
| Chapter 3, 6, 7 | Chapter 4, 5, 7, 12, 16 |
| Chapter 3 | Chapter 7 |

# Media

## Scope and Sequence

| Media | Level K | | | | | | Level 1 | | | | | | Level 2 | | | | | | Level 3 | | | | | |
|---|---|---|---|---|---|---|---|---|---|---|---|---|---|---|---|---|---|---|---|---|---|---|---|---|
| | U1 | U2 | U3 | U4 | U5 | U6 | U1 | U2 | U3 | U4 | U5 | U6 | U1 | U2 | U3 | U4 | U5 | U6 | U1 | U2 | U3 | U4 | U5 | U6 |
| Collage | 6 | 2 | 2, 3 | | 1 | 3 | 3 | | 5 | | | 3, 4 | 5 | 5 | | | | | | 4 | | | | |
| Drawing | 2, 4, 5 | 4, 5 | 1, 4, 5 | 1 | 2 | 1, 2 | 1 | 1–3, 5 | 1, 4 | | 2, 6 | 1, 5 | | | | 2, 3 | 2–4, 6 | 4 | 1, 2, 5, 6 | 3 | 1 | 1 | 3, 5 | 6 |
| Fiber Arts | | | | 4, 6 | | | | | | | 5 | | | | | | 5 | | | | | | 6 | 2 |
| Mixed Media | | 6 | | 3, 4 | 3 | | 5 | | | 5 | 1 | 2 | 2, 6 | 2 | 2, 3 | 6 | | | | 6 | 4, 6 | | | 4 |
| Painting | 1 | | 6 | | | | 1, 2, 4 | 4 | 3, 6 | 6 | | | 3, 4 | 6 | 1, 4–6 | | | 1, 3 | 3 | 2 | 2, 3, 5 | 4 | | |
| Photography | | | | | | | | | | | | | | | | | | | | | | | | |
| Printmaking | | 3 | | | | | | | | | 4 | | | | | 1 | | | | 1 | | | | 1 |
| Three-Dimensional Forms | | | | 2, 5, 6 | 5 | 4, 6 | | | 1–4 | 3 | | 6 | 1 | 1, 3, 4 | | 4 | 1 | 5 | 4, 5 | | 2, 3 | 4, 6 | 1, 5 | |
| Technology | 3 | 1 | | | | 5 | 6 | 6 | 2 | | | | | | | 5 | | 2, 6 | | | | 5 | 2 | 3 |

*Numbers indicate lesson numbers within a given unit.

| Level 4 | | | | | | Level 5 | | | | | | Level 6 | | | | | | Level 7 | Level 8 |
|---|---|---|---|---|---|---|---|---|---|---|---|---|---|---|---|---|---|---|---|
| U1 | U2 | U3 | U4 | U5 | U6 | U1 | U2 | U3 | U4 | U5 | U6 | U1 | U2 | U3 | U4 | U5 | U6 | Exploring Art | Understanding Art |
|  | 6 | 3 |  |  |  | 1 |  | 4 | 2 |  |  | 5 | 6 |  |  |  | 1 | Chapter 1, 6, 10 | Chapter 10 |
| 1–6 | 3, 4 | 2 |  |  | 1, 2, 4, 5 | 2, 4, 5 | 1, 4 | 1, 5 | 1, 4 | 3 | 2 | 1 | 3 | 1, 2, 4 | 3–5 | 1, 2, 5 |  | Chapter 2, 7, 11, 14 | Chapter 3, 15, 16 |
|  |  |  |  |  | 3, 6 |  |  |  | 2 | 4 |  | 2 |  |  |  |  | 3, 5 | Chapter 1, 2, 3, 13 | Chapter 7, 8, 10, 12 |
|  | 1, 5 |  | 4, 5 |  |  | 1, 4 |  |  |  |  |  | 1 |  |  |  | 6 | 4 | Chapter 5, 13 | Chapter 2, 3 |
|  |  | 4–6 |  |  |  | 2, 5 |  | 2, 3 | 3 | 3 | 4, 5 | 1 | 5 | 1, 2, 4 | 5 | 1 |  | Chapter 2, 3, 4, 5, 6, 9, 11, 14 | Chapter 1–8, 10, 11, 13–17 |
|  |  |  | 3 |  |  | 6 |  |  |  |  |  |  |  |  |  |  | 2 | Chapter 10 | Chapter 1, 17 |
|  |  |  |  |  |  |  |  |  |  |  | 3 |  |  |  |  |  |  | Chapter 3, 4, 8 | Chapter 1, 3, 6, 8, 14–17 |
|  |  |  | 1–3 |  |  |  | 5, 6 | 6 | 5, 6 | 6 |  |  | 3, 4 | 3, 6 | 6 | 3 | 6 | Chapter 2, 3, 4, 5, 7, 12, 13 | Chapter 1, 2, 3, 5–13, 15–17 |
|  | 2 | 1 | 6 | 6 |  | 3 |  | 2 |  |  | 6 |  |  |  | 5 | 2 | 4 | Chapter 4, 11, 15 | Chapter 3, 17 |

# Program Glossary

## A

**active lines** *noun* Lines that show action and add energy and movement to a work of art. Diagonal, zigzag, and curved lines are examples of active lines.

**additive sculpture** *noun* When something is added to either relief or freestanding sculpture

**alternating pattern** *noun* Can repeat a motif, but change position; alter spacing between motifs or add a second motif

**analogous color scheme** *noun* Uses colors that are side by side on the color wheel and have a common color

**analogous colors** *noun* Colors that sit side by side on the color wheel and have a common hue. Violet, blue-violet, blue, blue-green are examples of analogous colors.

**angle** *noun* A shape formed when two lines extend in different directions from the same point

**animal forms** *noun* A three-dimensional representation of an animal

**ant's view** *noun* Viewers feel they are looking up, toward an object or figure.

**appliqué** *noun* An art form in which cutout fabrics are attached to a larger surface

**approximate symmetry** *noun* A special kind of formal balance where both sides of a design are almost exactly the same. One example is the human face: each side is almost the same as the other.

**arc** *noun* Any portion of a curved line from a circle

**architects** *noun* Artists who design buildings, cities, and bridges using three-dimensional forms

**architecture** *noun* The art of designing and planning buildings, cities, and bridges

**armature** *noun* A framework for supporting material used in sculpting

**art form** *noun* A type of art

**assemblage** *noun* A sculpture technique in which a variety of objects is assembled to create one complete piece

## B

**asymmetrical balance** *noun* Another name for informal balance

**asymmetry** *noun* Another name for informal balance. Something asymmetrical looks balanced even if it is not the same on both sides.

**atmospheric perspective** *noun* The effects air and light have on how we perceive an object

**axis** *noun* A real or imaginary line across the center of a work of art

**background** *noun* The area of the picture plane farthest from the viewer

**balance** *noun* The principle of design that deals with visual weight in an artwork

**bird's-eye view** *noun* Or aerial view; viewers feel they are looking down on a scene.

**black** ▬

**blending** *noun* A shading technique that creates a gradual change from light to dark or dark to light

**blind contour drawing** *noun* A drawing that is made by looking at the object being drawn, not at the paper.

**blob** *noun* A type of free-form shape

**body forms** *noun* Three-dimensional representations of a person

**body proportions** *noun* The size relationship of one part of the body to another

**brass** *noun* A metal made by combining copper and zinc

**bright colors** *noun* colors that appear to reflect light

**broken (line)** *noun* A line that is made of a series of dashes, not solid

**building** *noun* a structure where we live, work, meet, or play

## C

**calm lines** *noun* Lines that give a work of art a quiet and peaceful mood. Horizontal and vertical lines are calm lines.

**carving** *noun* Art made by cutting into the surface of the medium.

**central axis** *noun* A real or imaginary dividing line that can run in two directions, vertically and horizontally

**circle** *noun* A round, geometric shape made when all points are placed the same distance from a center point.

**close-up view** *noun* Viewers feel they are right next to an object, or are a part of the action in a picture.

**coil** *noun* A long roll of clay joined into a circle or spiral. Clay coils are used to make pottery.

**collage** *noun* A two-dimensional work of art made up of pieces of paper and/or fabric to create the image.

**collograph** *noun* A printmaking technique where cut papers or thin boards are arranged to create an image on a stiff printing plate.

**color** *noun* 1. The art element that is created from reflected light; 2. In balance: a brighter color has more visual weight than a dull color; 3. In perspective: bright-colored objects seem closer, while dull or pale objects appear farther away.

**color intensity** *noun* The brightness or dullness of a color

**color scheme** *noun* A plan for organizing the colors used in an artwork

**color spectrum** *noun* The effect that occurs when light passes through a prism and separates into a band of colors in the order of red, orange, yellow, green, blue, and violet.

**color wheel** *noun* Shows the color spectrum bent into a circle

**column** *noun* A supporting pillar on a building

**complementary color scheme** *noun* Uses one set of complementary colors; for example, red and green, blue and orange, and yellow and violet

**complementary colors** *noun* Colors that are opposite each other on the color wheel

**complex geometric shapes** *noun* Shapes made by combining simple geometric shapes such as triangles, squares, and rectangles. Some examples of complex geometric shapes are diamonds, pentagons, trapezoids, hexagons, parallelograms, and octagons.

**contour** *noun* The edges and surface ridges of an object

**contour hatching** *noun* A shading technique that follows the form of an object

**contour lines** *noun* Continuous, unbroken lines that show the edges and surface ridges of an object or figure

**contrast** *noun* 1. A technique for creating a focal point or area of interest in a work of art using differences in elements; 2. In emphasis: contrast occurs when one element stands out from the rest of the work; 3. showing differences between things

**converging** *adj.* (*verb*) Coming together at one point or place

**converging lines** *noun* One of the six perspective techniques. Parallel lines seem to converge or move toward the same point as they move away from you.

**cool colors** *noun* Green, violet, and blue. They suggest coolness and move away from the viewer.

**cool hues** *noun* Blue, green, and violet. Cool hues are associated with cool things like snow, water, and grass.

**cross-hatching** *noun* A shading technique created when sets of parallel lines cross or intersect

**culture** *noun* Another word for custom

**curling** *verb* Hold one end of a long strip of paper. Grip the middle of the paper strip next to the side of a pencil. With a quick motion, pull the strip firmly across the pencil.

**curved** *adj.* Lines that bend and change gradually or turn inward to form spirals

**curved (line)** *noun* A line that changes directions slowly and bends in arcs

**curving movement** *verb* Using curved lines to move the viewer's eyes through a work of art and make the viewer feel that objects in the work of art are moving along curves

# D

**dark lines** *noun* Created by using less water for watercolor paints

**dark value** *noun* A value that has more black added to it

**decorative** *adj.* Serving to make more beautiful; to adorn with ornaments

**depth** *noun* 1. The appearance of distance; 2. How far something extends toward or away from the viewer.

**detail** *noun* One of the six perspective techniques. Objects with fuzzy, blurred edges appear farther away than those with clear sharp edges.

**diagonal** *noun* (*adj.*) Lines that are slanted. They look as if they are falling or rising. They make things look active.

**diagonal movement** *verb* Using diagonal lines to move the viewer's eyes through a work of art and make the viewer feel that objects in the work of art are moving along diagonals

**dimension** *noun* A measurement of the amount of space an object takes up in one direction

**diorama** *noun* A display of a scene using sculpted, miniature figurines

**directional lines** *noun* How a line moves: diagonally, vertically, or horizontally

**distortion** *noun* A deviation from normal or expected proportions

**dominant** *noun* (*adj.*) The part of the work of art that seems more important to the viewer. Dominant elements have been emphasized.

**dominant element** *noun* The element in a work of art that is noticed first.

**dull colors** Colors that are not bright

# E

**earthenware** *noun* Ceramics made out of clay and fired at a low heat

**elongate** *verb* To stretch out or make long

**embroidery** *noun* The art of decorating designs with needle and thread

**emphasis** *noun* The principle of design that stresses one area in an art work over another area

**even balance** *adj.* Both halves are equal. Left side and right side are the same.

**exaggerate** *verb* To make much larger than actual size

**exaggeration** *noun* To increase or enlarge beyond what is expected or normal

# F

**facial proportions** *noun* The relationship of one feature of a face to another feature

**faraway view** *noun* Or eye-level view; viewers feel they are standing far away from the scene.

**fiber** *noun* A material used to make baskets and cloth. Grass, yarn, and straw are kinds of fibers.

**flowing lines** *noun* Create a feeling of calm and gracefulness. Flowing lines are fluid; they change direction and size.

**flowing rhythm** *noun* Created when curved lines or shapes are repeated

**focal point** *noun* The point where the receding lines meet. It is the first part of a composition to attract the viewer's attention.

**foreground** *noun* The area of the picture plane that is closest to the viewer

**form** *noun* A three-dimensional object that is measured by height, width, and depth

**formal balance** *noun* Occurs when equal or similar elements are placed on opposite sides of a central axis

# Program Glossary (continued)

**free-form forms** *noun* Three-dimensional forms with irregular edges often found in nature

**free-form shapes** *noun* Two-dimensional images made of straight or curved lines or a combination of both

**freestanding** *noun* Forms that can be seen from all around

**freestanding sculpture** *noun* A three-dimensional work of art that can be viewed on all sides because it is surrounded by space

**fringing** *verb* Make parallel straight cuts along the edge of a piece of paper to create a ruffled look.

**frontal proportions** *noun* A front view of the head that is divided by three horizontal lines across the central axis

**futurists** *noun* A group of Italian artists during the early twentieth-century who repeated and overlapped shapes and lines to create the illusion of movement

## G

**geometric forms** *noun* Mathematically precise forms based on geometric shapes

**geometric shapes** *noun* Mathematically precise shapes: circle, square, and triangle

**gesture** *noun* An expressive movement

**gesture drawings** *noun* Quick drawings used to capture the position or pose of the body

**gesture lines** *noun* Lines drawn to capture the movement of a person, an animal, or an object in a painting or drawing

**gesture sketch** *noun* Quick drawings used to capture the position or movement of the body

**guide lines** *noun* Lines used by artists to create both full-face and profile portraits more accurately

## H

**hand tools** *noun* Simple instruments for carving or sculpting

**harmony** *noun* The principle of art that creates unity by stressing similarities of separate but related parts

**hatching** *noun* A shading technique that looks like a series of parallel lines

**height** *noun* A vertical measurement, or how tall something is

**high-intensity color** *noun* A pure hue such as red

**highlights** *noun* Small areas of white or light value to show the brightest spots

**horizon line** *noun* The point at which the earth and sky meet. The horizon line is always at the viewer's eye level.

**horizontal** *noun* (*adj.*) A line that moves from side to side

**hues** *noun* The spectral colors, or colors of the rainbow. Hues do not include black or white. Hues are red, orange, yellow, green, blue, and violet.

## I

**informal balance** *noun* A way of organizing parts of a design so that unlike objects have equal visual weight

**installation** *noun* An artwork that was created for a specific place, such as a gallery or outdoor location

**intensity** *noun* The brightness or dullness of a color

**interior designers** *noun* Artists who decorate the inside of a building

**intermediate colors** *noun* Colors made by mixing a primary color and a secondary color. There are six intermediate colors—red-orange, yellow-orange, yellow-green, blue-green, blue-violet, and red-violet.

**intermediate hues** *noun* Yellow-green, red-orange, blue-green, made by combining a primary hue with either of the secondary hues that are adjacent on the color wheel

**invented texture** *noun* Created when an artist uses lines or other elements to make a textural look without any specific texture in mind

**irregular** *adj.* Does not follow a rule or pattern

**isolation** *noun* An object is emphasized by its placement apart from other objects.

## J

**jeweler** *noun* An artist who designs and makes jewelry

**jewelry** *noun* Three-dimensional artwork that is made for people to wear

## K

**kinetic movement** *noun* Actual or real movement

**kinetic sculpture** *noun* A three-dimensional form that actually moves in space

## L

**landscape** *noun* a picture of the outdoors

**light lines** *noun* Created by adding more water to watercolor paints

**light value** *noun* A value that has more white added to it

**line** *noun* A mark drawn by a tool such as a pencil, pen, or paintbrush as it moves across a surface

**line variety** *noun* The different possibilities in the character of lines. For example, lines can be long or short, thick or thin, rough or smooth, and broken or solid.

**linear perspective** *noun* A system used to create the illusion of depth on a flat surface

**lines** *noun* One of the six perspective techniques. Parallel lines seem to converge or move toward the same point as they move away from the viewer.

**location** *noun* Artists can emphasize an object by placing it closer to the center of the piece.

**low-intensity color** *noun* A dull hue made by mixing a color with its complement

## M

**mandala** *noun* A radial design divided into sections or wedges, each of which contains a different image

**maquette** *noun* A small model for a larger sculpture

**mask** *noun* A three-dimensional art form of sculpted faces

**matte** *noun* A dull, sometimes rough finish

**medium** *noun* The supply an artist uses to create art. Some media are clay, paint, or wood.

**middle ground** *noun* The area of the picture plane that is usually toward the center

**minimal details** *noun* Used in gesture sketches to complete the drawing

**mix a neutral color** *verb* Mix a neutral color with another color to change its value

**mixed-media** *noun* An art object that has been created from an assortment of media or materials

**mobile** *noun* A moving sculpture in which shapes are balanced and arranged on wire arms and suspended from the ceiling to move freely in the air currents

**monochromatic** *adj.* A color scheme that is made up of one color and the tints and shade of that color

**monochromatic color scheme** *noun* Uses only one color and the values of that color

**monotonous** *adj.* Lack of variety; boring

**monumental sculptures** *noun* Sculptures that are larger than human forms

**motif** *noun* A unit that is made up of objects or art elements that can be repeated

**movement** *noun* The principle of art that leads a viewer's eyes throughout a work of art

**mural** *noun* A painting done on a wall

# N

**negative space** *noun* The empty space that surrounds objects, shapes, and forms

**neon** *noun* A special kind of light that can be made to be many bright colors

**neutral color scheme** *noun* Uses black, white, and a variety of grays

**neutral colors** *noun* Black, white, and gray; give hues a range of values

**nonobjective** *adj.* Art that has no recognizable subject matter

# O

**one-point linear perspective** *noun* A system used to create the illusion of depth on a flat surface where all receding lines meet at one point

**opaque** *adj.* Does not let light through

**outline** *noun* a line drawn around the edge of an object

**overlap** *verb* To place one object on top of another object and partially cover the first object up

**overlapping** *noun* 1. One object covers a portion of another object. 2. In perspective: one of the six perspective techniques; the object covering another will appear closer to the viewer, creating a feeling of depth.

# P

**painting** *noun* An art form using paint on a flat surface

**paper sculpting techniques** *noun* Six different techniques used to create paper sculptures: scoring a straight line, scoring a curve, pleating, curling, fringing, tab and slot.

**parallel lines** *noun* Lines that move in the same direction and always stay the same distance apart

**pattern** *noun* A repeated surface decoration

**perception drawing** *verb* Looking at something carefully and thinking deeply about what you see as you draw

**perspective** *noun* The method used to create the illusion of depth in two-dimensional art: overlapping, size, placement, detail, color, converging lines

**perspective techniques** *noun* The six techniques an artist uses to create the illusion of depth in two-dimensional art: overlapping, size, placement, detail, color, converging lines

**photograph** *noun* A picture taken using light-sensitive film and a camera

**picture plane** *noun* The surface of a drawing or painting

**placement** *noun* One of the six perspective techniques. Objects placed lower in the picture appear to be closer than those placed near eye level. There are three areas on a picture plane: foreground, middle ground, and background.

**pleating** *verb* Fold piece of paper from edge to edge. Then fold the same amount of paper in the other direction. Continue folding the paper back and forth in this manner.

**point of view** *noun* The angle at which the viewer sees an object

**portrait** *noun* A two- or three-dimensional artwork created in the image of a person or animal

**posed** *verb* Arranged in a special way

**position** *noun* In balance: a larger, positive shape and a small, negative space can be balanced by a small, positive shape and a large, negative space.

**positive space** *noun* Refers to any object, shape, or form in two- and three-dimensional art

**primary colors** *noun* Red, yellow, and blue. They cannot be made by mixing colors.

**primary hues** *noun* Red, yellow, and blue, used to mix the other hues on the color wheel

**print** *noun* An image created by using a stamp or printing plate. When artists make prints, they can make many identical images.

**printing** *verb* Pressing a shape from one thing to another many times

**printing plate** *noun* A plate that holds the image that will be used to create a print

**prism** *noun* A wedge-shaped piece of glass that bends light as it passes through

**profile** *noun* A side view of a person or animal

**profile proportions** *noun* A side view of the head that is divided by three horizontal lines

**proportion** *noun* The principle of art that is concerned with the size relationship of one part to another

# Program Glossary (continued)

## R

**radial balance** *noun* A type of balance that occurs when the art elements come out, or radiate, from a central point

**rainbow** *noun* An arc of spectral colors, usually identified as red, orange, yellow, green, blue, indigo, and violet, that appears in the sky opposite the sun

**random pattern** *noun* Occurs when the motif is repeated in no apparent order

**ratio** *noun* A comparison of size between two things

**real texture** *noun* Texture you can feel

**realistic scale** *noun* When an artist creates a work of art where everything fits together and makes sense in size relation

**rectangle** *noun* A four-sided geometric shape made of all right angles and whose opposite sides are equal in length.

**regular pattern** *noun* Occurs when identical motifs are repeated with an equal amount of space between them

**relief** *noun* A type of sculpture where forms project from a flat background

**relief sculpture** *noun* A sculpture in which objects stick out from a flat surface

**repeated lines** *noun* Used to give the feeling of movement or motion in a gesture drawing

**repetition** *noun* Lines, shapes, colors, or textures that are repeated throughout an artwork

**rest** *noun* The negative space between repetitions of the motif

**rhythm** *noun* The principle of design that organizes the elements in a work of art by repeating elements and/or objects

**rough** *noun* *(adj.)* A surface that has ridges; not smooth

**rough (line)** *noun* A line that has jagged, uneven edges

## S

**sail** *noun* A type of free-form shape

**scale** *noun* Size as measured against a standard reference

**score** *verb* The repeated scratching of the clay surface at the area that another scored piece will be attached

**scoring a curve** *verb* Gradually cut bending curves in the paper with the point of the scissors

**scoring a straight line** *verb* Hold a ruler in the center of a piece of paper. Run the point of the scissors along the edge of the ruler to cut the paper in a straight line.

**sculpture** *noun* Three-dimensional art

**sculpture model** *noun* The study or detailed example of what the sculpture will look like when completed

**secondary colors** *noun* Orange, green, and violet. These colors are made by mixing two primary colors.

**secondary hues** *noun* Orange, green, and violet; the result of mixing two primary hues

**self-portrait** *noun* A two- or three-dimensional artwork that an artist makes of him or herself

**sets of complementary colors** *noun* There are three sets on the color wheel: red and green, blue and orange, and yellow and violet.

**shade** *noun* Any hue blended with black

**shading** *noun* A technique for creating dark values or darkening an area by repeating marks such as lines or dots

**shadows** *noun* Shaded areas in a painting or drawing

**shape** *noun* A two-dimensional area that is measured by height and width

**shape reversal** *noun* Occurs when an object, shape, or form is positive space in one image and then in another image becomes negative space

**shiny** *noun* Bright from reflected light

**silhouette** *noun* The shape of a shadow

**simulated texture** *noun* Imitates real texture, see also visual texture

**size** *noun* 1. in perspective: objects that are closer look larger than objects that are farther away; 2. In balance: a large shape or form will appear to be heavier than a small shape, and several small shapes can balance one large shape.

**slip** *noun* A mixture of clay and water that is creamy to the touch and is used to attach two scored pieces of clay together

**smooth** *noun* A surface free from roughness; even

**smooth (line)** *noun* A line that has even edges

**solid (line)** *noun* A line that has no breaks, gaps, or holes

**space** *noun* The art element that refers to the areas above, below, between, within, and around an object

**spectral color scheme** *noun* Uses all the colors of the rainbow: red, orange, yellow, green, blue, and violet

**spectral colors** *noun* The colors of the light spectrum: red, orange, yellow, green, blue, and violet

**spectrum** *noun* The range of colors that it is possible to see; the rainbow

**splash** *noun* A type of free-form shape

**square** *noun* A four-sided geometric shape where all sides are the same length and all angles are right angles

**statue** *noun* Three-dimensional art that is a body form

**still life** *noun* The arrangement of common inanimate objects from which artists draw or paint

**stippling** *noun* A shading technique using dots to show value

**stitchery** *noun* Art made with yarn on cloth

**storyteller doll** *noun* A Native American sculpture that shows one person relating the history of the culture to many children

**style** *noun* A unique quality of an object

**subordinate** *noun* The parts of the artwork that seem less important. Subordinate objects are not emphasized.

**subtractive sculpture** *noun* When an artist carves pieces away from a form

**surrealism** *noun* An art movement that emphasized art in which dreams, fantasy, and the subconscious served as inspiration for artists

**symmetrical** When two sides of a work of art are mirror images of each other

**symmetry** *noun* A type of formal balance in which two halves of a balanced artwork are identical, mirror images of each other

# T

**tactile texture** *noun* The texture that can be felt

**texture** *noun* 1. The art element that refers to the way something feels; 2. In balance: a rough texture has an uneven pattern of highlights and shadows. For this reason, a rough surface attracts the viewer's eyes more easily than a smooth, even surface.

**thick (line)** *adj.* Wide

**thick line** *noun* Created by beginning with a thin line and gradually pressing the brush down

**thin (line)** *adj.* Narrow

**thin line** *noun* Created when a brush is held vertically to paper and touched lightly with the tip of the brush

**three-dimensional** *adj.* Has measurements in three directions: height, width, and depth

**three-dimensional patterns** *noun* Patterns that have depth and are formed on the surface of a sculptural form

**three-dimensional rhythm** *noun* A principle of design that indicates movement by the repetition of elements in a form

**tint** *noun* Any hue blended with white

**transparent** *adj.* Allows light to pass through so objects on the other side can be seen

**triangle** *noun* A three-sided geometric shape

**two-dimensional** *adj.* Shapes that are flat and can be measured by length and width

**two-dimensional decoration** *noun* Flat decoration produced on the surface of a work of art

# U

**unity** *noun* The feeling of wholeness in a work of art. Artists use repetition and grouping to show that different parts of a work belong together.

**unrealistic scale** *noun* When an artist makes size relationships that do not make sense

# V

**value** *noun* The lightness or darkness of a hue

**value contrast** *noun* The lightness or darkness stands out from the value that surrounds it

**vanishing point** *noun* The point on the horizon line where all parallel receding lines meet

**variety** *noun* The principle of art which is concerned with difference or contrast

**vertical** *noun* (*adj.*) Lines that move straight up and down. They make things look tall, steady, and calm.

**visual movement** *noun* Occurs when the eye is pulled through a work of art by a rhythm of beats and rests

**visual rhythm** *noun* The feeling of movement created when artists repeat colors, shapes, lines, and textures to lead the viewer's eyes through a work of art

**visual texture** *noun* Or simulated texture, imitates real texture. It is the illusion of a three-dimensional surface.

**visual weight** *noun* cannot be measured on a scale; it is measured by which objects the viewer's eyes see first.

# W

**warm colors** *noun* Red, yellow, and orange. They suggest warmth and come toward the viewer.

**warm hues** *noun* Red, orange, and yellow. Warm hues are associated with warm things such as fire or sunshine.

**weave** *verb* To interlace or interweave strips or strands of material

**width** *noun* A horizontal measurement, or how long across something is

# Z

**zigzag** *noun* (*adj.*) A line that is made by joining diagonal lines

# Program Index

# Program Index (continued)

# Program Index (continued)

# Program Index (continued)

# T